Computer-Aided Manufacturing

Second Edition

Computer-Aided Manufacturing

Second Edition

TIEN-CHIEN CHANG
Purdue University

RICHARD A. WYSK
Texas A&M University

HSU-PIN WANG
University of Iowa

PRENTICE HALL
Upper Saddle River, New Jersey 07458

Library of Congress Cataloging-in-Publication Data

Chang, Tien-Chien,
    Computer aided manufacturing / Tien-Chien Chang, Richard A. Wysk,
Hsu-Pin Wang, —2nd ed.
      p.   cm.
    Includes bibliographical references and index.
    ISBN–0–13–754524–x
    1. Computer integrated manufacturing systems. 2. CAD/CAM systems.
  3. Flexible manufacturing systems. I. Wysk, Richard A.,
II. Wang, Hsu-Pin, III. Title.
TS155.6.C48 1998
670′.285—dc21   97-25852
                                        CIP

Publisher: TOM ROBBINS
Acquisitions editor: ALICE DWORKEN
Production editor: ROSE KERNAN
Editor-in-chief: MARCIA HORTON
Cover designer: BRUCE KENSELAAR
Director of production and manufacturing: DAVID W. RICCARDI
Managing editor: BAYANI MENDOZA DE LEON
Manufacturing buyer: DONNA SULLIVAN

The author and publisher of this book have used their best efforts in preparing this book. These efforts include the development, research, and testing of the theories and programs to determine their effectiveness. The author and publisher make no warranty of any kind, expressed or implied, with regard to these programs or the documentation contained in this book. The author and publisher shall not be liable in any event for incidental or consequential damages in connection with, or arising out of, the furnishing, performance, or use of these programs.

Printed in the United States of America
10 9 8 7

ISBN 0-13-754524-X

Prentice-Hall International (UK) Limited, *London*
Prentice-Hall of Australia Pty. Limited, *Sydney*
Prentice-Hall Canada Inc., *Toronto*
Prentice-Hall Hispanoamericana, S.A., *Mexico*
Prentice-Hall of India Private Limited, *New Delhi*
Prentice-Hall of Japan, Inc., *Tokyo*
Simon & Schuster Asia Pte. Ltd., *Singapore*
Editora Prentice-Hall do Brasil, Ltda., *Rio de Janeiro*

To our families

*Our families endured the long hours we spent
on this book. Without their understanding and support,
this book would not be a reality.*

Contents

Preface

The paradigm of engineering is undergoing a major evolution throughout the world. The use of computers and the Internet has changed the way that we engineer and manufacture products. Among the recent trends in manufacturing are trends where products are subject to a shorter product life, frequent design changes, small lot sizes, and small in-process inventory restrictions (just-in-time, JIT). The result of these trends is that today more than 90% if our products are manufactured in lots of less than 50 parts. These low lot quantities have eliminated many applications of dedicated production lines that were so effective in producing the inexpensive goods of the 1950–1960s.

The first step employed to remain competitive with our international counterparts was the application of Computer-Aided Design (CAD) and Computer-Aided Manufacturing (CAM) to design and manufacture sophisticated products. Today, we routinely employ CAD systems to design products low- to medium-volume batch quantities. Linking CAD, CAM and Manufacturing Resource Planning (MRP) had produced a concept known as Computer-Integrated Manufacturing (CIM) systems. CIM systems are beginning to appear throughout the United States and in other competitive countries. Rather than creating and maintaining several separate engineering databases, there is a move underway to share information within a company and even throughout several companies. The Internet provides us with the physical connection to share design, marketing and manufacturing information. We now look toward the advent of Distributed Design and Distributed Manufacturing using Agile Networking as a means to produce products for the 21st century.

Employing numerical control (NC) and robotics in industry offers one potential solution to many manufacturing flexibility problems. This implementation, however, brings with it a variety of other problems. Robots and NC machines are designed to be flexible, self-contained, and capable of operating in a "standalone" or Aintegrated@ environment. Integrating this hardware into manageable systems has become a major focus of machine-tool makers and industry. Communication protocols for these systems are just beginning to evolve (manufacturing applications= protocol, MAP), and control software for scheduling for efficient operation is still engineered on a per-system basis.

Further integration of the manufacturing component with design and business systems is also a key to our manufacturing success. These communication and control issues, coupled with a variety of sensing issues, are critical to the success of flexible automation in the United States.

This book focuses on the science, mathematics and engineering of these new engineering methods. It is dedicated to making sure that the U.S. will remain the most efficient manufacturing nation in the world. The purpose of this book is to provide a comprehensive view of manufacturing with a focus on design, planning for manufacturing, automation, flexible automation, and computers in manufacturing. Unlike other CIM books, this book attempts to provide a strong science-base and analytical background for manufacturing planning, control, and design—the basic elements of a computer-aided manufacturing (CAM) system. The book is an excellent professional reference and also is an excellent text for CAM instruction. The Second Edition expands on the view provided in the First Edition by adding chapters on Tooling and Fixturing and Concurrent Engineering. The Second Edition also expands on the principal focus of its predecessor. One of the major features of the Second Edition is that examples have been added throughout the book to help reinforce the principles being presented. These examples should help both the students using the book as well as the professional by illustrating hard to understand application problems.

In keeping with the integration and agile networking focus of the book, the authors have created web pages with course notes, presentation slides and other materials that can be used with the book. These course notes are located on the authors home pages at:

1) http://www.personal.psu.edu/faculty/w/p/wp6/wp6.html

2) http://cam.ecn.purdue.edu/

These pages link to other teachers and researchers in the CIM area. It is our intent to continue to maintain and update these pages so if anyone teaching from the book creates new material, we will create the required links to access the material.

The book can be used for a variety of courses. In fact, covering all the material in the book requires at least two semesters. It is organized so that the first eleven chapters can be used for a course in automation, numerical control, and robotics. Chapters 12 through 16 focus on manufacturing-systems issues and fit well into a course of that title. Various combinations of chapters can be used for a course entitled computer-aided manufacturing to allow the instructor flexibility.

A Computer-Integrated Manufacturing-Student Manual and related software are also available to supplement the book. The software and manual provide work exercises for the student using a personal computer rather than having to program on shop-floor equipment. These materials are available from Delmar Inc. in Albany, N.Y. Software is available from the authors.

This book marks the end of countless hours spent by faculty and students at several universities. Although it would be impossible to mention all those who contributed to the book, we would like to thank several people for their time and effort in making the book a reality. Specifically, we would like to thank Drs. Ravi Mittal at North Carolina State University and Chen Zhou at the Georgia Institute for their contributions to Chapter 5—Tooling and Fixturing. Most of the chapter came directly from materials that they provided. Drs. David Wu, currently at Lehigh, and Hyunbo Cho, currently at the POSTECH Institute in South Korea contributed both to the organization and writing of Chapter 15, another chapter without parallel in the literature.

Several of our colleagues and outside reviewers read the manuscript and provided invaluable suggestions, among them, Drs. Sanjay Joshi at The Pennsylvania State University, and Jeffrey Smith at Texas A&M University. Special thanks are also due to Myra Winters and Holly Reese for their work on both the typing and editing of the materials. Finally, we would like to thank our families for tolerating us during the difficult parts of our writing.

Tien-Chien Chang
Richard A. Wysk
Hsu-Pin Wang

1

Introduction to Manufacturing

Technics and civilization as a whole are the result of human choices and aptitudes and strivings, deliberate as well as unconscious, often irrational when apparently they are most objective and scientific; but even when they are uncontrollable, they are not external. . . . No matter how completely technics relies on the objective procedures of the sciences, it does not form an independent system, like the universe. . . . The machine itself makes no demands and holds out no promises: it is the human spirit which makes demands and keeps promises. . . .

—Lewis Mumford, *Technics and Civilization*

1.1 INTRODUCTION

The wealth of a nation depends on its ability to retrieve natural resources and manufacture goods. Although the efficiency of the distribution system and service system is also important, the creation of goods is the most fundamental component of economic wealth. A simple and naive way of measuring the living standard of a culture is to divide the total goods produced (dollars sold) by the population. Of course, we know the matter is not so simple, because uneven distribution of wealth is indeed the norm everywhere. There are rich nations and poor nations, and rich people and poor people. However, the bottom line for creating national wealth is still to rely on the ability to manufacture. From history, we see that humanity has enjoyed an improvement in the standard of living over time. However, for thousands of years, the improvement has been relatively minor. Our first major improvement occurred during the stone age, when humans learned how to use hand tools. Actually, the ability to use hand tools distinguishes humans from other animals. Hand tools enable people to make simple things instead of waiting for nature to provide them. Hand tools are extensions of our hands. The next major improvement was not long ago: The Industrial Revolution brought another jump in the standard of living, and the development of machine tools. Machine tools are a principle product of the Industrial Revolution. They added power and precision to humans. With machine tools, humans can produce goods faster and more precisely. Human productivity has increased drastically, and industrial goods have replaced handmade products. They are both less expensive and of higher quality.

Europeans, with their newly invented machines, were able to expand their influence throughout the world. At the time of the Industrial Revolution, products were still custom made with manually operated machine tools. Parts interchangeability, developed by Eli Whitney, brought another major improvement to manufacturing. By combining jigs and gauges developed for interchangeable manufacture, and the concept of the production/assembly line and mass production became a reality in the twentieth century. Never before in human history had humanity enjoyed such an improvement in the standard of living than in the twentieth century. Mass production and scientific management of manufacturing helped to produce more, better, and less expensive goods. Automated (mechanically controlled) machines and systems (i.e., transfer lines) out-produced tens of hundreds of human workers. Mass-produced identical goods were plentiful and inexpensive. However, variety was limited due to the high cost of change-over in the manufacturing system. As Henry Ford so aptly put it, "You can have any color Model T that you'd like—as long as it's black."

Shortly after World War II, with the increasing demand for more complex parts, numerical-control (NC) machine tools were invented. NC replaced the need of the co-ordinated control of skilled machine operators, a skill that takes years to master. Since the 1950s, more scientific and technological developments have occurred than through-out human history. One of the most important developments is the invention of the digital computer. In discrete-product manufacturing, computers are essential to the development of NC, robotics, computer-aided design (CAD), computer-aided manufacturing (CAM), and flexible manufacturing systems (FMSs). These new computer-based technologies enable us to produce small-batch products at low cost. Many human decision-making functions are replaced or assisted by computers. Thus, they further increase human productivity. The development of artificial intelligence (AI) and expert systems provides us with limited intelligence for our manufacturing systems. Computers can not only replace manual labor, but now they can also perform some mental processing.

From both the product demand and manufacturing batch size, we also see a trend. Before the Industrial Revolution, demand was low and products were all custom-made. Few products were available and their prices were uniformly high. Machine shops produced primarily small-batch products. From the turn of the century to the 1950s, the world was transformed from a society with few industrial products for few people to abundant products for everybody. Demand for industrial products grew fast, and to respond to the demand, mass-production techniques were developed. The lower product cost further stimulated demand. However, the desire to have more product variety has changed production from high volume to medium- and small-batch quantities once again. Finally, in the 1980s, intense international competition has mandated that products be made quickly and inventory be kept to a minimum. Small-batch dynamic production environs are needed. The production technology that has resulted produces better, inexpensive products in response to rapid demand changes. On the other hand, demand drives the development of a new production technology. In the modern manufacturing industry, survival is predicated on automation while maintaining its flexibility.

Automation should provide good quality and low cost, and flexibility, all necessary to adapt to changes of the product and demand. It seems obvious that the solution is to apply computer-aided manufacturing (CAM) at the shop floor. Computer-aided manufacturing can be defined as "the applications of computers in manufacturing." CAM thus includes a larger number of functions, ranging from FMS scheduling to machine control. Of course, for the total corporation, the solution is computer-integrated manufacturing (CIM), which includes not only manufacturing functions, but also business and other engineering functions. CAM is part of the CIM solution. In this book, we include discussions of some of the key technologies of CAM, for example, the programmable logic controller (PLC), NC, robotics, computer-aided process planning (CAPP), flexible manufacturing systems (FMSs), and some supporting technologies, such as group technology (GT), CAD, AI, and manufacturing systems planning tools.

Today's new engineering thrusts include agile engineering, virtual manufacturing systems, rapid prototyping, and nanotechnologies. The first three thrusts are changes that are being made in the way that we engineer products so that we can be more flexible to changes in designs and more responsive to customer needs/requests. Agile engineering concepts are a set of integration linkages that allow cross-functional activities to occur transparently for the designer, process engineer, and production engineer. As the term *agile* implies, agile engineering is focused at rapid response to customer and product changes. An agile manufacturing system is one that can quickly/instantly respond to product changes (demand and design). In a *virtual enterprise,* a variety of manufacturing resource entities (possibly even competitors) will be assessable to a designer, for example, ownership of manufacturing resources is available to *virtually* anyone that wants to use them. In a *virtual enterprise,* if a special plating or manufacturing process is required to bring a new product to fruition, the designer would have access to existing manufacturing facilities with these processes to address and use them as though they were in his own shop facility. Scheduling and refining the operation of these resources will be as if they were in a local shop facility.

Rapid prototyping refers to a broad set of engineering topics that are intended to be item 1 of a new design. For many products, it is necessary to produce a physical item so that fit, accessibility, and other interrelated product aspects can be determined. Historically, first item production has occurred in a "tool or model shop" with highly skilled machinists and technicians. Even with these highly skilled workers, the time required to fabricate the first item has been exceptionally high (especially if custom tooling or fixturing is required). Rapid prototyping is the process that allows the "first of" to be produced more quickly and inexpensively. Although rapid prototyping normally refers to the fabrication of a physical product, it also can refer to creation of software (especially control software). The processes that are normally used in physical rapid prototyping include layered deposition of material, for example, laser sintering. These "layered-methods" processes have been referred to a 3-D copying because layers of materials are deposited in 2-D form and then built up to make a 3-D object.

Nanotechnologies are a new set of processes that produce very small features and products. Nanotechnologies utilize processes that can be focused at atoms and molecules. "Drilling" with nanotechnology processes can create a hole molecule by molecule, thus producing an exceptionally accurate (and small) hole.

By no means can all CAM technologies be addressed in a single volume with any depth. We instead provide a concise, yet comprehensive, discussion of each topic. Ample references are provided at the end of each chapter for further study in the individual areas. Before we begin the discussion on CAM, it is necessary that we discuss the fundamentals of manufacturing. CAM technologies and examples are applied to the processes, systems and definitions provided from this discussion.

1.2 BASIC DEFINITIONS FOR MANUFACTURING SYSTEMS

Today, the terms manufacturing, manufacturing engineering, and manufacturing systems have been widely used in both industry and academia. However, the general definitions of related terminologies are still not standardized. In this section, several important terms in the area of manufacturing systems are defined.

1. *Manufacturing* is a set of correlated operations and activities, which includes product design, material selection, planning, production, inspection, management, and marketing of the products, for the manufacturing industries.

2. *Manufacturing production* is a series of processes adopted to fabricate a product, and such processes exclude the activities for designing, planning, and controlling the production.

3. *Manufacturing processes* are the lower-level manufacturing activities used to make products. There are traditional machining processes, for example, turning, milling, and grinding, and more advanced nonchipping processes, for example, electrochemical machining (ECM) and electrodischarge machining (EDM).

4. *Manufacturing engineering* involves the design, operation, and control of manufacturing processes (planning, scheduling, as well as control of the manufacturing production and batch quality). It is the heart of design, planning, and control of the manufacturing systems and requires knowledge from other disciplines, such as electrical engineering, mechanical engineering, materials engineering, chemical engineering, and systems/information engineering.

5. *Manufacturing system* is an organization that comprises several interrelated manufacturing subsets. Its objective is to interface with outside production functions in order to optimize the total productivity performance of the system, such as production time, cost, and machine utilization. The activities of these subsets include design, planning, manufacturing, and control. These subsets are also connected with production functions outside the system, such as accounting, marketing, financing, and personnel.

Figure 1.1 illustrates the relationship between the subsets and functions outside of a manufacturing system. The activity in a manufacturing system initiates from the designing of a product, then proceeds with the planning of manufacturing processes, and develops control strategies for the system. After the planning and control operations are verified, the raw material can then be processed and output (product) is produced. The output of the manufacturing systems can be classified in two categories:

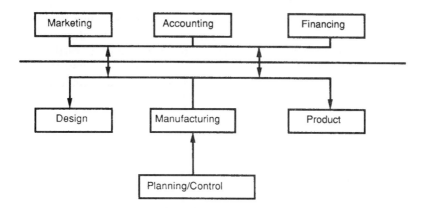

Figure 1.1   Manufacturing-system diagram.

(1) physical output, or product, and (2) manufacturing performance information that can be used as feedback to the system for adaptive adjustment of the machinery and control mechanisms.

1.3 DESIGN ACTIVITIES FOR MANUFACTURING SYSTEMS

Product design is the first step of the manufacturing activity that deals with the conceptualization and planning of the physical and functional characteristics of a product. An ideal design always stresses the ease of machining and assembly. In other words, the purpose of engineering design is to study how to design a product so that manufacturing cost and time can be reduced while preserving the functional requirements of a product. The major subsets (Figure 1.2) included in the design activities follow:

1. *Design conceptualization* and *function identification* are two vital elements of design. The designer begins by gathering all the appropriate technical information about the proposed product, for example, the materials, components, processes, and configurations that are required to satisfy the need. In other words, the function requirements of a product should be identified and asserted. Suh and Rinderle (1982) suggest an axiomatic approach for manufacturing design that can be treated as a general guideline for designers:

Axiom 1: Always maintain the independence of product functional requirements.
Axiom 2: Minimize the information content of any functional requirements and constraints.

These Axioms and other techniques will be discussed in detail in Chapter 14.

2. *Product modeling* establishes the analytical and graphical representation of a product, which can preserve and communicate the product configuration and functional requirements in an effective manner. Computer-aided design (CAD) is a popular modeling method and is detailed in Chapter 3.

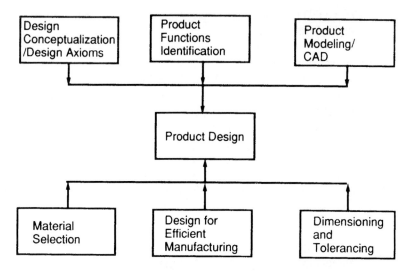

Figure 1.2   Design activities of the manufacturing system.

3. *Material selection* is a key issue in engineering design. It involves more than selecting a proper material that has the properties (part performance) to meet the functional requirements. The material is also closely connected with the processing (part manufacturing) of the raw material into a final product. Several sources of information on material properties are available such as [Lynch (1974), American Society for Metals (1978), and Reinhart (1987)].

4. *Design for efficient manufacturing* is the most convoluted portion of design activities. As the assembly parts illustrate in Figure 1.3, an improvement is made by having a rounded corner or chamfer on the insert. This modification results in easing the positional requirements for the assembly process.

5. *Dimensioning* and *tolerancing* of a product are intimately connected to the selection of machinery and a manufacturing process with proper capabilities. Tolerancing overspecification is one of the most common mistakes made by design engineers. It is a prevailing trend that engineering designers obtain a background in manufacturing processes before they dimension and specify a product. This will be discussed in detail in Chapter 2.

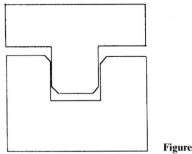

Figure 1.3   Assembly.

1.4 PLANNING AND CONTROL ACTIVITIES FOR MANUFACTURING SYSTEMS

The performance of a manufacturing system can be guaranteed only by detailed preliminary planning and the legitimate control and feedback of the system. Without these control mechanisms, it is meaningless to have a plan. The planning and control activities for manufacturing systems can be categorized based on specific factors, specifically the physical resource, information/knowledge, and time. Material-requirements planning (MRP), capacity planning, facility planning, inventory control, and tool management are planning and control activities for physical resources. Production scheduling is the planning and control of manufacturing resources over time. As to manufacturing information/knowledge control, it comprises the information communication and manufacturing database management. All these planning and control activities are interrelated, and each component is discussed in the following (refer to Figure 1.4):

1. *Material-requirements planning* works as an initiator for the manufacturing system. When management determines the master production-schedule requirements (the MRP process unit integrates this information with the existing plant-capacity status and generates purchase orders, work orders, and schedule notices), based on the raw material required (bill of material) and subassembly sequences determined by the engineering designer, and the inventory status reported from the storage warehouse manager, work orders and scheduling notices are sent to the shop floor control manager to prepare for production.

2. *Capacity planning* comprises the information that is required to accomplish the production goal, such as identifying the number of machines, persons, material-handling resources, tooling, and so on. The availability of shifts per work day, the work days per

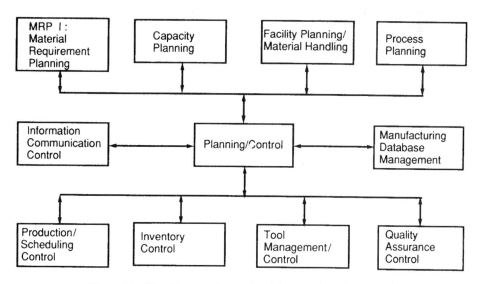

Figure 1.4   Planning/control activities of the manufacturing system.

week, overtime, subcontracting, and machine/tool/material-handling device requirements are fed back to the MRP control unit, which adjusts the work orders, purchase
orders, and schedule notices.

3. *Facility and material-handling device planning* are planning activities for selecting and arranging the physical layout of the manufacturing facilities, the material-
handling devices, and the storage space. For several decades, group technology (GT) has
gained increasing acceptance in this area. For small-to-medium production, GT cellular
layout can reduce the part routing time and reduce part fixturing during transfer from
machine to machine.

4. *Inventory control* deals with the control of (economic) inventory levels and the
reorder point for any raw material, semifinished, and finished parts. Also, the control of
work in process (WIP) is another key element of this area. The philosophy of just-in-
time (JIT) is a prevailing trend for reducing the WIP as well as the inventory. An ideal
inventory-control mechanism guarantees no delays of the material supply.

5. *Tool management* is a vital activity that is frequently neglected by the manufacturing engineer. It deals with tracking of tool location, cutting elapsed time, times for re-
conditioning, and so on. Minimizing tool breakage is a critical task of this control module.

6. *Scheduling* deals with the dispatching of job orders. Several rules such as FIFO
(first in, first out), SPT (shortest-processing-time), and LIFO (last in, first out) are
commonly used to schedule activities at workstations. The mean flow time, make span,
machine utilization, and due-date constraints are measures of performance for the
manufacturing system.

7. *Quality control* is the process that ensures the final acceptability of a product.
Quality control deals with activities ranging from inspection and related procedures to
sampling procedures used in manufacturing.

8. *Manufacturing information management* deals with the flow and allocation of
information concerning manufacturing resources and functions. Included here are resources such as workers, machines, materials, tooling, and so on. This information is necessary for virtually all other manufacturing functions. Computer databases for
managing manufacturing information can save storage space and standardize the information format, which is the major step for computer-integrated manufacturing.

9. *Information* and *communication* are especially important for large and
computer-integrated manufacturing systems. Several different types of electronic communication protocol are available for different considerations. Manufacturing Applications Protocol (MAP) is an electronic hierarchical manufacturing-control protocol
gaining rapid acceptance. Hierarchical control is suitable for many manufacturing systems, both manual and computer-controlled.

1.5 MANUFACTURING CONTROL

Manufacturing control encompasses a large variety of activities in a factory environment. At the factory level of operations, control usually refers to the coordination of a
variety of activities to ensure profitable operation. Materials management and capacity

planning are principal control functions at this level. At the less-aggregate centers of a manufacturing facility, such as a production center, the major focus of control is on the coordination of activities to maximize cell utilization and minimize inventory levels. At the cell level, control becomes involved with the scheduling of individual parts onto machines. Scheduling is a major component of cell control, although many other activities are part of cell control. When manufacturing engineers talk about control, this is the type of control that is normally addressed.

Two traditional control levels also exist below the cell. At the cell level, a given fixed time to produce a part is usually taken as a given to produce a schedule. However, a variety of speeds, feeds, tooling, tool paths, and so on, can be used for material processing. The selection and application of these variables form the primary focus of the workstation controller. Below the workstation resides the basic manufacturing process, which is the basis for all production. At the process level, motors, switches, feedback devices, and so on, must be controlled in order to attain the desired machine kinematics required to produce a part. An overview of a manufacturing control system architecture is shown in Figure 1.5.

The impact of layout dictates many characteristics of a manufacturing system. Each layout brings certain advantages and disadvantages to the production floor. The control of these systems (cells) also can be quite different. For instance, in a product layout where a single product is to be produced, a significant amount of planning and analysis must be performed before the system becomes operational. A line balance must be conducted to assign operations to the processing machines in order to distribute

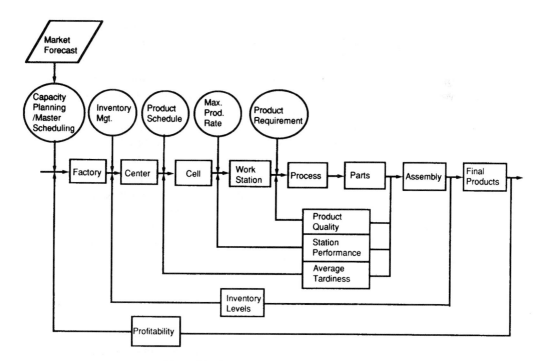

Figure 1.5   Manufacturing-system control loop.

operations as equally among the machines as is possible. Once the system is set up, the control is relatively easy because the only thing that needs to be controlled is the input station. Parts flow through the system at the rate of the slowest processing station.

The advent of today's modern flexible manufacturing systems has brought a wealth of control problems to the manufacturing engineer. In years past, many transfer lines operated automatically. However, these systems were product layout systems, and control from adjacent machine to adjacent machine was all that was necessary to control the entire system. Today's flexible manufacturing systems allow for a large selection of parts to be produced, and part transfer can be quite random. The sequence of operations and control of the required queues must be taken into account. In the job shop of the past, the machinist performed many of the scheduling activities required of today's control computer. Transferring the informal control to computer-controlled systems has proved to be a very difficult problem.

Controlling a programmable machining system has proved to be an exceptionally difficult problem for a variety of reasons. One problem that has been encountered in the development of these systems is protocol and interfacing. The time required to connect computer-controlled machines has in some cases been extreme. A set of standards, called MAP (manufacturing automation protocol), has been developed and is being used to reduce interface time. The sequencing of parts in the system in order to minimize make span or flow time is also a problem. Efficient generalized algorithms for scheduling have not yet been developed. These topics are covered in detail as definitions and requirements for control are provided throughout this book.

1.6 THE ORGANIZATION OF THE BOOK

The specific aim of this book is to provide a comprehensive view of computer-aided manufacturing (CAM) from a manufacturing engineering perspective. The main emphasis is the understanding of the principles of and relationships among the various components in CAM. It is tailored to those wanting to obtain state-of-the-art knowledge of CAM. Specifically, the objectives of this book are as follows:

- to provide in-depth knowledge about the various components of CAM systems
- to provide knowledge of state-of-the-art CAM technologies
- to develop skills in constructing and implementing CAM models
- to develop skills in evaluating CAM technologies
- to examine the relationship between CAD and CAM.

This book consists of 16 chapters; each addresses a specific issue of CAM. The following is a brief overview of the major focus of each chapter.

Chapter 1, "Introduction to Manufacturing," covers the basics of manufacturing. A general introduction to manufacturing systems (their planning and control) is given.

Chapter 2, "Part-Design Specification," lays a foundation of engineering design for manufacturing engineers. Specifically, this chapter provides the manufacturing engineer with knowledge about engineering representation and interpretation, as well as state-of-the-art CAD software and hardware. Because the purpose of manufacturing is to realize a design, it is essential to understand the design specification.

Chapter 3, "Computer-Aided Design," introduces the reader to the basics of *computer-aided design.* Representation schema and geometric modeling are described along with examples of CAD systems.

Chapter 4, "Process Engineering," addresses important issues such as machining processes, machining parameters, and process optimization, which are of major concern to most manufacturing engineers. This chapter serves as an introduction for other chapters on numerical control and computer-aided process planning.

Chapter 5, "Tool Engineering," provides fundamental knowledge of jig and fixture principles along with an overview of tooling considerations for machining operations. Tooling and fixturing are rapidly becoming the limiting resource in flexible manufacturing. This chapter overviews the basic elements of these constraints.

Chapter 6, "Fixed Automation," provides fundamental knowledge about fixed automation, which is still used in many mass-production environments. In contrast, flexible automation is discussed in Chapter 15. Many of the same computer-controlled devices are shared by fixed and flexible automation. Economical justification of automation is also discussed in this chapter.

Chapter 7, "Programmable Logic Controllers," covers almost everything that a manufacturing engineer needs to know about PLCs, which are powerful tools for automation and have been used extensively in industry. This chapter starts with an introduction to relay devices and why PLCs replaced them. It also details both the hardware and software aspects of PLCs.

Chapter 8, "Data Communication and Local-Area Networks in Manufacturing," provides up-to-date knowledge about what is perhaps the most important element in CAM. The data communication network in a CAM system is similar to the nervous system of a human body. The entire manufacturing information system is built on the network. Without it, manufacturing information cannot be communicated amongst the various component stations in the CAM system. The focus of this chapter includes data communication standards, communication components, local area networks, and manufacturing automation protocol (MAP).

Chapters 9 and 10, "Fundamentals of Numerical Control" and "Numerical-Control Programming," provide knowledge covering hardware, software, and control issues of modern NC. The three levels of NC programming instruction, manual part programming, computer-assisted part programming, and part programming with CAD, are discussed in detail. Analytical models for optimizing NC tool paths are also presented.

Chapter 11, "Industrial Robotics," discusses various issues of applying robotics technology in a manufacturing setting. Robots are the basic element in a CAM system. The basic operating principles of robotics are presented. The various issues of integrating robots with other automated equipment (e.g., computer vision) during the implementation stage is a focus of discussion.

Chapter 12, "Group Technology," presents information about that area. Group technology is the realization that many problems are similar, and that by grouping similar problems, a single solution can be found, thus saving time and effort. The potential benefits of group technology in manufacturing and how it impacts the design and planning of CAM systems are discussed. Various group-technology implementation techniques are presented with examples.

Chapter 13, "Process Planning," discusses computer-aided process planning (CAPP). CAPP is a key building block that bridges CAD and CAM. Commonly used CAPP approaches include variant and generative methods. The basics of both methods and various issues during implementation are discussed in detail.

Chapter 14, "Concurrent Engineering" discusses the interactions of engineering decision making, product engineering, process engineering, and facilities engineering. A parallel approach to conducting these activities is presented.

Chapter 15, "Integrated Computer-Aided Manufacturing," discusses integration issues of CAM systems. This chapter begins with a discussion on controlling a simple flexible manufacturing cell (FMC) and ends with an expert systems approach for controlling relatively complex flexible manufacturing systems (FMSs).

With the advent of computerized manufacturing systems comes the need to efficiently and accurately model the performance of such systems. Chapter 16, "The Planning of Manufacturing Systems," presents various models for manufacturing resource planning, capacity planning, machine-requirement planning, manpower planning, and space-requirement planning.

REVIEW QUESTIONS

1.1. Discuss the advantages and disadvantages of using transfer-line technology in a high-tech manufacturing facility.

1.2. Discuss the mechanical designer's role in a manufacturing facility.

1.3. Manufacturing systems planning and design are economically driven engineering functions. Discuss how classical engineering economic analysis is used and some of the problems related to "time-value" decisions.

1.4. Discuss the Department of Commerce statistic that 95% of all parts made in the United States are produced in lots of 50 or less. Toward what focus should this statistic direct us?

1.5. You and a group of close friends have recently patented a small NC drilling machine (for home use). You are currently planning on starting your own manufacturing operation. A marketing analyst has come back to you and said that because of the newness of the product line, "demand for the next 10 years may be between 50 and 50,000 units per year." The selling price for the drill was placed in the range of $1000 to $2500. If you were to manufacture the product yourself, the cost would range from $300 to $775 based on a production rate of 50 to 50,000 units per year as well as the production system design. Discuss your approach to beginning this company. (Include advantages and disadvantages as well as financing.)

1.6. Describe the environment where each of the three production systems would be most advantageous.

1.7. What is computer-aided manufacturing?

1.8. What are major developments of CAM technology?

1.9. What is the trend of manufacturing? Describe it in terms of market changes, technological development (both on products, and processes), managerial organization and philosophy shift, and social changes (use brain generation, green movement, and so on).

1.10. List five direct and five indirect applications of computers in manufacturing.

1.11. Briefly discuss the evolution of manufacturing.

1.12. What is a manufacturing workstation? What is a cell?

REFERENCES/BIBLIOGRAPHY

AMERICAN SOCIETY FOR METALS (1978). *Metals Handbook.* Materials Park, OH: ASM International.

GROOVER, M. P. (1987). *Automation, Production Systems, and Computer-Aided Manufacturing.* Englewood Cliffs, NJ: Prentice Hall.

HITOMI, K. (1979). *Manufacturing Systems Engineering.* London: Taylor and Francis.

KOREN, Y. (1983). *Computer Control of Manufacturing Systems.* New York: McGraw-Hill.

LYNCH, C. T. (1974). *CRC Handbook of Materials Science.* Cleveland, OH: CRC Press.

RANKY, P. (1989). *Computer Integrated Manufacturing.* Englewood Cliffs, NJ: Prentice Hall.

REINHART, T. J. (1987). *Engineering Material's Handbook.* Materials Park, OH: ASM International.

SUH, N. P., and J. R. RINDERLE (1982). "Qualitative and Quantitative Use of Design and Manufacturing Axioms," *Annals of CIRP,* 31, 333–338.

2

Part Design Specification

Before a product can be manufactured, it must be designed. The design process can be divided into five basic steps: (1) design conceptualization, (2) design synthesis, (3) design analysis, (4) design evaluation, and (5) design representation. Based on product requirements (functional requirements), a solution (design) is conceptualized. The initial solution is usually rather aggregate. It normally contains the general elements of the product, but lacks specification detail. The synthesis step adds more detail to the initial concept. In this stage, the geometry is laid out and design parameters and dimensions are assigned to the product. Steps 1 and 2 rely heavily on the creativity of a designer, and little scientific basis exists for these activities (perhaps with the exception of the axiomatic approach proposed by Suh, 1982).

During the first two steps, many design ideas are formed in the designer's head. As the design takes a more definite shape, a sketch is frequently used to help clarify the idea. When the design task is carried out by a group of people, a common, understandable representation must be used in order for all involved to share in the development. The solution is then analyzed and evaluated in order to identify viable and, eventually, the best alternative. Before the design is released for manufacture, it is necessary to perform the following: detailing of the design, which includes the selection of standard components; the determination of dimensions and tolerances; the determination of special manufacturing notes; and the final drafting. The design representation step includes both the rough sketch and the design layout detail.

In order for a part to be properly manufactured, a detailed part representation with information pertinent to manufacturing must be received before any manufacturing activity can begin. In this chapter, the various procedures used to specify a part design are discussed. The chapter begins with a general discussion on engineering design, followed by a discussion of interpreting an engineering drawing. In Chapter 3, a presentation of CAD systems, techniques, and models is presented.

2.1 ENGINEERING DESIGN

Engineering design is the partial realization of a designer's concept. The designer normally cannot directly transform a concept into a physical item. Instead, the designer conveys the idea to others through an alternate medium, such as an engineering drawing, and then the manufacturing engineer or machinist produces the design (Figure 2.1). When a farmer needed a tool prior to the Industrial Revolution, he normally went to a blacksmith and told the blacksmith the shape and size of the tool required. Because most tools were simple and did not require significant accuracy, the blacksmith would get a pretty good picture of a hoe or a plow through the verbal description. If the blacksmith still did not understand, the farmer could sketch the tool on the dirt floor of the blacksmith shop.

As product requirements and designs became more complex, a picture became necessary to relate the information to others. Multiview orthographic drawings have long been adopted by engineers as the standard tool to represent a design. Design information can be passed from the designer to others who are well trained in reading such drawings. The object a designer draws on paper can be interpreted and reconstructed in a viewer's mind. The ability to transform an object from one medium to another (e.g., from a two-dimensional, three-view drawing to a three-dimensional picture) and an understanding of the rules of drawing are prerequisite to pass design information from the designer to others without error.

There are several methods available to represent an engineering drawing. The conventional method is drafting on paper with pen or pencil. Manual drafting is tedious and requires a tremendous amount of patience and time. Recently, computer-aided drafting (CAD) systems have been implemented to improve drafting efficiency. The major objective of these systems is to assist the draftsman with tedious drawing and redrawing. Partially completed or completed drawings from a graphics tablet or screen can be stored in a computer and retrieved when needed.

Most CAD systems store drawings in a three-dimensional representation. Points (vertices), lines (edges), and curves are represented in (X, Y, Z) space. When a drawing is requested, a series of transformations are performed on the data, and a drawing is presented either in two- or three-dimensional perspective or in sectional views. The resultant drawing can then be drawn physically using a plotter, or simply displayed on

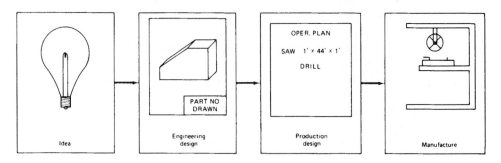

Figure 2.1   Evolution/realization of a product.

a cathode-ray tube (CRT). These types of internal representations can be used not only for design drafting, but also for engineering analysis, such as finite-element analysis.

In the 1980s, the term "geometric modeling" in CAD became common. Geometric modeling is a technique for providing computer-compatible descriptions of the geometry of a part. Conventional CAD systems employ geometric models that use surface-oriented, three-dimensional representations of the part. Recent advances in CAD have focused on the development of bounded-shape models for three-dimensional representations. In these bounded-shape models, individual surfaces are structured together to define the complete shell (boundary of the shape). Operations then can be applied to manipulate the shape. Chapter 3 will provide an introduction to basic CAD concepts and systems.

2.2 DESIGN DRAFTING

Engineering drawing is an abstract universal language used to represent a designer's idea to others. It is the most accepted medium of communication in all phases of industrial and engineering work. In ancient times, before multiview drawing standards were adopted, perspective drawings were normally employed. The great master of art during the Renaissance, Leonardo da Vinci, designed several machines and mechanical components (which still amaze contemporary designers) using perspective sketches (Figure 2.2) Today, pictorial drawings are still used to supplement other deisgn representations. The basic engineering drawing provides a complete and unambiguous representation of a part or product.

2.2.1 Multiview Drawing

In today's modern manufacturing industry, several types of drawings are acceptable. However, the standard is still the multiview drawing (Figure 2.3). A multiview drawing usually contains two or three views (front, top, and side). Each view is an orthographic projection of a plane. In the United States and Canada, the third-angle projection is the system used (see Figure 2.4). In the figure, the four quadrants of the Y-Z plane (called the I, II, III, and IV angles) are illustrated. For the third-angle projection, we always place the object in the third quadrant and project the object in three planes. This is done by projecting the object onto the frontal, horizontal, and profile planes. The projection on the frontal plane (X-Y) is fixed and the image is called the front view. With the projected image, the horizontal plane (X-Y) is rotated 90° clockwise on the X axis, the result is a top view of the object. The profile plane (Y-Z) is rotated 90° clockwise about the Y axis to obtain a right-hand side view. Hidden lines are shown by using dashed lines on the drawing.

2.2.2 Partial View

When a symmetrical object is drafted, two views are sufficient to represent it (typically, one view is omitted). A partial view can be used to substitute one of the two views (Figure 2.5). Sectional and auxiliary views are also commonly used to present part detail.

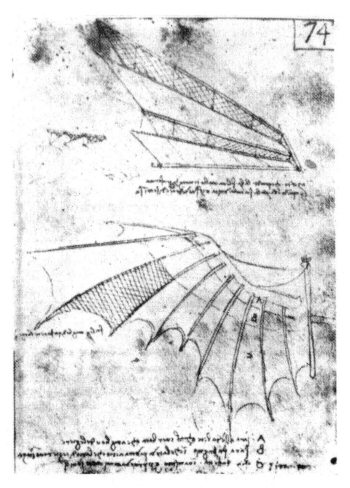

Figure 2.2   Idea sketch prepared by Leonardo da Vinci (1452–1519). (Courtesy of Institut de France.)

Sectional views, Figure 2.5(b), are extremely useful in displaying the detailed design of a complicated internal configuration. If the section is symmetrical around a center line, only the upper half needs to be shown. The lower half is typically shown only in outline. Casting designers often employ sectional views to explode detail. When a major surface is inclined to all three projection planes, only a distorted picture can be seen. An auxiliary plane that is parallel to the major surface, Figure 2.5(a), can be used to display an undistorted view.

2.2.3 Dimension and Tolerancing

A drawing is expected to convey a complete description of every detail of a part. However, dimensioning is as important as the geometric information. In manufacturing, a drawing without dimensions is only worth as much as the paper on which it is

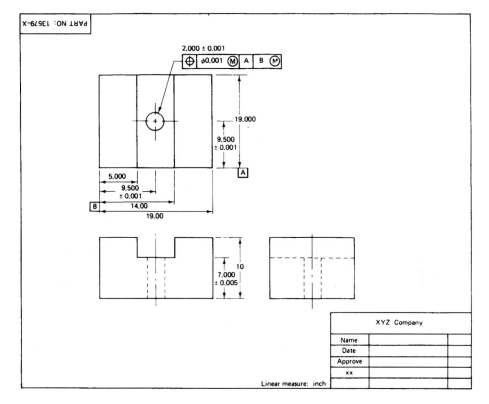

Figure 2.3   Multiview drawing of a bracket.

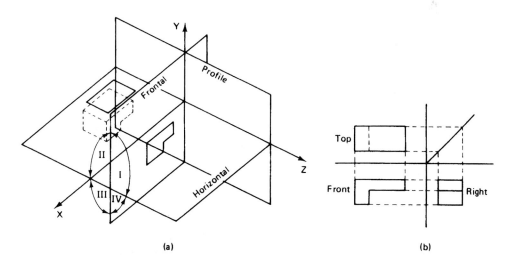

Figure 2.4   Third-angle projection.

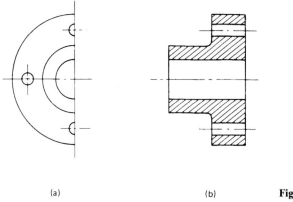

(a)   (b)   **Figure 2.5**   Partial views.

drawn. Dimensions convey the required size, whereas tolerances convey the required precision.

According to the American National Standards Institute (ANSI) standards, the following are the basic rules that should be observed in dimensioning any drawing:

1. Show enough dimensions so that the intended sizes and shapes can be determined without calculating or assuming any distances.
2. State each dimension clearly, so that it can be interpreted in only one way.
3. Show the dimensions between points, lines, or surfaces that have a necessary and specific relation to each other or that control the location of other components or mating parts.
4. Select and arrange dimensions to avoid accumulations of tolerances that may permit various interpretations and cause unsatisfactory mating of parts and failure in use.
5. Show each dimension only once.
6. Where possible, dimension each feature in the view where it appears in profile and where its true shape appears.
7. Wherever possible, specify dimensions to make use of readily available materials, parts, tools, and gauges. Savings are often possible when drawings specify (a) commonly used materials in stock sizes, (b) parts generally recognized as commercially standard, (c) sizes that can be produced with standard tools and inspected with standard gauges, and (d) tolerances from accepted published standards.

Most designers are well aware of the impact of the mechanisms that they choose in creating a product. Frequent scrutiny is made of the number of parts required to achieve a function. Designers are also constantly concerned with the performance of the design. Unfortunately, dimensioning and tolerancing often is an afterthought of the process even though the dimensioning and tolerancing of a part frequently implies information critical to the manufacture of a part. This information can effect the choice of process(es) to be used, tooling to be used, fixtures and fixture location, and machines required to produce a part. In the following sections, we will discuss some of the other specifics often neglected.

2.2.3.1 Conventional tolerancing.   Because it is impossible to produce the exact dimension specified, a tolerance is also used to show the acceptable variation in a dimension. The higher the quality a product has, the smaller the tolerance value specified. Tighter tolerances are translated into more careful production procedures and more rigorous inspection. There are two types of tolerances: bilateral tolerance and unilateral tolerance (Figure 2.6) Unilateral tolerances, such as $1.00^{+0.00}_{-0.05}$, specify dimensional variation from the basic size (i.e., decrease) in one direction in relation to the basic size; for example,

$$1.00^{+0.00}_{-0.05} = 0.95 \sim 1.00$$

The basic location where most dimension lines originate is the reference location (datum). For machining, the reference location provides the basis from which all other measurements are taken. By stating tolerances from a standard reference location, cumulative errors can be eliminated.

Most mechanical parts contain both working surfaces and nonworking surfaces. Working surfaces are those for items such as bearings, pistons, and gear teeth, for which optimum performance may require control of the surface characteristics. Nonworking surfaces, such as the exterior walls of an engine block, crankcase, or differential housings, seldom require surface control. For surfaces that require surface control, control surface symbols can be used. Figure 2.7 illustrates how these symbols are used.

Although many designers frequently ignore or arbitrarily specify surface-finish requirements, these specifications can dictate secondary or tertiary machining

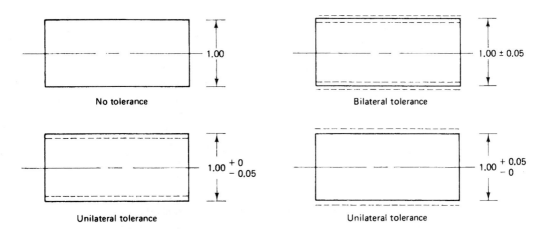

Figure 2.6   Tolerancing: bilateral and unilateral. Dashed lines show the tolerance limits.

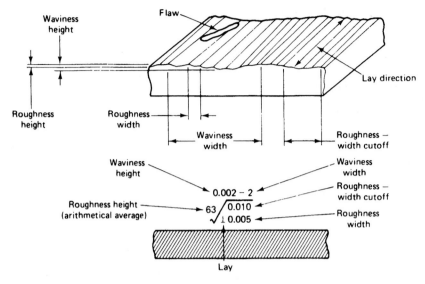

Figure 2.7   Surface control symbols.

requirements and significantly increase product cost. It is not unusual in the U.S. aerospace industry to find part surfaces with surface control requirements of $\sqrt{63}$ or less that are used by parts inspectors onto which to etch their identification and inspection dates. Although traceability is a critical characteristic of all components in an aircraft, this specification adds a secondary operation to the surface preparation, and the vibratory etching degrades the surface to fall outside the specification callout. Permanent ink applied with a rubber stamp onto a cast (or unprepared) surface will usually provide adequate identification for traceability.

Figure 2.7 connotes far more than just the arithmetic average roughness of a surface. In some design instances, the lay direction, waviness width, waviness height, and roughness width can be critical, especially for some parts-mating applications. For these applications, each of these attributes can be specified. The interpretation of the specifications is straightforward. The roughness width corresponds to the channel width that a production tool imparts on the workpiece surface. The roughness width cutoff corresponds to the minimum width of surface that yields the proper roughness value. The waviness width corresponds to the minimum length of workpiece to evaluate surface waviness.

In the specification, several surface characteristics are specified. The roughness height is the roughness value as normally related to the surface finish. It is the average amount of irregularity above or below an assumed centerline. It is expressed in microinches (μin. $= 0.000001$ in.) or, in the metric system, in micrometers (μm $= 0.000001$ m). Recommended roughness heights are given in Table 2.1. Lay is another property of a machined surface. It indicates the direction of the predominant pattern of surface ir-

TABLE 2.1 RECOMMENDED HEIGHT VALUES

Roughness value (μin.)	Type of surface	Purpose
1000	Extremely rough	Used for clearance surfaces only where good appearance is not required
500	Rough	Used where vibration, fatigue, and stress concentration are not critical and close tolerances are not required.
250	Medium	Most popular for general use where stress requirements and appearance are essential
125	Average smooth	Suitable for mating surfaces of parts held together by bolts and rivets with no motion between them
63	Better-than-average finish	For close fits or stressed parts except rotating shafts, axles, and parts subject to extreme vibration
32	Fine finish	Used where stress concentration is high and for such applications as bearings
16	Very fine finish	Used where smoothness is of primary importance, such as high-speed shaft bearings, heavily loaded bearings, and extreme tension members
8	Extremely fine finish produced by cylindrical grinding, honing, lapping, or buffing	Use for such parts as surfaces of cylinder
4	Superfine finish produced by honing, lapping, buffing, or polishing	Used on areas where packings and rings must slide across the surface where lubrication is not dependable

regularities produced by the tool. Lay symbols are listed in Figure 2.8. An example of using control surface symbols is shown in Figure 2.9.

Conventional methods of dimensioning only provide information concerning size and surface condition. A component can be produced without a guarantee of interchangeability. For example, in Figure 2.10, both components (b) and (c) satisfy the

$=$	Parallel to the boundary line of the nominal surface indicated by the symbol
$\perp$	Perpendicular to the boundary line of the nominal surface indicated by the symbol
X	Angular in both directions to the boundary line of the nominal surface indicated by the symbol
M	Multidirectional
C	Approximately circular relative to the center of the nominal surface indicated by the symbol
R	Approximately radial relative to the corner of the nominal surface indicated by the symbol

Figure 2.8 Lay symbols.

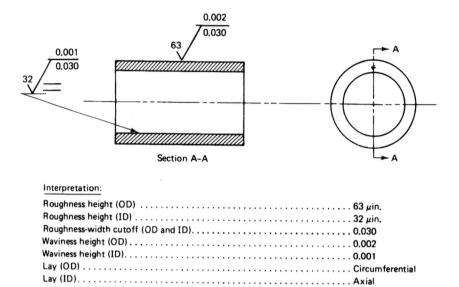

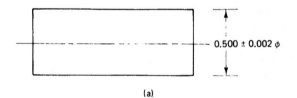

Interpretation:

Roughness height (OD) . . . . 63 μin.
Roughness height (ID) . . . . 32 μin.
Roughness-width cutoff (OD and ID). 0.030
Waviness height (OD) 0.002
Waviness height (ID). 0.001
Lay (OD) . . . . Circumferential
Lay (ID). . . . . Axial

Figure 2.9 Application and interpretation of the surface roughness symbols.

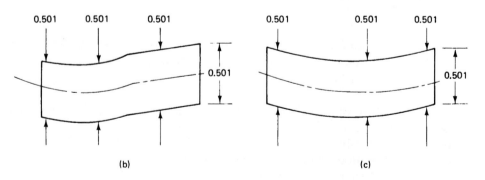

Figure 2.10 Illustration of some additional part conditions.

dimension specified in (a), that is, the diameter of components (b) and (c) is 0.501 in. over the entire length of the component. Obviously, both (b) and (c) are not desirable. However, as specified, both (b) and (c) meet specifications.

2.2.4 Geometric Tolerancing

Geometric tolerancing specifies the tolerance of geometric characteristics. Basic geometric characteristics as defined by the ANSI Y14.5M 1982 standard include

Straightness	Perpendicularity
Flatness	Angularity
Roundness	Concentricity
Cylindricity	Runout
Profile	True position
Parallelism	

Symbols that represent these features are shown in Table 2.2. To specify the geometric tolerances, reference features—planes, lines, or surfaces—can be established. A datum is a plane, surface, point(s), line, axis, or other information source on an object. Datums are assumed to be exact, and from them, dimensions similar to the reference-location dimensions in the conventional drawing system can be established. Datums are used for geometric dimensioning and frequently imply fixturing location information. The correct use of datums can significantly effect the manufacturing cost of a part.

Symbolic modifiers are used to clarify implied tolerances. The maximum material condition (MMC) can be used to constrain the tolerance of the produced dimension and the maximum designed dimension. It can be defined as the condition of a part feature where the maximum amount of material is contained. For example, maximum shaft size and minimum hole size can be illustrated, as shown in Figure 2.11. Least material condition (LMC) specifies the opposite of the maximum material condition. They can be applied only when both of the following conditions hold:

1. Two or more features are interrelated with respect to the location or form (e.g., two holes). At least one of the features must refer to size.
2. MMC or LMC must directly reference a size feature.

When MMC or LMC is used to specify the tolerance of a hole or shaft, it implies that the tolerance specified is constrained by the maximum or least material condition as well as some other dimensional feature(s). For MMC, the tolerance may increase when the actual produced feature size is larger (for a hole) or smaller (for a shaft). Because the increase in the tolerance is compensated by the deviance of size in production, the final combined hole-size error and geometric tolerance error will still be larger than the anticipated smallest hole. Figure 2.12 illustrates the allowed tolerance under the produced hole size. The allowed tolerance is the actual acceptable tolerance limit; it varies as the size of the produced hole changes. The specified tolerance is the value

TABLE 2.2 GEOMETRIC TOLERANCING SYMBOLS

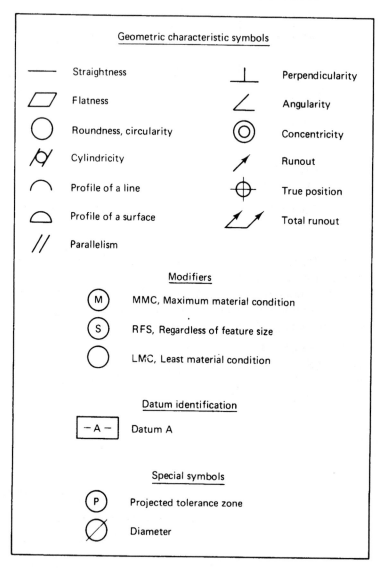

specified on the drawing. Hole size D is the specified value, and D' is the produced hole size, which is measured from the actual hole produced. The silhouette of the part at MMC produces a virtual part.

The third modifier is "regardless of feature size" (RFS). It is the default modifier when MMC or LMC is not specifically called out. When RFS is used, the tolerance does not change. Table 2.3 shows the application of three modifiers applied to the hole and shaft shown in Figure 2.11.

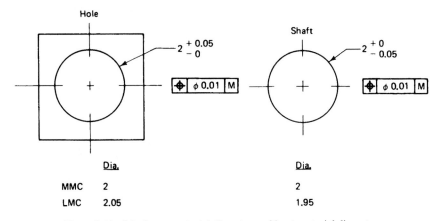

	Dia.	Dia.
MMC	2	2
LMC	2.05	1.95

Figure 2.11   Maximum material diameter and least material diameter.

2.2.4.1 Straightness (ASME Y14.5-1994).   Straightness is a condition where an element of a surface, or an axis, is a straight line. A straightness tolerance specifies a tolerance zone within which the considered element or derived median line must lie. A straightness tolerance is applied in the view where the elements to be controlled are represented by a straight line.

Straightness of a Derived Median Line
(a) *Definition.* A straightness tolerance for the derived median line of a feature specifies that the derived median line must lie within some cylindrical zone whose diameter is the specified tolerance.

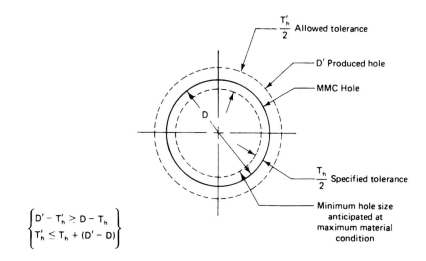

$$\begin{cases} D' - T'_h \geq D - T_h \\ T'_h \leq T_h + (D' - D) \end{cases}$$

Figure 2.12   Allowed tolerance under the produced hole size.

TABLE 2.3 MAXIMUM OUT-OF-TRUE POSITION ALLOWABLE UNDER THREE MODIFIERS

	Maximum out-of-true position allowable					
	Hole[a]			Shaft[b]		
Produced Size	MMC Ⓜ	LMC Ⓛ	RFS Ⓢ	MMC Ⓜ	LMC Ⓛ	RFS Ⓢ
1.95	Out-of-diameter tolerance range			0.05	0.02	0.01
1.96				0.04	0.03	0.01
1.97				0.03	0.04	0.01
1.98				0.03	0.04	0.01
1.99				0.02	0.05	0.01
2.00	0.01	0.06	0.01	0.01	0.06	0.01
2.01	0.02	0.05	0.01			
2.02	0.03	0.04	0.01	Out-of-diameter tolerance range		
2.03	0.04	0.03	0.01			
2.04	0.05	0.02	0.01			
2.05	0.06	0.01	0.01			

[a] $\varnothing\ 2.00^{+0.05}_{-0}$ ⊕ | 0.01 | Ⓜ

[b] $\varnothing\ 2.00^{+0}_{-.05}$ ⊕ | 0.01 | Ⓜ

A straightness zone for a derived median line is a cylindrical volume consisting of all points $\vec{P}$ satisfying the condition:

$$\left| \hat{T} \times (\vec{P} - \vec{A}) \right| \leq t \neq 2$$

where

$\hat{T}$ = direction vector of the straightness axis

$\vec{A}$ = position vector locating the straightness axis

t = diameter of the straightness tolerance zone

This feature is illustrated in Figure 2.13 for a cylindrical surface and Figure 2.14 for a planar surface.

(b) *Conformance.* A feature conforms to a straightness tolerance t_0 if all points of the derived median line lie within some straightness zone as defined above with $t = t_0$. That is, there exist $\hat{T}$ and $\vec{A}$ such that with $t = t_0$, all points of the derived median line are within the straightness zone.

(c) *Actual value.* The actual value of straightness for the derived median line of a feature is the smallest straightness tolerance to which the derived median line will conform.

Straightness of Surface Line Elements

(a) *Definition.* A straightness tolerance for the line elements of a feature specifies that each line element must lie in a zone bounded by two parallel lines that are separated by the specified tolerance and that are in the cutting plane defining the line element.

A straightness zone for a surface line element is an area between parallel lines consisting of all points $\vec{P}$ satisfying the condition:

$$|\hat{T} \times (\vec{P} - \vec{A})| \le t \ne 2$$

and

$$\hat{C}_P \cdot (\vec{P} - \vec{P}_S) = 0$$
$$\hat{C}_P \cdot (\vec{A} - \vec{P}_S) = 0$$
$$\hat{C}_P \cdot \hat{T} = 0$$

where

$\hat{T}$ = direction vector of the center line of the straightness zone
$\vec{A}$ = position vector locating the center line of the straightness zone
t = size of the straightness zone (the separation between the parallel lines)
$\hat{C}_P$ = normal to the cutting plane defined as being parallel to the cross product of the desired cutting vector and the mating surface normal at $\vec{P}_S$
$\vec{P}_S$ = point on the surface, contained by the cutting plane

Figure 2.13 illustrates a straightness tolerance zone for surface line elements of a cylindrical feature. Figure 2.14 illustrates a straightness tolerance zone for surface line elements of a planar feature.

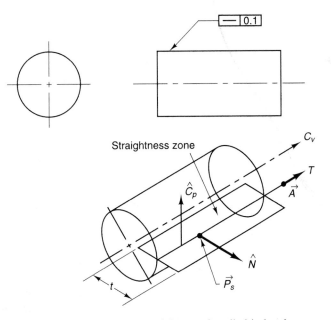

Figure 2.13 Evaluation of straightness of a cylindrical surface.

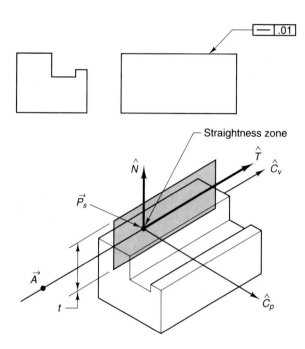

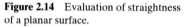

Figure 2.14   Evaluation of straightness of a planar surface.

(b) *Conformance.* A surface line element conforms to the straightness tolerance t_0 for a cutting plane if all points of the surface line element lie within some straightness zone as defined before with $t = t_0$. That is, there exist $\hat{T}$ and $\vec{A}$ such that with $t = t_0$, all points of the surface line element are within the straightness zone.

A surface conforms to the straightness tolerance t_0 if it conforms simultaneously for all toleranced surface line elements corresponding to some actual mating surface.

(c) *Actual value.* The actual value of straightness for a surface is the smallest straightness tolerance to which the surface will conform.

2.2.4.2. Flatness.   Flatness is the condition of a surface having all elements in one plane. A flatness tolerance specifies a tolerance zone defined by two parallel planes within which the surface must lie.

(a) *Definition.* A flatness tolerance specifies that all points of the surface must lie in some zone bounded by two parallel planes which are separated by the specified tolerance.

A flatness zone is a volume consisting of all points $\vec{P}$ satisfying the condition:

$$\left| \hat{T} \times (\vec{P} - \vec{A}) \right| \le t \ne 2$$

where

$\hat{T}$ = direction vector of the parallel planes defining the flatness zone
$\vec{A}$ = position vector locating the midplane of the flatness zone
t = size of the flatness zone (the separation of the parallel planes)

(b) *Conformance.* A feature conforms to a flatness tolerance t_0 if all points of the feature lie within some flatness zone as defined before, with $t = t_0$. That is, there exist $\hat{T}$ and $\vec{A}$ such that with $t = t_0$, all points of the feature are within the flatness zone.

(c) *Actual value.* The actual value of flatness for a surface is the smallest flatness tolerance to which the surface will conform.

2.2.4.3 Circularity (roundness).   Circularity is a condition of a surface where:

(a) for a feature other than a sphere, all points of the surface intersected by any plane perpendicular to an axis are equidistant from that axis;

(b) for a sphere, all points of the surface intersected by any plane passing through a common center are equidistant from that center.

A circularity tolerance specifies a tolerance zone bounded by two concentric circles within which each circular element of the surface must lie, and applies independently at any plane described in (a) and (b) above.

(a) *Definition.* A circularity tolerance specifies that all points of each circular element of the surface must lie in some zone bounded by two concentric circles whose radii differ by the specified tolerance. Circular elements are obtained by taking cross-sections perpendicular to some spine. For a sphere, the spine is 0-dimensional (a point), and for a cylinder or cone, the spine is 1-dimensional (a simple, nonself-intersecting, tangent-continuous curve). The concentric circles defining the circularity zone are centered on, and in a plane perpendicular to, the spine.

A circularity zone at a given cross-section is an annular area consisting of all points $\vec{P}$ satisfying the conditions:

$$\hat{T} \cdot (\vec{P} - \vec{A}) = 0$$

and

$$\left| \|\vec{P} - \vec{A}\| - r \right| \le t \ne 2$$

where

$\hat{T}$ = for a cylinder or cone, a unit vector that is tangent to the spine at $\vec{A}$. For a sphere, $\hat{T}$ is a unit vector that points radially in all directions from $\vec{A}$

$\vec{A}$ = position vector locating a point on the spine

r = radial distance (which may vary between circular elements) from the spine to the center of the circularity zone ($r > 0$ for all circular elements)

t = the size of the circularity zone

Figure 2.15 illustrates a circularity zone for a circular element of a cylindrical or conical feature.

(b) *Conformance.* A cylindrical or conical feature conforms to a circularity tolerance t_0 if there exists a 1-dimensional spine such that at each point $\vec{A}$ of the spine, the circular element perpendicular to the tangent vector $\hat{T}$ at $\vec{A}$ conforms to the circularity tolerance t_0. That is, for each circular element, there exist $\vec{A}$ and r such that with $t = t_0$, all points of the circular element are within the circularity zone.

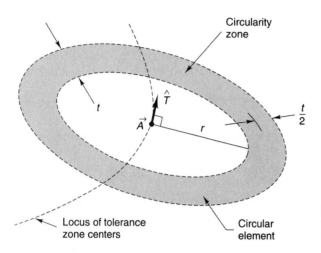

Circularity zone

$\hat{T}$

$\vec{A}$

r

t

$\dfrac{t}{2}$

Locus of tolerance zone centers

Circular element

Figure 2.15 Illustration of a circularity tolerance zone for a cylindrical or conical feature.

A spherical feature conforms to a circularity tolerance t_0 if there exists a point (a 0-dimensional spine) such that each circular element in each cutting plane containing the point conforms to the circularity tolerance t_0. That is, for each circular element, there exist $\hat{T}$, r, and a common $\vec{A}$ such that with $t = t_0$, all points of the circular element are within the circularity zone.

(c) *Actual value.* The actual value of circularity for a feature is the smallest circularity tolerance to which the feature will conform.

2.2.4.4 Cylindricity.
Cylindricity is a condition of a surface of revolution in which all points of the surface are equidistant from a common axis. A cylindricity tolerance specifies a tolerance zone bounded by two concentric cylinders within which the surface must lie. In the case of cylindricity, unlike that of circularity, the tolerance applies simultaneously to both circular and longitudinal elements of the surface (the entire surface). Note: The cylindricity tolerance is a composite control of form that includes circularity, straightness, and taper of a cylindrical feature.

(a) *Definition.* A cylindricity tolerance specifies that all points of the surface must lie in some zone bounded by two coaxial cylinders whose radii differ by the specified tolerance.

A cylindricity zone is a volume between two coaxial cylinders consisting of all points $\vec{P}$ satisfying the condition:

$$\left\| \hat{T} \times (\vec{P} - \vec{A}) \right\| - r \leq t \neq 2$$

where

$\hat{T}$ = direction vector of the cylindricity axis
$\vec{A}$ = position vector locating the cylindricity axis
r = radial distance from the cylindricity axis to the center of the tolerance zone
t = size of the cylindricity zone

(b) *Conformance.* A feature conforms to a cylindricity tolerance t_0 if all points of the feature lie within some cylindricity zone as defined before with $t = t_0$. That is, there exist $\hat{T}, \vec{A}$, and r such that with $t = t_0$, all points of the feature are within the cylindricity zone.

(c) *Actual value.* The actual value of cylindricity for a surface is the smallest cylindricity tolerance to which it will conform.

2.2.4.5 Profile control.

A profile is the outline of an object in a given plane (two-dimensional figure). Profiles are formed by projecting a three-dimensional figure onto a plane or taking cross-sections through the figure. The elements of a profile are straight lines, arcs, and other curved lines. With profile tolerancing, the true profile may be defined by basic radii, basic angular dimensions, basic coordinate dimensions, basic size dimensions, undimensioned drawings, or formulas.

(a) *Definition.* A profile tolerance zone is an area (profile of a line) or a volume (profile of a surface) generated by offsetting each point on the nominal surface in a direction normal to the nominal surface at that point. For unilateral profile tolerances, the surface is offset totally in one direction or the other by an amount equal to the profile tolerance. For bilateral profile tolerances, the surface is offset in both directions by a combined amount equal to the profile tolerance. The offsets in each direction may, or may not, be disposed equally.

For a given point $\vec{P}_N$ on the nominal surface there is a unit vector $\hat{N}$ normal to the nominal surface whose positive direction is arbitrary; it may point either into or out of the material. A profile tolerance t consists of the sum of two intermediate tolerances t_+ and t_-. The intermediate tolerances t_+ and t_- represent the amount of tolerance to be disposed in the positive and negative directions of the surface normal $\hat{N}$, respectively, at $\vec{P}_N$. For unilateral profile tolerances, either t_+ or t_- equals zero; t_+ and t_- are always nonnegative numbers.

The contribution of the nominal surface point $\vec{P}_N$ toward the total tolerance zone is a line segment normal to the nominal surface and bounded by points at distances t_+ and t_- from $\vec{P}_N$. The profile tolerance zone is the union of line segments obtained from each of the points on the nominal surface.

(b) *Conformance.* A surface conforms to a profile tolerance t_0 if all points $\vec{P}_S$ of the surface conform to either of the intermediate tolerances t_+ or t_- disposed about some corresponding point $\vec{P}_N$ on the nominal surface. A point $\vec{P}_S$ conforms to the intermediate tolerance t_+ if it is between $\vec{P}_N$ and $\vec{P}_N + \hat{N}t_+$. A point $\vec{P}_S$ conforms to the intermediate tolerance t_- if it is between $\vec{P}_N$ and $\vec{P}_N - \hat{N}t_-$. Mathematically, this is the condition that there exists some $\vec{P}_N$ on the nominal surface and some u, $-t_- \le u \le t_+$, for which $\vec{P}_S = \vec{P}_N + \hat{N}u$.

(c) *Actual value.* For both unilateral and bilateral profile tolerances, two actual values are necessarily calculated: one for surface variations in the positive direction and one for the negative direction. For each direction, the actual value of profile is the smallest intermediate tolerance to which the surface conforms. Note that no single actual value may be calculated for comparison to the tolerance value in the feature control frame, except in the case of unilateral profile tolerances.

2.2.4.6 Orientation tolerances.   Angularity, parallelism, perpendicularity, and in some instances profile are orientation tolerances applicable to related features. These tolerances control the orientation of features to one another.

In specifying orientation tolerances to control angularity, parallelism, perpendicularity, and in some cases profile, the considered feature is related to one or more datum features. Relation to more than one datum feature is specified to stabilize the tolerance zone in more than one direction.

Tolerance zones are total in value requiring an axis, or all elements of the considered surface to fall within this zone. Where it is a requirement to control only individual line elements of a surface, a qualifying notation, such as EACH ELEMENT or EACH RADIAL ELEMENT, is added to the drawing. This permits control of individual elements of the surface independently in relation to the datum and does not limit the total surface to an encompassing zone.

Where it is desired to control a feature surface established by the contacting points of that surface, the tangent plane symbol is added in the feature control frame after the stated tolerance.

Angularity is the condition of a surface or center plane or axis at a specified angle (other than 90°) from a datum plane or axis.

Parallelism is the condition of a surface or center plane, equidistant at all points from a datum plane or an axis, equidistant along its length from one or more datum planes or a datum axis.

Perpendicularity is the condition of a surface, center plane, or axis at a right angle to a datum plane or axis.

Mathematically, the equations describing angularity, parallelism, and perpendicularity are identical for a given orientation zone type when generalized in terms of the angle(s) between the tolerance zone and the related datum(s). Accordingly, the generic term *orientation* is used in place of angularity, parallelism, and perpendicularity in the definitions. See Appendix A.

An orientation zone is bounded by a pair of parallel planes, a cylindrical surface, or a pair of parallel lines. Each of these cases is defined separately below. If the tolerance value is preceded by the diameter symbol then the tolerance zone is a cylindrical volume; if the notation EACH ELEMENT or EACH RADIAL ELEMENT appears, then the tolerance zone is an area between parallel lines; in all other cases, the tolerance zone is a volume between parallel planes by default.

Planar Orientation Zone.

(a) *Definition.* An orientation tolerance that is not preceded by the diameter symbol and that does not include the notation EACH ELEMENT or EACH RADIAL ELEMENT specifies that the toleranced surface, center plane, tangent plane, or axis must lie in a zone bounded by two parallel linear planes separated by the specified tolerance and basically oriented to the primary datum and, if specified, to the secondary datum as well.

A planar orientation zone is a volume consisting of all points $\vec{P}$ satisfying the condition:

$$\left|\hat{\boldsymbol{T}} \cdot (\vec{\boldsymbol{P}} - \vec{\boldsymbol{A}})\right| \le \frac{t}{2}$$

where

$\hat{\boldsymbol{T}}$ = direction vector of the planar orientation zone
$\vec{\boldsymbol{A}}$ = position vector locating the midplane of the planar orientation zone
t = size of the planar orientation zone (the separation of the parallel planes)

The planar orientation zone is oriented such that, if $\hat{\boldsymbol{D}}_1$ is the direction vector of the primary datum, then

$$\left|\hat{\boldsymbol{T}} \cdot \hat{\boldsymbol{D}}_1\right| = \begin{cases} |\cos \Theta| \text{ for a primary datum axis} \\ |\sin \Theta| \text{ for a primary datum plane} \end{cases}$$

where Θ is the basic angle between the primary datum and the direction vector of the planar orientation zone.

If a secondary datum is specified, the orientation zone is further restricted to be oriented relative to the direction vector, $\hat{\boldsymbol{D}}_2$, of the secondary datum by

$$\left|\hat{\boldsymbol{T}} \cdot \hat{\boldsymbol{D}}_2\right| = \begin{cases} |\cos \alpha| \text{ for a secondary datum axis} \\ |\sin \alpha| \text{ for a secondary datum plane} \end{cases}$$

where $\hat{\boldsymbol{T}}'$ is the normalized projection of $\hat{\boldsymbol{T}}$ onto a plane normal to $\hat{\boldsymbol{D}}_1$, and $\boldsymbol{\alpha}$ is the basic angle between the secondary datum and $\hat{\boldsymbol{T}}'$. $\hat{\boldsymbol{T}}'$ is given by

$$\hat{\boldsymbol{T}}' = \frac{\hat{\boldsymbol{T}} - (\hat{\boldsymbol{T}} \cdot \hat{\boldsymbol{D}}_1)\hat{\boldsymbol{D}}_1}{\left|\hat{\boldsymbol{T}} - (\hat{\boldsymbol{T}} \cdot \hat{\boldsymbol{D}}_1)\hat{\boldsymbol{D}}_1\right|}$$

Figure 2.16 shows the relationship of the tolerance zone direction vector to the primary and secondary datums. Figure 2.17 illustrates the projection of $\hat{\boldsymbol{T}}$ onto the primary datum plane to form $\hat{\boldsymbol{T}}'$.

(b) *Conformance.* A surface, center plane, tangent plane, or axis S conforms to an orientation tolerance t_0 if all points of S lie within some planar orientation zone as defined before with $t = t_0$. That is, there exist $\hat{\boldsymbol{T}}$ and $\vec{\boldsymbol{A}}$ such that with $t = t_0$, all points of S are within the planar orientation zone. Note that if the orientation tolerance refers to both a primary datum and a secondary datum, then $\hat{\boldsymbol{T}}$ is fully determined.

(c) *Actual value.* The actual value of orientation for S is the smallest orientation tolerance to which S will conform.

2.2.4.7 Cylindrical orientation zone.

(a) *Definition.* An orientation tolerance that is preceded by the diameter symbol specifies that the toleranced axis must lie in a zone bounded by a cylinder with a diameter equal to the specified tolerance and whose axis is basically oriented to the primary datum and, if specified, to the secondary datum as well.

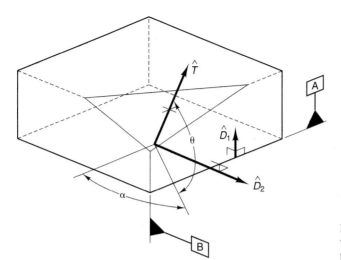

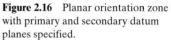

Figure 2.16 Planar orientation zone with primary and secondary datum planes specified.

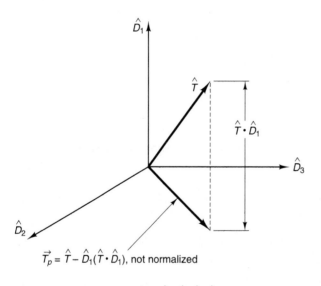

$$\vec{T_p} = \hat{T} - \hat{D_1}(\hat{T} \cdot \hat{D_1}), \text{ not normalized}$$

$$\text{Normalized, } T' = \frac{\vec{T_p}}{|\vec{T_p}|} = \frac{\hat{T} - \hat{D_1}(\hat{T} \cdot \hat{D_1})}{|\hat{T} - \hat{D_1}(\hat{T} \cdot \hat{D_1})|}$$

Figure 2.17 Projection of tolerance vector onto primary datum plane.

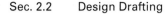
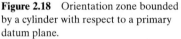
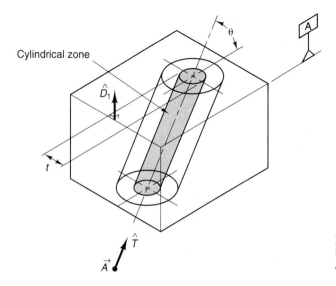

Figure 2.18 Orientation zone bounded by a cylinder with respect to a primary datum plane.

A cylindrical orientation zone is a volume consisting of all points $\vec{P}$ satisfying the condition

$$\left| \hat{T} \times (\vec{P} - \vec{A}) \right| \leq t \neq 2$$

where

$\hat{T}$ = direction vector of the axis of the cylindrical orientation zone

$\vec{A}$ = position vector locating the axis of the cylindrical orientation zone

t = diameter of the cylindrical orientation zone

The axis of the cylindrical orientation zone is oriented such that if $\hat{D}_1$ is the direction vector of the primary datum, then

$$\left| \hat{T} \cdot \hat{D}_1 \right| = \begin{cases} \left| \cos \Theta \right| & \text{for a primary datum axis} \\ \left| \sin \Theta \right| & \text{for a primary datum plane} \end{cases}$$

where Θ is the basic angle between the primary datum and the direction vector of the axis of the cylindrical orientation zone.

If a secondary datum is specified, the orientation zone is further restricted to be oriented relative to the direction vector, $\hat{D}_2$, of the secondary datum by

$$\left| \hat{T}' \cdot \hat{D}_2 \right| = \begin{cases} \left| \cos \alpha \right| & \text{for a secondary datum axis} \\ \left| \sin \alpha \right| & \text{for a secondary datum plane} \end{cases}$$

where $\hat{T}'$ is the normalized projection of $\hat{T}$ onto a plane normal to $\hat{D}_1$, and α is the basic angle between the secondary datum and $\hat{T}'$. $\hat{T}'$ is given by

$$\hat{T}' = \frac{\hat{T} - (\hat{T} \cdot \hat{D}_1)\hat{D}_1}{|\hat{T} - (\hat{T} \cdot \hat{D}_1)\hat{D}_1|}$$

Figure 2.18 illustrates a cylindrical orientation tolerance zone.

(b) *Conformance.* An axis S conforms to an orientation tolerance t_0 if all points of S lie within some cylindrical orientation zone as defined before with $t = t_0$. That is, there exists $\hat{T}$ and $\vec{A}$ such that with $t = t_0$, all points of S are within the orientation zone. Note that if the orientation tolerance refers to both a primary datum and a secondary datum, then $\hat{T}$ is fully determined.

(c) *Actual value.* The actual value of orientation for S is the smallest orientation tolerance to which S will conform.

2.2.4.8 Linear orientation zone

(a) *Definition.* An orientation tolerance that includes the notation EACH ELE-MENT or EACH RADIAL ELEMENT specifies that each line element of the toler-anced surface must lie in a zone bounded by two parallel lines that are (1) in the cutting plane defining the line element, (2) separated by the specified tolerance, and (3) are ba-sically oriented to the primary datum and, if specified, to the secondary datum as well.

For a surface point $\vec{P}_S$, a linear orientation zone is an area consisting of all points $\vec{P}$ in a cutting plane of direction vector $\hat{C}_P$ that contains $\vec{P}_S$. The points $\vec{P}$ satisfy the conditions

$$\hat{C}_P \cdot (\vec{P} - \vec{P}_S) = 0$$

and

$$|\hat{T} \times (\vec{P} - \vec{A})| \le t \neq 2$$

where

$\hat{T}$ = direction vector of the center line of the linear orientation zone
$\vec{A}$ = position vector locating the center line of the linear orientation zone
$\vec{P}_S$ = point on S
$\hat{C}_P$ = normal to the cutting plane and basically oriented to the datum reference frame
    t = size of the linear orientation zone (the separation between the parallel lines)

The cutting plane is oriented to the primary datum by the constraint

$$\hat{C}_P \cdot \hat{D}_1 = 0$$

If a secondary datum is specified, the cutting plane is further restricted to be oriented to the direction vector of the secondary datum $\hat{D}_2$, by the constraint

$$|\hat{C}_P \cdot \hat{D}_2| = |\cos \alpha| \text{ for a secondary datum axis}$$

$$|\hat{C}_P \cdot \hat{D}_2| = |\sin \alpha| \text{ for a secondary datum plane}$$

The position vector $\vec{A}$, which locates the center line of the linear orientation zone, also locates the cutting plane through the following constraint:

$$\hat{C}_P \cdot (\vec{P}_S - \vec{A}) = 0$$

If a primary or secondary datum axis is specified, and the toleranced feature in its nominal condition is rotationally symmetric about that datum axis, then the cutting planes are further restricted to contain the datum axis as follows:

$$\hat{C}_P \cdot (\vec{P}_S - \vec{B}) = 0$$

where $\vec{B}$ is a position vector that locates the datum axis. Otherwise, the cutting planes are required to be parallel to one another.

The direction vector of the center line of the linear orientation zone, $\hat{T}$, is constrained to lie in the cutting plane by

$$\hat{C}_P \cdot \hat{T} = 0$$

The center line of the linear orientation zone is oriented such that, if $\hat{D}_1$ is the direction vector of the primary datum, then

$$|\hat{T} \cdot \hat{D}_1| = \begin{cases} |\cos \Theta| & \text{for a primary datum axis} \\ |\sin \Theta| & \text{for a primary datum plane} \end{cases}$$

where Θ is the basic angle between the primary datum and the direction vector of the linear orientation zone.

Figure 2.19 illustrates an orientation zone bounded by parallel lines on a cutting plane for a contoured surface.

(b) *Conformance.* A surface, center plane, or tangent plane S conforms to an orientation tolerance t_0 for a cutting plane $\hat{C}_P$ if all points of the intersection of S with $\hat{C}_P$ lie within some linear orientation zone as defined before with $t = t_0$. That is, there exist $\hat{T}$ and $\vec{A}$ such that with $t = t_0$, all points of S are within the linear orientation zone.

A surface S conforms to the orientation tolerance t_0 if it conforms simultaneously for all surface points and cutting planes $\hat{C}_P$.

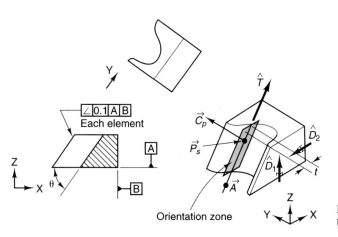

Orientation zone

Figure 2.19   Orientation zone bounded by parallel lines.

Note that if the orientation tolerance refers to both a primary datum and a secondary datum, then $\hat{\boldsymbol{T}}$ is fully determined.

(c) *Actual value.* The actual value of orientation for S is the smallest orientation tolerance to which S will conform.

2.2.4.9 Runout tolerance.

Runout is a composite tolerance used to control the functional relationship of one or more features of a part to a datum axis. The types of features controlled by runout tolerances include those surfaces constructed around a datum axis and those constructed at right angles to a datum axis.

Surfaces constructed around a datum axis are those surfaces that are either parallel to the datum axis or are at some angle other than 90° to the datum axis. The mathematical definition of runout is necessarily separated into two definitions: one for surfaces constructed around the datum axis, and one for surfaces constructed at right angles to the datum axis. A feature may consist of surfaces constructed both around and at right angles to the datum axis. Separate mathematical definitions describe the controls imposed by a single runout tolerance on the distinct surfaces that comprise such a feature. Circular and total runout are handled later in this chapter.

Evaluation of runout (especially total runout) on tapered or contoured surfaces requires establishment of actual mating normals. Nominal diameters, and (as applicable) lengths, radii, and angles establish a cross-sectional *desired contour* having perfect form and orientation. The desired contour may be translated axially and/or radially, but may not be tilted or scaled with respect to the datum axis. When a tolerance band is equally disposed about this contour and then revolved around the datum axis, a volumetric tolerance zone is generated.

Circular Runout

Surfaces Constructed at Right Angles to a Datum Axis

(a) *Definition.* The tolerance zone for each circular element on a surface constructed at right angles to a datum axis is generated by revolving a line segment about the datum axis. The line segment is parallel to the datum axis and is of length t_0, where t_0 is the specified tolerance. The resulting tolerance zone is the surface of a cylinder of height t_0.

For a surface point $\vec{\boldsymbol{P}}_S$, a circular runout tolerance zone is the surface of a cylinder consisting of the set of points $\vec{\boldsymbol{P}}$ satisfying the conditions

$$\left| \hat{\boldsymbol{D}}_1 \times (\vec{\boldsymbol{P}} - \vec{\boldsymbol{A}}) \right| = r$$

and

$$\left| \hat{\boldsymbol{D}}_1 \cdot (\vec{\boldsymbol{P}} - \vec{\boldsymbol{B}}) \right| \le \frac{t}{2}$$

where

r = radial distance from $\vec{\boldsymbol{P}}_S$ to the axis
$\hat{\boldsymbol{D}}_1$ = direction vector of the datum axis
$\vec{\boldsymbol{A}}$ = position vector locating the datum axis

$\vec{B}$ = position vector locating the center of the tolerance zone

t = size of the tolerance zone (height of the cylindrical surface)

(b) *Conformance.* The circular element through a surface point $\vec{P}_s$ conforms to the circular runout tolerance t_0 if all points of the element lie within some circular runout tolerance zone as defined before with $t = t_0$. That is, there exists $\vec{B}$ such that with $t = t_0$, all points of the surface element are within the circular runout zone.

A surface conforms to the circular runout tolerance if all circular surface elements conform.

(c)*Actual value.* The actual value of circular runout for a surface constructed at right angles to a datum axis is the smallest circular runout tolerance to which it will conform.

Surfaces Constructed Around a Datum Axis

(a) *Definition.* The tolerance zone for each circular element on a surface constructed around a datum axis is generated by revolving a line segment about the datum axis. The line segment is normal to the desired surface and is of length t_0, where t_0 is the specified tolerance. Depending on the orientation of the resulting tolerance zone will be either a flat annular area or the surface of a truncated cone.

For a surface point $\vec{P}_s$, a datum axis $[\vec{A}, \hat{D}_1]$, and a given mating surface, a circular runout tolerance zone for a surface constructed around a datum axis consists of the set of points $\vec{P}$ satisfying the conditions:

$$\frac{\hat{D}_1 \cdot (\vec{P} - \vec{B})}{|\vec{P} - \vec{B}|} = \hat{D}_1 \cdot \hat{N}$$

and

$$\left| |\vec{P} - \vec{B}| - d \right| \le \frac{t}{2}$$

$$\hat{N} \cdot (\vec{P}_s - \vec{B}) > 0$$

where

$\hat{D}_1$ = direction vector of the datum axis

$\vec{A}$ = position vector locating the datum axis

$\hat{N}$ = surface normal at $\vec{P}_s$ determined from the mating surface

$\vec{B}$ = point of intersection of the datum axis and the line through $\vec{P}_s$ parallel to the direction vector $\hat{N}$

d = distance from $\vec{B}$ to the center of the tolerance zone as measured parallel to $\hat{N}$ ($d \ge t/2$)

t = size of the tolerance zone as measured parallel to $\hat{N}$

Figure 2.20 illustrates a circular runout tolerance zone on a noncylindrical surface of revolution.

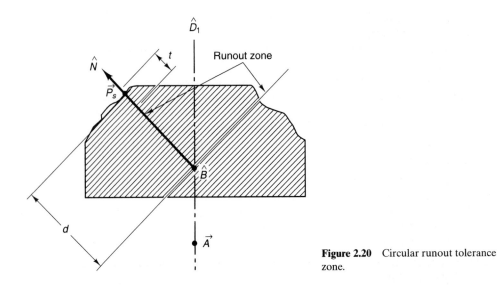

Figure 2.20   Circular runout tolerance zone.

(b) *Conformance.* The circular element through a surface point $\vec{P}_s$ conforms to the circular runout tolerance t_0 for a given mating surface if all points of the circular element lie within some circular runout tolerance zone as defined before with $t = t_0$. That is, there exists d such that with $t = t_0$, all points of the circular element are within the circular runout tolerance zone.

A surface conforms to a circular runout tolerance t_0 if all circular elements of the surface conform to the circular runout tolerance for the same mating surface.

(c) *Actual value.* The actual value of circular runout for a surface constructed around a datum axis is the smallest circular runout tolerance to which it will conform.

Total Runout

Surfaces Constructed at Right Angles to a Datum Axis

(a) *Definition.* A total runout tolerance for a surface constructed at right angles to a datum axis specifies that all points of the surface must lie in a zone bounded by two parallel planes perpendicular to the datum axis and separated by the specified tolerance.

For a surface constructed at right angles to a datum axis, a total runout tolerance zone is a volume consisting of the points $\vec{P}$ satisfying

$$|\hat{D}_1 \cdot (\vec{P} - \vec{B})| \leq t \neq 2$$

where

$\hat{D}_1$ = direction vector of the datum axis
$\vec{B}$ = position vector locating the midplane of the tolerance zone
t = size of the tolerance zone (the separation of the parallel planes)

(b) *Conformance.* A surface conforms to the total runout tolerance t_0 if all points of the surface lie within some total runout tolerance zone as defined before with $t = t_0$. That is, there exists $\vec{B}$ such that with $t = t_0$, all points of the surface are within the total runout zone.

(c) *Actual value.* The actual value of total runout for a surface constructed at right angles to a datum axis is the smallest total runout tolerance to which it will conform.

Surfaces Constructed Around a Datum Axis

(a) *Definition.* A total runout tolerance zone for a surface constructed around a datum axis is a volume of revolution generated by revolving an area about the datum axis. This area is generated by moving a line segment of length t_0, where t_0 is the specified tolerance, along the desired contour with the line segment kept normal to, and centered on, the desired contour at each point. The resulting tolerance zone is a volume between two surfaces of revolution separated by the specified tolerance.

Given a datum axis defined by the position vector $\vec{A}$ and the direction vector $\hat{D}_1$, let $\vec{B}$ be a point on the datum axis locating one end of the desired contour, and let r be the distance from the datum axis to the desired contour at point $\vec{B}$. Then, for a given $\vec{B}$ and r, let $C(\vec{B}, r)$ denote the desired contour. (Note: Points on this contour can be represented by $[d, r + f(d)]$, where d is the distance along the datum axis from $\vec{B}$.) For each possible $C(\vec{B}, r)$, a total runout tolerance zone is defined as the set of points $\vec{P}$ satisfying the condition

$$|\vec{P} - \vec{P}'| \leq t \neq 2$$

where

$\vec{P}'$ = projection of $\vec{P}$ onto the surface generated by rotating $C(\vec{B}, r)$ about the datum axis

t = size of the tolerance zone, measured normal to the desired contour.

(b) *Conformance.* A surface conforms to a total runout tolerance t_0 if all points of the surface lie within some total runout tolerance zone as defined before with $t = t_0$. That is, there exist $\vec{B}$ and r such that with $t = t_0$, all points of the surface are within the total runout tolerance zone.

(c) *Actual value.* The actual value of total runout for a surface constructed around a datum axis is the smallest total runout tolerance to which it will conform.

2.2.4.10 Free state variation.   Free-state variation is a term used to describe distortion of a part after removal of forces applied during manufacture. This distortion is principally due to weight and flexibility of the part and the release of internal stresses resulting from fabrication. A part of this kind, for example, a part with a very thin wall in proportion to its diameter, is referred to as a non-rigid part. In some cases, it may be required that the part meet its tolerance requirements while in the free state. In others, it may be necessary to simulate the mating part interface in order to verify individual or related feature tolerances. This is done by restraining the appropriate features. The restraining forces are those that would be exerted in the assembly or functioning of the part. However, if the dimensions and tolerances are met in the free state, it is usually not necessary to restrain the part unless the effect of subsequent restraining forces on the concerned features could cause other features of the part to exceed specified limits.

2.3 DESIGN INTERPRETATION

The specification of an engineering design carries with it a tremendous amount of detail. Tolerance specification may be the job of an inexperienced draftsperson who may not be aware of the interpretation and impact of details. These geometric details may increase the production cost of a part by as much as an order of magnitude. In the following sections, we will provide details and examples of tolerancing a mechanical product. The interpretation will be followed by defining the inspection requirements and interpretations for the parts.

2.3.1 Tolerancing

Two types of tolerancing schemes are allowed in the specification of geometric entities: parametric and geometric. Parametric tolerancing is what most engineers and draftspersons are taught in basic engineering drawing. The term parametric is used because limiting conditions, or *control parameters,* are defined based on normal Cartesian (or polar) dimensions. Figure 2.21 illustrates the use of parametric tolerancing.

2.3.1.1 Parametric tolerancing.   In parametric tolerancing, datum surfaces are a function of the location of dimension arrows on the drawing. When a dimension is specified from another dimensioned surface, the tolerances for the surfaces *stack* (become additive). Figures 2.22(a) to 2.22(c) illustrates the stacking of dimensions expressed sequentially. In Figure 2.22(a), each face is specified as a function of the previous face. The first flat is specified as $1.000 \pm .010$. This implies that the second face can be from 0.990 to 1.01 from the left side of the part (labeled datum B in the figure). Because the next face is specified from the second face, the tolerance of the first flat convolutes the second flat. The face labeled datum C can be from 1.975 to 2.025 from face datum A. Finally, the total width of the block can be from 2.970 to 3.030. In general, dimensions chained together in this manner accumulate as

$$\max d_n = \sum \max d_i$$

In the case of Figure 2.22(b), the tolerances stack differently. Because the entire width is specified, the width of the block is acceptable if the dimensions are from 2.990 to 3.010. Face datum B now can be from 0.975 to 1.025 from datum A, and surface datum C from 1.983 to 2.017 from datum A, and so forth. In Figure 2.22(c), the leftmost surface labeled datum A becomes an implicit datum, because all measurements are made with respect to it.

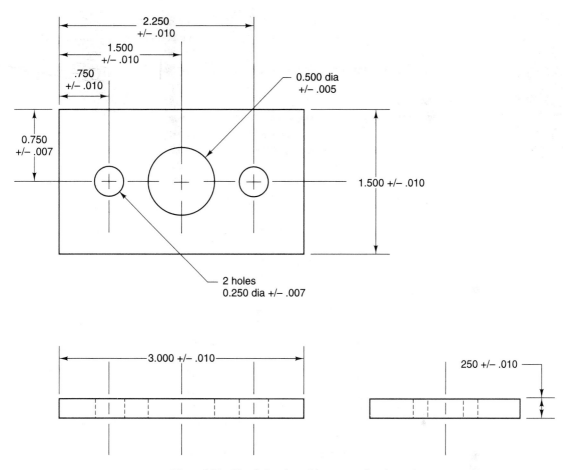

Figure 2.21   Simple bracket with parametric tolerancing.

Figure 2.23(a) to 2.23(c) again illustrates the chaining of errors for the parts shown in Figures 2.22(a) to 2.22(c). The figures represent the accumulation of errors as they are specified on the drawings. The chaining of the tolerances always should be viewed critically because the surface relationships affect the manufacturing (both sequence and process) and fixturing of the part. It is necessary to know that the tolerances will accumulate, and therefore reducing them is a poor substitute for correct specification. Special care should be taken in specifying tolerances, because they effect both the functionality and the manufacturability of a part.

2.3.1.2 Geometric tolerances.   The basic definitions for geometric tolerances were specified in Section 2.2.5. Geometric tolerances were created to eliminate deficiencies in the parametric tolerancing scheme. Geometric tolerancing is normally used to describe attributes of specific geometric features. The feature as we refer to it here

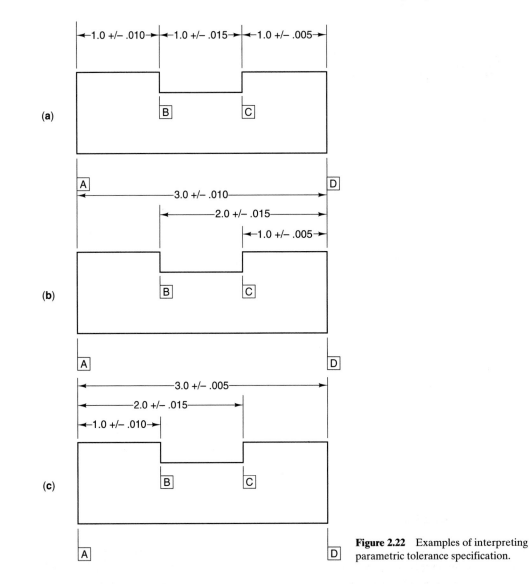

Figure 2.22 Examples of interpreting parametric tolerance specification.

qualifies a geometric entity, for example, roundness or cylindricity of a hole, true position of a geometric feature, and so on. Geometric tolerancing allows a designer to state allowable deviations in geometric form, where parametric tolerancing allows only Cartesian (and sometimes polar) implementation. In the following section, we will provide a set of examples and interpretations using both parametric and geometric tolerancing.

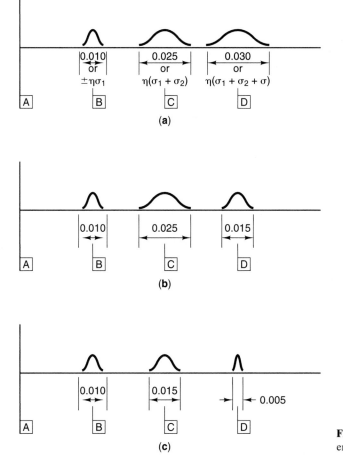

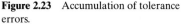

Figure 2.23   Accumulation of tolerance errors.

2.3.2 Tolerancing Examples

Figure 2.21 contains a sample bracket dimensioned using parametric specifications. Because parametric tolerances use translation to create the allowable range of inaccuracy, the part essentially grows or shrinks along the dimension axis. Figure 2.24 shows the acceptable ranges of tolerances for each feature on the bracket. An interesting note considering the holes on the bracket is that they must fit into a rectangular start point as defined by the center hole specification. Any center point located within the 0.014×0.020 rectangle (as defined by ± 0.007 and ± 0.010 specification) is an acceptable start point. If we were to create the maximum material condition (MMC) specification for the part (the silhouette into which we can fit a mating component), the silhouette of the holes would not be round, but would look as shown in Figure 2.24.

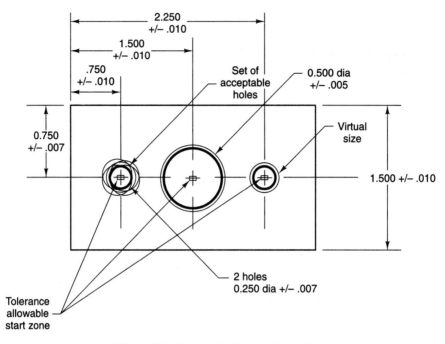

Figure 2.24   Interpreting the virtual part size.

Figure 2.25 contains a similar part with specification for square holes instead of the round ones in Figure 2.21. Again, the MMC interpretation of the holes is shown in Figure 2.26. The translation of square holes produces a larger but still square hole image. For prismatic features (like square holes and boxes), parametric tolerances are quite intuitive; however, for symmetrical features, the resultant specification may not provide an interpretation that a designer is seeking.

Figure 2.27 contains essentially the same part shown in Figure 2.21, but with geometric tolerance specification. The tolerances for the symmetric features (holes) are now specified using form geometry symbols, for example, $\oplus$, $\bigcirc$, and $\not\bigcirc$. The hole features in the figure are specified as MMC entities. This means that a *virtual size* for assembly is specified. This *virtual size* is specified as the MMC for all of the part features, and represents the minimum opening for all such labeled entities. For female features such as hole features, the virtual size is specified as

$$\xi_v = \xi_s - \tau_s - \gamma_s$$

where

ξ_v = virtual size of the feature
ξ_s = nominal size specification of the feature

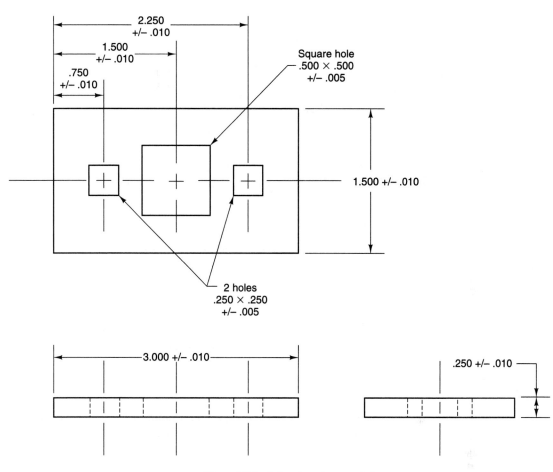

Figure 2.25 A drawing of square holes.

τ_s = negative tolerance specification

γ_s = form geometric value

For male features such as a shaft, the virtual size is specified as

$$\xi_v = \xi_s + \tau_s + \gamma_s$$

For the small holes shown in Figure 2.20, the virtual size of the holes is

$$\xi_v = 0.250 - 0.007 - 0.007 = 0.236$$

For the large hole, the virtual size is

$$\xi_v = 0.500 - 0.005 - 0.010 = 0.485$$

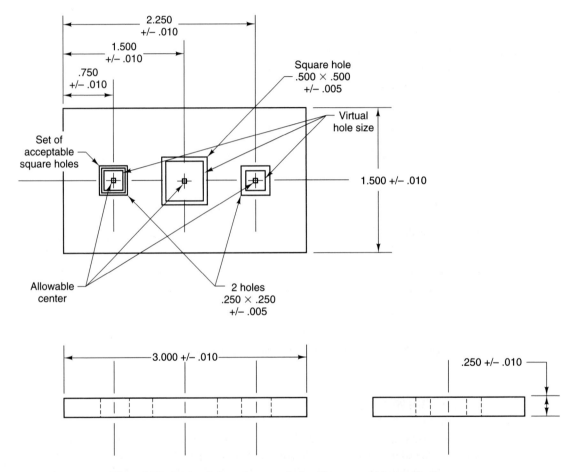

Figure 2.26   Interpretation of a square hole with a parametric specification.

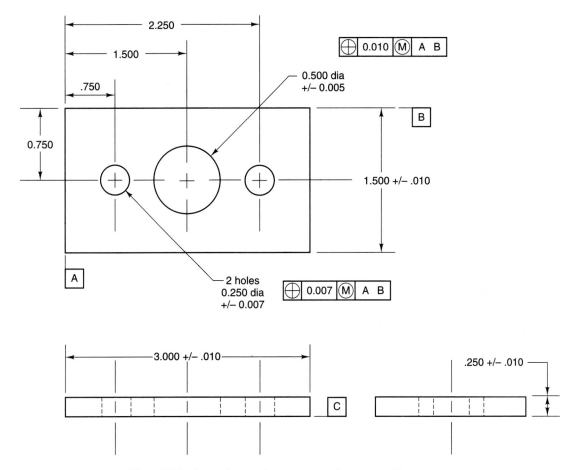

Figure 2.27   A part drawn using geometric tolerance specifications.

2.4 INSPECTION AND MEASUREMENT

The parts shown in Figures 2.21 and 2.27 look very similar but would potentially require different methods to manufacture as well as to inspect. We will discuss how the parts are produced in later chapters. The specification does dictate much of how the part can be produced, how the part can be fixtured, or how the part can be inspected.

The part in Figure 2.21 would require the use of conventional inspection equipment such as a vernier caliper or micrometer (inside and outside). If a large quantity of parts were to be produced and inspected, a set of gauges would most probably be used. The gauges that could be used to inspect the part would be a set of GO and NO GO gauges used to qualify the size for each of the holes. The small-hole GO gauge would be 0.243 inch. The NO GO gauge would be 0.257 inch. Similarly for the large hole, a GO gauge of 0.495 inch would be used and should fit into the hole, and a NO GO gauge of

0.505 inch should not fit into the hole. The length, width, and height of the bracket would also require measurement using either a vernier caliper or a set of GO and NO GO snap gauges. The position of the holes also would need to be checked, using either an optical comparator or a dowel and a vernier caliper. Each hole would be inspected independently from the leftmost and topmost surfaces because they are the implicit datum surfaces (dimensioned from) for the hole features.

The individual features for the part in Figure 2.27 will be inspected in a similar manner to the features for the part in Figure 2.21. The upper and lower feature size tolerances are the same and even the same gauges could be used in the inspection. Inspection for the location of the holes becomes far more simple and less time-consuming because geometric tolerances with MMC specifics (this is only true for MMC specifications) are used for the part. A GO gauge consisting of the mating component for the virtual part is all that is necessary to qualify the location of the holes. This gauge is shown in Figure 2.28. You should note from Figure 2.28 that the nominal tolerances for the

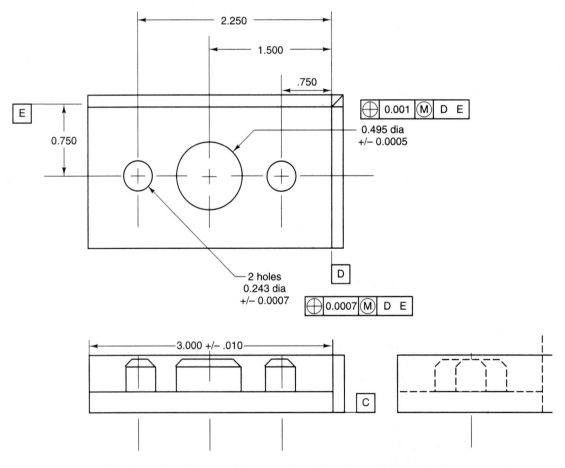

Figure 2.28   Location gauge to inspect hole position of a part in Figure 2.20.

gauge used to inspect the part are set using the *10 times rule* where the tolerances are 10 times tighter.

The parts used to illustrate how tolerances are interpreted are simple examples of engineered products. The point that the reader should glean from these examples is how tolerances are applied to drawings and features on the drawings. Datum surfaces on drawings usually become locating surfaces for fixturing and inspection. Designers and detailers frequently specify conditions that make manufacture and qualification of a product much more difficult than is necessary.

2.5 CONCLUDING REMARKS

In this chapter, we have discussed the basics of engineering drawing. Various methods of representing drawings along with drawing specifications were discussed. We have long used some form of icons to represent designs. We have evolved to a precise representation for the ideas that we convey as engineering drawings. As we fully immerse ourselves into the era of computer-aided design, we look to develop methods that can be automatically interpreted as well as compactly represented. We must be exceptionally careful that we fully understand the implications of our design and specification decisions. In this chapter, we presented both the standards to represent engineering specification as well as interpretations of the specification. In the chapters on process planning and tool engineering, we will look back to the detail specified on an engineering drawing to define methods for manufacture as well as methods to locate and support the product while it is being manufactured.

REVIEW QUESTIONS

2.1. What are the five major steps in a design process? Briefly explain each one.

2.2. What are internal representation and external representation in design?

2.3. Discuss how a design idea is represented in a designer's mind, that is, in the form of an equation, line drawing, and so on.

2.4. Discuss the advantages and disadvantages of using a three-dimensional solid model in mechanical part design.

2.5. Prepare a three-view drawing of the part shown in Figure 2.29.

2.6. What are the methods used in diameter inspection?

2.7. What kind of tolerance specification is necessary for the mating part shown in Figure 2.30 in order to ensure proper assembly?

2.8. What tolerance specifications are important for a tool holder for a NC machine?

2.9. Show the setup required for inspecting the part in Figure 2.31. If a part being inspected has the dimension shown in Figure 2.32, is it acceptable? Why?

2.10. Show that the unspecified dimensional tolerance is always the sum of all tolerances of the dimensions used to calculate this unspecified dimension. You may use Figure 2.33 to show your proof.

4 holes 1/4" at 3.5" pitch circle

through slot

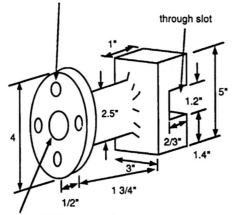

1"

2.5"

1.2"

5"

2/3"

1.4"

4

3"

1 3/4"

1/2"

through hole, 2" dia

Figure 2.29

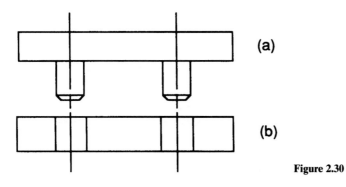

(a)

(b)

Figure 2.30

2.000 ±0.001 $\oplus$ $\varnothing$0.001Ⓜ A B

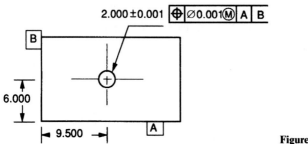

B

6.000

9.500

A

Figure 2.31

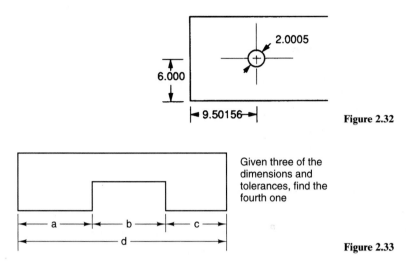

Figure 2.32

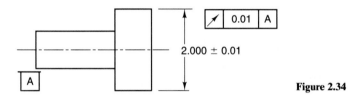

Given three of the dimensions and tolerances, find the fourth one

Figure 2.33

2.11. What does the tolerance specification in Figure 2.34 mean (illustrate with a figure)?

Figure 2.34

2.12. Given Figures 2.35(a) and 2.35(b), show their corresponding hole center tolerance zones. [Draw the shapes of each tolerance zone and its size; for (b), assume the produced hole is at MMC.]

2.13. What are the allowable true position tolerances of the hole in Figure 2.35(b)?

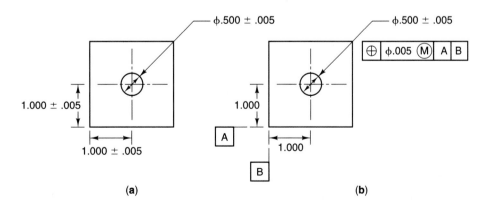

Figure 2.35

Produced hole size	Tolerance
0.495	
0.497	
0.500	
0.505	
0.508	

2.14. The tolerance of a hole is specified:

$\varnothing$ $1.000^{+0.003}_{-0.003}$ $\boxed{\oplus}$ $\boxed{\varnothing\ 0.03\ \text{Ⓜ}\ \boxed{\text{A}}\ \boxed{\text{B}}\ \boxed{\text{C}}}$

Show the true position tolerance value at the following produced hole size: 0.995, 0.997, 0.999, 1.000, 1.001, 1.002, 1.003, and 1.005

2.15. Why do we use MMC and LMC? Should RFS be sufficient for all applications?

2.16. Show the differences between (a) straightness and flatness, (b) roundness and cylindricity, and (c) runout and total amount. You may use figures to illustrate the differences.

2.17. The part in Figure 2.36 is made using two setups. Show whether all tolerances specified can be made.

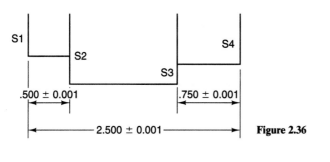

Figure 2.36

```
Setup I: Clamp on the left-hand side
  10 Turn up to S3
  11 Face S4
Setup 2: Clamp on the right-hand side
  20 Turn up to S2
  21 Face S1
```

Assume the process accuracy is 0.0005 in. The setup accuracy is 0.0005 in. Can the correct part be produced? Show your calculations.

REFERENCES/BIBLIOGRAPHY

EARLE, J. H. (1990). *Engineering Design Graphics,* 6th ed. Reading, MA: Addison-Wesley.

FOSTER, L. W. (1994). *Geo-Metrics III: The Application of Geometric Tolerancing Techniques.* Reading, MA: Addison-Wesley.

GOOLDY, G. (1995). *Geometric Dimensioning and Tolerancing.* Englewood Cliffs, NJ: Prentice Hall.

SUH, N. P. (1982). "Qualitative and Quantitative Analysis of Design and Manufacturing Axioms," *CIRP Annals,* 31, 333–338.

VOELCKER, H. B. (1993). "A Current Perspective on Tolerancing and Metrology," *Manufacturing Review,* 6, 4.

VOELCKER, H. B. and A. A. G. REQUICHA (1977). "Geometric Modeling of Mechanical Parts and Processes," *Computer,* 10, 12, 48–57.

3

Computer-Aided Design

Computer-aided design (CAD) can be most simply described as "using a computer in the design process." In the design process, a computer can be used in both the representation and the analysis steps. The application of CAD for representation is not limited to drafting. Three-dimensional, wire-frame modeling, boundary representation (B-rep) modeling, and solid modeling are representation methods available to CAD users. To aid in engineering analysis, there are packages that perform kinematic simulation, circuit analysis and simulation, and finite-element modeling. The application domain includes mechanical engineering applications, architecture and construction engineering applications, electronic circuits, printed-circuit board layout, IC layout, and so on. CAD systems frequently consist of a collection of many application modules under a common (not always) database and graphics editor.

CAD systems can be classified in several ways:

BY SYSTEM HARDWARE

Mainframe
Minicomputer
Engineering workstation
Microcomputer

BY APPLICATION AREA

Mechanical engineering
Circuit design and board layout
Architectural design and construction engineering
Cartography

BY MODELING METHOD

Two-dimensional drafting
Three-dimensional drawing

Sculptured surface

Three-dimensional solid modeling

In this section, the basic technology used in CAD and its applications are discussed in order to provide an overall picture of CAD.

3.1 A BRIEF HISTORY OF CAD

Before we present the basics of CAD, it is appropriate to give a brief history. CAD is a product of the computer era. It originated from early computer graphic systems, to the development of interactive computer graphics. Two such systems include the Sage Project at the Massachusetts Institute of Technology (MIT), and Sketchpad (Sutherland, 1963). The Sage Project was aimed at developing CRT displays and operating systems. Sketchpad was developed under the Sage Project. A CRT display and light pen input were used to interact with the system. This, coincidentally, happened at about the same time that NC and APT (Automatically Programmed Tool) first appeared. Later, X–Y plotters were used as the standard hard-copy output device for computer graphics. An interesting note is that an X–Y plotter has the same basic structure as an NC drilling machine except that a pen is substituted for the tool on the NC spindle.

In the beginning, CAD systems were no more than graphics editors with some built-in design symbols. The geometry available to the user was limited to lines, circular arcs, and the combination of the two. The development of free-form curves and surfaces, such as Coon's patch, Ferguson's patch, Bezier's patch, and B-spline, enables a CAD system to be used for sophisticated curves and surface design. Three-dimensional CAD systems allow a designer to move into the third dimension. Because a three-dimensional model (model is the data abstraction in a computer) contains enough information for NC cutter-path programming, the linkage between CAD and NC can be developed. So called turnkey CAD/CAM systems were developed based on this concept and became popular in the 1970s and 1980s.

The 1970s marked the beginning of a new era in CAD—the invention of three-dimensional solid modeling. In the past, three-dimensional, wire-frame models represented an object only by its bounding edges. They are ambiguous in the sense that several interpretations might be possible for a single model. There is also no way to find the volumetric information of a model. Solid models contain complete information; therefore, not only can they be used to produce engineering drawings, but engineering analysis can be performed on the same model as well. Solid modelers such as PADL-1 and PADL-2 (Voelcker and Requicha, 1977), Synthavision, BUILD-1 and BUILD-2 (Braid, 1973), COMPAC, EUCLID, GLIDE, and so on, were developed in the 1970s. Later, many commercial systems and research systems were developed. Quite a few of these systems were based on the PADL and BUILD systems. Although they are powerful in representation, many deficiencies still exist. For example, such systems have extreme computation and resource (memory) requirements, an unconventional way of modeling objects, and a lack of tolerancing capability have all hindered CAD applications.

It was not until the mid-1980s that solid modelers made their way into the design environment. Today, their use is as common as drafting and wire-frame model applications.

CAD implementations on personal computers (PCs) have brought CAD to the masses. This development has made CAD available and affordable. CAD originally was a tool used only by aerospace and other major industrial corporations. The introduction of PC CAD packages, such as, AutoCAD, VersaCAD, CADKEY, and so on, has made it possible for small companies and even individuals to own and use CAD systems. By 1988, more than 100,000 PC CAD packages had been sold. Today, PC-based solid modelers are available and are becoming increasingly popular. Because rapid developments in microcomputers have enabled PCs to carry the heavy computational load necessary for solid modeling, many solid modelers now run on PCs, and the platform has become less of an issue. With the standard graphics user interface (GUI), CAD systems can be ported easily from one computer to another. Most major CAD systems are able to run on a variety of platforms. There is little difference between mainframe, workstation, and PC-based CAD systems.

3.2 THE ARCHITECTURE OF CAD

A CAD system consists of three major parts:

1. Hardware: computer and input/output (I/O) devices
2. Operating system software
3. Application software: CAD package

Hardware is used to support the software functions. A wide range of hardware are used in CAD systems. This hardware will be discussed later. The operating system software is the interface between the CAD application software and the hardware. It supervises the operation of the hardware and provides basic functions such as creating and removing operating tasks, controlling the progress of tasks, allocating hardware resources among tasks, and providing access to software resources such as files, editors, compilers, and utility programs. It is important not only for CAD software, but for non-CAD software.

The application software is the heart of a CAD system. It consists of programs that do 2-D and 3-D modeling, drafting, and engineering analysis. The functionality of a CAD system is built into the application software. It is the application software that makes one CAD package different from another. Application software is usually operating-system-dependent. To transport a CAD system running in one operating system to another operating system is not as trivial as recompiling the software. Therefore, attention must be given to the operating system as well. Details of application software are also discussed in Section 3.5.

A general architecture of a CAD system is shown in Figure 3.1. The application software is at the top level and is used to manipulate the CAD model database. The graphics utility system performs the coordinate transformation, windowing, and display control. Because there may be several different I/O devices used, device drivers are

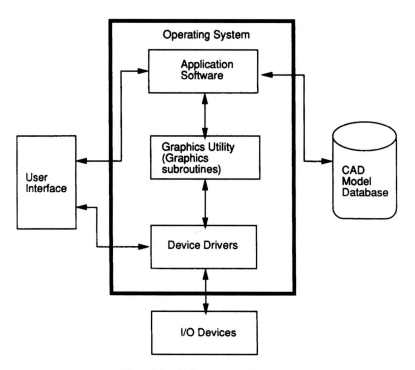

Figure 3.1   CAD system architecture.

used to translate the data into and out of the specific data format used by each device. They also control the devices. The operating system is run in background to coordinate the entire operation. Finally, a user interface links the human and the system.

3.3 MODELING OBJECTS

Before we discuss specific applications of CAD, it is worthwhile to study the information and knowledge built into CAD systems. In this section, object modeling and CAD operation are discussed. The model of an engineering object consists of geometry, topology, and auxiliary information. Geometry includes points, lines, circles, planes, cylinders, and other surfaces. It defines the basic shape characteristics. Topology represents the relationships of the geometry of an object. For example, a tube is an object with a through axial hole. Its geometry is very different than a doughnut. However, it has the same topology as a doughnut. Topology is very important in solid models. In addition to its shape, an engineering object also possesses some other attributes. Dimensions, tolerances, and surface finish are some important attributes.

CAD is a tool used not only to represent an engineering model, but also to manipulate it. To construct or display a model, geometric transformations and view transformations are needed. In this section, various aspects of object modeling and manipulation are discussed.

3.3.1 Basic Geometry

A component must be modeled before it can be drawn. In a conventional drafting system, a component is modeled using simple two-dimensional geometry (Figure 3.2). A drawing consists of line segments, circles, and curves. Points are also used to help locate other geometries. For example, a line can be defined by the coordinates of its two end points, one end point and an angle, the tangent line to two circles, and so on. In conventional manual drafting, a draftsperson uses drafting instruments such as rulers, triangles, T-squares, scales, and different templates to layout the geometry. Additional ways to define a specific geometric entity give more flexibility to the draftsperson and make the final model more accurate. The model does not contain the definition itself.

A model can also be configured using an APT-like (circles, lines, points, and so on; see Chapter 9) language to define geometric features. This type of model is stored in a data structure (e.g., the structure in Figure 3.3). The data structure is designed so that geometric manipulation is made possible and efficient. Some of the basic manipulation operations include adding a geometry entity, deleting a geometry entity, modifying the attributes or parameters of a geometry, and transforming (rotating, scaling, translating) all or part of the entire model. In addition to the basic geometry, many attributes must

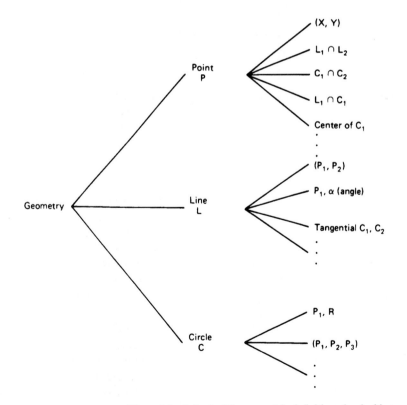

Figure 3.2   Subset of the geometric definitions for drafting.

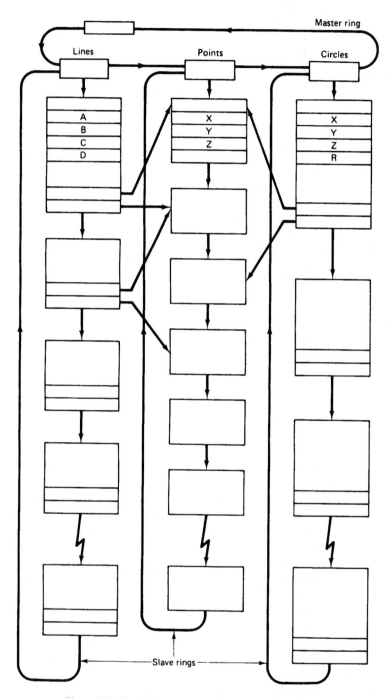

Figure 3.3   Typical data structure for geometric entities.

be included in the model. Text data are also necessary for definition. Some of the attributes of the text include line style (solid or dashed), line thickness, color, and so on. Text data are used to annotate a drawing. Data, such as dimension and tolerance, drafting notes, and so on, are essential to a drawing and must be included. The drawing (Figure 3.4) obtained using such a system is basically the same as that created by a draftsperson.

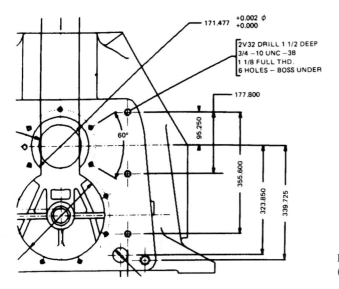

Figure 3.4   Drawing from a CAD system. (Courtesy of Schlumberger CAD/CAM.)

Modeling a part in two dimensions cannot satisfy the need of many engineering applications. Furthermore, an orthogonal or perspective drawing cannot be made directly from a 2-D model. Adding the third dimension is not as easy as it first appears. Because the display is always flat (two-dimensional), it lacks the third dimension to work on. A drawing shown on a display is always a projection. To select any geometry on a display, a user can either type in the 3-D coordinates or specify the "layer" on which the geometry resides, and then interactively select the geometry. A "layer" is an imaginary display plane defined by a user. Each layer resides on a different Z depth.

Even with the third dimension added to a model, it still only represents the skeleton of a part. There is no way to tell, among all the surfaces, which can be constructed by a loop of edges (lines and curves), which ones are on the part and which ones are not. Therefore, no effective hidden line or hidden surface removal can be performed. Face information has to be added to the model so that hidden lines can be removed and "features" assembled.

Any object can be modeled using a set of primitives. A convenient primitive is a polyhedron (Figure 3.5). A polyhedron is a bounded object with n faces. Each face is a planar polygon (Figure 3.6) that can be modeled by using an ordered list of the vertices (points) or by a similar list of its edges (lines). Wire-frame displays then can be generated using the edges of the polyhedron. However, the hidden lines or hidden surfaces

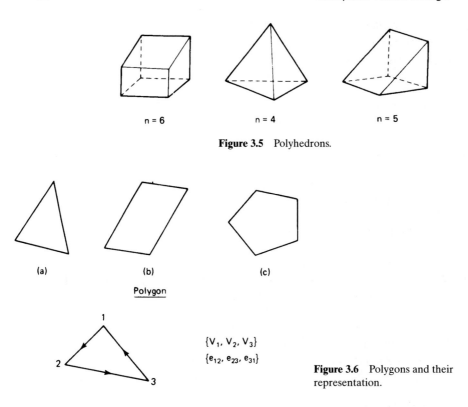

Figure 3.5   Polyhedrons.

$\{V_1, V_2, V_3\}$
$\{e_{12}, e_{23}, e_{31}\}$

Figure 3.6   Polygons and their representation.

cannot be removed from the display without defining faces on the object. Faces can hide edges, whereas edges cannot hide other edges.

3.4 CAD HARDWARE

3.4.1 Computers

There are two major types of hardware used in a CAD system: computer and input/output (I/O) devices. In the early days of CAD, some commercial CAD systems used proprietary computers. Today, nearly all CAD software runs on a general-purpose computer.

Depending on the complexity of the CAD package, it may require a mainframe computer, a minicomputer, or simply a microcomputer. In general, the more functionalities a CAD system provides, the more powerful the computer needed. Three-dimensional solid modelers require much more computing than do two-dimensional drafting systems; thus, they need more powerful computers. Systems that integrate engineering analysis or simulation packages generally are more computation-intensive. A powerful computer not only speeds up the response of a CAD system, but also can support multiple users without significant performance degradation.

Several other parameters and components concerning the computer also have to be considered. These are random-access memory (RAM) capacity

permanent disk-storage capacity

special graphics accelerator

tape backups

RAM is the actual physical memory (vs. virtual memory) of a computer. A small memory capacity means slow processing due to frequent swapping between the physical memory and the virtual memory on disk. Because CAD is extremely storage-demanding, disk capacity is important. Small disk capacity limits the system to the storage of only a few drawings. CAD is graphics-based and requires tremendous data processing. A graphics accelerator can drastically increase the performance of the system. Another component, the hard disk, is typically the major cost of a computer system. Therefore, it is not cost-justifiable to store all drawings on line on disk. Magnetic tape is still the most economical medium to use for off-line data storage. It is necessary for a CAD system to have a tape backup subsystem.

Currently, all levels of computers are used in CAD systems. Personal computers are used in low-cost, 2-D drafting applications, and with the new power of these computers, they are also being used for some 3-D solid modeling applications. Engineering workstations have been the mainstay in CAD, and are usually a single-user CAD workstation in a network. Minicomputers are used in multiuser CAD systems. Mainframes are used for large multiuser CAD systems to support real-time simulation and engineering analysis. Sometimes, in a large corporation, all levels of CAD systems are implemented. All these systems are linked together through a hierarchical computer network.

3.4.2 Input/Output (I/O) Devices

Figure 3.7 shows the typical I/O devices used in a CAD system. Input devices are generally used to transfer information from a human or storage medium to a computer where "CAD functions" are carried out. A keyboard is the standard input device used to transmit alphanumeric data to the system. Function keypads are also used to make input easier. Joysticks, track balls, and mouses are also used to manipulate a cursor. They can be used to position the graphic cursor (e.g., cross hair) on a monitor and feed back the location of an object on the monitor to the computer. Using these devices allows an operator to address terminal locations interactively. Joysticks and track balls are not used widely in CAD systems because of the difficulty in reaching an accurate position. Mouses have been used extensively with windows and pull-down menus. They are easy to use for pointing; however, using a mouse to trace a curve is not an easy task.

A light pen can also be used for interactive graphics (locational information is fed back discretely to the computer). A light pen is used to pick up items directly on the monitor display. It has been used since the beginning of interactive computer graphics and CAD. However, because it has to be used directly on the screen, the user must hold the pen in an elevated position. This can be tiring after an extended period of time.

There are three basic approaches to input an existing drawing: (1) model the object on a drawing, (2) digitize the drawing, or (3) scan the object. Digitizing is usually much easier than modeling. A digitizer is a device that translates the X–Y locations on a drawing into a digital signal and feeds that signal to a computer. Graphics scanners scan

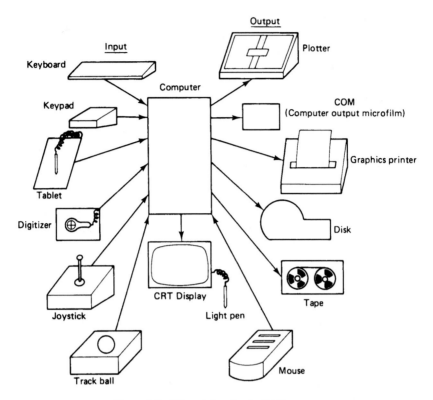

Figure 3.7   I/O peripherals of a CAD system.

a drawing and convert it to a CAD-system-readable format. Some scanners have built-in character-recognition software that can convert characters on paper into ASCII codes. Another input device is a sketch pad called a graphics tablet. A graphics tablet is a special flat surface on which a user draws with a stylus. The location of the stylus is sent to the computer. The tablet is an absolute coordinate device. It is easy to implement overlay menus on the tablet and pull down menus on the screen to improve the operation. Currently, the tablet is the most popular input device used in CAD other than the keyboard.

The standard output device for CAD is a monitor display. Modern monitor displays are raster-scan display monitors. Similar to a TV monitor, an electron gun (Sony Trinitron uses three guns for three basic colors) sends an electronic beam to the front of the monitor. Each display dot is called a pixel (picture element). For color displays, each pixel is represented by three closely located dots with red, green, and blue colors. The electronic beam selects the color elements and the intensity of each color element. The resolution of the monitor is determined by the number of pixels displayable on the screen (i.e., 640×480, 1024×1024) and the pixel dot size (.24 pitch, .32 pitch, and so on). The color or gray-scale resolution is determined by the number of different colors or gray scales displayable at each pixel, usually measured in bits. A 1-bit display can turn each pixel either ON or OFF. A gray scale has at least 2 bits which allow three light intensities plus an OFF (2^2). Usually, displays are 4 bits (16 colors), 8 bits (256 colors), 16 bits (thousands of colors), and 24 bits (millions of colors). The electronic beam sweeps the screen from the top to the bottom line by line. Because the dot is lit for only a very short period of time, the sweep must be done very quickly in order not to have a flickering image. The refresh rate is a measure of how many times the monitor is redrawn in one second.

The computer does not draw directly on the monitor. Connecting the computer to the monitor is usually a RGB (red, green, blue) cable. Three separate signal lines are connected. On the graphics board in the computer are circuits to generate the analog signals required to drive the monitor. There is also a frame buffer that serves as memory to store the image. Each pixel on the screen has a corresponding address in the frame buffer. The data in the frame buffer are converted into the appropriate analog signal and sent to the monitor at the refresh rate. Separately, the computer writes directly to the frame buffer the image it intends to draw. The greater the display size and number of colors, the more frame buffer is needed. The frame buffer on the graphics board is made of random-access memory (RAM).

3.5 CAD SOFTWARE

CAD software is what gives a CAD system its functionality and personality. Software can be classified based on the technology used:

1. 2-D drawing
2. Basic 3-D drawing
3. Sculptured surfaces
4. 3-D solid modeling
5. Engineering analysis

Some of the commonly available functions provided by CAD software are

1. Picture manipulation: add, delete, and modify geometry and text
2. Display transformation: scaling, rotation, pan, zoom, and partial erasing
3. Drafting symbols: standard drafting symbols
4. Printing control: output device selection, configuration, and control
5. Operator aid: screen menus, tablet overlay, function keys
6. File management: create, delete, and merge picture files

Each of the CAD system classifications is discussed in what follows.

3.5.1 2-D Drawing

Two-dimensional (2-D) drawing systems correspond directly to traditional engineering drawings. Basically, they are designed as a substitute for manual drafting. The early CAD systems are mostly of this type. Even today, for many users, it is still the most familiar tool to use. Applications of 2-D drawing systems include

1. Mechanical part drawing
2. Wiring diagram
3. Printed-circuit board design and layout
4. Pattern nesting (sheet metal and garment)
5. Facilities layout
6. Architectural design and construction engineering
7. Graphics art, technical publication
8. Cartography

Nearly all CAD systems support 2-D drawing in one way or another. Even 3-D systems usually can produce 2-D drawings from their 3-D database.

3.5.2 Basic 3-D Drawing

Basic 3-D drawing systems include 3-D wire-frame, $2\frac{1}{2}$-D drawing, and cartography. A 3-D wire-frame model describes the edges and outlines of curves; see Figure 3.8(a). A $2\frac{1}{2}$-D model is a 2-D model with a constant Z-axis dimension. Some cartography models can use digitized terrain data to produce contour and/or 3-D drawings. Basic 3-D models are easy to generate and work with, are simple to store and manipulate in computers, and are useful as visual aids. However, because there is no information on the surfaces nor the inside or outside of the object, the notion of solidity is not conveyed.

For example, the object represented by a wire-frame model in Figure 3.8(a) can be (b), or (c), or (d). A wire-frame model is ambiguous. The absence of surfaces also makes it difficult to support fully automatic hidden-line or hidden-surface removal routing.

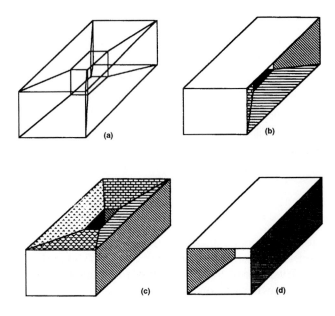

Figure 3.8 Ambiguity of a wire-frame model.

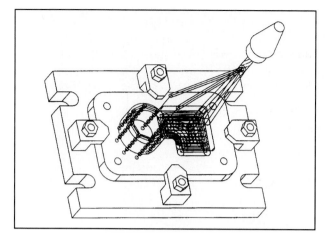

Figure 3.9   NC tool-path generation and simulation. (Courtesy of Gerber Systems Technology.)

Despite these limitations, 3-D wire-frame models are useful for many applications. Some of the applications include the following:

MECHANICAL ENGINEERING

1. Part design
2. Assembly design
3. NC tool path (Figure 3.9)
4. Robot programming

ARCHITECTURAL ENGINEERING AND CONSTRUCTION

1. Building design
2. Structural analysis
3. Piping layout and analysis
4. Site planning
5. Interior design

ELECTRICAL AND ELECTRONIC ENGINEERING

1. Integrated-circuit (IC) chip layout
2. Printed-circuit-board layout

CARTOGRAPHY

1. Map preparation

Many of the so-called CAD/CAM systems are 3-D wire-frame systems with interactive NC tool-path generation capability. Many 3-D wire-frame systems allow users to add faces to the model; therefore, hidden-surface routines can be used.

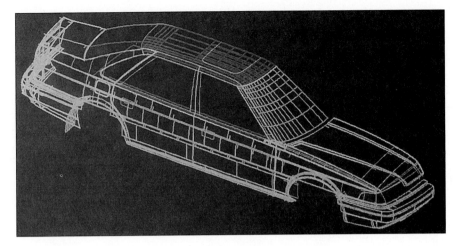

Figure 3.10   Surface model from "CAD CAM: From Principles to Practice", by Chris McMahon and Jimmie Browne. (Courtesy Addison-Wesley.)

3.5.3 Free-Form Curves and Surface Modeling

Basic 3-D models can only model simple geometries such as points, lines, circles, planes, and analytical surfaces. Some curves and surfaces that are produced by free-hand drawing belong to a separate class. In most 2-D design systems and graphics packages, free-form curves are available and integrated. Among them, the most popular is Bezier's curve. B-spline curves are also available in some systems. Free-form surfaces, also called sculptured surfaces, are usually available in more sophisticated packages. Figure 3.10 shows a surface model. They are usually used for the following applications:

1. Die and mold design and manufacturing
2. Automobile, ship, and aircraft body design
3. Commercial artwork

A free-form surface may be designed directly on a computer using control points or obtained through surface fitting from a digitized data set. In the first case, an interactive design session allows the designer to sculpture the model through moving control points on the screen. In the later case, either from an existing object or a clay model sculptured by hand, a scanner digitizes the surface points and feeds them into a math model for surface fitting.

Commonly used free-form surface models are bicubic surfaces, such as Bezier's surface (16 control points), B-spline surface (> 16 control points), nonuniform rational B-spline surface (NURB) (control points, knot spacing, and point weights). More details are presented in later sections of this chapter.

3.5.4 3-D Solid Modeling

All the CAD modeling methods discussed so far can produce only drawings. There is no volume information stored in the model. For many applications, it is essential that the volume information can be derived from the design model. 3-D solid modeling is a solution to this requirement. A 3-D solid model not only captures the complete geometry of an object, but it also can differentiate the inside and the outside of the space occupied by the object in three-dimensional space. By using this property, the volume of the object and the intersection between two objects can be calculated. Many other volume-related properties can also be obtained from the model. Hidden-surface/line removal and a shaded image can be produced as well.

When classifying a solid model, its internal representation is usually used. The internal representation is how a computer stores the model. It is different from the external representation, which is how the picture or image is displayed. There are six different types of solid internal representation schemes (see Figure 3.11):

1. Primitive instancing
2. Spatial occupancy enumeration (SOE)
3. Cell decomposition
4. Constructive solid geometry (CSG)
5. Boundary representation (B-rep)
6. Sweeping

Primitive instancing is one kind of solid representation; see Figure 3.11(a). It can be used to represent a family of objects. This family of objects is parameterized. An object instance can be defined by assigning values to the parameters. It can be used effectively to represent standard parts with different dimensions. GT coding can be also considered as an application of pure primitive instancing (Requicha, 1980). The model is extremely concise because it only has a model name and a set of parameters. For this reason, it is difficult to do geometric operation directly on the pure primitive instancing model. The model must be converted into another model, such as a B-rep model, before any operation can be performed.

Spatial occupancy enumeration (SOE) is a technique that records all spatial cells that are occupied by the object; see Figure 3.11(b). SOE is equivalent to storing the physical object in sections. To describe the object accurately, very small cells must be used. The massive memory required for even small objects makes this representation virtually useless in general engineering design. The required memory equals the object volume divided by the cell volume. When many engineering applications require 0.001 in accuracy, the volume of each cell is 10^{-9} in.^{3} Even a small engineering object requires an enormous amount of memory storage.

Cell decomposition is a general class of spatial occupancy enumeration. The representation is difficult to create. A solid is decomposed into simple solid cells with no holes, whose interiors are pairwise disjoint; see Figure 3.11(c). A solid is the result of "gluing" component cells that satisfy certain "boundary-matching" conditions. Because cell size is a variable, it requires many fewer cells and thus less memory than that for SOE. Boolean operations are used to manipulate objects. The operation can be difficult to perform.

Constructive solid geometry (CSG) is a superior system for creating 3-D models. Using primitive shapes (Figure 3.12) as building blocks, CSG employs Boolean set operators ($\cup$ union, $-$ difference, and $\cap$ intersection) to construct an object; see

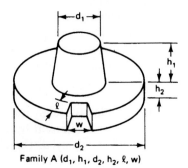

Family A (d_1, h_1, d_2, h_2, ℓ, w)

(a) Pure primitive instancing

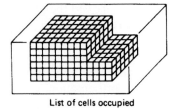

List of cells occupied

(b) Spatial occupancy enumeration

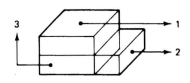

Cells 1, 2, and 3

(c) Cell decomposition

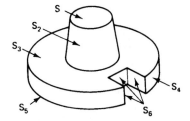

(d) CSG: (Δ · dif · Δ) · un · (<img> · dif · <img>)

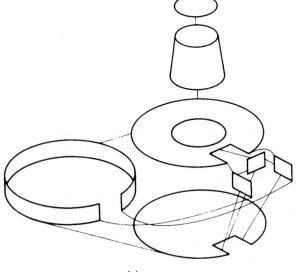

(e) Boundary:

Figure 3.11   Three-dimensional representation sketches.

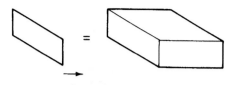
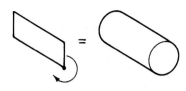

Translation sweep   Rotation sweep

Tool

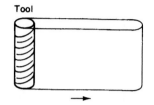

Translation sweep of a tool

(f) Sweeping

Figure 3.11   (Continued)

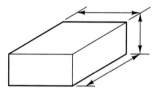

Block   Cylinder

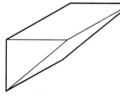

Wedge   Sphere

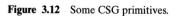

Cone   Torus   **Figure 3.12**   Some CSG primitives.

Figure 3.13. A CSG model is represented by a tree structure (Figure 3.14). At the terminals are primitives with dimensions (size of the primitive) and a coordinate transform (location and orientation of the primitive). At the nodes are Boolean operators. CSG models are not unique. The same object may be modeled using different primitives and operation sequences (Figure 3.15).

A CSG model may be displayed by using the ray-tracing technique. Parallel rays cast toward the object either hit the object or miss the object. When a ray hits the object, it reflects the light back to the observer. Depending on the lighting, object texture, and the intersection angle between the ray and the object surface, the light reflection can be calculated. The reflection is displayed on the screen. Because a simple ray has the form of $x = a, y = b$, the intersection can be calculated very easily and often implemented in firmware (burned into a chip installed in the computer or terminal). Ray tracing can be done on individual primitives. Then the proper Boolean operation is done to determine the final result. Therefore, there is no need to convert the CSG tree model into some other model before it is displayed.

An alternative way of displaying the object that is more frequently used is to convert the CSG tree into B-rep first, and then the B-rep is drawn. The process is called "boundary evaluation." Because B-rep has many useful properties, the conversion not only makes the display easy, but also provides other benefits. Figure 3.16 illustrates the CSG operations. The user of a CSG system has to work only with the primitives and Boolean operators. The rest is taken care of by the modeler.

Boundary representations (B-rep) are also used to identify an object. In these systems, objects are represented by their bounding faces. Faces are further divided and represented by edges and vertices; see Figure 3.11(e). A set of operators, called Euler operators, are available to build a B-rep from the ground up. To build a B-rep model by hand is very tedious. Most B-rep models are derived from a CSG model through boundary evaluation. More details of the B-rep will be presented in Section 3.7.

Sweeping is another powerful modeling tool for certain types of geometry. There are two types of sweeping: translation and rotation; see Figure 3.11(f). Translation sweeping of a rectangle produces a box. Rotation sweeping of the same rectangle produces a cylinder. Rotation sweeping can be used to create turned parts. In some design systems, an arbitrarily drawn face can be swept along either a line or a curve (translation sweeping). Very complex shapes can be created through this process. A manufacturing application of sweeping is NC cutting simulation. The removal volume can be represented by the sweeping of a tool.

Currently, the majority of 3-D solid modelers are based on either CSG or B-rep representations. CSG data input is the most popular. Often, many face types can be used in the solid model. The 3-D solid models discussed so far are called "manifold" models (2-manifold). In a 3-D manifold model, the dimensionality is maintained. The B-rep of an object consists only of bounded faces with no loose edges or faces. Each edge is bounded by exactly two vertices and is adjacent to exactly two faces. Each vertex belongs to one disk (traveling from one adjacent face to another, it will never cross the vertex itself). The manifold model does not allow any dangling faces or edges. It satisfies the Euler formula (Section 3.7.1). However, there are also "nonmanifold" modelers. A nonmanifold model allows additional faces and edges to exist in a solid model. To

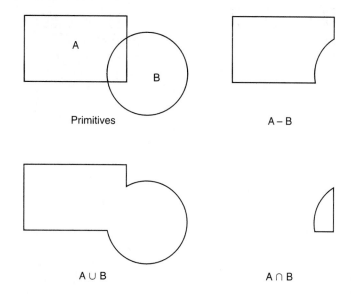

Primitives   A – B

A ∪ B   A ∩ B

Figure 3.13   Boolean operators.

a. Part

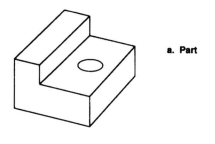

b. CSG Tree

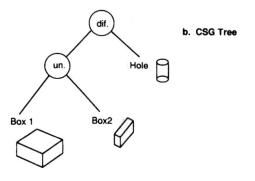

Hole = CYL(...) AT(...)   c. Instructions to construct part
Box1 = BLO(...) AT(...)
Box2 = BLO(...) AT(...)
Box = Box1 UN Box2
Part = Box DIF Hole   **Figure 3.14**   CSG example.

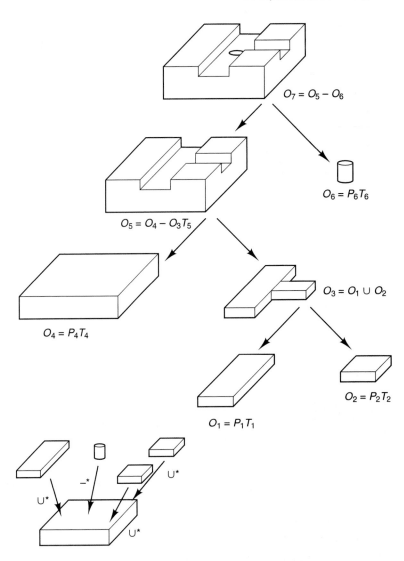

Figure 3.15   Alternative CSG models of an object.

track the inside and outside is more complex. A nonmanifold modeler such as ACIS (used in many CAD systems including AutoCAD R13) allows much more flexibility. More of the design intention can be saved in the design model.

When solid-model representation is complete, engineering analysis can be performed directly with the model. The solid-model representation also provides a common linkage among design, analysis, and manufacturing. The existence of solid modelers is essential for automated manufacturing environs.

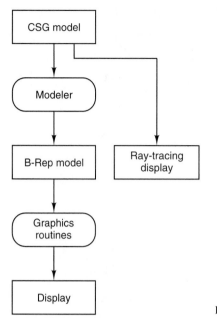

Figure 3.16 CSG operations.

3.5.5 Engineering Analysis

Engineering analyses commonly conducted on a design include finite-element analysis (FEA), volume and weight calculations, kinematic simulation, and circuit analysis and simulation. The most widely used group of methods for analysis is finite-element analysis, which is widely used in the following:

1. Static and dynamic analysis of complex structures such as aircraft, bridges, buildings, cars, dams, and so on
2. Fluid flow, diffusion and consolidation problems
3. Lubrication problems
4. Heat conduction and thermal stresses

   In finite-element analysis, a complex body is decomposed into basic elements, each having a geometric shape and made of a single material (Figure 3.17). The physical characteristics of each element can be determined by classical theories. The problem is then solved as a set of simultaneous equations for all the elements. Therefore, the first step in finite-element analysis is to partition the model of an engineering object into discrete elements. A CAD system can be used to design the object and help in automatic mesh generation. After the analysis results are returned by the software, the CAD system can display the results graphically to permit the visual interpretation of analysis results.

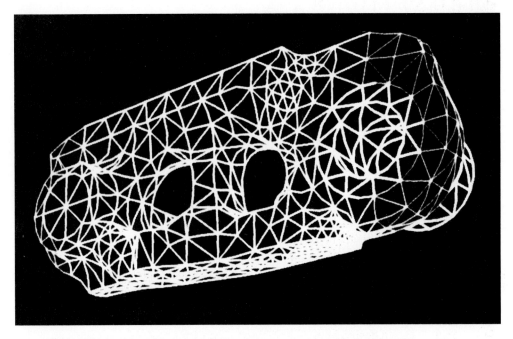

Figure 3.17   Finite-element analysis. (a) A finite-element model is constructed from a part design stored in the database (in this case, a wheel). (b) The nodes and elements are interactively constructed from the part-design geometry. (Courtesy of Structural Dynamics Research Corporation.)

3.6 CAD SYSTEM EXAMPLES

In the previous sections, engineering design and computer-aided design were discussed. In this section, examples of using CAD systems are shown. Two different CAD systems, CATIA and AutoCAD, are used. CATIA is a mainframe-based CAD system marketed by IBM. AutoCAD is a personal-computer-based system developed and marketed by AutoDesk. They are both very popular but represent CAD systems implemented on two extreme levels of computers. Their functionalities are introduced in this section.

3.6.1 CATIA

CATIA is a computer-aided design and computer-aided manufacturing (CAD/CAM) graphics system marketed by IBM. It consists of a base module, which provides the basic interactive graphics functions, and several application modules. The application modules include the following:

   3-D design: for 3-D design
   Drafting: for drafting
   Advanced surfaces: for sculptured-surfaces design
   Solid geometry: for solid geometry design

Kinematics: for kinematics simulation

Building design: for architectural design

Library: for custom symbols and objects define, storage, and classify

Numerical control: for NC part programming

Robotics: for design, stimulation, and programming robot cells

A common database is shared among all applications. Preprocessors and post-processors are available to translate between CATIA and IGES (initial graphics exchange specification) data format.

CATIA runs on IBM 308X, 303X, and 43XX computers under the VM/CMS operating system. It can be configured either with one terminal or two terminals per workstation (Figure 3.18). When two terminals are used, one is used as an alphanumeric terminal and the other one for graphics display. A processor associated with the terminal is used to relieve the central processor of display transformations, coloring, and shading. IBM 5080 and IBM 3270 terminals are normally used.

The design data are organized into projects, models, sheets, and libraries. With this organization, a large design project can be managed effectively. Projects are used to include all the designs in a project. Models contain all the parts and their relations for a device being designed. Sheets are individual drawings to be printed. Libraries contain commonly used design symbols and components for the project. A user is usually working on a part (called an element in CATIA) in a model under a project. An element may be of the space (3-D) or draw (2-D) type. Each element is placed on one of the 256 layers. A layer filter can be used to display or plot one or many element layers simultaneously so that parts can be displayed selectively. Each element consists of basic geometry (points, lines, circles, curves, and surfaces), solids, text, and attributes. Dimensions can be added to the drawings automatically.

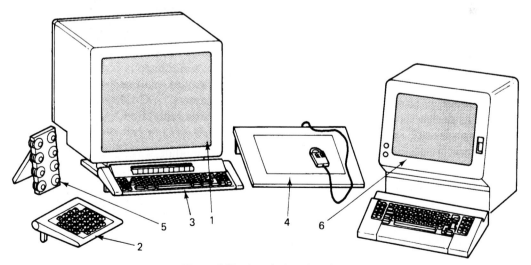

Figure 3.18   A typical workstation configuration.

Multiple-screen windows can be opened to allow the user to work on different views or different elements at the same time. On-screen window menus display frequently used commands. The user can use a programmable functional keyboard, a regular keyboard, or a tablet to enter commands. A dial device with eight dials can perform dynamic coordinate transformations. Pictures on the screen can be rotated, scaled, and paned dynamically through the dials. A local graphics processor associated with the workstation handles the transformation tasks.

Drawings developed on a CATIA system are shown in Figures 3.19 and 3.20.

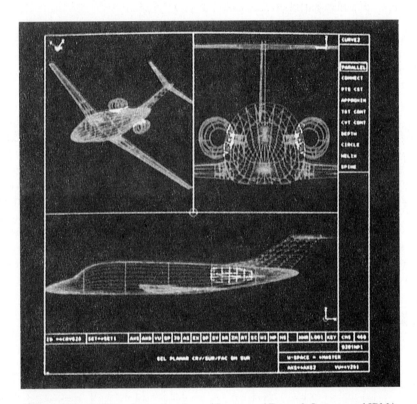

Figure 3.19   CATIA advanced surfaces. (Courtesy of Dassault Systems and IBM.)

3.6.2 AutoCAD

AutoCAD is one of the most successful CAD packages of the 1980s and the 1990s. It began as a PC-based drafting package running under the MS DOS environment. However, it gradually evolved into a full-blown CAD system. It supports nearly all the advanced functions found in more expansive packages and runs on most computer platforms. However, AutoCAD is still a single-user design package (only one user can work on the same design data file at a time). AutoCAD supports a standard file exchange

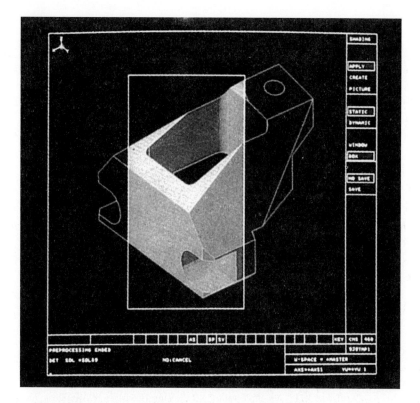

Figure 3.20   CATIA solid geometry (Courtesy of Dassault Systems and IBM.)

format—DXF—and an interface language—AutoLisp. Many add-on applications have been written for AutoCAD. Special applications can use application-specific interfaces and the underlying AutoCAD geometry and functions. Through DXF, the design data file also can be transferred into other applications including NC tool-path generation packages for part programming.

The most basic functions of AutoCAD are the 2-D drafting functions. 2-D geometry such as lines, circles, curves, and so on can be defined. A 2-D profile also can be extruded into a $2\frac{1}{2}$-D object. The extruded object is a wire-frame of the object. AutoCAD also allows a 3-D wireframe to be defined. To cover the wire-frame model, faces can be added to the model. This creates a shell of the object. Hidden-line/surface algorithms can be applied to create realistic pictures. Many menu functions are used to help simplify the design process. Annotation and dimensioning are also supported. Text and dimension symbols can be placed anywhere on the drawing, at any angle, and at any size. A sample drawing is shown in Figure 3.21.

A screen menu or a tablet menu (Figure 3.22) helps the user select the right command. The menus are user-configurable. The user also can define symbols (shapes) using lines, arcs, and circles, and save them in files. Predefined shapes can be loaded in and used in a drawing.

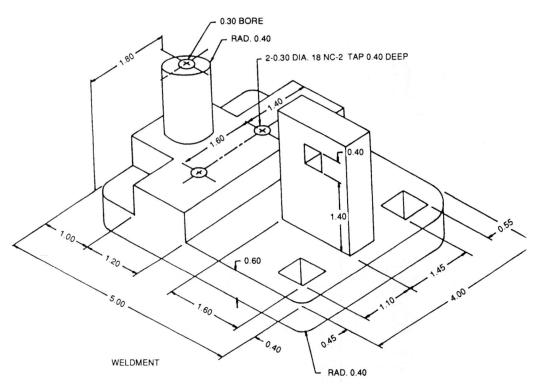

Figure 3.21   A sample AutoCAD drawing. (Courtesy of AutoDesk, Inc.)

In addition to the drafting functions, AutoCAD also includes a true 3-D solid-modeling capability. In Release 13 (the most recent at the time of this writing), the solid modeler is ACIS, a nonmanifold solid modeler. The 3-D solids created by AutoCAD are integrated into the overall design data. A CSG-based user interface is available to the user. 3-D primitives used in the design include BOX, WEDGE, CYLINDER, CONE, SPHERE, and TORUS. Primitives can also be created from 2-D entities using EXTRUDE (translation sweep) and REVOLVE (rotation sweep) commands. Boolean operators, UNION, SUBTRACT, and INTERSECTION, are used to construct solids from primitives. Other commands such as CHAMFER (chamfering), FILLET (fillet a corner), and SLICE (slice an object into two) modify the model. The surface area can be calculated using the AREA command. The mass property including mass, volume, bounding box, centroid, moments of inertia, products of inertia, radii of gyration, and principle moments are calculated using the MASSPROP command. Given two solids, the INTERFERE command can find the portion of the solids that overlap in the space. The resultant solid can be displayed as a 2-D drawing (projection), a 3-D wire frame, or a shaded image. An application program called AutoVision can be used for surface-texture mapping or for lighting a design to create realistic images of objects such as a machine, an office, a building, or a landscape. It does both rendering of a picture and

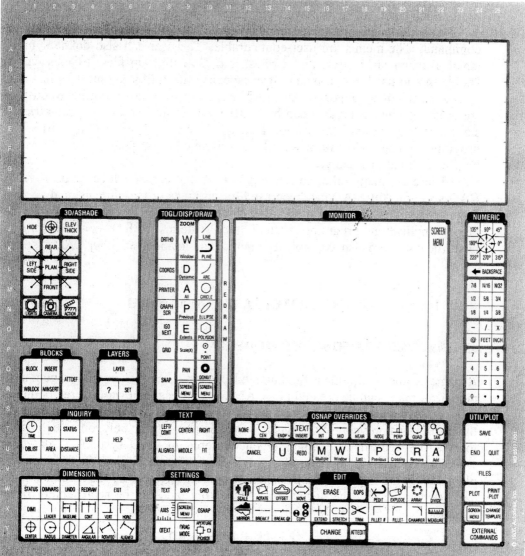

Figure 3.22   AutoCAD tablet menu. (Courtesy of Auto Desk, Inc.)

animation of a sequence of motion through a model. A sample rendered image is shown in Figure 3.23.

Figure 3.23   Auto Vision rendered image. (Courtesy of AutoDesk, Inc.)

INTERMEDIATE ANALYSIS

3.7 FUNDAMENTALS OF GEOMETRIC MODELING

A plane is one of the most fundamental elements used in creating a geometric model. A plane can be created in a CAD system in several ways (three points on it, and so on). A plane typically represents a face of a part, and the bounded edges of the face form a polygon. For regular prismatic parts, these polygons are joined to form a polyhedron. The difficulty encountered in CAD systems is detecting whether the inside or outside of a polyhedron is being displayed. The side of a plane facing the interior of a part cannot be seen. However, the side of a plane can be identified by the normal to a face. Any face can be represented by the equation

$$ax + by + cz + d = 0 \tag{3.1}$$

where a, b, c, and d are parameters of the face. If P represents the face, it can be characterized by its normal and a constant, $P = [a\ b\ c\ d]^T$. We can also map a vertex (from three-dimensional space to four-dimensional space) in order to obtain a homogeneous representation. This can be written in vector form as

$$V = (x, y, z, w) \tag{3.2}$$

where w can be any number. However, w is usually set to one. The inside or outside then can be represented by

$$V \cdot P < 0 \quad \text{or} \quad V \cdot P > 0 \tag{3.3}$$

3.7.1 Topology

Surface topology represents the basic relationships of the geometry of an object. For example, in Figure 3.24, the topology of a tetrahedron is shown using a tree structure. The basic topological relationships always remain the same for any tetrahedron, even though tetrahedrons can be of different size and may be oriented differently. The analogy of the tetrahedron can be expanded to any polyhedron. Any polyhedron can be characterized by its

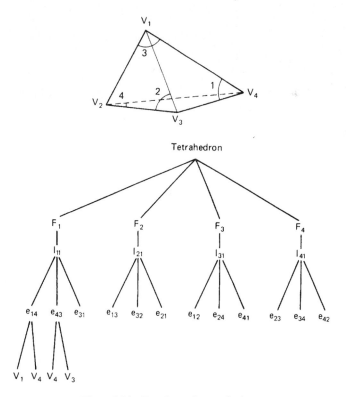

Figure 3.24 Topology of a tetrahedron.

1. geometry

2. topology

3. auxiliary information

Both geometry and topology are necessary in order to manipulate and display the object. Some additional information may also be necessary to display the object or for other purposes (e.g., engineering analysis, manufacturing, and so on). Such additional information is typically stored in an auxiliary information buffer. A complete model for a polyhedron is shown in Figure 3.25.

The topology of two-dimensional engineering drawings does not make much sense, and its study is unwarranted. However, the study of the topology of three-

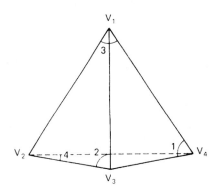

Geometry		$ax + by + cz + d > 0$ outside	
V_1	(x_1, y_1, z_1)	F_1	(a_1, b_1, c_1, d_1)
V_2	(x_2, y_2, z_2)	F_2	(a_2, b_2, c_2, d_2)
V_3	(x_3, y_3, z_3)	F_3	(a_3, b_3, c_3, d_3)
V_4	(x_4, y_4, z_4)	F_4	(a_4, b_4, c_4, d_4)

Topology

Faces		Edges	
F_1	V_1, V_4, V_3	$V_1 V_2$	$V_1 V_4$
F_2	V_1, V_3, V_2	$V_2 V_3$	
F_3	V_1, V_2, V_4	$V_3 V_4$	
F_4	V_2, V_3, V_4	$V_1 V_3$	
		$V_2 V_4$	

Auxiliary information

Color

Dimensions

Etc.

Figure 3.25 Complete representation of a tetrahedron.

dimensional solid models is important. Given a solid model, how does one know if it represents a valid or invalid engineering object? This question comes up often when one is manipulating a model. The mathematician, Euler, developed a formula that holds true only for valid (correct) geometric objects. Euler's formula states that given a polyhedra without any holes, the sum of faces and vertices equals the number of the edges plus 2:

$$F - E + V = 2 \tag{3.4}$$

where F, E, and V are the numbers of faces, edges, and vertices, respectively. For objects with holes, a generalized formula, Euler-Poincaré is applied:

$$V - E + F - (L - F) - 2(S - G) = 0 \tag{3.5}$$

where L is the number of edge loops, S is numbers of shells, and G is the number of genus (holes). Because B-rep models represent vertex, edge, and face explicitly in the data structure, the preceding formula can be used to check the validity of a solid.

Example 3.1

The boundary model of the object shown in Figure 3.26 consists of 6 faces, 8 vertices, and 12 edges. By applying Equation (3.4),

$$6 - 12 + 8 = 2$$

The object shown in Figure 3.27 has a square through hole at the center. It consists of 10 faces, 16 vertices, 24 edges, 12 loops (each face has 1 loop, and the top and the bottom faces have 2 loops, one inner, one outer), 1 shell, and 1 genus. By applying Equation (3.5),

$$16 - 24 + 10 - (12 - 10) - 2(1 - 1) = 0$$

For an object with curved surfaces, it is not as straightforward. For example, a cylinder is represented by two circles and a straight edge (Figure 3.28). The circle has one vertex that is both the beginning and the end vertex. The cylindrical face is bounded by two circular edges and one linear edge. There are 2 vertices, 3 edges (2 circles plus a

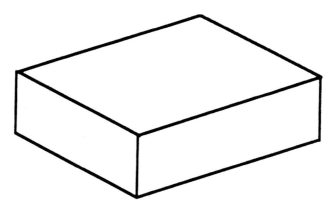

Figure 3.26

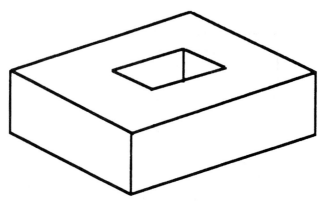

Figure 3.27

line), and 3 faces (two flat faces bounded by circles, and one cylindrical face bounded by the edge). Thus, $3 - 3 + 2 = 2$.

It is worth noting that the Euler formula is only a necessary condition for a valid 3-D object. The preceding formula is valid for 2-manifold models. A manifold object must satisfy the Euler formula. However, an object that satisfies the Euler formula may be nonmanifold (with dangling face). For example, a cube with a dangling rectangular face has 10 vertices, 15 edges, and 7 faces. Thus, $10 - 15 + 7 = 2$.

3.7.1.1 Loops.   A loop represents an oriented set of close and connected edges. For a face with a hole or protrusion inside, there is only one outer loop. However, when there are holes or protrusions inside, the face has more than one loop (Figure 3.29). In a B-rep model, loops are represented explicitly. A proper B-rep model has a structure of object-face-loop-edge-vertex (Figure 3.30).

By counting the number of inner loops, one can estimate the number of holes and protrusions. It is a property useful in feature recognition.

For a nonmanifold model, an empty shell within a solid is allowed (a manifold model has only one shell). The data structure includes the shell above the face. Some modelers also allow disjoint objects to be considered.

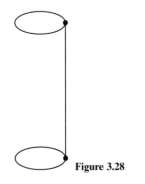

Figure 3.28

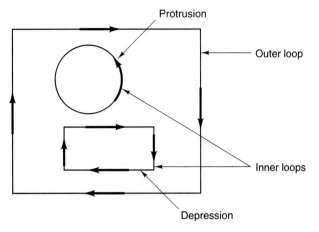

Figure 3.29   Loops.

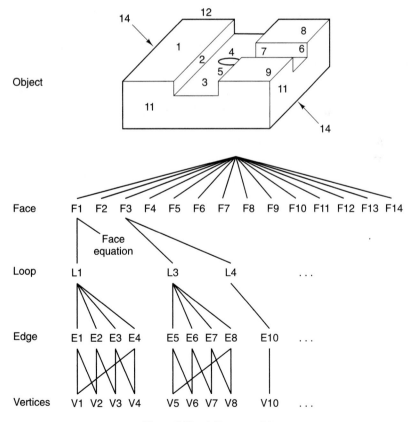

Figure 3.30   A B-rep model.

3.7.2 Curves

Thus far, only planar polygons have been discussed. The representation required for curved surfaces and curves is more complex. There are two types of curves: analytical curves and free-form curves. Analytical curves are those that are normally represented by a known equation. The definition of an analytical curve is exact. Free-form curves are those that do not have a known equation. Only a few control points are known. There are two ways to represent curves: (1) as functions of variables x, y, and z, and (2) as functions of another parameter (such as t). The parameter does not have a unit. In the first case, the curve is called a nonparametric curve; in the second case, a parametric curve. Nonparametric curves can be presented by either implicitly or explicitly. An implicit form sets the equation to zero:

$$f(x, y, z) = 0 \tag{3.6}$$

An explicit form sets one variable as a function of the rest of the variables:

$$z = f(x, y) \tag{3.7}$$

Analytical curves are usually represented in this way. For example, a circle is written as (implicit form)

$$(x - x_0)^2 + (y - y_0)^2 = r^2 \tag{3.8}$$

where

$$x_0, y_0 = \text{center of the circle}$$

$$r = \text{radius}$$

Some commonly used analytical curves are conic sections, as shown in Figure 3.31. They are represented in implicit forms. The implicit form is concise; however, it is difficult to calculate the intersection of two curves or to draw the curve directly using the implicit form. Converting one implicit equation into an explicit equation during the intersection calculation simplifies the calculation. However, this still does not solve the drawing problem. For example, the explicit form of a circle is

$$y = y_0 \pm \sqrt{r - (x - x_0)^2} \tag{3.9}$$

The range of x values is $x_0 - r \le x \le x_0 + r$. When incrementing the x value in this range, each x value yields two y values. A commonly used algorithm for drawing circles takes a different form

$$x = r \cos \theta + x_0 \tag{3.10}$$

$$y = r \cos \theta + y_0$$

where $0 \le \theta \le 2\pi$.

This is in a parametric form of a circle.

Ellipse:

$$\frac{x^2}{a^2} + \frac{y^2}{b^2} - 1 = 0$$

Parabola:

$$y^2 - 4ax = 0$$

Hyperbola:

$$\frac{x^2}{a^2} - \frac{y^2}{b^2} - 1 = 0$$

A parametric curve has the following general form:

$$x = f(t)$$
$$y = g(t) \qquad t_{min} \le t \le t_{max} \tag{3.11}$$
$$z = h(t)$$

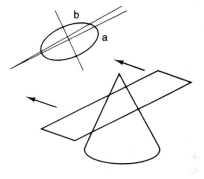

Ellipse

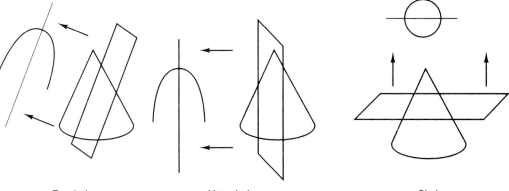

Parabola   Hyperbola   Circle

Figure 3.31   Quadratic polynomial functions.

Alternatively, a circle may be parametrized as

$$x(t) = r\frac{1 - t^2}{1 + t^2}$$
$$\qquad\qquad -1 \le t \le 1 \qquad\qquad (3.12)$$
$$y(t) = r\frac{2t}{1 + t^2}$$

Example 3.2

Represent a circle with center $(10,10)$ and a radius of 5 in (a) implicit form, (b) explicit form and, (c) parametric form.

Solution:

(a) Implicit form:

$$(x - 10)^2 + (y - 10)^2 = 25$$

(b) Explicit form:

$$y = 10 \pm \sqrt{25 - (x - 10)^2}$$

(c) Parametric form (for a quarter circle):

$$x = 5\frac{1 - t}{1 + t^2}$$
$$\qquad\qquad -1 \le t \le 1$$
$$y = 5\frac{2t}{1 + t^2}$$

For a free-form curve, it is difficult to identify the form of the curve equation (i.e., circle, parabola, and so on). A different approach is taken for free-form curves. First, most of the geometric shapes can be approximated by a polynomial equation. When the shape is very complex, it may be decomposed into several segments of polynomial curves. The polynomial curve is in parametric form (x, y, and z are functions of a parameter). To design a free-form curve, it is necessary to find the coefficients of the general polynomial equation. Of course, it is impossible to design a shape by assigning coefficients, because there is no physical connection between the two (shape and coefficients). An intermediate step has to be taken, which will be discussed shortly in the curve design.

Before one can assign the coefficients, one has to determine the order of the polynomial to be used. In engineering design, a third-degree polynomial will satisfy most of the applications. A third-degree polynomial curve is also called a cubic curve. A general cubic parametric curve has the following form:

$$x(t) = a_x t^3 + b_x t^2 + c_x t + d$$
$$y(t) = a_y t^3 + b_y t^2 + c_y t + d \qquad 0 \le t \le 1 \qquad (3.13)$$
$$z(t) = a_z t^3 + b_z t^2 + c_z t + d$$

or

$$r(t) = at^3 + bt^2 + ct + d \qquad 0 \le t \le 1 \quad (3.14)$$

or

$$r(t) = CT^t \qquad 0 \le t \le 1 \quad (3.15)$$

where

$$r(t) = \begin{bmatrix} x(t) \\ y(t) \\ z(t) \end{bmatrix}$$

$$C = [a \ \ b \ \ c \ \ d] = \begin{bmatrix} a_x & b_x & c_x & d_x \\ a_y & b_y & c_y & d_y \\ a_z & b_z & c_z & d_z \end{bmatrix}$$

$$T = [t^3 \ \ t^2 \ \ t \ \ 1]$$

The tangent of the curve can be found [based on Equation (3.14)]:

$$\dot{r}(t) = \frac{dr(t)}{dt} = 3at^2 + 2bt + c \qquad (3.16)$$

Example 3.3

Find the tangent line of a curve at $x = 1$.

$$y = 10 + 5x + x^2$$

Solution: At $x = 1, y = 16$,

$$\text{Slope} = \frac{dy}{dx}\bigg|_{x=1} = 5 + 2x|_{x=1} = 7$$

$$\text{Tangent line} = \frac{y - 16}{x - 1} = 7$$

$$y = 16 + 7(x - 1)$$

Example 3.4

Find the tangent vector of a parameter curve at $x = 1$.

$$r(t) = \begin{bmatrix} 1 \\ 2 \\ 1 \end{bmatrix} t^3 + \begin{bmatrix} 0 \\ 3 \\ -1 \end{bmatrix} t^2 + \begin{bmatrix} 4 \\ -2 \\ 3 \end{bmatrix} t + \begin{bmatrix} 5 \\ 8 \\ 9 \end{bmatrix} \qquad 0 \le t \le 1$$

Solution:

$$\frac{dr(t)}{dt}\bigg|_{t=1} = \begin{bmatrix} 3 \\ 6 \\ 3 \end{bmatrix} t^2 + \begin{bmatrix} 0 \\ 6 \\ -2 \end{bmatrix} t + \begin{bmatrix} 4 \\ -2 \\ 3 \end{bmatrix} = \begin{bmatrix} 3 + 0 + 4 \\ 6 + 6 - 2 \\ 3 - 2 + 3 \end{bmatrix} = \begin{bmatrix} 7 \\ 10 \\ 4 \end{bmatrix}$$

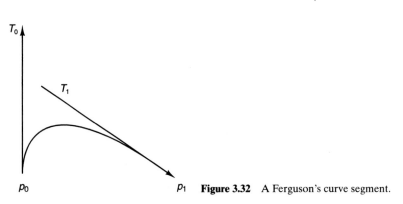

Figure 3.32 A Ferguson's curve segment.

In order to define a long curve with curve segments, one must be able to control the end points of the curve and the tangent at the end points. By setting the end point of the first segment at the beginning point of the second curve, one can make a continuous curve without break. This is also called the zero order (1st degree) continuity. In order to make the final curve smooth, the tangent at the end point of the first curve must be on the same direction as the tangent at the beginning of the 2nd curve. This is the 1st order (2nd degree) continuity. By doing so, one can create a continuous and smooth curve. With this in mind, several curve definitions have been developed. Here we will discuss Ferguson's curve, Bezier's curve, a B-spline curve, and a NURB curve.

3.7.2.1 Ferguson's Curve. Ferguson's curve $r(t)$ is defined by two end points and two tangents at the end points (Figure 3.32). Following are the conditions for the curve definition:

$$r(0) = p_0$$
$$r(1) = p_1$$
$$\dot{r}(0) = T_0 \quad\quad (3.17)$$
$$\dot{r}(1) = T_1$$

where p_0, p_1, T_0, and T_1 are begin and end points, and corresponding tangent vectors.

$$\dot{r}(t) = \frac{dr(t)}{dt}$$

By substituting Equation (3.17) into Equations (3.14) and (3.16),

$$p_0 = r(0) = d$$
$$p_1 = r(1) = a + b + c + d$$
$$T_0 = \dot{r}(0) = c$$
$$T_1 = \dot{r}(1) = 3a + 2b + c$$

Therefore,

$$a = 2p_0 - 2p_1 + T_0 + T_1$$

$$b = -3p_0 + 3p_1 - 2T_0 - T_1$$

$$c = T_0$$

$$d = p_0$$

$$r(t) = \begin{bmatrix} p_0 & p_1 & T_0 & T_1 \end{bmatrix} \begin{bmatrix} 2 & -3 & 0 & 1 \\ -2 & 3 & 0 & 0 \\ 1 & -2 & 1 & 0 \\ 1 & -1 & 0 & 0 \end{bmatrix} \begin{bmatrix} t^3 \\ t^2 \\ t \\ 1 \end{bmatrix} \tag{3.18}$$

The end points and the tangents at the end points are explicitly defined, so one can easily design a continuous and smooth curve using several curve segments. However, it is difficult to relate the tangent vectors to the overall shape of the curve.

3.7.2.2 Bezier's curve.   Dr. Bezier invented the Bezier's curve (1972) while working at the French automaker Renault. Since then, it has become the most popular curve design method used in graphics packages and CAD systems. A cubic Bezier's curve is a cubic curve defined by four control points (Bezier's curve can be generalized to higher- or lower-order curves) (Figure 3.33). A nice feature of Bezier's curve is that

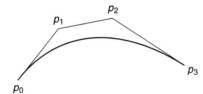

Figure 3.33   Bezier's curve segment.

it is close to the polygon (characteristic polygon) formed by the control points. This property is important because it helps the designer to relate the shape of the desired curve with the location of the control points. The relationship between the control points and the curve follows:

$$r(0) = p_0$$

$$r(1) = p_3$$

$$\dot{r}(0) = 3(p_1 - p_0) \tag{3.19}$$

$$\dot{r}(1) = 3(p_3 - p_2)$$

where $p_0, p_1, p_2,$ and p_3 are four user-defined control points.

By substituting Equation (3.19) into Equations (3.14) and (3.16),

$$p_0 = r(0) = d$$
$$p_3 = r(1) = a + b + c + d$$
$$3(p_1 - p_0) = \dot{r}(0) = c$$
$$3(p_3 - p_2) = \dot{r}(1) = 3a + 2b + c$$

Therefore,

$$a = p_3 - 3p_2 + 3p_1 - p_0$$
$$b = 3p_2 - 6p_1 + 3p_0$$
$$c = 3p_1 - 3p_0$$
$$d = p_0$$

$$r(t) = \begin{bmatrix} p_3 & p_2 & p_1 & p_0 \end{bmatrix} \begin{bmatrix} 1 & 0 & 0 & 0 \\ -3 & 3 & 0 & 0 \\ 3 & -6 & 3 & 0 \\ -1 & 3 & -3 & 1 \end{bmatrix} \begin{bmatrix} t^3 \\ t^2 \\ t \\ 1 \end{bmatrix} \quad 0 \le t \le 1 \quad (3.20)$$

It can also be expressed in a polynomial form:

$$r(t) = \sum_{i=0}^{3} B_i^3(t)p_i \quad 0 \le t \le 1 \tag{3.21}$$

where the $B_i^3(t)$ are called cubic Bernstein polynomials (or Bernstein blending functions). They blend the control points together to form the curve.

$$B_0^3(t) = (1 - t)^3$$
$$B_1^3(t) = 3t(1 - t)^2$$
$$B_2^3(t) = 3t^2(1 - t)$$
$$B_3^3(t) = t^3$$

It can be written as

$$B_i^3(t) = \frac{3!}{i!(3 - i)!} t^i (1 - t)^{3-i} \tag{3.22}$$

To generalize Bezier's curve to degree-n we blend $n + 1$ control points together.

$$r(t) = \sum_{i=0}^{n} B_i^n(t)p_i \quad 0 \le t \le 1 \tag{3.23}$$

where

$$B_i^n(t) = \frac{n!}{i!(n - i)!} t^i (1 - t)^{3-i}$$

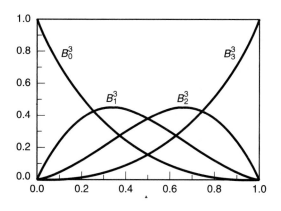

Figure 3.34   A plot of the blending function values.

From the equation, one also can see that at any location on the curve $r(t)$, between t from 0 to 1, the blending function values are not zero (Figure 3.34). This means that by changing any of the control points, the shape of the entire curve changes, except at the beginning ($t = 0$) and the end ($t = 1$) points. To maintain the zero-order continuity (1st degree), the first point (p_0^2) of the 2nd curve segment must be the same as the fourth point (p_3^1) of the 1st curve segment (Figure 3.35). For 1st-order continuity (2nd degree), points $p_2^1, p_3^1, p_0^2,$ and p_1^2 must be colinear.

Example 3.5

Bezier's curve is defined by four control points: (3,0,1), (4,0,4), (8,0,4), and (10,0,1). Find the equation of the curve.

Solution:

From Equation (3.20),

$$
r(t) = \begin{bmatrix} 10 & 8 & 4 & 3 \\ 0 & 0 & 0 & 0 \\ 1 & 4 & 4 & 1 \end{bmatrix} \begin{bmatrix} 1 & 0 & 0 & 0 \\ -3 & 3 & 0 & 0 \\ 3 & -6 & 3 & 0 \\ -1 & 3 & -3 & 1 \end{bmatrix} \begin{bmatrix} t^3 \\ t^2 \\ t \\ 1 \end{bmatrix}
$$

$$
= \begin{bmatrix} -5 & 9 & 3 & 3 \\ 0 & 0 & 0 & 0 \\ 0 & -9 & 9 & 1 \end{bmatrix} \begin{bmatrix} t^3 \\ t^2 \\ t \\ 1 \end{bmatrix}
$$

$$
= \begin{bmatrix} -5t^3 + 9t^2 + 3t + 3 \\ 0 \\ -9t^2 + 9t + 1 \end{bmatrix}
$$

$$
0 \le t \le 1
$$

A plot of the curve is shown in Figure 3.36. To plot such a curve, starting from $t = 0$, one increments the t value by a small quantity, Δt. For each new t value, find $r(t)$ and draw from

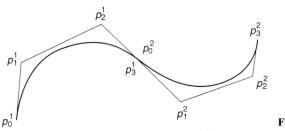

Figure 3.35   Two curve segments.

the current position to the new $r(t)$ position. The equation is very simple, so the computer can draw the curve very quickly.

3.7.2.3 B-spline Curve.   B-spline curves are also very popular since they offer more flexibility than Bezier's curves. A B-spline curve is defined by a set of control points. A B-spline curve (nonuniform) is a general case of the Bezier's curve. It is usually defined in a Cox-deBoor recursive function:

$$r(t) = \sum_{j=0}^{L} N_j^n(t)p_j \qquad t_i \leq t \leq t_{i+1} \tag{3.24}$$

where

$$N_j^n(t) = \frac{t - t_i}{t_{i+n-1} - t_i} N_i^{n-1}(t) + \frac{t_{i+n} - t}{t_{i+n} - t_{i+1}} N_{i+1}^{n-1}(t)$$

$$N_i^1(t) = \begin{cases} 1, t \in [t_i, t_{i+1}] & \text{and} \quad t_i < t_{i+1} \\ 0, \text{otherwise} \end{cases}$$

L = number of control points
n = degree of the curve

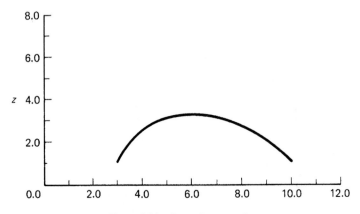

Figure 3.36   Curve for example.

To simplify the algebraic manipulations, a difference operator ∇ is introduced:

$$\nabla_i = t_{i+1} - t_i \tag{3.25}$$

$$\nabla_i^k = \nabla_i + \ldots + \nabla_{i+k-1} = t_{i+k} - t_i \tag{3.26}$$

Therefore,

$$N_j^n(t) = \frac{t - t_i}{\nabla_i^{n-1}} N_i^{n-1}(t) + \frac{t_{i+n} - t}{\nabla_{i+1}^{n-1}} N_{i+1}^{n-1}(t)$$

The difference operator ∇ defines the knot span. The t_i are knots. A nonuniform B-spline is one that has nonconstant knot spans. The cubic uniform B-spline (uniform knot spacing) blending function values are shown in Figure 3.37. This shows that control points have only a local effect. A long curve can be represented by a large number of control points. Any change to a control point will affect only the local region.

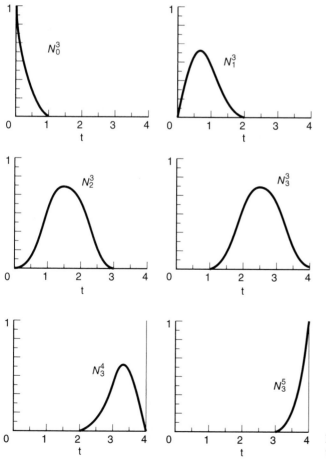

Figure 3.37   Cubic B-spline blending function values.

Bezier's curve is a special case of a uniform B-spline. For a Bezier's curve, $\nabla_i = 1$, $\nabla_j = 0$ for all $j \neq i$. $t_{i-2} = t_{i-1} = t_i = 0$, and $t_{+1} = t_{i+2} = t_{i+3} = 1$. One can prove that $N_j^n(t) = B_i^n(t)$, and Equation (3.24) becomes Equation (3.23).

In the curve, the order of the curve is defined by variable n. For a cubic curve, $n = 3$. A cubic B-spline curve can be defined by L number of control points as long as $n = 3$. L can be any number greater than 3. A complex curve can be defined using just one curve instead of several curve segments.

3.7.2.4 Rational curves.   A rational number is the one with a form a/b. A point in 3-D can be represented by its x, y, z coordinates, or by a vector containing these three coordinates. For example, point p is represented by $[x\ y\ z]$, which is a vector and also co-ordinates of the point. A homogeneous vector is one that has four components $[x\ y\ z\ h]$, and is a four-dimensional vector. The variable h is in the fourth dimension. To project the four dimensional vector to the plane, $h = 1$, the preceding vector can be converted into $[x/h\ y/h\ z/h\ 1]$, a rational form. Then h can be considered as a weight. If $h \neq 0$, the two vectors are identical points in 3-D. The conversion is called the normalization of the vector. Similarly, vector $[x\ y\ z\ 1]$ is the same as vector $[xw\ yw\ zw\ w]$. Without going into any detail, a rational curve is one that adds weight w to each control point. When substituting $[x_i w_i\ y_i w_i\ z_i w_i\ w_i]$ for p_i in Equation (3.21), and normalizing the resultant curve, a rational Bezier's curve can be found:

$$r(t) = \frac{\Sigma B_i(t)w_i p_i}{\Sigma B_i(t)w_i} \tag{3.27}$$

The end condition of the curve does not change. However, the shape of the curve can be changed by changing the weights. When w_i is positive, the curve can move from a straight line all the way to the characteristic polygon. This is a very nice property, because it allows better control of the curve. It is widely used when parametrizing conic sections.

3.7.2.5 NURB Curves.   The non-uniform rational B-spline curve combines features of all of the preceding curves. All these curves can be considered special cases of a NURB curve. A NURB curve is defined by its control points, knot spacing, and weights. A NURB curve can be found by substituting ordinary control points with weighed control points into Equation (3.24). NURB is flexible; however, it is also very complex to use. Too much control is not always a good thing. For most applications, it is too hard to use and too complex to compute. Yet, it can best fit a complex shape. NURB curves are widely available in CAD systems.

3.7.3 Surfaces

There are analytical surfaces and free-form surfaces used in engineering design. Spherical, cylindrical, conic, and so on, surfaces are analytical surfaces that are represented by known equations. There are other surface types that are constructed using curves. One way to construct a surface is through sweeping. A tabulated cylinder is the result of the translational sweep of a curve. Surfaces of revolution result from the rotational sweep of a curve. Another way to construct a surface is through blending. Two

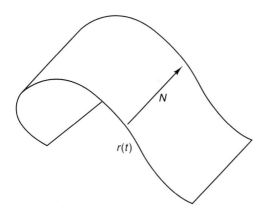

Figure 3.38   A tabulated cylinder.

curves can be blended to form a ruled surface. Finally, there are free-from surfaces, also called sculptured surfaces, that are defined using control points. In this section, we will introduce a few common surface types.

3.7.3.1 Tabulated cylinders.   A tabulated cylinder (Figure 3.38) is a surface created using a curve, $r(t)$ and a vector, N. The equation is expressed as

$$r(t,s) = r(t) + s N \qquad 0 \le t,\ s \le 1 \tag{3.28}$$

Curve $r(t)$ can be any parametric curve, even a line segment. A line segment can be written as $r(t) = tp_1 + (1 - t)p_0$. For example, to create a planar surface, one may sweep a line:

$$r(t,s) = [tp_1 + (1 - t)p_0] + sN \qquad 0 \le t, s \le 1$$

3.7.3.2 Surfaces of Revolution.   A surface of revolution is defined by a curve, $r(t)$, with rotational sweep around an axis (Figure 3.39). If a line instead of a curve is used, the result will be a cylindrical or conic surface. The surface equation for the example in Figure 3.39 is

$$r(t,\theta) = \begin{bmatrix} x(t) \cos \theta \\ x(t) \sin \theta \\ z(t) \end{bmatrix} \tag{3.29}$$

$$r(t) = \begin{bmatrix} x(t) \\ 0 \\ z(t) \end{bmatrix}$$

3.7.3.3 Ruled surfaces.   A ruled surface is the result of blending two curves, $r_0(t), r_1(t)$ (Figure 3.40). The surface is defined as

$$r(t, s) = r_0(t) + s[r_1(t) - r_0(t)] \qquad 0 \le t, s \le 1 \tag{3.30}$$

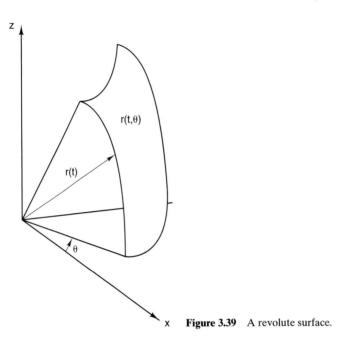

Figure 3.39 A revolute surface.

Curve $r(t)$ can be any parametric curves. Ruled surfaces are commonly found in engineering products to create a surface between two curves.

3.7.3.4 Free-form surfaces.
Free-form surfaces are based on free-form curves. Expanded from the Bezier, B-spline, and NURB curves, there are the Bezier, B-spline, and NURB surfaces. To blend points together to form a surface, two parameters t and s are needed.

$$r(t,s) = \sum_i \sum_j B_i(t)B_j(s)p_{ij} \qquad 0 \le t,\ s \le 1 \qquad (3.31)$$

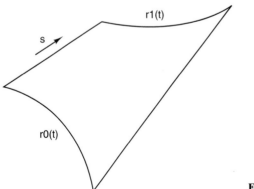

Figure 3.40 A ruled surface.

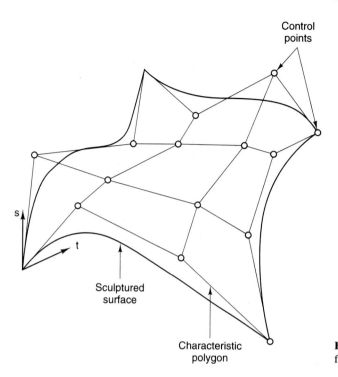

Figure 3.41   Characteristic polygon and surface of a bicubic Bezier's surface.

$B_i(t)$ and $B_j(s)$ are both the same as defined in Equation (3.23), except different indices and parameters are used. A bicubic Bezier's surface is shown in Figure 3.41. It is bicubic because on both t and s directions are found cubic polynomials. Each surface is called a surface patch and can be used to construct a large surface. A surface patch is defined by 16 control points (4×4). The four corners of the surface are located at p_{00}, p_{03}, p_{30}, and p_{33}. The continuity and smoothness conditions must be satisfied. At any given point on the surface, there is a tangent plane. On the tangent plane are two principal tangents along the t and the s directions. The two principal tangents can be found by doing partial derivatives with respect to t and s:

$$\frac{\partial r(t,s)}{\partial t} = \sum_i \sum_j \frac{dB_i(t)}{dt} B_j(s) p_{ij} \tag{3.32}$$

$$\frac{\partial r(t,s)}{\partial s} = \sum_i \sum_j B_i(t) \frac{dB_j(s)}{ds} p_{ij} \tag{3.33}$$

The surface normal is thus

$$N = \frac{\partial r(t,s)}{\partial t} \times \frac{\partial r(t,s)}{\partial s} \tag{3.34}$$

Other free-form surfaces can be defined using the same method introduced in this section.

3.7.4 Geometric Transformation

In order to manipulate a modeling object in the space, geometric transformations are used. For example, when a 3-D solid modeling system to build an object is used, the primitives used are located at the origin of the coordinate system. Before applying Boolean operators to combine them, we must position and/or rotate the primitives. A coordinate transformation is performed on each primitive. In another application, displaying an object on the screen, one also has to transform the object from 3-D to 2-D. Often, it is also desirable to reposition and rotate the viewpoint to obtain a better view. Again, coordinate transformation is the tool to accomplish these tasks.

There are two kinds of geometric transformation, that of transforming the object and that of transforming the coordinate system. Transforming the object moves the object within the existing coordinate frame (coordinate system), such as moving the primitives in solid modeling. Transforming the coordinate system moves the coordinate system, and then the object is viewed from the new coordinate frame, such as finding a better view or doing a 2-D orthogonal projection. The transformation methods are the same for both cases, except the signs are changed. In this section, we will discuss both kinds of transformation approaches.

Basic transformation includes translation (moving), and rotation. For view transformation, there are also scaling and mirror imaging. Mathematically, these transformations are represented in a matrix form, T. Any point p in a 3-D Cartesian coordinate frame is defined by its homogenous coordinates $[x\ y\ z\ 1]$. To transform the point into a new point p',

$$p' = p\ T \tag{3.35}$$

where T is a 4×4 matrix.

To translate a point by $[a\ b\ c]$ on X, Y, and Z axes (Figure 3.42), it is obvious that $p' = p + [a\ b\ c\ 0]$. The transformation matrix is (we use T_{to} to denote that it is for object transformation):

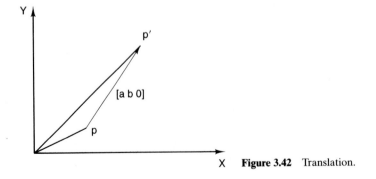

X   **Figure 3.42**   Translation.

$$T_{to} = \begin{bmatrix} 1 & 0 & 0 & 0 \\ 0 & 1 & 0 & 0 \\ 0 & 0 & 1 & 0 \\ a & b & c & 1 \end{bmatrix} \tag{3.36}$$

Therefore,

$$p' = [x \quad y \quad z \quad 1] \begin{bmatrix} 1 & 0 & 0 & 0 \\ 0 & 1 & 0 & 0 \\ 0 & 0 & 1 & 0 \\ a & b & c & 1 \end{bmatrix} = [x + a \quad y + b \quad z + c \quad 1]$$

We may use Figure 3.43 to illustrate the rotation about the Z axis. The right-hand rule is used to determine the direction of the rotation. In the figure, point p is rotated counterclockwise. When applying right-hand rule, let the thumb point in the positive Z direction. The fingers point in the positive rotational direction. The rotation in the figure is, therefore, a positive rotation. Thus, p is represented by (x,y) and p' by (x',y'). The following expressions hold true:

$$x' = l \cos (\theta + \alpha)$$

$$y' = l \sin (\theta + \alpha)$$

$$l = x/\cos (\alpha)$$

where l is the magnitude of vector p.

$$x' = l \cos (\alpha + \theta)$$

$$= \frac{x}{\cos \alpha} (\cos \alpha \cos \theta - \sin \alpha \sin \theta)$$

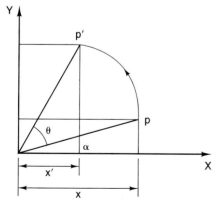

Figure 3.43   Rotation about the Z axis.

$$= x \cos \theta - x \frac{\sin \alpha}{\cos \alpha} \sin \theta$$

$$= x \cos \theta - y \sin \theta$$

$$y' = l \sin (\alpha + \theta)$$

$$= \frac{x}{\cos \alpha} (\sin \alpha \cos \theta + \cos \alpha \sin \theta)$$

$$= x \frac{\sin \alpha}{\cos \alpha} \cos \theta + x \sin \theta$$

$$= y \cos \theta + x \sin \theta$$

$$= x \sin \theta + y \cos \theta$$

In matrix form,

$$[x' \quad y' \quad z'] = [x \quad y \quad z] \begin{bmatrix} C & S & 0 \\ -S & C & 0 \\ 0 & 0 & 1 \end{bmatrix}$$

where

$$C = \cos \theta$$

$$S = \sin \theta$$

In homogeneous coordinates, the 3×3 transformation matrix for rotating about the Z axis can be written as

$$T_{zo}(\theta) = \begin{bmatrix} C & S & 0 & 0 \\ -S & C & 0 & 0 \\ 0 & 0 & 1 & 0 \\ 0 & 0 & 0 & 1 \end{bmatrix} \tag{3.37}$$

Similarly, one can derive the equations for rotating about the X and the Y axes.

$$T_{yo}(\theta) = \begin{bmatrix} C & 0 & -S & 0 \\ 0 & 1 & 0 & 0 \\ S & 0 & C & 0 \\ 0 & 0 & 0 & 1 \end{bmatrix} \tag{3.38}$$

$$T_{xo}(\theta) = \begin{bmatrix} 1 & 0 & 0 & 0 \\ 0 & C & S & 0 \\ 0 & -S & C & 0 \\ 0 & 0 & 0 & 1 \end{bmatrix} \tag{3.39}$$

Transforming the coordinate frame is just the opposite of transforming the object. To translate the coordinate frame by $[a \ b \ c]$ is the same as translating the point $[-a \ -b \ -c]$ (Figure 3.44). To rotate the coordinate system by an angle θ is the same as rotating

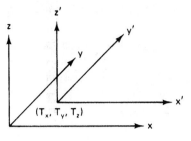

$$T_t = \begin{bmatrix} 1 & 0 & 0 & 0 \\ 0 & 1 & 0 & 0 \\ 0 & 0 & 1 & 0 \\ -T_x & -T_y & -T_z & 1 \end{bmatrix}$$

Translation

$$V' = V\,T_t$$
$$V = [x \ y \ z \ 1]$$

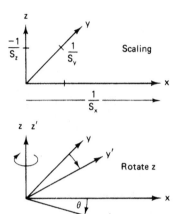

Scaling

$$T_s = \begin{bmatrix} S_x & 0 & 0 & 0 \\ 0 & S_y & 0 & 0 \\ 0 & 0 & S_z & 0 \\ 0 & 0 & 0 & 0 \end{bmatrix}$$

Rotate z

$$T_{r_z} = \begin{bmatrix} \cos\theta & +\sin\theta & 0 & 0 \\ -\sin\theta & \cos\theta & 0 & 0 \\ 0 & 0 & 1 & 0 \\ 0 & 0 & 0 & 1 \end{bmatrix}$$

Rotate y

$$T_{r_y} = \begin{bmatrix} \cos\theta & 0 & -\sin\theta & 0 \\ 0 & 1 & 0 & 0 \\ \sin\theta & 0 & \cos\theta & 0 \\ 0 & 0 & 0 & 1 \end{bmatrix}$$

Rotate x

$$T_{r_x} = \begin{bmatrix} 1 & 0 & 0 & 0 \\ 0 & \cos\theta & \sin\theta & 0 \\ 0 & -\sin\theta & \cos\theta & 0 \\ 0 & 0 & 0 & 1 \end{bmatrix}$$

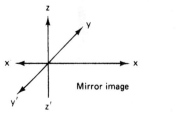

Mirror image

$$T_m = \begin{bmatrix} -1 & 0 & 0 & 0 \\ 0 & -1 & 0 & 0 \\ 0 & 0 & -1 & 0 \\ 0 & 0 & 0 & 1 \end{bmatrix}$$

Figure 3.44 Transforming the coordinate frame.

the point by an angle $-\theta$. For coordinate-frame transformation, there are also scaling and mirroring, as shown in Figure 3.44.

The 4×4 transformation matrices are called homogenous coordinate-transformation matrices. To perform a series of transformations, one can concatenate individual transformation matrices together (matrix multiplication). For example, to translate a point by T_t, rotate it about the X axis by θ, and the transformation matrix $T = T_t T_x(\theta)$. $p' = pT$. Pay special attention to the order of vector/matrix multiplication. The transformation that is performed first should always be multiplied by the vector first.

When we transform an object, we need to transform every vertex in the object. Only at the beginning of the operation do we build the combined transformation matrix by concatenating all the necessary transformation matrices. It is this combined matrix that is applied to all vertices in the object.

Example 3.6

A point [1 1 1 1] is translated by [4 2 0], rotated about the Z axis by $45°$, and then rotated about the X axis by $30°$.

The new coordinates of the point are:

$$p' = pT$$

$$T = T_{to}(4,2,0)T_{zo}(45°)T_{xo}(30°)$$

$$T = \begin{bmatrix} 1 & 0 & 0 & 0 \\ 0 & 1 & 0 & 0 \\ 0 & 0 & 1 & 0 \\ 4 & 2 & 0 & 1 \end{bmatrix} \begin{bmatrix} 0.707 & 0.707 & 0 & 0 \\ -0.707 & 0.707 & 0 & 0 \\ 0 & 0 & 1 & 0 \\ 0 & 0 & 0 & 1 \end{bmatrix} \begin{bmatrix} 1 & 0 & 0 & 0 \\ 0 & 0.866 & 0.5 & 0 \\ 0 & -0.5 & 0.866 & 0 \\ 0 & 0 & 0 & 1 \end{bmatrix}$$

$$= \begin{bmatrix} 0.707 & 0.61226 & 0.3535 & 0 \\ 0.707 & 0.61226 & 0.3535 & 0 \\ 0 & -0.5 & 0.866 & 0 \\ 1.414 & 3.6736 & 2.121 & 1 \end{bmatrix}$$

$$p' = \begin{bmatrix} 1 & 1 & 1 & 1 \end{bmatrix} \begin{bmatrix} 0.707 & 0.61226 & 0.3535 & 0 \\ 0.707 & 0.61226 & 0.3535 & 0 \\ 0 & -.5 & 0.866 & 0 \\ 1.414 & 3.6736 & 2.121 & 1 \end{bmatrix}$$

$$= \begin{bmatrix} 1.414 & 4.398 & 3.694 & 1 \end{bmatrix}$$

Now, fix the point, but translate the origin of the coordinate frame to [4 2 0], rotate the coordinate frame about the Z axis by $45°$, and then rotate it about the X axis by $30°$. Use the equation presented in Figure 3.44.

$$T = T_t(4,2,0)T_{rz}(45°)T_{rx}(30°)$$

$$T = \begin{bmatrix} 1 & 0 & 0 & 0 \\ 0 & 1 & 0 & 0 \\ 0 & 0 & 1 & 0 \\ -4 & -2 & 0 & 1 \end{bmatrix} \begin{bmatrix} 0.707 & -0.707 & 0 & 0 \\ 0.707 & 0.707 & 0 & 0 \\ 0 & 0 & 1 & 0 \\ 0 & 0 & 0 & 1 \end{bmatrix} \begin{bmatrix} 1 & 0 & 0 & 0 \\ 0 & 0.866 & -0.5 & 0 \\ 0 & 0.5 & 0.866 & 0 \\ 0 & 0 & 0 & 1 \end{bmatrix}$$

$$= \begin{bmatrix} 0.707 & -0.61226 & 0.3535 & 0 \\ 0.707 & 0.61226 & -0.3535 & 0 \\ 0 & 0.5 & 0.866 & 0 \\ -4.242 & 1.2245 & -0.707 & 1 \end{bmatrix}$$

$$T = \begin{bmatrix} 1 & 1 & 1 & 1 \end{bmatrix} \begin{bmatrix} 0.707 & -0.61226 & 0.3535 & 0 \\ 0.707 & 0.61226 & -0.3535 & 0 \\ 0 & 0.5 & 0.866 & 0 \\ -4.242 & 1.2245 & -0.707 & 1 \end{bmatrix}$$

$$= \begin{bmatrix} -2.828 & 1.725 & 0.159 & 1 \end{bmatrix}$$

Coordinate-transformation matrices and the operators are easily implemented in computer programs. Appendix 3.A provides C codes for coordinate transformation.

3.7.5 View Transformation

The next graphical issue to be discussed concerns the development of a methodology to display a three-dimensional object on a two-dimensional CRT display or plotter. In engineering drawing, there are either orthographic drawings (multiview or single view) or perspective drawings. The same basic approaches are applied to computer-generated drawings. For an orthographic projection, only two coordinates (e.g., X and Y) are displayed (the third coordinate, e.g., Z, is ignored). For a multiview (say, three-view) display, each view is a simple two-dimensional orthographic drawing. The front, top, and side views can be generated by simply discarding the y, z, and x coordinates, respectively. To produce a single-view orthographic drawing, one can rotate the object about the X axis by 45° followed by a rotation about the Z axis by 45°. The z coordinate of the object is then discarded.

To construct a perspective drawing, a geometric transformation is required. A perspective drawing can be generated by projecting each point of an object onto a plane (called a display screen, as shown in Figure 3.45), which is characterized by d,

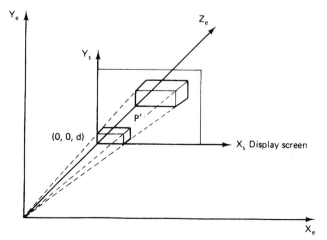

Figure 3.45   Perspective projection of an object on a display screen.

the distance from the eye. The X_s and Y_s axes of the display screen are parallel to the X_e and Y_e axes of the eye coordinate system. The transformed projection is shown in Figure 3.46. Point $P(x, y, z)$ in the eye coordinate system can be projected onto the display screen as (x_p, y_p). By using the relationships of two similar triangles, x_p and y_p can be found.

$$\frac{x_p}{d} = \frac{x}{z} \quad \text{and} \quad \frac{y_p}{d} = \frac{y}{z} \tag{3.40}$$

$$x_p = \frac{x}{z/d} \quad \text{and} \quad y_p = \frac{y}{z/d}$$

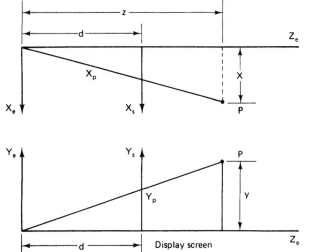

Figure 3.46   Perspective projection of a point (x, y, z).

3.8 CAD DATA EXCHANGE

Each CAD system has its own proprietary data format. To transfer data from one CAD system to another, a translation software has to be written. When the number of CAD systems increase, the number of translators must also increase. Using a specialized translator is uneconomical, and difficult to manage.

$$N = C\binom{n}{2} = \frac{n!}{2!(n-2)!}$$

where

$$n = \text{The number of CAD systems}$$

$$N = \text{The number of translators (two-way translation)}$$

The following table shows the value of N as n increases:

n	N
2	1
3	3
4	6
5	10
6	15

Data exchange not only happens between CAD systems, it also happens between CAD and CAM packages. A standard data exchange format (intermediate data format) will reduce the need for translators. When such a data file is used, each CAD system needs only one preprocessor and one postprocessor (one set of translators). The preprocessor imports the data into the system and the postprocessor outputs the file into standard format (Figure 3.47). Many CAD data-exchange formats have been developed by various countries and organizations. However, the most widely accepted formats are IGES and PDES. Both are international standards. DXF is one format that is not even a national standard, but due to the wide acceptance of AutoCAD, it has been accepted by many CAD vendors. In this section, we will discuss these three data-exchange formats.

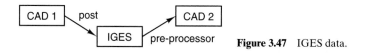

Figure 3.47   IGES data.

3.8.1 DXF Format

The DXF (Drawing Transfer File) format was developed by AutoDesk for its product, AutoCAD. Due to the popularity of AutoCAD, the DXF format has been used by many other software for graphics data exchange. A DXF file is an ASCII data file containing the following sections:

```
Header section
Tables section
        linetype, layer, style, view
Block section
        blocks
ENTITIES section
        drawing entities
```

For example, a line entity is represented in DXF as

```
0
LINE
10
(X1 value)
```

```
11
(y1 value)
20
(x2 value)
21
(y2 value)
0
```

When a drawing is represented, a lot of other data has to be included. For example, Figure 3.48 contains the definition of the simple drawing of Figure 3.49. The DXF file was generated by Canvas™ 3.5.1 on a Macintosh computer.

3.8.2 IGES

The Initial Graphics Exchange Standard was developed in 1980 as the standard CAD data-exchange format. It was accepted as an ANSI American national standard and later as an ISO international standard. IGES is developed for 2-D, 3-D, and surface-modeling data exchange. Almost all CAD systems support IGES. IGES has the following general structure.

```
Flag section
Start
Global: pre/post processor info
Directory entry: one for each entity, line type, color, and so on
Parameter data: parameters associated with each entity
Terminate
```

Geometric entities are coded in the directory entry, such as 100 circular arc, 102 composite curve, and 110 line. Most 2-D and 3-D geometries, including NURB surfaces are supported. Each entity has associated parameters stored in the parameter data section. For example, for a line entity:

DIRECTORY DATA

110   10

PARAMETER DATA

110, 1.0, 1.0, 0.0, 2.0, 2.0, 0.0

Figure 3.50 shows the IGES data file for the same drawing in Figure 3.49. Both the DXF and the IGES files were output from Canvas™ software (Deneb Software Inc).

3.8.3 PDES

Since before IGES was accepted as an international standard, several standards groups have been working on defining a new standard: Product Description Exchange for STEP. The word "STEP" used to be "Standard." PDES development was initiated in the US, and STEP is an European effort. When the two standard groups joined force, PDES

0	0	9	50	40	0	DWGMGR
SECTION	9	$SNAPUNIT	0.0	9.0	77	70
2	$LIMMAX	10	VPORT	41	0	0
HEADER	10	0	70	2.891304	78	0
9	-0.0556	20	2	42	0	ENDTAB
$ACADVER	49	0	0	50.0	0	0
1	0.0833	9	VPORT	43	ENDTAB	ENDSEC
AC1006	49	$SNAPSTYLE	2	0.0	0	0
9	-0.0556	70	*ACTIVE	44	TABLE	SECTION
$AXISMODE	0	0	70	0.0	2	2
70	ENDTAB	9	0	50	LTYPE	BLOCKS
0	0	$SPLINESEGS	10	71	70	0
9	TABLE	70	0.0	0	7	ENDSEC
$AXISUNIT	2	8	20	42	0	0
10	LAYER	9	0.0	0.2	LTYPE	SECTION
0.0625	70	$SPLINETYPE	11	3	2	2
20	1	70	1.0	txt	CONTINUOUS	ENTITIES
0.0625	0	6	21	4	70	40
9	LAYER	0	1.0	0	64	0.2778
$CECOLOR	2	ENDSEC	12	ENDTAB	3	49
62	LAYER1	0	13.01087	0	Descriptive	0.1389
7	70	SECTION	22	TABLE	Text	49
9	0	2	4.5	2	72	-0.1389
$CELTYPE	62	TABLES	13	VIEW	65	0
6	7	0	0.0	70	73	LTYPE
CONTINUOUS	6	TABLE	23	0	0	2
9	7	2	0.0	0	40	DASH2
$CLAYER	20	CONTINUOUS	14	ENDTAB	0	70
8	10	0	1.0	0	0	64
Layer1	9	ENDTAB	24	TABLE	LTYPE	3
9	$GRIDMODE	0	1.0	2	2	Descriptive
$EXTMIN	70	TABLE	15	UCS	DASH1	Text
10	0	2	0.0	70	70	72
0	9	STYLE	25	0.0	64	65
20	$GRIDUNIT	70	0.0	51	3	73
0	10	1]	16	0.0	Descriptive	2
9	0.125	0	0.0	71	Text	40
$EXTMAX	20	STYLE	26	0	72	0.1944
10	0.125	2	0.0	72	65	49
7	9	STANDARD	36	100	73	0.1389
20	$MIRRTEXT	D	1.0	73	2	49
10	70	70	17	1	0	-0.0556
9	1	0	0.0	74	0	0
$LIMMIN	9	40	27	1	ENDTAB	LTYPE
10	$SNAPMODE	0.0	0.0	75	0	2
0	70	41	37	0	TABLE	DASH3
20	0	1.0	0.0	76	2	70

Figure 3.48   The DXF file for the drawing of Figure 3.45.

64]	70	20	-0.0556	40	Descriptive	6
3	64	8.0972	49	0.6667	Text	CONTINUOUS
Descriptive	3	30	0.0833	49	72	62
Text	Descriptive	0	49	0.3333	65	7
72	Text	11	-0.0556	49	73	10
65	72	1.8194	0	-0.1111	6	1.2847
73	65]	21	LTYPE	49	40	20
2]	73	9	2	0.1111	0.6667	7.7569
40	0	31	DASH5	49	49	30
0.3611	LINE	0	70	-0.1111	0.3333	0
49	8	0	64	0	49	40
0.2778	LAYER1	CIRCLE	3	LTYPE	-0.0556	0.3542
49	6	4	Descriptive	2	49	0
-0.0833	CONTINUOUS	40	Text	DASH6	0.0833	ENDSEC
0	62	0.4722	72	70	49	0
LTYPE	7	49	65	64	8	EOF
2	10	0.2778	73	3	LAYER1	
DASH4	0.9028	49	4			

Figure 3.48   (*Continued*)

changed its name. PDES is an ambitious project. The goal is to define a standard file format that all information necessary to describe a product from design to production is
included. It also supports multiple-application domains, that is, mechanical engineering,
electronics, and so on. The following information is included in the PDES standard:

Feature
CSG
B-rep
Function
Process plan

It is obvious that the standard has to cover a lot more than does IGES. It takes a long
time to develop the standard. At the time of this writing, part of the standard has just
been released. Due to the limited space, we will not give any more details.

Figure 3.49   A line and a circle.

```
IGES file generated from a Canvas™ drawing by the IGES tool,version 3.0 S0000001
.4,from Deneba Software Inc. S0000002,,10HUntitled-1,14HUntitled-1.igs,10HCanvas
3.0,13HIGES Tool 1.0,32,38, G00000016,99,15,10HUntitled-1,1,1,4HINCH,32767,1.7639,
13H961016.142254,1.0D-8, G00000029.7222,30HBy Krishnan, Revised by Rieger,20HDeneba
Software Inc.,7,0; G0000003
     304     1          1                          0 0 2 0D0000001
     304                1    2                            D0000002
     304     2          3                          0 0 2 0D0000003
     304                1    2                            D0000004
     304     3          5                          0 0 2 0D0000005
     304                1    2                            D0000006
     304     4          7                          0 0 2 0D0000007
     304                1      2                          D0000008
     304     5          9                          0 0 2 0D0000009
     304                1    2                            D0000010
     304     6          11                         0 0 2 0D0000011
     304                1    2                            D0000012
     110     7     1    1    1                     0 0 0 1D0000013
     110     227   1    1                                D0000014
     104     8     1    1    1                     0 0 0 1D0000015
     104     227   1    2    1                            D0000016
304,2,0.1389,0.1389,1H2;                          1P0000001
304,2,0.1389,0.0556,1H2;                          3P0000002
304,2,0.2778,0.0833,1H2;                          5P0000003
304,4,0.2778,0.0556,0.0833,0.0556,1HA;            7P0000004
304,4,0.3333,0.1111,0.1111,0.11111,1HA;           9P0000005
304,6,0.3333,0.0556,0.0833,0.0556,0.0833,0.0556,2H2A;        11P0000006
110,0.9028,8.0972,0,1.8194,9,0;               13P0000007
104,0.1254,0,0.1254,-0.3223,-1.9459,7.7383,0,1.2785,8.1111,    15P0000008
1.2847,8.1111;                                15P0000009
S0000002G0000003D0000016P0000009                       T0000001
```

Figure 3.50   IGES file for the drawing of Figure 3.46.

3.9 CONCLUDING REMARKS

With the advent of the computer age, information automation has become a reality. We are able to use computers to assist in the design, analysis, representation, and manufacturing of engineering objects. Compared with what our ancestors had, the new tool, CAD, is much more powerful. It allows us not only to pass information more quickly and accurately, but also opens the door of integration and automation.

Since the invention of computer-aided drafting, over the past 30 years, we have had tremendous progress in CAD. Engineering objects can not only be represented by their bounding edges, but also by the space they occupy. Many engineering applications can use the same design model. Therefore, integration of an overall design/manufacturing system becomes feasible.

The development of CAD, the techniques used in CAD systems, and the application areas were discussed. This knowledge helps a manufacturing engineer to carry on work in process planning and NC programming.

REVIEW QUESTIONS

3.1. What are internal representation and external representation in design?

3.2. Discuss how a design idea is represented in a designer's mind, that is, in the form of an equation, line drawing, and so on.

3.3. Discuss the advantages and disadvantages of using a three-dimensional solid model in mechanical part design.

3.4. Prepare a three-view drawing of the part shown in Figure 3.51.

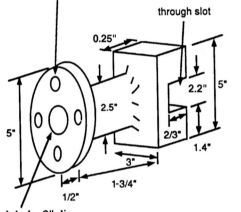

through hole, 2" dia.   **Figure 3.51**

3.5. What are the major classifications of CAD based on applications?

3.6. What are the advantages of using CAD for engineering design?

3.7. What are the differences between a wire-frame model and a solid model?

3.8. For NC part-programming purposes, one has to know the exact surface being machined. Which CAD representation scheme(s) is appropriate for this application?

3.9. Show mathematically that the B-Rep file in Figure 3.24 is a valid solid. (Use Euler's formula.)

3.10. Write a computer program to draw a circle of arbitrary accuracy. (Circles usually are approximated by line segments; see Figure 3.52. The number of chords used to approximate a circle determines the closeness of the plotted circle to the real circle.) Include your algorithm, a program listing, and testing results. To test your program, draw three circles:

Circle one: center (2,2) radius 2, tolerance 0.1
Circle two: center (4,2) radius 3, tolerance 0.05
Circle three: center (5,5) radius 4, tolerance 0.5

Tolerance is the maximum error between the true circle and the chord approximating the circle.

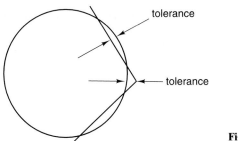

tolerance

tolerance

Figure 3.52

3.11. Write a program to plot a Bezier's surface; see Figure 3.53. Define your own control points. To draw a curve, move the pen to the beginning point and then plot to each subsequent points using a loop:

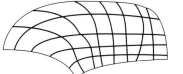

Figure 3.53

```
n=ceil(1/dt);
dt=1.0/n;
t=0.0;
printf("0 %f %f %f\n",x,y,z); /* set x,y,z to the first point coordinates */
for(i=0; i<=n; i++)
    t=t+dt:
    bezierCurve(t,&x,&y,&z);/*now calculate z,y,z*/
    printf("1 %f %f %f\n",x, y,z);
{
```

To draw a surface, you will need two loops.
Given *t* and *s*, bezierSurface returns the surface point. Note that the inner loop always uses a smaller increment. This ensures a smoother curve.

```
typedef struct point{
  float x:
  float y:
  float z:
} point:
```

FILE *fout;

```
/* input 16 control points and store them in a global array*/
fout=fopen("output.dat"."w"):
dt=0.15;
ds=0.05;
n=ceil(1/dt);
dt=1.0/n;
m=ceil(1/ds);
ds=1.0/m;
t=0.0;
for(i=0;i<=n;i++){ /* draw the s curves*/
  s=0.;
  bezierSurface(t,s,&pt); /* calculate x,y,z*/
  fprintf(fout,"0 %f %f %f\n",pt.x.pt.y.pt.z);
  for(j=0;j<m;j++){ /* draw a curve on the s
  direction*/
    s=s+ds;
    bezierSurface(t,s,&pt); /* calculate x.y.z*/
    fprintf(fout,"1 %f %f %f/n".pt.x.pt.y.pt.z);
  }
  t=t+dt:
}

                          s=0.;
                          for(i=0:i<=n:i++){ /* draw the t curves*/
                          t=0.;
                          bezierSurface(t,s,&pt); /* calculate x,y,z.*/
                          fprint(fout,"0 %f %f %f\n".pt.x.pt.y.pt.z):
                          for(j=0;j<m;j++){ /* draw a curve on the t
                          direction */
                          t=t+ds;
                          bezierSurface(t,s,&pt); /* calculate x,y,z*/
                          fprint(fout,"1 %f %f %f\n".pt.x.pt.y.pt.z);
                          }
                          s=s+dt:
                          }

                          /* you need to write the program to calculate
```

3.12. A rule surface is created by blending two curves r_0, r_1.

$$r(t,s) = r_0(t) + s[r_1(t) - r_0(t)]$$

where r_0, r_1 can be any parametric curves. To draw a rule surface, the following procedure may be used:

```
int n;
float s,t,dt;

n=10;
dt=1/(float)n; /* Assume that the range of t and s are between 0 and 1 */
s=0.0
for(i=0;i<n;i++){
s=s+dt;
t=0.0;
for(j=0;j<n;j++){
  t=t+dt;
```

```
      compute and draw a curve along t.
}
t=0.0
for(i=0;i<n;i++){
t=t+dt;
s=0.0;
for(j=0;j<n;j++){
  s=s+dt;
  compute and draw a curve along t.
}
}
```

Write a computer program to draw a rule surface of your design. Define your own r_0 and r_1. Both curves should be of the same type, for example, a Bezier's curve.

3.13. What are differences among 2-D, 2½-D, wire-frame, surface, and solid models? What are their applications?

3.14. For NC part-programming purposes, one has to know the exact surface being machined. Which CAD representation scheme(s) is appropriate for this application?

3.15. Show a B-rep of the part shown in Figure 3.54.

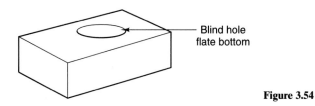

Blind hole
flate bottom

Figure 3.54

3.16. Prove that your B-rep of Review Question 3.15 is a valid three-dimensional object.

3.17. How will you construct a CSG tree for the part shown in Figure 3.54? Use generic terms to describe your primitives.

3.18. Draw a wire-frame model of the part shown in Figure 3.54. What are pros and cons of using a wire frame in mechanical design?

REFERENCES/BIBLIOGRAPHY

BEZIER, P. (1972). *Numerical Control—Mathematics and Applications*, trans. A. R. Forrest. London: John Wiley.

BRAID, I. C. (1973). *Designing with Volumes.* Cambridge: Cambridge University, CAD Group.

CHOI, B. K. (1991). *Surface Modeling for CAD/CAM.* Elsevier, Amsterdam.

DING, Q., and B. J. DAVIES (1987). *Surface Engineering Geometry for Computer Aided Design and Manufacturing.* Ellis Horwood, U.K.

ENCARNACAO, J. and E. G. SCHLECHTENDAHL (1983). *Computer Aided Design, Fundamentals and System Architectures.* Berlin: Springer-Verlag.

FARIN, G. E. (1995), *NURB Curves and Surfaces: From Projective Geometry to Practical Use*. A. K. Peters, Mass.

GORDON, W. J. and R. F. RIESENFELD (1974). "B-Spline Curves and Surfaces," in R. E. Barnhill and R. F. Riesenfeld, Eds., *Computer Aided Geometric Design.* New York: Academic Press, pp. 95–126.

GRAYS, J. C. (1967) "Compound Data Structures for Computer Aided Design: A Survey," in *Proceedings of the ACM National Conference.* Washington, DC: Thompson, pp. 355–365.

IBM (19XX). *General Presentation of CATIA.* City: IBM.

KENT, D. (1996), "The AutoCAD Reference Guide: Release 13." New York: Springer.

MAJCHRZAK, A., T. C. CHANG, W. BARFIELD, R. EBERTS, and G. SALVENDY (1987). *Human Aspects of Computer-Aided Design.* London: Taylor and Francis.

MANTYLA, M. (1986). *An Introduction to Solid Modeling:* Computer Science Press, Rockville, MD.

MITCHELL, M., Y. WANG, S. RYAN, and B. MARTIN (1990). *Data Model Development and Validation for Product Data Exchange*, NISTIR[3] 88-4078, Gaithersburg, MD: National Institute for Standard and Technology.

MORTENSON, M. E. (1985). *Geometric Modeling.* New York: John Wiley.

NEWMAN, W. M., and R. F. SPROULL(1979). *Principles for Interactive Computer Graphics,* 2nd ed. New York: McGraw-Hill.

RAKER, D., and H. RICE (1986). *Inside AutoCAD.* Thousand Oaks, CA: New Riders.

REQUICHA, A. A. G. (1980). "Representations of Rigid Solid: Theory, Methods, and System," *Computing Surveys,* 12(4), 437–464.

REQUICHA, A. A. G., and H. B. VOELCKER (1982). "Solid Modeling: A Historical Summary and Contemporary Assessment," *IEEE Computer Graphics and Applications,* 2(2), 9–24.

STOVER, R. (1984). *An Analysis of CAD/CAM Applications.* Englewood Cliffs, NJ: Prentice Hall.

SUTHERLAND, I. E. (1963), *SKETCHPAD: A Man-Machine Graphical Communication System,* SJCC 1963. Baltimore: Spartan Books.

VOELCKER, H. B., and A. A. G. REQUICHA (1977). "Geometric Modeling of Mechanical Parts and Processes," *Computer,* 10(12), 48–57.

WILLIAMS, R. (1971) "A Survey of Data Structures for Computer Graphics Systems," *Computer Surveys,* 3(1), 1–21.

APPENDIX 3A: C CODES FOR COORDINATE TRANSFORMATION

```
typedef double matrix[4][4];/* 4x4 matrix*/
typedef struct vector {
        double x;
        double y;
        double z;
        }vector;


/*example main program

The following program does the computation shown in example 3.6
The transformation matrices are based on coordinate frame transformation.*/ void
main()
```

```
{
        vector p,pprime;
        matrix Tt,Trx,Trz,T,T1;

        p.x=1; p.y=1;p.z=1;

        /*transforming the object*/
        tranMat(-4,-2,0,Tt);
        rotMat(-45,'z',Trz);
        rotMat(-30,'x',Trx);
        mulMat(Tt,Trz,T1);
        mulMat(T1,Trx,T);
        vXMat(p,T,pprime);          /*pprime holds the result*/

        /*transforming the coordinate frame*/
        tranMat(4,2,0,Tt);
        rotMat(45,'z',Trz);
        rotMat(30,'x',Trx);
        mulMat(Tt,Trz,T1);
        mulMat(T1,Trx,T);
        vXMat(p,T,pprime);

}


/*-------------------------------------------
 vector times matrix
        output is vin*m */
void
vXMat(vin,m,vout)
vector vin,*vout;
matrix m;
{
        (*vout).x=vin.x*m[0][0]+vin.y*m[1][0]+vin.z*m[2][0]+m[3][0];
        (*vout).y=vin.x*m[0][1]+vin.y*m[1][1]+vin.z*m[2][1]+m[3][1];
        (*vout).z=vin.x*m[0][2]+vin.y*m[1][2]+vin.z*m[2][2]+m[3][2];
}
/*-----------------------------------
        multiply two matrices
        mout=ml x m2*/
void
mulMat(m1,m2,mout)
matrix m1,m2,mout;
{
        int i,j,k;
        double x;

        for(i=0;i<4;i++){
                for(j=0;j<4;j++){
                        x = 0.0;
```

```
                for(k=0;k<4;k++){
                        x=x+m1[i][k]*m2[k][j];
                }
                mout[i][j]=x;
        }
    }

}
/*-----------------------------------
        Build a 4x4 view transformation matrix,
        rotate the coordinate system
        rotate ang degrees about axis. Return the matrix by mat
        axis is 'x', 'y', or 'z' */
void
rotMat(ang,axis,mat)
double ang;
char axis;
matrix mat;
{
        double pi=3.1415926;
        double rad;
        double sa,ca,negsa;

        ang=ang/180.*pi;
        sa=sin(ang);
        negsa=-sa;
        ca=cos(ang);
        identM(mat);
        if(axis=='x'|| axis=='X'){
                        mat[1][1]=ca;
                        mat[1][2]=sa;
                        mat[2][1]=negsa;
                        mat[2][2]=ca;}
        else if(axis=='y'|| axis=='Y'){
                        mat[0][0]=ca;
                        mat[0][2]=negsa;
                        mat[2][0]=sa;
                        mat[2][2]=ca;}
        else if(axis=='z'|| axis =='Z'){
                        mat[0][0]=ca;
                        mat[0][1]=sa;
                        mat[1][0]=negsa;
                        mat[1][1]=ca;}
        }

/*-----------------------------------
        Build an identity matrix */
void
identM(m)
```

```
matrix m;
{
        int i,j;
        for(i=0;i<4;i++){
                for(j=0;j<4;j++){
                        m[i][j]=0.0;
                }
        m[i][i]=1.0;
        }
}
/*------------------------------------
        build a translation matrix m*/
void
tranMat(x,y,z,m)
double x,y,z;
matrix m;
{
        identM(m);
        m[3][0]=-x;
        m[3][1]=-y;
        m[3][2]=-z;
}
```

APPENDIX 3B: MATRIX OPERATIONS

A matrix is defined by n rows and m columns of numbers. Each element in the matrix is represented as a_{ij}. The matrix A is said to be a $n \times m$ matrix.

$$A = \begin{bmatrix} a_{11} & a_{12} & a_{13} & a_{14} \\ a_{21} & a_{22} & a_{23} & a_{14} \\ a_{31} & a_{32} & a_{33} & a_{34} \end{bmatrix} \quad \text{(a 3} \times \text{4 matrix)}$$

Scalar Matrix Operations

$$kA = \|ka_y\|$$
$$A/k = \|a_{ij}/k\|$$

For example;

$$5 \begin{bmatrix} 1 & 2 \\ 3 & 4 \end{bmatrix} = \begin{bmatrix} 5 \times 1 & 5 \times 2 \\ 5 \times 3 & 5 \times 4 \end{bmatrix} = \begin{bmatrix} 5 & 10 \\ 15 & 20 \end{bmatrix}$$

$$\begin{bmatrix} 1 & 2 \\ 3 & 4 \end{bmatrix} / 2 = \begin{bmatrix} .5 & 1 \\ 1.5 & 2 \end{bmatrix}$$

Vector Matrix Operations

Row vector x, matrix A:

$$xA = \left[\sum_{i=1}^{n} x_i a_{i1} \cdots \sum_{i=1}^{n} x_i a_{im} \right]$$

The number of elements in x must be the same as the number of rows in A. For example

$$[1 \quad 2] \begin{bmatrix} 3 & 0 & 1 \\ 0 & 2 & 2 \end{bmatrix} = [3 + 0 \quad 0 + 4 \quad 1 + 4] = [3 \quad 4 \quad 5]$$

Column vector y, matrix A:

$$Ay = \begin{bmatrix} \sum_{j=1}^{m} a_j y_{1j} \\ \cdots \\ \sum_{j=1}^{m} a_{nj} y_j \end{bmatrix}$$

The number of elements in y must be the same as the number of columns in A. For example,

$$\begin{bmatrix} 1 & 2 & 3 \\ 4 & 5 & 6 \end{bmatrix} \begin{bmatrix} 3 \\ 2 \\ 1 \end{bmatrix} = [3 + 4 + 3 \quad 12 + 10 + 6] = [10 \quad 28]$$

Matrix Matrix Operations

Addition, subtraction: Two matrices must be of the same size.

$$A + B = \|a_{ij} + b_{ij}\|$$
$$A - B = \|a_{ij} - b_{ij}\|$$

For example,

$$\begin{bmatrix} 1 & 2 \\ 3 & 4 \end{bmatrix} + \begin{bmatrix} 3 & 2 \\ 1 & 4 \end{bmatrix} = \begin{bmatrix} 1 + 3 & 2 + 2 \\ 3 + 1 & 4 + 4 \end{bmatrix} = \begin{bmatrix} 4 & 4 \\ 4 & 8 \end{bmatrix}$$

Multiplication: Column number of the 1st matrix must be the same as the row number of the 2nd matrix.

$$A \times B = \left\| \sum_{k=1}^{n} a_{ik} b_{kj} \right\|$$

Where A is an $m \times n$ matrix, and B is a $n \times r$ matrix. The result is an $m \times r$ matrix. For example,

$$\begin{bmatrix} 1 & 2 \\ 3 & 2 \\ 2 & 1 \end{bmatrix} \times \begin{bmatrix} 1 & 1 & 2 \\ 3 & 2 & 1 \end{bmatrix} = \begin{bmatrix} 1+6 & 1+4 & 2+2 \\ 3+6 & 3+4 & 6+2 \\ 2+3 & 2+2 & 4+1 \end{bmatrix} = \begin{bmatrix} 7 & 5 & 4 \\ 9 & 7 & 8 \\ 5 & 4 & 5 \end{bmatrix}$$

Transpose:

$$A^T = \|a_{ji}\|$$

For example,

$$\begin{bmatrix} 1 & 2 & 3 \\ 4 & 5 & 6 \\ 7 & 8 & 9 \end{bmatrix} = \begin{bmatrix} 1 & 4 & 7 \\ 2 & 5 & 8 \\ 3 & 6 & 9 \end{bmatrix}$$

Some basic laws:

$$A + B = B + A$$

$$(A + B) + C = A + (B + C)$$

$$A(B + C) = AB + AC$$

$$A(BC) = (AB)C$$

Determinant of a Matrix

$$\begin{bmatrix} a_{11} & a_{12} & a_{13} \\ a_{21} & a_{22} & a_{23} \\ a_{31} & a_{32} & a_{33} \end{bmatrix}$$

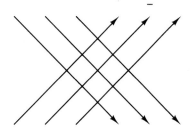

$$\begin{matrix} a_{11} & a_{12} & a_{13} & a_{11} & a_{12} \\ a_{21} & a_{22} & a_{23} & a_{21} & a_{22} \\ a_{31} & a_{32} & a_{33} & a_{31} & a_{32} \\ & & + & & \end{matrix}$$

$$\det A = \begin{matrix} a_{11}a_{22}a_{33} + a_{12}a_{23}a_{31} + a_{13}a_{21}a_{32} \\ - a_{31}a_{22}a_{13} - a_{32}a_{23}a_{11} - a_{33}a_{21}a_{12} \end{matrix}$$

For example,

$$\det \begin{bmatrix} 1 & 2 & 3 \\ 2 & 3 & 3 \\ 4 & 2 & 0 \end{bmatrix}$$

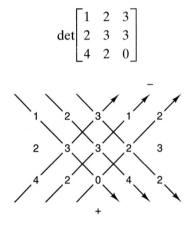

$$\begin{aligned} \text{determinant} &= 1 \times 3 \times 0 + 2 \times 3 \times 4 + 3 \times 2 \times 2 - 4 \times 3 \times 3 - 2 \times 3 \times 1 \\ &\quad - 0 \times 2 \times 2 \\ &= 0 + 24 + 12 - 36 - 6 - 0 \\ &= -6 \end{aligned}$$

For a 2×2 matrix,

$$\det \begin{bmatrix} 1 & 2 \\ 3 & 4 \end{bmatrix} = 1 \times 4 - 3 \times 2 = -2$$

4

Process Engineering

Manufacturing is the activity that transforms raw materials into a finished product. The finished product is typically specified on an engineering design (either a drawing on paper or in a CAD model). Selecting the manufacturing processes to transform the raw material into a finished part specification is based on matching the design requirements with the manufacturing process capabilities. Process capability is historic and scientific knowledge for each process. It is worthwhile to note that processes and machine tools are not equivalent. A process denotes a certain way an operation is carried out. For example, a drilling process denotes an operation that creates a hole by gradually removing material from a workpiece. There are many variations of drilling processes. A twist drill uses the two rotating chisel edges on the tool tip to cut the material while the flutes transport the cut material out of the hole being created. A paddle drill, on the other hand, employs no flutes for chip removal.

There are three levels of process capability: a universal level, a shop level, and a machine level. The universal-level process capability is our current ability to produce a product without regard to the individual shop or machines that perform the process. On the universal level, we say that a twist drill can produce a round hole with a certain accuracy. This statement is applicable to all twist drill processes; whether they are performed in company A or company B is not considered. Such universal-level process capability is normally presented in handbooks and textbooks. It represents an aggregate measure of the process capability.

The second process capability level is the shop level, where additional processing detail is considered. Although one generally can say that a twist drill operation can produce a certain hole diameter with a certain accuracy, at the shop level, we !ook at a specific machine or improved cutter requirements that can produce a much smaller hole or obtain better accuracy. This capability may not be achievable by other companies. Or, perhaps, the equipment is older and not as well maintained; thus, the capability is lessened. In either case, the shop-level capability represents the capability of the best machine in the shop. Shop-level capabilities are those published by companies for internal use.

The machine-level capability addresses the ability of a specific machine to achieve specific goals. Although the shop has certain capabilities, it does not necessarily follow that each machine in the shop has the same capability. For example, one may find an old milling machine in the same shop with a high-precision milling machine. Also a sophisticated jig may be used to provide accurate location for a bolt hole set. The capabilities are definitely different per machine and potentially different per setup. Statistical quality-control techniques usually are used to obtain the accuracy capability data. Machine-level capability information is important for selecting the specific machine to perform a specific process.

Some important process-capability parameters include the following:

1. The shapes and sizes a process can produce
2. The dimensions and geometric tolerances that can be obtained by various processes
3. The material removal rate
4. The relative cost
5. Other cutting characteristics/constraints

Process capability does not necessarily imply that all process selection or machine selection is based on these parameters. However, the more information considered in selecting a process, the more complete will be the result. For conventional process planning (when human planners are used), all process-capability information comes either in the form of experience or in handbook tables and guides. A computer-aided process-planning system functions based on this process-capability information. It is essential for a manufacturing engineer/process planner to know the process capability. In a computer-integrated manufacturing environment, process-capability information has to be captured and represented as computer-usable data so it can be used for decision making.

The basic mechanisms of process selection are discussed in Chapter 13. Process capability and its representation methods are discussed in this chapter.

4.1 EXPERIENCED-BASED PLANNING

It is always true that the accumulation of experience is knowledge. Most of our knowledge comes either from our own experience or is passed on to us by others and is based on their experience. This is also true in the context of manufacturing processes. If we go back to the example of the farmer and blacksmith in Chapter 2, we can make a point of how experience works in a manufacturing environment. When the farmer verbally specified or drew a picture of the hoe he wanted, the blacksmith must have had a manufacturing method (process plan) in mind; otherwise, he would not have been able to make the hoe. The process plan the blacksmith created was neither a written one nor a complete one. However, in his mind, he knew that he had some scrap iron in the back of his shop that he could use for the hoe. After retrieving the material, he heated it in his furnace until it was red hot (hot working). He then completed the forging cycle by hand and hammer. Had the farmer asked, "How did you know how to convert your scrap to my hoe?" the answer most assuredly would have been something like, "I've been in the trade for 30 years—experience told me."

Even in this computer age, many process-planning activities still rely on the experience of process planners. Where do process planners obtain their experience? From earlier training as machinists (most typical), from books, or from discussions with colleagues. This kind of information can be passed from person to person and generation to generation. However, there are some problems associated with such a planning base.

1. Experience requires a significant period of time to accumulate.
2. Experience represents only approximate, not exact knowledge.
3. Experience is not directly applicable to new processes or new systems.

Because of these problems, we need to seek other ways to represent our process-capability knowledge base so that it might be preserved and installed as a decision-support system in a computer.

4.1.1 Machinist Handbooks

One way to store process-capability information is to print it in handbooks. This has long been a standard manufacturing practice. Process-capability information is usually presented in tables, figures, or listed as guidelines. Large manufacturers typically prepare their own handbooks for internal use. Therefore, the knowledge is kept, but has traditionally been "proprietary." Handbooks can serve both as a reference and as a guide for process selection. Figure 4.1 represents some typical information of process capability (surface-finish ranges). The surface-finish chart shows the limiting extremes of several processes. For example, a flat surface of 8 μin. surface finish can be machined by grinding, polishing, and lapping. It can be rarely achieved by milling, yet a surface finish of 8 μin. is possible using a finish milling cut. Other information, such as process accuracy, can be found in similar tables or charts (see Table 4.1). In Table 4.1, an accuracy class 10 for drilling is considered highly accurate, but for reaming, it is only considered moderately accurate. The information in these books is very general and not specific to any shop. These manuals represent universal process capabilities.

Some process-capability information is presented as listed guidelines or tables, so that process planners can follow some general rules. Such guidelines are published in a shop to guide personnel in preparing process documents. These guidelines are not generally portable to other shops. We call such information shop-level process-capability information. For example, the following guidelines can be applied to produce holes.

I. Diameter ≤ 0.5 in.:	If the diameter is less than 0.5 in.
A. True position ≥ 0.010:	and greater than 0.010 in.
1. Tolerance > 0.010:	and the diametric tolerance is greater than 0.010 in.
Drill the hole	then drill.
2. Tolerance ≤ 0.010:	and the diametric tolerance is less than 0.010 in.
Drill and ream	then drill and ream.

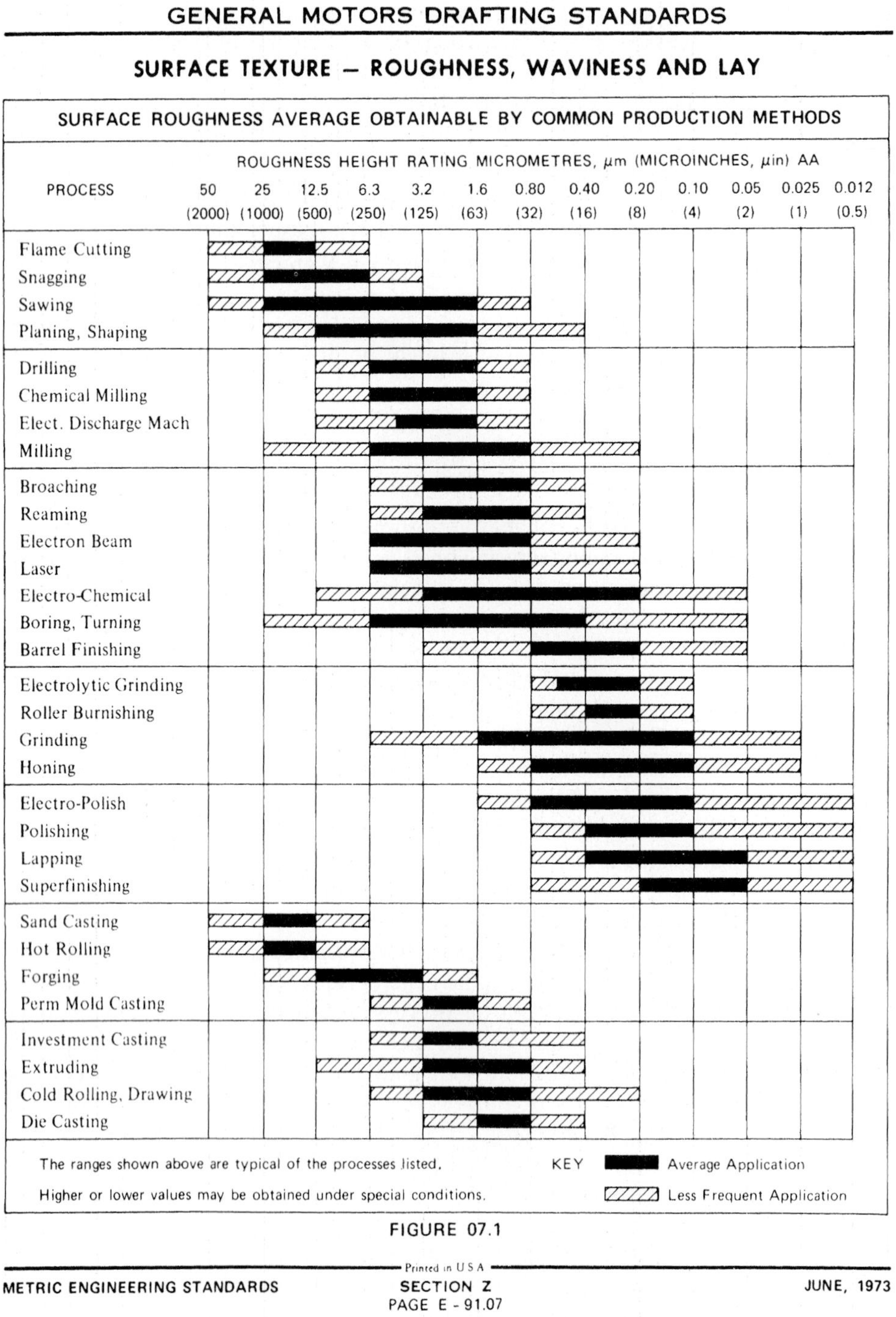
GENERAL MOTORS DRAFTING STANDARDS
SURFACE TEXTURE — ROUGHNESS, WAVINESS AND LAY
SURFACE ROUGHNESS AVERAGE OBTAINABLE BY COMMON PRODUCTION METHODS
ROUGHNESS HEIGHT RATING MICROMETRES, μm (MICROINCHES, μin) AA
PROCESS
50 (2000)
25 (1000)
12.5 (500)
6.3 (250)
3.2 (125)
1.6 (63)
0.80 (32)
0.40 (16)
0.20 (8)
0.10 (4)
0.05 (2)
0.025 (1)
0.012 (0.5)
Flame Cutting
Snagging
Sawing
Planing, Shaping
Drilling
Chemical Milling
Elect. Discharge Mach
Milling
Broaching
Reaming
Electron Beam
Laser
Electro-Chemical
Boring, Turning
Barrel Finishing
Electrolytic Grinding
Roller Burnishing
Grinding
Honing
Electro-Polish
Polishing
Lapping
Superfinishing
Sand Casting
Hot Rolling
Forging
Perm Mold Casting
Investment Casting
Extruding
Cold Rolling, Drawing
Die Casting
The ranges shown above are typical of the processes listed.
Higher or lower values may be obtained under special conditions.
KEY
Average Application
Less Frequent Application
FIGURE 07.1
Printed in U S A
METRIC ENGINEERING STANDARDS
SECTION Z
PAGE E - 91.07
JUNE, 1973

Figure 4.1 Surface-finish ranges. (Courtesy of General Motors Corporation [taken from GM Drafting Standsrds].)

TABLE 4.1   PRINCIPLES OF MACHINING BY CUTTING, ABRASION, AND EROSION

Classes (according to ISO): columns 1 to 3 … 14 to 16 are *of accuracy*; columns 1 … 14 are *of surface quality*.

Machining method	1 to 3	4	5	6	7	8	9	10	11	12	13	14 to 16	1	2	3	4	5	6	7	8	9	10	11	12	13	14
I. CHIP REMOVING PROCESSES																										
Turning				•	•	○	○	○	x	x	—	—	—	—	—	x	x	○	○	•						
Boring				•	•	○	○	○	x	x	—	—	—	—	—	x	x	○	○	•						
Drilling						•	○	x	x	—					—	—	x	x	○	•						
Reaming		•	•	○	○	x	x	—	—								—	x	○	○	•	•				
Peripheral milling			•	•	○	○	x	x	—	—				—	—	x	x	○	○	•	•					
Face milling			•	•	○	○	x	x	—	—				—	—	x	x	○	○	•	•					
Planing and shaping				•	○	○	○	x	x	—				—	—	x	x	○	○	•	•					
Broaching		•	•	○	○	x	x	—	—	—	—						—	x	○	○	•	•				
II. ABRASION PROCESSES																										
A. *Using abrasive tools*																										
Centre-type cylindrical grinding			•	○	○	x	x	—	—								—	x	x	○	•	•				
Centreless cylindrical grinding			•	○	x	x	x	—	—								—	x	x	○	○	•				
Internal grinding			•	○	○	x	x	—	—								—	x	x	○	○	•				
Surface grinding			•	○	○	x	x	—	—	—							—	x	x	○	○	•				
Abrasive belt grinding				•	○	○	x	x	—	—						—	x	x	○	○	•					
Surface honing		•	•	○	○	x	—	—										—	—	x	x	○	•			
Shaft and internal honing	•	•	•	○	○	x	—											—	—	x	x	○	○	•		
Superfinish	•	•	○	○	x	x	—											—	—	x	○	○	•	•		
B. *Using loose abrasive*																										
Lapping		•	•	○	○	x	x	—										—	—	x	○	○	•	•		
Mechanical polishing	•	•	○	○	x	x	—	—										—	—	x	x	○	○	•	•	
Vibratory and barrel finishing				•	•	•	○	○	x	x	—					—	—	x	x	○	•					
Abrasive-blast treatment				•	•	•	○	○	x	x	—	—				—	—	x	○	○	•	•				
Ultrasonic machining				•	•	○	○	x	x	—						—	x	○	○	•	•					

Accuracy
- — rough
- x fairly accurate
- ○ accurate
- • highly accurate

Surface quality
- — rough
- x fairly smooth
- ○ smooth
- • very smooth

Source: Courtesy of Peter Peregrinus Limited, taken from J. Kaczmarek, *Principles of Machining by Cutting, Abrasion, and Erosion*, 1977.

B. True position ≤ 0.01:   and less than 0.01 in.
    1. True position ≤ 0.01:   then drill and finish bore.
       Drill, then finish bore
    2. Tolerance ≤ 0.002:   and the diametric tolerance is less than
                                                  0.002 in.

       Drill, semifinish bore,   then drill, semifinish and finish bore.
       then finish bore
II. 0.05 in. < diameter ≤ 1.00:
    etc.

4.2 PROCESS-CAPABILITY ANALYSIS

Now that different process knowledge representation methods have been discussed, we can return our focus to the "knowledge" represented in our system. This knowledge includes the process capabilities that we discussed earlier in the chapter. Again, this knowledge base is limited to chip-metal removal processes.

Before any decision can be made (whether it be experience-, table-, or tree-based), the information required to make the decision must be complete. This information includes a process-by-process breakdown of the following elements:

1. Shape(s) that a process can generate
2. Size limitation (boundaries of the tooling, machine tools, fixtures)
3. Tolerances (both dimensional and geometric)
4. Surface finish (as a limiting value or functional expression)
5. Cutting force
6. Power consumption

The first four elements are capabilities and the last two are limitations. The limitations form the constraints that the machinery is bounded by during processing. The shape elements imply/define the basic geometry producible by a process (see Table 4.2). With little training, virtually anyone can develop a set of shapes that can be produced by a process. However, this feature is perhaps the most difficult task to achieve using a computer, that is, reasoning the shape capability in its natural form (geometry and topology), especially for sophisticated components. Many researchers are still working on this problem (Joshi and Chang, 1988). A feasible alternative is to represent shape by a code. Human judgment can be used to identify machined surfaces and assign codes to them. The matching of shape capability and machined surface may not be automatic, but can be significantly simplified.

For internal machining processes (holes, and so on), the size capability is constrained by the available tool size. For external machining, size is constrained by the available machine table size (machine cube). The other capabilities and limitations can be expressed mathematically. These expressions are straightforward to program on a computer if the "exact" equations and constraints can be found.

TABLE 4.2 SHAPE CAPABILITY

Process	Shape capability
Turning	External surfaces that can be generated by rotating a line or curve around an axis
Boring	Hole
Drilling	Hole
Reaming	Hole
Face milling	Flat surface
Peripheral milling	Flat surface, slot
Shaping and planing	Flat surface
End milling	Hole, flat surface, curved surface, slot
Grinding	Flat surface, hole, external cylindrical surface
Honing	Hole
Taping	Internal thread

4.2.1 Process Boundaries

One way to represent process capabilities is to use process boundaries. A process boundary is interpreted as the limiting size, tolerances, and surface finish for a process. It is expressed as the best- (or worst-) case result of a process. Such a result can be obtained by careful control of the cutting conditions and process parameters (feed, speed, depth of cut). Figure 4.2 is a typical process-boundary table.

Boundary	Hole-processing processes	Plane-producing processes
Smallest tool size	S_n	S_s
Largest tool size	L_{fn}	L_s
Negative tolerance	$A_1(\text{Dia.})^{n_1} + B_1$	$A_1(\text{Dia.})^{n_1} + B_1$
Positive tolerance	$A_2(\text{Dia.})^{n_2} + B_2$	$A_2(\text{Dia.})^{n_2} + B_2$
Straightness (holes)	$A_3(\text{Len./Dia.})^{n_3} + B_3$	$A_3 = \dfrac{\text{depth of cut} \times \text{length}}{\text{Dia.}} + B_3$
Parallelism	$A\left(\dfrac{\text{Len.}}{\text{Dia.}}\right) + B$	$A_5\left(\dfrac{\text{Len.}}{\text{Dia.}}\right) + B_5$
Roundness (holes); angularity (planes)	$R_n A_4$	$A_s A_4$
Depth limit	$D_n A_6 \cdot \text{Dia.}$	$A_6(\text{Dia.}) + B_6$
True position	A_7	
Surface finish	A_8	A_8

Figure 4.2 Process-boundary table (Wysk, 1977).

Size boundaries are determined by available tool sizes or machine-table sizes. This limitation is purely a function of the production system. In a small custom machine shop, the largest chuck for the lathes may be 10 in. in diameter. Therefore, the upper part size boundary for turning is a 10-in.-diameter workpiece. However, in a shipyard, the largest lathe may be able to accommodate up to a 3-ft-diameter component. The upper boundary for turning would be 3 ft instead of 10 in. Other process boundaries are also system-dependent.

For instance, dimensional tolerance is affected by many variables (e.g., tool diameter, machine-tool accuracy, vibration, thermal effect). Several sources (Eary and Johnson, 1962; Trucks, 1974) have developed tables, charts, and functions that show tolerance dependency as a function of surface size and perhaps other variables such as material or operational parameters. Scarr (1967) suggested that the tolerance for all hole-making processes can be expressed in a general form:

$$\text{Tol} = A(D)^n + B \qquad (4.1)$$

where

  Tol = tolerance
   A = coefficient of the process
   n = exponent describing the process
   B = constant describing the best tolerance attainable by the process
   D = hole diameter

The diameter-tolerance capability is related to the tool diameter. Other factors that affect diameter tolerance are taken into account by constant B. This general form also can be used to represent other processes. The values of coefficients A, B, and n in the equation can be obtained through experimentation. A regression analysis can be done using the measurements taken from the process. The estimated value of the tolerance capability may not be precise, but it provides a first-cut estimation. Again, it is worth noting that A, B, and n are system-dependent (i.e., no universal parameters can be found).

Straightness and parallelism tolerance for holes define the axial tolerance. Again, many factors affect these tolerances. A theoretical prediction is not possible, so we need to find a reasonable empirical model. To find such an empirical model, first, we would like to find an expression that can estimate the major cause of error. From the general form of such an expression, empirical data can be used to find the coefficients. The major cause of error on straightness and parallelism is tool deflection. A tool can be modeled most simply as a cantilever beam (Figure 4.3). The deflection of the beam is

$$\delta = \frac{Pl^3}{3EI} \qquad (4.2)$$

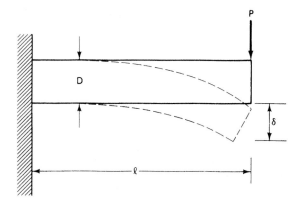

Figure 4.3   Cantilever beam.

where

E = modulus of elasticity
I = moment of inertia
l = beam length
P = force

and

$$I = \frac{\pi D^4}{64} \qquad \text{(for cylindrical beam or tool)} \qquad (4.3)$$

$$\delta = \frac{64Pl^3}{3ED^4} = \frac{CP}{D}\left(\frac{l}{D}\right)^3 \qquad (4.4)$$

where C is a constant.

Roughly, the error caused by deflection can be expressed as a coefficient multiplied by the length/diameter ratio raised to some exponential power. Because no machine is perfect, a constant is necessary to represent the effect of other errors. The final form of straightness and parallelism tolerances can be written as

$$\text{Tol} = A\left(\frac{l}{D}\right)^n + B \qquad (4.5)$$

where A, n, and B are experimentally determined values.

Flatness error, in surface production, is generally caused by the deflection of the tool and machine inaccuracy. Machining accuracy is a function of the machine-tool repeatability, backlash, deflection, distortion, and machine-spindle/tool alignment. If the machine is rigid, the tool can be again assumed to be a cantilever beam.

Cutting-force variables (width and depth cut, feed, number of cutter teeth), the length and diameter of the cutter, as well as today's shop practices, all affect surface flatness. Equation 4.6 is an empirical equation that has been used to estimate surface flatness [Wysk 77].

$$\text{Flatness} = A\left(\frac{a_p ld}{w}\right)^n + B \tag{4.6}$$

where

a_p = depth of cut
l = cutter length
d = cutter diameter
w = width of cut

Roundness error of a hole-making process is a function of machine rigidity, material, tool geometry, and so on. Little quantifiable information is available. However, experimental results can be used to find the boundaries for each process. The same is true for angularity and true position. Constant values or functional values can be used to model these characteristics.

Surface finish can be analytically expressed as a function of tool geometry and feed. The theoretical surface-finish heights for different tool geometries are shown in Figure 4.4. In the figure, h is the maximum height irregularity and f is the feed. The arithmetic mean value of surface finish, R_a, is defined as the sum of the areas above and below a line that equally divides these two areas (Figure 4.4). For a pointed tool, because $\triangle ABC = \triangle CDE$,

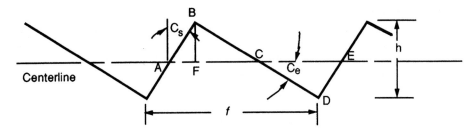

Figure 4.4   Arithmetic mean surface finish.

$$AC = CE = \frac{f}{2} \tag{4.7}$$

$$\text{Height of } \triangle ABC = \text{height of } \triangle CDE = \frac{h}{2}$$

$$\overline{AF} = \frac{h}{2}\tan C_s \tag{4.8}$$

$$\overline{CF} = \frac{h}{2}\cot C_e \tag{4.9}$$

$$\overline{AF} + \overline{CF} = \frac{f}{2} = \frac{h}{2}(\tan C_s + \cot C_e) \tag{4.10}$$

$$h = \frac{f}{\tan C_s + \cot C_e} \tag{4.11}$$

$$\Delta ABC = \Delta CDE = \frac{(f/2)(h/2)}{2} = \frac{fh}{8} \tag{4.12}$$

$$\text{Total area} = \Delta ABC + \Delta CDE = \frac{fh}{4} \tag{4.13}$$

$$R_a = \frac{\text{total area}}{f} = \frac{h}{4} \tag{4.14}$$

$$= \frac{f}{4(\tan C_s + \cot C_e)} \tag{4.15}$$

For a rounded tool (of tip radius r) with a small feed,

$$R_a = \frac{0.0321f^2}{r} \tag{4.16}$$

For a rounded tool with a large feed, Equation (4.16) also provides a reasonable approximation. However, these equations only estimate the surface finish under perfect cutting conditions; no consideration is given to other factors that affect cutting. Only the effect of feed is considered. Cook and Chanderamani (1964) showed that surface finish is affected by cutting speed as well as depth of cut. Other factors such as the sharpness of the cutter, vibration, and so on, also contribute to the roughness of the surface. The actual surface-finish value may be more than twice the theoretical value. The surface-finish boundary, however, should be the best attainable surface finish. Because feed and speed are control variables instead of process attributes, only a point estimator is used to predict the surface-finish capability. This point estimator can be taken from an existing data table, such as that shown in Figure 4.1.

Table 4.3 gives some example process-boundary data taken from Wysk (1977). As mentioned before, there is no universal process-boundary data. Each machine tool has its own unique process capability.

TABLE 4.3   PROCESS-BOUNDARY DATA

	Twist drilling	Rough face milling
Length	$\leq 12.0D$	NA
D	$0.0625 \leq$	NA
D	≤ 2.0	NA
Tol +	$0.007D^{0.5} \leq$	$0.002 \leq$
Tol −	$0.007D^{0.5} + 0.003 \leq$	$0.002 \leq$
Straightness	$0.0005\left(\frac{l}{D}\right)^3 + 0.002$	NA
Roundness	$0.004 \leq$	NA
Parallelism	$0.001\left(\frac{l}{D}\right)^3 + 0.003$	$50 \leq$
True position	$0.008 \leq$	NA
Surface finish	$100 \leq$	$50 \leq$
Flatness	NA	$0.001 \leq$
Angularity	NA	$0.001 \leq$

INTERMEDIATE MATERIALS

4.3 BASIC MACHINING CALCULATIONS

Before we start the topic of process capability, it is worthwhile to discuss the basic calculations of machining. Our discussion is limited to drilling, turning, and milling. Calculations for other conventional machining processes can be derived from the ones discussed.

4.3.1 Feed and Feed Rate

Feed, f, can be defined as the relative lateral movement between the tool and the workpiece during a machining operation. It corresponds to the thickness of the chip produced by the operation shown in Figure 4.5. In turning and drilling operations, it is defined as the advancement of the cutter per revolution of the workpiece (turning) or tool (drilling). The typical unit is ipr (inch per revolution). In milling, it is defined as the advancement of the cutter per cutter-tooth revolution; the unit is inch per revolution per tooth. Feed rate, V_f, is defined as the speed of feed; the unit is ipm (inch per minute).

$$V_f = fnN \tag{4.17}$$

where

n = number of teeth in the cutter for milling; $n = 1$ for drilling and turning

N = rotation speed of the cutter (drilling and milling) or workpiece (turning) in rpm

4.3.2 Cutting Speed

The cutting speed, V, can be defined as the maximum linear speed between the tool and the workpiece. The cutting speed for drilling, turning, and milling can be determined as a function of the workpiece or the tool diameter, D, and the rotation speed, N.

$$V = \frac{\pi D N}{12} \tag{4.18}$$

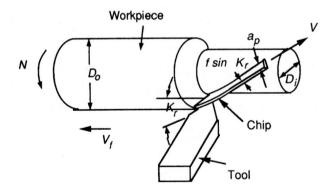

Figure 4.5   Chip formation.

where

V = speed, feet per minute
D = diameter, inches
N = rotational speed, rpm

4.3.3 Depth of Cut

The depth of cut is determined by the width of the chip (Figures 4.5 and 4.6). During the roughing operation, the depth of cut is usually much greater than that of the finishing operation. For turning, it is one-half the difference between the inner and the outer diameters of the workpiece.

$$a_p = \frac{D_o - D_i}{2} \tag{4.19}$$

where

a_p = depth of cut, inches
D_o = outer diameter, inches
D_i = inner diameter, inches

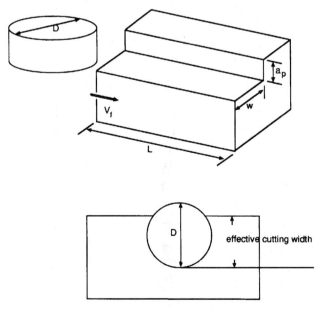

Figure 4.6   Face milling.

4.3.4 Metal-Removal Rate

The metal-removal rate (MRR) is a measurement of how fast material is removed from a workpiece. It can be calculated by multiplying the cross-sectional area of the chip by the speed. A large metal-removal rate (MRR) produces a short processing time and a low MRR yields a long processing time. However, the MRR also affects the life of a cutter. The effect of the metal-removal rate to tool life is discussed later. The unit of the metal-removal rate is usually expressed as cubic inches per minute. A different formula is used for different processes. For drilling, the cross-sectional area of the chip is $\pi D^2/4$.

$$MRR = \frac{\pi D^2}{4} V_f = \frac{\pi D^2}{4} fN \tag{4.20}$$

where

D = drill diameter, inches
V_f = feed rate, inches per minute
f = feed, inches per revolution
N = rotational speed, rpm

Because

$$N = \frac{12V}{\pi D} \tag{4.21}$$

$$MRR = \frac{\pi D^2}{4} f \frac{12V}{\pi D} = 3DfV \tag{4.22}$$

For turning, the chip width is $(D_o - D_i)/2$, where D_o and D_i are outer and inner workpiece diameters, respectively. The cross-sectional area is $\pi(D_o^2 - D_i^2)/4$. Therefore, the metal removal rate is

$$MRR = \frac{\pi(D_o^2 - D_i^2)}{4} V_f = \frac{\pi(D_o^2 - D_i^2)}{4} fN \tag{4.23}$$

$$N = \frac{12V}{\pi(D_o + D_i)/2} \tag{4.24}$$

$$MRR = 6(D_o - D_i)fV \tag{4.25}$$

For milling processes, the chip cross-sectional area is (Figure 4.6)

$$A = a_p w \tag{4.26}$$

$$MRR = a_p w V_f = a_p w fnN \tag{4.27}$$

$$N = \frac{12V}{\pi D}$$

$$MRR = \frac{12a_p wn}{\pi D} fV \tag{4.28}$$

where

a_p = depth of cut, inches
w = width of cut, inches
n = number of teeth on the cutter
D = cutter diameter, inches
f = feed, inches per tooth per revolution
V = speed, feet per minute

4.3.5 Machining Time

Machining time is the total amount of time it takes to finish processing a workpiece. Machining time is a function of workpiece size, depth of cut, feed, and speed. It can be calculated by dividing the tool-path length by the feed speed. The tool-path length is determined by the length of the workpiece, overtravel of the tool for clearance, and the number of passes required to clear the volume. For drilling, one-pass turning, and milling,

$$t_m = \frac{L + \Delta L}{V_f}$$
(4.29)

where

t_m = machining time, minutes
L = hole depth, inches
ΔL = clearance height or overtravel, inches
V_f = feed speed, inches per minute

For multiple-pass turning, the number of passes can be calculated as

$$n_p = \left| \frac{D_o - D_i}{2a_p} \right|^+$$
(4.30)

where

n_p = number of passes
D_o = raw-material diameter, inches
D_i = finished-part diameter, inches
a_p = depth of cut
$|x|^+$ = round off x to the next integer number

For milling processes,

$$n_p = \left| \frac{\Delta h}{a_p} \right|^+ \left| \frac{w}{\alpha D} \right|^+$$
(4.31)

where

Δh = total height of material to be removed, inches

w = workpiece width, inches

α = cutter overlapping factor = effective cutting width/tool diameter ≤ 1.0

D = cutter diameter, inches

Example 4.1

A workpiece of 3-in. diameter is to be machined on a lathe to 2.7-in. diameter. The total length of the workpiece is 10 in. It is recommended from the handbook that a feed of 0.01 ipr, a cutting speed of 200 fpm, and a maximum depth of cut of 0.1 in. be used. A 0.25-in. overtravel should be used for cutter clearance. How long will it take to finish the part?

Solution: The spindle speed N is

$$N = \frac{12 \times 200}{\pi 3} = 254 \text{ rpm}$$

$$V_f = 0.01 \times 254 = 2.54 \text{ ipm}$$

Because the required depth of cut is greater than the maximum allowable depth of cut, multiple passes are necessary.

$$n_p = \left|\frac{3 - 2.7}{2 \times 0.1}\right|^+ = 2 \text{ passes}$$

$$t_m = 2\left(\frac{10 + 0.25}{2.54}\right) = 8.07 \text{ min}$$

4.3.6 Tool Life

A tool's useful life can be ended by one of two mechanisms: erosion (wear) and breakage (catastrophic failure). The two major wear zones are crater wear (on the tool face) and the flank wear (Figure 4.7). Crater wear is caused by the high temperatures generated on the rake face combined with high shear stresses. When there is excessive crater wear, the cutting edge is weakened. The tool can no longer support the cutting force; catastrophic tool failure is the result. Flank wear is the result of the frictional action between the tool flank and the workpiece. It is a gradual wear. Catastrophic tool failure is usually quite unpredictable and a phenomenon that one tries to minimize; therefore, tool life is usually defined as the cut time a new tool undergoes before a certain flank wear is reached. Permissible values of flank wear have been recommended by the International Standards Organization (ISO, 1972). They appear in Table 4.4.

F. W. Taylor (1906) was the first to develop a generalized tool-life equation. He observed that using a constant feed when tool life and cutting speed were plotted on a log–log graph would result in a straight line. Such a relationship can be expressed as

$$\frac{V}{V_r} = \left(\frac{t_r}{t}\right)^n \tag{4.32}$$

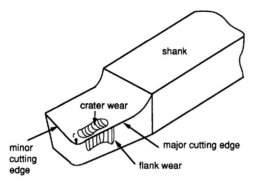

shank

crater wear

minor
cutting
edge

major cutting edge

flank wear

Figure 4.7   Cutter wear.

where

n = constant
V = cutting speed
t = tool life
V_r = reference cutting speed given tool life t_r

Figure 4.8 shows the results of tool-life experiments plotted on a log-log graph. By rearranging Equation (4.32), we obtain

$$t = \frac{t_r V_r^{1/n}}{V^{1/n}}$$

$$= \frac{C}{V^\alpha} \tag{4.33}$$

where

$\alpha = 1/n$
$C = t_r V_r^{1/n}$

Table 4.5 shows C and α for some metals, tool signatures, and sizes of cut.

Example 4.2

When cutting steel with a high-speed steel (HSS) cutter, the tool life at a cutting speed of 100 sfpm (surface feet per minute) is 60 minutes; at 150 sfpm, it is 30 minutes. What is the tool-life equation of the cutter on the material?

Solution:

$$\frac{100}{150} = \left(\frac{30}{60}\right)^n$$

$$0.667 = (0.5)^n$$

TABLE 4.4   AVERAGE PERMISSIBLE VALUES OF LATHE TOOL (FLANK) WEAR

Tool point material	Tool type	Workpiece material	Type of turning	Permissible values of VB in mm	
				In dry turning	In turning with coolant
High-speed steel (HSS)	For external straight turning	Steel and malleable cast iron	Rough, medium accurate, and accurate	0.5–1.0 0.3–0.5	1.5–2.0
		Grey cast iron	Rough, medium accurate, and accurate	3–4	—
	Boring and undercutting tools	Steel and malleable cast iron	Rough, medium accurate, and accurate	0.3–0.5	1.5–2.0
		Grey cast iron	Rough, medium accurate, and accurate	1.5–2.0	—
	Cutoff and parting tools	Steel and malleable cast iron	Rough, medium accurate, and accurate,	0.3–0.5	0.8–1.0
		Grey cast iron	Rough, medium accurate, and accurate	1.5–2.0	
	Form tools	Steel	Rough, medium accurate, and accurate	—	0.4–0.5
	Threading tools	Steel	Rough finish	—	2.0
				—	0.3
Sintered carbides	All types of tools	Steel	Rough, medium accurate, and accurate	0.8–1.0	—
		Grey cast iron	Rough and medium accurate ($s > 0.3$)	0.8–1.0	—
			($s < 0.3$)	1.4–1.7	—
Sintered metal oxides	All types of tools	Steel and cast iron	Medium accurate and accurate	0.8	—

Courtesy of Peter Peregrinus Limited, taken from J. Kaczmarek, *Principles of Machining by Cutting, Abrasion, and Erosion,* 1976.

$$n = \frac{\ln 0.667}{\ln 0.5} = \frac{-0.405}{-0.693} = 0.58$$

$$\frac{V}{150} = \left(\frac{30}{t}\right)^{0.58}$$

$$\left(\frac{V}{150}\right)^{1/0.58} = \frac{30}{t}$$

or

$$t = \frac{169{,}317}{V^{1.724}}$$

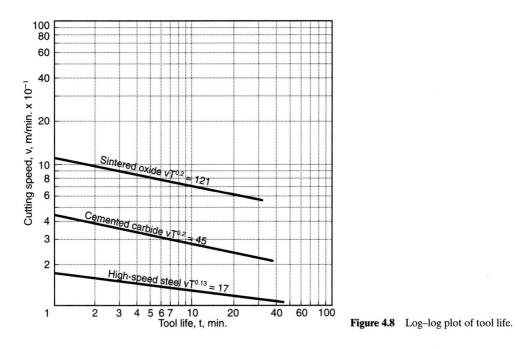

Figure 4.8 Log–log plot of tool life.

Later research confirmed that feed and depth of cut also contributed to the tool life. An expanded Taylor tool-life equation of the following form resulted:

$$t = \frac{\lambda C}{V^{\alpha_T} f^{\beta_T} a_p^{\gamma_T}} \tag{4.34}$$

where

λ, C = constants for a specific tool/workpiece combination

$\alpha_T, \beta_T, \gamma_T$ = exponents for a specific tool/workpiece combination

The influence of V on tool life is much greater than the influence of f. The depth of cut has the least influence on tool life. However, the last tool-life expression is based on the flank wear of the tool. For high-speed steel and carbide tools operating under normal conditions, flank wear is the major cause of tool deterioration. For ceramic tools, breakage is more significant than flank wear. A tool may fail before any significant flank wear can be detected. One must be also aware that a tool-life equation holds only when all cutting conditions such as tool geometry, material, workpiece material, cutting fluid, and so on, are held constant.

4.3.7 Machining Force and Power Requirements

Machining force and power requirements are not limiting values in process selection, but become important considerations in selecting process parameters (feed, speed, and depth of cut). Force and power are functions of process parameters. When using the

TABLE 4.5 SOME TYPICAL VALUES FOR C AND IN TOOL-LIFE EQUATION $VT^n = C$

Tool	Work Material	f (ipr)	α_p (in.)	C	n
High C steel	Yellow brass	0.013	0.100	1400	0.1
HSS	Gray cast iron	0.026	0.050	800	0.1
HSS	SAE 1035 steel	0.013	0.050	610	0.11
HSS	SAE 1045 steel	0.013	0.100	850	0.11
HSS	SAE 3140 steel	0.013	0.100	810	0.16
HSS	SAE 4350 steel	0.013	0.100	360	0.11
HSS	SAE 4350 steel	0.026	0.100	215	0.11
HSS	Monel metal	0.013	0.100	790	0.08
HSS	Monel metal	0.026	0.150	590	0.07
T64 carbide	SAE 1040 steel	0.025	0.062	3720	0.16
T64 carbide	SAE 1060 steel	0.025	0.125	3070	0.17
T64 carbide	SAE 1060 steel	0.025	0.250	2600	0.17
T64 carbide	SAE 1060 steel	0.042	0.062	2375	0.16
T64 carbide	SAE 1060 steel	0.062	0.062	1860	0.16
High C steel	Bronze	0.013	0.100	1080	0.109
HSS	SAE B1112 steel	0.013	0.050	1040	0.109
Stellite	SAE 3240 steel	0.031	0.187	1000	0.19

Source: Adapted from Boston, 1951, p. 150.

same tool, machine, and workpiece material, in general, the greater the volume of work material removed per unit time, the greater the power required. Reduced feed, speed, or depth of cut can reduce both the cutting force required and the power consumed. Because force and power are constrained by the machine output, it is necessary to know the power requirements of a cutting process as a function of the process parameters.

4.3.7.1 Machining forces.   In orthogonal cutting, the resultant force, F_r, applied to the chip by the tool lies in a plane normal to the tool cutting edge (Figure 4.9). F_c is the major cutting force and F_t is the thrust force. The cutting force can be expressed roughly as a product of the specific cutting resistance, k_s, and the cross-sectional area of undeformed chip.

$$F_c = wh_ck_s \tag{4.35}$$

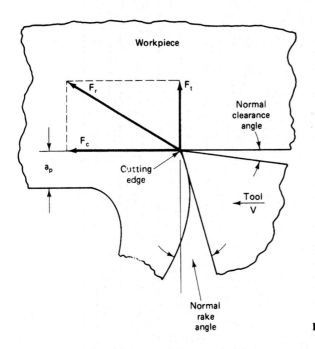

Figure 4.9   Cutting-force geometry.

$$F_t = bwh_ck_s \tag{4.36}$$

where

> F_c, F_t = cutting force, lbf
>> b = coefficient empirically determined by tool geometry
>> w = width of undeformed chip, inches
>> h_c = thickness of undeformed chip, inches
>> k_s = specific cutting resistance

    Because the major cutting force is usually much greater than the thrust force, it is of more interest to us. Because the thickness of the chip, a_p, is determined by the feed and the width of the chip is determined by the depth of cut, Equation (4.35) can be written as

$$F_c = K \cdot f^\alpha \cdot a_p^\beta \tag{4.37}$$

where

> F_c = major cutting force, lbf
> K = constant
> f = feed, ipr
> a_p = depth of cut, inches
> α, β = coefficients

Through experiments, it has been shown that α and β do not equal 1. When f versus F_c or a_p versus F_c are plotted on a log–log graph, straight lines result.

4.3.7.2 Cutting power.   The cutting-power consumption, P_c, can be calculated as the product of the cutting speed, v, and the cutting force, F_c. Thus,

$$P_c = \frac{F_c V}{33,000} \qquad (4.38)$$

where

P_c = power, horsepower
F_c = cutting force, lbv
V = cutting speed, fpm

Example 4.3

When a low-carbon steel is cut, it is found that the cutting-force equation is

$$F_c = 140,000 f^{0.8} a_p^{0.9}$$

If the selected cutting speed is 120 fpm, the feed is 0.01 ipr, and the depth of cut is 0.25 in., what is the required cutting horsepower? Assume the machine efficiency is 0.85.

Solution:

$$F_c = 140,000(0.01)^{0.8}(0.25)^{0.9} = 1009 \text{ lbf}$$

$$P_m = \frac{1009 \times 120}{33,000} = 3.67 \text{ hp}$$

$$\text{Horsepower} = \frac{3.67}{0.85} = 4.310 \text{ hp at the machine}$$

It can also be estimated by multiplying a specific cutting energy by the metal-removal rate.

$$P_c = p_s(\text{MRR}) \qquad (4.39)$$

where

p_s = specific cutting energy, hp $\cdot$ min/in.^{3}
MRR = metal-removal rate, in.^{3}/min

Specific cutting energy is a function of the hardness of the workpiece material and the mean value of the undeformed chip thickness. Figure 4.10 shows the approximate values of the specific cutting energy, p_s, for various materials and operations. Undeformed chip thickness for turning is $f \sin k_r$, for drilling is $(f/2)\sin k_r$, and for face

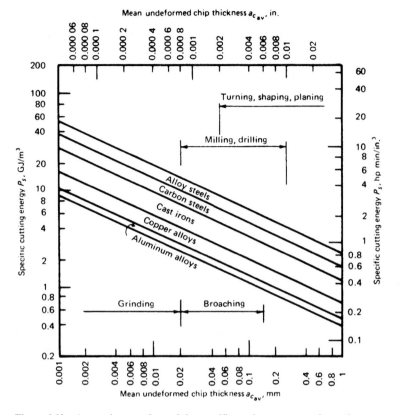

Figure 4.10   Approximate values of the specific cutting energy, p_s, for various materials and operations. (Reprinted from *Fundamentals of Metal Machinging Tools,* G. Boothroyd, 1975, by permission of Hemisphere Publishing Corporation, formerly Scripta Book Company.)

milling is V_f/Nn_t, where k_r is the major cutting edge angle, f is the feed, V_f is the feed rate, N is the rotation speed (rpm), and n_t is number of teeth on the cutter.

Equations for cutting force, power, surface finish, tool life, and machine time are summarized in Tables 4.6 and 4.7. The equations for F_c contain an empirically determined coefficient, K_F, to account for several factors that affect cutting force. K_F must be determined for all tool–work material combinations, process types, tool-wear conditions, workpiece hardness, tool geometry, and speed.

4.3.8 Process Parameters

So far, we have discussed process capabilities, cutting force, and power. However, surface finish, force, and power constraints are directly affected by the process parameters—feed, speed, and depth of cut. Therefore, process selection becomes an iterative

TABLE 4.6 SUMMARY OF EQUATIONS FOR CUTTING OPERATIONS[a,b]

Operation	Machining Time, t_m	Tool life, t	Cutting force, F_c	Power, P_m	Surface finish, R_a (4)
Turning Boring	$\dfrac{l_w}{f \cdot n_w}$	$K_T \cdot v^{\alpha_T} \cdot f^{\beta_T} \cdot a_p^{\gamma_T}$	$K_F \cdot f^{\beta_F} \cdot a_p^{\gamma_F}$	$\dfrac{F_c \cdot v}{6120 n_m}$	$\dfrac{32 \cdot f^2}{r_e}$
Facing Parting	$\dfrac{D_m}{2 \cdot f \cdot n_w}$ $\dfrac{b_w}{f \cdot n_t}$				
Shaping & planing					
Drilling & reaming	$\dfrac{l_w}{f \cdot n_t}$	$K_T \cdot v^{\alpha_T} \cdot f^{\beta_T} \cdot a_p^{\gamma_T} \cdot D_t^{\delta_T}$	$K_F \cdot f^{\beta_F} \cdot a_p^{\gamma_F} \cdot D_t^{\delta_F}$ (2)	$\dfrac{M \cdot n_e}{9.74 \times 10^5 \, \eta_m}$	$\dfrac{64 \cdot 2 f^2}{D_t}$ (5)
Slab Milling[a]	$\dfrac{l_w + k\sqrt{a(D_t - a)}}{f \cdot n_t}$ (1)		$K_F \cdot f^{\beta_F} \cdot a_c^{\gamma_F} \cdot D_t^{\delta_F} \cdot b_w \cdot z$		$\dfrac{64 \cdot 2 f^2}{D_t + e}$
Side & face milling		$K_T \cdot v^{\alpha_T} \cdot a_f^{\beta_T} \cdot a^{\gamma_T} \cdot D_t^{\delta_T} \cdot b_w^{\varepsilon_T} \cdot z^{\zeta_T} \cdot \lambda_\beta^{\eta_T}$			
Face milling	$\dfrac{l_w + D_t}{f \cdot n_t}$	$K_T \cdot v^{\alpha_T} \cdot a_f^{\beta_T} \cdot a_p^{\gamma_T} \cdot D_t^{\delta_T} \cdot b_w^{\varepsilon_T} \cdot z^{\zeta_T}$	$K_F \cdot v^{\alpha_F} \cdot a_f^{\beta_F} \cdot a_p^{\gamma_F} \cdot d_t^{\delta_F} \cdot b_w^{\varepsilon_F} \cdot z^{\zeta_F}$	$\dfrac{F_c \cdot v}{6120 \eta_\mu}$	$K_a \cdot a_t^{14}$
Broaching	$\dfrac{l_t}{v}$	$K_T \cdot v^{\alpha_T} \cdot a_f^{\beta_T}$	$K_F \cdot a_f^{\beta_F} \cdot D_m \cdot z_c$ (3)		$\cdots$

(1) $k = \begin{cases} 1, \text{ case (a)} \\ 2, \text{ case (b)} \end{cases}$

(2) Same formula holes for torque M.

(3) Valid for broaching of round holes only.

(4) Valid for ideal conditions only; however, empirical formulas are available for specific cases in turning operations.

(5) Eccentricity e will be equal to zero in ideal conditions.

$$n_w = \frac{v}{nD_w} \qquad n_t = \frac{v}{nD_t}$$

[a]An explanation of the notation used in this table is given in Table 3.6.

[b]From Armorego, 1968; Boothroyd, 1975; and Kaczmarek, 1976.

Source: Coelho [1980].

TABLE 4.7 NOTATION FOR TABLE 4.6

a, a_c, a_f, a_p	Depth of cut
b_w	Width of workpiece
D_m	Diameter of the machined surface
D_t	Diameter of the tool
f	Feed
K_F, K_T, K_R	Constants for cutting-force, tool-life, and surface-roughness empirical equations, respectively
l_t	Length of tool or broach
l_w	Length of surface to be machined
n_r	Frequency of reciprocation (strokes/min)
n_t	Tool-spindle speed (rpm)
n_w	Rotational frequency of the workpiece (rpm)
r_ε	Tool-nose radius
v	Cutting speed
z	Number of teeth on the cutting tool
z_c	Number of teeth cutting simultaneously in a tool
$\alpha_T, \beta_T, \gamma_T, \varepsilon_T, \eta_T, \delta_T$	Cutting speed, feed, depth of cut, tool diameter, machined surface width, number of teeth in the cutting tool, and tool cutting-edge inclination (L^0) exponents for cutting-force, surface-roughness, and tool-life equations, respectively
n_m	Overall efficiency of the machine-tool motor and drive systems
e	Tool cutting-edge inclination

procedure: First, a process is selected, and then the machining parameters are adjusted to accommodate the system constraints. The selection of the machining parameters, however, affects the time and cost required to produce a component. These parameters are not arbitrary, nor are they constant for different operations. Process parameters are the basic control variables for a machining process. The earliest study on the economical selection of process parameters was conducted by F. W. Taylor (1906). As a result of his effort and the later efforts of many others, machining data handbooks (Metcut Research Associates, 1980) and machinability data systems (Parsons, 1971) have been developed to recommend process parameters for efficient machining. These handbooks contain recommended feeds and speeds for different tooling, work material, tool diameter, depth of cut, and so on, combinations. The parameters recommended are good, but not necessarily the best or the most appropriate. An example is shown in Table 4.8, where the figure, feeds, and speeds for a 30-to-60 min tool life for high-speed steel (HSS) tools (for carbide insert, 1 to 2 h) are recommended.

Several machinability systems are currently marketed that recommend sets of parameters that optimize machining cost, time, or production rate or that simply retrieve data tables or calculated values. The FAST system (Parsons, 1971) is an example of a table-value retrieval system. An early General Electric (GE) system used a mathematical model developed by W. W. Gilbert (1950) to calculate one parameter given all others. In Gilbert's model, speed, material, coolant, workpiece surface condition, tool geometry, flank wear, workpiece hardness, tool life, feed, depth of cut, and so on, were represented as a mathematical function. A so-called machinability computer (a slide rule-like device) using Gilbert's model was marketed by GE in the late 1950s (General Electric, 1957).

TABLE 4.8 EXAMPLE OF DRILLING DATA

Feed[a] values are given as **ipr / mm·rev** and speed[a] as **fpm / m·min**; hole diameters are given in **in / mm**.

Material	Hardness Bhn	Condition	Speed[a] fpm / m·min	1/16 in 1.5 mm	1/8 in 3 mm	1/4 in 6 mm	1/2 in 12 mm	3/4 in 18 mm	1 in 25 mm	1 1/2 in 35 mm	2 in 50 mm	Tool material grade AISI or C	Tool material grade ISO
Alloy steels, wrought high-carbon	50 R$_c$ to 52 R$_c$	Quenched and tempered	10 / 3	— / —	0.0005 / 0.013	0.001 / 0.025	0.002 / 0.050	0.002 / 0.050	0.003 / 0.075	0.003 / 0.075	0.004 / 0.102	T15, M42[b]	S9, S11[b]
	52 R$_c$ to 54 R$_c$	Quenched and tempered	75 / 23	— / —	— / —	0.001 / 0.025	0.001 / 0.025	0.0015 / 0.038	— / —	— / —	— / —	C-2	K10
	54 R$_c$ to 56 R$_c$	Quenched and tempered	60 / 18	— / —	— / —	0.001 / 0.025	0.001 / 0.025	0.0015 / 0.038	— / —	— / —	— / —	C-2	K10
High-strength steels, wrought 300M 4340Si H11	225 to 300	Annealed	50 / 15	0.001 / 0.025	0.003 / 0.075	0.004 / 0.102	0.007 / 0.18	0.010 / 0.25	0.012 / 0.30	0.015 / 0.40	0.018 / 0.45	M10, M7, M1	S2, S3

TABLE 4.8 (*continued*)

Material	Hardness Bhn	Condition	Speed[a] fpm	Speed[a] m/min	Feed[a] ipr/mm·rev — 1/16 in / 1.5 mm	1/8 in / 3 mm	1/4 in / 6 mm	1/2 in / 12 mm	3/4 in / 18 mm	3/4 in / 18 mm	1 in / 25 mm	1½ in / 35 mm	2 in / 50 mm	Tool material grade AISI or C	ISO
4330V 98BV40 H13 4340 D6ac	300 to 350	Normalized	35	11	—	0.002 / 0.050	0.004 / 0.102	0.006 / 0.15	—	0.009 / 0.23	0.010 / 0.25	0.014 / 0.36	0.017 / 0.45	M10, M7, M1; S2, S3; T15, M42[b]	
	350 to 400	Normalized	30	9	—	0.002 / 0.050	0.004 / 0.102	0.006 / 0.15	—	0.008 / 0.20	0.010 / 0.25	0.012 / 0.30	0.015 / 0.40	S9, S11[b]; T15, M42[b]	
	43 Rc to 48 Rc	Quenched and tempered	20	6	—	0.002 / 0.050	0.003 / 0.075	0.004 / 0.102	—	0.004 / 0.102	0.004 / 0.102	0.004 / 0.102	0.004 / 0.102	S9, S11[b]; T15, M42[b]	
	48 Rc to 50 Rc	Quenched and tempered	15	5	—	0.001 / 0.025	0.002 / 0.050	0.003 / 0.102	—	0.003 / 0.102	0.004 / 0.102	0.004 / 0.102	0.004 / 0.102	S9, S11[b]; T15, M42[b]	
	50 Rc to 52 Rc	Quenched and tempered	10	3	—	0.0005 / 0.013	0.001 / 0.025	0.002 / 0.050	—	0.002 / 0.050	0.003 / 0.075	0.003 / 0.075	0.004 / 0.102	S9, S11[b]; C-2	
	52 Rc to 54 Rc	Quenched and tempered	75	23	—	—	0.025	0.025	—	0.038	0.038	0.038	0.038	K10	K10

[a]For holes more than two diameters deep, reduce speed and feed.

[b]Any premium HSS (T15, M33, M41–M47) or (S9, S10, S11, S12).

Source: From the *Machining Data Handbook*, 3rd ed. (by permission of the Machinability Data Center, © 1980 by Metcut Research Associates Inc.).

More recently (from 1960 to present), machinability systems have become computer-based to take advantage of the computational power to include optimization models. For example, a later version of the GE data system contains optimum feed and speed for minimum cost and time using an unconstrained optimization scheme to identify the optimal tool life. Although most commercial machinability data systems use unconstrained optimization, several research papers have appeared that focus on constrained models. This class of problems is discussed in the following sections.

4.4 PROCESS OPTIMIZATION

Before we discuss process optimization, we must first understand the basic tool-life equation. A faster metal-removal rate results in both reduced tool life and reduced machining time. However, whenever a tool has been worn past some practical limit, it must be replaced. Therefore, there is a trade-off between increased machining rate and machine idle time, which results in frequent tool changes.

Machining optimization models can be classified as single-pass and multipass models. In a single-pass model, we assume that only one pass is needed to produce the required geometry. In this case, the depth of cut is fixed. In a multipass model, this assumption is relaxed and a_p also becomes a control variable. Any multipass model can be reconstructed into a single-pass model.

4.4.1 Single-Pass Model

In a single-pass model, processing time per component, t_{pr}, can be expressed as the sum of machining time, t_m, material-handling time, t_h, and tool change time, t_t.

$$t_{pr} = t_m + t_h + t_t \left(\frac{t_m}{t} \right) \qquad (4.40)$$

where $(t_m/t)^{-1}$ represents the number of parts that can be produced before the tool requires changing.

Equations for t_m and t are found in Table 4.6. The depth of cut, a_p, in the equations is constant. The production cost per component, C_{pr}, can be written as

$$C_{pr} = \frac{C_b}{N_b} + C_m \left[t_m + t_h + \frac{t_m}{t} \left(t_t + \frac{C_r}{C_m} \right) \right] \qquad (4.41)$$

where

C_b = setup cost for a batch
C_m = total machine and operator rate (including overhead)

C_r = tool cost (for a HSS tool, it is the cost of regrinding for a tungsten carbide tool, TCT, steel; it is the cost of one insert cutting edge)

N_b = batch size

An optimization model for machining is as follows:

$$\min t_{pr} \quad \text{(for time)} \tag{4.42a}$$

or

$$\min C_{pr} \quad \text{(for cost)} \tag{4.42b}$$

subject to

1. Spindle-speed constraint:

$$n_{\min} < n_w < n_{\max} \quad \text{(for workpiece)} \tag{4.43a}$$

$$n_{t,\min} < n_t < n_{t,\max} \quad \text{(for tool)} \tag{4.43b}$$

2. Feed constraint:

$$f_{\min} < f < f_{\max} \tag{4.44}$$

3. Cutting-force constraint:

$$F_c < F_{c,\max} \tag{4.45}$$

4. Power constraint:

$$P_m < P_{\max} \tag{4.46}$$

5. Surface-finish constraint:

$$R_a < R_{a,\max} \tag{4.47}$$

Equations for n_w, n_t, F_c, P_m, and R_a are given in Table 4.6.

Many solution procedures can be used to solve the previous model. Berra and Barash (1968) and later Wysk (1977) used an iterative search procedure that approached optimum. Groover (1976) used an "evolutionary operations" procedure, which is somewhat similar to a Hooke–Jeeves search procedure. Hati and Rao (1976) applied a sequential unconstrained minimization technique (SUMT) (Fiacco and Mc-Cormick, 1968) in conjunction with the Davidson–Fletcher–Powell (D–F–P) algorithm to solve the problem. Dynamic programming (DP) and other mathematical programming methods have also been used.

Example 4.4

In a turning operation, the length of the part is 10 in., the diameter of the raw material is 3 in., and the diameter of the finished part is 2.9 in. The overtravel for the cut is 0.5 in. The recommended feed rate is 0.1 ipr. The time to load and unload a part is 2 min. The time for a cutter change is 3 min. The tool life can be expressed as $t = (1.7 \times 10^5)/V^{1.7}$.

(a) What is the unconstrained minimum time cutting speed?

(b) The operator rate is \$20/h and the machine rate is \$15/h. The cutter costs \$3 each. What is the minimum cost-cutting speed? Ignore the batch size and the batch setup cost.

Solution:

(a)

$$\eta \, (\text{rpm}) = \frac{12V}{\pi D}$$

$$D = \frac{3 + 2.9}{2} \approx 3$$

$$\eta \, (\text{rpm}) = \frac{12V}{3\pi} = 1.273V$$

$$V_f = f \cdot \text{rpm} = 0.1 \cdot 1.273V = 0.1273V$$

$$t_m = \frac{L + \Delta L}{V_f} = \frac{10 + 0.5}{0.1273V} = \frac{82.48}{V}$$

$$t_{pr} = t_m + t_h + t_t \left(\frac{t_m}{t}\right)$$

$$= \frac{82.48}{V} + 2 + 3\left[\frac{82.48/V}{(1.7 \times 10^5)/V^{1.7}}\right]$$

$$= 82.48V^{-1} + 2 + 0.001456V^{0.7}$$

$$\frac{dt_{pr}}{dV} = -82.48V^{-2} + 0.0010192V^{-0.3} = 0$$

$$0.0010192V^{-0.3} = 82.48V^{-2}$$

$$V^{1.7} = 80,926$$

$$V^* = 769 \text{ sfpm}$$

$$t_{pr}^* = \frac{82.48}{769} + 2 + 0.001456(769)^{0.7}$$

$$= 2.26 \text{ min}$$

(b)

$$C_{pr} = \frac{C_b}{N_b} + C_m\left[t_m + t_h + \frac{t_m}{t}\left(t_t + \frac{C_t}{C_m}\right)\right]$$

$$= \frac{20 + 15}{60}\left\{82.48V^{-1} + 2 + 82.48V^{-1}\left(\frac{V^{1.7}}{1.7 \times 10^5}\right)\left[3 + \frac{3}{(20 + 15)/60}\right]\right\}$$

$$= 0.5833\,(82.48V^{-1} + 2 + 0.00395V^{0.7}) = 48.11V^{-1} + 1.1666 + 0.0023V^{0.7}$$

$$\frac{dC_{pr}}{dt} = -48.11V^{-2} + 0.00161V^{-0.3} = 0$$

$$V^{1.7} = 29{,}882$$

$$V^* = 428 \text{ sfpm}$$

$$C_{pr}^* = \frac{48.11}{428} + 1.1666 + 0.0023(428)^{0.7}$$

$$= 1.438$$

Example 4.5[a]

This example shows the integer-transformation technique used in solving a milling-process optimization problem.

A low-carbon steel is machined by a milling process. The tool material is HSS. See Figure 4.11. The problem is to select the optimal parameters: n, d, R, Z, and V_p. The tool change time is equal to 80 s and the milling process is subject to the following constraints.

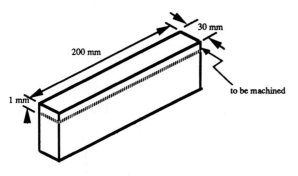

200 mm

30 mm

1 mm

to be machined

Figure 4.11 Workpiece for Example 4.5.

Machine power: $P_{\max} = 7.5$ kW
Cutting force: $F_{\max} = 60$ kg
Tool life: $T_{\min} = 30$ min
                             $T_{\max} = 60$ min
Spindle speed: $N_{\min} = 1$ rpm
                             $N_{\max} = 1200$ rpm

The tool-life equation (Wysk, 1977) can be stated as

$$T = \frac{C_v^3 (2R)^s}{V^\alpha (V_f/nZ)^\beta d^\gamma Z^{0.3} W^\delta} \tag{4.48}$$

where

$V =$ cutting velocity, m/min
$V_f =$ feed velocity, mm/s

For a milling operation using HSS tool and low-carbon steel material with ultimate tensile strength UTS $\cong 400$ MN/m², the model parameters are

$$C_v = 35.4, \qquad a = 3.03, \qquad b = 1.212, \qquad \gamma = 0.909, \qquad S = 1.364, \qquad d = 0.303$$

[a]This example is taken from Chang et al., 1982.

Equation (4.48) can be rewritten as

$$T = \frac{1.14 \times 10^5 R^{1.364} n^{1.212} Z^{0.909}}{V^{3.03} V_f^{1.212} d^{0.909} W^{0.303}} \qquad (4.49)$$

and

$$R = \frac{25.6}{4} Z = 6.4Z \qquad (4.50)$$

$$V = \frac{2\pi Rn}{1000} \times 60 = 2.413 Zn \qquad (4.51)$$

$$m = \frac{T \times 60}{T_c} \qquad (4.52)$$

$$T_c = \frac{L}{V_f} \qquad (4.53)$$

Substituting Equations (4.50) and (4.52) into Equation (4.49) yields

$$T = \frac{0.996 \times 10^5}{V_f^{1.212} d^{0.909} W^{0.303} n^{1.818} Z^{0.757}}$$

and including $W = 30$ mm, $d = 1$ mm, and $L = 200$ mm,

$$T = \frac{3.55 \times 10^4}{V_f^{1.212} n^{1.818} Z^{0.757}} \qquad (4.54)$$

Substituting Equations (4.54) and (4.53) into Equation (4.52) yields

$$m = \frac{1.066 \times 10^4}{V_f^{0.212} n^{1.818} Z^{0.757}}$$

and

$$V_f = \left(\frac{1.066 \times 10^4}{mn^{1.818} Z^{0.757}}\right) 4.717$$

$$= \frac{9.98 \times 10^{18}}{m^{4.717} n^{8.576} Z^{3.571}} \qquad (4.55)$$

The objective function is

$$T_T = T_c + T_t$$

or, in expanded form,

$$T_T = \frac{L}{60 V_f} + \frac{80}{60m}$$

$$= \frac{m^{4.717} n^{8.576} Z^{3.571}}{2.99 \times 10^{18}} + \frac{1.333}{m} \qquad (4.56)$$

The objective function is subject to the following constraints:

$$F = 1.46.6(2R)^{-1.1713}W^{1.1786}V^{-5557}d^{0.9128}\left(\frac{V_f^{0.7509}}{nZ}\right) \le 60 \text{ kg} \qquad (4.57)^a$$

$$P = \frac{60FV}{6010.2} \le 7.5 \text{ kW} \tag{4.58}$$

$$30 \le T \le 60 \text{ min} \tag{4.59}$$

$$1 \le n \le 1200 \text{ rpm} \tag{4.60}$$

$$2 \le Z \le 24 \tag{4.61}$$

$$1 \le m \tag{4.62}$$

Rewriting Equations (4.57) to (4.59) gives

$$F = 146.6(2 \times 6.4Z)^{-1.1713}(30)^{1.1796}(2.413nZ)^{-0.556}(1)^{0.9128}.$$

$$\left(\frac{9.959 \times 10^{18}}{m^{4.717}n^{9.58}Z^{4.57}}\right)^{0.7509} = \frac{4.605 \times 10^{16}}{m^{3.542}n^{7.749}Z^{5.158}} \le 60 \text{ kg} \tag{4.57a}$$

$$P = \frac{1.1 \times 10^{15}}{m^{3.542}n^{6.749}Z^{5.158}} \le 7.5 \text{ kW} \tag{4.58a}$$

$$30 = \frac{m^{5.717}n^{8.576}Z^{3.57}}{2.99 \times 10^{18}} \le 60 \tag{4.59a}$$

Bounds of m can be found by the force constraint:

$$\frac{1.6 \times 10^4}{n^{2.188}Z^{1.456}} \le m \tag{4.57b}$$

By the power constraint:

$$\frac{10^4}{n^{1.905}Z^{1.174}} \le m \tag{4.58b}$$

By the tool-life equation:

$$\frac{3.09 \times 10^3}{n^{1.5}Z^{0.624}} \le m \le \frac{3.48 \times 10^3}{n^{1.5}Z^{0.624}} \tag{4.59b}$$

Bounds of n can be found by machine characteristics:

$$1 \le n \le 1200$$

By Equation (4.57b) and the right-hand side of Equation (4.59b):

$$n \ge 2.47Z^{-0.49}$$

[a]Derived from Cincinnati Milling Machine Co. (1951).

By Equation (4.58b) and the right-hand side of Equation (4.59b):

$$n \geq 1.74 Z^{-0.29}$$

By the right-hand side of Equation (4.59b), $m > 1$,

$$n \leq 229.6 Z^{-0.416}$$

Because $W = 30$, it is preferred to have $2R > 30$; thus,

$$R = 6.4Z$$

$$Z \geq 2.34 \approx 3$$

By obtaining an optimum m,

$$\frac{\partial T_T}{\partial m} = \frac{m^{3.717} Z^{3.57} n^{8.576}}{6.34 \times 10^{17}} - \frac{1.333}{m^2} = 0$$

$$m^* = \frac{1367}{Z^{0.624} n^{1.5}}$$

$$\frac{\partial^2 T_T}{\partial m^2} > 0; \text{ consequently, } T_T \text{ is strictly convex}$$

Because m^* is always bounded by Equation (4.59b),

$$m^* = \left(\frac{3.09 \times 10^3}{Z^{0.624} n^{1.5}} \right)^- \qquad \text{(round off to the lowest integer)}$$

Therefore, Z and n should lie on their respective upper/lower bounds. In this case,

$$Z^* = 3 \qquad \text{and} \qquad n^* = 1$$

The results can be summarized as

$R = 19.2$ mm
$Z = 3$
$W = 30$ mm
$d = 1$ mm
$V_f = 13.2$ mm/min
$V = 7.239$ m/min
$n = 1$
$m = 1556$
$T_T = 0.02$ min

4.4.2 Multipass Model

Multipass models also consider the depth of cut as a control variable. Let a_p be the height of material to be removed, and n the number of passes. The time required per component can be written as

$$t_{pr} = t_h + \sum_{i=1}^{n_p} \left[t_m^i + \left(\frac{t_m^i}{t} \right) t_t \right] \tag{4.63}$$

where t_m^i is the time required for machining pass i.

The cost per component is

$$C_{pr} = \frac{C_b}{N_b} + C_m t_h + \sum_{i=1}^{n_p} C_{pr}^i \tag{4.64}$$

where

$$C_{pr}^i = C_m \left[t_m^i + \frac{t_m^i}{t} \left(t_t + \frac{C_r}{C_m} \right) \right] \tag{4.65}$$

$$a_t = \sum_{i=1}^{n_p} a_p^i \tag{4.66}$$

and superscript i represents the ith pass.

An additional constraint is also required in the formulation.

6. Depth-of-cut constraint:

$$a_{p,\min} < a_p^i < a_{p,\max} \tag{4.67}$$

The additional variable, a_p, makes the solution procedure more difficult than for a single-pass problem. In solving this class of problem, Challa and Berra (1976) used a modified Rosen gradient-search method. Philipson and Ravandaran (1978) and Subbarao and Jacobs (1978) both used goal programming to deal with the problem. Iwata et al. (1977) introduced a dynamic programming (DP) procedure to solve a multistage machining-optimization problem. Hayes et al. (1981) and Chang et al. (1982) transformed certain variables, such as depth of cut, into the discrete domain. The number of passes then can be obtained iteratively using a DP procedure to optimize the feed and speed. There is no general solution method that can be used for all problems.

Figure 4.12 shows the contours of unit cost and the feasible region for an example single-pass problem. In the figure, the bounding constraints as well as the objective function are plotted. The bounding constraint for the example is the surface finish. If the surface-finish constraint is relaxed, the force constraint becomes binding.

Tool: ISO SNMA 120408-P20

Holder: ISO PBSNR 2525

Material: SAE 1045 CD

Machine: Engine lathe

feed $\sim$ 0.05 – 2.5 mm/rev
speed $\sim$ 20 – 1600 rpm
power = 7.5 kW
machine efficiency = 0.80

$$t^* = \left(\frac{1}{n}-1\right) \frac{L}{L+e} \left(t_c + \frac{C_e}{C_m}\right) = 10 \text{ min}$$

C_m = \$0.25/min	t_h = 1.35 min/pc
C_e = \$0.50/edge	t_i = 0.2 min/pass
C_b = \$7.20/batch	t_c = 1 min/edge
D = 100 mm	L = 250 mm
e = 50 mm	N_b = 25
p = 0.1 a_p = 3 mm	K = 0.3

$$vt^{0.2} f^{0.3} a_p^{0.18} = 220$$

$$F_c = 250\, V^{-0.12} f^{0.75} a_p\, f\ 170 \text{ kp}$$

$$P_e = F_c v/6120 \leqslant 6 \text{ kW}$$

$$R_a = 2.43 \times 10^4\, v^{-1.52}\, f \leqslant 1.25\ \mu m$$

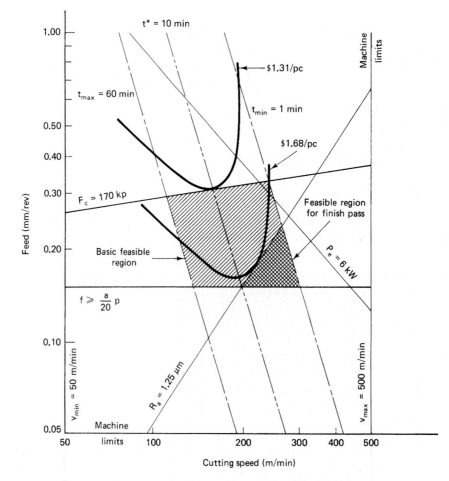

Figure 4.12   Contours of unit cost and the feasible region.

4.5 CONCLUDING REMARKS

There are two types of information that go into a process-planning system: design and process knowledge. Design representation was discussed in Chapter 2. In this chapter, process knowledge was discussed. Process planning can be said to be a procedure that matches the knowledge of the processes with the requirements of the design. Process capability is the producibility knowledge for a process. It is the basic mechanism of the process-planning system. However, a logical structure is necessary in order to carry out the matching procedure. This chapter provides both process capability and decision logic. In the next chapter, we discuss combining process planning and product design.

REVIEW QUESTIONS

4.1. It is desirable to produce a part with a surface finish of 3-μin. AA. If the surface has already been machined to dimension, what process(es) are needed to finish the surface? (*Hint:* Use Figure 4.1.)

4.2. It can be seen from Figure 4.1 and Table 4.1 that the grinding process is more accurate and can also produce a better surface finish than the milling process. Therefore, why aren't milling operations replaced by grinding operations? What factors should be considered before selecting a process?

4.3. Make a decision-table model for the following course-scheduling activity. Calculus is required before statistics can be taken, and two semesters of statistics are required before graduation. However, Professor Smith is the best statistics instructor, and unless taking her course postpones graduation, you will wait until she teaches the course.

4.4. Derive the ideal surface roughness for a tool with a round nose.

4.5. A hole of 1-in. diameter and 2.5-in. depth is to be drilled. The suggested feed is 0.05 ipr and the speed is 200 fpm. What are the feed speed, spindle rpm, MRR, and cutting time? Assume the clearance height is 0.2 in.

4.6. A part of 10-in. diameter and 20-in. length is to be turned down to 9.4 in. for the entire length. The suggested feed is 0.04 ipr and the speed is 450 fpm. The maximum allowable depth is 0.2 in. What are the feed speed, spindle rpm, MRR, and cutting time? Assume the overtravel is 0.5 in.

REVIEW PROBLEMS

4.1. The end of the part described in Review Question 4.6 is to be faced. The spindle rpm is set so as not to produce a cutting speed higher than the suggested speed (450 fpm). What are the feed speed, spindle rpm, MRR, and cutting time?

4.2. A volume 10 in. long, 5 in. wide, and 0.5 in. thick is to be removed by a face-milling cutter. The cutter is 3 in. in diameter and has six teeth. The maximum depth of cut is 0.3 in. What are the feed speed, spindle rpm, and cutting time?

4.3. When a 0.5-in. high-speed steel (HSS) drill on SAE 3140 steel at a feed of 0.03 ipr is used, the tool-life equation can be expressed as

$$t = \frac{6.16 \times 10^{15}}{V^{6.25}}$$

The hole drilled is 2 in. deep. If the selected speed is 200 fpm, how many holes can be drilled before we need to change the drill?

4.4. When a HSS tool is used to turn a stainless-steel shaft, the cutting force can be predicted:

$$F_c = 151,000 f^{0.85} a_p^{0.96}$$

The recommended speed is 200 fpm and the feed is 0.03 ipr. The diameter of the workpiece is 3 in. and the final diameter is 2.8 in. The part is 4 in. long. A 10-hp motor is used to drive the machine. The machine efficiency is 0.90. What is the maximum depth of cut based on the power-consumption constraint? How long will it take to finish the workpiece?

4.5. Assume the workpiece in Review Question 4.6 is made of alloy steel. What is the required cutting power? Use Figure 4.10.

4.6. In Review Problem 4.3, if the part loading/unloading time is 2 min, the tool change time is 3 min., what is the minimum-time cutting speed? What is the cutting time per hole?

4.7. In Review Problem 4.6, the operator and machine rates are $30/h. Each drill bit costs $2. What is the minimum-cost cutting speed? What is the cost per hole?

4.8. Derive the general expression for the unconstrained minimum-time cutting speed and the maximum-cost cutting speed.

4.9. The rate of profit, P, is defined as

$$P = \frac{S - C_{pr}}{t_{pr}}$$

Derive the expression for maximum-profit-rate cutting speed, V^*.

4.10. The processing time for single-pass model is given in Equation (4.40). The depth of cut, a_p, is a constant; therefore, the tool-life equation can be rewritten as

$$t = \frac{C'}{V^\alpha f^\beta}$$

Let the length of cut be L. If the maximum spindle speed is V_{max} and the maximum feed is f_{max}, what are the optimum cutting speed and feed?

4.11. Develop a method to solve the constrained optimization model for turning. Try to use the integer-transformation method illustrated in the milling optimization example.

4.12. Prepare a process plan for the part shown in Figure 2.14. First, assume that 10 parts will be made. What if 100,000 parts were made? How does this affect the process plan?

4.13. Find the general form of the tool life equation for Example 4.4.

REFERENCES/BIBLIOGRAPHY

ARMOREGO, E. J. and BROWN, R. H., *The Machining of Metals*, Prentice Hall, Englewood Cliffs, NJ, 1968.

BERRA, P. B. (1968). *Investigation of Automated Planning and Optimization of Metal Working Processes.* Ph.D. thesis, Purdue University, West Lafayette, Indiana.

BERRA, P. B., and M. M. Barash (1968). *Investigation of Automated Plating and Optimization of Metal Working Processes,* Report 14. West Lafayette, IN: Purdue University, Purdue Laboratory for Applied Industrial Control.

BOOTHROYD, G. (1975). *Fundamentals of Metal Machining and Machine Tools.* New York: McGraw-Hill.

BOSTON, O. W. (1951). *Metal Processing.* New York: John Wiley.

CHALLA, K., and P. B. BERRA (1976). "Automated Planning and Optimization of Machining Procedures—A Systems Approach," *Computers and Industrial Engineering,* 1(1), 35–36.

CHANG, T. C., R. A. WYSK, R. P. DAVIS, and B. CHOI. (1982). "Milling Parameter Optimization Through a Discrete Variable Transformation," *International Journal of Production Research,* 20(4), 507–516.

CINCINNATI MILLING MACHINE Co. (1951). *A Treatise on Milling and Milling Machines.* Cincinnati, OH: CMM.

COELHO, P. L. F. (1980). *The Machining Economics Problem in a Probabilistic Manufacturing Environment.* Unpublished M.S. thesis, Virginia Polytechnic Institute and State University, Blacksburg, Virginia.

COOK, N. H., and K. L. CHANDERAMANI (1964). "Investigation on the Nature of Surface Finish and Its Variation with Cutting Speed," *Journal of Engineering for Industry,* 86 (134), 134–140.

DeVor, R. E., W. J. ZDEBLICK, V. A. TIPNIS, and S. BUESCHER (1978). "Development of Mathematical Models for Process Planning of Machining Operations NAMRC—VII," in *Proceedings of the Sixth North American Metalworking Research Conference.* Dearborn, MI: Society of Manufacturing Engineers.

EARY, D. F., and G. E. JOHNSON (1962). *Process Engineering for Manufacturing.* Englewood Cliffs, NJ: Prentice Hall.

FIACCO, A. V., and G. P. McCORMICK (1968). *Nonlinear Programming.* New York: John Wiley.

GENERAL ELECTRIC (1957). *Operation Manual for the Carboloy Machinability Computer,* Manual MC-101-B. Detroit: General Electric Company, Metallurgical Processes Department.

GILBERT, W. W. (1950). "Economics of Machining," in *Machining: Theory and Practice.* Metals Park, OH: American Society for Metals.

GILBERT, W. W., and W. C. TRUCKENMILLER (1943). "Nomograph for Determining Tool Life and Power When Turning with Single-Point Tools," *Mechanical Engineering,* 65, 893–898.

GROOVER, M. P. (1976). *A Survey on the Machinability of Metals,* SME Technical Paper, Series MR76-269. Dearborn, MI: Society of Manufacturing Engineers, Dearborn, MI.

——— (1996). *Fundamentals of Modern Manufacturing: Materials, Processes, and Systems.* Englewood Cliffs, NJ: Prentice Hall.

GROOVER, M. P., A. M. GUNDA, and R. J. JOHNSON (1976). "Determination of Machining Conditions by a Self-Adaptive Procedure," in *Proceedings of the Fourth North American Metalworking Research Conference.* pp. 267–271.

HATI, S., and S. RAO (1976). "Determination of the Optimum Machining Conditions—Deterministic and Probabilistic Approaches," *Journal of Engineering for Industry,* 98(2), 354–359.

HAYES, G. M., JR., R. P. DAVIS, and R. A. WYSK (1981). "A Dynamic Programming Approach to Machine Requirements Planning," *AIIE Transactions,* 13(2), 175–181.

IWATA, K., et al. (1977). "Optimization of Cutting Conditions for Multi-pass Operations Considering Probabilistic Nature in Machining Processes," *Journal of Engineering for Industry,* 99(2), 210–217.

JOSH, S., and CHENG, T. (1988). "Graph-based Huevistics for Recognition of Machined Features from a 3D Solid Model," *Computer Aided Design,* 20(2), 58–66.

KACZMERK, J. (1976). *Principles of Machining by Cutting, Abrasion, and Erosion,* trans. A. Voellnagel and E. Lepa. Stevenage, England: Peter Peregrinus.

KALPAKJIAN, S. (1995). *Manufacturing Engineering and Technology,* 3rd ed. Reading, MA: Addison-Wesley.

LUDEMA, K. C., R. M. CADDELL, and A. G. ATKINS (1987). *Manufacturing Engineering, Economics and Processes.* Englewood Cliffs, NJ: Prentice Hall.

MCDANIEL, H. (1970). *Decision Table Software—A Handbook.* Princeton, NJ: Brandon/Systems Press.

METCUT RESEARCH ASSOCIATES, INC. (1980). *Machining Data Handbook,* 3rd ed. Cincinnati, OH: Machinability Data Center.

NIEBEL, B. W., A. DRAPER, and R. A. WYSK (1989). *Modern Manufacturing Process Engineering,* New York: McGraw-Hill.

PARSONS, N. R., ed. (1971). *N/C Machinability Data Systems.* Dearborn, MI: Society of Manufacturing Engineers.

PHILIPSON, R. H., and A. RAVANDARAN (1978). "Application of Goal Programming to Machinability Data Optimization," *Journal of Mechanical Design,* 100(2), 286–291.

SCARR, A. J. T. (1967). *Metrology and Precision Engineering.* London: McGraw-Hill.

SUBBARAO, P., and C. JACOBS (1978). "Application of Nonlinear Goal Programming to Machine Variable Optimization," in *Proceedings of the Sixth North American Metalworking Research Conference.* Dearborn, MI: Society of Manufacturing Engineers, 298–303.

TAYLOR, F. W. (1906). "On the Art of Cutting Metals," *Transactions of the American Society of Mechanical Engineers,* 28, 31.

TIPNIS, V. A., M. FIELD, and M. Y. FRIEDMAN (1975). *Development and Use of Machinability Data for Process Planning Optimization,* SME Technical Paper, Series MD75-517. Chicago, IL.

TRUCKS, H. E. (1974). *Designing for Economic Production.* Dearborn, MI: Society of Manufacturing Engineers.

WYSK, R. A. (1977). *Process Planning Systems,* MAPEC Module. West Lafayette, IN: Purdue University, School of Industrial Engineering,

5

Tooling and Fixturing

5.1 INTRODUCTION

In order to process parts, certain conditions must be realized. For example in order to assemble two items, one item is normally held firmly by some type of clamping device (a vise, a hand, and so on) while the second item is moved to the required assembly position with the proper orientation. The items are then joined together (screwed, snapped, slid, and so on) to form an assembly. If the parts are to be screwed together, then some additional processing resources (tooling—in this case a wrench or screwdriver) may also be required. The methods and resources used to assist in processing can significantly affect the efficiency and profitability of a process. In this chapter, we will present a discussion of the methods and resources required to process a part. We refer to this detail as tool engineering.

The trend toward flexibility in manufacturing systems has brought a new focus to tool engineering. For high-volume, long-run production items, significant time and effort were spent for custom tooling and fixturing. It was not uncommon for several months of engineering and manufacturing to precede the first production item. Much of today's emphasis on small-batch, custom manufacturing has led to the use of standard tooling and workholding devices that can be used for a variety of products. This chapter will again focus on machining and will begin with a discussion of tools. An introduction to fixtures and fixture design will then be presented.

F. W. Taylor was an early pioneer of tool engineering. His 1906 paper still provides many principles used in industry today. Although many of Taylor's principles are still used, the structures and characteristics of modern machining facilities have changed a great deal. Higher-powered, more rigid, multitool capacity, numerically controlled machines with a variety of available cutting tools have added significant complexity to tool engineering. In Taylor's time, there were not many tool materials available, and their performance was relatively easy for the operator to command. In the case of mass production, dedicated tests could be conducted to find the optimal performance. These circumstances are no longer globally true today. Beyond high-speed steel (HSS) and the original carbides, industry currently uses ceramics, cermets, cubic boron nitride (CBN), diamond tool materials, a variety of coatings, and ion and physical vapor-deposition (PVD) implementation techniques. These tools come with different geometries for different operations and various mounting configurations for many available toolholders. It is extremely difficult for a process planner or an operator to select the best tool geometry and the optimal application parameters. The situation in which a machinist grinds a tool from a HSS blank or brazed carbide is rare today. New tools and tool materials are developed routinely.

Over the years, thousands of man-hours and millions of research dollars have been spent to reveal the secrets of the metal-cutting process in the hope of predicting the process performance for a given operation. Metallurgical, microstructural, thermal, and mechanical aspects of the process have been investigated. Although important progress has been made to improve the understanding of the metal-cutting process, the ultimate goal of predicting process performance from setup and the material involved is still just a vision. It is unlikely that we will mathematically describe the process in general in the near future.

Despite the rapid developments of other system components in manufacturing systems, there has been little progress in tool management. This is primarily due to the number of variables involved and limited understanding of the processes. Direct and indirect performance measures of tool life are usually modeled as a function of primary machining parameters, speed, feed and depth of cut, and possibly some simplified tool geometry and workpiece variables, be it Taylor's exponential form or some other form (e.g., polynomial). Nonetheless, the metal-cutting process takes place at high temperature and pressure; the chemical, physical, and mechanical phenomena are beyond what a few parameters can describe. Moreover, the metal-cutting process appears random in nature. Any tool-life model can only give approximate values for average tool life. The variation of tool life is usually high: the coefficient of variation is as high as 0.3. Practitioners often indicate that tool-life consistency is more important than peak performance.

With the development of modern machining systems and new material-handling systems and especially the introduction of flexible manufacturing systems (FMSs), setup times have been greatly reduced. The percentage of time in cut has increased dramatically. In addition, the power and the rigidity of the machine tools have been improved tremendously. These new technologies upgrade system capability. However, the capital investment for these systems is much higher. The utilization of equipment is crucial for improving system productivity. Due to the increasing percentage of time in cutting, high system cost, less human attendance, and relatively low knowledge for the increased process complexity, technical operation management is more and more critical for improving machining industry productivity.

5.2 TOOL CHARACTERISTICS

In metal cutting, a proper tool must be identified for any operation. The technical involvement of the decision increases with the increasing number of possible tool selections and workpiece materials. Determining factors in selecting tool material, geometry, and construction include setup characteristics; material; shape and size of the workpiece; design requirement; operation type (roughing or finishing); and others. For a given setup and tool combination, machining-parameter selection (feed, speed, and depth of cut) must also be made. Although machining handbooks, which offer excellent application guides, are available (even in software form today), the selection of parameters is still no easy task. The suggested data in handbooks are based on isolated laboratory tests using standard specimens. Many restrictive factors, like setup rigidity, machine-tool quality, force, and power are carefully controlled. The environment determined by site, machine tool, and fixtures in the factory floor is often different from those encountered in laboratory tests. Performance is strongly dependent on environment variables, so the suggested data can be only used as a guide or starting point. The data pertinent to a specific application environment must be collected and documented to produce reliable performance guidelines. Even when applied to similar conditions, the suggested parameters tend to be conservative.

A metal-cutting process is the removal of unwanted metal using a wedge-shaped tool. Material is removed from a workpiece in the form of chips so as to obtain a desired surface. The cutting tool is made of a harder substance, and when forced against a workpiece, the edge of the tool deforms and removes a thin layer of material. A machine tool supplies the power, force, and necessary cutting tool movement at the proper speed with certain degrees of freedom. Fixtures are used to hold the workpiece firmly, conveniently, and accurately.

In manufacturing, the term *machining* is used to cover all the chip-making processes, for instance turning, milling, drilling, and boring. These operations are also classified as secondary processes, as opposed to primary processes, which are forming, rolling, forging, and casting. Common features of cutting tools are discussed in the following sections.

5.2.1 Tool Geometry

In metal cutting, the chip represents the volume of plastically deformed material removed from the workpiece surface. The deformation process normally takes place at a very high rate. High strain rates occur in both the chip and in the newly formed surface on the workpiece. A large amount of energy input must be provided to perform metal-cutting operations. The geometry of the tool point is one of the most important factors in determining the way in which the metal deforms, which in turn determines temperature, stress, and force on the tool. It also affects the interaction between the tool surfaces and work material. The fundamental geometric features of a turning tool can be characterized by the elements and parameters shown in Figure 5.1. The rake face is the surface on which the chip is formed and flows away from the workpiece. The highest temperature and stress on the cutting tool occurs on the rake face. The clearance face, or flank, intersects the rake face to form the cutting edge. Due to elastic deformation on the finished workpiece surface, friction and rubbing take place at the region of the flank closest to the cutting edge. The cutting action at the area closest to the end cutting edge formed by the side end clearance face and the rake face is similar to that of the side clearance face except that less cutting action takes place on that part of the tool point. In order to strengthen the tip of the tool and improve heat dissipation, a radius is used to connect the side clearance and end clearance faces. The nose radius also can

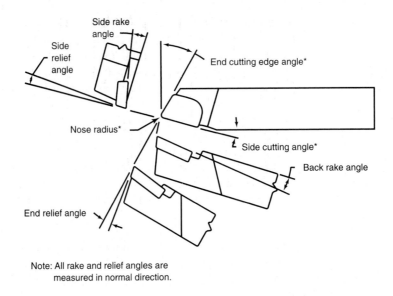

Note: All rake and relief angles are
measured in normal direction.

Figure 5.1   Turning-tool geometry (Niebel, Daper, and Wysk, 1989).

improve the theoretical surface roughness. When cracking, rubbing, ploughing, chatter-
ing, and other effects in the process are very small, the theoretical surface roughness can
be approximated by the side cutting angle, end cutting angle, nose radius, and the feed
rate. A large nose radius can generate better surface finish.

The influence of tool geometry is illustrated by using a metal-cutting diagram,
as shown in Figure 5.2. Deformation takes place primarily in three zones: the primary
deformation zone, the secondary zone, and the clearance zone. The influence of fundamental tool geometry parameters can be addressed with respect to these three zones.
The initial, and major, deformation takes place in the primary zone. The compressed
material plastically sheared along a certain direction is primarily determined by properties of workpiece material and tool rake angle. The shear angle, ϕ, is an important
characteristic of the metal-cutting process. It determines the strain rate in the removed
material. In general, the lower the shear angle, the higher the strain and the higher the
plastic deformation. This induces more heat, higher stress, and larger force. During the
process, the square-shaped, shaded area *klmn* deforms into *pqrs*. The shear angle ϕ is
related to rake angle and work material properties. For a given material, this relation
can be approximated by

$$tan\ \phi = \frac{R \cos \alpha}{1 - R \sin \alpha} \tag{5.1}$$

where α is the rake angle, and R is the chip thickness ratio t_2/t_1. When α is increased, R
is reduced. As a result, ϕ is an increasing function of α. This means that a higher α value
commonly results in a high shear angle, lower strain, lower energy input, and lower compression stress.

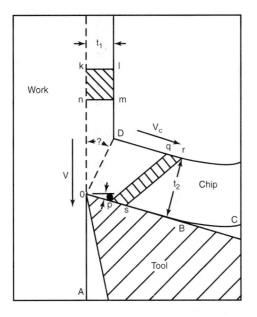

Figure 5.2   Metal-cutting diagram (Niebel, et al., 1989).

In the secondary zone, the deformed chip moves along the rake face under pressure to exit the cutting area. A small portion of the heat generated in the primary zone and part of the heat generated by the interaction between the chip and tool surface dissipate into the tool body. This heat raises the temperature around the tool edge. Due to high temperature and compression stress, the contact between the tool and work surface is nearly complete near the cutting edge. Sliding is virtually impossible under most cutting conditions. A flow zone is formed above the tool surface. This is demonstrated in Figure 5.3. It is similar to the flow of fluid over a surface and has a very complicated nature. There is no simple relationship (as in the case of classical Coulomb friction) between the forces normal and parallel to the contact surface. The equivalent friction force is usually very high. That is partially why a restricted contact on the rake face (also called land-edge chamfer) can greatly reduce the force and temperature in the process. The temperature on the rake face can be so high that it is often the limiting factor of the material-removal rate. This is a major driving force in improving hot hardness and wear resistance of tool materials. Figure 5.3 shows the typical temperature contours when cutting low-carbon steels with carbide tools. The high-temperature region is where the crater wear takes place. The temperature and stress are related to the rake angle. A high side rake angle allows a chip to move on the rake face more freely so as to reduce contact length and shear stress. However, a high α value reduces the tools strength, and the tool becomes less shock-resistant. It also reduces the tool's ability to dissipate heat, because a reduced included angle will have lower heat-transfer capacity. In certain operations, a slight change of rake angle may weaken the tool edge. However, a dramatic increase in rake angle may actually improve the process because of a significant drop in cutting force, stress, and temperature.

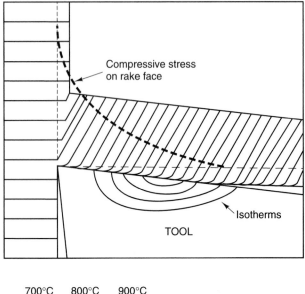

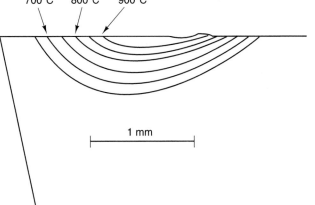

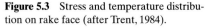

Figure 5.3 Stress and temperature distribution on rake face (after Trent, 1984).

In the clearance zone, the elastic/plastic deformed, newly formed surface on the workpiece recovers when leaving the tool edge. The expanded surface pushes against the clearance face and creates friction between these two surfaces, resulting in flank wear. The length of contact, heat generated, and friction force decrease with clearance angle. However, as in the case of the rake angle, an increased clearance angle can reduce the strength and heat-dissipation capability of the tool.

Other tool geometry parameters also have significant influence on metal-cutting processes. The side cutting edge angle (or lead angle) can change the force ratio along X and Z directions (Figure 5.4). Varying the side cutting edge angle should be considered when processing a part that lacks rigidity. The included angle formed by clearance and back clearance faces contributes to the tool strength and its heat-dissipation ability. It also affects surface finish when the nose radius is not large enough to form the

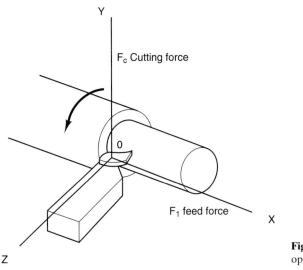

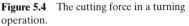

Figure 5.4   The cutting force in a turning operation.

machined surface completely. The size of the tool holder and insert can also affect the tool performance. The back rake angle can control the direction of chip flow. The orientation combined by rake and inclination angle determines either positive or negative entry in the milling operation. Figures 5.5 and 5.6 show the geometric features of milling and drilling tools. ISO (International Standards Organization) and ANSI identification systems for toolholders and indexable inserts have been defined to classify these parameters. When standard toolholders and inserts are used, the geometry feature is determined by the combination selected.

5.2.2 Tool Material

The most commonly used cutting-tool materials in machining industry today are HSS, carbides, ceramics, CBN, and diamonds. These materials have different characteristics and are suitable for different cutting applications. These are discussed in the following sections.

5.2.2.1 High-speed steel.   The introduction of high-speed steel was the first revolution in tool materials. Improved performance over carbon steel was made possible by the retention of hardness and compression strength at higher temperature (up to 600°C). Although more advanced tool materials, including carbides, ceramics, CBN, and diamond, are harder and more wear-resistant at higher temperatures, HSS is still one of the most important tool materials in use today. This is due to its higher strength and machinability. Its hardness at room temperature is close to that of carbides. These properties make it a top contender for high-volume, low-speed operations and interrupted operations. Higher rake angles, as compared to those of carbides, ceramics, and CBN, can be used in most processes. This is important for some low-machinability work materials such as nickel-based high-temperature alloys or for operations lacking rigidity.

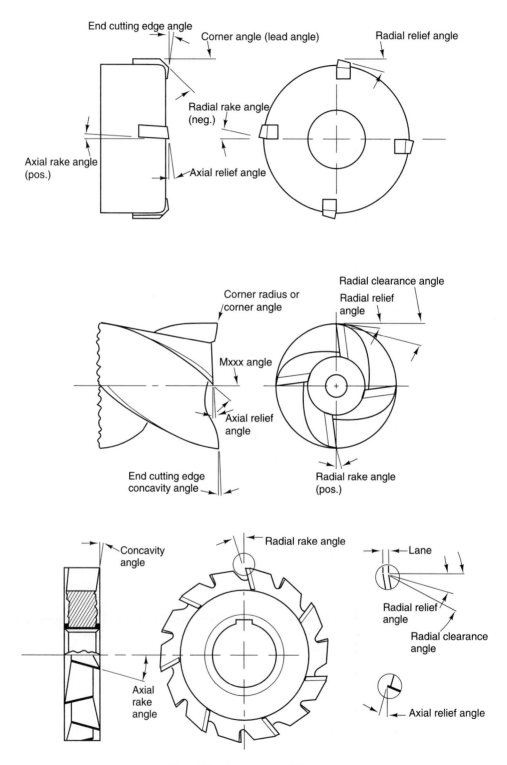

Figure 5.5   Geometry of milling tools.

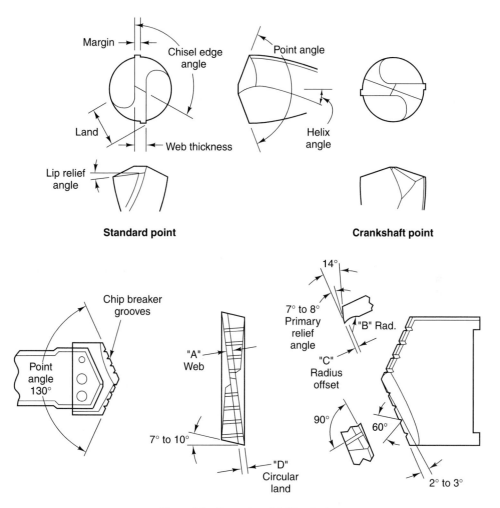

Figure 5.6   Geometry of drilling tools.

Because HSS can be machined in an annealed state, it is suitable for complex tool forms such as gear cutters, slotting tools, end mills, and twist drills.

Basically, there are three types of high-speed steels: tungsten, molybdenum, and ones that contain cobalt (see Table 5.1). Tungsten carbide, including T1 and T2 industrial grades, are similar to ones originally developed by Taylor. T2 is tougher than T1. The second type HSS has higher strength due to added molybdenum. Grades M1, M2, M3, M7, and M10 are widely used in general-purpose operations and fine-edge tools. The addition of cobalt to Type 3 HSS provides higher hot hardness and wear resistance. However, it is difficult to grind. It is more suitable for cutting hard work materials (with a hardness level of 350 BHN).

Both tungsten and molybdenum HSS can be hardened to 64–66 Rc and are recommended for machining of materials with hardness up to 350 BHN. The heat

TABLE 5.1 HIGH-SPEED STEELS AND THEIR
APPLICATIONS

Type	Application
1. Tungsten High-Speed Steels	
T1	General-purpose
T2	General-purpose—higher strength
2. Molybdenum High-Speed Steels	
M1	General-purpose
M2	General-purpose
M3 Class 1	Fine-edge tools
M3 Class 2	Fine-edge tools
M4	Abrasion-resistant
M7	Fine-edge tools—abrasion-resistant
M10	General-purpose—high-strength
3. High-Speed Steels Containing Cobalt	
M6	Heavy cuts—abrasion-resistant
M30	Heavy cuts—abrasion-resistant
M33	Heavy cuts—abrasion-resistant
M34	Heavy cuts—abrasion-resistant
M36	Heavy cuts—abrasion-resistant
M41	Heavy cuts—abrasion-resistant
M42	Heavy cuts—abrasion-resistant
M43	Heavy cuts—abrasion-resistant
M44	Heavy cuts—abrasion-resistant
M46	Heavy cuts—abrasion-resistant
M47	Heavy cuts—abrasion-resistant
T4	Heavy cuts
T5	Heavy cuts—abrasion-resistant
T6	Heavy cuts—abrasion-resistant
T8	General-purpose—hard material
T15	Extreme abrasion-resistant

treatment of the tungsten type is simpler than that of the molybdenum type, but the molybdenum type is tougher. Molybdenum's toughness is slightly reduced, though, and is advantageous only in machining of harder materials if both performance and preparation are considered. Types M3 and M4 contain more vanadium, providing increased wear resistance, but make the material harder to grind.

New developments in HSS tools include the advent of powder metallurgy processing and the use of coatings. Powder metallurgy has great potential for tools of larger size because it produces uniform material structure consistently and economically. Chemical vapor deposition (CVD) coating of thin layers (10 μm) of refractory titanium carbide (TiC), titanium nitride (TiN), hafnium nitride (HfN), alumina (A1$_2$O$_3$), and titanium carbonitride (TiCN) on HSS tools are widely adopted in commercial tools today. These coatings add high-temperature hardness, compressive strength, and wear resistance to very tough HSS substrates. Such coatings can also improve tool life by 300–400% or higher. Alternately, tool life can be maintained when the cutting speed is increased by 25% or more. The surface finish also can be improved at lower cutting speed, due to the elimination of the built-up edge. The speed limitation in the use of these coated tools is primarily due to the HSS substrate. At very high temperatures, HSS under the coating deform and alter cutting conditions.

5.2.2.2 Carbides.

Carbides are tool materials made of very hard and fine grains of carbide powder that are sintered (or bonded, cemented) together by a tougher metal, usually cobalt, nickel, or molybdenum. The most commonly used carbide substances are: tungsten (WC), titanium (TiC), and tantalum (TaC). These cemented materials have good thermal conductivity (which is very important to dissipate heat in metal cutting) and a very fine structure.

Straight tungsten carbide was first introduced in the 1920s. It is still one of the most widely used tool materials today for cast irons and nonferrous metals. Tungsten carbide contains cobalt contents of 4 to 12% by weight. The carbide grain size ranges from 0.5 to 10μm. The hot hardness, wear resistance, and toughness are dependent on the composition and grain size. The hardness and compressive strength decrease with increasing cobalt content and grain size. However, the transverse rupture strength, a measure of toughness, increases with the cobalt content and grain size. The quality of carbide particles and the sintering process are also very important to tool performance. There should be very few holes or nonmetallic inclusions in the material. The carbon content must be controlled within very tight tolerances.

Tungsten carbide has proven to be very successful in cutting cast iron and nonferrous metals at much higher speed than HSS tools can achieve. However, they are less effective in cutting steel. In steel cutting, the temperature on the tool surface is very high, at which diffusion wear dominates the wear process. Tungsten carbide does not offer high diffusion wear resistance, which results in a faster crater wear on the rake face and a rapidly increasing wear land. This led the investigation of carbides of the transition elements in Groups IV, V, and VI of the Periodic Table. The most successful additives have been tantalum, titanium, and niobium carbide bonded with cobalt, nickel, or molybdenum. These tools were used to cut steels beginning in the 1930s. The content of bonding material, hardness, and grain size is in the same range as straight tungsten carbide. TiC and TaC content greatly improves the diffusion wear resistance. However, it also reduces the toughness. For this reason, TiC and TaC content is kept relatively low, 4–20% for TiC and up to 20% for TaC. TaC is believed to cause less reduction in toughness and to increase high-temperature strength. However, it is much more expensive because it is a rare metal. These carbides also reduce thermal conductivity, which is a drawback. The major advantages of adding TiC and TaC content are high-temperature, compressive-strength, diffusion wear resistance. These tool materials can be used at a speed of up to three times faster than that of straight tungsten carbides in cutting steels. Even the addition of 5% TiC is very effective. The quality and performance of steel grade carbides are affected by many more variables than that of straight tungsten.

Researchers and manufacturers have been investigating composition, grain size, and sintering processes to make the best tools for certain operations. A very large number of commercial steel grades are available.

The ISO carbide identification system arranges the grades according to applications. The P series designates steel cutting grades. The K series is for cast iron and nonferrous metals grades. The M series can be used in both cases. In America, industrial codes C1 through C8 are used to group manufacturers products based on carbide content. C1 to C4 are straight tungsten carbide bonded with cobalt. Because straight tungsten carbide is recommended for cast iron and nonferrous metals, these are related to the K series in ISO identification. C5 to C8 are WC–TiC–TaC–Co type carbides. These are corresponding to the ISO P series. C8 also includes TiC bonded with molybdenum or nickel. These tools are more wear resistant at high speed, but the reliability and consistency is not as good as WC–TiC–TaC–Co tools. In ISO groups, the series number increases in order of increasing hardness and decreasing toughness in each series. The relation is the same in industrial codes.

Each manufacturer offers a wide range of carbide grades for a variety of machining operations. It is the manufacturer's responsibility to assign an industrial code or ISO group to their product. There are considerable differences in composition, structure, and properties between grades offered by different manufacturers in each category. We also find that there are usually many manufacturers' grades that fall into a single ISO group or industrial code, although in some cases, one grade may be recommended for several groups or codes (see Table 5.2).

As with HSS, the CVD coating techniques are used in carbide substrates. The result is improved tool life by a factor of 2 to 3 and/or speed by 25 to 50%. Due to higher hot hardness of carbides, the potential of coating is better utilized than the HSS substrate. In recent years, physical vapor deposition (PVD) has also been introduced. The PVD process takes place at a lower temperature (up to 500°C), which results in lower residual stress as compared to the CVD process (ranges from 850–1050°C). The coated layer is thinner, providing a sharper coated edge than CVD inserts. The thin layer also makes the tool life more predictable, which is very desirable in tool management. However, the coated layer does not adhere to the substrate as strongly as CVD coatings. Kennametal's KC710 is a PVD coated carbide suitable for interrupted operations that require a sharp edge.

5.2.2.3 Ceramics and ultrahard materials.

Ceramic tool material are high hardness and high melting-point refractory oxides. The first successful tool material of this kind is pure alumina. Ceramic tools are usually cold pressed, although hot pressing is also possible, and are white in color. Kennametal's K060 and Greenleaf's GEM9 are pure alumina ceramics. Alumina tools can be used at much higher speeds than carbides. At feed rates of 0.25 mm/rev, there is no excessive wear for long periods of time cutting carbon steel at a speed as high as 6000 m/min. The material is, however, very brittle. It can only be used for cast iron or steel with hardness lower than 32 Rc. A negative rake angle is always used. It cannot be used in interrupted operations. Coolant cannot be applied because of low thermal shock resistance. But despite its limitation, this is the most economical ceramic tool material available.

TABLE 5.2 INSERT CODES FROM SEVERAL TOOLMAKERS

TOOL MATERIAL	CEMENTED CARBIDE								COATED CARBIDE						CERAMICS			TIC	CBN	ULTRA FINE
OPERATION	TURNING, MILLING								TURNING				MILLING		TURNING		MILL-ING	Turning Milling	Turning Milling	END MILL
WORK MATERIAL	Iron Non-Ferrous Metal				Steel				Steel		Iron		Steel	Iron	Steel	Iron	Iron	Steel	More Than HRC45	Steel Iron
Code \ Mfg.	C-1	C-2	C-3	C-4	C-5	C-6	C-7	C-8	Al_2O_3	TiN/TiC	Al_2O_3	TiN/TiC			Cold Press	Hot Press	Hot Press			
ADAMAS	B	A AM PWX	AM PWX		434 499 THER-MILL	499	548	Micro-cut Micro-Mill		CNC	Ploxide	CNC						T80 T80 T50		
CARBOLOY	820 44A	883	895 905	999	370 375 395 390	370	350	320	570	550 515 516 518	570 549	523	570 518	570 518				210		
CARMET	CA3 CA12	CA443 CA4	CA7	CA8	CA740 CA730 CA720	CA720	CA711	CA704	CA740 CA-9740	CA-9443					CA-W	CA-8	CA-8			
DeALL	DO1 DO30	DO2 DO20	DO3	DO4	DO15 DO35	DO16 DO36	DO17 DO34	DO18		DO40 DO42 DO44			DO46		DO80	DO85	DO85			
EX-CELL-O	E8	E6 XLO28	E5 XLO28	E3	10A 8A	8A 8A 80S	6AX XLO61	6AX 30S		XL612 XL602			XL202	XL822 XL212				XL88 XL88 XL88		
FIRTH-STERLING	H91 H17 H	H21 HA HTA	HTA HF	HF	T04 T14 NTA TXM	T22 T24	T25 TXL		CC46	TC+4 HN-14 TC+ HN+	TC+4 HN-14 TC+ HN+							WF SOJ		
GREENLEAF	G01 G10	G23 G25 G02	G23 G25 G30	G40	G52 G50	G53 G54	G70 G74		G1	Ti5 Ti6 GA5 GA6	G1	GA2 Ti2			GEM1 GEM9	GEM2 GEM3	GEM2 GEM3	G80		
INGERSOL		KM1	KM1		P25 Gx	P20	P10		CP1	CM3	CP1	CM3								
ISCAR	IC28	IC2	IC20	IC4	IC54 IC50 IC50M	IC50M IC70	IC70 IC78		IC848	IC856 IC757	IC848	IC424						IC100T IC80T IC60T		
KYOCERA															A65 A82	A65 A82		TC30 TC50		
KENNAMETAL	K1	K8 C735	K68 K8	K11	K420 K21	K4M K2B84	K45 K5M	K7M	KC910 KC950	KC810 KC850	KC910 KC950	KC250 KC210	KC810 KC850	KC250	K060	K090	K090	K165	KD120	
NEW-COMER	N10	N22 N25	N30	N40	N52 N55	N60	N70 N72	N80	NA02	NT5 NT6	NA02	NT2	NT55	NT25				N9J N95		
NTK															CX3	HC2	HC2	T3N T4N N20		
SANDVIK	H20	HM H20 H1P	H1P H10	H05	S6 SM30 S4	SM S2	S1P	S1P	GC415 GC435 GC015	GC-1025 GC135	GC415 GC015	GC315	GC315 GC120	GC320 GC310						CB50
SECO	HX	HX SU41	H13		S6 S80M	S25M S4 S2	S1F S10M	S1G	TP15	TP35 TP25	TP15 TX10			T15M						
VALENITE	VC1 VC111	VC2 VC24 VC28 VC37	VC3	VC4	V56 VC125 VC55 VC	VC6	VC7 VC76	VC8	VO1 VO5	VN5 VN8 V90 V99	VO1 VO5	VN2 VN8 V88 V91			V34	V32	V32	V83		
VR-WESSON	2A68 VR54	2A5 VR82	VR82 2A7	2A7	WS WM VR77	VR75 26	WH VR73	VR71		650 660 670		630			VR97	VR100	VR100			
WALMET	WA1 WA50 WA110	WA2 WA35 WA107 WA69	CBD WA3	WA4	WA54 WA5 WA37	WA6 WA47	WA47 WA7 WA73	WA8	T5		T2									
WENDT-SONIS	CO22 CO12	CO2	CO3 CO23	CO4	CY17 CY12	CY16	CY14	CY31	918	714 715 716 U225	918	U222 027								

Cermet, an alumina and titanium-carbide composite, is a hot-pressed tool material. The added TiC increases the toughness of the tool. It can be used for roughing and interrupted operations, and continuous coolant can be applied. Cermet can be used for steel and cast iron with hardness up to 65 Rc. Kennametal's K090 and Greenleaf's GM2 are two commercial examples of cermet tools.

A relatively new material, Sialon (Si–Al–O–N), is another ceramic, made of silicon nitride (Si_3N_4) plus alumina. This material has a property that lies between cermets and coated carbides. It can be used for roughing cast iron at ceramic cutting speed using a feed rate normally associated with coated carbides. It also can be used for roughing nickel-based alloy at a higher speed (125–250 m/min) or higher feed rate (0.1–0.3 min/rev) than either cermet or carbide inserts. This material has a very high hardness value of up to 94 Rc.

Another new ceramic material, WG-300, was developed by Greenleaf Corporation. It is a ceramic composite reinforced matrix with silicon carbide single crystals called "whiskers." Due to its high purity and lack of grain boundaries, the whiskers grow under carefully controlled conditions, approaching the theoretical maximum strength. Cemented with a fine-grain alumina matrix, the whiskers act like rods, adding strength to brittle alumina. In addition, the thermal conductivity and thermal shock resistance are also enhanced, permitting the use of coolant in all operations. Substantial savings can be achieved in cutting of hardened steels up to 65 Rc; hard cast irons, and nickel-based aircraft, high-temperature alloys. The speed can be increased about 10 times more than the ones used for carbides. However, the speed increase is not dramatic for commonly used, easy-to-cut materials.

Ceramic tools offer two advantages over carbides and HSS tools: faster material-removal rate and high tip accuracy. However, their application in industry is still not widespread. The first reason is that extra care must be exerted in the handling of these tools because of their brittle nature. Another reason is that, in some operations, the setup constitutes a fixed portion of total time, and further reduction in the direct cutting time by using carbide tools may not have a significant impact on overall performance.

Cubic boron nitride (CBN) is a synthetic crystal not found in nature. CBN consists of two interpenetrating face-centered cubic lattices. The crystal, like diamond, has a very rigid structure. Kennametal's KD120 polycrystalline cutting edge is composed of cubic boron nitride fused to carbide. Its hardness and chemical inertness at high temperatures permit the machining of hardened steel at speeds four to five times faster than coated carbides. This is usefull for machining of tool steels, bearing steels, and chilled iron. It also can be used for difficult-to-cut, high-temperature alloys at speeds up to 300 m/min. Coolant can be used for a more satisfactory performance.

The polycrystalline diamond tools are aggregates of randomly oriented small synthetic diamond crystals. These tools are extremely hard and wear-resistant. Kennametal's KD100 belongs to this category. It can be applied to nonferrous and abrasive materials like A390 aluminum, hybrid composites, and glass-fiber reinforced plastics.

CBN and diamond tool materials are very expensive. The cost of a tip can be 10 times that of a carbide or ceramic insert. Careful justification is necessary to take advantage of these tool materials.

5.2.2.4 Summary of tool materials.   In general, the tool materials listed here are in increasing order of hardness, wear resistance, and cost, and in decreasing order of toughness. In any application, trade-offs are necessary to find the best choice for a particular application.

5.3 MACHINABILITY OF WORK MATERIALS

The term *machinability* is a widely used term in both research and industry. In *Metals Handbook,* American Society for Metals, (1985), it is defined as "the relative ease for a material to be machined." To the people engaged in a particular set of operations, it has a clear meaning, such as the number of components produced per hour or per tool, or the relative ease in achieving surface or dimensional specifications. However, the criteria used for various tests can be different. A material with good machinability by one criterion may have poor machinability by another criterion. Unlike most material properties, there is no generally accepted criterion used for its measurement. The term tends to reflect the interests of the user. The most commonly used criteria in practice are as follows:

1. *Tool life:* The amount of material removed by a tool under standard conditions before the tool performance becomes unacceptable or the tool is worn by a standard amount. The main criterion for the ISO standard is basically tool life.

2. *Limiting material-removal rate*: This is often the criterion for ultrahard work materials.

3. *Surface finish achieved*: It is usually one of the dominant factors in machining of ductile materials.

4. *Chip control*: In machining of some ductile materials, this can be the most significant factor in certain operations.

5. *Force and power consumption:* The force can be the limiting factor when the setup lacks rigidity. When cutting "easy-to-machine" types of materials at a very high speed and high volume, the available power is often the limiting factor.

5.3.1 Machinability Tests

The machinability index in the *Metals Handbook* (American Society for Metals, 1985) and many other industry reports are the results of machinability tests. The long-term absolute machinability standard became available in 1977 (ISO 3685–1977). Until then, the test conditions and criteria were determined by individual researchers. This resulted in a vast amount of machinability data that were impossible to correlate for a cohesive body of data. The ISO standard test indicates the relative merit (as of tool life) of two or more work-tool combinations for a range of cutting conditions. The test material should be mounted between centers or between the chuck and center. It should have a length-to-diameter ratio of less than 10 to 1. The tool material should be HSS, P30, P10, K20, or K10. Four sets of machining conditions are recommended. These conditions are intended to cover anything from light to heavy roughing operations. At least four speeds should be used that ideally result in tool life of 5, 10, 20, or 40 min. The tool failure criteria for HSS are

1. catastrophic tool failure, i.e., breakage
2. 0.3-mm average flank-wear land width if flank wear is even
3. 0.6-mm maximum flank wear if flank wear is irregular, scratched, chipped, or badly grooved.

For carbide grades, the first criterion is crater depth of $(0.06 + 0.3f)$ mm, where f is the feed in mm/rev. The criteria for ceramic tools are the same as with HSS. Of the failure modes, flank wear is by far the most commonly used, except in high-speed machining of cast iron, where the most significant failure mode is cratering.

In addition to long machinability tests, there are many types of short-term tests often conducted for a particular tool material combination. Czaplicki (1962) proposed a relationship between cutting speed, which results in a 60-min tool life, and chemical content as

$$V_{60} = 161.5 - 141.4\% \text{ C} - 42.4\% \text{ Si} - 39.2\% \text{ Mn} \\ - 179.4\% \text{ P} + 121.4\% \text{ S (m/min)} \tag{5.2}$$

Boulger, Moorhead, and Govey (1951) determined a relationship of the relative machinability index (MI; base 100) as

$$\text{MI} = 146 - 400\% \text{ C} - 1500\% \text{ Si} + 200\% \text{ S} \tag{5.3}$$

Henkin and Datsko (1963) developed a relation using dimensional-analysis techniques based on the material's physical properties:

$$V_{60} \propto \frac{B}{LH_B}\sqrt{1 - \frac{A_r}{100}} \tag{5.4}$$

where B is the thermal conductivity, L is a characteristic length, H_B is Brinell hardness, and A_r is the percentage reduction in tensile test. Similar work by Janitzky (1944) yielded the expression

$$V_{60} \propto \frac{D}{H_B A_r} \tag{5.5}$$

where D is a constant dependent on the size of cut. However, the application of these relationships is restricted to materials of the same type and thermal history. A more common form of machinability empirical relation was developed by Gilbert and cited by Olson (1985):

$$V = \frac{ABCDEFGPQ^{0.25}}{H^{1.72}T^n R^{0.16} f^{58} d^2} \tag{5.6}$$

The parameter definitions and typical values are summarized in Table 5.3. Equation (5.6) is a very powerful relation, especially when adapted to a given system with known products.

TABLE 5.3 PARAMETERS AND TYPICAL VALUES FOR
EQUATION (5.6)

Para.	Factor	Typical Values	
V	Cutting speed	Selected speed in ft/min	
A	Tool material	HSS: 180,000 Ceramics: 1,500,000	Carbides: 300,000
B	Coolant	Dry: 1.0 Soluble oils: 1.25	Cutting oils: 1.15
C	Material	Carbon steel: 0.8 Alloy steels: 1.1 Free-machining brass: 2.0 Magnesium alloys: 0.9	Free-machining steel: 1.05 Cast irons: 0.75 Aluminum alloys: 0.85
D	Micro structure	Austenitic: 0.7 Coarse spher.: 1.4	Most steel: 1.0
E	Surface	Sand cast: 0.7 Heat treatment: 0.8–0.95	Sand cast, blast: 0.75 clean surface: 1.0
F	Tool type	Single-point turning: 1.0 Drill, form tools: 0.7	Boring, milling: 1.0 Reamers: 0.8
G	Tool profile	Sharp, 0° entering; 1.0 High entering: 1.5	High radius: 1.5
P	Tool material	HSS: 1.0 Ceramics: 8.0	Carbides: 5.0
Q	Flank wear	About 0.3 mm	Depends on tool material
H	Hardness BHN		
R	Number of points	Single point: 1.0	Equal number for multiples
T	Tool life	A few minutes to a few hundred minutes	
n	Taylor expansion	HSS: 0.125 Ceramics: 0.68	Carbides: 0.25
f	Feed rate	inch/rev	
d	Depth of cut	inch	

In addition to these nonmachining tests, actual machining tests are also conducted in practice. There are constant-pressure tests in which a constant feed force is maintained. Accelerated tests in which a higher-than-normal speed is used to shorten test time, and so on.

Most machinability assessments are for single-point turning operations. Constant pressure and other types of tests have also been carried out for various processes, including drilling operations. Tool failure results from either catastrophic failure or some measure of drill-tip wear. There is a high possibility, particularly in small-diameter drills, of drill breakage. Drill length has a strong impact on drill breakage. Because there are a variety of milling operations, the chip equivalent concept (Colding, 1961) is often used to relate machinability to milling operations. However, as already indicated, machinability is highly dependent on process and on cutting conditions. It is difficult to relate results from one process to another unless the processes involved are practically the same.

The machinability of several basic types of work materials for all criteria will be discussed in following sections. The influence of some physical and mechanical properties of materials are as follows:

1. Material with high yield strength and work-hardening ability requires more power input, exerts higher compression stress, and, in general, generates higher temperature on the tool surface.
2. In addition to high-energy input, machining ductile material also results in poor surface finish.
3. Material with high-fracture toughness tends to generate long chips that are hard to break.
4. Material with high work-hardening capability requires more energy on the share plane. The tool may constantly cut against the work-hardened surface left by a previous cut.
5. Good thermal conductivity can reduce tool-surface temperature.
6. Material that tends to react chemically with the tool material at high temperatures can deteriorate tools.

5.3.2 Steels

Steels with very low carbon (commercially pure iron and steels with carbon content up to 0.15%C) have poor machinability by all criteria, because of their high ductility. A very low shear angle and large contact area on the rake face have been observed. The chips tend to adhere to the tool surface and may become hard to break, which often causes trouble. The high strain generates more heat, which requires more energy input and results in a higher temperature on the tool surface. Surface finish is also difficult to control because of rubbing.

The added alloys to low-carbon steel improve machinability in certain instances, depending on the additive elements and quantity. The increased carbon content decreases the ductility of steel, so that the energy consumption and required force are reduced. A more significant improvement can be achieved in surface finish. Although the heat generated becomes lower, the compression stress on the rake does not change much, because the contact area is also reduced. The highest tool-temperature point on the rake face moves closer to the tool edge. The added carbon content also improves the work material strength and hardness. For steels with a carbon content of greater than 0.30%, the power input and tool-surface temperature increases for steel of lesser carbon content for the same machining conditions. The surface finish improves as the carbon content goes up to 0.35%, but if the carbon content goes above 0.35%, the quality of the surface finish begins to go down again.

Other added alloys to low-alloy steels (manganese, chromium, and so on) increase the strength and hardness of steel. In general, the tool wear rate increases with alloy content, but other machining characteristics remain unchanged. Machinability is also strongly affected by heat treatment. As a general rule, the material should be treated to the minimum hardness requirement.

One important problem in cutting steel is tool-life variations. When cutting steel with steel-grade carbides at high speeds, major variation in tool life is attributed to the nonmetallic inclusions that attach to the rake face and form an unstable glassy barrier. Although the phenomenon is not as pronounced in WC-Co or HSS tools, these tool materials do not cut steel effectively. This gives rise to free-machining steels.

5.3.3 Free-Machining Steels

Free-machining steels are typically alloys of steel and sulfur, lead, or other suitable alloying agent. The addition of 0.1 to 0.3% S or 0.1 to 0.35% Pb or a small amount of Bi (bismuth), Se (selenium), Te (tellurium), and P (phosphorus) can greatly reduce force, power input, tool-surface temperature, and tool wear rate. Surface finish and chip control can also be improved. Most importantly, the tool performance is more consistent, because of less sensitivity to detailed heat history. The difference in tool life may be very large for the material with standard specifications but quite different for nonfree-machining steels. However, the mechanical properties of free-machining steels are not as good as regular steel, and they cost more. A compromise can be made among material cost, operation cost, and product performance. The manganese content of these steels must be high enough to ensure that all the sulfur present is in the form of MnS.

5.3.4 Stainless Steels

There are three major types of stainless steels with respect to microstructure: austenitic, ferritic, and martensitic. These materials have higher tensile strength and greater spread between yield and fracture strength than low-alloy steels. The energy input and the temperature on the tool surface are also higher than ordinary steels. Due to their high alloy content, they contain abrasive carbide phases. Both of these characteristics produce faster tool wear.

In addition to the preceding properties, austenitic stainless steels also possess strong work-hardening capability and low thermal conductivity. These severely reduce the machinability measures for all criteria. Not only will higher temperature be encountered, but the chips tend to bond to the tool surface and are hard to break.

Specifically, problems arise when the tool edge is cutting into a work-hardened surface, left by a previously machined surface. Because of this, a sharp tool, a reasonable feed rate, and a reasonable depth of cut are recommended to avoid excessive wear caused by continuously cutting a work-hardened surface. In order to improve the generally low machinability of austenitic stainless steels, sulfur, selenium, and tellurium are added to reduce ductility. These are called free-machining stainless steels. They are more expensive and the additives reduce the corrosion resistance slightly.

5.3.5 Cast Irons

Flake graphite and spheroidal graphite (SG) cast irons have good machinability with respect to all criteria. The graphite flakes and spheres initiate fracture on the shear plane at very frequent intervals. The process experiences a low tool wear rate, high MRR, low force, and low power consumption. Good surface finish can be easily achieved. The chips fall in very short segments for flake graphite and easy-to-break longer segments for SG. Tool life decreases mainly with hardness. In recent years there have been more applications for using ceramic tools at a very high speed. Due to the high production rate and high surface finish achieved, additional grinding operation can be eliminated. Another ceramic tool application on cast irons is for chilled irons with hardness of 430 HV at speeds up to 50 m/min. CBN can also be used for cast-iron hardness range from 55–58 Rc (600–650 HV) at speeds up to 80 m/min. A higher clearance angle is recommended for SG cast iron to eliminate extremely ductile flow-zone material from clinging to the flank.

5.3.6 Nickel-Based Alloys

Nickel-based alloys are among the most difficult to machine materials, because of their very strong work-hardening capability and hard abrasive-carbide phases. At much lower speeds than cutting steels, the tool temperature can reach the point at which plastic deformation and diffusion can take place. Because of this work hardening, the feed rate is very important. When it is too low, the tool is continuously cutting through work-hardened material generated by previous cut. Conversely, at high feed rates, even if the theoretical surface finish is acceptable, the stresses on the tool may be too high and can cause catastrophic tool failure. As a compromise between two extremes, a feed rate of 0.18 to 0.25 mm is recommended. In order to eliminate rubbing effects, a positive rake should be used. WC-Co grades of carbide can be used at speeds up to 60 m/min. Steel-cutting grade tools fail more rapidly, and even coatings have shown little advantage. However, in recent years, ceramics, CBN, and Sialon tools have been found to be more effective in cutting nickel-based, high-temperature alloys. The surface speed can be as high as 250 m/min.

5.3.7 Aluminum Alloys

Pure aluminum is very ductile. The chip tends to adhere to the tool surface and it can be very hard to break the stringy chip. It is difficult to achieve a good surface finish, especially at low cutting speeds. However, aluminum alloys have good machinability in almost all criteria. Cast-aluminum alloys with silicon as the main alloying element are the most important casting group. These alloys contain abrasive silicon particles, which can reduce tool life, and therefore are more economically machined at lower cutting speeds and feeds than other types of aluminum alloys. The addition of copper can improve not only material strength, but tool life as well. Due to reduced ductility, the chips are easier to control. The aluminum–magnesium and aluminum–zinc–magnesium alloys all have good machinability. The cutting speed can go up to 300 m/min for HSS tools and 2000 m/min for WC–Co carbides. The machinability of wrought aluminum can be improved by addition of low-melting-point insoluble metals, tin, bismuth, and lead. The flank wear is most pronounced in cutting aluminum alloys and is usually the measure of tool failure.

5.3.8 Copper and Its Alloys

Pure copper is similar to other pure metals and has poor machinability. Unlike other pure metals, however, copper with a very low alloy content is widely used in electronic components and fittings. The cutting speed of these small-size components are usually limited by spindle speed (up to 140–220 m/min). A built-up edge does not occur in this type of application. The tool forces are very high due to the large contact area on rake face and the low shear angle. However, the surface finish and chip control can become a problem. For this reason, high-conductivity coppers are regarded as one of the most difficult materials to machine. In drilling deep holes, for example, the forces are often high enough to break the drill. The addition of lead, sulfur, and tellurium improves the machinability after cold working. For most operations, the important concern is chip control.

5.4 MACHINING OPERATIONS

Machining is used as a general term to cover several operations. Generally, turning is the process in which a tool cuts a rotating workpiece held in the chuck. It can be further classified as facing, cut off, contouring, and so on. Figure 5.7 shows common turning operations. These operations can be performed in a conventional lathe, turret lathe, screw machine, and turning centers. In turning operations, the workpiece is held to a rotating spindle. Standard workholding devices called "chucks" are used to locate and support the workpiece. In a milling operation, a rotating tool is placed in contact with a stationary workpiece. Milling operations are performed on vertical and horizontal milling machines, gear-cutting machines, and machining centers. Milling operations can be classified as face milling, end milling, and slotting. Figure 5.8 shows these operations. Important concepts in milling are conventional milling (or up milling) and down milling. In conventional milling, the feed direction is against the cutting force. Constant pressure can be maintained, so backlash has no major effect on the process. However, the cutter usually starts by cutting a very thin layer of material. As explained earlier, the cutter can virtually rub against the workpiece surface, which can reduce tool life and cutting stability. Nevertheless, modern machines have an antibacklash mechanism in the drive system. Up milling introduces no such trouble in the process. The advantage to

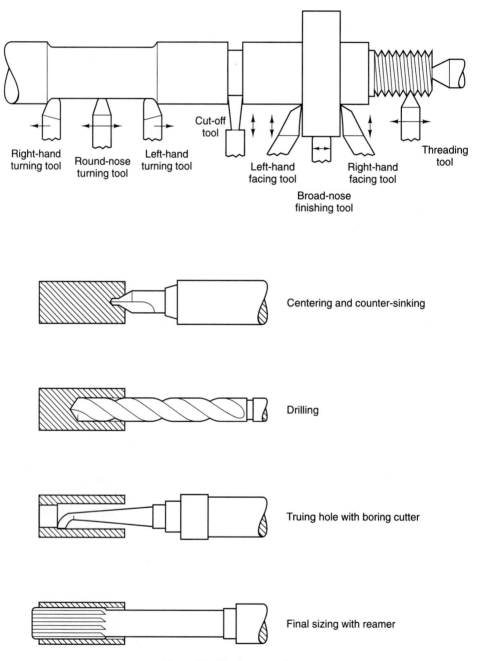

Right-hand
turning tool

Round-nose
turning tool

Left-hand
turning tool

Cut-off
tool

Left-hand
facing tool

Right-hand
facing tool

Broad-nose
finishing tool

Threading
tool

Centering and counter-sinking

Drilling

Truing hole with boring cutter

Final sizing with reamer

Figure 5.7   Turning operations.

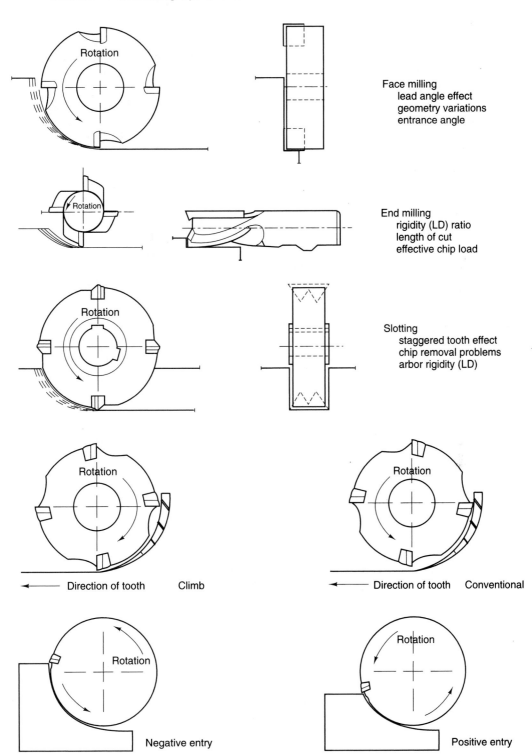

Figure 5.8 Milling operations.

conventional milling is more pronounced in materials with high ductility and work-hardening capability. Milling is an interrupted operation that usually demands higher tool toughness, honed edge, or negative land on the rake face. Another machining operation, drilling, is a process in which a fixed-diameter cutting tool is fed into a work-piece. The nominal size of the hole is the same as the nominal size of the tool. Drilling can be performed on a lathe, milling machine, or a drilling machine. Drilling and turning operations are illustrated in Figure 5.7.

5.5 WORKPIECE HOLDING PRINCIPLES

Fixtures are used to locate and constrain a workpiece in machining and other manufacturing operations. To ensure that the workpiece is produced according to the specified shape, dimensions, and tolerances, it is essential that it is appropriately located and clamped on the machine tool. The configuration of a machining fixture depends not only on workpiece characteristics, but also on the sequence of machining operations, magnitude and orientation of the expected cutting forces, capabilities of the machine tool, and cost considerations. A fixture could be specially designed and fabricated for each workpiece (dedicated fixtures), or a fixture could be constructed from standardized fixturing elements chosen from a catalog (modular fixtures). Usually, it is expensive to design and build a fixture for each individual type of workpiece, so it is often considered satisfactory to select readily available fixturing elements from a catalog. Each fixturing element has a specific function, and a number of elements can be combined to build a complete fixture.

The traditional approach to designing fixtures for prismatic parts has been for the human designer to look at the workpiece drawing and to analyze the geometrical features from the viewpoint of obtaining the desired orientation and restricting the necessary degrees of freedom. A fixture designed from these initial considerations is further modified to conform to the machining sequence and to the configuration of the machine tool on which the part is manufactured. Other external issues, such as the mechanism for loading and unloading the workpiece (human/robot), setup times, chip disposal, and so on, will also influence the fixture design process. The ability to come up with a feasible solution will depend on the designer's experience, the designer's ability to recall fixture designs for similar workpieces, his or her knowledge of material-removal operations, and the workpiece's material properties. Obtaining a suitable design in this manner can be called *nonalgorithmic,* because it involves trial and error.

5.5.1 Fixtures and Jigs

General principles in the practice of fixture design are more or less agreed upon; however, a systematic structured design procedure does not exist. The relationship among the chosen locating and clamping scheme and the machining sequence, process parameters, and workpiece characteristics has not been adequately analyzed. A unified treatment of these issues is the key to building fixtures. A survey of common principles in workholding and terminologies will be presented.

In general, a workholding device serves three primary functions: location, clamping, and support. The workpiece has to be correctly positioned, with respect to the tool, in order to maintain the specified tolerances: *location*. This position of the workpiece must be maintained while it is being subjected to cutting forces: *clamping*. Finally, the deflection of the workpiece, due to the tool and the clamping forces, must be minimized: *support*. Total workpiece control involves both linear equilibrium (balance of forces) and rotational equilibrium (balance of moments). Correct placement of locators, supports, and clamps enables this equilibrium to be achieved. In addition to the three primary functions, fixtures may also perform the operations of centralizing and guiding. Where appropriate, as found in specialized fixtures called jigs, a special guiding system leads the tool to its precise position relative to the work. An abstract description of the individual functions of a fixture is shown in Figure 5.9. To guarantee the exact relationship between the tool and the work, four important relationships or "couplings" must be controlled (Weck and Bibring, 1984). As shown in Figure 5.10, these are the relationships among: (1) tool and tool holder, (2) tool holder and machine, (3) workpiece and clamp, and (4) clamp and machine. Among other criteria, certain practical considerations that indicate a good design are as follows:

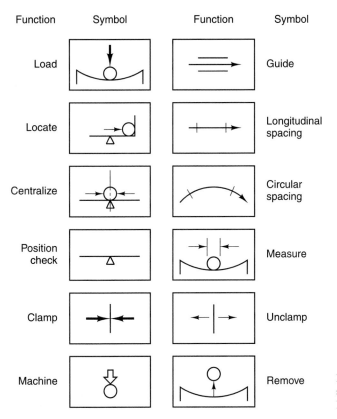

Figure 5.9   Functions of fixtures and their symbolic representation (Weck and Bibring, 1984).

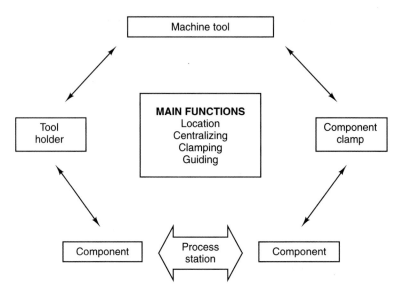

Figure 5.10   Four key fixturing relationships (Weck and Bibring, 1984).

1. Locating and clamping methods should reduce idle time of the machine tool to a minimum.
2. The configuration of the locators and clamps should not interfere with the swept volume of the cutter. Collision avoidance between the cutting tool and fixturing elements is imperative for the safety of the operator, and to prevent damage to the machine tool or cutter.
3. Adequate clearance, in the form of channel ways, should be provided to allow for good chip clearance. This implies that awkward corners, wherein chips tend to collect, should be avoided. Similar considerations dictate the ease with which coolants will be able to access the cutting edges.
4. The design should be robust in order to withstand intermittent cutting and avoid vibration effects.
5. The design should be foolproof, that is, within reason, it should be impossible to insert the workpiece incorrectly in the fixture.

Table 5.4 summarizes the general considerations in fixture design.

5.5.2 Location

Location establishes a desired relationship between the workpiece and the fixture, which in turn establishes the relationship between the workpiece and the cutting tool. Weck and Bibring (1984) define "locating" as using faces of the component as reference planes. A free body in space has six degrees of freedom, that is, a linear and rotational motion for each of the X, Y, and Z axes. These 6 basic motions can occur in 2 directions

TABLE 5.4 FIXTURE DESIGN CONSIDERATIONS

1. Locating considerations
   - (a) Radial
   - (b) Concentric
   - (c) From surfaces
   - (d) From points
   - (e) Other
2. Positioning considerations (relation to tool and orientation in the fixture)
   - (a) Indexing (linear and circular)
   - (b) Rotating
   - (c) Sliding
   - (d) Tilting
3. Clamping considerations
   - (a) Rapidity
   - (b) Amount of clamping forces
   - (c) Direction of clamping forces
   - (d) Actuation (manual, power)
4. Supporting considerations
   - (a) Relation to tool forces
   - (b) Relation to clamping pressure
   - (c) Relation to thin-walled sections of workpiece
5. Loading considerations (including manual lifting and sliding; hoisting; unloading chutes, magazines)
   - (a) Rapidity
   - (b) Ease
   - (c) Safety
6. Coolant considerations
   - (a) Direction
7. Chip considerations
   - (a) Accumulation
   - (b) Disposal

Source: Wilson and Holt (1962).

each for a total of 12 degrees of motion are possible. Usually, locators will eliminate as many degrees of freedom as are possible while still being able to perform the operation with the required accuracy. The most common method of location is 3–2–1, or the six-points principle. The first plane, which usually has the largest surface area, establishes the primary locating plane (3-plane), and is located by three points [Figure 5.11(a)]. The

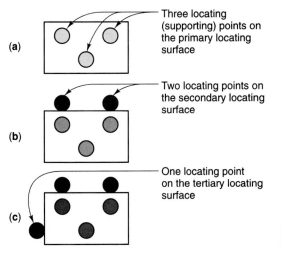

(a) — Three locating (supporting) points on the primary locating surface

(b) — Two locating points on the secondary locating surface

(c) — One locating point on the tertiary locating surface

Figure 5.11 3–2–1 location: (a) 3-Plane, (b) 2-Plane, and (c) 1-Plane (Hoffman, 1987).

surface with the next largest amount of area generally establishes the secondary locating plane (2-plane) and is located with two locators [Figure 5.11(b)]. The final locator is placed on the tertiary plane (1-plane), to complete the location of the part [Figure 5.11(c)]. The 3-plane restricts two rotational motions and one linear motion, the 2-plane restricts one rotational and one linear motion, and the 1-plane restricts one linear motion.

The type of location is governed by the type of feature and the number of faces being machined. Locating arrangements for different production requirements are shown in Figure 5.12. To machine one face, control of dimension a is required, and hence, only one locating plane is necessary. Two locating planes are required for machining an open slot, as dimensions a and b need to be controlled. Full location (three planes) is necessary for milling a blind slot, as dimensions a, b, and c need to be controlled. The 3–2–1 principle is ideal for prismatic or rectangularly shaped workpieces

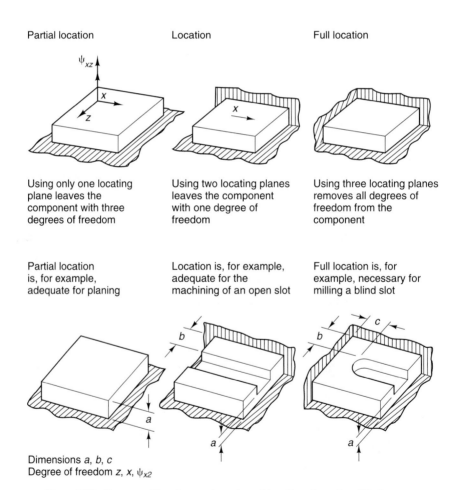

Partial location   Location   Full location

Using only one locating plane leaves the component with three degrees of freedom

Using two locating planes leaves the component with one degree of freedom

Using three locating planes removes all degrees of freedom from the component

Partial location is, for example, adequate for planing

Location is, for example, adequate for the machining of an open slot

Full location is, for example, necessary for milling a blind slot

Dimensions a, b, c
Degree of freedom z, x, ψ_{x2}

Figure 5.12   Degrees of freedom and number of locating planes for differing production requirements (Darvishi and Gill, 1988).

only. For simple cylindrical or conical shapes, just five locators are needed, because one rotation is stopped purely by friction (Figure 5.13).

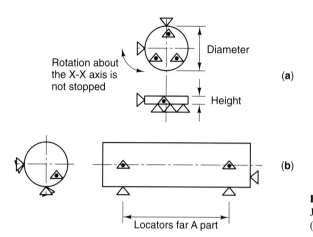

Figure 5.13 Workpiece control (Eary and Johnson, 1962); (a) short cylinder, (b) long cylinder.

By the act of location, a machinist establishes a relationship between the features of the workpiece that are being machined in the given setup, and other features being used as a reference, in order to locate the workpiece at the desired position in the machine-tool coordinate system. To determine the reference features or surfaces of the workpiece, it is vital to examine how the workpiece dimensions are specified on the blueprint. Incorrect placement of locators will cause the workpiece to go out of tolerance. It is important to (1) select the correct surfaces for placement of the locators, and (2) position the locators correctly on the surface selected.

Excess of locators exist when more than six locators are provided for a prismatic workpiece in a single fixture. Four points of location, all on one surface, allow a workpiece to be clamped on slightly different planes, which may be enough to throw the workpiece out of tolerance. A locator directly opposite another locator is also harmful, because the distance between the two locators may not be large enough to allow for size variation of the workpiece.

Location may involve centering. Whereas locating normally brings one surface of the workpiece into proper position relative to the fixture, centering is applied to two surfaces. It usually locates a plane or an axis within the part. A centralizer is a combination of fixed and movable locators that provide positive contact and pressure without clearance. Typical combinations of locators and centralizers are shown in Figure 5.14. Double centering is accomplished whenever an axis is located. Locating requirements are achieved by providing plane location, concentric location, or radial location (Figure 5.15). In general, the following principles in location are commonly applicable:

1. Stability of the workpiece is best when the locators have the largest overall distance between them. This also diminishes the effect of surface irregularities, dirt,

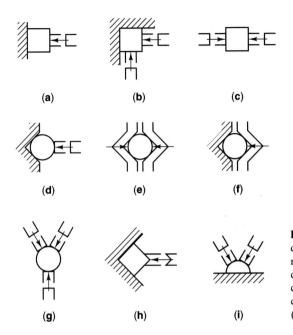

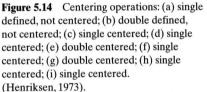

Figure 5.14 Centering operations: (a) single defined, not centered; (b) double defined, not centered; (c) single centered; (d) single centered; (e) double centered; (f) single centered; (g) double centered; (h) single centered; (i) single centered. (Henriksen, 1973).

and locator wear, on the position of the workpiece. However, locator spacing cannot be unduly large, in order to minimize workpiece deflection.

2. The center of gravity of the workpiece should be as low as possible and close to the centroid of the three locators in the 3–2–1 system.

3. Good dimensional control is achieved when locators are placed on one of the two surfaces, to which the dimension is shown, on the part drawing. When the drawing specifies close tolerances on parallelism, perpendicularity, or concentricity, more than one locator must be placed on one of the two surfaces to which the tolerance applies (Eary and Johnson, 1962).

4. Locating surfaces should not be larger than is necessary for proper support and wear. It is hard to keep larger surfaces clean and free of chips, which could cause inaccuracies. If possible, the locating surfaces should be completely covered by the workpiece, so that chips cannot fall on the locating points.

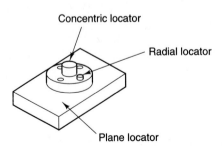

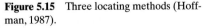

Figure 5.15 Three locating methods (Hoffman, 1987).

5. Ideally, locating surfaces should be fixed. Movable surfaces should be used for clamping only.

6. Buttons and pins—rather than flat surfaces—are preferable for locating, as they are easier to keep clean and afford easier adjustment for wear. Locating pins from previously drilled holes should be hardened and ground and have sufficient clearance for chips and burrs. These pins should locate from only one diameter, when used with counterbored holes.

7. Foolproofing the locating arrangement is desired, so that it is not possible to place the part in an improper position (Hamner, 1982).

5.5.3 Supporting and Clamping

Once positioning of the workpiece is accomplished by the locating arrangement, further control of the workpiece is necessary. The function of any clamping device is to apply and maintain a sufficient counteracting holding force to a workpiece while it is being machined. The workpiece may deflect, within elastic limit, due to the cutting forces, clamping forces, or its own weight. Excessive clamping and cutting forces may also cause distortion of the workpiece, that is, deflection beyond the elastic limit. As defined by Eary and Johnson (1962), a support is a device to limit or stop the deflection of a workpiece. Supports are either fixed, adjustable, or equalizing. The fixed support is placed away from the locating plane, against the locators, so that the workpiece will not contact the support.

Under the influence of cutting forces, the workpiece is permitted to deflect and contact the fixed support, thus limiting deflection. An adjustable support is suitable for uneven surfaces typical for castings. This type of support is kept away from the workpiece during location but adjusted to contact the workpiece after it has been clamped. Equalizing supports are connected units in which the depression of one point causes the other points to rise and maintain contact.

The clamping arrangement must force the workpiece to make contact with all locators, if not already so. Clamps must also maintain the workpiece contact at all locators, in spite of cutting-force variations, inertia forces, dead weight, and vibrations in the MFTW (machine–fixture–tool–workpiece) system. To ensure correct clamping of the workpiece, the following points may be considered.

1. The design must permit the clamps to act against the locators, so as to minimize the deflection due to clamping forces. For geometries where clamping forces cannot be applied opposite the locators, supports may be used to control the deflection caused by clamping forces. A recent method of clamping the workpiece is SAFE (self-adapting fixture element), which uses flat contact areas of hardened steel balls that are free to swivel within their sockets (Smith, 1982; Drake, 1984; Kuznetsov, 1986a). The balls automatically accommodate irregularities in the workpiece surface and provide contoured support without causing distortion.

2. The clamping scheme should be such that maximum cutting forces are directed toward the solid part of the fixture body and not toward the clamp.

3. Cutting forces should be absorbed by a fixed locator/support and not by friction between the work and the clamp.

4. Workpiece surface quality may dictate placing the clamps on noncritical surfaces.

Power clamping, which uses hydraulic or air/hydraulic-actuated components to provide the clamping force, is widely used ("Fast Clamping," 1975). A number of U.S. companies provide off-the-shelf components for power clamping systems (Carr Lane, 1988; De-Sta-Co, 1988; Owatonna Tool Co., 1988; Vektek, 1988). For a description of the various clamp designs used for NC machines, refer to Kuznetsov (1975).

5.6 PART SETUP OR ORIENTATION

The features of a workpiece are machined in a certain sequence, as given in its process plan. These features (pockets, slots, holes, and so on) are located on different sides (faces) of the workpiece. Usually, all the features cannot be accessed (machined) while the workpiece is in a given orientation. An *orientation,* or *setup,* refers to a unique locating, supporting and clamping configuration. Every machining operation has a fixturing configuration that is best for the operation but may not be a practical solution. One would like to find a subset of such feasible fixturing configurations whereby all the operations can be performed within those configurations. Therefore, it is necessary that the machining operations be grouped into setups. Grouping depends on the geometry of the individual features and availability of cutting tools. Each setup will have a so-called primary positioning face, usually the 3-plane, on which the workpiece rests, and also the remaining positioning planes (2-plane and 1-plane). In addition, a setup will also have a unique clamping scheme. Thus, each orientation requires a separate fixture. Because changing from one setup to another involves unclamping/removing the workpiece from one fixture and locating/clamping it into another fixture, the number of setups (fixtures) should be minimized to get the best accuracy.

The face of the workpiece, used as reference for any machining operation in a given setup, may be called the *machining reference face.* In some cases, the machining reference face could also serve to maintain the stability of the part. Inui et al. (1985, 1987) have given some guidelines on how an initial selection of the candidates for the machining reference face may be done. Subsequently, the authors' system evaluates candidate faces for stability of the machined part when it is resting on any one of the candidate faces. Candidates with stability not good enough to support the part are eliminated from consideration. It is recommended that the workpiece be supported by a face with as few bounding faces as possible. Other resting faces of the workpiece are determined in the same manner.

A number of rules for part orientation planning have been proposed and formalized (Ferreira et al., 1985; Ferreira and Liu, 1988). One example of such a rule, as incorporated in a rule-based system by the authors is: "A workpiece is stable in an orientation if the vertical projection of its center of gravity passes through the convex hull of its support (base) face." A convex hull is obtained by connecting the outer most vertices of a part. A number of "basic" and "optimizing" objectives are identified to search for solutions in a given situation. Depending on the particular manufacturing environment, the objectives can change. For example, in large-scale production, a maximum number of operations should be performed in one setting. However, ease of workpiece restraint is the primary objective in small-batch sizes. For machining to tight tolerance specifications, the attainable accuracy will dictate the orientation of the workpiece. Stability in the resting position, against gravity, becomes important for large and heavy workpieces.

Guidelines for setup selection, based on orientation and tolerance relationships, have been proposed by Boerma and Kals (1988, 1989). Their procedure incorporates the dual objectives of (1) reducing the number of "critical" tolerances in the geometrical relations between features belonging to the different setups, and (2) keeping the number of setups to a minimum. In order to compare the significance of the different kinds of tolerances in the relations between features, a nondimensional "tolerance factor" is introduced. It is assumed that the smallest tolerance factor determines the maximum permissible rotation and translation errors of the part during fixturing. The two features, related by the smallest tolerance factor, determine the two orientations of the setup base. The third orientation is selected based on the tolerance-factor relationship of a third feature with either of the first two. The procedure is somewhat simplistic because it ignores all tolerance relationships, except tolerances of position, parallelism, and perpendicularity.

5.7 FIXTURING FOR NC MACHINING

For a fixture to be cost effective, it has to be used for large-batch sizes or be adaptable to different part geometries. Welded fabrications are commonly used as fixtures in production shops; but such custom-built fixtures are relatively expensive and can be limited to a single application. To eliminate the need for single-purpose fixtures, the use of standardized fixtures is quite popular. Tombstone tooling blocks, angle plates, parallels, V-blocks, riser blocks, and subplates are the basic components of standardized fixtures (Gouldson, 1982; Boyes, 1986). A tooling block or a base plate can be mounted precisely on the machine table. These components have a predetermined grid pattern of tapped holes to accept studs, clamps, and other fixture components, as shown in Figure 5.16. The built-up fixture can be removed and replaced exactly in the same position on one or more machines. There is also the provision of a tram hole, which is a bushing in the fixture base, at some known distance from the part location point. The tram hole establishes that point on the fixture from which all part dimensions are based.

Subplates can aid in setup time reduction, because they are usually designed and manufactured for the customer's machining center. A subplate needs to be aligned with the machine axes, using an indicator in the machine spindle, only during the initial installation. Once the subplate is locked into position, the indicator is not used again. Each modular component of the fixture, which is dowel-pinned and screwed to the subplate, is accurately aligned with the machine axes.

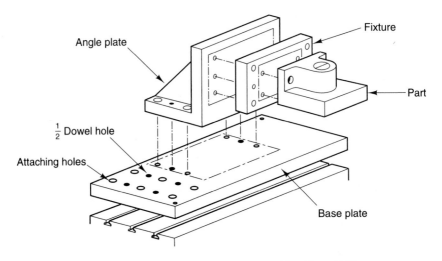

Figure 5.16   Assembly of standard fixtures (Gouldson, 1982).

The design of the fixture also depends on whether it is a first-operation fixture or a second-operation fixture (Gouldson, 1982). A first-operation fixture is used for a workpiece where no machining has yet been performed. These fixtures may be constructed using adjustable supports and locators in conjunction with a predetermined target point or line. If possible, a premachining operation is carried out on a conventional machine to establish a datum surface or locating holes. A second-operation fixture is used where some machining has taken place, so that reference surfaces or holes exist, which position the part with respect to the fixture and the fixture with respect to the machine table. Such fixtures are comparatively easier to design because an adequate reference surface is already available. Case studies on fixtures designed for NC machine tools can be found in Hatschek (1977).

A flexible manufacturing system (FMS) involves a group of CNC machine tools that perform a number of operations and manufacture many different parts. A material-handling system, such as an industrial robot, can transfer parts from one machine tool to another, provided the part geometry is not complicated. For heavier components and complex geometries, pallets are used. Fixtures are mounted on pallets that travel from one machine tool to another. Pallets, with the work material already loaded in fixtures, are held in the magazines of flexible manufacturing modules (FMMs), or in a central buffer store, from where they are delivered to the machines in the desired sequence (Karyakin, 1985). Multisided or cubic fixturing is frequently used where machine up time is important and the workpieces are relatively simple (Kellock, 1986). In a FMS, 2 to 12 components of the same type or different types can be loaded at one time for palletized transportation. Such an environment precludes the use of special-purpose fixtures from the cost viewpoint, because a large number of such dedicated fixtures would be required. This has lead to extensive research in adaptable, or flexible, fixturing.

A flexible (adaptable) fixture has been defined as a single device that holds parts of various shapes and sizes that are subjected to the wide variety of external force fields and torques associated with conventional manufacturing operations (Gandhi and Thompson, 1985a). Flexibility is a property of the fixturing device that makes it conform to the workpiece geometry. Flexible fixtures offer the following advantages (Thompson, 1984): (1) reduction in lead time and effort required for designing special fixtures; (2) lower overhead cost of storing a multiplicity of fixtures, which are required to effect rapid changeover between different manufacturing operations; and (3) simpler programming requirements. Designs of various "resettable" fixtures for use in a FMS have been proposed (Eremin, Lysenko, and Nemytkin, 1988). These fixtures have a common location scheme for a group of workpieces, and just resetting of the clamping element is required when a new workpiece is introduced. Some special problems encountered in building fixtures for the automated factory have been outlined by Bagchi and Lewis (1986). Zimmerman (1984) and Kuznetsov (1986) describe case studies on fixtures designed and built for use in FMSs. Noaker (1988) observes that, even though there has been ongoing R&D in flexible fixturing systems over the last 5 years, the most successful systems for tough problems have cost as much as the capital equipment.

Many different approaches have been tried in flexible fixturing, as shown in Figure 5.17. A number of individuals (Thompson, 1984; Gandhi and Thompson, 1985a; Grippa, Thompson, and Gandhi, 1988; Youcef-Toumi and Buitrago, 1988) have surveyed flexible-fixturing methodologies. Broadly, there are two major groups in flexible fixtures: discrete contact and continuous contact. In the discrete-contact type, there are a finite number of contact points that can be arranged in space to give different configurations. Continuous contact is one in which the number of contact points is infinite, such

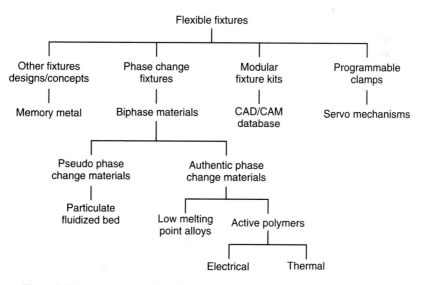

Figure 5.17   An overview of flexible fixturing methodologies (Gandhi, Thompson, and Maas, 1986).

as line or area contact. A point contact would completely constrain the motion in a direction normal to the workpiece surface only. Motions parallel to the workpiece surface would not be completely constrained, because of the limited friction in point contact. Surface contact would not only constrain the motion of the workpiece along the three axes, but also would constrain the applied moments. The following sections outline the salient features of some flexible-fixturing techniques.

5.7.1 Modular Fixtures

By incorporating a system of interchangeable and reusable components, it is possible to accommodate a wide variety of workpieces. Modular tooling systems use a system of individual components, which are assembled on a base, to suit the workpiece that requires fixturing. These systems are typically used for prototype tooling, short production runs for limited part quantities, or as a backup workholder to replace dedicated tooling that requires repair. By using a number of standard parts, and by eliminating the use of special parts as much as possible, the time required to design a complete workholder can be significantly reduced. The assembly time is also a fraction of the time required to build a dedicated fixture. Many companies have eliminated the use of dedicated fixtures, except where they are absolutely essential, and found considerable savings in modular tooling systems (Koch, 1988a, 1988b).

Modular fixtures permit the design of a fixture parallel with part design, because most modular system components can be accessed and retrieved from a CAD database. For example, elements of the CATIC modular fixturing system have been coded and stored in a database called PALCO-FIXTURE (Ranky, 1983). This fixture database incorporates graphics information and mating-surface descriptions for each element. Modifications in the modular fixture, due to alterations in the part geometry, are comparatively simple. Depending on the basic construction, modular fixturing is classified into three major systems: subplate system, T-slot system, and dowel-pin system.

Subplate systems are comprised of a baseplate or subplate to which all other components are attached. A subplate can be a simple plate, which is either drilled or tapped to accept threaded fasteners; or it can be machined with T-slots to accept nuts and bolts. The subplate may also be mounted vertically and may be single-sided or multisided. Subplate systems do not typically include accessories such as locators, supports, and clamps; these must be purchased separately. Common applications of subplate systems are for large parts, irregular parts, or short runs of simple parts. Parts can be mounted directly on the subplate, or the subplate can be used as a mounting device for other workholders such as box parallels, V-blocks, toolmaker's knees, and slotted angle plates. The Challenge System, ATCO System, Matrix Positioning System, Mid-state System, and Stevens Modular Tooling Systems are the premier systems in this category (Hoffman, 1987).

T-slot modular systems are rectangular, square, or round base plates across which T-slots are machined exactly perpendicular and parallel to each other. Round base plates usually have tangential and radial slots. T-slot systems are a complete fixturing set or system, that is, each element within the set is designed to be used to completely build or assemble an entire workholder. The advantage of T-slot systems is in the flexibility of positioning the various component parts. Principal systems in this category are the Halder system (Krauskopf, 1984; Erwin Halder KG, 1987), CATIC modular fixturing system (Lewis, 1983; Xu et al., 1983), Warton Unitool system (Hoffman, 1987), Block Build Jig system 64 (Horic, 1988), and Cessloc system (Hoffman, 1987).

Dowel-pin modular tooling systems are the newest form of modular component tooling. Examples of this category are the QU-CO system (Qu-Co, 1987), Bluco Technik Modular system (Quinlan, 1984) SAFE system (Smith, 1982), and Yuasa Modula-Flex Fixturing system (Hoffman, 1987). All these systems use some combination of precisely positioned dowel holes along with tapped holes to accurately align, locate, and secure fixturing elements. These holes are arranged in a rectangular pattern in a base plate and larger structural elements. Like the T-slot systems, dowel-pin systems incorporate all locating and workholding elements into a single set. However, this set does not include the base plate, which the user can buy or machine separately. Dowel-pin systems have the advantage of consistently accurate placement of each fixturing element at fixed coordinate points, so these systems are ideally suited for use with CAD, NC machining, inspection systems, and for assembly by robots. Special T-slot overlay elements are available for dowel-pin patterns, giving both T-slot flexibility and dowel-pin accuracy (Quinter, 1988).

In addition to the base plates or mounting plates, modular fixturing elements include locating and supporting elements, mounting blocks, and clamping elements. The locating and the supporting elements closely resemble those used in conventional jigs and fixtures. Mounting blocks are a form of locating and supporting elements that are primarily used to position locators or clamping devices at specific heights off the mounting base. The commonly used clamping elements are strap clamps and screw clamps. Generally, all fixturing elements are made of high-grade alloy steel to tolerances of ±0.005 to ±0.01 mm in flatness, parallelism, and size. These tolerances assure accurate alignment and referencing. Modular fixtures are increasingly using some type of power clamping based on air or oil pressure. Devices for power clamping are clamping cylinders, swing clamps, rotating or pivoting clamps, retracting clamps, toe clamps, and power toggle clamps. Power-operated positioning and supporting devices are also commercially available.

A cost comparison for FMSs showed that modular fixturing yielded up to 75% savings over dedicated fixturing (Lewis, 1983). Significant reductions in lead times were also observed. Cost equations for economic justification of modular fixtures have been developed (Xu et al., 1983; Friedman, 1984).

5.7.2 Phase-Change Fixtures

This fixture type exploits the property of some materials to change from liquid to solid and back to fluid again. The workpiece is immersed to the desired depth in the material while it is still liquid. The special material is then changed to solid by altering certain conditions, and machining of the workpiece is carried out. To remove the workpiece from the fixture, the immersion material is liquified again. These materials may be of two kinds, those that undergo a pseudo phase change, like particulate fluidized beds, and those that undergo a true phase change, like low-melting-point alloys. The evaluation of phase-change materials is based on the following properties (Gandhi and Thompson, 1984): (1) The phase change must be rapid, reversible, and uniform in space and time; (2) there should be no adverse effect on the geometry or surface properties of the workpiece; and (3) the power required to initiate the change of phase must be carefully quantified. Particulate fluidized bed fixtures (Gandhi and Thompson, 1985a, 1985b, 1986; Thompson and Gandhi, 1989) are based on the two-phase property of a particulate fluidized bed. As shown in Figure 5.18, the fixture consists of a porous bottom container that is filled with a spherical particle material. When air is supplied at a controlled rate through the porous base, the particulate bed achieves a fluid state of dynamic equilibrium, permitting the workpiece to be immersed. On switching off the air supply, the particles compact under gravity, thereby fixing the workpiece. After machining, the air supply is switched on and the workpiece is removed. This fixture falls in the intermediate category between the discrete-contact and the continuous-contact type of flexible fixtures. The degree of performance of this kind of fixture can be measured by its ability to resist extraction forces in the vertically upward direction, because lateral movement of the workpiece is already constrained by the compacted particulate bed. Experiments (Gandhi, 1986) indicate that extraction force F may be maximized by maximizing the depth of immersion, using a bed material of the largest specific weight, and by choosing a bed material with a high coefficient of friction for the given workpiece material. Mathematical models for calculation of extraction force F and computer simulations to examine the role of different bed-material parameters and loading conditions have been presented (Gandhi and Thompson, 1985b, 1985c; Thompson and Gandhi, 1989).

Low-melting-point alloys have been used to partially encapsulate the workpiece prior to machining. These bismuth-based alloys, which have melting points as low as 47° C, tend to expand on solidification. This technique has been applied to the manufacture

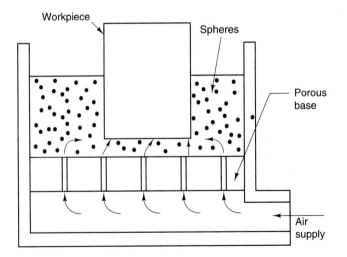

Figure 5.18   Schematic of a fluidized bed fixture (Ghandi, 1986).

of awkwardly shaped high-tolerance components, such as gas turbine and compressor blades (Nyamekye and Black, 1987), and for grinding wedges for milling cutters (Kellock, 1986). An injected metal encapsulation machine is the main feature of this system. The workpiece, which may be an unmachined blade, is precisely positioned with locators into a cavity in the machine prior to the injection of a molten alloy. As soon as the alloy solidifies, the encapsulated blade is ejected from the injection machine. The block of alloy is thus cast in a shape that gives the reference and clamping surfaces required during machining. After machining, the capsule is mechanically cracked open and the alloy is reused. Because a different die is required for each workpiece, the use of low-melting-point alloys is generally quite expensive.

Electrically induced phase-change fixturing (EPF) is an innovative concept that employs modern polymeric materials like polycrylonitile as the medium undergoing the phase change (Gandhi and Thompson, 1985b). In these materials, a phase change is induced by an electric field. This class of fixtures has the advantage of a limited compliance in the solid phase, which is beneficial in robot assembly.

5.7.3 Flexible Fixturing Requirements

Among other less common fixturing schemes are the Multi-Leaf Vise and the Petal Collet (Thompson, 1984), electromagnetic chucks (Kellock, 1985), magnetic cubical fixtures (Kellock, 1986), and electrostatic fixtures (Tazetdinov, 1969). A survey of various magnetic force applications in workholding has been conducted ("Magnetic Work Holding," 1974). Although the choice of a flexible-fixturing technique will depend on the application, it should satisfy certain requirements, in order to function successfully in a flexible manufacturing cell. Some key requirements are as follows (Youcef-Toumi and Buitrago, 1988, 1989):

1. *Reconfiguration of conformable surface:* The intermediate medium, between the rigid part of the fixture and workpiece surface, should have the dual properties of compliance and stiffness, with a quick "phase" change between the two.

2. *Clearance from machining paths:* Flexible fixtures, by their nature, tend to occupy larger surface areas of the workpiece in certain locations. Therefore, the design of the fixturing layout is more critical than in conventional fixtures.

3. *Clearance for workpiece loading/unloading:* The workpiece must be located and referenced to fixed supports, before the conformable surfaces of the fixture approach, to adapt to the workpiece surface. Thus, there should be provision of some initial reference surfaces to place the workpiece in the future.

4. *Ease of operation by a robot manipulator:* An example of this property can be found in modular fixtures where special mating surfaces and locking devices guarantee positive location of the modules, thereby significantly reducing the accuracy requirements of the robot.

5. *Actuation:* The fixture should be self-contained, that is, it should contain at least one actuation element that provides the fixturing force. Actuating forces could also be provided by a robot.

5.8 ERRORS DUE TO LOCATION, CLAMPING, AND MACHINING

Tolerances are specified on a drawing, because it is not possible to manufacture a part exactly to the specified dimensions. The zone, in which the outline of the finished part is to lie, is provided by the tolerance specification. A prismatic part may be considered to be placed in a system of three mutually perpendicular planes that are called *datums*. A datum is a theoretical plane from which dimensions are specified. The surface in contact with the datum is called the *datum surface*. Tolerances control not only the dimensions, but also the geometrical properties of the part, such as flatness, perpendicularity, parallelism, straightness, runout, and surface roughness. It is the primary objective of the process planner to produce the part to the desired tolerance (accuracy), and therefore any fixture design procedure will have to take tolerances into consideration.

Location (mounting) errors have a significant effect on workpiece accuracy. These errors may be considered to be the inaccuracy of the workpiece position with respect to the pallet surface, cutting toolholder, machine tool guideways, and so on. Rigidity of the locating elements and of the workpiece material will also give rise to mounting errors. For an analysis of rigidity effects, refer to the work of Shuleshkin and Gromov (1960). Another important source of inaccuracy is the nonsimultaneous application of clamping forces on the workpiece. Both mounting and clamping errors combine to result in tilting and turning moments and also shear forces that displace the workpiece with respect to the desired position. Bazrov (1982) has formulated criteria to show how the overall accuracy attained in machining is influenced not only by the precision mounting of the workpiece, but also by the choice of coordinate systems employed for setting the pallet, cutting tool, fixture elements, and so on. Analyses and experiments to study the influence of the sequence of clamping forces on the accuracy of the workpiece have been conducted by various investigators. Bazrov and Sorokin (1982) established how a rational sequence of clamping forces, force magnitudes, and friction coefficients may be selected to adjust the workpiece displacement in the desired direction. Experiments by Batyrov (1984, 1986) show that adverse quality of the surfaces in contact between the fixture and the workpiece may enhance the errors caused by clamps being actuated in a particular sequence.

For a part being produced on a machining center, the operations performed most commonly are side milling, end milling, and hole making. Knowledge of the process mechanics of each of these processes is vital to the fixture design process. Whereas a clamping force is static and fixed in both direction and magnitude, the cutting force is dynamic, with a magnitude and point of application that vary during the machining operation. These will require the development of rules or strategies to ensure that the position and orientation of clamps and supports will suffice to locate and hold the workpiece, so that it does not deflect more than a certain "critical" deflection. This "critical" deflection limit will depend on workpiece material properties and machining parameters. During the metal-removal operation, the workpiece deflects and assumes a certain profile. This is due to the bending and torsional deflection produced in the workpiece by the machining operation. After machining, the workpiece will "spring back" and assume a profile that will differ both from its original and from the one assumed during machining.

It is this final profile that will determine the acceptability of the workpiece in terms of the specified tolerances on its blueprint.

5.9 SUMMARY

In this chapter, the basics of tool engineering have been presented. Although several analytical models for jig and fixture design have evolved over the past decade, fixture design is still an "art" that can dictate the profitability of a manufacturing process. Tooling and fixturing also impose some of the most rigid flexibility constraints in today's flexible manufacturing environment.

REVIEW QUESTIONS

1. Define the following terms: rake face, flank face, rake angle, cutting edge, and shear angle.
2. Describe the situations in which positive and negative rake angles are used.
3. What are the major causes of rake wear and flank wear?
4. What is the purpose of coating HSS tools? What kind of materials are used in coating?
5. What are the most commonly used carbide substances for tools?
6. Why is a negative rake angle always used with ceramic tools?
7. What are the advantages of using ceramic tools?
8. What are the most commonly used criteria used in measuring machinability?
9. How does one determine that a tool has failed?
10. What is free-machining steel?
11. What is a jig and what is a fixture? What are they used for?
12. List important considerations in fixture design.
13. What is the 3–2–1 principle?
14. What are the 6 points in 3–2–1 used for?
15. After the six points have been determined, how do we ensure that the workpiece will not move?
16. What is the relationship between locating points and datum surfaces?
17. What is the basic principle in selecting supporting methods?
18. What is the principle in selecting clamping arrangements?
19. What is a modular fixture?
20. What are the advantages and disadvantages of using modular fixtures?
21. What kind of fixture is used in a flexible manufacturing system? What are the differences between this kind of fixture and conventional fixtures?
22. Design a fixture for the following operation: The flat surface of a disk 4 inches in diameter and 0.5 inch tall is to be milled. The disk is made of steel.
23. Design a fixture to hold the part shown in Figure 2.29.
24. Ten thousand of the parts shown in Figure 2.22 are to be machined. The true position tolerance is 0.001 inch. The operation needed is to drill the two holes. Design a jig/fixture for the process.

REVIEW PROBLEMS

1. Design a drilling fixture for the part shown in Figure 2.14. Assume that 5000 parts will be produced on a radial drill.

2. If the part shown in Figure 2.14 was to be a very low-volume part (only four to five parts were to be produced), what kind of fixture would be used?

3. Suppose the same part shown in Figure 2.14 was to be produced in high volume (more than a million), what kind of holding device and machine would be used?

REFERENCES/BIBLIOGRAPHY

AMERICAN SOCIETY FOR METALS (1985). *Metals Handbook,* New York.

APPLIED POWER, INC. (1988). *S.A.F.E. by Enerpac,* Product Catalog. Butler, WI: API.

BAGCHI, A., AND R. L. LEWIS (1986). "On Fixturing Issues for the Factory of the Future," in *Proceedings of the 1986 ASME International Computers in Engineering Conference and Exhibition.* New York: NY: American Society of Mechanical Engineers, 2:197–202.

BATYROV, U. D. (1984). "Factors Affecting Setting Errors of Pallet Fixtures," *Soviet Engineering Research,* 4(4), 67–69.

———. (1986). "More Accurate Clamping of Pallet Fixtures," *Soviet Engineering Research,* 6(9), 58–60.

BAZROV, B. M. (1982). "Selection of Support and Reference Surfaces (Locations) for Mounting the Exchangeable Elements of the MFTW System," *Soviet Engineering Research,* 2(5), 94–98.

BAZROV, B. M., and A. I. SOROKIN (1982). "The Effect of Clamping Sequence on Workpiece Mounting Accuracy," *Soviet Engineering Research,* 2(10), 92–95.

BOERMA, J. R., and H. J. J. KALS (1988). "FIXES, A System for Automatic Selection of Set-Ups and Design of Fixtures," *Annals of the CIRP,* 37(1), 443–446.

———. (1989). "Fixture Design with FIXES: The Automatic Selection of Positioning, Clamping and Support Features for Prismatic Parts," *Annals of the CIRP,* 38(1), 399–402.

BOULGER, F. W., H. A. MOORHEAD, and T. M. GOVEY (1951). "Superior Machinability of MX Steel Explained," *Iron Age,* 1678, 90–95.

BOYES, W. E., ED. (1986). *Low-Cost Jigs, Fixtures and Gages for Limited Production.* Dearborn, MI: Society of Manufacturing Engineers.

CARR LANE (1988). *Product Catalog.* St. Louis: Carr Lane Manufacturing Co.

COLDING, B. N. (1961). "Machinability of Metals and Machining Cost," *International Journal of Machine Tool Design Research,* 1, 220–248.

CZAPLIKI, L. (1962). "L'usinabilite et al coupe des metaux," *Res. Soc. Roy. Belge Ingeniere,* 12, 708–730.

DARVISHI, A. R., and K. F. GILL (1988). "Knowledge Representation Database for the Development of a Fixture Design Expert System," *Proceedings of the Institute of Mechanical Engineers,* Part B, 202(B1), 37–49.

DE-STA-CO. (1988). *The World of Clamping,* Product Catalog. Troy, MI: De-Sta-Co.

DRAKE, A. (1984). "Fixture Design: Working with Modules," *Manufacturing Engineering,* 92(1), 35–38.

EARY, D. F., and G. E. JOHNSON (1962). *Process Engineering for Manufacturing,* Englewood Cliffs, NJ: Prentice Hall.

EREMIN, A. V., N. V. LYSENKO, and S. A. NEMYTKIN (1988). "Designing Fixtures for FMSs." *Soviet Engineering Research,* 8(1), 84–86.

ERWIN HALDER, K. G. (1987). *Halder Modular Jig and Fixture System* 70, Parts Catalog. Berlin, West Germany: Erwin Halder KG.

"Fast Clamping, More Machining—They Go Together" (1975). *Automation,* 22, 42–44.

FERREIRA, P. M., B. KOCHAR, C. R. LIU, and V. CHANDRA (1985). "AFIX: An Expert System Approach to Fixture Design," in *Computer Aided Intelligent Process Planning, ASME Winter Annual Meeting.* New York: American Society of Mechanical Engineers, pp. 73–82.

FERREIRA, P. M., and C. R. LIU (1988). "Generation of Workpiece Orientations for Machining Using Rule-Based System," *Robotics and Computer-Integrated Manufacturing,* 4(3/4), 545–555.

FRIEDMANN, A. (1984). "The Modular Fixturing System, A Profitable Investment," in *Proceedings of the International Conference on Advances in Manufacturing.* Dearborn, MI: Society of Manufacturing Engineers, pp. 165–173.

GANDHI, M. V., and B. S. THOMPSON (1984). "Phase-Change Fixturing for FMS," *Manufacturing Engineering,* 93(6), 79–80.

———. (1985a). "Flexible Fixturing Based on the Concept of Material Phase-Change," in *Proceedings of the CAD/CAM, Robotics and Automation International Conference.* Tucson, AZ: pp. 471–474.

———. (1985b). "The Integration of CAD and CAM in Adaptive Fixturing for Flexible Manufacturing Systems," in *Proceedings of the 1985 ASME International Computers in Engineering Conference and Exhibition.* New York: American Society of Mechanical Engineers, 1:301–305.

———. (1985c). "Phase Change Fixturing for Flexible Manufacturing Systems," *Journal of Manufacturing Systems,* 4(1), 29–39.

GANDHI, M. V., B. S. THOMPSON, and D. J. MAAS (1986). "Adaptable Fixture Design: An Analytical and Experimental Study of Fluidized-Bed Fixturing," *Transactions of the ASME, Journal of Mechanisms, Transmissions, and Automation in Design,* 108(1), 15–21.

GILBERT, W. W. (1950). "Economics of Machining," *Machining Theory and Practice,* New York.

GOULDSON, C. J. (1982). "Principles and Concepts of Fixturing for NC Machining Centers," in W. E. Boyes, Ed., *Jigs and Fixtures,* 2nd ed. Dearborn, MI: Society of Manufacturing Engineers, pp. 331–349.

GRIPPO, P. M., B. S. THOMPSON, and M. V. GANDHI (1988). "A Review of Flexible Fixturing Systems for Computer Integrated Manufacturing," *International Journal of Computer Integrated Manufacturing,* 1(2), 124–135.

HAMNER, J. R. (1982). "Tool Designer's Notebook," in W. E. Boyes, Ed., *Jigs and Fixtures,* 2nd Ed. Dearborn, MI: Society of Manufacturing Engineers, pp. 3–10.

HATSCHEK, R. L. (1977). "Workholding," *American Machinist,* 121(7), Special Report 697, SR-1 to SR-12.

HENKIN, A., and J. DATSKO (1963). "The Influence of Physical Properties on Machinability," *Journal of Engineering for Industry,* November, 321–327.

HENRIKSEN, E. K. (1973). *Jig and Fixture Design Manual.* New York: Industrial Press.

HOFFMAN, E. G. (1987). *Modular Fixturing.* Lake Geneva, WI: Manufacturing Technology Press.

HORIC, T. (1988). "Adaptability of a Modular Fixturing System to Factory Automation," *Bulletin of the Japan Society of Precision Engineering,* 22(1), 1–5.

INUI, M., H. SHUZUKI, F. KIMURA, and T. SATA (1985). "Generation and Verification of Process Plans Using Dedicated Models of Products in Computers," in *Knowledge-Based Expert Systems for Manufacturing, ASME Winter Annual Meeting.* New York: American Society of Mechanical Engineers, pp. 275–286.

———. (1987). "Extending Process Planning Capabilities with Dynamic Manipulation of Product Models," in *19th CIRP International Seminar on Manufacturing Systems.* University Park: Pennsylvania State University, pp. 273–280.

JANITZKY, E. J. (1944). "Machinability of Plain Carbon, Alloy and Austenitic Steels and Its Relation to Yield Stress Ratios When Tensile Strengths Are Similar," *Transactions of the ASME,* 66, 649–652.

KARYAKIN, V. N. (1985). "Tooling and Fixtures for Flexible Manufacturing Systems," *Soviet Engineering Research,* 5(11), 45–48.

KELLOCK, B. (1985). "Maintaining a Grip on Changing Needs," *Machinery and Production Engineering,* 143(3681), 47–53.

———. (1986). "Never Forget You Have a Choice," *Machinery and Production Engineering,* 144(3699), 65–69.

KOCH, D. H. (1988). "Modular Fixtures Build Fast, Hold Fast," *Tooling and Production,* 54(7), 55–56.

———. (1988). *Undedicated Fixturing,* SME Technical Paper TE88-104. Dearborn, MI: Society of Manufacturing Engineers.

KRAUSKOPF, B. (1984). "Fixtures for Small Batch Production," *Manufacturing Engineering,* 92(1), 41–43.

KUZNETSOV, Y. I. (1975). "Clamping Devices for NC Machines," *Machines and Tooling,* 46(9), 45–48.

———. (1986a). "Automated Fixtures for Flexible Manufacturing Systems," *Soviet Engineering Research,* 6(7), 49–51.

———. (1986b). "A Range of Resettable Fixtures," *Soviet Engineering Research,* 6(10), 74–75.

LEWIS, G. (1983). "Modular Fixturing Systems," in *Proceedings of the 2nd International Conference on Flexible Manufacturing Systems.* London: pp. 451–461.

MACHINABILITY DATA CENTER (1980). *Machining Data Handbook,* 3rd ed. Cincinnati: Metcut Research Associates.

"Magnetic Work Holding" (1973–1974). *Singapore Polytechnic Engineering Society (S. P. E. S.) Annual Journal,* 11, 125–130.

NIEBEL, B. W., A. B. DRAPER, and R. A. WYSK (1989). *Modern Manufacturing Process Engineering.* New York: McGraw-Hill.

NOAKER, P. M. (1988). "Workholding: Firm but Flexible," *Production,* 100(8), 50–55.

NYAMEKYE, K., and J. T. BLACK (1987). "Rational Approach in the Design Analysis of Flexible Fixtures for an Unmanned Cell," in Society of Manufacturing Engineers, Dearborn, MI, *15th North American Manufacturing Research Conference Proceedings,* pp. 600–607.

OLSON, W. W. (1985). *Machinability Data Bases for Metal Cutting,* NIST Technical Report, ARLCB-TR-85030. Washington, DC: U.S. Department of Commerce, National Institute of Standards and Technology.

OWATONNA TOOL CO. (1988). *OTC Hytec Catalog No. H-8401.* Owatonna, MN: OTC.

PIROVICH, L. Y. (1972). "Systematization of Fixtures for Unit-Construction-Type Machine Tools and Transfer Lines," *Machines and Tooling,* 43(5), 41–43.

QU-CO (1987). *Qu-Co Modular Fixturing System Catalog.* Union, OH: Qu-Co.

QUINLAN, J. C. (1984). "New Ideas in Cost-Cutting, Fast-Change Fixturing," *Tooling and Production,* 50(1), pp. 44–48.

QUINTER, K. (1988). "Modular Systems Expand the Fixture Continuum," *Tooling and Production,* 54(7), 57–58.

RANKY, P. (1983). *The Design and Operation of FMS.* London: IFS (Publications).

SHATZ, A. S., AND A. F. ISHCHUK (1971). "Machining Workpieces Located in Composite Fixtures," *Machines and Tooling,* 42(2), 27–28.

SHULESHKIN, A. V., AND N. V. GROMOV (1960). "Setting-up of 'Body Type' Work-Pieces for Increased Accuracy," *Russian Engineering Journal,* 40(6), 45–49.

SMITH, W. F. (1982). "A New Approach to Positioning and Holding Workpieces," in W. E. Boyes, Ed., *Jigs and Fixtures,* 2nd Ed. Dearborn, MI: Society of Manufacturing Engineers, pp. 169–175.

TAYLOR, F. W. (1906). "On the Art of Cutting Metals," *Transactions of the ASME,* 28, 31.

TAZETDINOV, M. M. (1969). "Electrostatic Fixtures," *Machines and Tooling,* 40(8), 48–50.

THOMPSON, B. S. (1984). *Flexible Fixturing—A Current Frontier in the Evolution of Flexible Manufacturing Cells,* ASME Technical Paper 84-WA/Prod-16. New York: American Society of Mechanical Engineers.

THOMPSON, B. S., M. V. GANDHI, AND D. J. DESAI, "Workpiece-Fixture Interactions in a Compacted Fluidized-Bed Fixture Under Various Loading Conditions," *International Journal of Production Research,* 27(2), 229–246.

TRENT, E. M. (1984). *Metal Cutting.* London: Butterworths.

VEKTEK (1988). *VEKTORFLO,* Product Catalog. Emporia, KS: Vektek, Inc.

WECK, M., and H. BIBRING (1984). *Handbook of Machine Tools,* Vol. 1. New York: John Wiley.

WILSON, F. W., and J. M. HOLT, JR., EDS. (1962). *Handbook of Fixture Design.* New York: McGraw Hill.

XU, Y., G. LIU, Y. TANG, J. ZHANG, R. DONG, AND M. WU (1983). "A Modular Fixturing System (MFS) for Flexible Manufacturing," *FMS Magazine,* 1(5), 292–296.

YOUCEF-TOURNI, K., and J. H. BUITRAGO (1988). "Design of Robot Operated Adaptable Fixtures," in *Proceedings of Manufacturing International '88.* Atlanta, GA: Society of Manufacturing Engineers, Dearborn, MI: 3:113–119.

———. (1989). "Design and Implementation of Robot-Operated Adaptable and Modular Fixtures," *Robotics and Computer-Integrated Manufacturing,* 5(4), 343–356.

ZIMMERMAN, H. (1984). *Considerations for Special Machines, Processes and Fixturing as Integrated into a Flexible Manufacturing System,* SME Technical Paper MS84-929. Dearborn, MI: Society of Manufacturing Engineers.

6

Fixed Automation

6.1 INTRODUCTION

Since the beginning of our industrial society, many inventions have been patented. From some of these inventions, whole new technologies have evolved. Whitney's concept of interchangeable parts, Watt's steam engine, and Ford's assembly line are but a few developments that are most noteworthy outgrowths of the Industrial Revolution. Ford's assembly line and his efforts to automate many assembly-line activities certainly changed our lives. Each of these developments has impacted manufacturing as we know it, and has earned these individuals deserved recognition in history. Efforts to mechanize and automate factory operations have made us more productive. However, the single development that has impacted manufacturing more quickly and significantly than any previous technology is the digital computer.

Today, only 40 years after its commercial development, the computer is used for a variety of manufacturing-control functions. Manufacturing facilities without a computer are the exception rather than the rule. Facilities employing as few as 100 people may have half that number of computers or computer-based controllers performing a variety of manufacturing activities. The modern factory environment has become an example of computer-controlled manufacturing. Facilities currently exist where parts are created on a computer (on a computer-aided design, or CAD system), production plans are created from the CAD data using an automated process-planning system, numerical-controlled part programs are created using the tool-path requirements on a CAD system, and parts are manufactured under the control of a computer. Manufacturing systems can generally be classified as flexible or fixed systems. They are also referred to as softwired or hardwired systems. Fixed systems are typically used for the production of high-volume products and are usually limited to the production of a single part or, at most, a few parts. Flexible systems are easily reprogrammable and are used in the production of a variety of parts.

Because industrial productivity is measured as the ratio of sales dollars output to man-hours input, industrial automation will continue to be a natural emphasis for engineers and managers. This evolution toward automation, however, must only come after the economics of automation can be justified. In general, dedicated automation systems are used to produce high volumes of parts, whereas low-volume products are normally produced on manufacturing systems that are capable of producing more than one part. Automated transfer lines are typically groups of specially designed machine components that are integrated into a system by way of specially designed parts-transfer and material-handling systems. Special machine systems, such as an automatic screw machine system, are specially designed systems that can be altered (via alternate cams, adjustable screw settings, special wiring, and so on) in order to produce a small family of parts (like screws). Stand-alone automatic machines, such as a numerical-control machine, are normally used to produce small batches of many different parts. Several factors other than variety and volume, such as part geometry and accuracy, affect the choice of manufacturing system. The specific system choice usually is determined by a detailed economic analysis. Table 6.1 contains a brief summary of system specifics for general manufacturing practice.

TABLE 6.1   MANUFACTURING SYSTEM CHARACTERISTICS

Type of system	Volume of parts	No. of different parts	Cost/piece	Flexibility of system
Transfer line	Highest	1 or 2	Lowest	Lowest
Special systems	High	1 to 12	Low	Low
Stand-alone automatic machines	Low–mid	Many	Moderate	High
Stand-alone manual machines	Low	Most	Highest	Highest

In this chapter, the basics of automated manufacturing and automatic mechanisms are discussed. The chapter provides an introduction to fixed-automation principles and introduces some mechanisms used in conventional as well as modern automation systems.

6.2 MANUFACTURED COMPONENT DESIGN

Although many designers use modern CAD systems to aid in the design process, the use of CAD does not change the design-process requirements. As in the past, the modern design engineer is still responsible to

1. develop the geometric detail required for the product (shape, dimension, tolerance, and so on)
2. perform the necessary analysis on the design
3. review and alter the design based on functional and economic (manufacturability) characteristics
4. communicate the design via an understandable drafting system.

Whether a CAD system is employed in the design or whether the designer uses a standard drafting table, each of these design steps must be addressed either formally or informally. As an example of these activities, suppose an engineer needs a special wrench to adjust a positioning nut that is located in a place that is inaccessible with a standard straight-shank tool. Several bends must be manufactured into a standard open-end wrench.

In order to obtain such a wrench in the most expeditious manner, the engineer would most likely walk to the tool fabrication shop and explain the needs to one of the machinists. If the number of bends required in the wrench is few and the bends simple, the engineer may simply explain the needs verbally. Based on this description, the machinist may understand the geometric requirements and select the material based on the physical requirements (maximum torque conditions, length of shaft, and so on). Without ever appearing in a drawing, the part may be designed and conveyed in the heads of the engineer and machinist and never take form on paper. As the part is being machined, the machinist may alter the initial conception of the part to ease manufacturing requirements.

As the complexity of the part increases, the likelihood of the process requiring a sketch or drawing also increases. If a very complex tool were necessary, then a fully specified engineering drawing would be required.

6.3 DESIGN FOR MANUFACTURE

Today more than ever, it is important for the product designer to understand the implications of decision making on the manufacturability of a product. For a commercial product to fair well in the marketplace, the design needs for the product first must be met. However, no company will survive in today's competitive market selling an equivalent product at a higher price. The key to any manufacturer's success is to develop a good product that is easily manufactured. Whether a product is produced manually or using automatic equipment, the key to successful production is good design. Typically, 80% of a product cost is committed by the designer.

The design should not be overspecified so as to include tight dimensional tolerances. The surface finish, for instance, should be specified to be the largest value possible that meets the functional needs. Deep holes (one with a length/diameter ratio of greater than 3.5) can and should be avoided in part through changing the hole diameter or modifying the hole length. Similarly, parts that must be assembled should be designed so that tolerance "stacks" do not introduce any assembly interference and so that assembly takes place in a logical manner.

The impact of design on manufacturing cannot be overstated. The company's profitability may be severely handicapped by specifying parts requiring secondary and tertiary operations when an alternative part requiring only a single operation suffices.

The design must be carefully thought out. Design simplification and design for manufacture should be part of every product's life cycle. These activities, in fact, may be the most important part of the engineering process.

Once a good design is created, it is time to produce the product in the most appropriate manner. Manual production for small lot sizes may still be the best alternative. Many operations, however, can be automated in order to lessen the amount of direct labor required for production. This automation may also lessen the variability of the part. In the next sections, we discuss some mechanisms for automation.

6.4 AUTOMATED MANUFACTURING

The scientific study of metal cutting and automation techniques is a product of the twentieth century. Two pioneers of these techniques were Fredrick Taylor and Henry Ford. During the early 1900s, the improving U.S. standard of living brought a new high in personal wealth. The major result was an increased demand for durable goods. This increased demand meant that manufacturing could no longer be treated as a blacksmith trade, and the use of scientific study was employed in manufacturing analysis. Taylor pioneered studies in "scientific management," where methods for production by both men and machines were studied. Taylor also conducted metal-cutting experiments at the Midvale Steel Company that lasted 26 years and produced 400 tons of metal chips. The result was the development of the Taylor tool-life equation, which is still used in industry today. This tool-life equation is still the basis of determining economic metal cutting and has been used in adaptive controlled machining.

Henry Ford's contributions took a different turn than Taylor's. Ford refined and developed the use of assembly lines for the major component manufacture of his automobile. Ford felt that every American family should have an automobile, and if it could be manufactured inexpensively enough, then every family would buy one. Several mechanisms were developed at Ford to accommodate assembly lines. The automation that Ford developed was built into the hardware, and he realized that significant demand was necessary to offset the initial development and production costs of such systems. Many of the automation techniques and mechanisms that Ford used on his early production and assembly lines are still in use today.

6.5 FIXED AUTOMATED MANUFACTURING SYSTEMS

As mentioned earlier in this chapter, manufacturing systems can generally be classified as fixed (hardwired) or flexible (softwired). These classifications are normally bestowed on both the processing equipment (machine tools, welders, and so on) and the material-handling system that integrates the processes. Each process or machine usually consists of dozens of mechanisms that create the required relative motion to complete an activity. These mechanisms include cams, ways and slides, pistons (pneumatic or hydraulic), vibratory devices, push rods, and screw mechanisms. Each of these mechanisms have particular characteristics that allow them to be coupled together to amplify force or speed and create/convert linear or rotary motion. When these mechanisms are mechanically fastened on a base relative to each other in order to perform a specific task, we refer to this type of mechanization as fixed, or hardwired. These mechanisms can be integrated to form a machine that performs a single dedicated function automatically or semiautomatically. We refer to these machines as hardwired, or fixed, machines.

An automated manufacturing system consists of a collection of these automatic or semiautomatic machines linked together by an "intrasystem" material-handling system. These systems have been around since before Henry Ford began to manufacture his Model T on his moving assembly line, and these automated systems have been used to produce machined components, assemblies, electrical components, food products, chemical products, and so on. The total number of products produced on a single system varies along with the production method. It is *not* the purpose of this book to deal with basic mechanical mechanisms and component design, so no further discussion of simple mechanisms is provided. A discussion of systems flow is presented first. This discussion is followed by an introduction to some specific mechanisms normally used for the transfer of materials from station to station.

Figure 6.1 contains the symbology for production flow diagrams along with a typical production system schematic diagram. The workstations in a production system can be manual, semiautomatic, or fully automatic. The automatic stations can be programmable or hardwired. Flow diagrams like the one shown in the figure are normally used to communicate the relationships of flow in a factory. They serve as an aggregate model

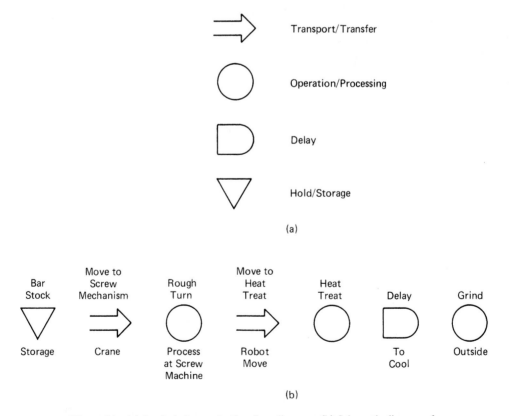

Figure 6.1   (a) Symbols for production flow diagrams. (b) Schematic diagram of a production system.

of the production environment and are frequently used in work simplification and analysis.

6.6 WORKPIECE HANDLING

In an automated manufacturing system that consists of more than one machine or processing station, a transfer mechanism between stations is required. The transfer mechanism must move a part from one machine to the next and orient and locate the part accurately enough so that the necessary processing can be performed with the required accuracy. Although many mechanisms can be used for the transfer, these mechanisms fall into the following three categories:

continuous transfer
intermittent or synchronous transfer
nonsynchronous or power-and-free transfer

The type of transference used normally dictates many of the other system characteristics. The control of the system for these basic transfer procedures also changes significantly, and many different mechanisms can be used to accommodate this transfer.

6.6.1 Continuous Transfer

As the name implies, in a continuous transfer system, the parts are moved at a constant speed through the system. Because the parts are constantly in motion, the processing stations must be able to follow a part's position. In order to accommodate this movement, station workheads are frequently set in rotary shells that are timed to rotate at the same speed as the transfer system. An example of this type of system is a beer bottling facility, where the bottles flow at constant speed through the system and are filled by a head that rotates to the speed of the line. Some automotive systems currently employ robots on continuous transfer systems. On these systems, timing marks are normally employed to signal and provide the robot with a reference position, and the program for the robot's activities accounts for the additional movement.

Continuous transfer systems are usually employed on relatively high-volume products with few options or product changes occurring over time.

6.6.2 Intermittent Transfer

Intermittent transfer, again, as the name implies, moves the parts through a system in an intermittent, or timed, discrete motion. All parts move at the same time, as was the case of the continuous transfer systems; however, the parts dwell motionless at the processing stations. This allows the processing stations to work on a part in a fixed position. However, this also requires that the processing stations wait idle for the transfer to occur.

6.6.3 Nonsynchronous Transfer

The use of continuous and intermittent transfer mechanisms requires that a good "line balance" is possible, that is, that all station workloads are approximately equal. If this is not the case, parallel workstations or additional shifts must be employed. Because of the imbalance, in-process queues are required, and the transfer of parts through the system must be conducted independently of other processing stations. Examples of non-synchronous systems include "power-and-free conveyors" used to cycle parts through a production facility and a robot moving parts between several processing stations.

6.7 HARDWARE FOR AUTOMATION

Automated production systems have been around for many years and have taken many different appearances. In general, an automated manufacturing system can be described as a collection of mechanical, electrical, and electronic components coupled together to perform one or more manufacturing tasks. In early automated systems, most of the functions were automated using a variety of mechanical devices. These mechanisms were integrated into a large system using cams, timing chains, and a variety of other mechanical integrating devices. The screw machine shown in Figure 6.2 was typical of mechanical automation. One general characterization of these systems was that they could normally be used only to produce one or a very few parts, and the setup time required to change over from one part to another was usually orders of magnitude greater than the cycle time. This type of automation could be used effectively to produce large lots of parts. Second-generation automation equipment integrated more flexible electric controls such as relays, timers, and counters into the system. These systems could be set up for different parts production far more quickly than the first-generation systems. Finally, today's manufacturing systems employ programmable electronic controls that, in some cases, can be set up for random parts sequences without incurring any setup time between parts. It is impossible within the scope of this book to present a treatise of mechanisms used for automation. Therefore, only two basic mechanisms are covered: one is a rotary mechanism and the other is a linear mechanism. Depending on the size of the components being manufactured, the number of operations required, the accuracy requirements, and the weight of the parts, either a rotary or linear system may be more appropriate. In general, if few operations are required on relatively small parts, then rotary transfer mechanisms are usually employed. In this case, parts are fixed on a rotary table and move intermittently through the system. A common device employed in these systems is the Geneva Mechanism shown in Figure 6.3. The Geneva Mechanism has several characteristics that make it ideal for use in automation.

6.7.1 The Geneva Mechanism

The Geneva Mechanism is a camlike mechanism that is widely used for both low- and high-speed machinery. It has widespread use where a spindle, turret, or worktable must

Figure 6.2 An automatic screw machine, typical of mechanical automation. (Courtesy of Tornos Bechler U.S. Corporation.)

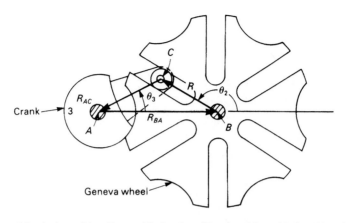

Figure 6.3   A six-position Geneva Mechanism. (Reprinted from *Modern Manufacturing Process Engineering* by Niebel et al., copyright © 1989, McGraw-Hill, Inc., by permission of the publisher.)

be indexed. Although the Geneva Mechanism shown in the figure has six slots, these mechanisms can have between three and a large number of slots or indexing positions (a more realistic upper limit for indexing positions is 12). A feature that makes these mechanisms most valuable is that the center lines of the drive crank and indexer are perpendicular at initial engagement and disengagement. This allows the use of constant-velocity motors without having to deal specifically with indexing table acceleration and deceleration problems. The indexing table is normally mounted on top of the Geneva wheel.

In designing these mechanisms, a known drive radius or indexing positioner radius and the number of indexing positions required are usually given and provide the logical starting point. As shown in Figure 6.4, the rotation required for an *n*-position table can be calculated as

$$Q_i = 2\pi/n \tag{6.1}$$

The indexer radius can then be expressed as

$$r_i = d \sin(Q_d/2) \tag{6.2}$$

The drive radius can also be expressed as

$$r_d = d \sin(Q_i/2) \tag{6.3}$$

The ratio of r_i to r_d then can be expressed as

$$\frac{r_i}{r_d} = \frac{\sin(Q_i/2)}{\sin(Q_d/2)} \tag{6.4}$$

and

$$0 \le q_i \le Q_i \quad \text{and} \quad 0 \le q_d \le Q_d$$

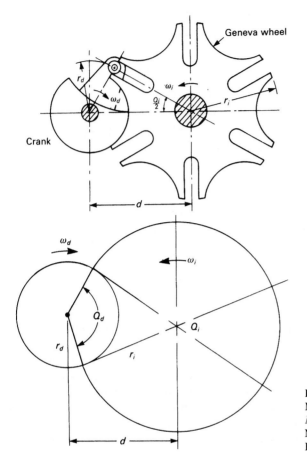

Figure 6.4 Nomenclature for a Geneva Mechanism. (Reprinted from *Modern Manufacturing Process Engineering* by Niebel et al., copyright © 1989, McGraw-Hill, Inc., by permission of the publisher.)

where

Q_i, Q_d = initial angle of indexer and drive crank

n = number of slots

q_i, q_d = instant rotation angle

This ratio is important for both the design as well as for the operation of the Geneva Mechanism. The ratio provides the ratio of drive to dwell time, and for a given dwell requirement, dictates the drive crank speed. For one rotation of the drive, only the q_d angle (drive angle) is driving the indexer. In the rest of the angle, the indexer dwells. The operation cycle time is the dwell time. The time t for the drive to make one rotation is the sum of the drive time, t_d, and the cycle time, t_c:

$$t = t_d + t_c$$

$$\frac{t_c}{t} = \frac{2\pi - Q_d}{2\pi}$$

The constant angular speed of the drive is

$$\omega_d = 2\pi/t \tag{6.5}$$

The drive motor rpm, N, is

$$N = \frac{1}{t} = \frac{2\pi - Q_d}{2\pi t_c} \tag{6.6}$$

Figure 6.5 illustrates the position of the roller in the slot during the drive cycle. From the figure, the indexing angle can be calculated as

$$\frac{a}{r_d} = \sin\frac{q_d}{2}$$

$$c = d - r_d \cos(q_d/2)$$

$$\tan\frac{q_i}{2} = \frac{\sin(q_d/2)}{d/r_d - \cos(q_d/2)} \tag{6.7}$$

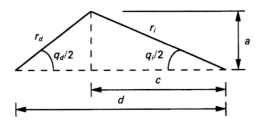

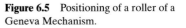

Figure 6.5   Positioning of a roller of a Geneva Mechanism.

The angular velocity of the wheel can be determined for any value of q_d by differentiating Equation (6.7) with respect to time. This produces

$$\omega_i = \omega_d \frac{(d/r_d)\cos(q_d/2) - 1}{1 + (d^2/r_d^2) - 2(d/r_d)\cos q_d} \tag{6.8}$$

The maximum wheel velocity occurs when the crank drive angle is zero, $q_d = 0$, or

$$\omega_i^{max} = \omega_d \frac{r_d}{d - r_d} \tag{6.9}$$

If a system is being planned that requires three stations and a station cycle time of 0.5 min, then the following can be computed for an indexer of 12-in. diameter. The indexing angle can be computed as

$$Q_i = \frac{2\pi}{3} = 2.094 \text{ rad} = 120°$$

The distance between drive and index centers is

$$d = \frac{r_i}{\cos(Q_i/2)} = \frac{12}{\cos 1.047} = 24 \text{ in.}$$

The drive diameter is

$$r_d = \sqrt{d^2 - r_i^2} = 20.78$$

The drive angle is

$$Q_d = 2(\pi/2 - Q_i/2) = 1.047 \text{ rad} = 60°$$

Since the nondrive time must correspond to the cycle time, the rotation of the drive motor can be calculated as

$$N = \frac{1}{t} = \frac{2\pi - Q_d}{2\pi t_c} = \frac{2\pi - 1.047}{2\pi \times 0.5} = 1.67 \text{ rpm}$$

In our case, the drive motor would rotate 1 revolution every 36 s. The ratio of time spent processing to time spent indexing would be 300:60 if a constant-speed motor were used.

6.7.2 The Walking Beam

Conveyors undoubtedly comprise the majority of linear transfer devices used today. However, conveyor systems can take on a variety of control characteristics, ranging from simple to programmable control. Chapter 7 discusses some of the merits of programmable applications. As a result, the walking-beam transfer device is illustrated as the linear device of choice. The walking beam is a reasonably simple device used for the intermittent transfer of parts to stations laid out in a linear manner. The power drive for the walking beam is typically a pneumatic or hydraulic two-stroke piston.

The walking beam is illustrated in Figure 6.6. As can be seen in the figure, the piston provides the horizontal as well as the vertical drive for the system. As such, the drive stroke of the piston must be greater than the distance that the transfer rail and parts travel. The action, as seen in the figure, begins by withdrawing the piston. The transfer rail moves backward until the rail makes contact with the back stop. The rail is then driven up by the walking beams until the rail falls to rest on the forward rest. The piston then drives the transfer rail forward until the forward stop is impacted. The forward stop inhibits the forward movement of the transfer rail, driving it back off the beams.

Figure 6.7 shows the geometry of the walking beam. To design a walking beam, the designer normally begins with the distance between workstations, d_s, and the required lifting height, h_z. A walking-beam size, b, is then selected (usually about 10 times the lifting height). From the geometry in the figure, the following can be determined

$$D_x = b \sin (90 - \beta) \tag{6.10}$$

$$h_z = b - b \cos (90 - \beta) \tag{6.11}$$

The minimum and maximum piston strokes then can be computed. The minimum piston stroke corresponds to the stroke required to lift the beam to a vertical position. This can be expressed as

$$S_{\min} = d_s + b \sin (90 - \beta) + b \sin (90 - \alpha) \tag{6.12}$$

The maximum piston stroke corresponds to that driven from stop to stop and can be expressed as

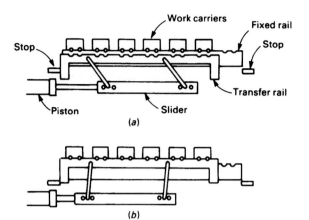

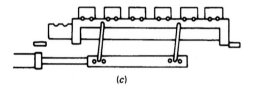

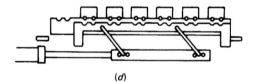

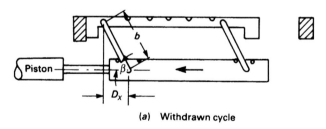

Figure 6.6   The walking beam. (Reprinted from *Modern Manufacturing Process Engineering* by Niebel et al., copyright © 1989, McGraw-Hill, Inc., by permission of the publisher.)

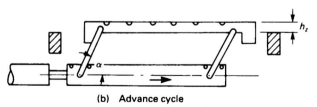

Figure 6.7   Geometry of a walking beam. (Reprinted from *Modern Manufacturing Process Engineering* by Niebel et al., copyright © 1989, McGraw-Hill, Inc., by permission of the publisher.)

$$S_{max} = d_s + 2[b \sin(90 - \beta) + b \sin(90 - \alpha)] \tag{6.13}$$

A piston whose stroke falls somewhere between these values is then specified.

The type of hardware selected for any manufacturing system usually depends on many parameters. The mechanisms described here are simple mechanisms that are frequently used in transfer devices. These mechanisms can be embellished in many ways to improve their performance. For instance, a Geneva Mechanism will frequently employ a motor and timer. By doing so, the efficiency of the transfer device can normally be improved. This control does add to the complexity of the system and may or may not be justifiable. This type of control is discussed in the next chapter.

6.8 ECONOMICS OF AUTOMATION

The purpose of any production system is to produce a product or family of products in the most economic manner possible. Automated production systems are no different than any other type of manufacturing system. In order to employ any form of automation, the automation must be economically justifiable. Automation has traditionally been most appropriate for high-volume long-life products. However, flexible automation equipment has brought automation to some relatively low-volume products. In general, automated manufacturing is employed to

  reduce labor cost
  improve product quality
  increase production rates
  reduce in-process inventory
  reduce material-handling cost and time
  increase manufacturing control

The key to any production system is to utilize those components that produce the required quality part at the minimum cost. This cost is determined by a number of factors that go into the design of the system.

Like any other engineering system, a production system must be economically justified before it is purchased. The justification is based on an after-tax analysis of the equipment and labor costs.

There are many ways to justify the use of automation in manufacturing. Although some industry projects are automated for a variety of reasons, including to increase safety, to improve the work environment, to increase quality, and so on, the basis for virtually all automation applications is the economic advantage that it brings. In this section, we discuss three of the most popular project economic-analysis methods. They are the *payback period,* the *before-tax cash-flow analysis,* and the *after-tax cash-flow analysis.* An example of each method is given after a brief description of the procedures. While we are discussing the economics, we would like to stress that a decision on automation should not be based on economic justification alone. Many factors should be considered that are difficult to quantify in terms of economics, for example, safety, quality, job satisfaction, and so on.

6.8.1 Payback Period

The payback-period method is used to estimate the number of years required to recover an initial equipment investment. Payback does not consider the time value of money. As you will see later, the payback-period method does not provide a precise evaluation of the project. It does, however, produce a quick indication on how attractive is a particular project. Payback may be the most widely used procedure in industry to cost justify projects. A commonly used indication of an acceptable project is to have a payback period (N) less than 1.5 years. That is, any equipment that is used in industry must pay for itself within 1.5 years of installation. Although the period for payback varies throughout industry, 1.5 years seems to be the most common meter used.

The payback period, N, can be defined as

$$N = C_0/S_a \qquad (6.14)$$

where

C_0 = initial investment
S_a = annual savings

Example 6.1

A machine shop currently employs 5 machine operators, 3 material handlers, and uses 10 conventional machine tools. Based on a shop modernization study, 6 of the 10 machine tools can be replaced by 2 machining centers. After the system is implemented, only 2 machine operators are needed. However, an NC programmer will have to be hired. Some of the loading/unloading work can also be done by 2 pick-and-place robots. It is suggested that an automated material-handling system also should be implemented. The material-handling system will replace the 2 material handlers. After a simulation study is conducted, it is shown that the new system can increase production by 50%. We are interested to know whether the project is cost justifiable to implement. All equipment costs include installation. The cost data are

Operator rate (including overhead): $30,000/year
NC programmer rate (including overhead): $40,000/year
NC machine cost: $70,000 and $100,000, respectively
Estimated salvage value of 6 existing machines: $60,000
Robot cost: $50,000
Automated material-handling-system cost: $50,000
Additional annual maintenance cost: $40,000/year

Solution:

C_0 = NC machine cost − salvage value of existing machines + robot's cost
    + automated material-handling-system cost

= $70,000 + $100,000 − $60,000 + $50,000 + $50,000

$$= \$210,000$$

$$S_a = \text{labor savings} - \text{programmer cost} - \text{maintenance cost}$$

$$= \$30,000 \times (3 + 2) - \$40,000 - \$40,000$$

$$= \$70,000$$

$$N = \frac{\$210,000}{\$70,000} = 3 \text{ years}$$

Although the payback period is long, there are other benefits that are not considered in the economic-justification process. For example, the new system brings with it greater production capacity, better quality, shorter product lead time, and so on. Not placing an economic value of these factors severely handicaps the justification of automation applications. The use of the payback method also is a deterrent to automation applications because the capital requirements for automation applications are usually high and a short payback term is normally not possible.

6.8.2 Before-Tax Cash-Flow Method

The cash-flow method considers the time value of money. Usually, the time value is represented by an interest rate (rate of return), i. The opportunity cost (or benefit) of possessing money for investment of loaning is also represented by i. We assume that if the money is not used in a specific project, it could be invested elsewhere with a rate of return equal to i^*, which is called the minimum attractive rate of return (MARR). There are several measures of merit used in cash-flow analysis. In the present-worth method, all the costs and savings are brought back to the beginning of the project. If the cash value of the project is greater than 0, then the project is profitable. Other commonly used measures of merit are *future worth, annual worth, internal rate of return,* and *external rate of return.* Except for the external rate of return, each of these methods gives the same answer. To consider the time value of money, one first draws a cash-flow diagram, as shown in Figure 6.8.

The figure shows that the initial investment is C_0, the annual revenue is R_{aj}, and the annual cost is C_{aj}. Therefore, the present worth (PW) is

$$\begin{aligned} \text{PW} &= C_0 + \sum [S_{aj}(P/F,i,j)] \qquad j = 1 \text{ to } n \\ &= C_0 + S_a(P/A,i,n) \qquad\qquad \text{if } S_a \text{ is constant} \end{aligned} \tag{6.15}$$

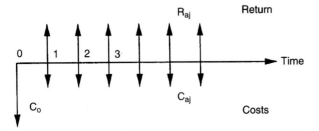

Figure 6.8   Cash-flow diagram.

where

$$S_{aj} = R_{aj} - C_{aj}$$

$(P/F,i,j)$ is the future-worth to present-worth conversion factor

$$(P/F,i,j) = \frac{1}{(1 + i)^j} \tag{6.16}$$

Values for $(P/F,i,j)$ can be found in almost any compounding interest table. $(P/A,i,n)$ is the annual-worth to present-worth conversion factor.

$$(P/A,i,n) = \frac{(1 + i)^n - 1}{i(1 + i)^n} \tag{6.17}$$

The before-tax present-worth method does not take into account the effect of taxation on the investment.

Example 6.2

Now we analyze the previous example using the present-worth method. Let us first assume that the project life is 10 years, and there is no annual adjustment for the operator and programmer rates. The salvage value of the proposed equipment after 10 years is 10% of the purchase value. The minimum attractive rate of return is 15%.

Solution:

$$\begin{aligned} PW &= -\$210{,}000 + \$70{,}000(P/A,15,10) + \$27{,}000(P/F,15,10) \\ &= -\$210{,}000 + (\$70{,}000 \times 4.8004) + (\$27{,}000 \times 0.2231) \\ &= \$132{,}052 \end{aligned}$$

Because PW is greater than 0, the project is said to be justifiable.

6.8.3 After-Tax Cash-Flow Method

The after-tax cash-flow method is similar to the before-tax analysis except that taxes are taken into consideration. There are two major items that affect the after-tax cash flow. One is the depreciation of capital equipment and the other is income tax. To perform an after-tax cash-flow analysis, one has to select from several depreciation methods for the equipment that is being purchased. The cash flow includes the before-tax cash flow (B), depreciation (D), taxable income (C), tax (T), and then the after-tax cash flow (A).

$$C = B - D \tag{6.18}$$

$$T = \text{tax rate} \times C \tag{6.19}$$

$$A = B - T \tag{6.20}$$

As mentioned, there are several depreciation methods acceptable by the Internal Revenue Service (IRS). The IRS has outlined several favorable depreciation procedures to encourage automation. These procedures allow for a short depreciation period for flexible manufacturing equipment and accelerated depreciation rates. However, for illustration purposes, we only show the straight-line depreciation method. We also ignore the additional first-year depreciation. For the current tax laws, refer to current IRS publications.

$$D = \frac{C - S}{n} \tag{6.21}$$

where

C = capital cost
S = salvage value
n = service life of the equipment

Example 6.3

We continue Example 6.2 and conduct an after-tax cash-flow analysis. Let us assume that the corporate income tax rate is 50%.

Solution:

$$D = \frac{\$270,000 - \$27,000}{10} = \$24,300$$

Year	B	D	$C = B - D$	$T = 0.5 \times C$	$A = B - T$
0	$-\$210,000$				$-\$210,000$
1–10	$\$70,000$	$\$24,300$	$\$45,700$	$\$22,850$	$\$47,150$
10	$\$27,000$			$\$13,500$	$\$13,500$

$$PW = -\$210,000 + \$47,150(P/A,15,10) + \$13,500(P/F,15,10)$$

$$= -\$210,000 + \$22,6338.86 + \$3011.85$$

$$= \$19,350.71$$

Although the after-tax present worth of the project is still positive, the value is much lower than that of the before-tax analysis. The specific results will depend on the specific application and company finances and tax policies.

6.9 CONCLUDING REMARKS

This chapter has presented an overview of the integration issues between design and manufacturing as well as the basics of integrated automation issues. Design and manufacturing are normally viewed as separate issues covered by two separate disciplines (mechanical and industrial, or manufacturing, engineering). The integration of these activities is paramount for the success of a modern industry. No product can compete effectively in the international marketplace unless design and production are integrated in an effective manner. Once these issues are completed, we can begin to look at automating the manufacturing function. This chapter has also presented some mechanisms used in automated manufacturing. An optimum amount of automation can be identified after product design has been completed. This optimum is a function of the quantity of products to be produced and several additional system specifics. A traditional engineering economic analysis is required to determine the best manufacturing alternative.

REVIEW QUESTIONS

6.1. When would it be appropriate to use a hardwired automated system as opposed to a softwired (programmable) automated system?

6.2. What are the basic functions that a process engineer must perform? How are they assisted by using a CAD system? How do these issues relate to the designer?

6.3. Create a schematic diagram of what an automated assembly system for an electric motor production line might look like. The major components of the motor are the motor frame, the armature, the magnetic coils, the end shields, and the fasteners. Assume whatever order you feel is logical.

6.4. Could a Geneva Mechanism be used for a production system in which the station times are unequal? Explain your answer.

6.5. Create a Geneva Mechanism for an eight-station automated table. The indexer diameter is set to 36 in. The station cycle time (time required for each station) is 40 s. Show both the engineering design and calculations.

6.6. Create a walking-beam mechanism for the system described in Review Question 6.3.

6.7. Design a walking-beam mechanism to move parts along the rail shown in Figure 6.9. State any assumptions that you feel necessary. The cycle time is 45 s.

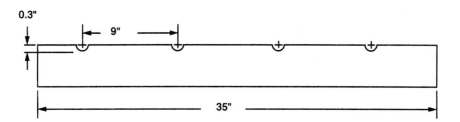

Figure 6.9   A rail to move part in a walking-beam mechanism.

6.8. A manufacturer is considering converting an existing system into a semiautomated facility. The system correctly consists of four drilling machines, three milling machines, and six lathes. Currently, machinists, who are paid $22.00/h (including overhead and fringe benefits), operate the machines. NC machining centers are being proposed to replace the drilling and milling machines. Each machining center performs the equivalent function of two drills and two mills combined. Furthermore, a single operator can run two machining centers simultaneously. A computer numerical control (CNC) turning center is also proposed to take the place of the lathes. A single CNC turning center can do the work of three conventional lathes. The cost of a machining center is $185,000 and the cost of a CNC turning center is $110,000. An NC programmer would be required to program the machines. One programmer could program all the machines. The cost of an NC programmer is $55.00/h. Use the payback, before-tax, and after-tax methods to decide what should be done. State all of the necessary assumptions.

REFERENCES/BIBLIOGRAPHY

BOOTHROYD, G., C. POLI, and L. E. MURCH (1982). *Automatic Assembly*. New York: Marcel Dekker.

NIEBEL, B. W., A. DRAPER, and R. A. WYSK, (1989). *Modern Manufacturing Process Engineering*. New York: McGraw-Hill.

THUESEN, G. J., and W. J FABRYCKY (1993). *Engineering Economy*, 8th ed. Englewood Cliffs, NJ: Prentice Hall.

WHITE, J. A., M. H. AGEE, K. E. CASE (1989). *Principles of Engineering Economic Analysis*, 3rd ed. New York: John Wiley.

7

Programmable Logic Controllers

7.1 INTRODUCTION

A manufacturing system consists of a group of machines along with material-handling, storage, and control devices. To automate the system, not only does the control device need to be automated, but the flow of information also needs to be automated. Today, when the word automation appears, most people get the notion of a system controlled by computers. However, this is not the only form of automation used in modern industry. Along with sophisticated computer controls, there are conventional control devices, such as mechanical controllers with cams and linkages, relay panels, NC controllers, and something called programmable logic controllers. In this chapter, the capabilities, programming, and applications of programmable logic controllers (PLCs) are discussed.

7.1.1 Functions of Controllers

The functions of controllers used in a manufacturing system can be classified as

1. on–off control
2. sequential control
3. feedback control
4. motion control

The most simple form of control is the on–off control. The controller switches a device on or off based on the state of a sensor. For example, a temperature controller uses a thermostat to turn on or off a furnace to heat a shop and a power switch turns a conveyor on or off. In many instances, a simple switch and some wiring are the only necessary controller components. When the control logic is a little more complex or the operating voltage and current are higher than the safety levels, relays are used.

Sequential controls are used to control a fixed sequence of events. Many manufacturing operations go through a fixed sequence of events. Each event takes a fixed time period to complete or may be terminated by a trigger from a sensor. A drum sequencer is a control device that was once used widely. It is very similar to a music box, that is, many spikes on a drum represent the events. However, a drum sequencer is used more for discrete event control; it basically turns a series of switches on and off in a certain pattern. For smoother and analog control, mechanical cams can be used.

For processes that require more precise control, a feedback device is required. For example, if it is desired to maintain a furnace at a very stable temperature, it is necessary to use the feedback of a temperature transducer to determine the amount of fuel injected into the burner. This control action must be done continuously or else the temperature will vary over time. Thus, a thermostat is not sufficient for this application. The characteristic of the burner must also be taken into consideration by the controller. Either a specially designed analog device or a computer-based controller is necessary.

The other type of control that is often used in factory processes is motion control. Quite often we would like to maintain the speed of the machine at a precise rpm. For example, in order to obtain a good quality part, an NC machine must run at a predefined feed and speed. Robot control is also an example of motion control. The details of NC machines and robotic control are discussed in Chapters 9, 10 and 11. Usually, a machine drive system consists of a motor and a transmission. Given any load change, the speed can be represented by a second-order differential equation. A motion controller is needed in order to move the machine to the desired position quickly and to maintain that speed.

7.1.2 Control Devices

Several types of control devices are used in industry to satisfy the previously mentioned control needs:

1. mechanical control
2. pneumatic control
3. electromechanical control
4. electronic control
5. computer control

Mechanical controls include cams and governors. Although they have been used for the control of very complex machines, to be cost effective, today they are used for simple and fixed-cycle task control. Some automated machines, such as screw machines, still use cam-based control. Mechanical control is difficult to manufacture and is subject to wear.

Pneumatic control is still very popular for certain applications. It uses compressed air, valves, and switches to construct a simple control logic, but is relatively slow. Because standard components are used to construct the logic, it is easier to build than a mechanical control. Pneumatic control is generally used for fixed automation, because reprogramming is not easy, it requires rewiring air ducts. Pneumatic control parts are subject to wear.

As does a mechanical control, an electromechanical control uses switches, relays, timers, counters, and so on, to construct control logic. It is similar to pneumatic control, except electric current is used instead of compressed air. It shares the same limitation as a pneumatic control. However, because electric current is used, it is faster and more flexible. The controllers built using electromechanical control are called relay devices.

Electronic control is similar to electromechanical control, except that the moving mechanical components in an electromechanical-control device are replaced by electronic switches, which work faster and are more reliable. The inherent problems of an electromechanical control also apply to an electronic control.

Computer control is the most versatile control system. The logic of the control is programmed into the computer memory using software. It not only can be used for machine and manufacturing-system control, but also for data communication. Very complex control strategies with extensive computations can be programmed. However, speed suffers when complex logic is handled by the computer. Even with modern super-microcomputers, some fast feedback-control applications may still need a special controller coupled with a computer. The difficulty of using a computer as a controller stems from two facts. The first is the interface with the outside world. Internally, the computer uses a low voltage (5 to 12 volts) and a low current (several milliamps). Machinery requires much higher voltages (24, 110, or 220 volts) and currents (measured in amps). The interface not only has to convert the voltage difference, but also must filter out the electric noise usually found in the shop. The interface thus must be custom built for each application. The second difficulty is software development. It is acknowledged by experts that software development is more difficult and more costly than hardware development. Knowledge of lower level language is usually needed for device-level programming. However, it is difficult to write the code and even more difficult to debug the software. Software development is a long and costly process. Developing computer controls requires good computer engineers.

In order to use the advantages of all these controllers and eliminate the difficulties, the programmable logic controller was invented. A PLC is a computer-based device that has standard interface modules. Initially, a PLC was a replacement for relay devices. They are programmed using a ladder diagram which is a standard electric wiring diagram. As PLCs become more flexible, high-level as well as low-level languages are available to PLC programmers. PLCs have the flexibility of computers as well as a standard and easy interface with processes and other devices. They are widely accepted in industry for controlling from a single device to a complex manufacturing facility.

7.1.3 Programmable Logic Controllers

Programmable logic controllers (PLCs) were first introduced in 1968 as a substitute for hardwired relay panels. The original intent was to replace a mechanical switching device (relay modules). Bedford Associates (now the Modicon division of Gould, Inc.) first coined the term and patented the invention. However, since 1968, the capabilities of the PLC have been enhanced significantly. Although the purpose of the original PLCs was to replace relay panels, modern PLCs have many more functions. Their use extends from simple process control to manufacturing system controls and monitoring.

They are used for high-speed digital processing, high-speed digital communication, high-level computer-language support, and, of course, for basic process control.

The National Electrical Manufacturing Association (NEMA) defines the programmable controller as "a digitally operating electronic apparatus which uses a programmable memory for the internal storage of instructions by implementing specific functions such as logic sequencing, timing, counting, and arithmetic to control, through digital or analog input/output modules, various types of machines or processes. The digital computer which is used to perform the functions of a programmable controller is considered to be within this scope. Excluded are drum and other similar mechanical sequencing controllers." This definition implies that a PLC is an electronic interface device used to perform logic operations on input signals in order to generate a set of desired output signals or responses. Input for a basic PLC typically comes from discrete signal devices, such as push buttons, microswitches, photocells, limit switches, and proximity switches, or analog devices, such as thermocouples, voltmeters, and potentiometers. Output from a basic PLC is normally directed to switching closures for motors, valves, motor starters, and so on. More sophisticated PLCs may also include a mathematics processor, a color graphics display, serial communication ports, and a local-area-network interface.

PLCs vary in size and power. Figure 7.1 shows a large PLC system. The main module measures 19 in. × 20 in. × 14.5 in. A large PLC can have up to 10,000 I/O points and support all the functions discussed earlier. There are also expansion slots to accommodate PC and other communication devices. For many applications, a small PLC is sufficient. Figure 7.2 shows a small PLC (Allen Bradley MicorLogix 1000). It measures only 4.72 in. × 3.15 in. × 1.57 in. It has 32 I/O points and a standard RS-232 serial commu-

Figure 7.1   A PLC system: CPU module (*left*) and an I/O rack (*right*) (Allen-Bradley PLC-3). (Courtesy of Allen-Bradley.)

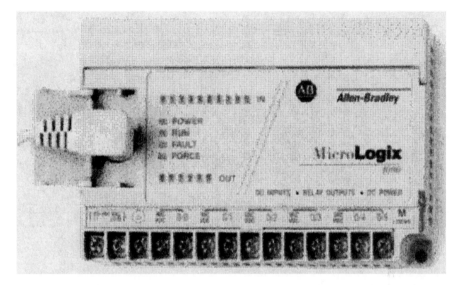

Figure 7.2   A small PLC (Allen-Bradley MicroLogix 1000; 4.72 in. × 3.15 in. × 1.57 in.). (Courtesy Allen-Bradley.)

nication port. The speed of PLCs is constantly improving. Even the low-end PLCs perform at high speed. One to two microsec/kbyte of memory speed is very common.

In this chapter, the fundamentals of programmable controllers, their programming, and applications are discussed. First, the basic devices used in relay modules are reviewed.

7.2 RELAY-DEVICE COMPONENTS

PLCs were primarily intended to replace relay devices, so it is appropriate to be familiar with the components used in relay devices. A relay device consists of a front display panel with switches, relays, timers, and counters. Each of these is discussed briefly in the following sections.

7.2.1 Switches (Contact)

A switch is a device that either opens or closes a circuit. Although there are numerous types and styles of switches, they can be classified into the following categories (Figure 7.3):

1. locking and nonlocking
2. normally open and normally closed
3. single throw and multiple throw
4. single pole and multiple pole
5. break-before-make (interrupt transfer) and make-before-break (continuity transfer)

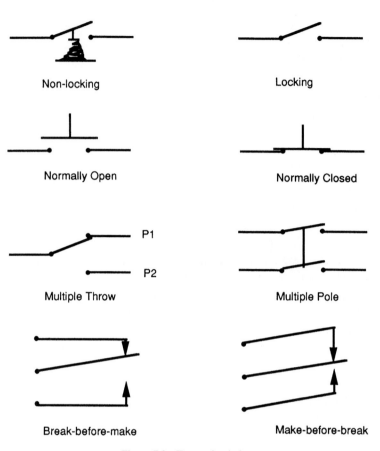

Figure 7.3　Types of switches.

A nonlocking switch returns to its initial state. A normally open switch contact is made by physically depressing the switch ("make" contact). Normally closed switches operate in the opposite manner: Contact is actively interrupted (break) from operation. A single-throw switch has two states: on and off. There are some switches that have three states: a release and two operating positions. One can select either a neutral circuit or connect to one of two circuits. This kind of switch is called a double-throw switch. A multiple-throw switch has several states. These switches all have a single pole (moving part), and, subsequently, are called single-pole switches. In order to close (or break) two or more contacts at the same time, multiple-pole switches are necessary. The most widely used multiple-pole switch is the double-pole switch.

For some circuits, contact can be made or broken several times in succession. There are two types of transfer contacts in which "makes" and "breaks" can be combined. A "break-before-make," or interrupt transfer, contact does as the name suggests—breaks one contact before another is made. When the switch is operated, there is a certain amount of time when the common spring is in contact with neither contact. Thus, a break-before-make results. A "make-before-break," or continuity transfer, contact provides the same function as a transfer contact. However, continuity always exists for one or the other contact.

Typical switches used in the control circuits include

selector switches

push-button switches

photoelectric switches

limit Switches

proximity switches

level switches

thumbwheel switches

slide switches

Among them, photoelectric switches and proximity switches are noncontact switches. A proximity switch changes its state when an object is moved in close proximity to the sensing face of the switch. Photoelectric switches are activated by a light beam. Usually, the switch includes a light source and a reflector. The light beam is reflected back to the switch sensor located beside the light source.

Switches are also rated by their currents and voltages. For industrial applications, standard switch ratings are

24 volts AC/DC

48 volts AC/DC

120 volts AC/DC

230 volts AC/DC

TTL level (transistor-to-transistor, ±5 V)

7.2.2 Relays

A switch whose operation is activated by an electromagnet is called a relay (Figure 7.4). The contact and symbology for relays is usually the same as for switches. A small current passes through the magnet, causing the pole to switch. Usually, the magnet is rated between 3 to 100 volts and a few hundred milliamps. Therefore, it is operated at very low power (current and voltage). A circuit carrying a much heavier rating can be switched using a relay, however, the two circuits are totally separated.

When a relay operates, the contacts do not all open or close instantaneously. There may be a delay of several milliseconds between the operation of two contacts of the same relay. In the design of a relay circuit, this delay must always be taken into account.

Based on the discussion, one can see that a relay is really a magnet-operated contact switch. The contact switch inside a relay also can be classified by the number of poles and throws. Although most relays are single throw, it is very common to have multiple-pole relays.

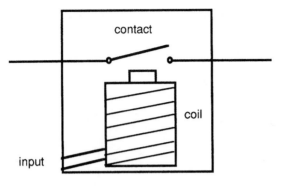

Figure 7.4   A relay.

7.2.3 Counters

Based on their structure, counters can be classified as mechanical or digital. Mechanical counters, such as an odometer, usually give readings as their output. Because mechanical counters are generally not used in a relay panel circuit, we do not discuss them. Digital counters output in the form of a relay contact when a preassigned count value is reached. A digital counter consists of a count register, an accumulator, and a relay contact (Figure 7.5). The count register holds the preassigned count value. The accumulator is used to either increment or decrement a count each time an input pulse is received. When the accumulator value equals the register value, the relay contact is activated.

The operation of a counter can be best shown by a timing diagram (Figure 7.6). The preassigned count register value is 5. There are up counters and down counters. An up counter counts starting from zero and increments the value when there is an input. A down counter, on the other hand, counts down from an initial value. They both serve the same purpose, to count a certain number of inputs and then output to a relay contact. A typical counter is characterized by the number of counting digits, the input electric rating, the reset system, the output contact rating, and the power source. Counters

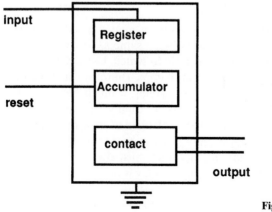

Figure 7.5   A counter.

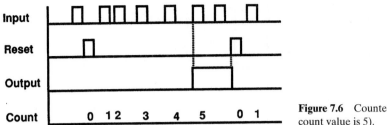

Input

Reset

Output

Count   0 1 2   3   4   5   0 1

Figure 7.6   Counter timing diagram (the count value is 5).

can be cascaded to form a larger counter. For example, an eight-digit counter can be made by cascading 2 four-digit counters. Input to a counter is normally activated from a contact. To initialize the counting, a reset input is used. The output contact is rated the same as a regular contact switch.

7.2.4 Timers

A timer, as its name implies, is used for some timing purpose. It consists of an internal clock, a count-value register, and an accumulator (Figure 7.7). In process control, a significant number of operations must be timed. For example, in a chemical process, the curing of certain products, the mixing of chemicals, and so on, all require a certain period of time to complete. In process control, synchronization of operations is also essential. There are two ways to synchronize operations, namely, event-triggered synch and time-controlled synch. Event-triggered synch can be achieved by using sensors and switches to detect the event. For time-controlled synch, each operation is given a fixed time period to finish; therefore, a clock or timer is necessary.

A timer starts timing after receiving a start signal. When a preassigned timing value is reached, it outputs a signal. The operation of a timer can be shown by a

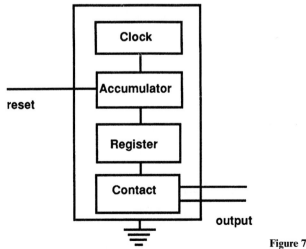

reset

output

Figure 7.7   A timer.

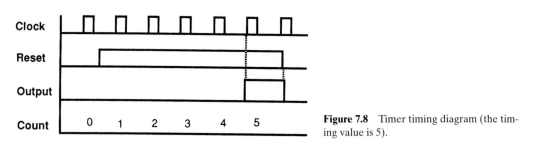

Figure 7.8 Timer timing diagram (the timing value is 5).

timing diagram (Figure 7.8). It is very similar to that of a counter, except that the counting pulses are generated internally in the timer. In the diagram, the preassigned timing value is 5 s. Each clock pulse represents 1 s.

Depending on the application, the timing diagram for other timers may have some small deviation. However, the basic principle is the same. Usually, timers are characterized by the following factors: features, such as size, mounting, and display type; time range; rated operating voltage; accuracy; contact rating; and output contact classification.

7.2.5 An Example of Relay Logic

For a control process, it is desired to have the process start (by turning on a motor) 5 s after a part touches a limit switch. The process is terminated automatically when the finished part touches a second limit switch. An emergency switch stops the process any time when it is pushed.

The circuit design for the process control is shown in Figure 7.9. In the diagram, LS_1 is the first limit switch. It is a normally open type. PB_1 is a pushbutton switch; it is normally closed. LS_2 is the second limit switch; it is normally closed. R_1 is a relay with a double-pole contact. R_2 is a relay connected to a motor. (The ladder diagram is discussed in greater detail in Section 7.4.1.) A wiring diagram for this circuit is shown in Figure 7.10.

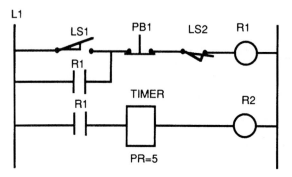

Figure 7.9 Ladder diagram for the circuit.

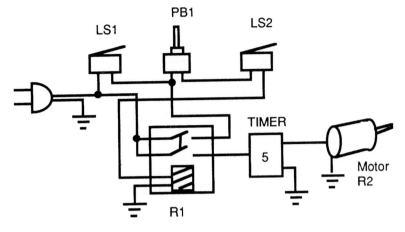

Figure 7.10   Wiring diagram.

7.3 PROGRAMMABLE CONTROLLER ARCHITECTURE

In the preceding sections, the basic components in a relay panel circuit and the design of a relay ladder diagram have been discussed. In the implementation of such a circuit, not only does the logic problem have to be thought out, but also the electrical compatibility and wiring layout have to be considered. Breadboarding a relay panel circuit is a tedious task; it requires a lot of careful planning and work. The debugging and changing of a circuit is even more difficult. Programmable logic controllers replace most of this wiring by software programming. Therefore, the task is made much easier. Because the wires and the moving mechanical components (relay contacts) are mostly replaced by software, the system is much more reliable. In this section, the basic architecture of programmable logic controllers is discussed.

Like a general-purpose computer, a programmable controller consists of five major parts: CPU (processor), memory, input/output (I/O), power supply, and peripherals (Figure 7.11).

7.3.1 The Processor

Although early PLCs used special-purpose logic circuits, most current PLCs are microprocessor-based systems. The processor (central processing unit, or CPU, as it is often called) scans the status of the input peripherals, examines the control logic to see what action to take, and then executes the appropriate output responses.

The microprocessor-based PLC has significantly increased the logical and control capacities of programmable logic controllers. High-end PLC systems allow the user to perform arithmetic and logic operations, more memory blocks, interface with computers, and a local-area network, functions, and so on.

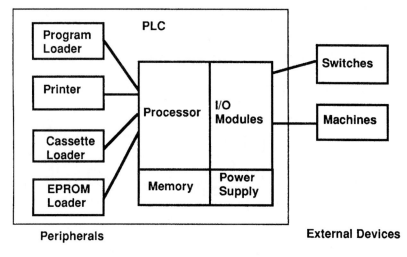

Figure 7.11 Programmable logic controller system structure.

7.3.2 Memory

The memory of the PLC is important because the control program and the peripheral status are stored there. Memory size in a PLC is measured in either bits, bytes, or words. Because many words of memory are required, it is usually measured in "k" increments (where 1k = 1024).

Although several types of memory are used in modern PLCs, memory can be classified into two basic categories: volatile, and nonvolatile. Volatile memory is that which loses state (the stored information) when power is removed. This may seem perfectly appropriate. However, you must remember that the program is stored in memory, and if the power fails (the plug is pulled, and so on), the program must be rekeyed in or reread into memory, a potentially time-consuming activity. Nonvolatile memory, on the other hand, maintains the information in memory even if the power is interrupted. Some types of memory used in a PLC include

1. ROM (read-only memory)
2. RAM (random-access memory)
3. PROM (programmable read-only memory)
4. EPROM (erasable programmable read-only memory)
5. EAPROM (electronically alterable programmable read-only memory)
6. Bubble memory

Of these memory types, the only volatile memory is RAM. (Oddly enough, it is probably the most commonly used memory.) The other memory types maintain their status even after power is lost. Many RAM-based memory systems use battery backups to preserve the contents of memory in case of power failure. These RAMs are built using CMOS technology. CMOS devices consume minimum amounts of power.

Memory can be further classified as read-only or read-write. Of the memory types listed, RAM and bubble memory are read-write. They can be easily changed by the processor. The other types of memory require additional hardware to alter or program.

PLC memories are usually expandable. Memory modules can be added. User memory ranges from less than 1k byte to several megawords.

7.3.3 Input and Output

The input and output (I/O) for a PLC is normally a set of modular plug-in peripherals (notice the difference between this definition and the one used in computer I/Os) (Figure 7.12). The I/O modules allow the PLC to accept signals from a variety of external devices, for example, limit switches, optical sensors, and proximity switches. The signals (two state signals for the devices mentioned, open or closed) are converted from an external voltage (115 VAC, 230 VAC, 24 VDC) to a TTL signal of ±5 VDC. The PLC processor then uses these signals to determine the appropriate output response. A 5 VDC signal is transmitted to the appropriate output module, which converts the signal to the appropriate response domain (115 VAC, 230 VAC, 24 VDC).

Normally, a peripheral-interface adapter (PIA) is used to transfer the status of the input peripherals to some prespecified memory location. The user defines the location of the peripheral on the I/O housing in the program. Each I/O location is assigned to a

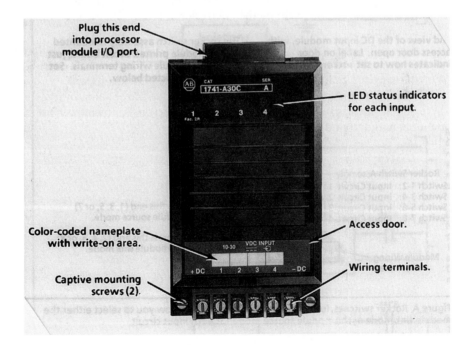

Figure 7.12 A simple input module.

specific memory location. This makes accessing input by the CPU a task of loading the contents of a specific memory into a storage register. Output changes are equally easy for the CPU to perform. The contents of a particular memory location is then altered. Due to the electrical differences between the CPU and external I/O peripheral, I/O points and internal memory are actually electrically isolated. In a more advanced design, a separate I/O processor is used to bring the external I/O status to an internal memory location.

I/O modules are typically housed in a rack separate from the PLC. Light indicators are usually included in the I/O module to provide the current state (ideal for troubleshooting). In addition, each module is normally fused and isolated from the processor. Some typical I/O modules include

1. AC voltage input and output
2. DC voltage input and output
3. numerical input and output
4. special-purpose modules, for example, high-speed timers and stepping motor controllers

For discrete I/Os, either DC or AC are most commonly used. A discrete input is usually connected to a switch. Internally, the input module always electrically isolates the external signal from the internal circuit. An LED (light emitting diode) indicator on each of the input points of the input module shows the logic state of the switch. A discrete output point is turned on or off by the controller. It is also electrically isolated from the internal circuit.

TTL inputs are used to connect to TTL-compatible devices, including solid-state controls and sensing instruments, and some photoelectric sensors. TTL outputs are connected to devices such as LED displays and other 5-VDC devices.

Analog inputs are usually used for sensor interface. Analog outputs are used to drive analog devices such as actuators, motors, and so on. Following is a list of both analog input and output devices.

ANALOG INPUTS

Flow sensors
Humidity sensors
Potentiometers
Pressure sensors
Temperature sensors

ANALOG OUTPUTS

Analog meters
Analog valves and actuators
DC and AC motor drives

Numerical I/O exchange multiple-bit data with the outside devices. Typical inputs include thumbwheel switches, bar-code readers, and encoders. Typical outputs include seven-segment displays, intelligent displays, and so on. For seven-segment displays, BCD code (Appendix 7A) are used.

There is a wide range of special-purpose I/O modules. Not every PLC provides the full range of special-purpose I/O modules. Usually, they are supported by midsize to large-size PLCs. A few of those special-purpose I/O modules follow:

- *Thermocouple input:* Low-level analog signal, filtered, amplified, and digitized before sending to the processor through the I/O bus.
- *Fast input:* 50- to 100-microsecond pulse-signal detection.
- *ASCII I/O:* Communicates with ASCII devices.
- *Stepper-motor output:* Provides direct control of a stepper motor.
- *Servo interface:* Controls DC servo motor for point-to-point control and axis positioning. May use either resolver or encoder interface (for more details, see Chapter 9).
- *PID control:* The proportional integral derivative is used for closed-loop process control. It is applied to any process that requires continuous closed-loop control. For an example, see Section 7.4.3.
- *Network module:* Provides LAN (Chapter 8) capability to the controller. It supports vendor-specific protocol, ethernet, or MAP. (Manufacturing Automation Protocol).

7.3.4 Power Supply

The power supply operates on AC power to provide the DC power required for the controller's internal operation. It is designed to take either 115 or 220 VAC. Some power supplies can take either voltage with a jumper switch for selection. The operation of I/O modules is also supported by the PLCs' power supply. However, separate power sources are required in order to close the circuits of switches, motors, and external devices. Figure 7.13 shows typical AC, DC, and TTL input connections.

In the rest of the text, whenever an input or output module is shown, the power connection will not be shown. However, it is implied that proper wiring is necessary. The same is true for output (Figure 7.14).

7.3.5 Peripherals

A number of peripheral devices are available. They are used to program the PLC, prepare the program listing, record the program, and display the system status. The following is a partial list of peripherals:

hand-held programmer (HHP)
CRT programmer
operator console
printer

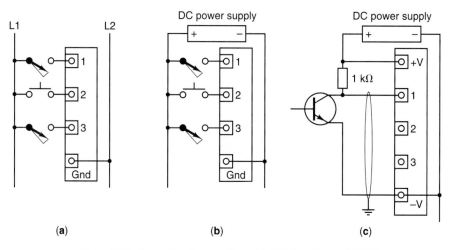

Figure 7.13 Power input connections: (a) AC, (b) DC, and (c) TTL.

simulator
EPROM loader
graphics processor
network communication interface
modular PC

Usually, programs are entered into a PLC by a hand-held program, a CRT pro-grammer, or a personal computer. A hand-held programmer is a low-cost programming device that can display only one or a few program statements (Figure 7.15). It is com-

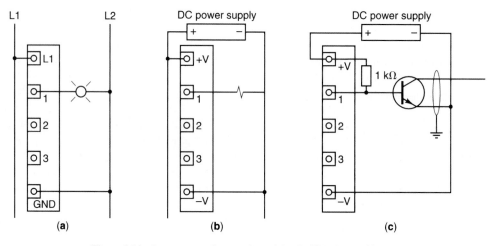

Figure 7.14 Power output connections: (a) AC, (b) DC, and (c) TTL.

Figure 7.15   An Allen-Bradley hand-held programmer for MicroLogix 1000. (Courtesy of Allen-Bradley.)

monly used on small low-cost PLCs, such as the one shown in Figure 7.2. A CRT programmer is a computer-based special CRT terminal (Figure 7.16). A special keyboard, which has keys representing ladder-diagram elements of PLC programs, makes programming easier. Programs can also be stored on a floppy disk. Most CRT programmers also allow users to track the operation of the PLC by highlighting the status of ladder-diagram elements in real time. Programmers are used only during the programming and debugging period. Programmers and loaders are not required during the regular operation of the PLC; therefore, they are shared among several PLCs. There is also software available to allow a regular personal computer to function as a programmer. Normally, a documentation-preparation function is also supported.

An operator console or operator display unit is used for operator data input or system monitoring. It can be a small numeric key pad with an LED display or a full-sized CRT display with a typewriter keyboard. A machine operator can enter

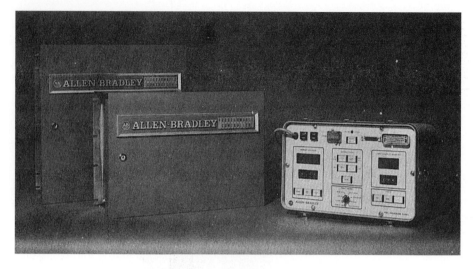

Figure 7.16   Intelligent CRT. (Courtesy Square D Co.).

machine-control parameters on the console. However, a PLC program cannot be changed with it. Some operator consoles use the touch screen to provide better user interface.

A printer is used to print PLC programs and operation messages. When a hard copy of the operating conditions or production statistics is needed, a printer is used to produce a report.

A simulator system is a board usually consisting of some lights and switches. It is used to debug a program. It can be connected to the PLC I/O module. PLC program logic can be tested by flipping switches and observing the lights.

An EPROM loader can load a program from an EPROM to a PLC's memory. Some models also allow programs in the PLC memory to be dumped to an EPROM. A cassette loader serves the same purpose, however, it becomes less popular.

Graphics processors are useful for operator interface, system simulation, and system monitoring. Some advanced PLCs provide a separate graphics processor and graphics monitor. Using interactive graphics, an application engineer can define the layout of the system. Each part of the display entities is mapped to one device in the physical system. The status information of the system can be read and used to update the display.

More advanced PLCs can also communicate with other computers or devices through a communications network. At this time, most major PLC manufacturers support Ethernet local-area network (LAN). A unified LAN (MAP proposed by General Motors) is also supported by nearly all control-device manufacturers. Using LAN, all PLCs and control devices can be linked to the same network and share the same resources. The basic components of a PLC have been discussed. Most PLCs have employed computer communication standards and, therefore, can be expanded easily or can communicate with a computer.

7.4 PROGRAMMING A PROGRAMMABLE LOGIC CONTROLLER

Programmable logic controllers were initially developed to replace relay devices. The programming language used was similar to that used by electrical technicians to design electric circuits—the ladder diagram. However, as PLCs grew more powerful and flexible, the limitations of the ladder diagram soon became apparent. Not only did the ladder diagram have no easy way to represent data manipulation, but it is also extremely difficult to write and debug a large and complex ladder diagram. In recent years, many high-end PLCs began to introduce high-level languages. Some of them are Englishlike, some use BASIC language or BASIC-like language, and some others developed PASCAL-like structured language. Often, code written in such high-level languages can coexist with the ladder-diagram program. An international effort to standardize the PLC programming language has resulted in an IEC 1131-3 standard that was published in 1993 [Lewis, 1995]. Under IEC 1131-3, the ladder diagram, structured text, function block diagram, instruction list, and sequential function chart are all included in the standard. Before the standard was fully adopted, each PLC vendor had developed its own language. In this section, we will try to follow the IEC standard.

What language to use for an application depends on several factors. First, most current PLCs use a vendor-specific language. For a chosen PLC, the choice becomes limited. Often it is only between a high-level language and the ladder diagram. Ladder diagrams were designed to solve logic problems involving simple timing, counting, and sequencing. For these applications, a ladder diagram can be easily written. However, if math functions or communications are required, ladder-diagram programming is very difficult, if not impossible.

Because the ladder diagram is still the most basic, this section begins with a brief introduction to ladder-diagram programming. A few programming examples are also given. High-level language programming using the IEC 1131-3 standard will follow. Finally, some discussion on advanced PLC functions and their programming will be discussed. One such function is PID control, which is widely used in the process industry.

7.4.1 Ladder Diagram

A ladder diagram (also called contact symbology) is a means of graphically representing the logic required in a relay logic system. Ladder diagrams have long preceded the PLC and still represent the basic logic required by a relay device or PLC. The fundamental ladder diagram consists of a series of inputs, timers, and counters. Most simply, the ladder diagram represents the actions required (relay closure) as a function of a series of inputs that are either on or off. Each ladder-diagram element is represented using some standard symbols; some commonly used ones are shown in Figure 7.17.

A ladder diagram consists of two rails of the ladder and various control circuits, rungs (Figure 7.18). Each rung starts from the left rail and ends at the right rail. We can consider that the left rail is the power wire and the right rail is the ground wire. Power flows from the left rail to the right rail, and each rung must have an output to prevent a short. The output is connected to physical devices, such as motors, lights, and solenoids.

Limit switch	Normally open	LS ⬤⟋o
	Normally closed	LS ⬤—o
	Held open	⬤⟋o
	Held closed	⬤⟍o
Proximity switch	Open	◇⬤⟋o◇
	Closed	◇⬤—o◇
Toggle switch		⬤⟍o
Rotary selector	Nonbridging contacts	o o o RSS o⬤—⬤ o
	Bridging contacts	o o o RSS o⬤—⬤ o
Push button	Single circuit — Normally open	‾‾ PB o o
	Single circuit — Normally closed	o⊥o PB
	Double circuit	o⊥o PB o o
Contacts	Relay — Normally open	—||—
	Relay — Normally closed	—|/|—
Coils	Relays	—O— CR
	Solenoids	o—/\/—o SOL
Motor	DC armature	—(A)— MTR
Pilot lights		—(R)— LT

Figure 7.17   Some relay diagram symbols.

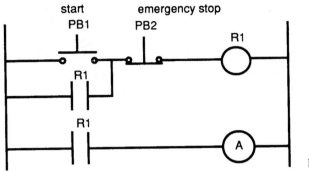

Figure 7.18   A ladder diagram.

To control the output, some switches are used on the rung to form the AND and OR logic. Different rungs are not connected except through the rails. Each rung can contain only one output.

Functionally, the components in a ladder diagram consist of those used internally to construct the logic, such as some relays, timers and counters, and those used to connect to the physical devices, such as switches and motors. The internal components are the ones replaced by a programmable logic controller (Figure 7.19).

Because of the operating-voltage difference and the logic-circuit requirement, the output is usually not connected to the motor or other devices directly. Instead, a relay is normally used. In Figure 7.18, PB_1 and PB_2 are the input push-button switches and R_1 *is the internal relay*. Motor-starter relay A is connected to a DC motor.

In the circuit of Figure 7.18, when push-button switch PB_1 is pushed, relay R_1 energizes and turns on the output circuit. In the circuit, the relay has a double-pole contact. The first contact forms a parallel circuit with PB_1. Even when PB_1 is released, current can still flow through rung 1. The second contact of R_1 is connected to A, turning A on or off.

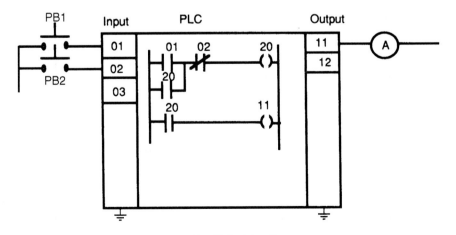

Figure 7.19   PLC wiring diagram.

In a hardwired relay circuit, current flows through all rungs simultaneously. However, in a programmable logic controller, the relay circuit is implemented in software and executed sequentially. Each ladder diagram element is assigned a working memory location (register). A PLC resolves the logic of a ladder diagram (program) rung by rung, from the top to the bottom. Usually, all the outputs are updated based on the status of the internal registers. Then the input states are checked and the corresponding input registers are updated. Only after the I/Os have been resolved is the program then executed. This process is run in an endless cycle. The time it takes to finish one cycle is called the *scan time*. The shorter the scan time, the faster the sample rate, and, thus, the faster the response to the event.

A scan cycle is illustrated in Figure 7.20. The reason that I/Os are done at the beginning of the cycle is that the program scan (execution) will not be interrupted by I/O changes. Input always affects the program right from the first rung and the output is always the result of the entire program execution from first to the last rung. If I/Os are read and written during the program scan, depending on the timing, the same set of input states may take effect at a different rung, thus creating different results. On a PLC, scan length depends on program length. In order to obtain a fixed scan time, some PLCs insert an idle state after the program execution. The idle time makes up the difference between the preset scan time and the I/O and program scan times. This gives a predictable scan time.

For some time critical applications, immediate I/O might be desirable. In this case, a special program code is used to force immediate input or output. The scan cycle is used regardless of the programming method used.

As shown in Figure 7.19, a PLC uses ladder logic programming. The program is very similar to a standard ladder diagram. In the following sections, we show how such programming is done. We use the term *ladder diagram* to denote the program normally input to a PLC. There are basically seven types of PLC instructions:

1. relay
2. timer and counter
3. program control
4. arithmetic
5. data manipulation
6. data transfer
7. others, such as sequencers

Figure 7.20 PLC scan.

Relay, and timer and counter instructions are the most fundamental because they correspond to what is on a ladder diagram, and are available on all PLCs. The other five types of instructions are available on more advanced PLCs. We limit our discussion to the first two types of instructions. We begin our discussion first with the logic of the PLC before discussing PLC instructions.

7.4.2. Logic

By using serial and parallel connections, various types of logic can be represented in a ladder diagram. The logic states of a component are either on (true, contact closure, energize) or off (false, contact open, deenergize). The ladder diagram takes input state from the input module and output results to the output module. In Figure 7.18, on rung 1, PB_1 and R_1 are in parallel; and they are connected with PB_2 and the R_1 coil in series. Complex control logic can be represented using this simple graphical logic. In this section, the fundamentals of logic construction are discussed. Ladder diagrams and equivalent logic representations are presented. Additional information on logic and truth tables can be found in Appendix 7B.

7.4.2.1 Basic logic.   The ladder diagram in Figure 7.21 depicts the most simple circuit logic. The output is solely determined by the input. Rung 1 uses a normally open contact, where the state of the output is the same as the state of the input. On rung 2, output R_2 has the opposite state of input PB_2. In the control diagram, when switch PB_2 is pushed, output R_2 is turned off.

NOT represents negation. AND and OR are logic operators. These symbols are used throughout the text.

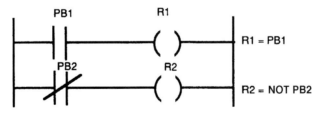

Figure 7.21   Basic Logic.

AND Logic.   As mentioned before, AND logic is achieved by connecting two components in series. The two rungs shown in Figure 7.22 consist of AND logic. AND logic is the most commonly used logic and is required in most applications. For example, in a punch-press control, the operator has a foot pedal to control the stroke of the punch. A safety guarding device, such as a photodiode detector, is also used to prevent the accidental triggering of the punch while part of the operator's body is under the punch. The circuit on rung 2 can be used for this process. Let PB_3 be the pedal switch, PB_4 be the photodiode detector, and R_2 be the control of the clutch.

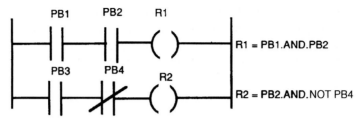

Figure 7.22   AND logic.

OR Logic.   OR is used when either one of two switches (or one or more switches out of several) is pushed and the logic output needs to be true. In Figure 7.23, either switch PB_1 or PB_2 can turn on output R_1.

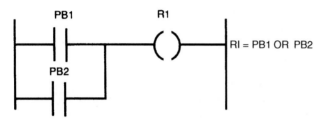

Figure 7.23   OR logic.

Combined AND and OR Logic.   A combination of AND and OR logic also can be included in one rung. For example, if we want to turn on R_1 when either (1) PB_1 is pushed or (2) PB_2 and PB_3 are pushed, the logic can be represented by an equation:

$$R_1 = PB_1 \quad \text{OR} \quad (PB_2 \quad \text{AND} \quad PB_3)$$

The corresponding rung is shown in Figure 7.24.

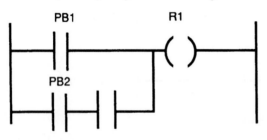

Figure 7.24   Combined AND and OR logic.

7.4.2.2 Relays.   A relay consists of two parts, the coil and the contact(s). The following are instructions (symbols) related to different coils and contacts.

   CONTACTS

   (a) normally open: -| |-
   (b) normally closed: -|/|-
   (c) positive transition—sensing: -|P|-
   (d) negative transition—sensing: -|N|-

A transitional contact output is a brief pulse. When the reference is triggered, it outputs only in one scan and functions like a one-shot. A positive transitional contact output is a pulse resulting when the reference makes a transition. A negative transitional contact occurs when the transition is from on to off.

COILS

(a) coil: -( )-

(b) negative coil: -(/)-

(c) set coil: -(S)-

(d) reset coil: -(R)-

(e) retentive memory coil: -(M)-

(f) set retentive-memory coil: -(SM)-

(g) reset retentive-memory coil: -(RM)-

(h) positive transition-sensing coil: -(P)-

(i) negative transition-sensing coil: -(N)-

The coil is the one shown in the previous examples. When the rung condition is true, the coil is energized (which, in turn, closes its normally open internal contacts). A negative coil works in the opposite way. When the rung condition is false, the coil is energized. The set coil latches the state of output. As soon as the rung condition turns true, the coil keeps the energized state, even though the rung condition becomes false. The reset coil is the only one that can deenergize the set coil. A retentive coil behaves as the normal coil, except that the state of the coil is retained on PLC power failure. A positive transition-sensing coil is set on for one scan when the power flow on the left-hand link changes from off to on. On the other hand, a negative transition-sensing coil is set on when the opposite happens.

7.4.2.3 Timers and counters

TIMERS

(a) retentive on delay: -(RTO)-

(b) retentive off delay: -(RTF)-

(c) reset: -(RST)-

The retentive-on-delay timer starts counting when the run condition is true. The retentive-off-delay timer starts counting when the rung condition is false. The timing value is specified on the timer symbol. The timing diagram of Figure 7.8 is for a retentive-on-delay timer.

COUNTERS

(a) counter up: -(CTU)-

(b) counter down: -(CTD)-

(c) counter reset: -(CTR)-

An up counter increments the accumulator value each time there is an input. The down counter decrements the accumulator value. The counter reset is used to reset the counter value.

7.4.2.4 Programming example. Now that we have some background knowledge about PLC programming, the following example shows its applications. In order to keep the example brief, the problem has been simplified.

Example 7.1. Robotic Material-Handling Control System

A robot is used to load/unload parts to a machine from a conveyor. The layout of the system is shown in Figure 7.25. The process can be described as following.

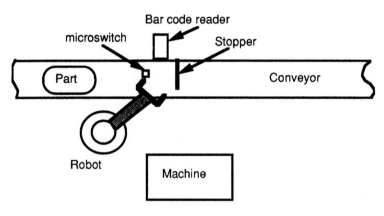

Figure 7.25   Cell layout.

A part comes along the conveyor. When it touches a microswitch, it is scanned by a barcode reader to identify it. If the part is the desired one, a stopper is activated to stop it. A robot picks up the part and loads it onto the machine if it is idle. Otherwise, the robot waits to unload the machine. The following is the assignment of control components:

ID	DESCRIPTION	STATE	EXPLANATION
MS_1	Microswitch	1	Part arrives
R_1	Output to bar-code reader	1	Scan the part
C_1	Input from bar-code reader	1	Right part
R_2	Output robot	1	Loading cycle
R_3	Output robot	1	Unloading cycle
C_2	Input from robot	1	Robot busy
R_4	Output to stopper	1	Stopper up
C_3	Input from machine	1	Machine busy
C_4	Input from machine	1	Task complete

The program and wiring diagram are shown in Figures 7.26 and 7.27, respectively.

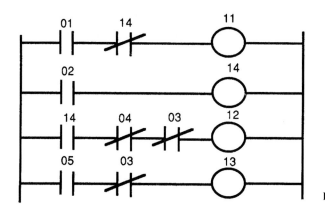

Figure 7.26   Program.

EXPLANATION OF THE PROGRAM

Rung 1. If a part arrives and no part is stopped, trigger the bar-code reader.

Rung 2. If it is a right part, activate the stopper.

Rung 3. If the stopper is up, the machine is not busy and the robot is not busy; load the part onto the machine.

Rung 4. If the task is completed and the robot is not busy, unload the machine.

7.4.3 Structured Text Programming

Structured text is a high-level language that can be used to express the behavior of functions, function blocks, and programs. In the IEC 1131-1 standard, structured text has a syntax very similar to PASCAL. In this section, a brief introduction to structured text programming is presented.

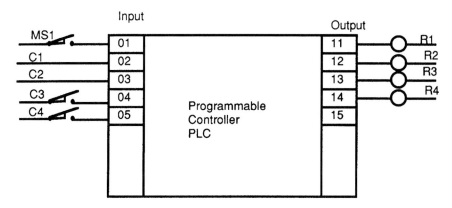

Figure 7.27   Wiring diagram.

Structured text is a strongly typed language. That means that all variables used in the program have to be declared before they can be used. The language also provides the following functionalities:

assignments
expressions
statements
operators
function calls
flow control, such as conditional statements and iteration statements

7.4.3.1 Data types.   IEC defines a wide range of data types. Before a variable can be used, it must be declared as one of the data types. Data types include the following:

SINT	short integer	1 byte
INT	integer	2 bytes
DINT	double integer	4 bytes
LINT	long integer	8 bytes
USINT	unsigned short integer	1 byte
UINT	unsigned integer	2 bytes
UDINT	unsigned double integer	4 bytes
ULINT	unsigned long integer	8 bytes
REAL	real	4 bytes
LREAL	long real	8 bytes
TIME	time duration	
DATE	calendar date	
TOD	time of day	
DT	date and time of day	
STRING	character strings	
BOOL	boolean	1 bit
BYTE	byte	1 byte
WORD	16-bit bit string	16 bits
DWORD	32-bit bit string	32 bits
LWORD	64-bit bit string	64 bits

User data type also can be derived from the built-in data types. When declared, they are placed inside a TYPE define statement.

```
TYPE    (*user-defined data types, this is a comment*)
        pressure    :       REAL;
        temp        :       REAL;
        part_count  :       INT;
END_TYPE;
```

The data type of structure is also allowed. For example, the following code declares a data structure called "data_packet", which contains four data elements: input, t, out, and count.

```
TYPE data_packet:
    STRUCT
        input :     BOOL;
        t     :     TIME;
        out   :     BOOL;
        count :     INT;
    END_STRUCT:
END_TYPE;
```

7.4.3.2 Variable declaration.   Variables are declared before they are used. There are global variables, local variables, input variables, output variables, input-output variables, external variables, and directly represented variables. Global variables are declared outside a program organization unit (POU), such as a function. Local variables are declared in a POU. Input variables are used as input parameters to a POU, and output variables are used as output parameters.

To declare a variable:

```
a, b, c :   REAL;
input   :   INT;
```

To declare special types of variables, a keyword corresponding to the variable type is used. VAR, VAR_INPUT, VAR_OUTPUT, VAR_IN_OUT, VAR_GLOBAL, and VAR_EXTERNAL are used for local, input, output, input-output, global, and external variables respectively. The declaration ends with a END_VAR keyword. For example, to declare a set of local variables, the following statements are used:

```
VAR
    I,j,k  :INT;
    v      :REAL;
END_VAR
```

7.4.3.3 Assignment statements.   An assignment statement has the following format:

```
A: = 1.234;
X: = Y;
```

7.4.3.4 Operators.   Operators include the following:

( )	parenthesized expression
function()	function
**	exponentiation
—	negation
NOT	Boolean complement
+−*/	math operators
MOD	modulus operation
<><=>=	comparison operators
=	equal
<>	not equal
AND, &	Boolean AND
XOR	Boolean XOR
OR	Boolean OR

7.4.3.5 Expressions and statements.   An expression contains one or more constants, variables, and/or functions linked by operators. An expression always produces a value of a particular data type. In a statement, there may be several expressions. A statement ends with a semicolon. The following are a few example statements:

```
y := a AND b;
v := (v1 + v2 + v3)/3
output := (light = open) OR (door = shut);
```

7.4.3.6 Conditional Statements. There are two types of conditional statements:

```
IF ... THEN ... ELSE ... END_IF;
```

and

```
CASE ... OF ... ELSE ... END_CASE;
```

The first conditional statement selects the statement to execute based on the result of the Boolean expression after IF. The second conditional statement switches the execution statement based on a integer value given after the CASE keyword. The following examples show how these two statements are used.

```
IF a > 100 THEN
        redlight := on;
ELSEIF a > 50 THEN
        yellowlight := on;
ELSE
        greenlight := on;
```

```
END_IF;

CASE dial_setting OF
     1 :    x := 10;
     2 :    x := 15;
     3 :    x := 18;
     4,5:    x := 20; (*either 4 or 5*)
ELSE
     x := 30;
END_CASE
```

7.4.3.7 Iteration statements.   Iteration statements are used to create looped execution. There are three types of iteration statements: FOR ... DO, WHILE ... DO, and REPEAT ... UNTIL. The FOR ... DO statement repeats a set of statements depending on the iteration variable after FOR. For example,

```
FOR I:= 0 to 100 BY 1 DO
     light[I] := ON;
END_FOR
```

The WHILE ... DO checks the Boolean expression after WHILE to decide when to exit the loop. For example,

```
I:= 0;
WHILE I < 100 DO
     I := I + 1;
     light[I]:= on;
END_WHILE
```

The REPEAT ... UNTIL is similar to the WHILE ... DO except the Boolean statement is placed after UNTIL.

```
I:= 0;
REPEAT
     I := I + 1;
     light[I] := on;
UNTIL I > 100;
END_REPEAT
```

7.4.3.8 Functions.   A function is a program unit that takes a set of inputs, does some operations, and then returns a value to the calling statement. A function is typed based on the data type of the return value. The following is an example of a function that adds two real numbers and returns the result:

```
FUNCTION add_num    :REAL
     VAR_INPUT
          I,J  :    REAL
```

```
                    END_VAR
                    add_num:= I + J;
                END_FUNCTION
```

In the preceding function, the VAR_INPUT section defines the input variables (argument list), and the output is returned through the function name.

To call a function, a function name is referenced with a set of input variables. For example, to call function "add_num":

```
                    x := add_num(1.2, 5.6);
```

This statement will return a value 6.8 and assign it to the variable x.

Built-in functions include math functions (ABS, SQRT, LN, LOG, EXP, SIN, COS, TAN, ASIN, ACOS, ATAN, ADD, MUL, SUB, DIV, MOD, EXPT, MOVE), logic functions (AND, OR, XOR, NOT), bit-string functions [SHL (shift bit string left), SHR (shift bit string right), ROL (rotate bit string left), ROR (rotate bit string left), and so on.]

7.4.3.9 Programs.   A program begins with the keyword PROGRAM and ends with END_PROGRAM. The structure of a program is similar to that of a function. However, the program body can be described using one of the IEC languages, including a ladder diagram. The following is an example program for the application in Example 7.1.

```
        PROGRAM Example7.1
            VAR_INPUT
                    MSI :       BOOL;
                    C1  :       BOOL;
                    C2  :       BOOL;
                    C3  :       BOOL;
                    C4  :       BOOL;
            END_VAR
            VAR_OUTPUT
                    R1  :       BOOL : FALSE;
                    R2  :       BOOL : FALSE;
                    R3  :       BOOL : FALSE;
                    R4  :       BOOL : FALSE;
            END_VAR

            R1:=MS1 AND (NOT R4);
            R2:=R4 AND (NOT C3) AND (NOT C2);
            R3:=C4 AND (NOT C3);
            R4:=C1;
        END_PROGRAM
```

7.4.4 Functional Block Programming

In the IEC 1131-3 standard, functional block (FB) is a well-packaged element of software that can be reused in different parts of an application or even in different projects.

Functional blocks are the basic building blocks of a control system and can have algorithms written in any of the IEC languages. A function block type contains two parts: (1) data declarations, and (2) an algorithm expressed using a structured text, a function block diagram, a ladder diagram, an instruction list, or a sequential function chart. A functional block also can be used directly in a ladder diagram.

A functional block for an upcounter is defined as shown in Figure 7.28)

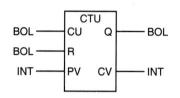

Figure 7.28   An up-counter function block.

The algorithm in structured text is as follows:

```
FUNCTION BLOCK CTU
    VAR_INPUT
        CU:BOOL R_TRIG;
        R:BOOL;
        PV:INT;
    END_VAR
    VAR_OUTPUT
        Q:BOOL;
        CV:INT;
    END_VAR
    IF R THEN
        CV := 0;
    ELSIF CU
            AND (CV<PV) THEN
        CV:= CV+1;
    END_IF;
    Q:= (CV>=PV);
END_FUNCTION_BLOCK
```

The CTU block counts the number of input CU. In the block, R is the reset, PV is a preset value, Q is the contact output, and CV is the counter value. When a signal from CU is detected, the CV value increments by one. When the CV value reaches the PV value, Q is set to true. When the R signal is detected, the CV value is reset to zero and Q is set to false.

The IEC 1131-3 standard defines a small number of basic function blocks. Counters, timers, real time clocks, edge detectors, and bistable are all predefined. More complex function such as the PID control block also can be defined. An example PID block is shown in Figure 7.29.

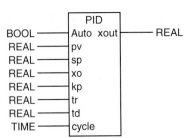

Figure 7.29   A PID-control function block.

The variables can be found in the control block diagram of Figure 7.30. The control algorithm is represented by the following equation.

$$V_{out} = K_p E + T_r \int E \, dt + T_d \frac{dE}{dt}.$$

A PID controller consists of three components: proportional control, integral control, and derivative control. It is commonly used in the process industry for closed-loop continuous-process control. For example, in a chemical-reaction control, SP may be the set temperature, XOUT may be the current going into a heating element, and PV may represent the temperature-sensor reading. It also can be used in the control of servo motors in a machine like a robot arm. In this case, SP will be the target rotational angle, XOUT will be the voltage signal sent to the servo motor, and PV will be the position-transducer feedback. KP, TR, and TD are gains for the proportional error, the integral, and the derivative control, respectively. The user must set these values. If AUTO is true, the function block calculates the value for XOUT. The "cycle" defines the time between function-block execution. XO is for manual output adjustment.

7.4.5 Instruction List

The instruction list (IL) is a low-level language that has a structure similar to an assembly language. Because it is simple, it is easy to learn and ideal for small hand-held

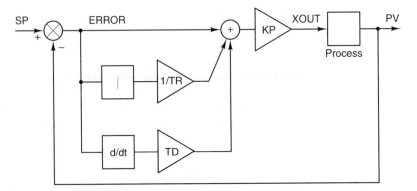

Figure 7.30   Block diagram of a PID controller.

programming devices. The instruction list has a simple syntax. Each line of code can be divided into four fields: label, operator, operand, and comment. Label and comment fields are optional. Basic operators include the following

OPERATOR	MODIFIERS	DESCRIPTION
LD	N	Load operand into register
ST	N	Store register value into operand
S		Set operand true
R		Reset operand false
AND	N, (	Boolean AND
&	N, (	Boolean AND
OR	N, (	Boolean OR
XOR	N, (	Boolean XOR
ADD	(	Addition
SUB	(	Subtraction
MUL	(	Multiplication
DIV	(	Division
GT	(	Greater than
GE	(	Greater than and equal to
EQ	(	Equal
NE	(	Not equal
LE	(	Less than and equal to
LT	(	Less than
JMP	C, N	Jump to label
CAL	C, N	Call function block
RET	C, N	Return from function or function block
)		Execute last deferred operator

Modifier "N" means negate, "(" defers the operator, and "C" is a condition modifier; the operation is executed if the register value is true.

By using the instruction list, the example in Figure 7.25 can be written as follows:

```
PROGRAM example7.1
    VAR_INPUT
        MSI  :      BOOL;
        C1   :      BOOL;
        C2   :      BOOL;
        C3   :      BOOL;
        C4   :      BOOL;
    END_VAR
    VAR_OUTPUT
        R1   :      BOOL:FALSE;
```

```
                    R2   :        BOOL:FALSE;
                    R3   :        BOOL:FALSE;
                    R4   :        BOOL:FALSE;
            END_VAR

            LD       MS1
            ANDN     R4
            ST       R1
            LD       R4
            ANDN     C3
            ANDN     C2
            ST       R2
            LD       C4
            ANDN     C3
            ST       R3
            LD       C1
            ST       R4


        END_PROGRAM
```

7.4.6 Sequential Function Chart

The sequential function chart (SFC) is a graphics language used for depicting sequential behavior. The IEC standard grew out of the French standard, Grafcet, which in turn is based on Petri-net. An SFC is depicted as a series of steps shown as rectangular boxes connected by vertical lines (Figure 7.31). Each step represents a state of the system being controlled. A horizontal bar indicates a condition; it can be a switch state, a timer, and so on. A condition statement is associated with each condition bar. Each step also can have a set of actions. The action qualifier causes the action to behave in certain ways. The indicator variable is optional; it is for annotation purposes.

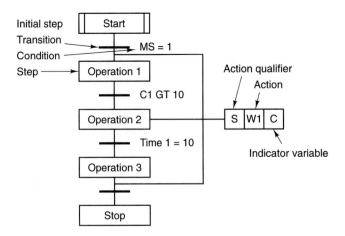

Figure 7.31 A sequential function chart.

The action can be described as part of the SFC, or on another diagram or page. The action qualifiers are as follows:

N   nonstored; executes while the step is active
R   resets a store action
S   sets an action active
L   time-limited action; terminates after a given period
D   time-delayed action
P   a pulse action; executes once in a step
SD   stored and time-delayed
DS   time-delayed and stored
SL   stored and time-limited

The example problem in Figure 7.25 can be written in a sequential function chart, as shown in Figure 7.32.

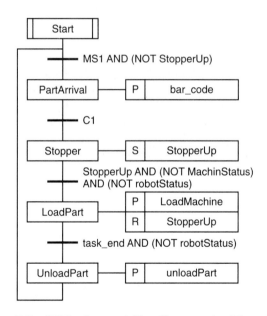

Figure 7.32   SFC for the material-handling example of Figure 7.25.

7.5 CONCLUDING REMARKS

By now you should be acquainted with the basic functions of a programmable logic controller. Because the expanded functions of a PLC vary in symbology and capability from vendor to vendor, they were not directly addressed. Instead, a hypothetical PLC symbology was used. After you learn the basic concepts, you should have little difficulty in using any PLC and expanding your PLC command library.

The PLC is an inexpensive flexible control device that is quickly becoming a standard control device for individual processes as well as for process integration; however, it is worthwhile to note that the PLC is not the only means of control. The conventional relay and computer control are two other alternatives. Although the PLC is both attractive and economic for most control applications, in some applications, relay logic and/or computer control may be more appropriate. We should not overlook any feasible tool.

The major advantages of the PLC over other devices are ease of programming interface and robustness. When an application requires only 10 or fewer relays, hardwired relay logic is probably more economical. When an application requires more complex control, then the PLC becomes a more attractive alternative.

When compared with computer control, the PLC is not as flexible. However, because the PLC is microcomputer-based and specifically designed for industrial control, it is much easier to use in the harsh shop environment, where a computer will not survive long. A PLC can operate without any problems; yet, if the application requires some function that a PLC does not support or a sampling rate that is greater than the shortest scan time can provide, then a computer is more desirable. If you have experience with computer interfacing and low level programming, you will appreciate how easy it is to use a PLC for control.

Actually, a PLC can be seen as a computer dedicated to process control. It has some standardized interface modules and runs a special interpretive control language. Following the advance of microcomputer technology and the development of interface and language, the PLC has become more like a computer. More and more mathematical functions have been added. Color graphics display, network capability, and so on, have totally changed the image of a PLC as a relay-panel substitute. In the future, we will see a greater use of PLCs for all kinds of manufacturing-systems control and device control. The failure to recognize and utilize these devices will undoubtedly handicap manufacturing, electrical, and mechanical engineers.

REVIEW QUESTIONS

7.1. Why is scan time critical to some applications?

7.2. What are the advantages of using a PLC over a relay-panel circuit?

7.3. What are the advantages of using a PLC over a microcomputer?

7.4. Design a ladder diagram that will latch the state of a switch LS_1. It is unlatched only when switch LS_2 is triggered. The state of switch LS_1 is shown by a pilot light, PL_1.

7.5. Design a ladder diagram to function XOR logic.

7.6. Design a PLC ladder diagram that will turn on light PL_1 5 s after push-button PB_1 is pressed. The light is turned off when the switch is released.

7.7. A two-axis modular robot is controlled by a PLC. Each axis is driven by a pneumatic cylinder. An output signal to the pneumatic cylinder causes it to extend (on state). When there is no signal, the pneumatic cylinder retracts (off state). The gripper is also driven by a pneumatic cylinder. The gripper open position is an off state and the closed position is an on state. In order to perform a task, the following sequence of operations must be performed:

SEQUENCE NO.	AXIS 1	AXIS 2	GRIPPER
0	off	off	off
1	on	off	off
2	on	off	on
3	on	on	on
4	off	on	on
5	off	off	on
6	off	off	off

The process beings when the start push button is on and a part triggers a limit switch. For safety, an emergency switch is used to shut off the entire system. Design a circuit and PLC ladder diagram for this application.

7.8. For the application described in Review Question 7.7, prepare a list of system components needed. Also prepare a programmable logic controller specification for the application. Assume that all the pneumatic cylinders are controlled by a 24-V signal.

7.9. Call a local PLC vendor and find out the cost of the cheapest PLC, relays, timers, and counters. What is the break-even point of switching from relays to a PLC (in terms of numbers of internal relays)?

7.10. Design a ladder diagram that has a light indicator connected to output 10 that flashes on six times for 1 s with a 2-s delay between flashes. A switch connected to 02 initiates and resets the program.

7.11. The ABC Company is in the toy business. It produces two types of toy cars, wooden cars and metal cars. A conveyor belt carries the product through the production floor (See Figure 7.33). Wooden cars are sensed by a photoelectric switch and metal cars are sensed by a proximity switch. Cars are pushed to diverters by means of solenoids. The conveyor belt is activated by a push button. However, in case of an emergency, the whole system is shut down by means of an emergency push button. Assume that wooden cars are diverted to diverter A by means of solenoid 1 and that metal cars are diverted to diverter C by means of solenoid 3. Write a ladder diagram for the control of this system. See Review Question 7.12 for a hint.

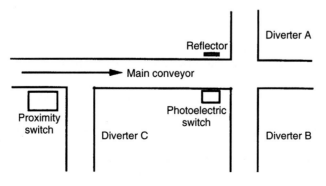

Figure 7.33   System layout.

7.12. From Review Question 7.11, the company increases the production of wooden toy cars. The production increase requires two diverters for the wooden cars. Both diverters have a capacity of four cars. Diverters *A* and *B* are controlled by solenoids 1 and 2, respectively. Assuming that the parts are removed when the diverters are full, draw a ladder diagram and test it on a simulation board.

ADDRESSES FOR INPUT DEVICES

SWITCH	ADDRESS
Motor start	1
Emergency stop	2
Photoelectric	3
Proximity	4

ADDRESSES FOR OUTPUT DEVICES

OUTPUT	ADDRESS
Solenoid 1	29
Solenoid 2	30
Solenoid 3	31
Motor	32

ADDRESSES FOR COUNTERS

OUTPUT	ADDRESS
Counter 1	901
Counter 2	902

Hint for Review Questions 7.11 and 7.12: There are two pieces representing the cars, a wooden piece and a metal piece. When the wooden piece is passed through the photoelectric switch output, 29 or 30 is on in the output module. When a metal piece is passed through the proximity switch, output 31 is turned on. However, notice that a metal piece is sensed by both the proximity switch and the photoelectric switch. That is not the case for wooden parts, which are only activated when the beam of light is broken.

The motor that controls the conveyor is represented by address 32. This means that whenever the motor start button is pressed, light 32 in the output module of the programmable controller is turned on. However, when the emergency stop is pressed, light 32 changes its status to off.

7.13. Figure 7.34 shows a PLC ladder diagram and a wiring diagram. Outputs 10, 11, and 12 are connected to lights. Fill in the state of the lights in the table.

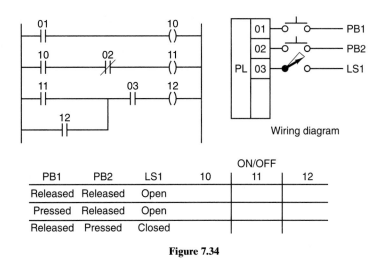

Wiring diagram

PB1	PB2	LS1	10	ON/OFF 11	12
Released	Released	Open			
Pressed	Released	Open			
Released	Pressed	Closed			

Figure 7.34

7.14. Design a ladder-diagram program to control a two-speed motor. The motor can be started only at a low speed. The motor can be switched to high speed only after 10 seconds of operation. The motor cannot be switched from high to low speed.

7.15. In a PE (proportional error) controller, the output is proportional to the error between the set point (SP) and the sensor feedback (PV).

$$xout = K(SP - PV)$$

For example, the goal is to maintain a certain temperature. The set point is the desired temperature and PV is the thermometer reading. However, to regulate the temperature, the controller has to provide more electrical current to the heating element. The Xout is the current.

Write a program in structured text for a functional block called PE control. The inputs are RUN, SP, PV. The output is Xout.

Note: Readers may solve the ladder-diagram programming problems in this chapter using structured text, functional blocks, instruction lists, or sequential function charts.

REFERENCES/BIBLIOGRAPHY

BERTRAND, R. M. (1996). *Programmable Controller Circuits*, Albany, NY.: Delmar Publishers.

CRISPIN, A. J. (1990). *Programmable Logic Controllers and Their Engineering Applications*. New York: McGraw-Hill.

GILLES, M. (1990)*Programmable Logic Controllers*. New York: John Wiley.

LEWIS, R. W. (1995). *Programming Industrial Control Systems Using IEC 1131-3.* London: Institution of Electrical Engineers.

OTTER, J. D. (1988). *Programmable Logic Controllers*. Englewood Cliffs, NJ: Prentice Hall.

SIMPSON, C. D. (1994). *Programmable Logic Controllers*, Englewood Cliffs, NJ: Prentice Hall.

STENERSON, J. (1993). *Fundamentals of Programmable Logic Controllers, Sensors, and Communications*, Englewood Cliffs, NJ: Prentice Hall.

APPENDIX 7A: NUMBERING SYSTEMS

Binary Number

A binary number consists of only two digits: 0 and 1. Any integer number can be represented by these two digits, for example, 10100110_2. To convert a binary number into decimal, one does the following:

$$
\begin{array}{cccccccc}
1 & 0 & 1 & 0 & 0 & 1 & 1 & 0 \\
2^7 & 2^6 & 2^5 & 2^4 & 2^3 & 2^2 & 2^1 & 2^0
\end{array}
$$
$$128 + 0 + 32 + 0 + 0 + 4 + 2 + 0 = 166_{10}$$

The weight of each digit is 2 to the power of the digit position minus 1. In a digital system, such as a computer, the state is either on or off, so a binary number can represent the state of a set of components. For example, computer memory is grouped into an 8-bit-unit, called a byte. Each bit can be either on or off (1 or 0). A byte, therefore, stores an 8-digit binary number.

To convert a decimal number into binary, one divides the decimal number by 2 repeatedly until the remainder is either 0 or 1.

$$25_{10}$$

remainder

$$\frac{25}{2} = 12 \quad + \quad 1$$

$$\frac{12}{2} = 6 \quad + \quad 0$$

$$\frac{6}{2} = 3 \quad + \quad 0$$

$$\frac{3}{2} = 1 \quad + \quad 1$$

$$\frac{1}{2} = 0 \quad + \quad 1$$

$$1\ 1\ 0\ 0\ 1_2$$

Octal Number

An octal number is based on eight digits: 0, 1, 2, 3, 4, 5, 6, and 7. Any integer number can be represented by these eight digits, for example, 374_8. Because the base, 8, is a power of 2, an octal number can be translated into binary easily.

3	7	4	Octal number
8^2	8^1	8^0	Octal weight of each digit
$2^2\ 2^1\ 2^0$	$2^2\ 2^1\ 2^0$	$2^2\ 2^1\ 2^0$	Binary weight of each digit
0 1 1	1 1 1	1 0 0	Binary representation

To do the conversion, each digit is converted into binary. The binary equivalent is the concatenation of the separately converted binary numbers. To convert into a decimal number, the same approach as binary–decimal conversion is used.

3	7	4	Octal number
8^2	8^1	8^0	Octal weight of each digit

$$3 \times 64 + \quad 7 \times 8 + \quad 4 = 252_{10}$$

To convert a decimal number into an octal number:

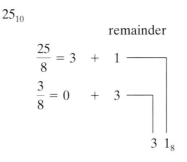

$$25_{10}$$

remainder

$$\frac{25}{8} = 3 \quad + \quad 1$$

$$\frac{3}{8} = 0 \quad + \quad 3$$

$$3\ 1_8$$

Hexadecimal Number

A hexadecimal number (hex) is based on 16 digits and/or symbols: 0, 1, 2, 3, 4, 5, 6, 7, 8, 9, A, B, C, D, E, and F. Any integer number is represented by these eight digits, for example, $2AF_{16}$. Because the base, 16, is 2 to the power of 4, each digit of a hexadecimal number represents four bits. A byte can be conveniently represented by two hexadecimal digits, a concise representation. The conversion from hex number of binary is also straightforward.

2	A	F	Hexadecimal number
16^2	16^1	16^0	Hex weight of each digit
$2^3\ 2^2\ 2^1\ 2^0$	$2^3\ 2^2\ 2^1\ 2^0$	$2^3\ 2^2\ 2^1\ 2^0$	Binary weight of each digit
0 0 1 0	1 0 1 1	1 1 1 1	Binary representation

To do the conversion, each digit is converted into binary. The binary equivalent is the concatenation of the separately converted binary numbers. To convert into a decimal number, the same approach as binary–decimal conversion is used.

2	A	F	Hex number
16^2	16^1	16^0	Hex weight of each digit
$2 \times 256 +$	$10 \times 16 +$	$15 = 687_{10}$	

To convert a decimal number into an hex number:

$$125_{10}$$

remainder

$$\frac{125}{16} = 7 \ + \ 13$$

$$\frac{7}{16} = 0 \ + \ 7$$

$$7\,D_{16}$$

Binary-Coded-Decimal (BCD) Number

One way to represent a decimal number is to represent individual decimal digit in binary separately. For example, the decimal number 25 is represented as

$$\frac{2 \quad 5}{010 \quad 101}$$

Typical applications of BCD codes include data entry (time, volume, weights, and so on) via thumbwheel switches, data display via seven-segment displays, and input from absolute encoders.

Binary Arithmetic

ADDITION

$$0 + 0 = 0$$
$$1 + 0 = 1$$
$$1 + 1 = 10$$

Example:

$$
\begin{array}{r}
10110 \\
+ \ \ 10011 \\
\hline
101001_2
\end{array}
$$

SUBTRACTION

$$1 - 0 = 1$$
$$1 - 1 = 0$$
$$0 - 1 = 1 \ \text{borrow 1}$$

Example:

$$
\begin{array}{r}
1\,0\,1\,1\,0 \\
-\ 1\,0\,0\,1\,1 \\
\hline
0\,0\,0\,1\,1_2
\end{array}
$$

MULTIPLICATION

$$0 \times 0 = 0$$
$$1 \times 0 = 1$$
$$1 \times 1 = 1$$

Example:

$$
\begin{array}{r}
1\,0\,1\,1\,0 \\
\times \quad\ \ 1\,1 \\
\hline
1\,0\,1\,1\,0 \\
1\,0\,1\,1\,0 \\
\hline
1\,0\,0\,0\,0\,1\,0
\end{array}
$$

Multiplication is basically a series of shift operations, and then add the result together.

Signed and Unsigned Binary Number

A binary number can be signed or unsigned. In a signed binary number, the most significant bit (leftmost) stores the sign. A negative binary number is stored in the *2's-complement form*. To obtain a 2's-complement form, first, all 1s are converted to 0's and 0's to 1's. The result is called the 1's complement. By adding 1 to the 1's-complement, the 2's-complement form is obtained.

ORIGINAL NUMBER	1's-COMPLEMENT	2's-COMPLEMENT
01001101	10110010 + 1 =	10110011
77_{10}		-77_{10}

An 8-bit signed binary number has the following range:

10000000	... 11111111	00000000	00000001 ... 01111111	
-128_{10}	... -1_{10}	0_{10}	1_{10} ...	127_{10}

APPENDIX 7B: TRUTH TABLES AND LOGIC GATES

Truth Table

A truth table shows the results of a logic operation. Logic operators include AND, OR, XOR, NOT, and so on. The following are truth tables:

AND

A	B	A AND B (AB)
0	0	0
0	1	0
1	0	0
1	1	1

OR

A	B	A OR B (A + B)
0	0	0
0	1	1
1	0	1
1	1	1

XOR

A	B	A XOR B
0	0	0
0	1	0
1	0	0
1	1	1

NOT

A	NOT A ($\bar{A}$)
0	1
1	0

Logic Gates

Logic gates are electronic switches that perform logic operations. For example, the output of an AND gate equals the logic AND of the inputs. Logic gates are operated at transistor-transistor logic (TTL) level, which is +5V and ground for logic 1 and 0.

AND GATE

AND Gate

OR GATE

OR Gate

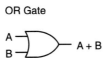

EXCLUSIVE OR GATE

Exclusive OR Gate

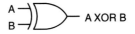

NAND GATE

NAND Gate

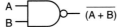

The output of the AB is negated $\overline{(A + B)}$

A	B	$\overline{(A + B)}$
0	0	1
0	1	1
1	0	1
1	1	0

The output of the AB is negated $\overline{(A + B)}$.

A	B	$\overline{(A + B)}$
0	0	1
0	1	1
1	0	1
1	1	0

NOR GATE

NOR Gate

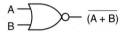

$$\overline{(A + B)}$$

8

Data Communication and Local-Area Networks in Manufacturing

In an automated manufacturing facility, there are typically several different types of machines and controllers. Machines are controlled by controllers, which are commonly computer-based. In order to maintain smooth operation, all of these devices must be coordinated. Communication between and among devices thus becomes essential. In a shop where devices cannot talk to each other, communication is normally carried out by human operators. A human operator typically goes to a machine, reads the display from its controller, and then goes to another machine and enters the data to its controller. This human-assisted communication is slow and can be prone to error. Fortunately, most modern controllers are computer-based, and thus have a built-in communication capability. They are able to send data and read data in one of several ways. At the lowest level, such communication may be conducted through discrete input and output points. That is, the machines communicate through an on/off signal. Because limited information (on/off) can be carried, this type of communication is normally used only for linking simple devices. A more popular way of communicating between two computers is through their serial communication ports. A byte (8 bits) of data is serialized and transmitted through a pair of wires (actually, at least three wires, one for transmit, one for receive, and one for ground). This method allows encoded data, such as text, numbers, and so on, to be transmitted from one device to another. Another similar approach is parallel communication, in which a wire is used for each data bit. A byte of data (rather than a bit) is normally sent via parallel communication. These methods of data communication are inexpensive to implement, but are limited by their communication speed and one-to-one communication topology. In recent years, local-area-network (LAN) techniques have become more popular in both shop floor and office automation. A local-area network is able to perform much faster communications than the previously mentioned (point-to-point) communication methods. It also allows many-to-many communication on the same network through the same cable. As the price of implementing local-area networks becomes relatively low, many factories are installing some type(s) of LAN.

Unfortunately, at the beginning there was little standardization in the way LANs were implemented. Devices manufactured by different vendors typically could not communicate with each other. A separate computer had to be dedicated to translate data between two networks from two different vendors, and sometimes even from the same vendor. According to a study (General Motors, 1984), 50% of the cost spent on shop-floor computers was spent on networks. This cost was far too high to be justifiable. In the early 1980s, GM spearheaded an effort to establish a common standard—Manufacturing Automation Protocol (MAP)—that defined the physical and logical communication standard for manufacturing facilities. MAP has since been adopted as the standard for the shop-floor intervendor device data communication. The International Standards Organization (ISO) is adopting MAP as the international standard, although many other communication protocols are still being used.

In this chapter, we discuss the fundamentals of computer data communication, local-area-networks, and the MAP standard. The purpose is to provide a comprehensive introduction to various data-communication methods employed on the shop floor today. This information coupled with that discussed in Chapters 6 and 7 and that to be discussed in Chapter 9 extensively describes modern manufacturing shop-floor automation.

8.1 FUNDAMENTALS OF DATA COMMUNICATION

8.1.1 Basic Concepts in Communication

Data communication as used here means passing data from one computer device to another. Internally, a digital computer-based device stores data in registers or RAM memory(Figure 8.1). Data are exchanged between memory locations or registers through a data bus. Depending on the computer architecture, the data bus can be either 8, 16, 32, or 64 bits wide. Usually, the bus size determines the size nomenclature of a CPU, that is,

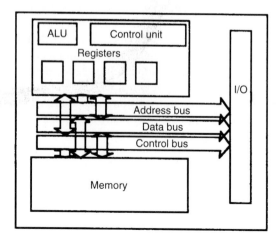

Figure 8.1   A simplified computer architecture.

8-bit, 16-bit, 32-bit or 64-bit. When there is a need to communicate with external devices, input/output (I/O) hardware is used. I/O can be performed through either isolated I/O or through memory-mapped I/O. Isolated I/O uses specially assigned I/O ports and locations assigned for I/O purposes. A limited number of such locations are available. Special I/O instructions that allow the input and output of data through those ports are available in the CPU instruction set.

In the case of memory-mapped I/O, a digital I/O device (IC chip) is assigned to a memory address and treated like any other computer memory location. To address a memory location, the address is placed on the address bus. The decoder decodes the address and enables the device (or the memory byte) to obtain the data. Only the device that is enabled by the decoder replies to the control signal, which came from a control bus. The control signals can be either *read* or *write*. Note that the I/O port previously mentioned also needs one of these digital I/O devices.

A digital I/O device can be a buffer, a latch, a bidirectional driver, a parallel interface adapter, or a serial interface adapter (i.e., UART, universal asynchronous receiver/transmitter, or USRT, universal synchronous receiver transmitter). Whenever a read or write access is addressed to that memory location, the I/O device responds to the instruction. To the CPU, operation is the same as that of an ordinary memory read or write. However, some synchronization with the external device is needed. The simplest I/O device can be a TTL buffer. Whenever the buffer is accessed, the state of the data bus is stored and made available to the external device(Figure 8.2). Other I/O devices work similarly to a buffer. Two of the most frequently used data-communication methods are serial data communication and parallel data communication. Before we discuss serial and parallel data communication, we need to discuss data-coding methods.

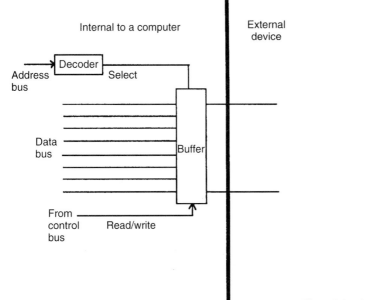

Figure 8.2   An I/O buffer.

8.1.2 Data Coding

Computers store data in a binary format, so everything in a digital computer has to be represented in binary. Unfortunately, only integer numbers have equivalent binary numbers. All other data, such as real numbers, text (alphanumeric), and graphics, do not have natural binary equivalents. A data-coding scheme is used to represent those data. To exchange data between two computers, the data must be in a form that is recognizable to both. Most computers store alphanumeric data in ASCII (American Standard Code for Information Interchange) form. Some manufacturing devices also use the EIA (Electronic Industries Association) form. Another code used only on IBM mainframes is the EBCDIC (Expanded Binary-Coded Decimal Interchange Code.) These codes include all letters, digits, punctuation marks, and control characters. Control characters are those nonprintable characters used to control printer devices, CRT displays, coordinate data communication, and to mark line breaks and the end of a file. For example, line feed (LF), carriage return (CR), backspace (BS), form feed (FF), escape (ESC), and delete (DEL) are some control characters. Each control character has a commonly accepted meaning. However, device vendors can use these control characters differently. These control characters are listed in the first two columns of the ASCII table shown in Table 8.1. Numerical data can be stored in ASCII or (as in most programming languages) in a different format. The ASCII table shows the characters represented and their codes. The first row of the table contains the high bits of the code, that is, the first 3 bits of the 7-bit code. The low bits are shown in the first column. For example, to find the ASCII code for LF, first, we locate LF in the table, which is in column 2. The high bits for column 2 are 000. The low bits for the row where LF is located are 1010. Therefore, the code for LF is 0001010_2. Uppercase and lowercase letters are distinguished by different codes. The differences are the high bits. For example, S is 1010011_2 and s is 1110011_2. To convert an uppercase letter to lowercase, an 0100000_2 (32_{10}) is added to the code.

In the codes of Table 8.1, a character is stored in 1 byte (7 bits are for the basic code and 1 bit for parity). The parity bit is used for error checking. A code may be set to be at even parity; in this case, the parity bit is set to make the total number of ones in the binary representation even. Parity can be even parity, odd parity, no parity, space parity, or mark parity. Even parity means that the total of the data bits plus the parity bit yields an odd number. Odd parity means that the total of the data bits plus the parity bit yields an odd number. When no parity is selected, the parity bit is not generated by the transmitting device and not checked by the receiving device. Space, or zero, parity means that the parity bit is always set to zero. Mark parity means that the parity bit is always set to one. For example, the ASCII code for character S is 1010011_2, which has four ones. In even parity, it is 01010011_2; in odd parity, it is 11010011_2. In space parity, the code is 01010011_2; in mark parity, it is 11010011_2. The parity bit can be inserted either by the hardware or software. The receiving end checks parity when it is used. An odd number of bit-transmission errors can be detected by this method. However, if there are an even number of errors, the transmission error will not be detected.

When a data file consists of only numbers, the numbers can be stored in binary format, which is the natural format of numbers. For example, the integer number 20 in binary format is 10100. Depending on the application, an integer number can be stored

TABLE 8.1 ASCII CODE CHART

Low Bits

	High Bits							
low	000	001	010	011	100	101	110	111
0000	NUL	DLE	SP	0	@	P	\	p
0001	SOH	DC1	!	1	A	Q	a	q
0010	STX	DC2	“	2	B	R	b	r
0011	ETX	DC3	#	3	C	S	c	s
0100	EOT	DC4	$	4	D	T	d	t
0101	ENQ	NAK	%	5	E	U	e	u
0110	ACK	SYN	&	6	F	V	f	v
0111	BEL	ETB	‘	7	G	W	g	w
1000	BS	CHN	(	8	H	X	h	x
1001	HT	EM	)	9	I	Y	i	y
1010	LF	SUB	*	:	J	Z	j	z
1011	VT	ESC	+	;	K	[	k	{
1100	FF	FS	,	<	L	\	l	|
1101	CR	GS	-	=	M	]	m	}
1110	SO	RS	.	>	N	^	n	~
1111	SI	US	/	?	O	_	o	DEL

in 2 or 4 bytes. When representing a number in ASCII code, the length of the code can depend on the size of the number. For the previous case, 2 bytes are needed. The first byte is for 2, which in ASCII is 0110010_2, and the other for 0, which in ASCII is 0110000_2 (Table 8.1). In ASCII, usually 8 bits are used to represent one character. Seven of the eight bits are used to represent the data and one bit for parity. With even parity, 2 is 10110010_2; with odd parity, the same character is represented by 00110010_2. Although it does not make any difference in the memory requirement whether a single-digit integer number is stored in binary format or in ASCII, it does make a difference for a multiple-digit integer number. For a number like 32767, 2 bytes are needed in binary format and 5 bytes are needed in ASCII. Also, before the number can be used, the computer must convert the ASCII-coded number into binary.

For data communication, either format may be used. However, formats normally do not mix. ASCII is still the most popular way of transferring text files, including NC part programs (the new BCL format is binary; see Chapter 10) and machine-control instructions. Most terminals, except some IBM terminals, use ASCII code. A keyboard transmits the corresponding ASCII code of the key typed to the computer, and the computer, in turn, transmits ASCII code of the data to be displayed on the CRT screen.

The encoding of graphics is different from that of the text. A picture can be represented by a bit map. Depending on the number of colors used, each pixel (picture element) is represented by a certain number of bits. This data can be either transferred in binary or encoded into ASCII using a conversion standard before transfer. Some applications have their own representation format. For example, the PostScript, GIF, JPEG, and TIFF formats are used for various communication requirements. For CAD applications, drawings and geometric models can be represented in IGES, PDES/STEP, and DXF formats. All these formats are encoded in ASCII. So far, graphics representation is still very application-specific.

8.1.3 Serial Data Communication

Serial data communication, as indicated by its name, is a way to communicate data in a serial fashion. A data byte is serialized and sent out on a line 1 bit at a time. Serial communication is the most widely used data-communication method. A serial communication port usually is built into many computers, machine controllers, telephone modems, and terminals. It is inexpensive and easy to program. The cable connection is also simple. In serial data communication, both communication devices need a serial port and a cable with at least three wires connecting them (Figure 8.3). Of the three required wires, one is for transmitting data (TX), another for receiving data (RV), and the third for ground (GND). In the figure, the wires for transmit and receive are crossed, so the receive pin of device 1 is connected to the transmit pin of device 2. The UARTs shown in Figure 8.3 convert output data from parallel to serial and input data from serial to parallel. Coordination with the UARTs is required to ensure data are transmitted or received properly. Several error-checking schemes are built into the UARTs.

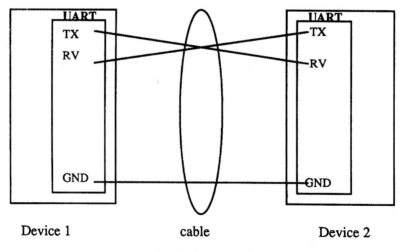

Figure 8.3 Serial communication.

On a serial communication line, data are transmitted as square waves (or very close to square waves). The state "zero" is represented by a positive voltage, and the state "one" is represented by a negative voltage. Positive voltages are between $+5$ to $+15$ volts for output and between $+3$ and $+15$ volts for input. Negative voltages are specified as being between -5 and -15 volts for output and between -3 and -15 volts for input. The most common signal is ± 5V. In order to coordinate both UARTs, the same signal frequency must be used. UARTs are asynchronous, which means clocks are set individually at the transmission and the receiving sides. A signal is resynchronized at the receiving side. The clock rate is also called the baud rate (equals bit per second) in most cases, however, some modern modems may pack more than one bit in a band. For example, 110 baud means 110 bits are transmitted/received per second. Most serial communications are set at either 110, 300, 1200, 2400, 4800, 9600, 14.4, 19.2, and 28.8 baud.

Data are sent 1 byte at a time. Such a byte is sent in a *frame*. In this frame, start and stop bits are used to signal the beginning and end of a data byte. An agreed-upon word length (5 to 8 bits), parity type (even, odd, none), baud rate, and start and stop bits (one or two) must be set at both ends identically. For every byte of data sent to an UART, parity is generated and the data bits are shifted into serial form. Start and stop bits are inserted, and the entire signal is sent out through the transmit wire. A complete frame for the letter S (ASCII 1010011_2) is shown in Figure 8.4. Note that when transmitting a byte, the least significant bit is sent first, whereas in writing, the most significant bit is always presented first. The rate of this transmission is set by the baud rate clock. On the receiving side, the start bit is detected by sampling the input line at the clock rate. After the start bit is detected, the parity is checked and the data bits are sent to a shift register to convert them back into a parallel byte format. The converted byte is held in an output register, ready to be sent to the data bus. When a byte of data is ready in the output register, it also sends out a control message. To the UART, the type of code is immaterial. For the purpose of explanation, we use only ASCII code in this chapter.

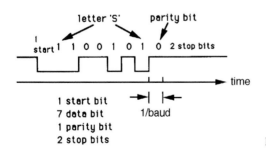

Figure 8.4   Transmitting the letter S.

The transmission length of a byte varies, depending on the number of start bits, stop bits, and data bits used. As a rule of thumb, it generally takes 10 bits to transmit a character, therefore, a simple formula to estimate the number of characters transmitted in a second (n) is

$$n = \frac{\text{baud rate}}{10}$$

In this formula, the delay between two consecutive bytes is not taken into account. The gap between 2 bytes varies. It depends on how fast the transmitting device can provide the next byte to the UART. The actual n is thus smaller.

Often, it is necessary to let the transmitting device know that the receiving device is ready to receive the next byte. This need occurs when the receiving device cannot respond as fast as the transmission. For example, a printer cannot print as fast as the computer can send the data. Under these circumstances, information must be sent back from the receiving device to the transmitting device to signal whether it is ready or not. This is called flow control, or handshaking, which may be done either by hardware or software. Hardware handshaking is done through a dedicated wire in the serial port (discussed in the next section). Software handshaking is done by sending a control character, such as DC1 and DC2. DC1 signals the device is ready and DC2 signals the device is busy.

8.1.3.1 Serial communication standards.

There are standards defining the physical (electrical and mechanical) and logical specifications of the serial connection. RS-232-C (also CCITT V.24, its international equivalent; CCITT stands for International Consultative Committee for Telephony and Telegraphy, and V stands for voice) and RS-422 are the two most commonly used standards in industry. RS-232-C, published in 1969 by the Electronic Industries Association (EIA), is still the most widely used serial communication standard. It was developed for modem (transmitting data through voice signal) communication; therefore, many idiosyncrasies of modem communication are in the specification. Devices are classified as data-terminal equipment (DTE) and data-communication equipment (DCE). The transmit and receive signal lines in DTE and DCE are swapped. Pin 2 of the DTE is for transmit and pin 3 for receive. For DCE, pin 2 is for receive and pin 3 for transmit. The DTE's port normally has a male connector whereas the DCE device typically uses a female connector. The connectors used most typically have 9 or 25 pins, and the most common connectors are the DB9 and DB25 connectors. Not all manufacturers comply with these pin and connector arrays, and it is not always obvious whether a given device is DTE or DCE. As a result, the communication of two devices is not necessarily plug-compatible. One still faces the problems of gender change (when two connectors of the same gender are to be connected) and pin swapping (e.g., when both pin 2's are for receive). Often the user must experiment with the connectors by swapping wires (one way to do it is to use a specially designed break-out box that allows the user to swap the wires easily). When connecting two devices for the first time, if there is no communication at all, the first thing to do always is to swap pins 2 and 3. If only garbage (unreadable) data are received, the causes may be baud rate, parity, start, stop bits, and data-bit length.

The definition of RS-232-C signals are shown in Table 8.2. Data Set Ready (for DCE) and Data Terminal Ready (for DTE) signals are used to indicate whether the equipment is ready to send or receive data. Many RS-232 interfaces assume the equipment is always ready and thus omit these signals. The DTE sends a Request to Send signal when it is ready to transmit data. When the DTE is ready to receive data, a Data Terminal Ready signal is sent. The DCE responds with a Clear to Send signal when it is ready to transmit the data. When a DCE is ready to receive data, a Data Set Ready

TABLE 8.2   EIA RS-232-C STANDARD

PIN	Name	< TO DTE	TO DCE >	FUNCTION	EIA	CCITT
1	FG			Frame Ground	AA	101
2	TD		>	Transmitted Data	BA	103
3	RD	<		Receive Data	BB	104
4	RTS		>	Request to Send	CA	105
5	CTS	<		Clear to Send	CB	106
6	DSR	<		Data Set Ready	CC	107
7	SG			Signal Ground	AB	102
8	CD	<		Carrier Detect	CF	109
9	—			Reserved	—	—
10	—			Reserved	—	—
11	—			Unassigned	—	—
12	(S)CD	<		Sec. Carrier Detect	SCF	122
13	(S)CTS	<		Sec. Clear to Send	SCB	121
14	(S)TD		>	Sec. Transmitted Data	SBA	118
15	TC	<		Transmitter Clock	DB	114
16	(S)RD	<		Sec. Received Data	SBB	119
17	RC	<		Receiver Clock	DD	115
18	—			Unassigned	—	—
19	(S)RTS			Sec. Request to	SCA	120
20	DTR		>	Terminal Ready	CD	108.2
21	SO	<		Signal Quality Detector	CG	110
22	RI	<		Ring Indicator	CE	125
23			>	Data Rate Selector	CH	111
				Data Rate Selector	CI	112
24	(E)TC		>	Ext. Transmitter Clock	DA	113
25	—			Unassigned	—	—

signal is sent. The RS-232 is usually for low-to-medium data rates. Equipment using the RS-232 interface is limited to 19.2 kilobaud. Cable length for RS-232-C communication is limited to 50 feet. Although a cable of even several thousand feet may work, the longer the cable, the lower the baud rate that can be used. This problem is due to distortion and attenuation of the signal.

RS-422 is a newer standard intended for a faster communication link; rates up to 10 megabaud are possible. It is for balanced circuits, and those used at higher speeds use two wires. The ones and zeros are signaled by changes in the polarity of the two wires with reference to each other instead of a single wire changing in polarity with reference to a signal ground. By using twisted-pair wires, RS-422 devices can communicate at 100 kbps (kilobits per second) at 120-m cable length and at 10 Mbps (megabits per second) at 12-m cable length. RS-423-A defines an unbalanced circuit. The speed for RS-423-A specification is 3 kbps at 1000 m and 300 kbps at 10 m. It is possible to interconnect RS-423-A and RS-232-C devices. Theoretically, RS-422 is not compatible with RS-232-C. However, RS-422 ports of some devices are compatible with RS-232-C because manufacturers have made some modifications to the standard. These devices are theoretically not RS-422 devices.

When two devices communicate, they may transmit and receive data simultaneously or alternatively. When they transmit and receive simultaneously, they are called full-duplex. When devices can only transmit or receive alternatively, they are called half-duplex. In the case of a terminal, when a half-duplex device is used, the transmitted data are echoed back to the terminal.

The type of communication discussed thus far takes place at the "physical layer," the most fundamental layer of communication. At the higher levels, there are several data-communication protocols. A data-communication protocol defines a logical convention for data transfer. These protocols enable data to be transferred easily and without error. Popular protocols include KERMIT, XMODEM, and YMODEM. They are used to transfer data files from one device to another. The file type, file name, file length, and so on, are transferred in a header data block. The file is divided into small chunks called blocks or packets. Each block has a fixed size with the header information added. An error-checking procedure is built into the protocol, so that transfer errors can be detected. When such an error is detected, the block is retransmitted. A handshaking method is used to synchronize the devices. For example, XON and XOFF (control characters) may be used to signal that the receiving device is ready or not ready for the next block of data. Many popular data-communication software packages support all popular protocols.

8.1.4 Parallel Data Communication

In parallel data communication, an entire byte is transmitted together. Data are said to be handled in parallel. It is a popular way to transfer data between the computer and outside devices such as sensors, actuators, and peripherals. However, it is less frequently used between computers transferring data. Typically, a programmable LSI (large-scale integrated) device is used as the parallel I/O interface. Such a device usually contains two or more 8-bit ports that can be programmed to be either input or output ports. A data-direction register is used to define the direction in which the data are to be transferred by the corresponding bits of the port. It is possible to program individual bits of a port to be either input or output. For example, a 1 in the data-direction register mean output, and a 0 means input. By setting 11110000 in the data-direction register, the first 4 bits of the port are set to be output and the last 4 bits to be input. When the data arrive, they are latched and saved in the buffer. Some other general features of a parallel port include status and control for handshaking, other control and timing signals for peripherals, and direct interface with the processor address, data, and control buses. A parallel-interface adapter block diagram is shown in Figure 8.5.

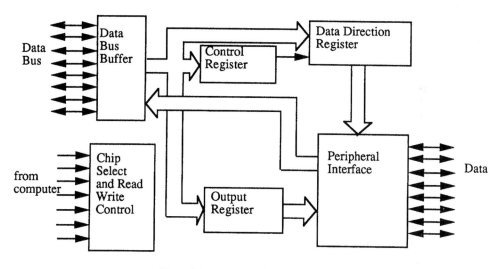

Figure 8.5   A parallel interface adapter.

A parallel interface is normally addressed as a set of memory locations. Each port contains a direction register, a data register, a control register, and two control lines. The control register determines the active logic connections in the device and also contains the data-ready or peripheral-ready bits.

One of the parallel interface standards is IEEE 488, the standard digital interface for programmable instrumentation. It is also known as the Hewlett-Packard Interface or the general-purpose interface bus (GPIB). It is used in networks of instruments. Most Hewlett-Packard instruments have built-in IEEE 488 interfaces.

The IEEE 488 is a bus of 24 lines. Of the 24 lines, 8 are for ground, 8 for data, and 8 for control. As mentioned, IEEE 488 is designed for a network instruments. Up to 15 devices can be connected to the bus. Which devices can talk or listen is specified by the control. All devices are connected to the 8 data lines. On the data lines, bits are transmitted in parallel and bytes are transmitted in serial. The 8 control lines are divided into 3 data transfer lines and 5 bus-management lines. Data-transfer lines consist of DAV (data valid), NRFD (not ready for data), and NDAC (no data accepted). These lines help synchronize the flow of information between the talking (transmitting) and the listening (receiving) devices. The bus-management lines coordinate the flow of information on the bus. The IFC line places the system in a known state. The ATN line indicates the nature of the information on the data lines. REN commands instruments to select remote operation. The SRQ line services requests. The EOI line indicates the end of a multiple-byte transfer sequence, or, in conjunction with ATN, executes a polling sequence.

In a network, one device is designated as the controller. The bus is controlled by this controller. In a typical communication cycle, first the ATN line is set low so all devices monitor the lines. The commands Untalk and Unlisten are sent to eliminate all previous connections. Then the commands Listen Address and Talk Address are placed on the data bus to configure the bus. The device addresses are built into the devices and assigned by the hardware manufacturers. At any given time, only one device is assigned as the talker, whereas several can be listeners. ATN lines are then set high so that data transmission can begin. After the transmission is completed, the talker returns control of the network to the controller.

The maximum data rate in an IEEE 488 network is 1 megabit per second. The maximum cable length is 2 meters times the number of devices or 20 meters, whichever is less.

8.1.5 Data-Transfer Techniques

The actual data transfer between the computer or control and external devices is carried out using one of three methods:

(a) polling

(b) interrupts

(c) direct memory access

The first two methods are used widely for data communication between two computers. Direct memory access is used mostly for computer and peripheral device communication, especially when large amounts of data need to be transferred, such as computer-to-hard-disk-drive communication.

(a) Polling. Polling means checking the status of the I/O ports. When there is only one I/O port being polled, a communication program checks the status of the port repetitively. When the output port is ready, it sends 1 byte to the port. When the input port is ready, the byte in the input port buffer is retrieved. The polling loop runs continuously and the status of the port(s) is checked at fixed intervals. Polling is simple and no additional hardware circuitry is required. Figure 8.6 shows a polling loop. However, polling also requires constant checking of the status, which is time-consuming (CPU time). In reality, most of the CPU time is spent checking I/O status. When there are multiple I/O ports with different data-transfer rates, the polling may not be fast enough to service the highest-data rate I/O port. Some data may get lost while the CPU checks other I/O ports. This polling loop also shares CPU time with other applications (the polling loop can run in background and may be active only during certain time intervals, which are set by a timer). It may slow down other applications.

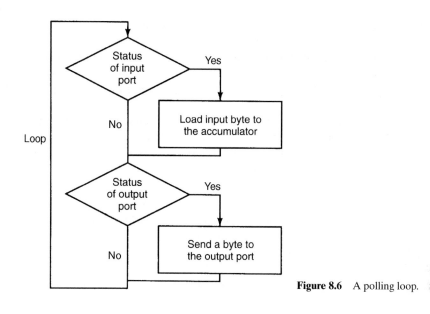

Figure 8.6   A polling loop.

(b) Interrupts. To reduce the overhead in polling, interrupts can be used. The idea is to eliminate the time spent by polling devices that do not need service at the time. Every CPU has a built-in hardware interrupt. When an interrupt signal is sent to the CPU interrupt line, the system saves the current register status and jumps to a memory location defined by either hardware or the user software. A routine at that location is executed. The routine is called an interrupt service routine. I/O routines can be written as interrupt service routines. By using interrupts, the I/O routine is called to read only when data are available to the buffer. Therefore, CPU time is not used to check the status unnecessarily. If interrupt I/O is used, hardware interrupt circuitry must be constructed to send the interrupt signal to the CPU. An interrupt service routine is written and stored in an appropriate memory location.

Priorities can also be assigned to different devices. The priorities are numbered as level 0, level 1, and so on. The lower the level, the higher the priority (Figure 8.7). For critical devices, a higher priority is assigned. the higher-priority interrupt can interrupt the lower-priority one, but not the other way around. Because I/O is normally slow, when interrupt I/O is used, the computer can perform other tasks. Polling and interrupts can be applied to either serial I/O or parallel I/O.

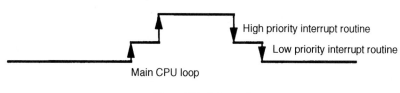

Figure 8.7   Interrupt.

8.2 LOCAL-AREA NETWORKS

In order for a computer-aided manufacturing facility to run smoothly, the many devices in the facility must be linked. Not only do data files, such as NC part programs, design data files, and so on, have to be exchanged between devices and computers, but control commands and device status information also have to be exchanged. The system operator needs the ability to directly log into each system device to maintain the system, check the status, alter the control, and up/down load the data files. The traditional serial or parallel I/Os are limited in this application because of the following aspects:

1. point-to-point communication requires $C_2^n = n!/(n - 2)!\,2$ connections; for example, for 50 devices, $C_2^{50} = 1225$
2. slow communication speed (up to 20 kbytes per second, higher when data compression is used)
3. limited transmission distance (about 10 m)

The development of computer-networking techniques has enabled a large number of computers to be connected. Computer networks can be classified as wide-area networks (WANs), local-area networks (LANs), and high-speed local networks local networks (HSLNs). A wide-area network is one serving a geometric area of more than 10 km. Such a network includes the popular Internet. Thousands of computers are connected in internet, enabling users to transfer files, mail electronic messages, and remotely log on to computers. HSLNs are designed for computer rooms, mainly for mainframe-to-mainframe communication and mainframe-to-disk-drive communication. They are confined to very short distances and extremely high speeds.

A local-area network is one that is confined to a 10-km distance (in practice, much shorter), in an office group, a building, a university campus, or a company. Devices in the network can perform the same type of data communication as does a wide-area network. In a LAN, the communication speed can be as high as 300 megabits per second. However, Ethernet, which became the most popular LAN in the 1980s, runs at 10 Mbps (or 100 Mbps fast Ethernet). It is significantly faster than an RS-232 serial communication connection (19.2 kbps). A comparison of a few network technologies is shown in Table 8.3. Note that CBX utilizes telephone service for data transmission. Several of the terms used in the table are explained in the following section.

A factory network fits the definition of a LAN, so a LAN is the network best suited for CAM. An ideal LAN has the following characteristics:

- high speed: greater than 10 Mbps
- low cost: easily affordable on a microcomputer and/or machine controller
- high reliability/integrity: low error rates, fault-tolerant, reliable
- expandability: easily expandable to install new nodes
- installation flexibility: easily installed in an existing environment
- interface standard: standard interface across a range of computers and controllers

TABLE 8.3   COMPARISON OF A FEW COMMUNICATION TECHNOLOGIES

	LAN	High Speed Local Network (HSLN)	Computerized Branch Exchange (CBX)
Transmission medium	Twisted pair Coaxial cable Optical fiber	CATV coax	Twisted pair
Topology	Bus, tree, ring	Bus	Star
Speed	1–100 Mbps	50 Mbps	9.6–64 kbps
Max distance	25 km	1 km	1 km
Switching technique	Packet	Packet	Circuit (no delay)
No. of devices supported	100's–1000's	10's	100's–1000's
Attachment cost	Low	High	Very low
Applications	Computers Terminals	Main frame to disk drive	Voice Terminal-t-terminal Terminal-t-host

In a local-area network, computers and controllers can communicate with each other. Terminals also can access any computer on the network without a physical hardwire. It is beneficial because the same terminal can now access all devices on the shop floor.

In this section, we discuss LAN technologies and LAN protocols.

8.2.1 Network Technology

A LAN consists of software that controls data handling and error recovery, hardware that generates and receives signals, and media that carry the signal. The software and hardware design are governed by a set of rules called a protocol. This protocol defines the logical, electrical, and physical specifications of the network. In order for devices in a network to communicate with each other, the same protocol must be followed. For a device to send a message across the network, the sender and the receiver must be uniquely identified. The message must be properly sent and error checking must be performed in order to ensure the correctness of the information. Similar to a parcel prepared for the Postal Service, the software has to package and identify the data with appropriate labels. The label contains the address of the destination and information concerning the contents of the message. The package is then converted into the appropriate electrical signals and waits to be transmitted. To transmit the signals, a conducting medium carries the electrical signals to the destination. Several techniques are used to accomplish this task. In this section, we discuss the packaging of the data (packet), the signal itself (bandwidth), the transmission media, and the network configuration.

8.2.1.1 Packet.   Data can be sent either byte by byte, in small units, or all together. In the case of byte-by-byte transfer, overhead is extremely high, because packed with each byte must be the sender and receiver address and some control information. When sending data all together in one package, we face congesting the network. Each message may occupy the network for a long time (the message can be a several hundred kilobyte data file), and an error causes the retransmission of the entire message. In order to utilize the network efficiently, packet switching was developed, in which a message is split into smaller units called packets. Packets are routed and carried separately through the network and later reassembled in sequence at the receiving end. To the user of the data, the entire message comes in sequence. For example, on the Ethernet, each packet may contain between 46 and 1500 bytes of data.

8.2.1.2 Transmission media.   Coaxial cable and twisted-pair wires are used in LANs. A coaxial cable is commonly seen in the household for cable TV connections. It is a cable consisting of a solid copper-core wire, wrapped by a mesh thin copper wires (Figure 8.8) (or, in inexpensive cable TV cable, aluminum foil). The wrapping wire is connected to the ground and serves as the noise insulator. There is an electric insulator between the center core and the wrapping wire. The exterior of the cable is a plastic insulator. A coaxial cable allows high-frequency analog signals to travel. A twisted-pair wire, as the name indicates, is a pair of twisted wires. The frequency of the signal carried by the twisted-pair wire is much lower than that of coaxial cable, and, thus, the transmission speed is slower. There are 50Ω and 75Ω coaxial cables.

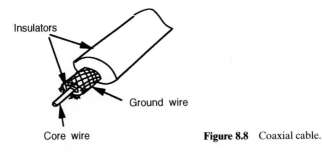

Insulators

Ground wire

Core wire   **Figure 8.8**   Coaxial cable.

8.2.1.3 Bandwidth.   Signals are transmitted on the cable, and these signals are modulated at certain frequencies. The range between the lowest and the highest frequency that can be carried on the communication line is called the bandwidth. The higher the bandwidth, the more information it can carry. There are two methods used in LAN: baseband and broadband. Baseband is a method of data communication in which different voltages representing binary 0 and 1 are directly applied to the communication line. The speed is limited and only one signal can be carried at a time. Broadband utilizes analog (radio) signals. A digital signal is modulated on one of the analog signals. The carrier-signal frequency is from 5 to 300 MHz, and higher frequencies are also possible. Each analog signal takes one frequency band (channel). Two channels can be separated easily by filtering the desired frequency. Because there are many channels, broadband technology allows the same cable to be used by several LAN subnetworks, TV signals, and so on, at the same time. Cable TV coaxial cable is normally used as the transmission media. More than 100 channels can be opened at the same time without interfering with each other. Each channel is able to transmit at least 5 Mbps. Needless to say, the total information transmitted is extremely high. In the near future, gigabits per second will be available.

8.2.1.4 Network topologies.   A network can be arranged in several ways. It may be arranged as a ring, a star, or a bus. Such arrangements can be made either physically or logically. Here we discuss only the physical arrangements. These topologies can be seen in Figure 8.9. The ring topology is simple; however, if the ring breaks, the entire network is down. Also, the cable must be routed back to where it begins. The star topology is easy to grow, however, the network relies on a server at the center of the star. All communication between nodes must go through the center. The bus topology is like the ring, only it does not require the cable to be routed back to where it begins. Nodes can be added easily into the network. However, the control is conceptually more difficult. In reality, the control of the bus network is no more difficult than the others. For this reason, the use of bus topology in LANs is popular.

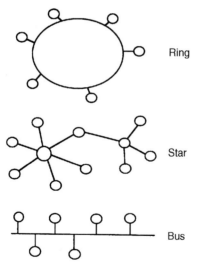

Ring

Star

Bus

Figure 8.9   Network topologies.

8.2.1.5 Medium-access control.   LANs use distributed control. This enables each device on the network to have equal access to the network and prevents catastrophic failure due to the failure of the master. The distributed control scheme is called the medium-access control. The most commonly used medium-access control methods are CSMA/CD (Ethernet bus), and token passing (token bus or token ring).

(a) CSMA/CD and Ethernet. CSMA/CD, carrier sense multiple access with collision detection, was developed by Xerox in the 1970s and implemented in Ethernet. Ethernet has since become the industry standard. Most engineering workstations and minicomputers use Ethernets. Many of the industrial controller vendors also support their version of Ethernet. There is a good chance that the reader has access to such a network. A bus topology is used in Ethernet (Figure 8.10). In the figure, four computers are connected to two separate buses. Each bus is a 50-ohm coaxial cable with a terminator at each end. This cable is specially made for Ethernet, and due to its relatively small demand, it is much more expensive than TV coaxial cable. A tap connects the computer to the bus. The tap must be placed at a multiple of a fixed interval (2 ft) on the cable. An Ethernet controller board in the computer translates the data to be sent or received. The data in digital form are then sent to the transceiver. The transceiver makes the physical and electrical connections onto the cable and transmits and receives digital signals to and from the cable. A repeater links two buses together to form a single bus. Whenever there is no signal on the bus, any device on the bus can start transmitting. Because it takes time for a signal to travel from one end of the network to the other, it is possible that one device will begin transmitting while there is a signal already on the bus. The CSMA/CD protocol resolves this problem.

In each device, there is built-in circuit that detects the collision of the signals on the bus. The procedure to resolve the collision is as follows.

(a) When a collision is detected by the transmitter, stop transmitting. Send a jam signal to assure that everyone knows there has been a collision.

(b) Each transmitter waits for a random amount of time and then transmits again.

Because the waiting time is random, the chance of having both devices transmitting at the same time again is low. This process is shown in Figure 8.11. The transmission time for a message from A is 1. At t_0, A begins to transmit. It takes a amount of time for the signal to reach B. At e, the time before the signal reaches B, B begins to transmit. B detects the collision of two signals only at a time $t_0 + a$. B stops transmission for a random amount of time β. The signal from B continues to travel until A detects it at a time $t_0 + 2a - e$. At this time, A stops transmission for a random amount of time α before it retransmits.

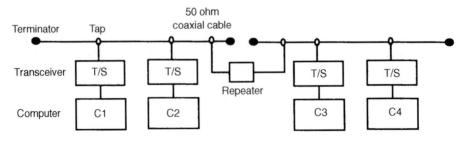

Figure 8.10   Ethernet.

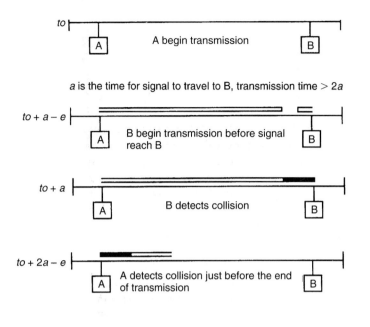

Figure 8.11 Collision detection.

CSMA/CD Ethernet uses a baseband coaxial cable as the medium. Operating speeds of 1, 5, 10, and 100 Mbps are possible. A typical Ethernet runs at 10 Mbps.

(b) Token Ring. A token ring network is one using a token for access control. A token is a unique bit pattern that is passed from one device to the other. The device that has the token is allowed to transmit; all others receive only. When no device is transmitting, the token circulates continuously in the ring. The ring is formed by linking the repeaters with ring segments. The token and the data packet travel in one direction (Figure 8.12). The repeater always receives data from one side and sends the identical data out to the other side. To transmit a message, the computer must wait for the token to arrive at its repeater. When the token arrives, it changes one of the bits to 1. This changes the free token to a busy token, so that the token is no longer available to other computers. The computer sends out the message with header information indicating the address of the receiving computer. The message goes through the repeaters in the ring in sequence. Each computer has a chance to read the message; however, only the ones addressed will copy the message to their memory. The message eventually travels back to the sender. At this time, the repeater of the sender is actually separated into two parts: one is a transmitter of the message and other is the sink of the message. Only when the message comes back to the sender, does it know that the transmission has been successful. The message length may be variable. When the message transmission is

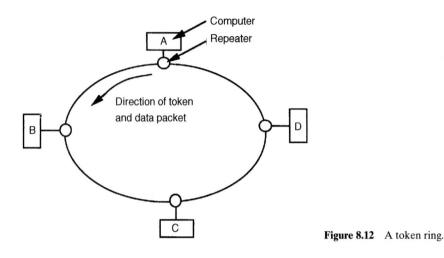

Figure 8.12   A token ring.

complete, the token is reinstated onto the ring by the transmitting computer. Because only the computer with the token can talk, there are no collision problems as in an Ethernet. The speed of a token ring is typically 1 or 4 Mbps.

(c) **Token Bus.** A token-bus network is a logical token ring implemented on a physical bus (Figure 8.13). Thus, it has the advantages of both the token ring and CSMA/CD. Like Ethernet, there is no need for a repeater, and the signal is available to all devices at the same time. The cable need not loop back to the initial device. A new device can be added to the network easily by tapping into the existing cable. For medium-access control,because a token is used, it eliminates the problem of signal collision, which is a problem in Ethernet. It is thus appropriate for real-time application, such as those applications on the shop floor.

In a token bus, each device is assigned a unique address. A token is passed from one device to another according to a logical ring sequence. The next device in the logical ring does not have to be physically adjacent. The ring is formed by assigning preceding and succeeding addresses to each address. A token is a packet with a zero data

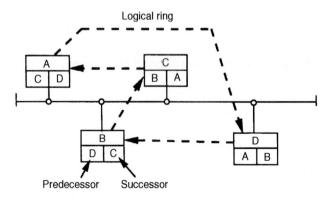

Figure 8.13   A token bus.

byte. In the packet, the source and destination addresses are given. When the token is broadcast through the bus, only the destination device accepts the token. If transmission is desired, the device with the token begins transmitting its message in packets. After the transmission is completed, the device sends the token to its successor. In Figure 8.13, the ring is formed by assigning each device an address: a predecessor address and a successor address. The ring has a sequence of *A–D–B–C.* By changing the address table, the sequence of the devices in the ring can be changed.

It is the responsibility of the device that has a free token to make sure the token is properly received by the next device. In case there is no response from the next device, a new successor is selected and the failed device address is removed from the logic ring. If one of the devices has failed, the token bus will still operate.

A token bus may use either a baseband or a broadband technology. Either baseband or broadband may have up to a 10-Mbps data rate. The communication medium used is 75-ohm coaxial cable. The manufacturing automation protocol (MAP) uses a token bus.

8.2.2 The ISO/OSI Model

Several LAN protocols have been developed. As mentioned before, a protocol is a set of rules that govern the operation of functional units to achieve communication. However, to ensure that data are transmitted properly, there are several tasks that must be performed. Assume the cell controller needs to check the status of NC machine 1. The application program in the cell controller issues an instruction such as "Machine 1 status" to machine 1. This message must be converted to a proper format that the network can carry. The final data must be modulated into electric signals, either digital or RF. Then the signals are properly sent through the network to the destination machine. The access control, network layout, media type, and so on, all play an important role in transmitting this data. On the receiving side, the data are decoded and sent to the machine-control executive. The message format may not be compatible with the NC machine-controller, command-language syntax. In order to establish painless communication, this incoming message must be translated into a compatible format. It can be seen even in this simple example that lots of tedious tasks have to be performed before the network is usable. A set of protocols has to be defined in order for the devices in the network to follow.

In the late 1970s, the International Standards Organization (ISO) began developing a model for LANs. The model is called the Open System Interconnect (OSI) model and it splits the communication process into seven layers (Figure 8.14). On each layer, standards can be set to satisfy the need. When a packet of data is sent from device *A* to device *B,* it goes down the layers. On each layer, a control message is appended to the data. The complete packet is then transmitted through the medium to device *B.* On each of the device *B* layers, the control message is stripped and proper actions are taken to convert the data into the proper format. This layered model allows the system designer to modularize the implementation task. Each layer can be developed independently and replaced without affecting the other layers. However, it is also very complicated, thus requiring significant software overhead. For a simple application, this may be

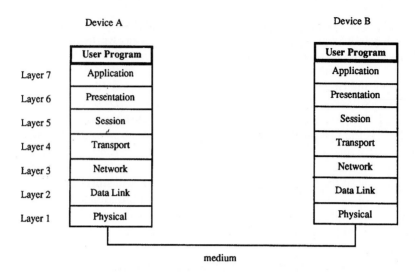

Figure 8.14   The seven-layer ISO/OSI model.

overkill. However, for data communication in a complex manufacturing facility, such an approach definitely has more benefit than cost.

The seven layers of the OSI model are as follows:

8.2.2.1 Physical layer.   This layer deals with the electrical and mechanical means of transmitting data. The physical layer includes cable, connector, voltage level, speed, bandwidth, and data-encoding method. For example, the RS-232 communication standard belongs to the physical layer. In the case of a LAN, the baseband and broadband technologies are on this layer.

8.2.2.2 Data-link layer.   This layer transfers frames across a single LAN and its functions include resolution of contention for use of the shared transmission medium, delimitation and selection of frames addressed to this node, detection of noise via a frame check sequence, and any error correction or retries performed within the LAN. It is used to improve the error frequency for messages moved between adjacent nodes. The data integrity transmitted between two devices in the same network is ensured on this layer. The ISO HDLC (high-level data-link control) standard is used on this layer. In HDLC, a frame begins and ends with an 8-bit flag. Between the flags are addresses of the destination, control information, variable-length data, and frame length. In LAN, this layer is divided into two operations: the resolution of contention is the medium-access control, and there is a logical link control.

8.2.2.3 Network layer.   The network layer provides the transparent transfer of data between transport entities. It is responsible for establishing, maintaining, and terminating connections. Between networks, the network layer has the responsibility for internetwork routing. A global unique node address is used by this layer.

8.2.2.4 Transport layer.   This layer ensures that data units are delivered error-free, in sequence, with no losses or duplications. It should provide a network-independent service to the upper layer.

8.2.2.5 Session layer.   The session layer controls the dialogue between applications during a communication session. The type of dialogue, whether it is two-way (simultaneous, alternate) or one-way dialogue, is defined. It provides a checkpoint and a resynchronizing capability. In case the dialogue breaks during the session, it provides a means to recover from the failure.

8.2.2.6 Presentation layer.   The presentation layer takes care of the syntax of the data exchanged between applications. For example, a device may use the EBCDIC code. A message sent from it to an ASCII device is translated by this layer. Other data syntax includes teletext, videotex, encryption, and virtual terminal.

8.2.2.7 Application layer.   This is the most difficult layer. It ensures that data transferred between any two applications are understood. Given the number of applications that exist, it is extremely difficult to define this layer. A standard for each application domain needs to be defined.

8.2.3 Manufacturing Automation Protocol (MAP)

Manufacturing automation protocol (MAP) is a LAN-protocol specification that was initially published by General Motors. It was developed especially for a factory environment. As mentioned before, many LAN standards have been developed over the past decade. Many combinations of different types of technologies may be used in building a LAN. Even when using the same LAN technologies, products from different vendors are not always compatible. Sometimes the networks for different products of the same vendor are not compatible. On the shop floor, it is quite common that products from different vendors are used. Each vendor has a particular strength in building certain products, so it is natural to put the best product in the shop. To connect these products directly in a communication network becomes a seemingly impossible task. For example, DEC minicomputers, which are widely used for cell control and process control, use DECnet, which is a version of Ethernet. IBM computers on the shop floor talk SNA (systems network architecture), Allen-Bradley PLCs use data highways, Texas Instruments has their TIway, and Gould Modicon's PLCs run Modbus. General Motors fell victim to this problem because it is one of the companies that has controllers and computers made by virtually every vendor. Facing the extremely high cost of building gateways (a dedicated computer that converts messages from one network to the other) between LANs of different vendors, GM jointly with all major computer and controller manufacturers developed the MAP protocol.

MAP is a collection of existing and emerging communication protocols, each of which has been developed by a standard setting body (Table 8.4). MAP adopted the ISO/OSI model because it has been accepted worldwide. MAP is a low-cost, multi-vendor, data-communication network. The MAP controller is used in machine tools,

TABLE 8.4   MAP 2.1 STANDARD

Layer	MAP Implementation
Layer 7 application	ISO FTAM {DP} 8571 File Transfer Protocol Manufacturing Messaging Format Standard (MMFS) MAP Directory Services MAP Network Management
Layer 6 presentation	NULL/MAP transfer
Layer 5 session	ISO Session{IS} 8327 Basic Combined Subset & Session Kernel, Full Duplex
Layer 4 transport	ISO Transport{IS} 8073 Class 4
Layer 3 network	ISO Internet{DIS} 8473 Connectionless, SubNetwork Dependent Convergence Protocol
Layer 2 data Link	ISO Logical Link Control {DIS} 8802/2 (IEEE 802.2) Type 1, Class 1 ISO/IEEE 802.4 Token Passing Bus Medium Access Control
Layer 1 physical	ISO Token Passing Bus{DIS} 8802/4 (IEEE 802.4) 10 Mbps Broadband

robots, programmable controllers, computers, and terminals. It makes it possible to plug equipment directly into the MAP network and communicate transparently with other devices. The layered approach also allows new technology to be incorporated when it becomes available. Thus, MAP is an evolving standard. As billions of dollars are invested in automation projects, the compatibility of data communication enables these investments to be utilized effectively and benefits to be realized quickly. Although there are already hundreds of thousands of controllers and computers installed in factories, it is not feasible to replace all the existing networks with MAP. Vendors are currently building gateways to link the MAP network with their own proprietary networks.

Another significant development is the office automation network, TOP (technical and office protocol), proposed by Boeing Computer Service. TOP and MAP share the standards on several layers. The difference is on the physical layer, where TOP is based on the CSMA/CD bus of Ethernet. A gateway can be built easily to bridge the two networks. With MAP and TOP, not only communication within a manufacturing shop can be ensured, but also a link to the corporation offices can be established. It becomes a total solution for the corporate communication need.

An integrated corporate communication network is depicted in Figure 8.15. In the overall network, networks of different types are linked through gateways. From the corporate network, the factory network is connected. The factory network is divided into the MAP backbone, several MAP subnetworks, and some vendor proprietary networks. Gateways bridges and routers are used to link those networks. These networks, offices, and factories can be located at different geological locations, even on different conti-

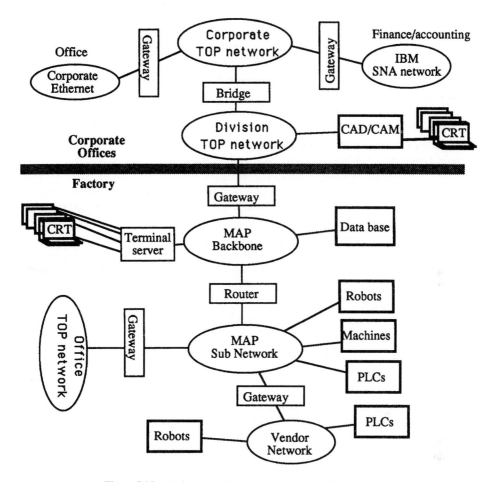

Figure 8.15   An integrated corporate communications network.

nents. The link can be by coaxial cable, telephone line, microwave, optical fiber, or satellite. Workers located at different sites can communicate with each other through the network. In the same manner, devices can be accessed remotely. With this technology, a global factory concept can be accomplished.

8.2.4 TCP/IP Protocols

Although MAP and TOP have been promoted as the network protocols for manufacturing and office automation, the most widely used network is probably the commercial Ethernet. With the installation of engineering workstations such as Sun, DEC, HP, Silicon Graphics, and RS6000, a common network has been established in most engineering offices. Most current engineering workstations run UNIX or an implementation of the UNIX operating system. Built into the UNIX operating system is Ethernet and the Internet protocols. A UNIX system can communicate locally with other UNIX machines on the network, as well as connect through a wide-area network (like the Internet) to other machines. When a gateway is established between the local network with a external network such as ArPAnet of NSFnet, and so on, nationwide and world-wide network service is provided.

A set of Internet protocols have been defined to enable machines to communicate with each other. The TCP/IP protocols, a product of the U.S. Department of Defense, are the most widely accepted protocols on the Internet. TCP/IP can trace its roots to the early 1970s to the ArPAnet project. IP, which stands for Internet Protocol, is a simple datagram protocol that uses globally assigned addresses to transmit data between two hosts. It allows data to be broken into small packets. When data are transferred over a wide network, the datagram may go through any number of gateways. Internet Protocol is a lower-level protocol. TCP (Transmission Control Protocol) is a connection-oriented protocol. It provides reliable flow-controlled data transfer between two nodes. TCP is built on top of the IP protocol. When a message is sent to a remote machine, a datagram is sent. The IP protocol is appropriate for this application. However, if a remote login terminal session is desired, a connection-oriented protocol, TCP is needed. Two of the popular communication applications, FTP and TELNET, are both built on top of the TCP protocol. FTP is a file-transfer application and TELNET is a remote-terminal session application.

TCP/IP corresponds to the ISO model on the network and the transport layer. Figure 8.16 shows the Internet protocol layering.

Transport Layer	TCP	UDP
Network Layer	IP	
Data-link Layer	Network interface	

Figure 8.16   Internet layering.

The physical layer can be the Ethernet as in all of the UNIX engineering workstation installations. For a wide-area network, the physical layer required to transmit the data from one host to another may be several different networks. The UDP (User Diagram Protocol) shown in the figure is a simple protocol that provides an additional data checksum for a datagram. It does little beyond what IP does. It is used in the Internet domain for datagram communication.

To establish communication between two hosts, first, a socket is established. A socket is an end point of communication. It is created by a system call with a specification of the destination. There is an associated data structure that stores all the necessary information for the communication and a data buffer. Data are broken into small pockets and sent to the socket with a specification of protocols. The TCP, IP, and Ethernet headers are added to the packet before the packet is transferred to the Ethernet cable. The TCP header includes source port, destination port, sequence number, acknowledg-

Ether	IP	TCP	Data

Figure 8.17 A packet.

ment number, checksum, urgent pointer, and additional flags. The IP header includes type of service, total message length, ID, fragment flags, header checksum, protocol, source and destination addresses, and so on. When the local network is not Ethernet, an appropriate protocol is used to replace the Ethernet header.

When a message is received by the destination host, the header information is stripped off the packet and the proper action is taken to ensure the correct data transfer. Out-of-sequence packets are kept until properly sequenced packets have arrived. When using an application such as FTP or TELNET, the user only need specify the destination host name (e.g., mars.ecn.purdue.edu). The protocols are transparent. When writing programs to access the network, a set of system function calls takes care of the communication.

For example, to initialize a TELNET session with the Science and Technology Information System (STIS) at the National Science Foundation, one would type

```
telnet stis.nsf.gov or telnet 128.150.195.40.
```

At the login prompt, log in as user *public*. The user then responds as if he or she is logged into a local terminal. The preceding *stis* is the name of the host where STIS is located. The domain name where *stis* is located is *nsf*. A government installation is indicated by *gov*. The Telnet application uses a host table on the local system to locate the Internet address. If the address is not found, a user may type the address directly, such as 128.150.195.40.

8.2.5 The Internet, Information Superhighway, Gopher, and the World Wide Web

Since the digital computer was first introduced some 50 years ago, computer visionaries have envisaged a concept of a universal database of knowledge: information that would be accessible to people around the world and link easily to other pieces of information so that any user could quickly find the things most important to themselves. It was in the 1960s when this idea was explored further, giving rise to visions of a "docuverse" that people could electronically sift through, revolutionizing all aspects of human–information interaction. Only now has the technology caught up with these visions, making it possible to implement them on a global scale (Hughes, 1994).

The Internet is the catch-all word used to describe the massive worldwide network of computers. The word "internet" literally means "network of networks." In itself, the Internet is comprised of thousands of smaller regional networks scattered throughout the globe. On any given day, the Internet connects roughly 20 million users in over 50 countries. The Internet is the beginning of what many writers have called the

Information superhighway. The Internet usually refers to the physical side of the global network, a giant mass of cables and computers (Hughes, 1994).

No one "owns" the Internet. Although there are companies that help manage different parts of the networks that tie everything together, there is no single governing body that controls what happens on the Internet. The networks within different countries are funded and managed locally according to local policies.

Having access to the Internet usually means that one has access to a number of basic services: electronic mail, interactive conferences, access to information resources, network news, and the ability to transfer files.

8.2.5.1 Gopher.

Gopher is an Internet service that was developed at the University of Minnesota by its Computer and Information Services group. It was initially intended so that users (clients) could browse and retrieve information from Gopher "servers" located elsewhere. Gopher servers currently operate on thousands of computer platforms throughout the world to provide a variety of information services to the Internet community. Event calendars, telephone (address and E-mail) directories, archived publications, and general guides are available from a variety of servers.

Gopher servers can be set up on a variety of computing platforms. For instance, servers are available for mainframes, UNIX workstations, Macintoshes, NeXTs, and PCs. The server software is available for each of these platforms from the University of Minnesota at no charge. Interestingly, one can even use a Gopher client to download the Gopher server software. To get the Gopher client software, you can anonymous ftp to

```
BOOMBOX.MICRO.UMN.EDU
```

The necessary software is in the *pub/gopher* directory. Instructions regarding the installation are included in the archived compressed software.

Gopher provides many advantages for the student and researcher. It makes library information remotely available and searching extremely efficient. It makes information maintenance much more dynamic, and most importantly, it saves money when used properly.

8.2.5.2 The World Wide Web.

The World Wide Web uses the Internet to transmit hypermedia documents between computer users internationally. No one "owns" the World Wide Web. People are responsible for the documents they author and make available publicly on the Web. Via the Internet, hundreds of thousands of people around the world are making information available from their homes, schools, and workplaces.

Although it is possible to use World Wide Web software without having to use the Internet, Internet access is necessary in order to make full use of and participate in the World Wide Web. The World Wide Web is officially described as a "wide-area hypermedia information retrieval initiative aiming to give universal access to a large universe of documents." What the World Wide Web (WWW, W3) project has done is provide users on computer networks with a consistent means to access a variety of media in a simplified fashion. By using a popular software interface to the Web called Netscape or

Internet Explorer, the Web project has changed the way people view and create information: It has created the first true global hypermedia network. The media supported by W3 includes text, pictures (GIF and JPG), drawings (PostScript), motion video (MPG, GL, and DL), and audio [Hughes, 1994].

The operation of the Web relies mainly on hypertext as its means of interacting with users. Hypertext is basically the same as regular text—it can be stored, read, searched, or edited—with an important exception: Hypertext contains connections within the text to other documents. For instance, suppose you were able to somehow select (with a mouse or with your finger) the word "hypertext" in the sentence before this one. In a hypertext system, you would then have one or more documents related to hypertext appear before you: a history of hypertext, for example, or Webster's definition of hypertext. These new texts would themselves have links and connections to other documents: Continually selecting text would take you on a free-associative tour of information. In this way, hypertext links, called hyperlinks, can create a complex virtual web of connections.

Hypermedia is hypertext with a difference—hypermedia documents contain links not only to other pieces of text, but also to other forms of media—sounds, images, and movies. Images themselves can be selected to link to sounds or documents. Hypermedia simply combines hypertext and multimedia.

Documentation concerning W3 can be obtained over the Internet. A PostScript copy of the documentation can be obtained by anonymous FTP to

```
ftp.eit.com
```

The publication can be found in */pub/web.guide*.

8.3 CONCLUDING REMARKS

So far in this chapter, we have discussed the different methods for data communication. All methods discussed have been implemented on the shop floor. Among them, RS-232-C serial communication is still the most widely used communication method. However, in a modern automated manufacturing facility, the need for higher speed and more reliable data communication renders serial communication undesirable. The development of LANs in the late 1970s has brought us a sound solution. Yet the lack of "one" standard has made it impossible for the user to plug devices from different vendors into a network. Expensive gateways need to be installed. The new MAP protocol provides a standard for all vendors to follow, thus making it possible to have plug compatibility. The standard has become mature during the 1980s. In the 1990s, we can expect to have much better communication capability in offices as well as in factories. This data-communication capability will serve as the infrastructure for the factory of the future. Because the technology is evolving rapidly, one must follow closely this new development. As students of computer-aided manufacturing, it is essential for us to understand the fundamentals of data communication, its current practice, and its future development.

REVIEW QUESTIONS

8.1. Convert the following message into ASCII code:

```
MACHINE 1 OFF
```

8.2. Convert the following messages into ASCII code with (a) even parity, (b)odd parity, (c) Space parity, and (d) Mark parity.

```
ON
OFF
idle
M/C 3
```

8.3. A part program of 8000 characters in length is to be transferred to a machine through a serial port running at 300 baud. What is the approximate time in seconds needed to complete the transfer? Assume there is a 10% delay overhead.

8.4. Describe the different techniques in data transfer and the pros and cons of each.

8.5. When connecting a terminal to a cell-control computer, we found only garbage (unreadable) text displayed on the screen. What are the possible causes? What kind of action can be taken to correct the error? Assume that both the terminal and the computer are in good operating condition.

8.6. Find what kind of communication ports are available on the CNC controller in your shop. What are the purposes of those ports? Are they being used now? What kind of devices are connected to them?

8.7. Find the setting of the terminal you use in the lab. What are the baud rate, numbers of start and stop bits, parity, and duplex?

8.8. Describe the incentive of installing LAN on a shop floor. Compare it with serial and parallel communication (point-to-point).

8.9. What is the motivation for using MAP protocol for shop-floor LAN?

8.10. Define the following terms: baseband, broadband, medium-access control, and packet.

8.11. What are the disadvantages of using CSMA/CD for LAN?

8.12. What is the ISO/OSI model? What is it for and where can it be applied?

8.13. What is the function of a bridge and a gateway in a multiple-network communication system?

REFERENCES/BIBLIOGRAPHY

CROWDER, R. (1988). "The MAP Specification," *Understanding MAP*, in V. A. Rizzardi Ed., pp. 16–19. Dearborn, MI: Society of Manufacturing Engineers.

DACONTA, M. C. (1996). *Java for C/C++ Programmers*. New York: John Wiley.

ELECTRONIC INDUSTRIES ASSOCIATION (1969). *EIA Standard RS-232-C: Interface Between Data Terminal Equipment and Data Communications Equipment Employing Serial Binary Data Interchange*. Washington, DC: EIA.

GENERAL MOTORS (1984). *General Motor's Manufacturing Automation Protocol, A Communication Network Protocol for Open Systems Interconnection.* Warren, MI: GM MAP Task Force.

GRAHAM, I. S. (1996). *The HTML Sourcebook: A Complete Guide to HTML 3.0.* New York: John Wiley.

HALSALL, F. (1996). *Data Communications, Computer Networks, and Open Systems,* 4th ed. Reading, MA: Addison-Wesley.

HUGHES, K. (1994). *Entering the World-Wide Web: A Guide to Cyberspace,* Enterprise Interaction Technologies electronic document. Palo Alto, CA.

KROL, E. (1993). *The Whole Internet: User's Guide & Catalog,* Sebastopol, CA: O'Reilly & Associates.

RIZZARDI, V. A. Ed. (1988). *Understanding MAP Manufacturing Automation Protocol.* Dearborn, MI: Society of Manufacturing Engineers.

SCHATT, S. (1996). *Understanding ATM.* New York: McGraw-Hill.

THOMAS, R. M. (1996). *Introduction to Local Area Networks.* San Francisco: Network Press.

VACCA, J.R. (1996) *VRML, Bringing Virtual Reality to the Internet.* Boston: AP Professional.

9

Fundamentals of
Numerical Control

It has been over 40 years since the first numerical-control (NC) machine tool was demonstrated. The invention of the NC machine tool is a major technological evolution in manufacturing. It has since changed the technology and image of the discrete product manufacturing industry. NC is the foundation for many modern manufacturing technologies, such as robotics, flexible manufacturing cell (FMC), flexible manufacturing system (FMS), CAD/CAM, and computer-integrated manufacturing (CIM). In this chapter, we will discuss the history and the hardware aspects of NC. In Chapter 10, the programming of NC machines will be discussed.

9.1 HISTORICAL DEVELOPMENT

When we trace back the history of machine-tool development, we can find evidence of some kind of machining (turning) as early as 700 B.C. (Rolt, 1967). However, it was not until the fifteenth century that people began machining metal. Eighteenth-century industrialization ushered in the demand of production-type machine tools. Machine shops were established to create more machines. However, there was little change in the principle and mechanism of machine tools and cutting tools used. Early in this century, F. W. Taylor invented a new tool metal—high-speed steel—and published his work on tool-life studies. Up to this point, what had been achieved was to use machines to reinforce human strength and to cut hard materials. The machines also provided humans with a means to measure the dimensions of the parts produced.

In the first two decades of this century, we saw attempts to mass fabricate products and automating production equipment. Screw machines, transfer lines, and assembly lines are but a few successful examples of the era. These automated machines were controlled by mechanical devices using cams and preset stops. The motion sequence is encoded in the contour of a cam. When the cam turns at a constant speed, a follower moves up and down the surface of the cam creating the desired displacement and velocity. In turn, the follower controls the motion of the machine table or tool carrier. These types of automation work well as long as the product is produced in large quantity and is not too complex in shape. Parts with complicated geometry or small demand still require the full attention of a skilled machinist. For most parts, current technology allows machines to replace skilled humans.

In the past two decades, we have witnessed the increasing use of electromechanical devices. Machine tools that were driven by a common power source (e.g., steam-engine-powered shop shaft) were fitted with their own motors. Certain operation sequences now can be controlled by mechanical, electromechanical, or pneumatic controllers. The 1930s and 1940s comprised an era of fixed automation. Toward the end of this period (the eve of the World War II), there was a race of arms production. More and more sophisticated military equipment was developed. A large number of sophisticated products were needed. The quantity prompted the demand of automation, and the sophistication prompted the demand of a more skilled labor force.

During the first half of the 1940s, World War II was fought, and the Cold War began. The arms race did not stop there. More sophisticated aircraft were developed, for both military and civilian use. There was a technology boom, and the U.S. Air Force found that sophisticated part contours were required in order to make airplanes fly higher and faster. It was (and in some cases still is) not uncommon to remove up to 95% of the metal from a workpiece in order to produce a lightweight and structurally sound aircraft part. These parts also have to be extremely accurate. Reducing the manufacturing cost of these sophisticated parts became a major goal in aircraft development. The concept of numerical control was born as part of this effort. The intent was to replace human skill and sophistication with a programmable machine.

Generally, the concept of numerical control is credited to John Parsons. In 1947, Parsons developed a jig bore that was coupled with a computer. Using punched cards, Parsons was able to control the machine's position. In 1949, the U.S. Air Force, encouraged by Parson's success, commissioned MIT to develop a prototype of a "programmable" milling machine. The history of NC development can be found in a book written by one of its project leaders, T. F. Reintjes (1991). In 1952, a modified three-axis Cincinnati Hydrotel milling machine was demonstrated, and the term *numerical control* was coined. The machine was controlled by a hardwired electro-mechanical controller. The program was punched on cards and fed to the controller. Since then, many improvements, in the machine and in the control have been made. Nearly all kinds of machine tools are equipped with NC controllers. A new class of machines called machining centers and turning centers that can perform multiple machining processes were developed. A mill-turn center that combines lathe features with second active spindle can turn as well as mill a part. Modern NC controllers are computer-based (CNC), many with interactive computer graphics interface and easy "on-machine" programming. Tool changers, pallet changers, and network communications are also available on many machines. Many such machines can run unattended after workpieces have been loaded. Some machines also have high-speed spindles ($> 20,000$ rpm), high-feed-rate drives (> 600 ipm), and high precision (< 0.0001-in. accuracy).

CNC controllers have been applied to nearly every kind of machine tool: lathes, milling machines, drill presses, grinders, and so on. Modern NC machines are accurate, fast, strong, versatile, and easy to use. This is accomplished through improvements in both machine hardware and in the controllers. There is a trend of putting more intelligence onto the machine tool. We can expect the NC machines of the future to include some kind of the planning and adaptive control capabilities.

Figure 9.1 shows a modern machining center for large parts. In the front is a pallet changer. Four pallets have been mounted and are ready for machining. On the right is a loading and unloading station, where an operator is mounting a workpiece onto a pallet. As soon as the workpiece is mounted, the pallet can be loaded onto the index table. Any one of the six pallets can be placed onto the machine table and is ready for machining. The machine is located at the far side of the pallet index table. A pallet carrying a large disklike workpiece is being machined. On the left-hand side of the machine is a carousel tool magazine on which many tools have been mounted. A system like this is capable of running unattended for a long period of time until all workpieces in queue have been completed. By using the tool changer, the machine is able to use one of the many tools stored in the tool magazine. The pallet changer serves as a queue for the workpiece. Very complex parts can be produced automatically.

9.2 PRINCIPLES OF NUMERICAL CONTROL

Controlling a machine tool using variable input, such as a punched tape or a stored program, is known as numerical control (NC). NC has been defined by the Electronic Industries Association (EIA) as "a system in which actions are controlled by direct insertion of numerical data at some point. The system must automatically interpret at least some portion of this data." A part program is that numerical data required to produce a part.

A numerical-control machine-tool system contains a machine-control unit (MCU) and the machine tool itself (see Figure 9.2). The MCU is further divided into two elements: the data-processing unit (DPU) and the control-loops unit (CLU) (Koren, 1983). The DPU processes the coded data read from the tape or other media and passes information on the position of each axis, its direction of motion, feed, and auxiliary function controls signals to the CLU. The CLU operates the drive mechanisms of the machine, receives feedback signals about the actual position and velocity of each of the axes, and announces when an operation has been completed. The DPU sequentially reads the data when each line has completed execution as noted by the CLU.

A DPU consists of some or all of the following parts:

- data-input device such as a paper-tape reader, magnetic-tape reader, RS-232-C port, and so on
- data-reading circuits and parity-checking logic
- decoding circuits for describing data among the controller axes
- an editor

A CLU, on the other hand, consists of the following:

- an interpolator that supplies machine-motion commands between data points for tool motion
- position-control-loops hardware for all the axes of motion, where each axis has a separate control loop

Figure 9.1 An NC system for large parts (Courtesy of Cincinnati Milacron).

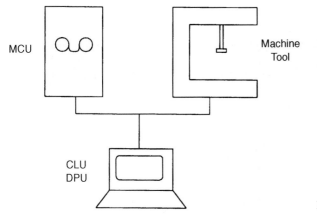

Figure 9.2 An NC machine system.

- velocity-control loops, where feed control is required
- deceleration and backlash takeup circuits
- auxiliary function control, such as coolant on/off, gear changes, and spindle on/off control

As mentioned previously, the motion control of NC machine tools is completed by translating NC codes into machine commands. The NC codes can be broadly classified into two groups, as shown in Figure 9.3: (1) commands for controlling individual machine components, such as motor on/off control, selection of spindle speed, tool

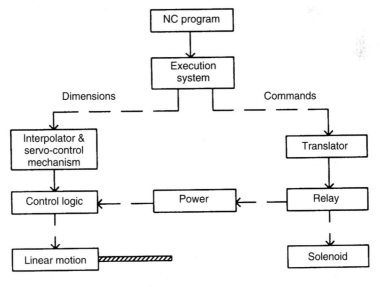

Figure 9.3 NC motion-control commands.

change, and coolant on/off control (these tasks are accomplished by sending electric pulses to the relay system or logic control network); and (2) commands for controlling the relative movement of the workpiece and cutting tools. These commands consist of such information as axis and distance to be moved at each specific time unit. They are translated into machine-executable, motion-control commands that are then carried out by the electromechanical control system.

9.3 CLASSIFICATION OF NUMERICAL CONTROL

NC machines can be classified as follows:

1. Motion control: point to point (PTP) and continuous (contouring) path
2. Control loops: open loop and closed loop
3. Power drives: hydraulic, electric, or pneumatic
4. Positioning systems: incremental and absolute positioning
5. Hardwired NC and softwired computer numerical control (CNC)

9.3.1 Motion Control: Point to Point and Continuous Path

There are two types of motion-control systems for NC machines, namely, point-to-point and continuous-path control. The function of a PTP motion-control system is to move the machine table or spindle to a specified position so that machining operations may be performed at that point. The path taken to reach the specific point is not defined by the programmer in such a system (Figure 9.4). Because this movement from one point to the next is nonmachining, it is made as rapidly as possible, usually at a rate of more than 100 ipm. Figure 9.5 illustrates some paths that may be taken between the two points *P* and *Q*. If the job is to drill the same-sized holes at points *P* and *Q*, the programmer does not need to specify the path used to reach the points. In most cases, however, path *B* is taken in a PTP NC machine. A PTP NC machine is able to perform simple milling

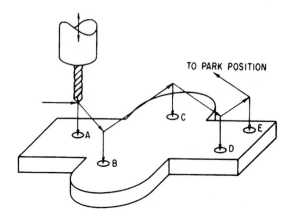

Figure 9.4   PTP motion control. (J. J. Childs, *Principles of Numerical Control,* 1982. Courtesy of Industrial Press.)

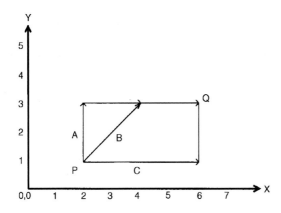

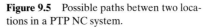

Figure 9.5 Possible paths betwen two locations in a PTP NC system.

operations if the machine is equipped with a feed-control mechanism. With most PTP machines, the only directions that are accurately controlled are straight lines parallel to the machine axes, that is, right and left, forward and backward. "Picture frames" can be easily done in such a manner on a PTP machine.

In a continuous (contouring) control system, the machine controls two or more axes simultaneously. The machine controls not only the destinations, but also the paths through which the tool reaches these destinations. In the process of machining, the tool contacts the workpiece, and desired shapes are made, as shown in Figure 9.6. Suppose that a slot is to be cut from left to right at 30°, as shown in Figure 9.7. Notice that as the table (or spindle) moves 4.330 in. to the right, it must move up 2.500 in. and travels 5.0000 in. on the diagonal. This type of cut requires the two driving motors to run simultaneously at two different speeds. This contouring control system is more expensive than PTP equipment.

Control of the travel rate in two (or more) directions, proportional to the distance moved, is called linear interpolation. If V_f if the desired velocity along the line of motion, the velocities along the two axes, V_x and V_y, are

$$V_x = \frac{\Delta x}{(\Delta x^2 + \Delta y^2)^{1/2}} V_f \qquad (9.1)$$

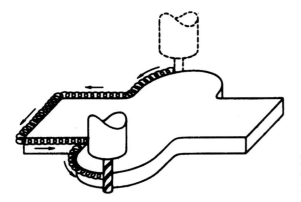

Figure 9.6 Continuous-path control. (J. J. Childs, *Principles of Numerical Control,* 1982. Courtesy of Industrial Press.)

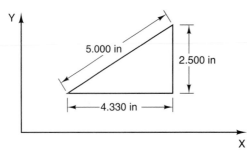

Figure 9.7 Continuous-path control using linear interpolation.

$$V_y = \frac{\Delta y}{(\Delta x^2 + \Delta y^2)^{1/2}} V_f \tag{9.2}$$

where Δx and Δy are displacements along the X and Y axes, respectively.

9.3.2 Control Loops

When there is position feedback, the NC system is considered to be a closed-loop system; otherwise, it is an open-loop system. Obviously, the advantage of a closed-loop system is its positioning accuracy. Because high precision is required of most NC machines, the majority of NC machines use a closed-loop control system. Most closed-loop systems control use servo motors (either DC or AC). A position transducer returns the current table position. When the table reaches the programmed position, the motor stops running.

Open-loop control can be found in some light application NC machines. Open-loop NC machines normally use stepping-motor drives. The stepping motor is controlled through a digital signal. Each pulse of the signal turns the motor a small fixed angle (step angle). This movement is also translated to the table to move a distance of one BLU (basic length unit).

9.3.3 Power Drives

The majority of modern NC machines use a DC or AC servo motor to drive its axes and the spindle. Their small size, ease of control, and low cost are a few of the advantages of servo motors. In some large machines, hydraulic drives are used. A hydraulic motor has a much larger power/size ratio. For the same size as a DC motor, it can drive a much larger load at a greater acceleration. However, difficult maintenance, increased noise, and a bulky off-the-machine hydraulic power supply have limited hydraulic drive use. Pneumatic drives are rarely used in NC positioning system due to the difficulty of maintaining a precise continuous motion and position. However, they can be used to drive the auxiliary devices attached to the machine.

9.3.4 Positioning Systems

Whether a machine uses an incremental or absolute positioning system depends on the position transducers used. When the transducer reports the absolute position of the machine table, the machine is an absolute positioning machine. However, modern NC machines also allow the user to choose the types of positioning system through software. Regardless of the hardware, a user may program the machine in an incremental, absolute, or mixed positioning system. The coordinates are tracked by the software. In an absolute-positioning-system NC machine, the coordinate origin also can be reset. A machine that allows its coordinate origin to be reset is called a floating-zero machine; others are called fixed-zero. Floating-zero machines have the advantage of allowing the user to program a part using the part coordinates and set the machine origin at the part coordinate origin.

9.3.5 NC and CNC

The difference between NC and CNC lies in controller technology. At the time when NC was invented, the computer was a rarity. The NC system was built using a dedicated vacuum-tube circuit, a transistor, and relay technology. Other than simply binary addition and substraction, these early controllers could not perform much of what a digital computer can. There was little system software per se. Every NC function had to be designed and implemented in hardware circuits. It was not until in the late 1960s when minicomputers became available on the shop floor (it was proposed in 1969) that a minicomputer was used to replace the hardwired NC controller. NC functions then could be implemented in software. However, minicomputers were still expensive compared to the cost of a machine tool. In the late 1970s and 1980s, microcomputers were introduced to NC. Microcomputers are small in size, low in cost, and high in performance. Many of today's CNC controllers are based on existing microcomputers. They use an industrial-grade, general-purpose computer as the hardware platform. The computer operating system, the development environment, and the existing software all can be used in an NC controller. On many CNC controllers, one can find data communication, color graphics, file management, editing, and so on. Some controllers even allow the user to include customized functions. CNC has also made the integration of machine tools with the rest of the manufacturing system possible.

Since the 1980s, no hardwired NCs have been produced. Today, when the term NC is mentioned, it normally means CNC.

9.4 NUMERICAL-CONTROL SYSTEM

The fundamental components that comprise a numerical-control installation and their functions are described in this section. Figure 9.8 shows a cutaway view of a horizontal NC machining center. The machine controller and the servo controls are located in a cabinet on the right side of the figure. The spindle, machine table, tool changer, tool magazine, and the three-axis leadscrew, ways, and motors can be seen in the figure. The major components of a numerical-control system are also shown in a block diagram in Figure 9.9.

The NC system controller consists of a mechanism for automatically reading the tape and the electronic hardware and software for converting the coded tape information into machine-tool instructions. The controller is the heart of the NC operation and

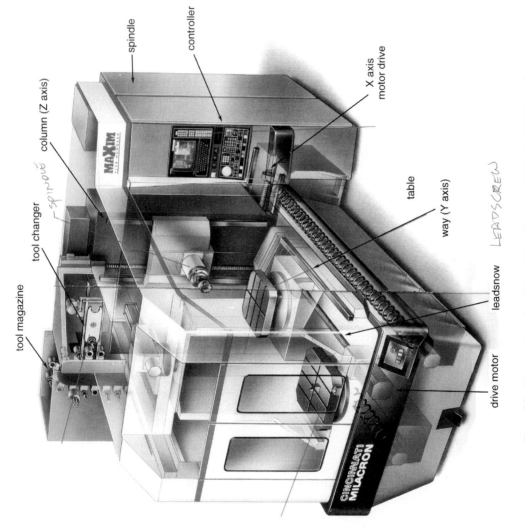

spindle

controller

column (Z axis)

X axis
motor drive

tool changer

spindle

tool magazine

table

way (Y axis)

leadsnow

LEADSCREW

drive motor

Figure 9.8 The structure of an NC machine. (Courtesy of Cincinnati Milacron).

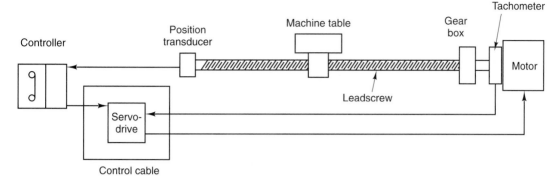

Figure 9.9   Major components comprising an NC machine tool.

constitutes a significant portion of the overall equipment cost of NC installation. The size of the machine has little effect on the size or complexity of the controller.

Between the controller and the machine are a number of nonelectronic items that are not normally found in conventional machine tools. The operator's console contains the necessary controls for operating the machine manually, thus offering the facility for "setting up" workpieces. The console may be on a pedestal, in a rolling cabinet, or in an overhanging pendant. The main distinction between this console and the "operator panels" on conventional machine tools is in the increased number of command switches and buttons, some of which may be duplicates of those on the panel of the controller.

Another major item of the system is the magnetics-control cabinet. This unit contains the magnetic relays and starting switches for controlling the flow of electrical power to the hydraulic and coolant pumps, spindle motor, and other electric devices. These devices within the magnetics box are controlled by signals from the controller.

The prime mover of an NC system is a motor. Although hydraulic motors are used in some machine tools, the majority of machine tools use electric motors. The electric motor is typically connected to a leadscrew (Figure 9.10, the center screw) through a gear box or coupling, with the machine table riding on two ways (Figure 9.10). As the leadscrew turns, the nut attached to the table and constrained from rotating moves the table along the ways. A tachometer is also attached to the motor spindle to give feedback to the servo drive. Based on the location feedback received from a position transducer and a speed command, the controller sends an analog signal to the servo drive, which in turn controls the motor rotation. A transducer is a device that transforms one physical phenomenon to another, for example, from table position to a digital signal.

As the leadscrew rotates, the feedback device, which may be attached to either end of the leadscrew or may reside entirely independent of the leadscrew (e.g., on a rotating table or motor shaft) records the movement and sends back a signal to the controller. The controller compares the signal with the input instructions as described by the tape, and continues to send signals to the servo drive until a balanced condition exists between the command signals as read from the tape and the feedback signals as generated by movement of the machine components.

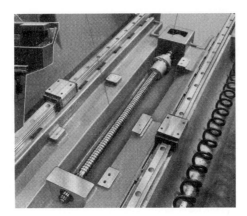

Figure 9.10   Leadscrew and machine ways (Courtesy of Cincinnati Milacron).

9.4.1 NC Accuracy and Repeatability

An NC machine is usually rated by the following factors: accuracy, repeatability, spindle and axis-motor horsepower, number of controlled axes, dimension of workspace, and features of the machine and the controller. The accuracy of the NC machine is the result of a combination of the control instrumentation resolution and hardware accuracy. The control resolution is the minimum length distinguishable by the control unit. It is called the basic length unit (BLU), and is determined primarily by the axis transducer and leadscrew that are used. Hardware inaccuracies are caused by physical machine errors. There are many sources of errors in a machine, caused by component tolerances. Such errors include inaccuracies in the machine elements, machine-tool assembly errors, spindle runout, and leadscrew backlash (see Section 9.4.4). Another type of error is related to machine operation. Tool deflection, whose magnitude is a function of the cutting force, produces dimensional error and chatter marks on the finished part. Thermal error, which can be more critical than the deflection error, is caused by thermal expansion of machine elements. The heat sources during machine operation include heat generated by the motor operation, cutting process, friction on the ways and bearings, and so on. Because the temperature on various parts of the machine differs, the error caused by the thermal effect is not uniform. Because thermal error is normally the greatest source of machine error, many methods are used to remove heat from a machine. Using cutting fluids, locating drive motors away from the center of a machine, and reducing friction from the ways and bearings are a few conventional techniques used. In precision machining, a strictly controlled environment is used to ensure a constant temperature. Machine accuracy is an absolute measurement. Normal accuracy is specified as the machine error plus one-half the control resolution. The manufacturer-rated machine accuracy does not include machine-operation-related error. The actual accuracy can vary significantly from the rated accuracy.

Repeatability is another measure of machine accuracy. It is a measure of how closely a machine repeats a given position command. If a machine always goes to a fixed position, then it is said to be highly repeatable, even if the position is very far from the command position. Repeatability is measured as the diameter of the circle enclosing a target area produced by many repeated experiments (Figure 9.11).

Spindle power and axis power are important in the operation of a machine. The type of material being processed and the material removal rate can be constrained by these factors. The number of axes of a machine determines the geometric complexity

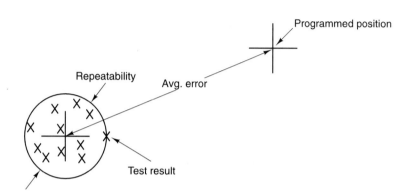

Figure 9.11   Accuracy and repeatability.

of the parts that the machine is able to produce. For most parts, a three-axis machine is sufficient, however, many aerospace and aircraft parts require four-, five-, and even six-axis machines. The additional axes make the construction of the machine, the control, and the programming of the part more difficult.

9.4.2 Prime Movers

The prime mover of a machine is the power source that moves the table and the spindle. It usually determines the range of the machine's performance capabilities and, in turn, its feasibility for various applications. The two major power sources are hydraulic and electric.

9.4.2.1 Hydraulic power drive.   A hydraulic power drive consists of a hydraulic motor (the prime mover), a hydraulic pump (which delivers hydraulic power to the motor), an electric motor (which drives the pump), and a servo valve (which controls the flow of hydraulic fluid). See Figure 9.12. Hydraulic power drives can deliver large torques and fast responses so that the machine moves with uniform speed. The power/size ratio is relatively large. Hydraulics are used for many large and heavy-duty

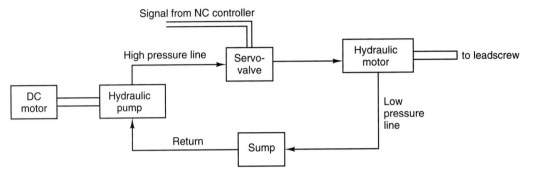

Figure 9.12   A hydraulic power drive.

machines. The major disadvantages of hydraulic power drives are high cost, additional peripherals required, noise, response lag due to delay caused by hydraulic fluid viscosity, and contamination from leaking fluid.

The rotational speed of a motor is determined by the power output of the motor divided by the amount of torque required to move the load. The output power of a hydraulic motor depends on the input power. There are two factors in the input: pressure and flow rate. The input pressure is set at the pump and remains constant. A DC motor is operated automatically to maintain the output of the hydraulic pump at this constant pressure. The control variable is therefore the flow rate. The flow rate of a hydraulic power drive is controlled by a servo valve. The opening and the closing of the valve are proportional to the signal level (voltage) sent from a NC controller. The faster one wants to turn the motor, the higher the signal level. The following calculations show these relationships.

The servo valve output flow rate is

$$q = k_v V \tag{9.3}$$

where

   q = output flow rate, in^3/s
   k_v = valve constant
   V = signal voltage, volt

The power of the motor is

$$pq = T_m \omega \tag{9.4}$$

where

   p = input pressure, psi
   q = input flow rate, in^3/s
   T_m = output torque, in. lb
   ω = angular speed, rad/s

The steady-state rotational speed of the motor is

$$\omega = Kq \tag{9.5}$$

where K is the motor constant.

9.4.2.2 Electric power drives.

Electric drives are most applicable for precision jobs or when close precision control is desired. Sophisticated motion-control features are typical of electrical NC machines. There are two major groups of electrical drives, namely, stepping motors and servomotors.

Stepping Motors.   Basically, a stepping motor is an electromechanical actuator that translates digital electrical signals into fixed mechanical rotation. Whereas conventional motors rotate continuously when energized, a stepping motor rotates in angular increments. Due to the ease of control, stepping motors have been used in a wide variety of applications, including NC, robots, printers, plotters, VCRs, and cameras,

Stepping motors are manufactured in a wide range of step angles and power capabilities. Sizes range from 1-in.-diameter pancake-type motors, producing less than 1 oz-in. of torque, to 7-in.-diameter units weighing 75 lb. These can produce more than 3 hp of usable shaft output power. Typical step angles vary from 0.72° to 90°, with 1.8°, 7.5°, and 15° being the most popular.

Figure 9.13 illustrates a stepping motor. The motor is driven by four signals. When the pattern of the signals shift, the motor rotates one step. The direction of rotation depends on the pattern-shifting direction. For example, if the current signal pattern is (Step 1) 1 0 1 0 to rotate clockwise one step, the next pattern should be 1 0 0 1. To step counterclockwise, a pattern 0 1 1 0 is required. The pattern can be generated directly by a microcomputer or in many cases by a dedicated stepping-motor controller board. A microcomputer sends one stepping signal and a direction signal. The controller converts the information into the four control bits.

The number of steps (displacement) is determined by the number of signals (pulses) received. The speed of a stepping motor is determined by the rate at which the

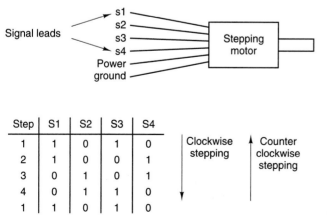

Step	S1	S2	S3	S4
1	1	0	1	0
2	1	0	0	1
3	0	1	0	1
4	0	1	1	0
1	1	0	1	0

Clockwise stepping

Counter clockwise stepping

Figure 9.13   A stepping motor.

signals (pulse rate) are received. For example, if we would like to turn a 1.8° step angle motor 2000 steps at 360 rpm, what is the number of pulses and pulse rate to be sent to the motor?

The number of pulses should be the same as the desired steps. Therefore, it is 2000 pulses.

$$360 \text{ rpm} = 360 \text{ rev/min/60 s/min} = 6 \text{ rev/s}$$

Number of steps per revolution, N:

$$N = 360°/1.8° = 200 \text{ steps/rev}$$
$$\text{Pulse rate} = 6 \text{ rev/s} \times 200 \text{ steps/rev} = 1200 \text{ pulses/s}$$

As mentioned previously, stepping motors are suitable for open-loop control. In general, the following conditions are for stepping-motor applications: (1) the torque requirement is from a fraction of an oz-in. to several thousand oz-in.; (2) the power required is less than 1 hp; (3) the speed range is from 0 to 300 rpm; and (4) the positional accuracy is from 1 to 5% of the motor step angle.

Because of its digital nature, the stepping motor provides many advantages: (1) It is directly compatible with digital methods; (2) it provides accurate positioning with noncumulative errors; (3) its construction is simple and rugged; and (4) it provides bidirectional rotation and control with no additional control complexity.

However, there are two areas where a stepping motor can run into operating problems: (1) Operating the motor at or near its natural resonance can lead to substantial ringing, which can result in loss of control. (2) In a certain speed range, stepping motors can develop spontaneous velocity modulations. These often continue to increase in amplitude until loss of synchronization occurs.

Servo Motors.   Servo motors are those controlled using a feedback mechanism. A transducer feedback and a speed control form a servo loop. There are two types of servo motors: DC and AC servo motors. A DC motor is controlled through a voltage change. When a higher voltage is applied to the motor, a large current flows through the motor coil, which in turn produces more torque and makes the motor run faster. An AC motor is a synchromotor, where the speed of the motor is determined by the frequency of the power source. The higher the power-source frequency, the faster the motor rotation. This is called frequency control. Because it is easier to control voltage changes, most of the early NC machines used DC motors exclusively. However, currently both DC and AC motors are used in a variety of NC equipment. In this chapter, however, we will limit our discussion to DC servo motors.

A DC motor consists of the following parts: stator (field), rotor (armature), commutator, bearing, and housing. The stator is an electromagnet that creates a strong field. There may be several sets of stator electromagnets, called poles. The rotor consists of several individual coils forming electromagnets. At any given time, only one rotor coil per pole is activated. By activating the rotor electromagnets in an order and ahead of the stator field, the rotor electromagnet is attracted to the field poles and keeps the rotor turning. The distribution of the electricity to the armature coil is done through commutators. Commutators are carbon brushes that touch the copper conductors on the rotor (Figure 9.14). The most popular DC motor is the permanent-magnet DC motor

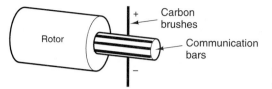

Figure 9.14   The commutator of a DC motor.

(PM DC motor). A PM DC motor uses permanent magnets to create the magnetic fields. Unlike an electromagnet, it provides a constant and reliable magnetic field. The speed of the motor is limited by the sliding of the brush against the commutation bars and the bearing rating.

When one puts a permanent magnet in the rotor and winding in the stator, a brushless DC motor results. Because there is no brush commutator to change the rotor-field direction, the commutation must be done on the stator coil through electronics.

A DC servo motor consists of a speed transducer, a DC motor and a servo drive (Figure 9.15). The speed transducer is a tachometer. A tachometer is a DC generator. At low speed, the tachometer output is low, the output of the differential amplifier is high, and thus the acceleration of the motor is high. When the desired speed has been reached, the tachometer feedback cancels the velocity command (a voltage), and motor acceleration stops. This ensures that the proper speed of the motor is controlled.

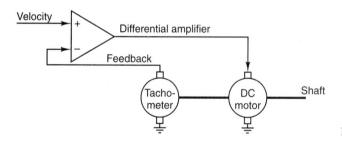

Figure 9.15   A DC servo-motor system.

9.4.3 Transducers

A transducer is a device that transforms one physical phenomenon to another. Two major kinds of transducers are used in NC systems: position transducers and speed transducers. A typical speed transducer is the tachometer that we mentioned earlier. As for position transducers, there are several different types used.

9.4.3.1 Speed transducer.   As mentioned, a tachometer is a DC generator. The output signal level of a tachometer is directly proportional to its rotational speed. It can be characterized by the following equation.

$$v = K_t \omega \qquad (9.6)$$

where

v = output voltage, volts

ω = shaft angular speed, rad/s

K_t = tachometer constant, volts/rad

9.4.3.2 Position transducer. Position transducers are used in closed-loop systems for position feedback. There are several types of position transducers. The most popular ones used in NC machines are encoders, resolvers, LVDTs or Linear Variable Differential Transformer, and inductosyns. All of these devices transform the position information into electrical signals. Due to its low cost and ease of use, encoders are most commonly used in NC machines.

Encoders. Encoders usually are arranged to measure angular displacement. They output digital signals. The construction of an encoder is rather simple. It consists of a light source, a glass disk with painted patterns, and a photoelectric sensor (Figure 9.16). The light emitted from the light source, usually a photodiode, can either pass or be blocked by the pattern on the glass. It is detected by the photoelectric sensor when the light passes through the glass. The output is a series of electric pulses. A Schmitt-trigger device is used to convert the output signal into a square-wave signal. The resolution of an encoder depends on the number of blackened cells painted on one ring (track) of the disk. For example, if an encoder has 100 blackened cells per track, the resolution is $360°/100 = 3.6°$. When the shaft turns one rotation, the encoder outputs 100 pulses.

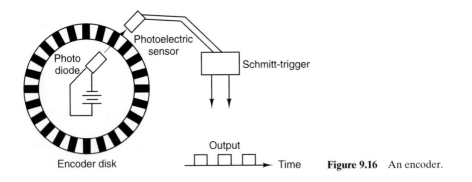

Figure 9.16   An encoder.

There are two types of encoders: incremental and absolute. Figure 9.16 illustrates the structure of an incremental encoder. The output is a series of pulses. There is no reference of the actual position. In order to determine the actual position, an external device must keep track of the output and accumulate the position count. For example, from a home position, the encoder registered two motions. The first motion outputs 1000 pulses and the second one outputs 300 pulses. The current position can be summed up to be $(1000 + 300)/100 = 13$ rotations. When connecting an incremental encoder to a DC motor, it acts somewhat like a stepping motor. The encoder resolution is equivalent to the stepping-motor resolution. However, a controller is needed to count the pulses received and to determine whether to continue the motor rotation or stop.

An absolute encoder is more complicated than an incremental encoder. It outputs a binary number denoting the rotational angle from a reference on the encoder shaft. Several tracks of patterns are painted on the disk. Each row of the pattern has coded position information.

The output of an incremental encoder can be characterized by the following equation.

$$f = K_e \omega \tag{9.7}$$

where

f = output pulse frequency, pulses/s
ω = input angular speed, rpm
K_e = encoder gain

The output of an absolute encoder is the shaft angle.

Resolvers.   A resolver (Figure 9.17) is similar to an AC generator, which is an analog device. There is an input AC signal and an output AC signal. The voltage level of both outputs are the same but the phases are different. The shaft angle can be measured directly by comparing the phase difference between the input and the output.

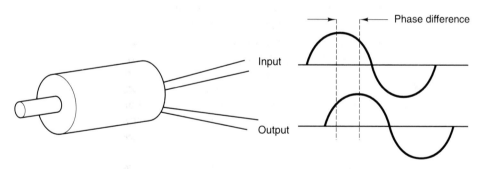

Figure 9.17   A resolver.

The output of a resolver is

$$v = V \sin(\omega t + \varphi) \tag{9.8}$$

where

V = input voltage, volts
φ = shaft angle
ωt = input signal phase

LVDTs. An LVDT (linear variable differential transformer; Figure 9.18) consists of a metal bar and a moving ring with coil windings. There is an input winding and an output winding. The input is an analog reference signal, and the output is also an analog signal. Depending on the relative position between the ring and the core (metal bar), the output level is changed. Position can be read directly from the signal. LVDTs are not as widely used as the other types of position transducers.

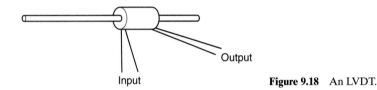

Input   **Figure 9.18** An LVDT.

Inductosyns. Inductosyn is a trade name of a position transducer produced by Farrand Controls. It is a direct position-reading transducer. It consists of two parts: a stator and a rotor (not necessary rotational). For linear measurement, the stator is a scale that can be attached to the machine bed, and the rotor is a slide that can be mounted to the machine table. For angular measurement, the stator and the rotor are both disks. The relative position between the rotor and the stator can be read directly from the rotor output. Because the output is the actual position of the machine table, it is more accurate than the indirect measurement of encoders and resolvers. In the latter case, the shaft rotation is translated to the linear motion of the table based on the physical connection. The error between the table position and the shaft is usually not considered.

9.4.4 Leadscrews

Another important component of an NC machine is the leadscrew (Figure 9.9). The rotational motion of the motors is converted to a linear motion by a leadscrew. The leadscrew is coupled with the machine table through a nut. The machine table is confined to a linear motion by two slides (ways). When the leadscrew turns, the machine table is forced to move along the slides. As discussed before, heat generated by the friction has to be reduced. A precision grounded ball-bearing leadscrew (Figure 9.19) is normally used in NC machines. To reduced backlash, the ball bearings are preloaded. Backlash is caused by the free play of the screw and the nut. When there is a gap between the screw thread and the nut thread, and the rotation is reversed, the threads are not engaged. Preloading the ball bearing ensures the proper contact between the leadscrew thread, ball bearing, and the nut screw thread.

The pitch of the leadscrew determines the resolution a machine can achieve. The pitch (p) is defined as the distance between adjacent screw threads (Figure 9.20), and is related to the number of teeth per inch (n):

$$n = 1/p \tag{9.9}$$

For each screw rotation, the nut advances a distance equal to the pitch.

Figure 9.19   Preloaded ball nut and leadscrew.

The machine BLU is determined by the leadscrew pitch and the position-transducer resolution. The rotational position-transducer resolution coupled to the leadscrew has N pulses per revolution resolution; then the BLU of the machine is

$$\text{BLU} = p/N \qquad (9.10)$$

For example, an NC machine uses a 0.1-in. pitch leadscrew and a 100-pulse/rev encoder. The BLU for the machine is

$$\text{BLU} = p/N = 0.1 \text{ in./rev}/100 \text{ pulses/rev} = 0.001 \text{ in.}$$

The same formula can be used in stepping-motor control. For example, if the same leadscrew is used in a stepping-motor system, and the stepping motor has 100 steps/rev; the BLU of this machine is the same as the preceding one

$$\text{BLU} = 0.1/100 = 0.001 \text{ in.}$$

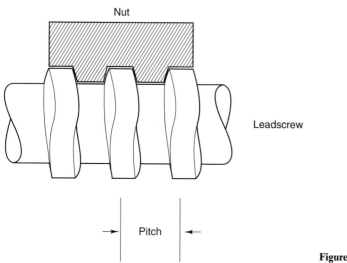

Figure 9.20   A typical screw thread.

Figure 9.9 illustrates one axis of an NC system. In the figure, a gear box is used between the motor and the position transducer. The gear box does not affect the resolution of the machine, because its influence is outside the position transducer and leadscrew loop.

9.4.5 Control Loops

There are open- and closed-loop NC systems. As discussed before, open-loop systems are normally used only on small and low-power machines. The majority of NC systems use closed-loop control. Figure 9.21 illustrates the concept of open-loop control. In this scheme, the controller is used as an on-line processor of programs and data to generate specific commands for the manipulation of machine and process actuators. Open-loop principles are also employed in the use of computers to manipulate electric or electro-hydraulic stepping motors for machine tool control. In an open-loop control system, the controller first converts the speed and displacement commands into pulse rate and pulse count. A timer is used to generate the desired pulse rate. The output of the timer is sent to the stepping motor and at the same time sent to a down counter. The counter is loaded with the pulse count. When the count value reaches zero, the pulse is stopped from reaching the motor. With this simple control scheme, the motor will rotate at the desired speed for a desired number of rotations. The following example illustrates the operation of an open-loop system.

In a system similar to the one shown in Figure 9.21, the BLU = 0.001 in. It is desired to move the table 5 in. at a speed (feed rate) of 6 ipm. The pulse rate and pulse count can be calculated as follows:

$$\text{pulse rate} = \text{speed/BLU} = 6 \text{ ipm}/0.001 \text{ ipp} = 6000 \text{ pulses/min}$$

$$= 6000/60 = 100 \text{ pulses/s}$$

$$\text{pulse count} = \text{distance/BLU} = 5/0.001 = 5000 \text{ pulses}$$

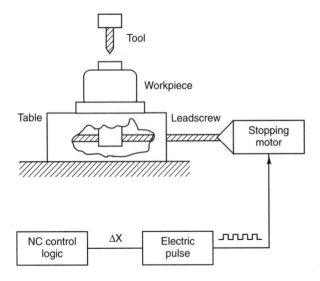

Figure 9.21 Open-loop control mechanism.

A timer is programmed to generate 100 pulses/s and the down counter is loaded with 5000 pulses. In order to completely automate a machine tool, it is inevitably necessary to develop control systems that have the capability of comparing a desired set of results with actual results and to take corrective action. This is the essence of closed-loop feedback control. The system shown in Figure 9.22 is an incremental system using an encoder as the feedback transducer and a proportional-error-control controller (the output control signal is proportional to the desired position and the feedback signal). In the figure, the DC motor, tachometer, gear box, encoder, and leadscrew are physically connected. The arrows show the direction of the control information flow. The input to the system is a reference signal that is the same as the one used in the stepping-motor drive. Certain number of pulses at certain pulse rate is sent to the up-down counter. When a pulse is received, the counter increments its value. The counter value (a binary number) is converted into an analog signal by a digital-to-analog converter (DAC). The magnitude of this signal determines the motor speed. One can see that the higher the reference pulse rate, the higher the counter value can be. A comparator/amplifier/motor/tachometer circuit makes sure that the motor accelerates to the desired speed (see discussions in Section 9.4.2). The motor shaft is connected to an encoder through a gear box. When the motor turns, the encoder returns pulses to the up-down counter. The counter value is decremented by the feedback encoder pulses. The higher the reference pulse rate, the higher the counter value, thus, the greater the motor acceleration. When the desired speed has been reached, the motor stops accelerating, but maintains its speed. When the motor turns, the counter value is decremented. When the destination is reached, the counter value should be zero and the motor stops. The motor accelerates at the beginning of the motion, reaches a steady-state speed, and then decelerates before stopping at the desired position.

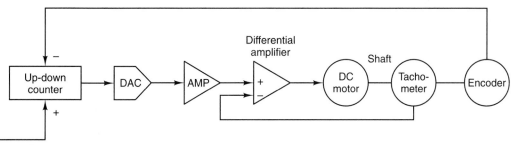

Figure 9.22   Closed-loop control mechanism.

9.4.6 Interpolation

So far our discussion has been limited to the control of a single axis. Normally at least two axes are needed to control a machine like a lathe or a drill press (for fixed-Z drilling applications). The majority of the applications require three-axis control. For a two-axis,

point-to-point machine, one can simply put two individual single axis controllers together. As long as the tool reaches the desired position, the exact path is not important.
For example, in Figure 9.23, the tool moves from (3,2) to 10,5). Both the X and Y axes
move at the same speed, and the resultant tool path is shown in the figure. The tool path
is acceptable for drilling operations, however, it is not for milling or turning. In order to
control the tool to move in a straight line, it is necessary to control the speed of each
axis, so that both axes reach the destination at the same time (Figure 9.24).

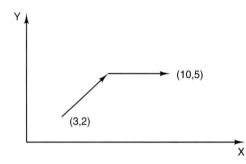

X   **Figure 9.23**   Point-to-point control path.

Using the preceding example, if the desired feed rate is 6 ipm, the speed components on the X and Y axes are [using Equations (9.1) and (9.2):

$$V_x = 6 \frac{10 - 3}{[(10 - 3)^2 + (5 - 2)^2]^{1/2}} = 6 \frac{7}{[49 + 9]^{1/2}} = 5.5149 \text{ in./min}$$

$$V_x = 6 \frac{5 - 2}{[(10 - 3)^2 + (5 - 2)^2]^{1/2}} = 6 \frac{3}{[49 + 9]^{1/2}} = 2.3635 \text{ in./min}$$

If BLU equals 0.001 in., the pulse rate in X is 5515 pulses/min, in Y is 2364 pulses/
min. Although this probably will work, there is no guarantee that the result is a perfect
line. Even though the velocity components are set correctly, there is no synchronization
beyond the start of the motion. In order to get as close to the desired line as possible,
both axes must be coordinated closely. This is called linear interpolation. Linear interpolation is available on nearly all NC machines.

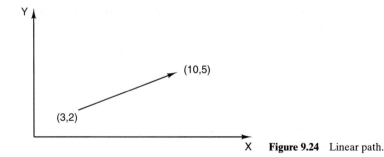

X   **Figure 9.24**   Linear path.

Circles are also frequently used in many parts. Circular arcs also can be used to approximate high-order curves. Although a circle can be approximated by line segments, it is more desirable to control the machine to interpolate a circle directly with minimum error. The function of a circular interpolator is to move the tool automatically on a circular arc without external approximation. There are also parabolic or other higher-order interpolators available on some specialized machines. Virtually all CNC machines provide both linear and circular interpolation capabilities.

The idea of interpolation is to generate a series of fixed-sized steps in order to approximate a geometric feature that is not directly attainable. The maximum deviation of the tool path is kept within one step. Because the interpolation is right above the servo level, speed is critical, and the process must not involve excessive computation. The computation unit must keep up with the maximum feed rate. Traditional NC interpolators were implemented directly in hardware. The speed is driven by a clock pulses. A simple differential equation approach is used in the interpolator design. The differential equations for complex shapes are implemented in a network of devices called digital differential analyzers (DDAs). When a DDA is used, there is no calculation needed. The controller can take directly the part program instruction and execute it. A replacement is a programmable timer. The timer can generate the desired pulse rate for each axis. In a modern CNC machine, interpolators are frequently implemented in software.

For higher-order curves that cannot be implemented easily in an on-line interpolator, off-line approximation algorithms are applied. Such algorithms break down the curve into either line segments or circular arcs before feeding them into a NC machine. One example of higher-order curves is a free-form curve or free-form surface (see Chapter 3). The approximation of such a curve is discussed in Chapter 10.

9.4.6.1 Linear interpolator.   A linear function of time can be represented as

$$x = at + b \qquad (9.11)$$

In a digital system, the time is divided into small increments called clock cycles (same as pulses), Δt. The linear function can be written in a difference form:

$$x_i = a \sum_{j=1}^{i} \Delta t + b = x_{i-1} + a\,\Delta t \qquad (9.12)$$

A simple device, a DDA (Figure 9.25), is built to carry out the preceding computation. The input to the DDA is clock pulses. Each time a pulse (frequency: f) is received, the value of the register (a value) is added to the accumulator. When the accumulator overflows, the overflow bit is output to the motor control up-down counter (x value). Δt is determined by the accumulator width.

$$\Delta t = \frac{1}{2^N} \qquad (9.13)$$

where N is the width of the accumulator (bits).

For example, an 8-bit accumulator has a $\Delta t = 1/256 = 0.00390625$. The index j in Equation (9.12) denotes the input pulse.

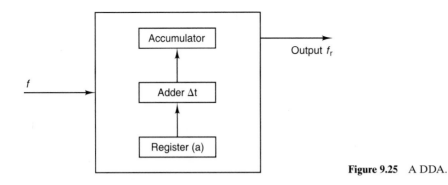

Figure 9.25 A DDA.

The relationship of the output frequency and the input frequency can be expressed as

$$f_r = \frac{af}{2^N} \tag{9.14}$$

where

f_r = output frequency, Hz
a = register value
N = accumulator width, bit
f = input clock frequency, Hz

To control two axes, two DDAs are used (Figure 9.26) with a single-input clock signal driving the two DDAs. Each DDA is loaded with appropriate register values. The output pulses are sent to the axis control up-down counters. Because a DDA acts like a pulse divider, to control the feed rate, one can simply add another DDA to the input (Figure 9.26).

The feed-rate control DDA can be developed as follows:

$$f = \frac{a_f f_c}{2^{N_f}} \tag{9.15}$$

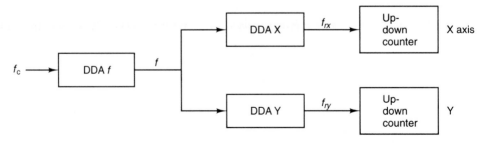

Figure 9.26 Two-axis control.

where

$$a_f = \text{DDA } f \text{ register value}$$
$$N_f = \text{DDA } f \text{ width}$$
$$f_c = \text{controller clock pulse}$$

The output to the axis control is

$$f_r = \frac{a_f f_c}{2^{N_f}} \frac{a}{2^N} = \frac{a a_f}{2^{N_f+N}} f_c \tag{9.16}$$

A conventional NC controller is not equipped to compute the speed components, V_x, and V_y, from the feed rate as we did earlier. A scheme can be implemented to take care of this deficiency. The a value for each axis is loaded with the BLU value of each incremental motion. By using our earlier example to move the tool from (3,2) to (10,5) at the 6-ipm feed rate, the following values are loaded in the DDAs:

$$a_x = (10 - 3) \text{ in./0.001 in./step} = 7000 \text{ steps}$$
$$a_y = (5 - 2) \text{ in./0.001 in./step} = 3000 \text{ steps}$$

From our earlier calculation, we know that f_{rx} has to be 5515 and f_{ry} 2364. They are computed as follows:

$$f_{rx} = V_f \frac{\Delta x}{(\Delta x^2 + \Delta y^2)^{1/2}}$$

from Equation (9.1) (all length units in BLUs). Combine Equations (9.1) and (9.16):

$$\frac{a_x a_f}{2^{N_f+N}} f_c = V_f \frac{\Delta x}{(\Delta x^2 + \Delta y^2)^{1/2}} \tag{9.17}$$

Because a_x is set to Δx, they both can be eliminated from Equation (9.17).

$$\frac{a_f}{2^{N_f+N}} f_c = \frac{V_f}{(\Delta x^2 + \Delta y^2)^{1/2}}$$

$$a_f = \frac{V_f}{(\Delta x^2 + \Delta y^2)^{1/2}} \frac{2^{N_f+N}}{f_c} \tag{9.18}$$

Notice that $2^{N_f+N}/f_c$ is a constant based on hardware design. If we set this value to A, then

$$a_f = \frac{A V_f}{(\Delta x^2 + \Delta y^2)^{1/2}} \tag{9.19}$$

If we load the feed-rate-control DDA (the a_f value) and each axis DDAs with the incremental displacement value, then the resultant motion will be at the desired feed rate. No additional internal computation is needed to compute the speed components. Actually, Equation (9.19) provides the definition of the inverse time code used in conventional NC feed-rate programming. Of course, in CNC machines, this is not necessary, because feed-rate conversion can be done easily via computer.

The following example illustrates the operation of a simplified DDA interpolator.

$$N = 3$$
$$\Delta x = 4 \text{ BLUs}$$
$$\Delta y = 3 \text{ BLUs}$$

Figure 9.27 illustrates the operation of the DDAs. First, the Δx value, 4 (binary 100), and the Δy value, 3 (binary 011), are loaded into the corresponding DDA registers. When the clock sends a pulse to the DDAs, they each add their register value to the accumulator. In the table, the X and the Y columns show the corresponding accumulator value in binary. At clock cycle 2, there is an overflow of DDA x, the X counter value is 1. At clock cycle 3, the Y counter also receives an overflow. The operation continues until the destination is reached at clock cycle 8. The diagram in Figure 9.27 shows the tool motion. Note that each motion is within 1 BLU, the best precision that any machine can achieve.

DDAs can also be simulated through software. The software can run either in a loop (not recommended) or be driven by an interrupt (see Chapter 8).

A DDA can also be replaced by a programmable timer. The input to the timer is a clock of frequency f. The register value is p, which is loaded by the CPU. The word length of the timer is N. The output frequency of the timer is

$$f_r = \frac{pf}{2^N} \tag{9.20}$$

$$p = \frac{f_r 2^N}{f} \tag{9.21}$$

Clock	X	X Counter	Y	Y Counter
1	100	0	011	0
2	000	1	110	0
3	100	1	001 →	1
4	000 →	2	100	1
5	100	2	111	1
6	000 →	3	010 →	2
7	100	3	101	2
8	000 →	4	000 →	3

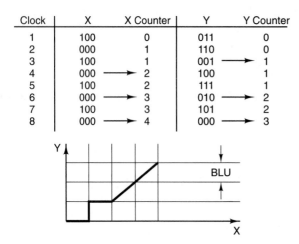

Figure 9.27   Linear interpolator example.

Example 9.1

Given the following data, calculate the register value.

$$BLU = 0.01 \text{ in.}$$
$$f = 1 \times 10^3 \text{ Hz}$$
$$\Delta x = 2 \text{ in.}$$
$$\Delta y = 3 \text{ in.}$$
$$v_f = 6 \text{ in./min}$$
$$N = 10$$

Solution:

$$v_x = \frac{6 \times 2}{\sqrt{2^2 + 3^2}} \frac{1}{0.001 \times 60}$$

$$= 55.5 \text{ BLU/s}$$

$$v_y = \frac{6 \times 3}{\sqrt{2^2 + 3^2}} \frac{1}{0.001 \times 60}$$

$$= 83.3 \text{ BLU/s}$$

$$f_{rx} = 55.5$$

$$f_{ry} = 83.3$$

$$p_x = \frac{55.5 \times 2^{10}}{1 \times 10^3}$$

$$= 57$$

$$p_y = \frac{83.3 \times 2^{10}}{1 \times 10^3}$$

$$= 85$$

9.4.6.2 Circular interpolator.   Circular interpolation can also be implemented in DDAs. The DDAs used in circular interpolation is modified from the ones used in linear interpolation. A circular arc is defined by a center P_0, and two end points, P_1 and P_2 (Figure 9.28). The angular position of the tool is ϕ is measured with respect to P_0. The feed rate is, therefore,

$$V_f = R \frac{d\phi}{dt} \tag{9.22}$$

where R is the radius of the circular arc.

$$x = R \cos \phi + x_0 \tag{9.23}$$

$$y = R \sin \phi + y_0 \tag{9.24}$$

$$R \cos \phi = x - x_0 \tag{9.25}$$

$$R \sin \phi = y - y_0 \tag{9.26}$$

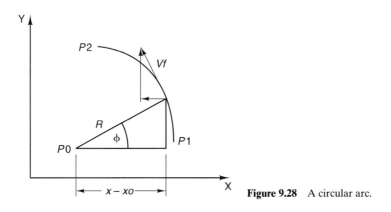

Figure 9.28   A circular arc.

The X and Y components of the feed speed can be found:

$$\frac{dx}{dt} = -R \sin \phi \frac{d\phi}{dt}$$

$$= -(y - y_0) \frac{d\phi}{dt} \tag{9.25}$$

$$\frac{dy}{dt} = R \cos \phi \frac{d\phi}{dt}$$

$$= (x - x_0) \frac{d\phi}{dt} \tag{9.26}$$

The dx/dt and dy/dt are values loaded into the DDAs. Because DDA registers are un-signed, absolute values $|y - y_0|$ and $|x - x_0|$ are used. From Equation (9.22), $d\phi/dt = V_f/R$. It is for the feedrate control. To move on a circular arc, the speed also changes where the rate of change of dx/dt and dy/dt can be found:

$$\frac{d^2x}{dt^2} = -R \cos \phi \frac{d\phi}{dt} \frac{d\phi}{dt}$$

$$= -\frac{dy}{dt} \frac{d\phi}{dt} \tag{9.27}$$

$$\frac{d^2y}{dt^2} = -R \sin \phi \frac{d\phi}{dt} \frac{d\phi}{dt}$$

$$= \frac{dx}{dt} \frac{d\phi}{dt} \tag{9.28}$$

The change over the arc if therefore defined by Equations (9.27) and (9.28). A DDA circuit can be designed using two modified DDAs (Figure 9.29). The DDA X is loaded with $|y_1 - y_0|$ and DDA Y with $|x_1 - x_0|$. The sign is added after the output is produced by changing the direction of the motor. Because the desired rate of change to DDA X equals $-dy/dt$, the output of DDA Y, when there is an output from DDA Y, the

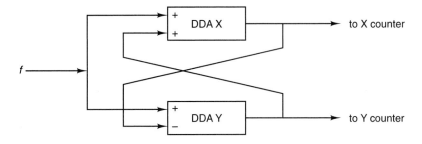

Figure 9.29   A circular interpolator.

DDA X register is incremented. Note that both dx/dt and d^2x/dt^2 have the same sign. Similarly, the DDA Y register value is affected by the output of DDA X. This time, the register value is decremented (the negative sign in dx/dt is carried out through the decrement operation).

The arc shown in Figure 9.28 is in quadrant I. In quadrant II, the value of $(x - x_0)$ is negative. Because the register is an unsigned binary, the sign has to be handled separately. Therefore, this circular interpolator does not work across two quadrants. When an arc extends across two quadrants, it must be broken into two segments. This hardware limitation is the reason that many NC machines must be programmed in separate quadrants. In CNC machines, through software interpolation, full-circle circular interpolation can be achieved.

The feed-rate control for circular interpolation is similar to that used in linear interpolation, except that the value is

$$a_f = \frac{V_f}{R} \frac{2^{N_f+N}}{f_c}$$

$$= \frac{10\,V_f}{R} \tag{9.29}$$

A numerical example is not given here, but can be constructed easily from the preceding discussion. The following data may be used: Cut a circular arc centered at $(0,0)$, from $(10,0)$ to $(0,10)$; the DDA register width is 4 bits. Initially, both a_x and a_y should be loaded with a value 10.

INTERMEDIATE ANALYSIS

9.5 ANALYSIS OF A DC MOTOR

A typical DC motor configuration is shown in Figure 9.30. A circuit diagram for a field-controlled DC motor is given in Figure 9.31. The torque of the DC motor is calculated as follows:

$$T_m = K_e I_a \Phi \tag{9.30}$$

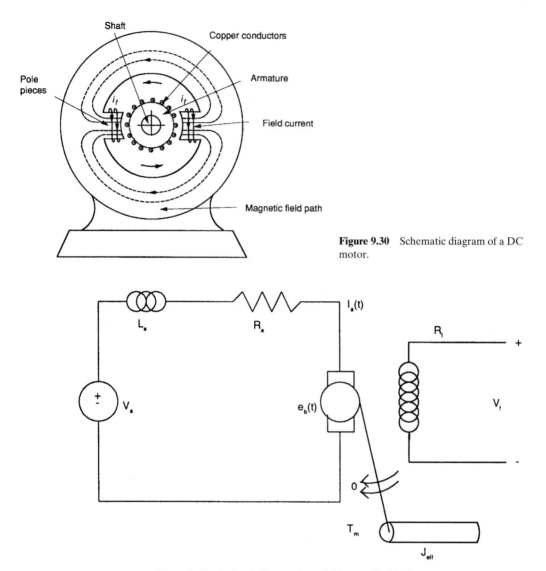

Figure 9.30 Schematic diagram of a DC motor.

Figure 9.31 A circuit diagram for a field-controlled DC motor.

and let

$$K_m = K_e \Phi$$
$$T_m = K_m I_a$$

where

T_m = motor torque, oz-in.
K_e = motor constant

I_a = armature current, amps

Φ = magnetic flux

$$e_b = K_b\omega \tag{9.31}$$

where

e_b = back emf generated by the motor coil, volts

K_b = constant

ω = motor rotation speed, rad/s

Therefore, from Kirchhoff's voltage law, we know

$$V_a = K_b\omega + R_aI_a + L_a\frac{dI_a}{dt} \tag{9.32}$$

where

V_a = armature voltage, volts

R_a = armature resistance, ohms

Then, the total torque required is

$$T = T_{rm} + T_l \tag{9.33}$$

where

T = total torque required, oz-in.

T_{rm} = torque required to turn the motor

T_l = torque required to turn the load

$$
\begin{aligned}
T_{rm} &= T_d + T_s \\
&= J_m\dot{\omega} + f_m\omega
\end{aligned} \tag{9.34}
$$

where

J_m = moment of inertia of the motor, oz-in.-s²/rad

f_m = viscous friction coefficient of the motor, oz-in.-s/rad

T_d = dynamic torque

T_s = static torque

$$T_l = J_l\dot{\omega} + f_l\omega \tag{9.35}$$

where

J_l = moment of inertia of the load

f_l = viscous friction coefficient of the load

The load is coupled to the motor shaft through a gear train. The gear train has a gear ratio $(\omega_l/\omega), n$.

$$T = (J_m + n^2 J_l)\dot{\omega} + (f_m + n^2 f_l)\omega \tag{9.36}$$

For a motor not connected to an external load, the torque is

$$T_m = T = J_m\dot{\omega} + f_m\omega \tag{9.37}$$

$$K_m I_a = J_m\dot{\omega} + f_m\omega \tag{9.38}$$

From Equation (9.32), we know that

$$R_a I_a + L_a \dot{I}_a = V_a - K_b\omega \tag{9.39}$$

By a Laplace transform,

$$R_a I_a(S) + SL_a I_a(S) = V_a(S) - K_b\omega(S)$$

$$I_a(S) = \frac{V_a(S) - K_b\omega(S)}{R_a + SL_a} \tag{9.40}$$

Also

$$K_m I_a(S) = SJ_m\omega(S) + f_m\omega(S) \tag{9.41}$$

By substituting Equation (9.40) with (9.41), we obtain

$$\frac{K_m V_a(S) - K_m K_b\omega(S)}{R_a + SL_a} = SJ_m\omega(S) + f_m\omega(S)$$

$$\omega(S) = \frac{K_m V_a(S)}{S^2 L_a J_m + (L_a f_m + R_a J_m)S + (R_a f_m + K_m K_b)}$$

$$= \frac{(K_m/L_a J_m)V_a(S)}{S^2 + [(L_a f_m + R_a J_m)/L_a J_m]S + (R_a f_m + K_m K_b)/L_a J_m} \tag{9.42}$$

Angular speed is therefore determined by the characteristic function

$$S^2 + \frac{L_a f_m + R_a J_m}{L_a J_m} S + \frac{R_a f_m + K_m K_b}{L_a J_m} \tag{9.43}$$

Let us assume that both the impedance and the friction are low, that is, $\omega_a \to 0$ and $f_m \to 0$. Equation (9.42) can be rewritten as

$$\omega(S) = \frac{K_m V_a(S)}{R_a J_m S + K_m K_b}$$

$$= \frac{(1/K_b)V_a(S)}{(R_a J_m/K_m K_b)S + 1} \tag{9.44}$$

Let

$$\tau_m = \frac{R_a J_m}{K_m K_b} \tag{9.45}$$

Then

$$\omega(S) = \frac{V_a(S)/K_b}{\tau_m S + 1} \tag{9.46}$$

Suppose that V_a is a step function, that is, $V_a = V$ at $t = 0$:

$$V(S) = \frac{V}{S}$$

$$\omega(S) = \frac{V/K_b}{S(\tau_m S + 1)}$$

$$= \frac{V/K_b}{S} + \frac{-\tau_m(V/K_b)}{\tau_m S + 1}$$

$$= \frac{1}{S}\frac{V}{K_b} - \frac{V/K_b}{S + 1/\tau_m} \tag{9.47}$$

By an inverse Laplace transform,

$$\omega(t) = \frac{V}{K_b} - \frac{V}{K_b}e^{-t/\tau_m} = \frac{V}{K_b}(1 - e^{-t/\tau_m}) \tag{9.48}$$

Therefore, τ_m is the time constant of the motor.

At steady state, $t \to \infty$:

$$\omega(t \to \infty) = \frac{V}{K_b} \tag{9.49}$$

Figure 9.32 shows the operation diagram of a DC motor. The block diagram of the motor is shown in Figure 9.33

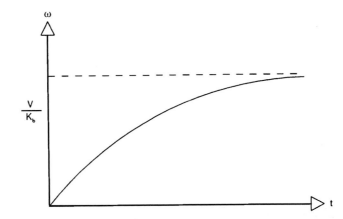

Figure 9.32   An operation diagram of a DC motor.

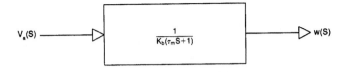

Figure 9.33   Block diagram of a DC motor.

Example 9.2

Given a DC motor with the following data, find the time constant and motor rotation $\omega(t)$.

$K_b = 0.9$ V-s/rad
$R_a = 0.3$ ohm
$J_m = 0.3$ lb-m-s^2
$K_m = 8$ lb-in./A
$V = 10$ V

$$\tau_m = \frac{R_a J_m}{K_m K_b} = \frac{(0.3) \cdot (0.3)}{(8) \cdot (0.9)} = 0.0125 \text{ s} = 12.5 \text{ ms}$$

$$\omega(t) = \frac{10}{0.9} (1 - e^{-t/0.0125}) = 11.1(1 - e^{-t/0.0125})$$

The 1 time diagram is shown in Figure 9.34

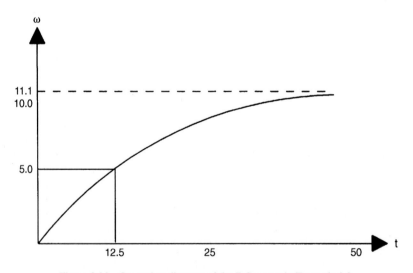

Figure 9.34   Operation diagram of the DC motor in Example 9.2.

9.6 ANALYSIS OF AN NC SYSTEM

Within the controller (see Figure 9.22), two distinct operations are usually performed: the difference or error between the operating point and the set point or error is calculated from

```
Error = set point - actual output
```

and a corrective action is determined by the solution of an equation or set of equations that has been established as characterizing a desirable way to control the system. The law governing the determination of this manipulation can be referred to as the control algorithm. These operations are illustrated in block-diagram form in Figure 9.35. In the following, we provide some mathematical formulation to characterize the system.

From the following equation as well as the block diagram in Figure 9.31,

$$\omega = \frac{V_a}{K_b(\tau_m S + 1)} \tag{9.50}$$

When the external load is considered,

$$V_a = V_c - K_s \frac{T_s(S)}{S} \tag{9.51}$$

$$V_c = K_a V_e \tag{9.52}$$

Consider the inner closed loop:

$$V_e = V_d - V_t \tag{9.53}$$

$$= K_d f - K_t \omega \tag{9.54}$$

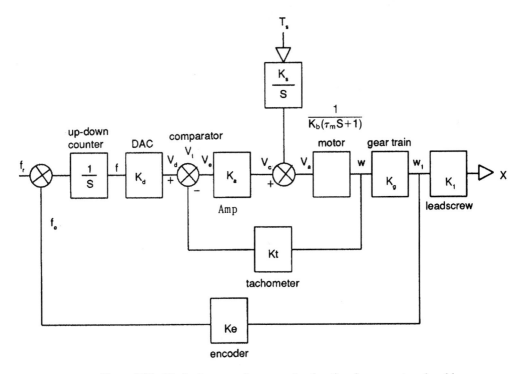

Figure 9.35 Block diagram of a computer function for computer closed-loop control.

The transfer function for the up-down counter is

$$f = (f_r - f_e)\frac{1}{S} \tag{9.55}$$

$$f_e = K_e\omega_l \tag{9.56}$$

$$\omega_l = K_g\omega \tag{9.57}$$

$$\omega = \frac{\omega_l}{K_g} \tag{9.58}$$

$$f = (f_r - K_e\omega_l)\frac{1}{S} \tag{9.59}$$

$$V_e = \frac{K_d}{S}(f_r - K_e\omega_l) - K_t\frac{\omega_l}{K_g} \tag{9.60}$$

By taking everything into consideration, the controller output, V_c, can be expressed as

$$V_c = \frac{K_aK_d(f_r - K_e\omega_l)}{S} - \frac{K_aK_t\omega_l}{K_g} \tag{9.61}$$

$$V_a = \frac{K_aK_df_r - K_sT_s(S)}{S} - \left(\frac{K_aK_dK_e}{S} + \frac{K_aK_t}{K_g}\right)\omega_l \tag{9.62}$$

$$\omega_l = \frac{K_g}{K_b(1 + S\tau_m)}\left[\frac{K_aK_df_r - K_sT_s(S)}{S} - \left(\frac{K_aK_dK_e}{S} + \frac{K_aK_t}{K_S}\right)\omega_l\right] \tag{9.63}$$

$$\frac{(K_g/K_b)[K_aK_df_r - K_sT_s(S)]}{S(1 + S\tau_m)}$$

$$= \frac{S(1 + S\tau_m) + (K_g/K_b)[K_aK_dK_e + (K_aK_t/K_g)(S)]}{S(1 + S\tau_m)}\omega_l \tag{9.64}$$

$$\omega_l(S) = \frac{(K_g/K_b)K_aK_df_r - (K_g/K_b)K_sT_s(S)}{S + S^2\tau_m + (K_g/K_b)K_aK_dK_e + (K_aK_t/K_b)(S)} \tag{9.65}$$

$$= \frac{(K_g/K_b)[K_aK_df_r/\tau_m - K_sT_s(S)/\tau_m]}{S^2 + (1 + K_gK_t/K_b)S/\tau_m + K_SK_aK_dK_e/K_b\tau_m} \tag{9.66}$$

The characteristic equation is

$$S^2 + 2\xi\omega_nS + \omega_n^2 = 0 \tag{9.67}$$

$$\omega_n = \left(\frac{K_gK_aK_dK_t}{K_b\tau_m}\right)^{1/2} \quad \text{(natural frequency)} \tag{9.68}$$

$$\xi = \frac{1 + K_a/K_t/K_b}{\tau_mK_aK_dK_cK_g/K_b} \quad \text{(damping factor)} \tag{9.69}$$

When $\xi = 1$, critically damped, and if f_r, a step function at $t = 0$, F equals

$$\omega_l(S) = \frac{(K_g/K_b)[(K_aK_d/\tau_m)f_r - (K_s/\tau_m)T_s(S)]}{S(S + \omega_n)^2} \tag{9.70}$$

$$\omega_l(t) = \frac{K_g}{K_b}\left[\frac{K_aK_d}{\tau_m}F - \frac{K_s}{\tau_m}T_s(S)\right]\left[\frac{1}{\omega_n^2}\frac{1}{S} - \frac{1}{\omega_n^2}\frac{1}{S + \omega_n} - \frac{1}{\omega_n}\frac{1}{S + \omega_n}\right] \tag{9.71}$$

$$= \frac{K_s}{K_b}\left[\frac{1}{K_l}F - \frac{K_s}{K_aK_dK_l}T_s(S)\right][1 - e^{\omega_n t} - \omega_n t e^{-\omega_n t}] \tag{9.72}$$

At steady state, $t \to \infty$,

$$\omega_l(t) = \frac{K_g}{K_b}\left[\frac{1}{K_l}F - \frac{K_s}{K_aK_dK_l}T_s(S)\right] \tag{9.73}$$

9.7 CONCLUDING REMARKS

In this chapter, a general overview of NC systems was presented. As should be noted from the text, NC machines are a complex integration of hardware, firmware, and software. The capabilities of these machines as well as their costs vary greatly. In the next chapter, we discuss programming NC machines.

REVIEW QUESTIONS

9.1. What are the major components of an NC machine system? Briefly describe the function of each.

9.2. What is point-to-point motion control? Contouring motion control? Describe the shapes of workpieces that can be machined by each of these control methods.

9.3. Write a computer program for the circular interpolation algorithm described in Section 9.4. The program should accept the following input: the center-point location, radius, type of tolerance specification, and maximum tolerance for the given tolerance type. The output should include the coordinates of all interpolated points.

9.4. What are the major power sources for NC machines. Describe the advantages and disadvantages of each.

9.5. There are four points, p_1, p_2, p_3, and p_4, and their coordinates are $(10,4,9)$, $(29,4,-10)$, $(-9,21,10)$, and $(4,10,5)$, respectively. We want to move the tool of an NC machine in a $p_1 \to p_2 \to p_3 \to p_4$ sequence. Write down the corresponding X-, Y-, and Z-axis dimensions in an NC part program if an incremental positioning system is used.

9.6. Given the same data of Review Question 9.5, what would be the X-, Y-, and Z-axis dimensions for an absolute positioning system?

9.7. Define accuracy and repeatability.

9.8. Two pulse dividers are used to control an X-Y table. One BLU equals 0.001 in. The input frequency is 1×10^4 Hz. The word length is 10 bits. In order to move the table from $(0,0)$ to

(4,5) (both coordinates in inches) at a speed of 8 ipm, what P values should be loaded into the X and Y pulse dividers? How many pulses should be sent to each axis?

9.9. A DC motor is connected to an external load directly. The moment of inertia of the load is 2 lb-m-s². Let $K_b = 0.9$ volt-S/rad, $R_a = 0.4$ ohm, $J_m = 0.4$ lb-m-s², $K_m = 8$ lb-in./A, and $f_m = f_1 = 0$. After applying 20 volts to the motor, what is the steady-state rotational speed of the motor? What is the time constant?

9.10. Design an NC system that yields a resolution of 0.0001 in. and a maximum feed speed (linear speed on X–Y axis) of 100 fpm. Specify the leadscrew pitch, encoder resolution, pulse-divider word length, and pulse-divider input frequency.

9.11. Referring to Figure 9.35, derive $\omega(t)$ as a function of V_d. Compare the time constant and the steady-state angular speed of a system with a tachometer to one without; see Equation (9.44).

9.12. Discuss the differences between an open-loop NC system and a closed-loop NC system.

9.13. Write a computer program to simulate a DDA-based linear interpolator.

9.14. Write a computer program to simulate a DDA-based circular interpolator.
  Hints for 9.13 and 9.14: Use a loop to simulate the clock cycle. Use IF statement to check whether a desired position has been reached.

9.15. What is a machining center? What is a turning center?

9.16. An NC machine uses a 200-pulse/rev encoder and a 10-teeth/in. leadscrew for its axis control. What is the BLU of the machine?

9.17. An NC machine has a resolution (BLU) of 0.001 in. To move the cutter from coordinates (1,1) to (3,4) at 18 ipm, how many pulses and at what rate would the controller send to the X and Y servo motors?

9.18. Show a DDA-based linear interpolator for the NC machine described in the Review Question 9.17. What p values should be loaded in the feed-rate control, and in the X and Y DDAs?

9.19. What are the sources of error in NC machining?

9.20. Design a circular interpolator (for the X and Y axes). Prove it works using a set of data you have chosen. You may do it by hand or with a computer. The interpolator can use only addition, subtraction, multiplication, and division operators. No trigonometric function is allowed.

9.21. Use a block diagram to show the structure of a closed-loop NC system (one axis only). Begin with the reference signal from the interpolator, and include all system components (motor, transducers, and electronic and mechanical elements).

REFERENCES/BIBLIOGRAPHY

CHILDS, J. J. (1982). *Principles of Numerical Control*. New York: Industrial Press.

ELECTRONIC ASSOCIATION OF AMERICA (1990). *Axis and Motion Nomenclature for Numerically Controlled Machines*, American National Standard, Washington, DC: EIA.

KELLY, M. R., and H. BROOKS (1988). *The State of Computerized Automation in U.S. Manufacturing*. Cambridge, MA: Harvard University, J. F. Kennedy School of Government.

KOREN, Y. (1983). *Computer Control of Manufacturing Systems.* New York: McGraw-Hill.

LIU, D. (1994). "Next Generation CNC Control: Object-Oriented, Software-Centric System on an Open System Architecture," in *Proceedings of Autofact '94.* SME, Dearborn, MI.

PRESSMAN, R. S., and J. E. WILLIAMS (1977). *Numerical Control and Computer-Aided Manufacturing.* New York: Wiley.

REINTJES, T. F. (1991). *Numerical Control: Making a New Technology.* London: Oxford University Press.

ROLT, L. T. C. (1967). *A Short History of Machine Tools.* Cambridge, MA: The MIT Press.

THYER, G. E. (1993). *Computer Numerical Control of Machine Tools,* 2nd ed. New York: Industrial Press.

10

Numerical-Control Programming

10.1 NC PART PROGRAMMING

10.1.1 Coordinate Systems

In an NC system, each axis of motion is equipped with a separate driving source that replaces the handwheel of the conventional machine. The driving source can be a DC motor, a stepping motor, or a hydraulic actuator. The source selected is determined mainly based on the precision requirements of the machine, as described in Chapter 9.

The relative movement between tools and workpieces is achieved by the motion of the machine tool slides. The three main axes of motion are referred to as the X, Y, and Z axes. The Z axis is perpendicular to both the X and Y axes in order to create a right-hand coordinate system, as shown in Figure 10.1. A positive motion in the Z direction moves the cutting tool away from the workpiece. This is detailed as follows:

Z AXIS

1. On a workpiece-rotating machine, such as a lathe, the Z axis is parallel to the spindle, and the positive motion moves the tool away from the workpiece (Figure 10.2).
2. On a tool-rotating machine, such as a milling or boring machine, the Z axis is parallel to the tool axis, and the positive motion moves the tool away from the workpiece (Figures 10.3 and 10.4).
3. On other machines, such as a press, a planing machine, or shearing machine, the Z axis is perpendicular to the tool set, and the positive motion increases the distance between the tool and the workpiece.

X AXIS

1. On a lathe, the X axis is the direction of tool movement, and the positive motion moves the tool away from the workpiece.
2. On a horizontal milling machine, the X axis is parallel to the table.

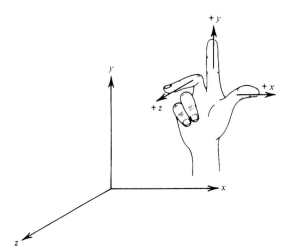

Figure 10.1 A right-hand coordinate system. (Y. Koren, *Computer Control of Manufacturing Systems,* McGraw-Hill, 1983.)

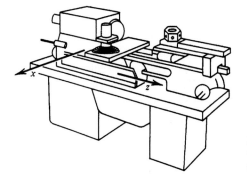

Figure 10.2 Coordinate system for a lathe. (Y. Koren, *Computer Control of Manufacturing Systems,* McGraw-Hill, 1983.)

3. On a vertical milling machine, the positive X axis points to the right when the programmer is facing the machine.

The Y axis is the axis left in a standard Cartesian coordinate system.

10.1.2 NC Program Storage Media

During the numerical-control process, numerals and symbols representing the motion of the NC machine, as well as manual operating commands, are passed to the machine-control unit (MCU). Numerical data and symbols are represented by holes in a punched tape or computer cards, magnetized domains on magnetic tape, or electronic impulses sent via computer networks. As long as the communication media are defined, an MCU can be designed to translate the information contained within the media and actuate servomechanisms to perform the required tasks.

The initiation of the NC process takes place by communication of data and symbols to the control unit. The ideal medium for communication and data storage packs

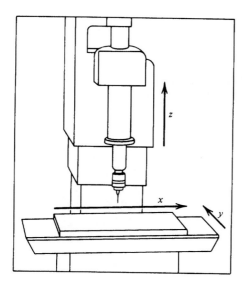

Figure 10.3   Coordinate system for a drill. (Y. Koren, *Computer Control of Manufacturing Systems,* McGraw-Hill, 1983.)

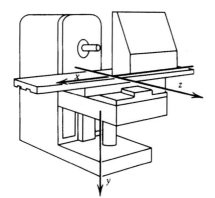

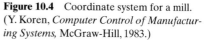

Figure 10.4   Coordinate system for a mill. (Y. Koren, *Computer Control of Manufacturing Systems,* McGraw-Hill, 1983.)

information into a dense, easily interpreted code that, after input to a reader, is sent to the MCU at high speeds.

There are several basic types of NC part program storage media: punched tape, magnetic tape, mylar tape, floppy disk, and a direct communication link (Pressman and Williams, 1979).

1. The punched card has provided an efficient and accurate means of data storage and transfer since it was first invented by Herman Hollerith in 1887. It is really simple to edit individual blocks of NC codes because a card can be extracted from the deck, retyped using a keypunch, and replaced. However, because of the low storage density, the data can be only input to the MCU at a much slower rate than other media types.

2. The majority of NC machines receives data from reels of 1-in.-wide tape containing holes. Figure 10.5 illustrated the characteristics of such a tape. A bit is defined

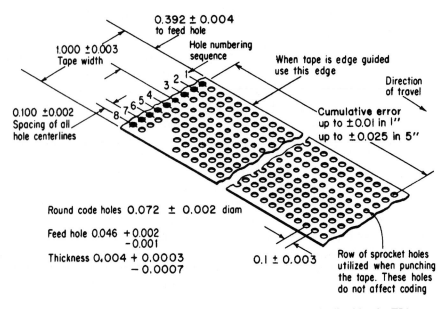

Figure 10.5   Numerical-control punched tape format at standardized by the EIA (J. J. Childs, *Principles of Numerical Control,* 1982. Courtesy of Industrial Press.)

as a condition of one of two possible states, that is, either on or off. With respect to the tape, this means the presence or absence of a hole, respectively. A character on the tape is a collection of holes positioned on one line across the tape (a character represents a number, a letter, or a symbol). A word is an ordered set of characters that can be used to cause a specific action of a machine tool. $X + 600$, for example, causes the movement of the machine head 600 units in the positive X direction. A block is a word or a group of words considered as a unit and generally offering one complete instruction for a specific machine movement. Blocks are separated by an end-of-block (EOB) character. The tape is read one block at a time when passing through the reader in a hardwired control system and read multiblock in a CNC system (Childs, 1982).

3. Modern magnetic tapes are made by coating a polyester or Mylar film with an iron-oxide coating. Such magnetic tapes have extremely high storage densities: 1600 to 6250 bytes per inch are common in computer applications. The symbolic code used to specify data is similar in many respects to codes used for paper tapes. However, magnetic tapes are prepared using computer-based methods; therefore, direct manual editing on the tapes is impossible. Also, because of the fragile nature of the medium, the applications of magnetic tapes are sometimes limited.

4. Floppy disks (3½ in. or 5¼ in.) are widely used in personal computers. CNC controllers are microcomputer-based devices, many of which use a standard personal-computer platform. Logically, floppy disks have been adopted for NC part program storage. Because several computer-assisted part programming software run on personal computers, data exchange is made easier, and database management is enhanced using standard computing platforms.

Modern CNC controllers provide several ways of transferring data. Perhaps the most typical data-communication methods used to transfer part program files is an RS-232C interface (see Chapter 8). An NC part program is stored in a file on a computer or a CNC controller. The file download (or upload) can be initiated by setting up a transfer mode on the CNC controller. On the other side of the communication cable is a computer that sends or receives data byte by byte. The operator must start and end the data-transfer process on both the CNC controller and the computer. Some machines use higher-level protocols to ensure an error-free data transfer. Two of the higher-level protocols used are Kermit and *X*modem. Kermit and *X*modem are widely accepted in the computer-to-computer telecommunication file-transfer process. These protocols allow the file transfer to be controlled by either the computer or the controller. The computer can send and retrieve data directly. Some machines also provide local-area network (LAN) instead of serial communication. Ethernet and MAP are two technologies used. Some CNC controllers allow the entire controller function to be initiated from a remote computer through the data-communication network.

10.1.3 Symbolic Codes

A BCD (binary-coded decimal) or ASCII (American Standard Code for Information Interchange) code is frequently used in NC applications.

- BCD: An eight-track punched tape is one of the more common input media for NC systems. Hence, all data in the form of symbols, letters, and numbers must be representable by eight binary fields. The BCD code has been devised to satisfy this requirement. In a BCD code, the numerals 0 through 9 are specified using only the first four tracks, quantities 1, 2, 4, and 8. Note that the four numbers 1, 2, 4, and 8, added together as needed make all numbers from 1 to 15. Letters, symbols, and special instructions are indicated by using tracks 5 through 8 in combination with the numeral tracks. A complete BCD character set, based on EIA Standard RS-244A, is illustrated in Figure 10.6. Each BCD character must have an odd number of holes. By punching a parity bit along with all even bit strings, all characters have an odd number of holes. If an even number of holes is detected, it is by definition an error, and a parity check occurs. This simple method provides some protection from input errors resulting in part damage.

- ASCII: ASCII was formulated to standardize punched-tape codes regardless of applications (Pressman and Williams, 1979). Hence, ASCII is used in computer and telecommunications as well as in NC applications. ASCII code was devised to support a large character set that includes uppercase and lowercase letters and additional special symbols not used in NC applications. Figure 10.6 illustrates the ASCII subset applicable to NC. Many new control systems now accept both BCD and ASCII codes. It is likely that the move toward ASCII standardization will progress as older NC equipment is replaced.

ISO Char	8	7	6	5	4	•	3	2	1	EIA Char	8	7	6	5	4	•	3	2	1		Meaning
0			o	o		•				0			o			•					Numeral 0
1	o		o	o		•			o	1						•			o		Numeral 1
2	o		o	o		•		o		2						•		o			Numeral 2
3			o	o		•		o	o	3				o		•		o	o		Numeral 3
4	o		o	o		•	o			4					o	•					Numeral 4
5			o	o		•	o		o	5				o	o	•			o		Numeral 5
6			o	o		•	o	o		6				o	o	•		o			Numeral 6
7	o		o	o		•	o	o	o	7					o	•		o	o		Numeral 7
8	o		o	o	o	•				8	o					•					Numeral 8
9			o	o	o	•			o	9	o			o		•			o		Numeral 9
A		o				•			o	a		o	o			•			o		Address A
B		o				•		o		b		o	o			•		o		?	Address B
C	o	o				•		o	o	c		o	o	o		•		o	o	?	Address C
D		o				•	o			d		o	o		o	•					Address D
E	o	o				•	o		o	e		o	o	o	o	•			o		Address E
F	o	o				•	o	o		f		o	o	o	o	•		o			Address F
G		o				•	o	o	o	g		o	o		o	•		o	o		Address G
H		o			o	•				h	o	o	o			•				?	Address H
I	o	o			o	•			o	i	o	o	o	o		•			o		Address I
J	o	o			o	•		o		j		o		o		•			o	?	Address J
K		o			o	•		o	o	k		o		o		•		o			Address K
L	o	o			o	•	o			l		o				•		o	o		Address L
M		o			o	•	o		o	m		o		o	o	•					Address M
N		o			o	•	o	o		n		o			o	•			o		Address N
O	o	o			o	•	o	o	o	o		o			o	•		o			Address O
P		o	o			•				p		o		o	o	•		o	o		Address P
Q	o	o	o			•			o	q		o		o		•					Address Q
R	o	o	o			•		o		r		o				•			o		Address R
S		o	o			•		o	o	s			o	o		•		o			Address S
T	o	o	o			•	o			t			o			•		o	o		Address T
U		o	o			•	o		o	u			o	o	o	•					Address U
V		o	o			•	o	o		v			o		o	•			o	?	Address V
W	o	o	o			•	o	o	o	w			o		o	•		o			Address W
X	o	o	o		o	•				x			o	o	o	•		o	o		Address X
Y		o	o		o	•			o	y	o		o	o		•				?	Address Y
Z		o	o		o	•		o		z	o		o			•			o		Address Z
DEL	o	o	o	o	o	•	o	o	o	Del	o	o	o	o	o	•	o	o	o	•	Delete (cancel an error punch).
NUL						•				Blank						•				•	Not punched. Can not be used in significant section in EIA code.
BS	o			o		•				BS	o			o	o	•				•	Back space
HT				o	o	•			o	Tab	o	o	o	o	o	•	o	o		•	Tabulator
LF or NL				o	o	•		o		CR or EOB	o					•					End of block
CR	o			o	o	•	o		o											•	Carriage return
SP	o		o			•				SP			o			•				•	Space
%	o		o			•	o		o	ER				o	o	•		o	o	•	Absolute rewind stop
(			o		o	•				(2–4–5)				o	o	•		o			Control out (a comment is started)
)	o		o		o	•			o	(2–4–7)		o			o	•		o			Control in (the end of a comment)
+			o		o	•		o	o	+		o	o		o	•				•	Positive sign
–			o		o	•	o		o	–		o				•				•	Negative sign
:			o	o	o	•	o													•	Colon
/	o		o		o	•	o	o	o	/			o	o		•			o		Optional block skip
.			o		o	•	o	o		.		o	o		o	•		o			Period (A decimal point)
#	o		o			•		o	o											•	Sharpe
$			o		o	•														•	Dollar sign
&	o		o			•	o	o		&					o	•	o	o		•	Ampersand
'			o		o	•	o	o	o											•	Apostrophe
*	o		o		o	•		o												•	Asterisk
,	o		o		o	•	o													•	Comma
;	o		o	o	o	•		o	o											•	Semicolon
<			o	o	o	•	o													•	Left angle bracket
=	o		o	o	o	•	o		o											•	Equal
>	o		o	o	o	•	o	o												•	Right angle bracket
?			o	o	o	•	o	o	o											•	Question mark
@	o	o				•														•	Commercial at mark
"			o			•		o												•	Quotation
{	o	o		o	o	•		o	o											•	Left brace
}	o	o		o	o	•	o		o											•	Right brace

Figure 10.6 EIA and ASCII codes for perforated tape used in NC applications. (Courtesy of FANUC Ltd.).

10.1.4 Tape Input Formats

The organization of words within blocks is called the tape format (EIA Standard RS-274) (Groover, 1980). Four tape formats are used for NC input (Pressman and Williams, 1979):

1. The fixed sequential format requires that each NC block be the same length and contain the same number of characters. This restriction enables the block to be divided into substrings corresponding to each of the NC data types. Because block length is invariant, all values must appear even if some types are not required.

2. The block-address format eliminates the need for specifying redundant information in subsequent NC blocks through the specification of a change code. The change code follows the block sequence number and indicates which values are to be changed relative to the preceding blocks. All data must contain a predefined number of digits in this format.

3. The tab sequential format derives its name because words are listed in a fixed sequence and separated by depressing the tab key (TAB) when typing the manuscript on a Flexowriter. Two or more tabs immediately following one another indicate that the data that would normally occupy the null locations are redundant and have been omitted. An example of tab sequential NC code is

```
T001 T01 T07500 T06250 T10000 T612 T718 T T EOB
T002 T T08725 T06750 T T T T EOB
T003 T T T T05000 T520 T620 T01 T EOB
```

(T represents a tab character.)

4. The word-address format places a letter preceding each word and is used to identify the word type and to address the data to a particular location in the controller. The X prefix identifies an *X*-coordinate word, an S prefix identifies spindle speed, and so on. The standard sequence of words in a block for a three-axis NC machine is

    N word
    G word
    X word
    Y word
    Z word
    F word
    S word
    T word
    M word
    EOB

A word-address NC code is

```
N001 G01 X07500 Y06250 Z10000 F612 S718 EOB
N002 X08752 Y06750 EOB
N003 Z05000F520 S620 M01 EOB
```

10.1.5 NC Words

A block of NC part program consists of several words. A part program written in this data format is called a G-code program. A G-code program contains the following words:

N, G, X, Y, Z, A, B, C, I, J, K, F, S, T, R, M

Through these words, all NC control functions can be programmed. An EIA standard, RS-273, defines a set of standard codes. However, it also allows for the customizing of certain codes. Even with this standard, there is still a wide variation of code format. A program written for one controller often does not run on another. It is, therefore, essential to refer to the programming manual for the target machine before a program is written. In this section, before the meaning of each word is explained, we will first analyze the requirements of an NC control.

10.1.5.1 Basic requirement of NC machine control.   To control a machine, it is necessary to begin by defining the coordinates of the tool motion. It is necessary to specify whether the motion is a positioning motion (rapid traverse) or a feed motion (cutting). The feed motion includes linear motion and circular motion. Linear motion requires the destination coordinates. When circular interpolation is used, the center of the circle must be given in addition to the destination. Before a cutting motion is called out, the spindle must be turned to the desired rpm and the feed speed must be specified. The spindle can rotate either clockwise or counterclockwise. Sometimes coolant is required in machining, and the coolant may be applied in flood or mist form. If an automatic tool changer is present, the next tool number has to be known to the controller before a tool can be changed to the machine spindle. The sequence to change the tool also needs to be specified. It is often desirable to aggregate a fixed sequence of operations such as drilling holes into a cycle. Using cycle codes can drastically reduce programming effort. Additional information is needed for specific cycle operations. Finally, there are other programming functions, such as units—inch or metric—positioning system—absolute or incremental, and so on. All of these activities can (and in some cases must) be controlled through the NC controller and related part program. These control functions and data requirements are summarized in what follows:

(a) Preparatory functions: the words specify which units, which interpolator, absolute or incremental programming, which circular interpolation plane, cutter compensation, and so on.

(b) Coordinates: define three translational (and three rotational) axes.

(c) Machining parameters: specify feed and speed.

(d) Tool control: specifies tool diameter, next tool number, tool change, and so on.

(e) Cycle functions: specify drill cycle, ream cycle, bore cycle, mill cycle, and clearance plane.

(f) Coolant control: specify the coolant condition, that is, coolant on/off, flood, and mist.

(g) Miscellaneous control: specifies all other control specifics, that is, spindle on/off, tape rewind, spindle rotation direction, pallet change, clamps control, and so on.

(h) Interpolators: linear, circular interpolation, circle center, and so on.

These control functions are programmed through program words (codes).

10.1.5.2 NC words.   A specific NC function may be programmed using an NC word or a combination of NC words. All functions can be programmed in one block of a program. Many CNC controllers allow several of the same "word" be present in the same block. Thus, several functions can be included in one block. This is normally done by using a word-address format, which is the most popular format used in modern CNC controllers. The sequence of the words within one block is usually not important, except for the sequence number that must be the first word in the block. In order to make a program more readable, it is a good practice to follow a fixed sequence. Each word consists of a symbol and a numeral. The symbol is either N, G, X, Y, and so on. Numerals follow as data in a prespecified format. For example, the format for an X word might be "3.4," which means three digits before the decimal point and four digits after the decimal are used. The function of each NC word (code) and their applications are discussed in what follows:

> *N-code.* A part program block usually begins with an "N" word. The N word specifies the sequence number. It is used to identify the block within the program. It is especially useful for program editing. For example, when the format is "4," a proper sequence number would be

> N0010

It is a good practice to program N values in increments of 10 or greater. This allows additional blocks to be inserted between two existing blocks.

G-code. The G-code is also called preparatory code or word. It is used to prepare the MCU for control functions. It indicates that a given control function is requested or that a certain unit or default be taken. There are modal functions and nonmodal functions. Modal functions are those that do not change after they have been specified once, such as unit selection. Nonmodal functions are active in the block where they are specified. For example, circular interpolation is a nonmodal function. Some commonly used G-codes are listed in the Table 10.1. Some of these functions are explained in what follows.

G00 is the rapid traverse code that makes the machine move at maximum speed. It is used for positioning motion. When G01, G02, or G03 are specified, the machine moves at the feed speed. G01 is linear interpolation; G02 and G03 are for circular interpolation. For circular interpolation, the tool destination and the circle center are programmed in one block (explained later). G04 (d well) is used to stop the motion for a time specified in the block. G08 and G09 codes specify acceleration and deceleration, respectively. They are used to increase (decrease) the speed of motion (feed speed) exponentially to the desired speed. Before an abrupt turn, decelerate the tool. Rapid acceleration in the new direction may cause a tool to break. The best accuracy can be obtained with acceleration and deceleration codes on and set to lower values. Most NC controllers interpolate circles on only

TABLE 10.1 G CODES

G00	Rapid traverse	G40	Cutter compensation—cancel
G01	Linear interpolation	G41	Cutter compensation—left
G02	Circular interpolation, CW	G42	Cutter compensation—right
G03	Circular interpolation, CCW	G70	Inch format
G04	Dwell	G71	Metric format
G08	Acceleration	G74	Full-circle programming off
G09	Deceleration	G75	Full-circle programming on
G17	X-Y Plane	G80	Fixed-cycle cancel
G18	Z-X Plane	G81–89	Fixed cycles
G19	Y-Z Plane	G90	Absolute dimension program
		G91	Incremental dimension

XY, *YZ*, and *XZ* planes. The interpolation plane can be selected using G17, G18, or G19. When a machine is equipped with thread-cutting capability, (G33–G35), the part program must specify the proper way to cut the thread. Codes G40–G43 deal with cutter compensation. They simplify the cutter-center offset calculation. More details of cutter compensation are discussed later in Section 10.2.2. Most canned cycles are manufacturer-defined. They include drilling, peck drilling, spot drilling, milling, and profile turning cycles. The machine-tool manufacturer may assign them to one of the nine G codes reserved for machine manufacturers (G81–G89). A user also can program the machine using either absolute (G90) or incremental (G91) coordinates. In the same program, the coordinate system can be changed. In order to simplify the presentation, most of the examples given in this chapter use absolute coordinates. Many controllers also allow the user to use either inch units (G70) or metric units (G71). Because hardwired NC circular interpolators work only in one quadrant and many CNC systems allow full-circle interpolation, a G74 code emulates NC circular interpolation for CNC controllers. G75 returns the CNC back to the full-circle circular interpolation mode.

X-, Y-, Z-, A-, B-, and C-Codes. These words provide the coordinate positions of the tool. *X*, *Y*, and *Z* define the three translational (Cartesian) axes of a machine. A, B, and C are used for the three rotational axes about the *X*, *Y*, and *Z* axes. For a three-axis machine, there can be only three translational axes. Most applications only require *X*, *Y*, and *Z* codes in part programs. However, for four-, five-, or six-axis machine tools, A, B, and C are also used. The coordinates may be specified in decimal number (decimal programming) or integer number (BLU programming). For a controller with a data format of "3.4," to move the cutter to (1.12, 2.275, 1.0), the codes are

```
X1.1200 Y2.2750 Z1.000
```

In BLU programming, the programmer also may need to specify leading zero(s), or trailing-zero formats. A leading-zero format means that zeros must be entered in the space proceeding the numeric value. In this format, the controller locates the decimal point by counting the digits from the beginning of a number. In trailing-zero format, it is reversed. The number specified is in the BLU unit. The data format "3.4" implies that a BLU equals 0.0001 in. (fourth decimal place). By using the data from preceding example, the leading-zero program would be

```
X00112 Y002275 Z001
```

In the trailing-zero format, the program looks like

```
X11200 Y22750 Z10000
```

For circular motion, more information is needed. A circular arc is defined by the start and end points, the center, and the direction. Because the start point is always the current tool position, only the end point, the circle center, and the direction need to be specified. I, J, and K words are used to specify the center. Usually, circular interpolation works only on either *X-Y*, *Y-Z*, or *X-Z* planes. When interpolating a circular arc on the *X-Y* plane, the I word provides the *X*-coordinate value of the circle center and the J word provides the *Y* coordinate value. X and Y words specify the end point. Clockwise or counterclockwise motions are specified by the G-code (G02 versus G03). There are many variations in circular interpolation programming. Each NC controller vendor has its own form and format. Also, they can depend on the combination of absolute or incremental, full-circle on or off modes. The following example is based on absolute programming with full circle on for a hypothetical controller.

F-Code. The F-code specifies the feed speed of the tool motion. It is the relative speed between the cutting tool and the workpiece. It is typically specified in in./min (ipm). From a machinability data handbook, feed is given in in./rev (ipr). A conversion has to be done either by hand or on-board the controller. Some controllers offer a G-code that specifies the ipr programming mode. When the ipr programming mode is used, the tool diameter and the number of teeth must be specified by the operator. The F-code must be given before G01, G02, or G03 can be used. Feed speed can be changed frequently in a program, as needed. When an F-code is present in a block, it takes effect immediately. To specify a 6.00-ipm feed speed for the cutting motion in Figure 10.7, one would program

```
N0100 G02 X7.000 Y2.000 I5.000 J2.000 F6.00
```

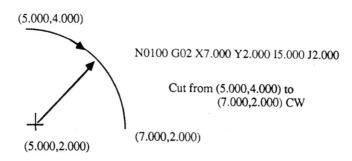

N0100 G02 X7.000 Y2.000 I5.000 J2.000

Cut from (5.000,4.000) to
(7.000,2.000) CW

Figure 10.7   Cutting a circular arc.

S-Code. The S-code is the cutting-speed code. Cutting speed is the specification of the relative surface speed of the cutting edge with respect to the workpiece. It is the result of the tool (or workpiece in turning) rotation. Therefore, it is programmed in rpm. The Machinability Data Handbook (Machinability Data Center, 1980) gives these values in surface feet per minute (sfpm), and conversion is required before programming is done. When a controller is equipped with a sfpm programming option, the operator must specify the tool diameter. The S-code is specified before the spindle is turned on. The S-code does not turn on the spindle. The spindle is turned on by an M-code. To specify a 1000-rpm spindle speed, the program block is

```
N0010 S1000
```

T-Code. The T-code is used to specify the tool number. It is used only when an automatic tool changer is present. It specifies the slot number on the tool magazine in which the next tool is located. Actual tool change does not occur until a tool-change M-code is specified.

R-Code. The R-code is used for cycle parameter. When a drill cycle is specified, one must give a clearance height (R plane) (see Figure 10.8). The R-code is used to specify this clearance height. In Figure 10.8, the drill cycle consists of five operations:
1. Rapid to location (1,2,2).
2. Rapid down to the R plane.
3. Feed to the Z point, the bottom of the hole.
4. Operation at the bottom of the hole, for example, dwelling.
5. Rapid or feed to either the R plane or the initial height.
The cycle may be programmed in one block, such as (cycle programming is vendor-specific)

```
N0010 G81 X1.000 Y2.000 Z0.000 R 1.300
```

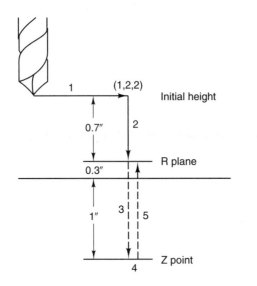

Figure 10.8 Drill cycle.

M-Code. The M-code is called the miscellaneous word and is used to control miscellaneous functions of the machine. Such functions include turn the spindle on/off, start/stop the machine, turn on/off the coolant, change the tool, and rewind the program (tape) (Table 10.2). M00 and M01 both stops the machine in the middle of a program. M01 is effective only when the optional stop button on the control panel is depressed. The program can be resumed through the control panel. M02 marks the end of the program. M03 turns on the spindle (clockwise). The spindle rpm must be specified in the same line or in a previous line. M04 is similar to M03, except it turns the spindle on counterclockwise. M05 turns off the spindle. M06 signals the tool-change operation. On a machine equipped with an automatic tool changer, it stops the spindle, retracts the spindle to the tool-change position, and then changes the tool to the one specified in the T-code. M07 and M08 turn on different modes of coolant. M09 turns off the coolant. M30 marks the end of the tape. It stops the spindle and rewinds the program (tape). On some controllers, more than one M-code is allowed in the same block.

TABLE 10.2 M-CODES

M00	Program stop	M06	Tool change
M01	Optional stop	M07	Flood coolant on
M02	End of program	M08	Mist coolant on
M03	Spindle CW	M09	Coolant off
M04	Spindle CCW	M30	End of tape

10.2 MANUAL PART PROGRAMMING

10.2.1 Part Programs

In manual part programming, the machining instructions are recorded on a document, called a part-program manuscript (see Figure 10.9) by the part programmer. The manuscript is essentially an ordered list of program blocks. The manuscript is either entered as a computer file or punched on a paper tape. Each symbol on the manuscript, alphanumeric or special characters, corresponds to a perforation(s) on the tape (or magnetic bit pattern on a disk) and is referred to as a character. Each line of the manuscript is equivalent to a block on the punched tape and is followed by an EOB (end-of-block) character. When it is stored in a computer file, a tape-image format is used.

Because a part program records a sequence of tool motions and operations to produce the final part geometry, one must prepare a process plan with setups and fixtures before writing the program (see Chapter 13). The workpiece location and orientation, features (holes, slots, pockets) to be machined, tools and cutting parameters used need to be determined. We will use an example to illustrate how a part is programmed.

Example 10.1

The part drawing shown in Figure 10.10 is to be machined from a 4-in. × 4-in. × 2-in. workpiece. The workpiece material is low-carbon steel. We will use a hypothetical 3-axis CNC machining center for the process. The process plan for the part is as follows:

THE NC PART PROGRAMMING MANUSCRIPT

Part name _____	MANUSCRIPT CONTOURING PROGRAM	Prepared by _____ Date _____
Part number _____		Checked by _____ Date _____
Sheet _____ _____		Machine _____
Remarks _____		Tape number _____

n	g	x	y	z	i	j	k	f	s	t	m	REMARKS

Figure 10.9   NC part-program manuscript.

1. Set the lower-left bottom corner of the part as the machine zero point (floating-zero programming).
2. Clamp the workpiece in a vise.
3. Mill the slot with a ¾-in. four-flute flat, end mill made of carbide. From the Machinability Data Handbook, the recommended feed is 0.005 in./tooth/rev and the recommended cutting speed is 620 fpm.
4. Drill two holes with a 0.75-in.-diameter twist drill. Use 0.18-ipr feed and 100-fpm speed.

Figure 10.11 shows the setup, fixturing, and cutter path. Write a part program for the part.

Solution   The cutting parameters need be converted into rpm and ipm.

Milling:

$$\text{rpm} = \frac{12V}{\pi D} = \frac{12 \times 620 \text{ fpm}}{\pi \times 0.75 \text{ in.}} = 3157 \text{ rpm}$$

$$V_f = nf \text{ rpm} = 4 \text{ tpr} \times 0.005 \text{ iprpt} \times 3157 \text{ rpm} = 63 \text{ ipm}$$

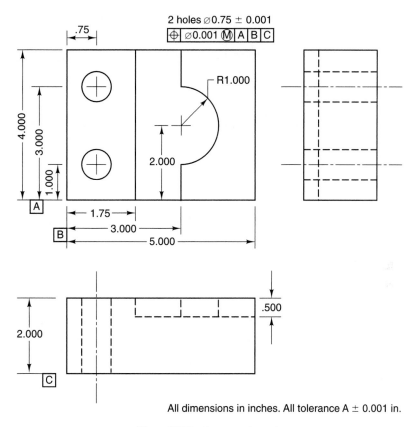

Figure 10.10   An example part.

Drilling:

$$\text{rpm} = \frac{12V}{\pi D} = \frac{12 \times 100 \text{ fpm}}{\pi \times 0.75 \text{ in.}} = 509 \text{ rpm}$$

$$V_f = f \text{ rpm} = 0.018 \text{ ipr} \times 509 \text{ rpm} = 9.16 \text{ ipm}$$

For the milling operation, the cutter is smaller than the slot, and two passes are required. The cutter first moves to p1′ (the prime denotes the upper point). There must be clearance between the cutter and the workpiece, so that the cutter will not touch the workpiece during rapid positioning. We will use 0.1 in. as the clearance. The cutter then plunges down to p1, which is on the slot bottom level. Both p2 and p3 are outside the workpiece to ensure the slot edges are completely cut. The center of the cutter overhangs the edge by 0.1 in. The cutter moves to p4 from p3 to clear the slot. p5 is the beginning of a circular interpolation and p6 is the end. From p6, the cutter moves to p7 to clear the center of the circular area, and then moves to p8. After the milling operation, a drill is installed in the spindle through an automatic tool change. The two holes are drilled using a drilling cycle.

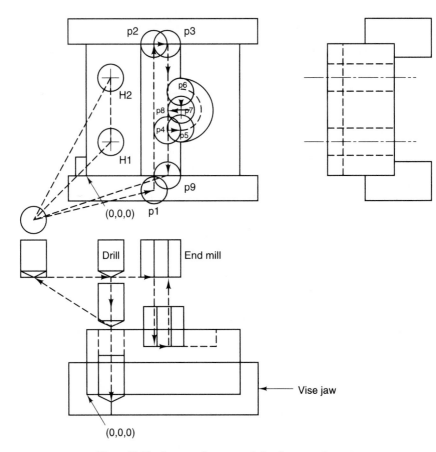

Figure 10.11   Setup and cutter path for the example part.

The coordinates of each point (cutter location) are

p1': $(1.75 + 0.375, -0.1 - 0.375,400) = (2.125,-0.475,4.000)$

p1: $(2.125, -0.475,2.000 - 0.5000) = (2.125,-0.475,1.500)$

p2: $(2.125,4.000 + 0.100,1.500) = (2.125,4.100,1.500)$

p3: $(3.000 - 0.375,4.100,1.500) = (2.625,4.100,1.500)$

p4: $(2.625,2.000 - 1.000 + 0.375,1.500) = (2.625,1.375,1.500)$

p5: $(3.000,2.000 - 1.000 + 0.375,1.500) = (3.000,1.375,1.500)$

p6: $(3.000,2.625,1.500)$

p7: $(3.000,2.000,1.500)$

p8: $(2.625,2.000,1.500)$

p9: $(2.625,-0.100,1.500)$

p9': $(2.625,-0.100,4.000)$

Combining the information from the process plan and the cutter-location data, a part program can be written. The program for the example part is shown in Figure 10.12. A step-by-step explanation is presented on the right-hand-side of the figure. The part program is

Part program	Explanation
N0010 G70 G90 T08 M06	Set the machine to the inch format and absolute dimension programming.
N0020 G00 X2.125 Y-0.475 Z4.000 S3157	Rapid to p1′.
N0030 G01 Z1.500 F63 M03	Down feed to p1, spindle CW.
N0040 G01 Y4.100	Feed to p2.
N0050 G01 X2.625	To p3.
N0060 G01 Y.1375	To p4.
N0070 G01 X3.000	To p5.
N0080 G03 Y2.625 I3.000 J2.000	Circular interpolation to p6.
N0090 G01 Y2.000	To p7.
N0100 G01 X2.625	To p8.
N0110 G01 Y-0.100	To p9.
N0120 G00 Z4.000 T02 M05	To p9′, spindle off, tool sign 2.
N0130 F9.16 S509 M06	Tool change, set new feed and speed.
N0140 G81 X0.750 Y1.000 Z-0.1 R2.100 M03	Drill hole 1.
N0150 G81 X0.750 Y3.000 Z-0.1 R2.100	Drill hole 2.
N0160 G00 X-1.000 Y-1.000 M30	Move to home position, stop the machine.

Figure 10.12   Part program for the part in Figure 10.10.

verified using a program called Mac CNCS, and the results are shown in Figure 10.13. The result in Figure 10.13 is the same as what is shown in Figure 10.11; thus, the program is correct. A three-dimensional view can also be found in Figure 10.14.

10.2.2 Tool-Radius Compensation

When machining a complicated workpiece, it is necessary to compensate (or position the tool further away from the desired cutting surface) in order to allow for the radius of the cutting tool. The geometry in Example 10.1 is relatively simple, and little calculation was required. However, when there are nonorthogonal lines or planes in the drawing, the calculations can become more complicated. Also, when a slightly different size cutter is used instead of the programmed cutter, the program becomes invalid. In this case, a new program must be written. The tool-radius compensation feature of modern CNC machines can eliminate the tool-offset calculation for the finish cut. Tool-radius compensations make it possible to program directly from the drawing's measurements. The actual tool size is then "keyed into" the CNC controller prior to the operation. The CNC controller performs the offset calculations automatically. Tool-radius compensation only modifies the existing path. Because the number of roughing passes and their path are determined by cutter size, tool-radius compensation cannot be used. We will illustrate some typical tool-radius compensation functions in what follows:

- G40: cancel tool-radius compensation.
- G41: compensation—left; Figure 10.15(a). Assume cutter is on the left-hand side of the line. The direction is established by the tool-motion direction.
- G42: compensation—right; Figure 10.15(b).

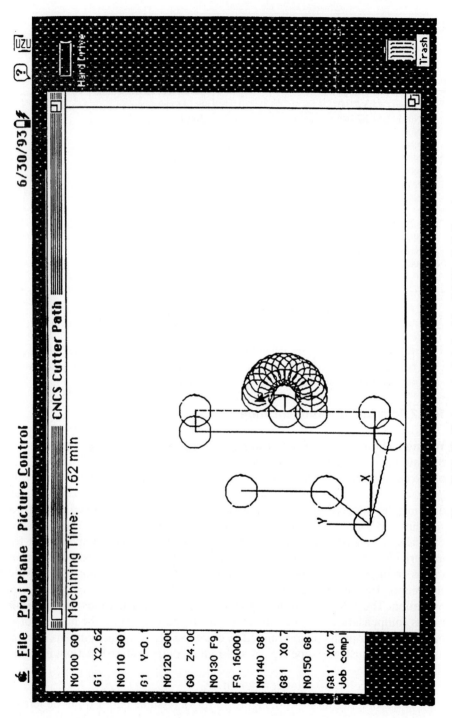

Figure 10.13 Verified cutter path (using Mac CNCS by T. C. Chang).

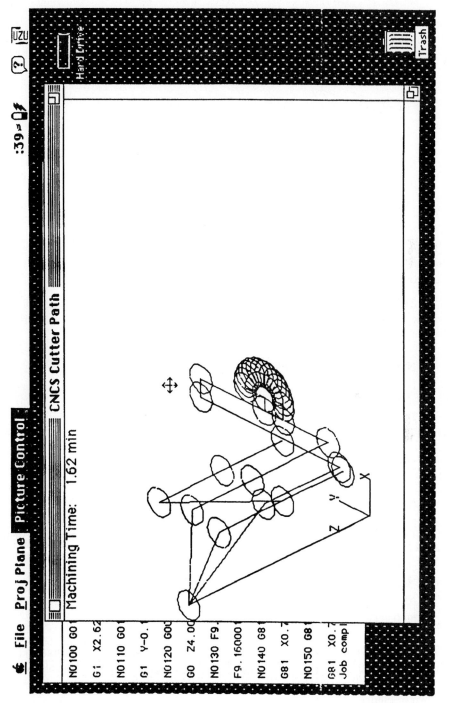

Figure 10.14 A three-dimensional cutter-path verification.

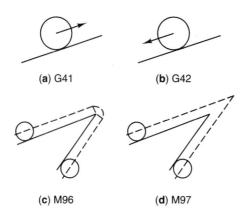

(a) G41   (b) G42

(c) M96   (d) M97

Figure 10.15 (a) Tool compensation—left, (b) tool compensation—right, (c) additional block for external curves, (d) go to machining point when cutting external curves.

- M96: additional block for external curves; Figure 10.15(c). The circular arc at the corner is inserted by the CNC controller.
- M97: go to machining point when cutting external curves; Figure 10.15(d).

An example on how to use these functions follows:

Start of Compensation. If G41 (or G42) and G01 are in the same block, there will be a gradual effect of the compensation, as shown in Figure 10.16(a). This is known as a ramp-up block and takes place at block N0010.

N0010 G01 G42 X0.500 Y1.700
N0020 G01 X1.500

If G41 (or G42) and G01 are in separate blocks from X and Y, the compensation is effective from the start of the block, as shown in Figure 10.16(b).

N0010 G41
N0020 G01 X0.500 Y1.700
N0030 G01 X1.500

Inside Corner. When the cutter path determines the geometry of an inside corner, it stops at the inside cutting point, as shown in Figure 10.16(c).

N0010 G41
N0020 G01 X1.500 Y2.000
N0030 G01 X0.000 Y1.600

Use of M96 and M97. If a step is to be cut using a cutting tool that is larger than the height of the step, M97 must be used. If M96 is used, the cutter will roll over the corner and into the material [see Figure 10.16(d)]. The following code creates the error shown in Figure 10.16(d).

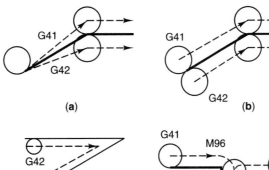

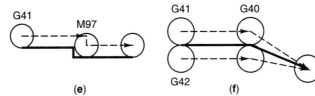

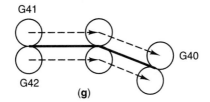

Figure 10.16   (a) Ramp on block, (b) tool compensation is effective from the start, (c) tool compensation at inside corner, (d) use of M96 improperly, (e) use of M97, (f) ramp off block, and (g) tool compensation is effective to the end point.

N0010 G41
N0020 G01 X1.000 Y1.000
N0030 G01 Y.800 M96
N0040 G01 X2.000

The correct program should be

N0010 G41
N0020 G01 X1.000 Y1.000
N0030 G01 Y0.800 M97
N0040 G01 X2.000

The result is shown in Figure 10.16(e).

Cancel Tool Compensation. If G40 is in the same block as *X* and *Y*, there will be a gradual cancellation of compensation. This is known as a ramp-off block, as shown in Figure 10.16(f)

```
N0060 G40 X2.000 Y1.700 M02
```

If G40 is in a block following the last motion, the compensation is effective to the end point (2.000,1.700); see Figure 10.16(g).

```
N0060 X2.000 Y1.700
N0070 G40 M02
```

Example 10.2

A 2.0-in. × 2.0-in. square is to be milled using a ½-in. end milling cutter. The drawing is given in Figure 10.17. Write an NC part program to make the square.

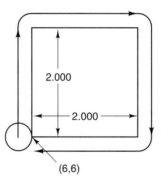

2.000

2.000

(6,6)

Figure 10.17 A 2-in × 2-in. square is to be milled using a 0.5-in. end-milling cutter.

Solution Let us set up the lower left corner of the square at (6.0,6.0). By using tool-radius compensation, the square can be produced by the program shown in Figure 10.18.

Part Program	Explanation
N0010 G41 S1000 F5 M03	Begin compensation, set feed and speed, spindle on
N0020 G00 X6.000 Y6.000	Move to lower left corner
N0030 G01 Z-1.000	Plunge down the tool
N0040 Y8.000	Cut to upper left corner
N0050 X8.000	Cut to upper right corner
N0060 Y6.000	Cut to lower right corner
N0070 X6.000	Cut to lower left corner
N0080 Z1.000	Lift the tool
N0090 G40 M30	End compensation, stop the machine

Figure 10.18 Part program and explanation for Example 10.2

10.3 COMPUTER-ASSISTED PART PROGRAMMING

In computer-assisted part programming, general-purpose computers are used as an aid in programming, and special-purpose, high-level programming languages perform the various calculations necessary to prepare the punched tape. The computer allows economical programming of the machining of complex parts that could not be manually programmed economically. The part programmer's job is divided into two tasks: First, define the configuration of the workpiece in terms of basic geometric elements via points, lines, surfaces, circles, and so on. Second, direct the cutting tool to perform machining steps along these geometric elements. Programming languages that are capable of running on general-purpose computers have been developed. These languages are based on common English words and mathematical notations and are easy to use.

An NC processor is a computer application program that accepts as input user-oriented language statements that describe the NC operations to be performed. Figure 10.19 illustrates a generalized flow chart for most NC processors. Commonality among the many types of NC devices that exist is obtained by designing NC processors to produce a common interface code called CL (cutter-location) data. The CL data, in turn, are used as the input to another computer application program called a postprocessor, which produces the code for the particular NC device utilized. This output is normally in the form of punched tape for convenient storage and reading by the device's controller during the step-by-step execution of the operation.

There are two major classes of part-programming languages (Smith and Evans, 1977):

1. *Machine-oriented languages* create tool paths by doing all the necessary calculations in one computer processing stage by computing directly the special coordinate-data format and the coding for speed and feed requirements.

2. *General-purpose languages* break down the computer processing into two stages, a processing stage and a postprocessing stage. The processing stage creates an intermediate set of data points called CL data. There are three steps in the processing stage.

   • *Translate input symbols.* This function translates symbolic inputs contained in the part program into a computer-usable form. It also establishes the link between the human operator and the computer.
   • *Arithmetic calculation.* The arithmetic calculation unit performs geometric and trigonometric calculations required to generate the part surface.
   • *Cutter offset calculations.* The cutter offset unit calculates the path of the center line of the cutter based on the part-outline information.

EIA RS-494B provides a new standard for computer numerical control that allows different machines to operate from the same input data. The name of this standard is "Standard for 32 Bit Binary CL Exchange (BCL) Input Format for Numerically Controlled Machines."

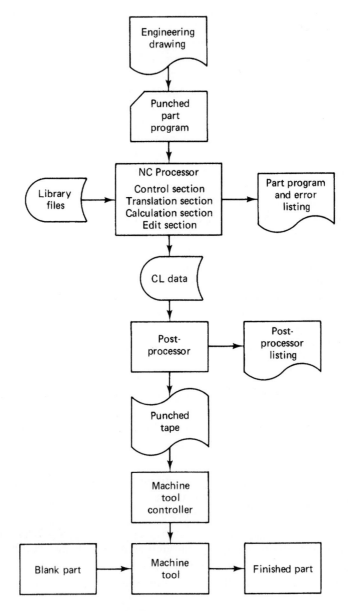

Figure 10.19 NC processor flow chart.

The BCL format represents NC machining input data as a series of records that are groups of 32-bit binary integer words. The content of these records closely parallels the content of CL data records defined in ANSI Standard X3.37 as prepared by ANSI Committee X3J7. The syntax and the semantics of records defined by this standard in most cases either conform to or are extensions of ANSI X3.37—1980 Programming Language APT. A BCL file is typically produced by a part-oriented post-processor called a BCL converter. Its primary functions are to retrieve CL data records, select the relevant portions of the data, convert the floating-point data to 32-bit integer data, format data into records, and produce a BCL program file and program listing. It performs only machine-dependent functions. The BCL format structure is as follows:

FILE HEADER (optional)

PARTNO record (optional)

UNITS record

DATA record

DATA record

DATA record

END OF FILE record

Figure 10.20 illustrates a sample BCL program. In this program, corresponding APT commands are listed for cross-reference. The code is shown in hexadecimal.

At the postprocessing stage, the CL data are converted by the computer to make them more specific for a particular machine-tool system and a punched tape (or floppy disk) is prepared. The output of the postprocessor is the NC tape (or the NC program on a floppy disk) written in an appropriate format for the machine in which it is to be used.

Since 1956, more than 100 NC part-programming languages have been developed. Some of them are special-purpose, machine-oriented languages. However, most of them are general-purpose. Some languages have stood the test of time, whereas many have not. We describe some of the more popular languages in common use today in the following.

10.3.1 APT

APT is an acronym for Automatically Programmed Tool. Initially developed in 1956 at MIT, it is the most popular part-programming language in the United States (Childs, 1982). APT has continued to evolve, and the Illinois Institute of Technology Research Institute (IITRI) has continued the development and administrative responsibility for the fourth version of APT. APT is the most powerful general-purpose part-programming system against which other systems are commonly compared and evaluated. Summary characteristics of APT are as follows (Illinois Institute of Technology Research Institute, 1967):

- Three-dimensional unbounded surfaces and points are defined to represent the part to be made.

LINE	BCL code	interpretation	APT source statement
E.1			PARTNO BCL SAMPLE
	6415 0002	PARTNO (record no. 2)	
	2042 434C	BCL	
	2053 414D	SAM	
	504C 4520	PLE	
E.2			UNITS/INCHES
	9409 0004	UNITS (record no. 4)	
	7FFF 012F	INCHES	
E.3			SPINDL/RPM, 1200, CLW
	8407 0006	SPINDL (record no. 6)	
	7FFF 004E	RPM	
	0067 1600	12000000	
	7FFF 003C	CLW	
E.4			COOLNT/FLOOD
	8406 0008	COOLNT (record no. 8)	
	7FFF 0059	FLOOD	
E.5			RAPID
	8005 000A	RAPID (record no. 10)	
E.6			GOTO/1,0,4.1
	9001 000C	GOTO (record no. 12)	
	0000 2710	10000	
	0000 0000	0	
	0000 A028	41000	
E.7			FEDRAT/FPM, 10
	83F1 000E	FEDRAT (record no. 14)	
	7FFF 0142	FPM	
	0001 86A0	100000	
E.8			GOTO/1,0,1
	9001 0010	GOTO (record no. 14)	
	0000 2710	10000	
	0000 0000	0	
	0000 2710	10000	
E.9			RAPID
	8005 0012	RAPID (record no. 18)	
E.10			GOTO/1.1,0,1
	9001 0014	GOTO (record no. 20)	
	0000 2AF8	11000	
	0000 0000	0	
	0000 2710	10000	
E.11			RAPID
	8005 0016	RAPID (record no. 22)	
E.12			GOTO/1.1,0,4.1
	9001 0018	GOTO (record no. 24)	
	0000 ZAF8	11000	
	0000 0000	0	
	0000 A028	41000	

Figure 10.20   Listing of BCL codes.

```
LINE  BCL code        interpretation           APT source statement
E.13                                           RAPID
      8005 001A RAPID (record no. 26)
E.14                                           GOTO/.9,0,4.1
      9001 001C GOTO (record no. 28)
      0000 2328 9000
      0000 0000 0
      0000 A028 41000
E.15                                           THREAD/SCALE, 1000000,
      840C 001E THREAD (record no. 30)         LEAD, .05, TURN
      7FFF 0019 SCALE
      000F 4240 1000000
      7FFF 0146 LEAD
      0000 C350 50000
      7FFF 0050 TURN
E.16                                           THREAD/ON
      840C 0020 THREAD (record no. 32)
      7FFF 0047 ON
E.17                                           GOTO/.9,0,1.2
      9001 0022 GOTO                           (record no. 34)
      0000 2328 9000
      0000 0000 0
      0000 2EE0 12000
E.18                                           THREAD/OFF
      840C 0024 THREAD (record no. 36)
      7FFF 0048 OFF
E.19                                           RAPID
      8005 0026 RAPID (record no. 36)
E.20                                           GOTO/1.1,0,1.2
      9001 0028 GOTO (record no. 40)
      0000 2AF8 11000
      0000 0000 0
      0000 2EE0 12000
E.21                                           SPINDL/OFF
      8407 002A SPINDL (record no. 42)
      7FFF 0048 OFF
E.22                                           COOLNT/OFF
      8406 002C COOLNT (record no. 44)
      7FFF 0048 OFF
E.23                                           GOHOME
      8011 602E GOHOME (record no. 46)
E.24                                           END
      8001 0030 END (record no. 48)
E.25
      8000 0032 END OF FILE (record no. 50)
```

Figure 10.20   (Continued)

- Surfaces are defined in a X–Y–Z coordinate system chosen by the part programmer.
- In programming, the tool does all the moving; the part is stationary.
- The tool path is controlled by pairs of three-dimensional surfaces; other motions, not controlled by surfaces, are also possible.
- A series of short straight-line motions are calculated to represent curved tool paths (linear interpolation).
- The tool path is calculated so as to be within specified tolerances of the controlling surfaces.
- The X, Y, and Z coordinates of successive tool-end positions along the desired tool path are recorded as the general solution to the programming problem.
- Additional processing (postprocessing) of the tool-end coordinates generates the exact tape codes and format for a particular machine.

An APT processor interprets and computes the cutter path, whereas a post-processor translates the cutter path to a format acceptable by a specific machine. There are five types of statements in the APT language.

1. *Identification statements.* These define a specific project.
2. *Geometry statements.* These define a scaler or geometric quantity.
3. *Motion statements.* These describe a cutter path, such as GOLFT.
4. *Postprocessor statements.* These define machining parameters such as feed, speed, coolant on/off and so on.
5. *Auxiliary statements.* These describe auxiliary machine-tool functions to identify the tool, part, tolerances, and so on.

Some of the APT geometry and motion statements are explained with examples as follows:

10.3.1.1 Geometry statements.   Geometry statements are used to define basic geometric entities such as points, lines, circles, and so on.

Points. A point can be defined by the following:

1. The specification of the X, Y, and Z coordinates of the point explicitly.

$$p_1 = \text{POINT}/x, y, z$$

2. The intersection of two lines; see Figure 10.21(a).

$$p_2 = \text{POINT}/l_1, l_2$$

3. The center of a circle; see Figure 10.21(b).

$$p_3 = \text{POINT}/\text{CENTER}, c_1$$

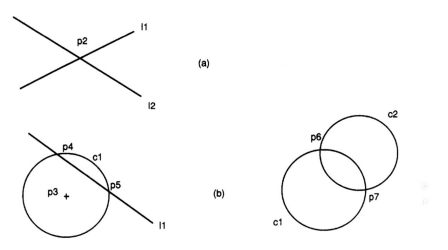

Figure 10.21   POINT statements.

4. The intersection of a line and a circle; see Figure 10.21(b).

$$p_4 = \text{POINT/YLARGE, INTOF}, l_1, c_1$$

$$p_5 = \text{POINT/XLARGE, INTOF}, l_1, c_1$$

5. The intersection of two circles; see Figure 10.21(c).

$$p_6 = \text{POINT/YLARGE, INTOF}, c_1, c_2$$

$$p_7 = \text{POINT/XLARGE, INTOF}, c_1, c_2$$

Lines.   A line can be defined by the following:

1. The specification of the coordinates of the two points connecting the line explicitly.

$$l_1 = \text{LINE}/x_1, y_1, z_1, x_2, y_2, z_2$$

2. The specification of the two points connecting the line; See Figure 10.22(a).

$$l_2 = \text{LINE}/p_1, p_2$$

3. A point and a line; see Figure 10.22(b).

$$l_3 = \text{LINE}/p_1, \text{PARLEL}, l_{20}$$

$$l_4 = \text{LINE}/p_1, \text{PERPTO}, l_{20}$$

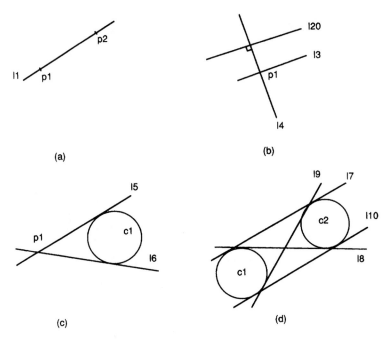

Figure 10.22　LINE statements.

4. A point and a circle; see Figure 10.22(c).

$$l_5 = \text{LINE}/p_1, \text{LEFT, TANTO}, c_1$$
$$l_6 = \text{LINE}/p_1, \text{RIGHT, TANTO}, c_1$$

5. Two circles; see Figure 10.22(d).

$$l_7 = \text{LINE/LEFT, TANTO}, c_1, \text{LEFT, TANTO}, c_2$$
$$l_8 = \text{LINE/LEFT, TANTO}, c_1, \text{RIGHT, TANTO}, c_2$$
$$l_9 = \text{LINE/RIGHT, TANTO}, c_1, \text{LEFT, TANTO}, c_2$$
$$l_{10} = \text{LINE/RIGHT, TANTO}, c_1, \text{RIGHT, TANTO}, c_2$$

Circles.　A circle can be defined by the following:

1. The specification of the X, Y, and Z coordinates of the center and the radius of the circle.

$$c_1 = \text{CIRCLE}/x, y, z, R$$

2. The specification of the center point and a radius; see Figure 10.23(a)

$$c_2 = \text{CIRCLE/CENTER}, p_1, \text{RADIUS}, R$$

3. A point and a line; see Figure 10.23(b).

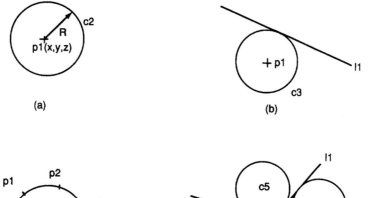

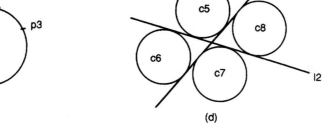

Figure 10.23   CIRCLE statements.

$$c_3 = \text{CIRCLE/CENTER}, p_1, \text{TANTO}, l_1$$

4. Three points; see Figure 10.23(c).

$$c_4 = \text{CIRCLE}/p_1, p_2, p_3$$

5. Two lines and a radius; see Figure 10.23(d).

$$c = \text{CIRCLE/} \left\{ \begin{array}{l} \text{XSMALL} \\ \text{XLARGE} \\ \text{YSMALL} \\ \text{YLARGE} \end{array} \right\}, l_1, \left\{ \begin{array}{l} \text{XSMALL} \\ \text{XLARGE} \\ \text{YSMALL} \\ \text{YLARGE} \end{array} \right\}, l_2, \text{RADIUS}, R$$

By using different combinations of above statements, four circles can be specified.

10.3.1.2 Motion Statements

From.   The FROM statement is used to define the starting point of certain motion.

$$\text{FROM/} \left\{ \begin{array}{l} p_1 \\ x, y, z \end{array} \right\}$$

Go.   The GO statement is used to define the destination of certain motion (see Figure 10.24). The difference between GOTO/ and GO/TO is obvious.

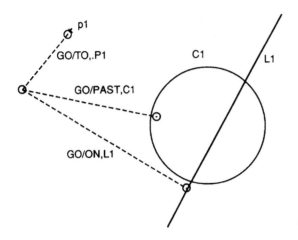

Figure 10.24 Motion statements—I.

$$\text{GOTO/}\left\{\begin{array}{c} p_1 \\ x, y, z \end{array}\right\}$$

$$\text{GOTO/}\left\{\begin{array}{c} \text{TO} \\ \text{PAST} \\ \text{ON} \end{array}\right\}, \left\{\begin{array}{c} p_1 \\ l_1 \\ c_1 \end{array}\right\}$$

Go Directions.   These statements are used to define the path of certain tool motion in order to avoid ambiguity.

1. GOLFT and GORGT; see Figure 10.25(a).

$$\text{GORGT/}l_1, \text{TO}, l_2$$

2. GOFWD and GOBACK; see Figure 10.25(b).

$$\text{GORG/}l_1, \text{TO}, l_2$$

$$\text{GOFWD/}l_1, \text{PAST}, c_1$$

3. GOUP and GODOWN; see Figure 10.25(c).

$$\text{GOUP/}l_4, \text{TO}, l_3$$

There are two other important features provided in the APT language:

* Macros: Individual macros similar to FORTRAN subroutines can be created to add to APT program routines. A library of frequently used routines and definitions can be created as special macros.
* Loops: Individual sections of an APT program can be repeated until a specified result is obtained.

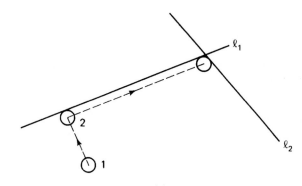

(a)

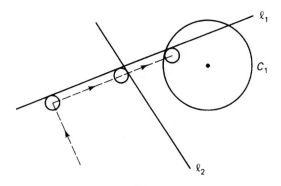

(b)

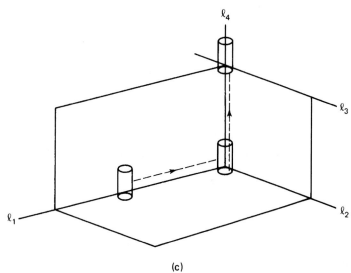

(c)

Figure 10.25   Motion statements—II

In addition to the basics just presented, APT also provides more geometric capabilities and advanced functions to handle complex parts. Other geometries supported by APT include the following:

- *Plane curves:* Ellipse, Hyperbola, GCONIC and LCONIC.

  An ellipse is defined by its center, major, and minor axes, and the angle between the major axis and the $+X$ axis. A hyperbola is defined in the same way as an ellipse. GCONIC is a general conic section, which includes circles, ellipses, hyperbolas, and parabolas. LCONIC defines loft conics, which is interpolated from a set of points.

$$\frac{x^2}{a^2} + \frac{y^2}{b^2} = 1 \quad \text{(ellipse)} \tag{10.1}$$

$$\frac{x^2}{a^2} - \frac{y^2}{b^2} = 1 \quad \text{(hyperbola)} \tag{10.2}$$

$$ax^2 + by^2 + cz^2 + dx + ey + f = 0 \quad \text{(GCONIC)} \tag{10.3}$$

- *Surfaces:* Quadratic surfaces, cylinders, tabulated cylinders, surfaces of rotation, ruled surfaces, and polyconic surfaces.

  Quadratic surfaces are commonly used in engineering design. A quadratic surface has the following form:

$$ax^2 + by^2 + cz^2 + dyz + ezx + fxy + gx + hy + iz + j = 0 \tag{10.4}$$

The APT statement for a quadric surface is

QADRIC/a, b, c, d, e, f, g, h, i, j

A cylinder (CYLNDR) in APT can be defined in many ways. There is an infinitely long cylinder. A tabulated cylinder (TABCYL) is a surface produced by the linear sweep of a curve. The curve in a tabulated cylinder is defined by a set of points (spline curve). The sweep is defined by a vector or using one of the three axes.

Surfaces of rotation include cones, spheres, and toruses.

A ruled surface (RLDSRF) is blended together by two spline curves. If we define r_p r_2 as two spline curves (each defined by a set of points), the ruled surface r is

$$r = \lambda r_1 + (1 - \lambda)r_2 \tag{10.5}$$

where λ is a parameter, $0 \leq \lambda \leq 1$.

A polyconic surface (POLCON) defines a surface using a series of cross-sectional curves. It is an extension of a ruled surface. The cross-sections of a polyconic surface are perpendicular to the longitudinal axis. Each section is approximated from a set of points by polynomial functions. The profile on the longitudinal axis is approximated by a polynomial function. Surfaces like aircraft wing profiles can be described by a polyconic surface.

- *Advanced functions:* Advanced functions include pattern cutting, pocket milling, and sculptured surface machining. The sculptured surface machining function is not typically available in APT. It is an add-on to the APT processor. The pattern-cutting function (PATERN) is especially useful in drilling hole patterns. Patterns can be either linear or circular. When combined with a set of modifiers for transformation and editing, it can describe very complex patterns.

  The pocket milling function (POCKET) automatically generates roughing and finishing paths for milling a pocket. A pocket is defined by a set of points. APT produces a contouring pattern that begins from the center of the pocket to the pocket boundary. The tool motion follows the sequence in which the points are defined. The pocket geometry is limited to convex polygons. A nonconvex pocket must be split into several convex pockets by the programmer. Figure 10.26 shows an example of the POCKET function.

  The PSIS statement is used to assign the part surface. The surface can be a planar surface defined by PLANE or one of the curved surfaces defined in the previous section. The APT processor uses an iterative method to locate the cutter onto the part surface while moving the cutter either along a line or in a pocket. The error created by the cutting is kept within the specified tolerance limit.

10.3.2 Other Part-Programming Languages

AUTOSPOT is a 2-D part-programming language developed at IBM. This processor allows point-to-point operations in two dimensions only. This type of operation requires the movement of a cutter to a discrete position, enables the performance of a desired machining function at that position (i.e., drilling, boring, and so on), and then enables these steps to be repeated.

ADAPT (Adaptation of APT) was the first attempt to adapt more commonly used APT routines for smaller computers. It was developed at IBM under a U.S. Air Force contract. It was constructed in a modular manner, providing greater flexibility to the user wanting to add and delete routines. It has full two-dimensional and some limited three-axis capabilities. It has routines for curve fitting, inclined planes, polygonal pockets, and macro definitions.

UNIAPT was developed by the United Computing Corporation of Carson, California. It was the first successful attempt to handle the full power of APT on a small computer. Externally, it is completely compatible with APT; it differs only in the internal design of the processor.

EXAPT (Extended Subset of APT) was developed jointly in West Germany around 1964 by several technical universities to make APT more appropriate to European conditions.

AUTOSPOT (Automatic System for Positioning Tools) was developed at IBM for three-axis, point-to-point motion control around 1962. It was subsequently combined with ADAPT to provide an effective language for both point-to-point and continuous-path applications.

COMPACT was developed by Manufacturing Data Systems, Ann Arbor, Michigan, to simultaneously service multiple users from a remote computer over telephone

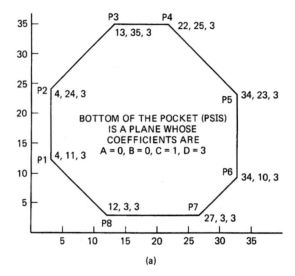

(a)

Pocket Part Program

```
 1 REMARK POCKET POLYGON COLLAPSE DEMONSTRATION TEST
 2 NOPOST $$ NO POSTPROCESSING FOR THIS TEST CASE
 3 CLPRNT $$ PRINT CUTTER CENTER DATA
 4 TOLER/.001 $$ TOLERANCE BAND
 5 $$ POINTS DEPINING POCKET PERIMETER
 6 P1 = POINT/4, 11, 3 $$ STARTING POINT OF POCKET DEFINITION
 7 P2 = POINT/4,24,3
 8 P3 = POINT/13,35,3
 9 P4 = POINT/22,35,3
10 P5 = POINT/34,23,3
11 P6 = POINT/34,10,3
12 P7 = POINT/27,3,3
13 P8 = POINT/12,3,3 $$ ENDING POINT OF POCKET DEFINITION
14 H = .01 $$ SCALLOP HEIGHT MAXIMUM
15 D = .38 $$ CONSTANT CUTTER DIAMETER
16 CR = .19 $$ CUTTER CORNER RADIUS
17 D2 = SQRTF((D * B) - B ** 2)$$ A BALL END MILL EFFECTIVE CUTTER RADIUS
18 CV = (4 * D2)/D $$ A MEASURE OF POCKETING CUT OFFSET
19 CUTTER/D, CR $$ BALL END MILL
20 FEDRAT/50 $$ MODAL FEED RATE
21 FROM/0,0 $$ STARTING CUTTER POSITION
22 GO TO/20,20,5 $$ MOVE CUTTER TOWARD AND OVER CENTER OF POCKET
23 PSIS/(PLANE/0,0,1,3) $$ BOTTOM PLANE OF POCKET
24 POCKET/D2,CV,CV,3,10,10,1,1,P1,P2,P3,P4,P5,P6,P7,P8 $$ STATEMENT
25 GO DLTA/0,0,2 $$ CLEARANCE POSITION OF CUTTER
26 GO TO/0,0,0 $$ END CUTTER POSITION
27 FINI $$ END OF PART PROGRAM
```

(b)

Figure 10.26   (a) A pocket to be machined using the IBM APT, and (b) the program listing for machining the pocket.

lines. The COMPACT system converts its language statements to machine-control codes in a single computer iteration, thus eliminating the postprocessing stage completely (Smith and Evans, 1977). COMPACT II, the latest version (together with APT), is the most popular part-programming language. It is also supported by most turnkey CAD/CAM systems. The COMPACT II program of Figure 10.26(b) was written to machine the part shown in Figure 10.27. The geometry describing the part and the machining motion generated by the program is illustrated in Figure 10.28.

In a COMPACT II program, a geometric entity is identified by its type and a number. For example, LN1 refers to line 1, PT1 refers to point 1. A "D" in front of a geometric name defines the geometry. To define line 1, DLN1 is used. In Figure 10.28, all the statements beginning with DLN, DPT, DCIR, are geometry definitions. Tool-change and speed and feed specifications are done using ATCHG (automatic tool-change) and MTCHG (manual tool-change) statements. MOVE is used to rapid traverse to a geometry; it is similar to the GO statement in APT. CUT does the same, except feed motion is used. To move around a circular arc, three statements are used: OCON, ICON, and CONT, which are outer contouring, inner contouring, and contouring, respectively. The DRL statement is used for hole-pattern drilling.

MAPT (Micro-APT) is a subset (a microcomputer version) of the APT language processor. Using MAPT, a manufacturing engineer specifies the geometry of a part to be machined, the motion of the tool (cutter), and the operations involved in producing the part. The MAPT system translates these instructions into numerical information that guides the machine tool to produce the part. Tool-center offsets are automatically calculated. Currently, MAPT is capable of three-axis programming.

MAPT is an interpretive language. Like the full-scale APT language processor, MAPT contains four classes of statements. With MAPT, the user can compile a MAPT

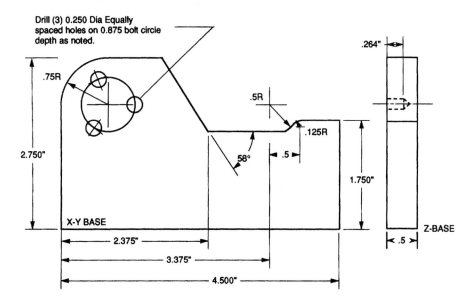

Figure 10.27   A part to be machined using the COMPACT II program of Figure 10.28(b).

```
MACHINE MILL
IDENT DEMONSTRATION PROGRAM
SETUP
BASE, 3XB, 8YB, 6ZB
DLN1, XB
DLN2, 2. 75YB
DPT1, .75XB, 2YB, ZB
DCIR1, PT1, .75R
DPT2, 2.375XB, 1.5YB, ZB
DLN3.PT2, 58CW
DLN4, 1.5YB
DPT3, 3.5XB, 1.5+.5YB,ZB
DCIR2.PT3,.5R
DPT4, 3.5+.5XB, 1.75-.125YB.ZB
DCIR3, PT4,.125R
DLN5, 1.75 YB
DLN6. 4. 5XB
DLN7, YB
DCIR4, PT1,.875DIA
ATCHG, TOOL1, .5TD. 6GL, 250FPM, .01IPR
MOVE, PASTLN1.PASTLN7, .6ZB
CUT, -.03ZB
OCON, CIR1, CW.S(180) .F(270)
CUT,PARLN2.PASTLN3
CUT.PARLN3.TOLN4
ICON.CIR2.CCW.S (TANLN4), F(TANCIR3)
OCON, CIR3.CW.S (TANCIR2), F(TANLN5)
CUT, PASTLN6
CUT, PASTLN7
CUT, PASTLN1
ATCHG, TOOL2, .25TD, 6GL, 800RPM, 011PR, 118TPA
DRL3, CIR4, CW, SO, 5ZB, 3DP
END
```

Figure 10.28   A sample COMPACT II part program.

source program line by line. The final CL data and error messages, if any, are printed out on the screen as the program compiles. The CL data can be plotted with user-defined geometry to verify the program. Paper tape or paper-tape-format data are generated by postprocessors for the target NC machine tools.

MAPT also contains a built-in screen editor with an on-line help facility. The user is able to obtain on-line assistance on both editor commands and MAPT language syntax. A MAPT source program can be created, compiled, edited, and then compiled again without leaving the MAPT working environment. A built-in graphics package allows the user to verify a program. It can also simulate the cutter path on a real-time basis. The verification plot of both the part geometry and tool path also can be attained on a digital plotter.

The MAPT program structure and syntax is presented in Figure 10.29. The details about the MAPT language are available in Wysk, Chang, and Wang (1988). A newer version that contains most of the APT features described in this chapter is also available from the authors.

During the past few years, significant changes have occurred that affect the NC environment. These require a reassessment of the adequacy of current NC processors. A program written in MAPT for the part shown in Figure 10.17 is

```
partno/example 10.2
fedrat/5.0
splindl/1000,cw
cutter/0.5
clprint/on
pt1 = point/6,6,0
pt2 = point/pt1,0,2,0
pt3 = point/pt2,2,0,0
I1 = line/pt1,p2
I2 = line/pt2,p3
I3 = line/pt3, parlel,11
14 = line/pt1,parlID,12
go/to,11
golft/11,past,12
gorgt/12,past,13
gorgt/13,past,14
gorgt/14,past,11
fini
```

In the program all points and lines are defined with respect to pt1. The part location can be changed easily by redefining the coordinates of pt1. The statement "clprint/on" prints the data value of each geometric entity and cutter location. It is used for de-bugging purposes. The tool motion commands consist of one GO statement and four GOLFT/GORGT statements. A MAPT "word" can be written in either uppercase or lowercase.

PART PROGRAM STRUCTURE AND SYNTAX

The MAPT program has the following structure
— Part Identification
    SYNTAX:
        PARTNO/part identification

— Environment Description
    CUTTER/dia
    INTO/tolerance
    OUTTO/tolerance
    TOLT/tolerance
    CLPRINT/{ON, OFF}
    PSIS/{pl-name, OFF}

— Geometric Definitions
    Point
        p-name = POINT/x, y, z
        p-name = POINT/p-name, dx, dy, dz
        p-name = POINT/l-name, l-name
        p-name = POINT/CENTER, c-name
    Line
        l-name = LINE/xl, yl, zl, x2, y2, z2
        l-name = LINE/p-name, p-name
        l-name = LINE/p-name, {LEFT RIGHT}, c-name
        l-name = LINE/p-name, parlel, l-name
        l-name = LINE/p-name, angle
        l-name = LINE/{LEFT RIGHT}, c-name, {LEFT RIGHT}, c-name
    Circle
        c-name = CIRCLE/x, y, r
        c-name = CIRCLE/l-name, {LEFT RIGHT}, {FAR NEAR}, l-name, r
        c-name = CIRCLE/p-name, RADIUS, r
        c-name = CIRCLE/p-name, TAN, l-name
        c-name = CIRCLE/p-name, p-name, p-name
    Plane
        p-name = PLANE/a, b, c, d

— Motion Statements
    Positioning Statements
        SETPT/x, y, z
        GODLTA/x value, y-value, z-value
    Start-Up Motion
        GO/{TO ON PASS}, {p-name l-name c-name}
    Continuous Motion
        GORGT/{l-name c-name}, {TO ON PAST}, {p-name l-name c-name}
        GOLFT/{l-name c-name}, {TO ON PAST}, {p-name l-name c-name}

—Postprocessor Commands
    FEDRAT/feedrate
    MACHINE/machine type
    COOLNT/{ON OFF}
    RAPID/speed
    SELECT/TOOL, tool#
    SPINDL/{OFF rpm, {CLW CCLW}}
    TORCH/{ON OFF}

—Termination
    FINI/

Figure 10.29   MAPT program structure and syntax.

- Based on the experiences reported by NC users, new requirements have been identified and have to be satisfied. Among these are the following:
  - NC machine tools have grown in complexity and capability, and their new functions need to be supported via NC processors and resultant postprocessors.
  - Most of the worldwide NC users support the standardization of an NC language so that it provides a common Englishlike language based on APT syntax and language, with subsets and modularized features therein. (Both ANSI and ISO have committees addressing this subject.)
- Computer hardware and programming technology have evolved considerably. Among the areas directly affecting current NC processors are the following:
  - The architecture of current NC processors has inhibited their ability to take advantage of new advances in computer hardware that may improve price/performance (i.e., new disk devices, increased core capacity, and so on).
  - The advent of new operating systems enables applications that properly utilize their functions to be smaller, more efficient, and more reliable. The current NC processors were developed prior to the existence of elaborate operating-system facilities and cannot be conveniently altered to take advantage of these improvements.
  - Many improvements in programming technology have resulted in more efficient methods for performing algorithmic operations, especially for geometric functions. Current NC processors may only selectively utilize these new techniques and at a sacrifice of efficiency.
- The concept of computer-aided manufacturing (CAM) is evolving. CAM encompasses the spectrum of manufacturing applications and utilizes the computer to integrate plant operations. NC processors are a vital application with CAM, however, current processors do not lend themselves to this environment and would be extremely difficult to extend to do so. For example:
  - Large disk files containing data required by several CAM applications need to be utilized by NC processors (i.e., material file, tool file, and so on) for the automatic calculation of feeds and speeds at the user's option.
  - CAM applications lend themselves to be used in a terminal-oriented environment to increase efficiency and reliability, thereby improving flow time.

It is clear from this discussion that computer-aided part programming has received a great deal of attention over the past 20 years. The languages developed can be of tremendous advantage to the part programmer. With the advent of computer-aided design (CAD), the geometric information needed for part programming is already resident in the computer. The new generation of computer-aided part-programming systems is capable of automatically generating some limited part programs. Future systems should be able to do this more effectively.

10.4 CAD PART PROGRAMMING

For a machine tool such as a mill or lathe, the part program describes the path that the cutter will follow, as well as the direction of rotation, rate of travel, and various auxiliary functions such as coolant flow. Traditionally, programs for NC machine tools have been created using one of the previously described methods; manual part program-ming or computer-assisted part programming. Simple programs are often created manually, perhaps with the aid of a calculator, and more complex programs are usually created using a computer and a part-programming language, such as APT. The manual method, while adequate for many simple point-to-point processes, requires the pro-grammer to perform all calculations required to define the cutter-path geometry and can be time-consuming. Errors made by the programmer are often not discovered until the program is tested graphically or on the machine tool, and error correction can be cumbersome. Also, because most machine tools have their own language, the pro-grammer is often working with different instruction sets, which further complicates part-program creation. The computer-assisted or part-programming language ap-proach simplifies the process because the programmer uses the same language for each program, regardless of the target machine tool. The language processor, which translates the part-programming language (such as APT) into the NC machine tool's instructions, also performs most of the calculations needed to describe the cutter path. Errors, however, are often not discovered until the program is tested.

Although the computer-assisted approach offers advantages over the manual approach, both require the programmer to translate geometric information from one form (usually an engineering drawing) into another, which has a significant potential for errors in the process.

Creation of NC programs from CAD provides yet another option by allowing the part programmer to access the computer's computational capabilities via an interactive graphics display console. This allows geometry to be described in the form of points, lines, arcs, and so on, just as it is on an engineering drawing, rather than requiring a trans-lation to a text-oriented notation. Use of a graphics display terminal also allows the sys-tem to display the resulting cutter-path geometry, allowing earlier verification of a program, which can avoid costly machine setups for program testing.

Most CAD/NC systems generally provide significant productivity gains. These systems allow the user to more rapidly define the geometry as well as to use powerful graphics display capabilities to quickly define, verify, and edit the actual cutter motion.

The part-programming operation typically starts with the receipt (by the manu-facturing department) of a design in the form of a CAD/NC drawing or model. After a review by a production planner, the tool design/selection process is completed, often with the assistance of the CAD system.

The programmer, using the part's geometric description as created by the design department and, perhaps, other geometric data produced later by the manufacturing department (clamps, appliances, and so on), now begins the part-programming process. If the programmer was not using any CAD/NC system, the first step would be to de-fine some or all of the part geometry. When using a CAD/NC system, this step is greatly simplified.

The programmer now generates a cutter path by selecting geometric elements with a digitizer (such as a light pen or mouse) attached to the display terminal. Various auxiliary and postprocessor commands are also entered at the terminal.

Once a cutter path is created, it can be replayed for verification. The computer assists the programmer by animating the entire path on the display terminal, show-ing the location of the cutter visually, and by displaying the X, Y, and Z coordinates.

Editing may be done interactively during the replay to correct errors or make changes to the program.

After verification, the various cutter passes are combined to form a program using a postprocessing command, provided by most of the CAD/NC systems. Information relating to the machine tool to be used is automatically extracted from the CAD/NC machine file on a storage medium such as magnetic disk, and merged with the program, which is then stored for processing by different postprocessors. Finally, the NC program is produced on punched tape or whatever medium is required by the NC machine tool.

Many manufacturers of discrete products have employed NC machine tools for decades. Whether it is a simple two-axis drill or a complex five-axis machining center, all NC machines require part programming. The preparation of paper tapes or tape images for NC machine tools is complex and time-consuming. It often takes 24, even 500, hours to program and prepare a paper tape for a part on a machine tool (Knox, 1983). Because part programmers have difficulty keeping up with the demand for new part programs, the tendency is to develop efficient procedures capable of replicating this human process and install these procedures on a CAD/CAM system.

Several CAD/CAM systems, such as CADAM, Computervision, and CATIA, have the capability of generating NC machining instructions based on the geometric definition of a workpiece.

10.4.1 Computervision System

Computervision has a relatively powerful NC package, called NC Vision, for the generation of NC instructions. A rough description of the procedure to generate an NC tool path (face-milling operation) using NC Vision follows (the entire NC tool-path planning process is conducted in an interactive mode):

- Create a part drawing using CADD4.
- Select the NC planning function from the menu.
- Select a milling cutter from the tool library. The library contains a complete set of tools for turning, milling, drilling, countersinking, and several other operations.
- After entering the NC planning mode, the user answers a series of questions, such as tool geometry, stepover, approach type, retraction type, and tolerance. NC Vision then generates a tool path for the planned part.

NC Vision is able to assist the user to generate and verify NC tool paths based on different algorithms.

10.4.2 CADAM System

The NC capability provided by CADAM is more limited than that of Computervision. For example, in milling a flat surface in CADAM, the user has to explicitly specify those points on which the tool stops or changes direction. CADAM then generates a tool path based on what the user has defined. As a result, the user is solely responsible for generating a "good" tool path.

10.4.3 CATIA System

CATIA utilizes a modeling scheme different from CADAM and Computervision. Basically, CATIA is a CAD package that has the capability of generating NC tool paths internally. CATIA provides a utility function that allows the user to convert a CATIA file to a tool path using a sophisticated NC planning function.

10.4.4 NC Programmer

NC Programmer is an AutoCAD-based NC part-program generator. The NC instruction-planning capability of NC Programmer is relatively primitive. First, the user needs to create a part drawing using AutoCAD and export the drawing to an ASCII data file. Second, in the NC instruction-planning mode, the user has to explicitly "tell" NC Programmer the starting and the ending locations of each tool path using a pointing device such as a mouse. NC Programmer then generates a NC part program entirely based on the instructions by the user.

Despite the fact that many CAD/CAM systems provide the facility that is able to generate NC tool path directly from CAD data, this area is far from fully developed. This can be addressed as follows:

1. *Geometric coverage.* The commercial CAD/NC packages are limited to very simple geometric shapes such as 2-D peripheral cut, pocket milling, and turned parts (Wang and Lin, 1987). More complicated features demand human interpretation, which is time-consuming. In order to automate the CAD/NC interface, more sophisticated feature-recognition algorithms are required.

2. *Optimization of NC tool path.* CAD/CAM systems are currently generating the cutter path for many NC operations. However, no mathematical model is available for creating an optimal path. By utilizing such a model, the minimum length of cut could be identified for all kinds of surface features. In the following section, a preliminary study on NC tool-path optimization, which was conducted exclusively for face-milling operations, is presented.

10.4.5 Interactive Part Programming

Interactive part programming can be done either on a CNC controller or on a personal computer. Because it is relatively easy to learn and inexpensive to purchase, many small shops opt for interactive part programming instead of a part-programming language or the more expansive CAD-based part programming. Interactive part programming is usually limited to 2½ D parts.

Because CNC controllers are computer-based, some vendors add interactive or graphical part-programming functions to the controller. A machinist can enter the part program interactively on the controller. The part geometry can be entered using a keyboard and special function keys. After the part geometry is defined, the machinist can define the cutter and its path. The graphics display on the controller shows both the part geometry defined and the final tool path. The controller guides the user through each step, little or no language syntax needs to be followed. Many advanced controllers provide this capability. One company, Hurco, produces controllers exclusively using interactive part programming. Using dual displays, a programmer works on the geometric display in one window and observes the text on the other. The user is able to program the machine while the machine is actively cutting a workpiece. Figure 10.30 shows the Hurco CNC controller.

Another type of interactive part programming is graphical part-programming software such as SmartCAM. SmartCAM is capable of handling two-dimensional geometries. Part shape is defined using lines, arcs, chamfers, and so on, where geometric objects are selected from a menu. End-point coordinates of each geometric object are entered after the system prompt. The part geometry is assumed to be the 2-D profile swept in the Z direction. The geometry also can be imported from other CAD systems in DXF (see Chapter 3) format. The user can select menu items to change the direction of cut, starting position, tool-path profile, and so on. The system is capable of generating cutter path for offset walls, simple pockets, pockets with islands, drill patterns, and turned profiles. Figure 10.31 shows the SmartCAM programming system.

10.4.6 Solid-Model-Based Cutter-Path Generation

Almost most of the cutter-path-generation packages use lines and arcs as the basic geometric entities (wire-frame model), some systems have begun to use solid models directly. When the cutter path is generated using a wire-frame model, there is no way of detecting interference between the tool and the part and the fixture. By using a solid model, the entire machining environment, including stock, part volume, tools, and fixtures, can be modeled and used to generate a collision-free cutter path. Gouge-avoidance algorithms can be used to check the entire tool and toolholder to ensure gouge-free machining. It is also possible to incorporate geometric reasoning rules and machining knowledge to select feeds, speeds, tools, and operation sequence. Machining knowledge is applied to each solid geometry feature to be machined. An optimal cutter-path algorithm can be written for each feature. Figure 10.32 shows a cutter-path simulation verifying a cutter path generated by the SDRC I-DEAS Master Series package. In the figure, it clearly shows the workpiece, fixtures, and the machine table. Any interference can be detected before the actual machining take place. Other example is a package called Strata by Spatial Technology. Strata is a feature-based NC cutter-path-generation package using an object-oriented solid modeler, ACIS. Strata contains optimum cutter-path-generation algorithms for many solid features.

10.5 NC CUTTER-PATH VERIFICATION

Before a part is machined, the part program needs to be verified. The purposes of verification are (1) to detect geometric error of the cutter path, (2) to detect potential tool interference, and (3) to detect erroneous cutting conditions. Geometric error is the most common problem. The machined part geometry must agree with the design specification. When a tool follows the programmed cutter path, it may not produce the exact part

Figure 10.30 On controller programming—Hurco Ultimax II. (courtesy of Hurco Machine Tool Company)

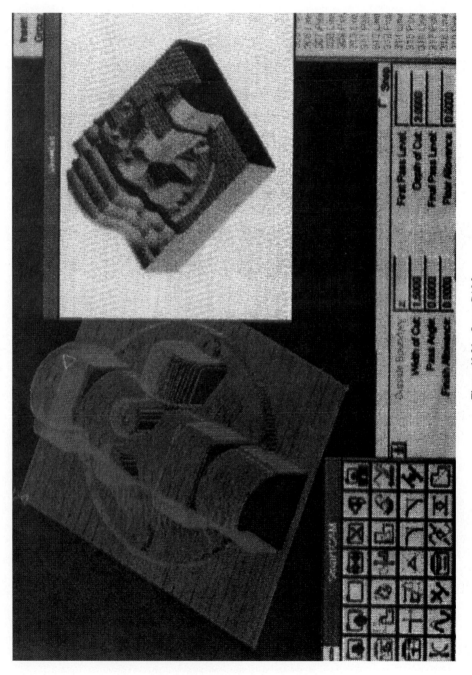

Figure 10.31 SmartCAM.

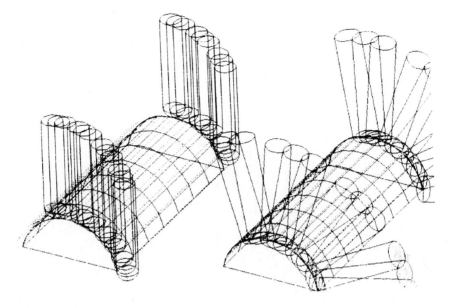

Figure 10.32   Solid-based machining from SDRC. (Courtesy of SDRC.)

surface the designer has specified. Although gross geometric errors do occur in some part programs (especially those written by less experienced part programmers), many errors occur because of local gauging and undercutting. These errors are more difficult to detect. Other types of errors are caused by the interference between the tool with the workpiece and the fixture elements. In three-axis machining, such errors often occur during rapid positioning motions. For five-axis machining, it can happen any time. It is difficult for the part programmer to detect the error during programming. The cutting condition is the specification of specific machining speed, feed, depth of cut, cutter geometry, and tool material on the workpiece material. The selection of tool and cutting parameters is experience-based. There is no guarantee that they are correct. In order to predict the cutting condition, one must have an exact process model. Unfortunately, this is the area for which we have least knowledge. In order to eliminate potential errors during actual machining, it is necessary that a part program be verified.

There are several ways to verify a part program. For instance, one may make a dry cut on the machine without the workpiece. A dry cut can detect gross programming mistakes, but not the detailed geometric ones. Another approach is to actually machine a prototype. Typically, a prototype part is machined in wax, machining plastic, wood, foam, or some other soft material. The actual geometry is then measured and compared with the design specification. Because material property is critical in determining the cutting condition, this approach can verify only the geometry.

When a part program is generated using a CAD-based system, a graphic output of the cutter path may be produced by the software. By visual inspection, cutter-path abnormalities may be detected. On a simple system, the cutter path is shown as a line drawing, sometimes overlaid on the part model. The exact final geometry is left for the user to imagine. Figure 3.9 shows such an approach in a commercial CAD/CAM system. In an advanced system, a solid model may be used to generate a realistic picture of the workpiece, tool, and the finished part. Real-time simulation of the cutting process can be displayed on screen. However, most simulations are purely geometry-based, where the cutting condition is not considered. One example of such a system is shown in Figure 10.33.

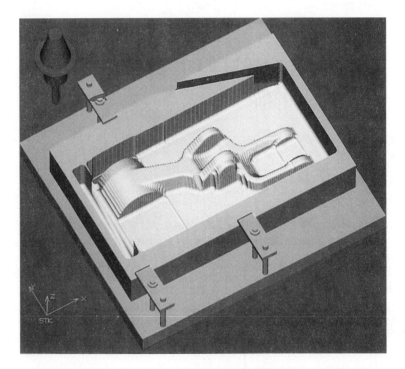

Figure 10.33   Cutter path verification using VeriCut (courtesy Vericut)

ADVANCED/INTERMEDIATE MATERIALS

10.6 ANALYTICAL GEOMETRY FOR PART PROGRAMMING

10.6.1 Cutter-Center Location and Tool Offset

The following examples show the mathematical foundation of a computed cutter path. The method illustrated is implemented in MAPT. The method uses homogeneous coordinate transformation to convert a complex geometry program into an easier one. Directions of a cutter motion and offset can be easily taken care of by this method. The reader may extend this idea to solve many other related problems.

Algebra provides the foundation for CL data generation. However, when one wants to implement some procedure to compute CL data, problems may occur. This is especially true when one tries to write computer programs for the computational procedure. Here is an example. Suppose that we want to find the cutter-center location after the following APT command is issued (see Figure 10.34).

$$\text{GO} \begin{Bmatrix} \text{LFT} \\ \text{RGT} \end{Bmatrix} / l_1, \begin{Bmatrix} \text{TO} \\ \text{ON} \\ \text{PAST} \end{Bmatrix}, l_2$$

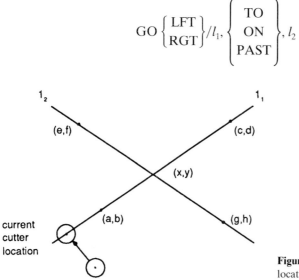

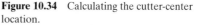

Figure 10.34   Calculating the cutter-center location.

We know that by solving the following simultaneous equations, we can obtain the X and Y coordinates.

$$l_1: \frac{x - a}{y - b} = \frac{a - c}{b - d} \tag{10.5}$$

$$l_2: \frac{x - e}{y - f} = \frac{e - g}{f - h} \tag{10.6}$$

However, in reality, problems occur when

1. $b - d = 0$ or $f - h = 0$
2. l_1 / l_2
3. $b - d \to 0, a - c/b - d \to \infty$
4. It is impossible to tell whether the tool goes to the left- or right-hand side of l_1 in order to determine the tool offset.

In the following, we present a new approach to find the exact location of the cutter center.

First, let us examine an ideal situation, where l_1 is on the Y axis and the current cutter location is at the origin of the X–Y coordinate system, as shown in Figure 10.35.

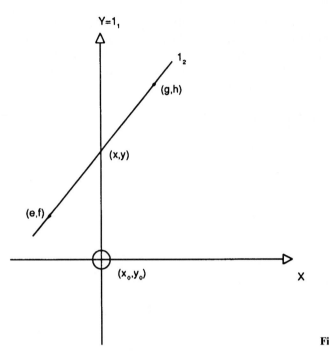

Figure 10.35 l_1 is lined up with the Y axis.

In this ideal case, the following procedure provides the solution for x and y.

1. If $|e - g| \leq \delta$, then there is no solution.
2. Otherwise,

$$x = 0$$

$$y = f + (-e)\frac{f - h}{e - g} \qquad (10.7)$$

Now the question is how to transfer a pair of arbitrary lines, that is, l_1 and l_2, to this ideal situation. Let us find the angle, θ, between the Y axis and l_1 so that l_1 is lined up with the Y axis (see Figure 10.36). The next step is to rotate about the Z axis for θ.
    The rotation transformation matrix is

$$RT_z(\theta) = \begin{bmatrix} \cos\theta & \sin\theta & 0 & 0 \\ -\sin\theta & \cos\theta & 0 & 0 \\ 0 & 0 & 1 & 0 \\ 0 & 0 & 0 & 1 \end{bmatrix} \qquad (10.8)$$

Chapter 3 contains a more detailed description of coordinate transformation. The following is the solution for procedure for a general case:

1. Find θ.
2. Translate the current cutter location to the origin of the X–Y coordinate system. Rotate θ about the Z axis.

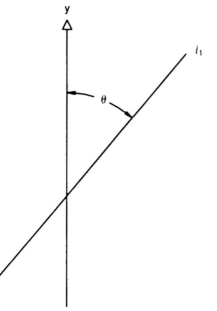

Figure 10.36   Rotating l_1 for θ

$$[e', f', 0, 1] = [e, f, 0, 1] \cdot \text{Tran}(a, b, c) \cdot RT_z(\theta)$$

$$[g', h', 0, 1] = [g, h, 0, 1] \cdot \text{Tran}(a, b, c) \cdot RT_z(\theta)$$

3. If $|e' - g'| \le \delta$, stop. (No solution is found.) δ is a very small number arbitrarily chosen by the user.

4. Find α for the tool-offset calculation (see Figure 10.37).

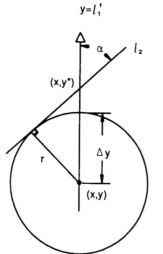

Figure 10.37   Calculating tool offset.

5. Calculate the tool offset:

$$x' = 0$$

$$y' = \left|\left(f' - e'\frac{f' - h'}{e' - g'}\right)\right| + (flag)\frac{r}{\sin \alpha} \qquad (10.9)$$

where

$$flag = \begin{cases} -1 & \text{for} & \text{TO} \\ 0 & \text{for} & \text{ON} \\ 1 & \text{for} & \text{PAST} \end{cases} l_2$$

6. Transform (x', y') back to the original coordinate system.

$$[x, y, 0, 1] = [x', y', 0, 1] \cdot RT_z(-\theta) \cdot \text{Tran}(-x_0, -y_0, 0) \qquad (10.10)$$

(x, y) is the solution.

The same procedure can be applied to find the cutter-center location for this command (see Figure 10.38).

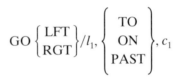

$$GO \begin{Bmatrix} LFT \\ RGT \end{Bmatrix} /l_1, \begin{Bmatrix} TO \\ ON \\ PAST \end{Bmatrix}, c_1$$

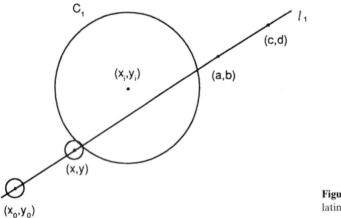

Figure 10.38   A different example for calculating cutter-center location.

The procedure that finds the cutter-center location is as follows (see Figure 10.39).

1. Find θ, the angle between l_1 and the Y axis.
2. Translate (x_0, y_0) and rotate θ about the Z axis.

$$[x_i', y_i', 0, 1] = [x_i, y_i, 0, 1] \cdot \text{Tran}(x_0, y_0, 0) \cdot RT_z(\theta) \qquad (10.11)$$

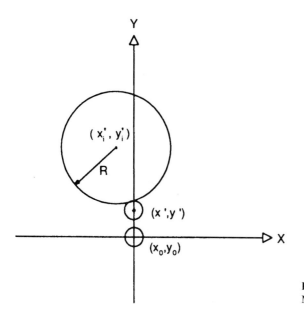

Figure 10.39   The tool path generated by a MAPT statement.

3. $R' = R + (\text{flag}) \cdot r$
where

$$\text{flag} = \left.\begin{Bmatrix} 1 & \text{TO} \\ 0 & \text{ON} \\ -1 & \text{PAST} \end{Bmatrix}\right\} c_1$$

If $|x_i'| > |R'|$, no solution is found.

4. Transform the solution back to the original coordinate system.

$$[x, y, 0, 1] = [x', y', 0, 1] \cdot RT_z(-\theta) \cdot \text{Tran}(-x_0, -y_0, 0) \tag{10.12}$$

(x, y) is the solution.

10.6.2 Computational Geometry

10.6.2.1 Parametric representation.   In preparing NC part programs, we have to deal with the geometry of many different objects. Under these circumstances, having the knowledge of computational geometry is helpful. In this section, we provide some basic formulas that can serve as a starting point for further study.

1. *Tangent of a curve.* The tangent of a curve $y = f(x)$ at point $p(x_1, y_1)$ is computed from the following equations; see Figure 10.40.

$$y = y_1 + f'(x_1)(x - x_1) \tag{10.13}$$

$$f'(x) = \frac{df}{dx}(x) \tag{10.14}$$

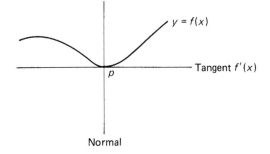

Normal

Figure 10.40   Tangent of a curve.

$$\frac{y - y_1}{x - x_1} = \frac{df}{dx} = \frac{dy}{dx} \tag{10.15}$$

2. *Tangent at point p.* The tangent at point p with parameter $v = v_1$ is calculated from the following equations; see Figure 10.40.

$$x = x(v_1 + \tau \dot{x}(v_1))$$
$$y = y(v_1 + \tau \dot{y}(v_1)) \tag{10.16}$$

where

τ = parameter for the new line

$\dot{x}(v_1) = dx/dt$ at $v = v_1$

$\dot{y}(v_1) = dy/dt$ at $v = v_1$

3. *Normal to a curve.* The normal to a curve is available from the following equations; see Figure 10.40.

$$x = x(v_1) - \tau \dot{y}(v_1)$$
$$y = y(v_1) - \tau \dot{x}(v_1) \tag{10.17}$$

4. *Parametric description of surfaces.* A plane passing through the point r_0 and containing the lines $\mathbf{r} = \mathbf{r}_0 + u\mathbf{r}_1$ and $\mathbf{r} = \mathbf{r}_0 + v\mathbf{n}_2$, where $\mathbf{n}_1$ and $\mathbf{n}_2$ are unit vectors, as shown in Figure 10.41.

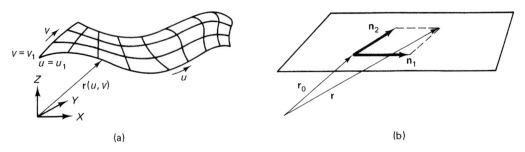

(a)   (b)

Figure 10.41   Parametric description of a surface.

5. *Tangent to a curve.* A tangent vector (unit vector) is defined as follows; see Figure 10.42.

$$T = \frac{d\mathbf{r}/du}{|d\mathbf{r}/du|} \tag{10.18}$$

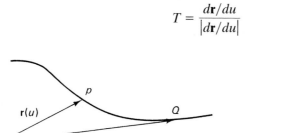

Figure 10.42   Tangent to a curve.

where

$$\left|\frac{d\mathbf{r}}{du}\right| \neq 0 \tag{10.19}$$

A tangent line at $u = u_0$ can then be expressed as

$$\mathbf{r}_t = \mathbf{r}(u_0) + \lambda \mathbf{T}(u_0) \tag{10.20}$$

Example 10.3

Find the tangent line for the following curve:

$$\mathbf{r} = u^3\mathbf{a} + u^2\mathbf{b} + u\mathbf{c} + \mathbf{d} \tag{10.21}$$

$$\frac{d\mathbf{r}}{du} = 3u^2\mathbf{a} + 2u\mathbf{b} + \mathbf{c} \tag{10.22}$$

$$u_0 = 0 \tag{10.23}$$

$$\frac{d\mathbf{r}}{du} = c \tag{10.24}$$

$$\mathbf{T}(0) = \frac{c}{|c|} \tag{10.25}$$

$$\mathbf{r}(0) = d \tag{10.26}$$

$$\mathbf{r}_t = \mathbf{d} + \frac{\lambda c}{|c|} \tag{10.27}$$

Therefore, the tangent line for

$$\mathbf{a} = \begin{bmatrix} 1 \\ 2 \end{bmatrix} \quad \mathbf{b} = \begin{bmatrix} 2 \\ 2 \end{bmatrix} \quad \mathbf{c} = \begin{bmatrix} 3 \\ 2 \end{bmatrix} \quad \mathbf{d} = \begin{bmatrix} 4 \\ 1 \end{bmatrix}$$

is

$$\mathbf{r}_t = \begin{bmatrix} 4 \\ 1 \end{bmatrix} + \frac{\lambda}{\sqrt{13}} \begin{bmatrix} 3 \\ 2 \end{bmatrix} \tag{10.28}$$

6. *Tool offset.* The tangent and normal vectors to a surface are calculated as follows; see Figure 10.43.

$$\mathbf{r} = \mathbf{r}(u, v) \tag{10.29}$$

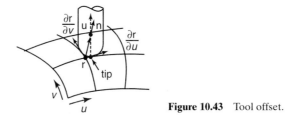

Figure 10.43   Tool offset.

At (u_0, v_0) $\partial\mathbf{r}/\partial u$ is a tangent vector to the curve $\mathbf{r} = \mathbf{r}(u, v_0)$, and $\partial\mathbf{r}/\partial v$ to the curve $\mathbf{r} = r(u_0, v)$. Given a unit normal vector,

$$\mathbf{n} = \pm \frac{[\partial\mathbf{r}/\partial u \times \partial\mathbf{r}/\partial v]}{|\partial\mathbf{r}/\partial u \times \partial\mathbf{r}/\partial v|} \tag{10.30}$$

When cutting the surface using a ball end-mill, $\mathbf{r}$ is the cutter contact point. The normal pass through the center of the tool. Since the tool is aligned with the z axis, the tip of the tool is right under the center. At $u = u_0$ and $v = v_0$, the tool tip coordinate $\mathbf{r}'$ is:

$$\mathbf{r}' = \mathbf{r}(u_0, v_0) + R(\mathbf{n} - \mathbf{u}) \tag{10.31}$$

where R is the tool radius, $u = \begin{bmatrix} 0 & 0 & 1 \end{bmatrix}$.

10.6.2.2 Sculptured surface machining.   Sculptured surfaces are usually machined on three-, four-, or five-axis machines. To machine a sculptured surface with a three-axis Cartesian machine, a flat end-milling cutter is used to remove most of the material on the surface. A ball end-milling cutter is then used to finish the surface by approximating the surface using line segments. Because the entire spherical surface of the ball end-milling cutter can be used for cutting, it can cut curved surfaces. At each step is a cutter contact point. The surface normal vector at the cutter contact point passes through the cutter center. The cutter path is defined by the cutter center points. The resultant surface produced by the cutter must be within the tolerance specified on the design. The smaller the tolerance, the more cutter path steps have to be taken. After the machining, usually grinding and polishing operations are used to smooth the surface. Because grinding and polishing are slow and expensive, it is important that machining is done properly, so that a minimum amount of secondary processes will be needed.

There are several ways to generate finishing cutter paths for a sculptured surface: APT type cutting, Cartesian cutting, and isoparameter cutting. In APT-type cutting, the sculptured surface is defined as the part surface (PSIS; see Section 10.3.1). Newton's method is used to find the tool position iteratively. In Cartesian cutting, the tool path is generated using the Cartesian coordinates mapped onto the part surface. For example, the cutter moves first in the X direction and then sidesteps in the Y direction (Figure 10.44). Because the part surface is defined in the parameter domain (u, v), it is difficult

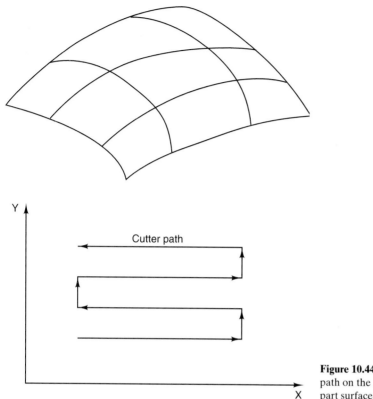

Cutter path

Figure 10.44   Cartesian cutting. The cutter path on the X–Y plane is mapped onto the part surface above.

to calculate the cutter contact point (given X and Y coordinates, find u and v). In isoparameter cutting, the cutter moves on u–v space either incrementing on u first and then on v, or vice versa. In this section, we will discuss only the isoparameter approach.

The following algorithm to be discussed is not optimal, however, it works well for simple surfaces. The objective of the cutter-path generation is to generate a minimum step cutter path that is within the tolerance limit. The control points describing the surface, the tool diameter, and the desired tolerance value are given in the figure.

Step 1. Select a direction u or v to move first. Set $u = 0$, $v = 0$, $i = 0$, and $j = 0$.

Step 2. Move along u (or v), and find step size Δu that satisfies the tolerance requirement (Figure 10.45). (The step-size algorithm will be presented later.)

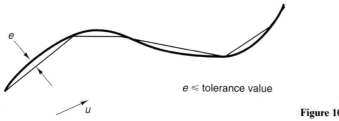

$e \leqslant$ tolerance value

Figure 10.45   Forward step size.

$u_{i+1} = u_i + \Delta u$, $r(u_{i+1}, v_j)$ is the cutter contact point. Find the cutter center at

$$r_{CL} = r(u_{i+1}, v_j) + \frac{dia}{2} \frac{\mathbf{n}(u_{i+1}, v_j)}{|\mathbf{n}(u_{i+1}, v_j)|}$$

Where dia is the tool diameter, $\mathbf{n}(u_{i+1} \geq v_j)$ is the surface normal at $r(u_{i+1}, v_j)$. Repeat the step until $u_{i+1} \geq 1$.

Step 3. Move (sidestep) Δv for the next curve. $v_{j+1} \geq v_j + \Delta v$. Make sure that the scallop height δ is less than tolerance (Figure 10.46). (The scallop-height calculation will be presented later.)

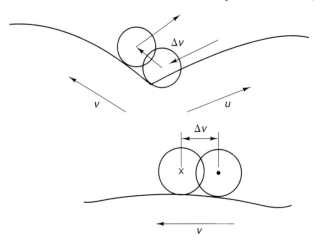

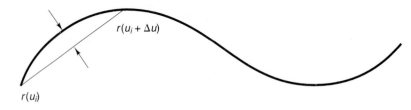

Figure 10.46   Step size.

Step 4. Repeat steps 2 and 3 until the entire surface has been machined ($v_{j+1} \geq 1$). When j is an odd number, set the initial u_0 to 1 and $u_{i+1} = u_i - \Delta u$. This makes a zig-zag cutter path.

Finding the Step Size.   (Figure 10.47)

$r(u_i + \Delta u)$

$r(u_i)$

Figure 10.47   Step size.

At constant $v,*$ the curve $r(u) = r(u, v^*)$.

Set an initial Δu, and find the maximum cordal deviation. If d^* is greater than the tolerance, reduce Δu and try again until d^* is within the tolerance.

Because the exact error is difficult to find, we may use a "quick-and-dirty" method to get a tool path (Figure 10.48). The method follows.

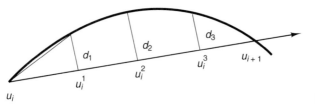

Figure 10.48   Error at each test point.

(a) Set Δu = constant

$$u_i = 0$$

(b) $u_{i+1} = u_i + \Delta u$. If $u_{i+1} \geq 1$, $u_{i+1} = 1$.
(c) Find three points: $r(u_i^1)$, $r(u_i^2)$, and $r(u_i^3)$.

$$u_i^j = u_i + j\frac{\Delta u}{4}$$

$$d_j = \left| \frac{[r(u_i^j) - r(u_i)][r(u_{i+1}) - r(u_i)]}{|r(u_{i+1}) - r(u_i)|} \right|$$

Because this is a curve in a surface, $r(u_i)$ should be $r(u_i, v^*)$, where v^* is the current v value. On a two dimensional map, the distance between a point and a line also can be calculated. Let the line equation be $ax + by + c = 0$. The point is located at (x_1, y_1).

$$d = \frac{ax_1 + by_1 + c}{\sqrt{a^2 + b^2}}$$

(d) If max (d_j) > tolerance, set $\Delta u = 0.75\ \Delta u$ and repeat step (c); otherwise, set the next step at $r(u_{i+1})$.
(e) If $u_{i+1} = 1$, end; otherwise, go to step (a).

Find the Sidestep.   At constant u^*, the curve $r(v) = r(u, v^*)$. Assume that the surface normals are the same at $r(v_i)$ and $r(v_{i+1})$ (Figure 10.49).

(a) Set Δv = constant.
(b) $v_{i+1} = v_i + \Delta v$
(c) $l = |r(v_{i+1}) - r(v_i)|$ (see Figure 10.50)

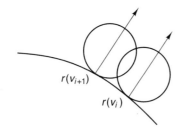

Figure 10.49   Tool at two adjacent paths.

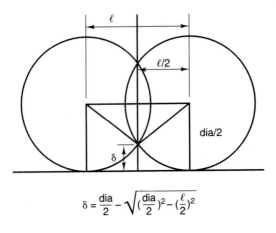

$$\delta = \frac{dia}{2} - \sqrt{(\frac{dia}{2})^2 - (\frac{\ell}{2})^2}$$

Figure 10.50   Approximate scallop height.

(d) $\delta = dia/2 - \sqrt{(dia/2)^2 - (l/2)^2}$

(e) If $\delta > 10$, set $\Delta v = 0.75\,\Delta v$ and go to step (b).

(f) Otherwise, v_{i+1} is the new step.

The preceding equation for calculating δ is approximate. There are several potential problems associated with the approach.

(a) The normal and curvature on the surface are changing. For the concave area, the estimated error is less than the actual error (Figure 10.51). For the convex region, the estimate is conservative (Figure 10.52).

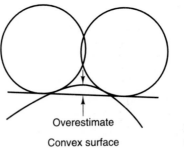

Overestimate

Convex surface

Figure 10.51   Overestimate on a convex surface.

(b) When the surface curvatures at two ends are very different the paths generated are either too close to each other, or, not close enough (Figure 10.53).

The procedure discussed before can find the "least-number-of-steps" solution. However, it is computationally expensive because of the search strategy employed. In order to improve the computational efficiency, a quick estimate approach may be more desirable. Using the initial step size Δu, we can find the error at u_i. If the error is smaller than the tolerance output, then position and increment u, $u_{i+1} = u_i + \Delta u$. If the error is

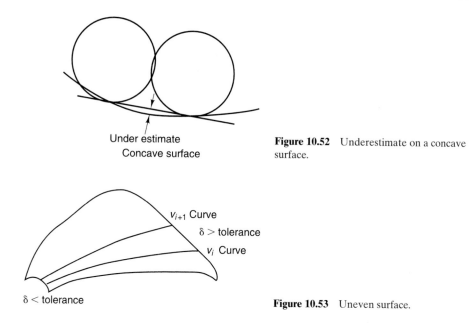

Under estimate
Concave surface

Figure 10.52   Underestimate on a concave surface.

v_{i+1} Curve

$\delta >$ tolerance

v_i Curve

$\delta <$ tolerance

Figure 10.53   Uneven surface.

greater than the tolerance, reduce Δu and check again. We may take smaller steps than necessary, but the computation is greatly simplified.

10.7 SUMMARY

Numerical-control (NC) machining has changed the appearance of an entire industry in a way that nobody would have dreamed, NC machining has impacted almost every aspect of manufacturing—accuracy, repeatability, flexibility, and economics—in a positive and profound manner. The soul of NC machining, NC programming, is introduced in this chapter. NC programming, depending on the level of automation, can be divided into (1) manual programming, (2) computer-assisted programming, and (3) automated generation of NC code (CAD/CAM). All three levels of NC programming were discussed, along with analytical aspects of NC. Although NC programming is moving toward the direction of fully integrated CAD/CAM, a modern manufacturing engineer should be equipped with the knowledge of manual programming and computer-assisted part programming, as they will still exist on the shop floor for years to come.

REVIEW QUESTIONS

10.1. Prepare an NC part program for making the slot shown in Figure 10.54. The cutter diameter is ³⁄₁₆ in. The start point is (0,0) at 2 in. to the left and 2 in. below the lower left corner of the part.

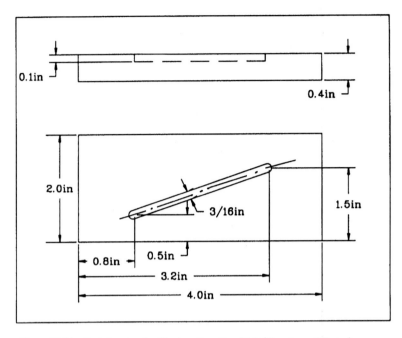

Figure 10.54   Part drawing for Review Question 10.1. (Courtesy of Terco.)

10.2. Prepare an NC part program for the part shown in Figure 10.55 The dimensions given in the figure are in millimeters. The tool diameter is 20 mm.

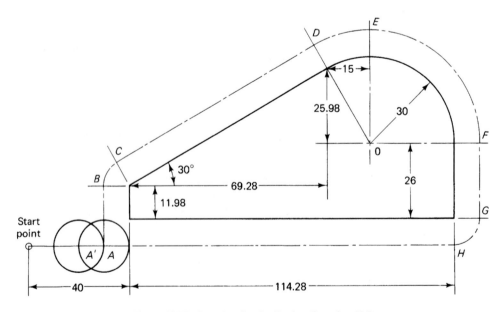

Figure 10.55   Part drawing for Review Question 10.2.

10.3. Prepare an NC part program for the part shown in Figure 10.56. The suggested cutting conditions are 6 ipm for the feed rate and 400 fpm for the speed. The cutter diameter is 5 in. The dimensions are all in inches.

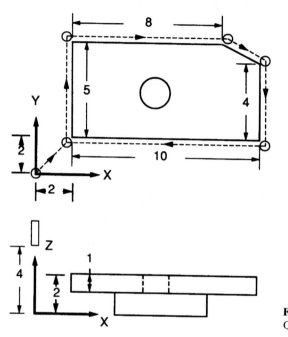

Figure 10.56 Part drawing for Review Question 10.3.

10.4. Prepare an NC part program for the part shown in Figure 10.57. The cutting conditions are the same as those given in Review Question 10.3. The dimensions are all in inches.

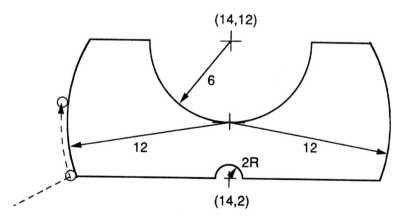

Figure 10.57 Part drawing for Review Question 10.4.

10.5. Prepare an NC part program for making a ball whose diameter is 2.8 in. The ball will be made out of a 3-in. × 3-in. × 3-in. cubic blank.

10.6. Write an APT part program for the part shown in Figure 10.58. The cutter diameter is 1 in., the suggested feed rate is 8 ipm, and the spindle speed is 764 rpm. The start is 2 in. to the left and 2 in. below the corner of the part.

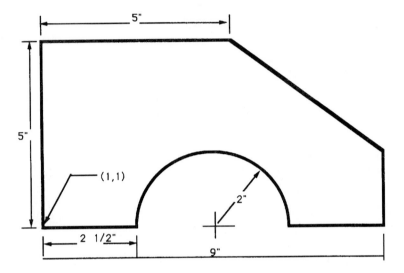

Figure 10.58   Part drawing for Review Question 10.6.

10.7. Prepare an APT part program for the part shown in Figure 10.55.

10.8. Turned parts are machined on lathes. A lathe usually has two axes, X and Z. To turn a part from a cylinder down to the part profile, one must first program the roughing passes and then the finish pass. The roughing passes remove most of the materials from the workpiece. Only a small layer of finishing allowance is left on the workpiece. The finishing cut is close to the part profile. For the part shown in Figure 10.59, the roughing passes are shown in

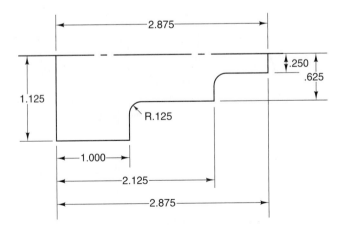

Figure 10.59   A turned part (half of the-cross section).

Figure 10.60. Assume that the cutter tip has a $\frac{1}{32}$-in. radius. Write a part program for the roughing and the finishing passes. The depth of cut for each roughing layer is 0.2-in. and finishing allowance is 0.1-in.

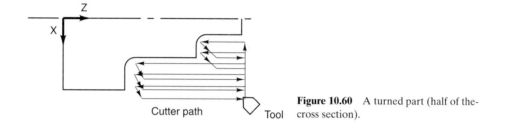

Figure 10.60   A turned part (half of the-cross section).

10.9. The profile of a turned part is defined by a Bezier's curve. The four control points are (0,0), (3,6), (6,−2), and (8,1). Write a program for the finishing cut. Use $\frac{1}{32}$-in. as the tool-nose radius. The tolerance allowed is 0.001-in.

10.10. Develop an algorithm for turning a profile consisting of lines and curves (see Figure 10.60). The algorithm must generate both rouging and finishing cuts. Implement your algorithm in a computer language you know.

10.11. Develop an algorithm to mill a rectangular pocket. Assume the corner radius is the same as the tool radius. Use the staircase approach for the pocketing.

10.12. Repeat Review Question 10.11 using the contouring approach.

10.13. Write a computer program to generate a cutter path for a Bezier's curve (Figure 10.61). The input consists of four control points, a cutter diameter, and tolerance. The output consists of a cutter path and graphics.

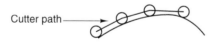

Figure 10.61   Bezier's curve cutting.

10.14. Write a computer program to generate cutter path for a Bezier's surface (Figure 10.62). The input consists of 16 control points, a tolerance = 0.1-in. and a direction of interpolation (t first or s first). The output consists of a cutter path, and verification graphics. The tool consists of a $\frac{1}{2}$-in. ball-nose end mill, 1-in. maximum depth, and $\frac{1}{4}$-in. maximum cut depth/pass. Set (0,0,0) to be the center of the 4-in.-diameter workpiece (floating-zero, decimal programming), for example,

```
N0100 G00 X0.000 Y0.000 Z1.000
```

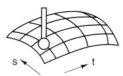

Figure 10.62   Bezier's surface cutting.

Show the derived equations, the flow chart, the source code listing, and three experimental results (data and graphics). The graphics must include both the surface plot and the cutter-path plot. Use the same control points and three different tolerances for the experiments. Use the algorithm introduced in the chapter to implement the program.

10.15. A rule surface is created by blending two curves, r_0 and r_1.

$$r(t, s) = r_0(t) + s[r_1(t) - r_0(t)]$$

where r_0 and r_1 can be any parametric curves. Write a program to generate a cutter path for a ruled surface.

REFERENCES/BIBLIOGRAPHY

CHILDS, J. J. (1982). *Principles of Numerical Control.* New York: Industrial Press.

CHOI, B. K. (1991). *Surface Modeling for CAD/CAM.* Amsterdam: Elsevier.

DING, Q., and B. J. DAVIES (1987). *Surface Engineering Geometry for Computer Aided Design and Manufacture.* West Sussex, England: Ellis Horwood.

ELECTRONIC INDUSTRIES ASSOCIATION. (1992). *32 Bit Binary CL (BCL) and 7 Bit ASCII CL (ACL) Exchange Input Format for Numerically Controlled Machines.* Washington, DC: EIA.

KOREN, Y. (1983). *Computer Control of Manufacturing Systems.* New York: McGraw-Hill.

KRAL, I. H. (1986). *Numerical Control Programming in APT.* Englewood Cliffs, NJ: Prentice Hall.

MACHINABILITY DATA CENTER. (1980). *Machining Data Handbook,* 3rd ed. Cincinnati, OH: Metcut Research Associates, Inc.

MARCINIAK, K. (1992). *Geometric Modelling for Numerically Controlled Machining.* Oxford: University Press.

PRESSMAN, R. S., and J. E. WILLIAMS (1979). *Numerical Control and Computer-Aided Manufacturing.* Aerospace Industries Association.

WANG, H. P., and A. C. LIN (1987). "Automated Generation of NC Part Programs for Turned Parts Based on 2-D Drawing Files," *International Journal of Advanced Manufacturing Technology,* 2(3), 23–36.

WYSK, R. A., T. C. CHANG, and H. P. WANG. (1988). *Computer Aided Manufacturing PC Application Software.* Albany, NY: Delmar Publishers.

YELLOWLEY, I., A. WONG, and B. DESMIT. (1987). "The Economics of Peripheral Milling," in *Manufacturing Engineering Transactions.* Society of Manufacturing Engineers, pp. 388–394, Dearborn, MI.

11

Industrial Robotics

11.1 INTRODUCTION

11.1.1 Background

With a pressing need to upgrade productivity, manufacturing industries are turning more and more toward computer-based flexible automation. Currently, many of our automated manufacturing tasks are carried out by hardwired automation designed to perform predetermined functions. The inflexibility of these handwired machines has led to a broad interest in the use of industrial robots. An industrial robot is a general-purpose computer-controlled manipulator consisting of several rigid links connected in series by revolute or prismatic joints. One end of the robot arm is attached to a supporting base and the other end is free and equipped with a gripper or a tool to manipulate objects or perform assembly or fabrication tasks.

The concept of robotics, although not referred to by that term until relatively recently, has captured human imagination for centuries. One of the first automatic animals—a wooden bird that could fly—was built by Plato's friend Archytas of Tarentum, who lived between 400 and 350 B.C. In the second century B.C., Hero of Alexandria described in his book, *De Automatis,* a mechanical theater with robotlike figures that danced and marched in temple ceremonies. In 1921, Karel Capek, the Czech playwriter, novelist, and essayist wrote the satirical drama *R.U.R.* (Rossum's Universal Robots), which introduced the word "robot" into the English language. The playwriter coined the word to mean "forced labor"; the machines in his play resembled people, but worked twice as hard.

Generally in manufacturing, robots, when compared to humans, yield more consistent quality, more predictable output, and are more reliable. Compared to automated machines, the robots' flexibility becomes quickly apparent when compared with the rigidness of hardwired automation. As previously mentioned, a robot is essentially an arm fixed to a base on which it can move. The accurate and flexible characteristics of motion depend on the sophistication of the robot's control system. In contrast, a hardwired automated machine is inflexible and generally has no redundant degrees of freedom to allow it to process products outside its narrow focus. Figure 11.1 shows that

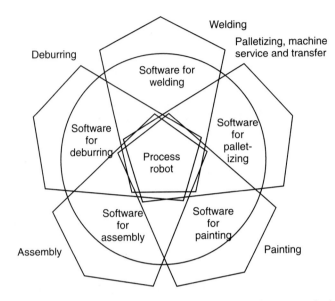

Figure 11.1   The use of appropriate software and hardware allows a standard robot to be customized to a specific task.

a robot can be reconfigured (through special software and hardware accessories) to perform a wide range of tasks. Therefore, it is generally considered that it makes economic sense to install a robot whose optional features are relatively low-priced when compared to the robot's base price, rather than a different, specialized machine for each task.

However, the robot, being a generalized device, has many redundant links and features, resulting in a slower process time and less accurate motions than a machine designed for specific tasks. Robots also have limited dexterity when compared with humans. If the tasks performed are in an uncertain environment, sophisticated sensors and controls are needed. The complexity of the control algorithm and high hardware and software costs may make the robotic application undesirable. Therefore, it is necessary to know the capabilities and limitations of robots before a robot is selected to be used in an application. The reprogrammable characteristic of robots, which makes them so attractive in a flexible manufacturing environment, actually may be a negative factor due to the high cost of program development. Since the introduction of industrial robots in the 1960s, there have been many successful applications reported. However, at the same time, many failures also occurred. One must recognize that the use of robotics is sound for the type of problem best suited for it. The technology is far from making a robot as capable as the one described in Capek's play. In this chapter, we discuss the capabilities and limitations of robots and show how to build an application. Some theoretical background on kinematics is also included. These materials provide a general background in industrial robotics.

11.1.2 Classification of Robots

The Robotics Institute of America defines a robot as "a reprogrammable multifunctional manipulator designed to move material, parts, tools, or other specialized devices through variable programmed motions for the performance of a variety of tasks." Robots like NC machines can be powered by electrical motors, hydraulic systems, or pneumatic systems. Controls for either device can be either open- or closed-loop. In fact, many developments in robotics have evolved from the NC industry, and many of the manufacturers of NC machines and NC controllers also manufacture robots and robot controllers.

Robots have been used in industry since 1965. Industrial robots are widely used in manufacturing and assembly tasks such as material handling, stock selection, welding, parts assembly, product inspection, paint spraying, machine loading, and unloading, foundry application, space and undersea exploration, and in handling hazardous and toxic materials. They can also work in complete darkness, poor light, and in noisy, hot, and confined environments.

A physical robot is normally composed of a main frame (or arm) with a wrist and some tooling (usually some type of gripper) at the end of the frame. An auxiliary power system, that is, a hydraulic power source, may also be included with the robot. A controller with some type of teach pendant, joystick, or keyboard is also part of the system.

Robots are usually characterized by the design of the mechanical system. Generally, there are six recognizable robot configurations: (1) Cartesian, (2) gantry, (3) cylindrical, (4) spherical, (5) articulated, and (6) SCARA.

1. *Cartesian Robots.* A robot whose main frame consists of three linear axes (joints) is called a Cartesian robot and is shown in Figure 11.2. The Cartesian robot

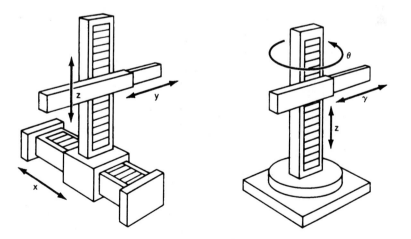

Figure 11.2   Rectilinear or Cartesian robot. (Reprinted by permission of the publisher, from *Robotics in Practice,* © Joseph F. Engelberger. Published by AMACOM, a division of American Management Association, New York. All rights reserved.)

derives its name from the coordinate system. Travel normally takes place linearly in three axes. The X, Y, and Z coordinates of a Cartesian robot can be easily derived from the joint variables, as shown in the following:

$$X = a \tag{11.1}$$

$$Y = b \tag{11.2}$$

$$Z = c \tag{11.3}$$

where a, b, and c are joint variables.

2. *Gantry Robots.* A gantry robot is a type of Cartesian robot whose structure resembles a gantry. This structure is used to minimize deflection along each axis (see Figure 11.3). Many large robots are of this type. The X, Y, and Z coordinates of a gantry robot can be derived using the same set of equations used for the Cartesian robot.

3. *Cylindrical Robots.* A cylindrical robot has two linear axes and one rotary axis. The robot derives its name from the operating envelope—the space in which a robot operates—that is created by moving the axes from limit to limit (see Figure 11.4). The X, Y, and Z coordinates of a cylindrical robot can be obtained from the joint variables using the following equations:

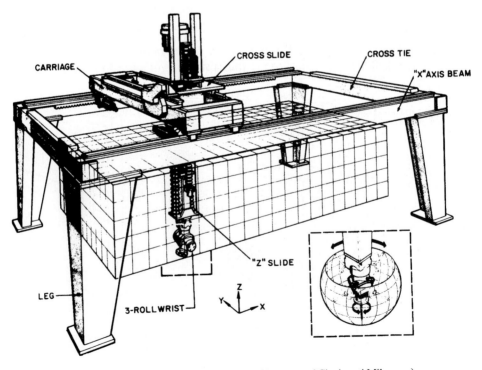

Figure 11.3   Gantry-configuration robot. (Courtesy of Cincinnati Milacron.)

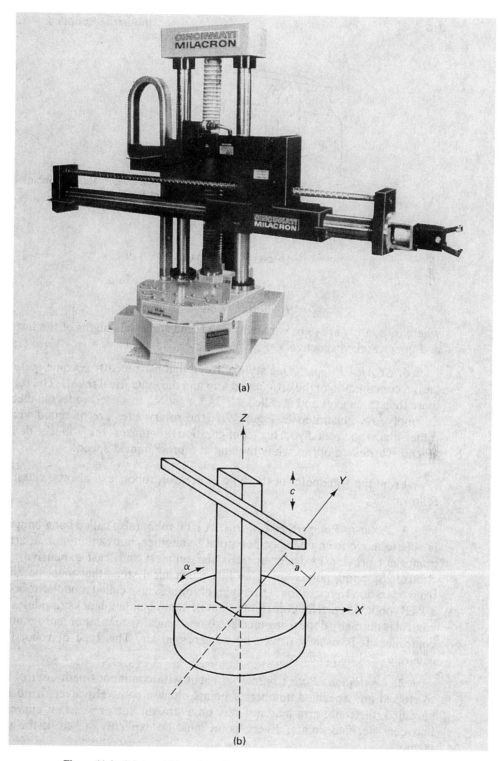

Figure 11.4   Joint variables of a cylindrical robot. (Part [a] courtesy of Cincinnati Milacron.)

$$X = a \cos \alpha \tag{11.4}$$

$$Y = a \sin \alpha \tag{11.5}$$

$$Z = c \tag{11.6}$$

where α, a, and c are joint variables.

4. *Spherical Robots.* A spherical robot has one linear axis and two rotary axes (see Figure 11.5). Spherical robots are used in a variety of industrial tasks, such as welding and material handling. The X, Y, and Z coordinates of a spherical robot can be obtained from the joint variables using the following equations:

$$X = a \cos \alpha \cos \beta \tag{11.7}$$

$$Y = a \sin \alpha \cos \beta \tag{11.8}$$

$$Z = a \sin \beta \tag{11.9}$$

where a, α, and β are joint variables.

5. *Articulated Robots.* An articulated robot has three rotational axes connecting three rigid links and a base, as shown in Figure 11.6. An articulated robot is frequently called an anthropomorphic arm because it closely resembles a human arm. The first joint above the base is referred to as the shoulder. The shoulder joint is connected to the upper arm, which is connected at the elbow joint. Articulated robots are suitable for a wide variety of industrial tasks, ranging from welding to assembly. As we have seen in other types of robots, the X, Y, and Z coordinates of an articulated robot can be obtained from the joint variables using the following equations:

$$X = [l_1 \cos \beta + l_2 \cos (\beta + \gamma)] \cos \alpha \tag{11.10}$$

$$Y = [l_1 \cos \beta + l_2 \cos (\beta + \gamma)] \sin \alpha \tag{11.11}$$

$$Z = l_1 \sin \beta + l_2 \sin (\beta + \gamma) \tag{11.12}$$

where α, β, are γ are joint variables, and l_1 and l_2 are the lengths of the lower arm and upper arm, respectively.

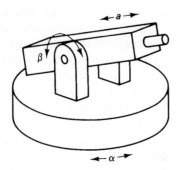

Figure 11.5   Joint variables of a spherical robot.

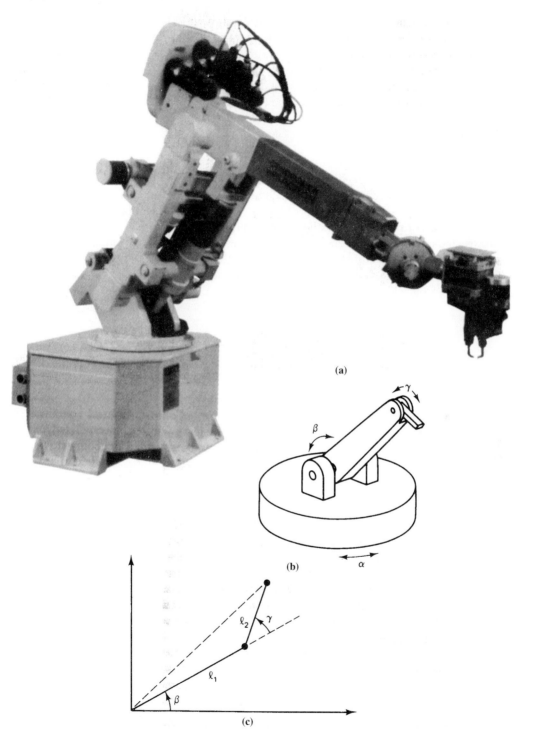

Figure 11.6 (a) An articulated robot and (b) and (c) its joint variables. (Part [a] courtesy of Cincinnati Milacron.)

6. *SCARA Robots.* One style of robot that has recently become quite popular is a combination of the articulated arm and the cylindrical robot. The robot has more than three axes and is called a SCARA robot. It is used widely in electronic assembly. As illustrated in Figure 11.7, the rotary axes are mounted vertically rather than horizontally. This configuration minimizes the robot's deflection when it carries an object while moving at a programmed speed.

From the standpoint of the type of control, robots can also be classified as follows:

1. *Point-to-Point (PTP) Control.* A PTP robot (also called a bang-bang robot) is able to move from one specified point to another, but cannot stop at arbitrary points not previously designed. It is the simplest and least expensive type of control. Stopping points are often just mechanical stops that must be adjusted from operation to operation. This type of robot is also called modular robot because a PTP robot is typically constructed out of some building blocks (modules). The control is normally done using an electromechanical sequencer or a programmable controller. It is usually driven by compressed air. This type of robot is fast, accurate, and inexpensive.

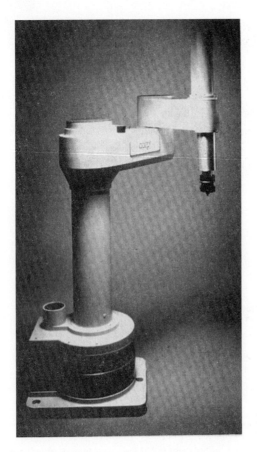

Figure 11.7   SCARA configuration robot. (Courtesy of Adept Technology, Inc.)

2. *Continuous-Path Control.* A robot with continuous-path control is able to stop at any specified number of points along a path. However, if no stop is specified, the robot arm may not stay on a straight line or a constant curved path between specified points. Every point must be explicitly stored in the robot's memory.

3. *Controlled-Path (Computed Trajectory) Control.* Control equipment on controlled-path robots can generate straight lines, circles, interpolated curves, and other paths with high accuracy. Paths can be specified in geometric or algebraic terms in some of these robots. Good accuracy can be obtained at any point along the path. Only the start and finish points and the path definition function are required for control.

11.1.3 Workspace Envelopes

The workspace envelope of a robot is constrained by its mechanical systems configuration. Each joint of a robot has a limit of motion range. By combining all the limits, a constrained space can be defined. A workspace envelope of a robot is defined as all the points in the surrounding space that can be reached by the robot or the mounting point for the end effector or tool. The area reachable by the end effector itself is usually not considered part of a work envelope. Clear understanding of the workspace envelope of a robot to be used is important because all interaction with other machines, parts, and processes only takes place within this volume of space.

Figures 11.8 to 11.11 show the workspace envelopes of Cartesian, cylindrical, spherical, and articulated robots, respectively. Because the workspace envelope is defined by the joint motion range, given the robot configuration and range limits, the workspace envelope can be derived. To derive the workspace envelope, robot kinematic equations, which are discussed in a later section, are used. Robot manufacturers

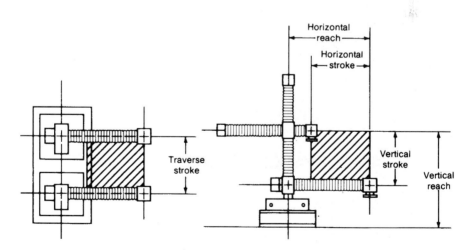

Figure 11.8 Work envelope: Cartesian coordinate robot. (Reprinted with permission of Macmillan Publishing Company from *Introduction to Robotics* by Arthur J. Critchlow. Copyright © 1985 by Macmillian Publishing Company.)

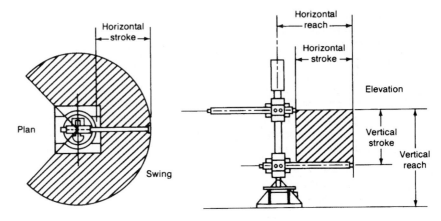

Figure 11.9 Work envelope: cylindrical coordinate robot. (Repinted with permission of Macmillan Publishing Company from *Introduction to Robotics* by Arthur J. Critchlow. Copyright © 1985 by Macmillan Publishing Company.)

also usually provide drawings of workspace envelopes similar to those shown in Figures 11.8 to 11.11

To design a robot application, the application workspace must be within the envelope. However, as discussed before, this envelope is defined by the end of the arm and does not take into consideration what tool may be attached to the arm. Also, it only defines the position or points that can be reached. The possible orientations of the tool at each point have to be found separately. Because the tool orientation is affected not only

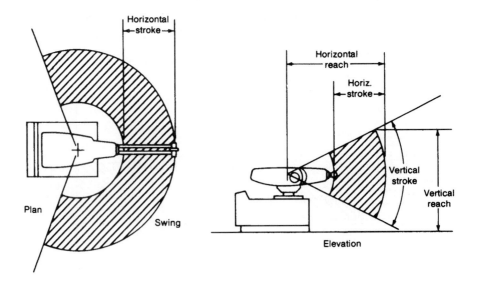

Figure 11.10 Work envelope: spherical or polar coordinate robot. (Repinted with permission of Macmillan Publishing Company from *Introduction to Robotics* by Arthur J. Critchlow. Copyright © 1985 by Macmillan Publishing Company.)

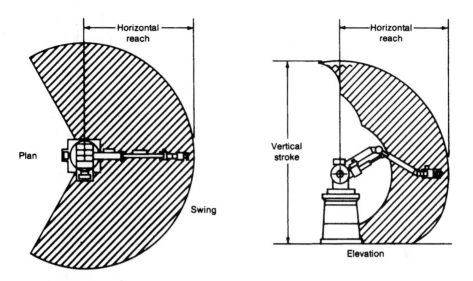

Figure 11.11   Work envelope: revolute or jointed coordinate (articulated) robot. (Repinted with permission of Macmillan Publishing Company from *Introduction to Robotics* by Arthur J. Critchlow. Copyright © 1985 by Macmillan Publishing Company.)

by the base's three axes, but also by the wrist joints and tool length, a kinematic equation including all these variables is needed.

Example 11.1

In a proposed manufacturing cell, a robot is used to load/unload two machines. The machines, feeder, buffer, and finished-part rack dimensions are shown in Figure 11.12. Design a layout of the cell.

Solution   A circular layout is adopted, because it maintains a relatively constant distance between each device and the robot. The selected robot can reach all of them. Figure 11.13 shows a proposed design. The robot workspace envelope is a circular area with a 7-ft diameter and a 270° sweep angle.

Example 11.2

Given the inside radius, r_1, and the outside radius, r_2, of the footprint of a cylindrical robot workspace (see Figure 11.14), calculate the maximum rectangular area that the robot can reach while fitting a maximum workbench in the robot workspace.

Solution   From Figure 11.14, we know

$$w = r_2 \cos \theta - r_1$$
$$l = 2r_2 \sin \theta$$
$$A = lw$$
$$= 2r_2 \sin \theta (r_2 \cos \theta - r_1)$$
$$\frac{dA}{d\theta} = \frac{d}{d\theta} (r_2^2 \sin^2 \theta - 2r_1 r_2 \sin \theta)$$

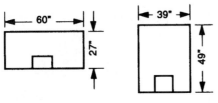

M/C 1   M/C 2

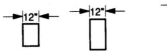

Feeder   Buffer   Finished
                                  part rack   **Figure 11.12**   Manufacturing cell device.

$$= 2r_2^2 \cos 2\theta - 2r_1r_2 \cos \theta$$

$$= 0$$

$$r_2 \cos 2\theta - r_1r_2 \cos \theta = 0$$

$$r_2(2 \cos^2 \theta - 1) - r_1 \cos \theta = 0$$

Let $\cos \theta = x$:

$$2r_2x^2 - r_1x - r_2 = 0$$

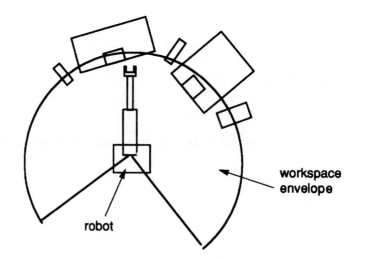

robot

workspace
envelope

Figure 11.13   Cell layout.

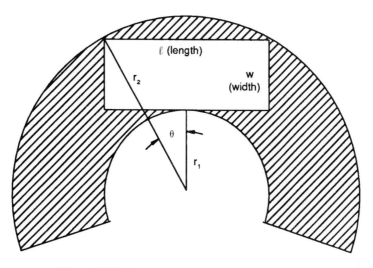

Figure 11.14   Footprint of a cylindrical robot workspace.

$$x = \frac{r_1 \pm \sqrt{r_1^2 + 8r_2^2}}{4r_2}$$

$$\theta = \cos^{-1}\left(\frac{r_1 \pm \sqrt{r_1^2 + 8r_2^2}}{4r_2}\right)$$

For example, if r_1 is 10 and r_2 is 100, the maximum rectangular area that the robot can reach is 8611.70.

11.1.4 Accuracy and Repeatability

Two very important terms in describing machine characteristics are accuracy and repeatability. The accuracy of a linear axis is one-half the control resolution plus the mechanical error (see Section 9.4.1). In a machine tool or a Cartesian coordinate robot where all three base axes are linear, the theoretical accuracy can be considered uniform throughout the entire workspace envelope. (Realistically, nothing is truly uniform; however, in an ideal condition, they are.) Robots of other configurations employ one or several rotational axes. The control resolution is on the angle of rotation. The accuracy is normally defined as the error in the Cartesian space. The linear error due to the resolution of a rotational axis, as shown in Figure 11.15, is a variable; $a_1 \neq a_2$. When combining the effect of several rotational and linear axes, the term accuracy no longer can be used.

Robots are usually characterized by their repeatability. Repeatability is a statistical term. It does not describe the error with respect to absolute coordinates; instead, it describes how a point is repeated. Figure 9.11 shows positional error and repeatability on a two-dimensional plane. Although a target is always missed by a large margin, if the same error is repeated, then we say that the repeatability is high and the accuracy is

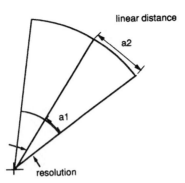

Figure 11.15   Resolution of a rotational axis.

poor. Robot repeatability is normally measured in thousandths of an inch. Positional accuracy depends on the position in the workspace envelope. For this reason, it is difficult to do robot off-line programming without using sensors.

11.2 POWER SOURCES, ACTUATORS, AND TRANSDUCERS

The actuators and transducers for building industrial robots are essentially the same as those for building NC machinery. The major power sources for robots are hydraulic, pneumatic, and electric.

Hydraulics can deliver large forces, so they are commonly used on large robots that have to move large payloads. Pneumatics is used on those robots whose payload requirements are low, but that require high-speed movement. Electric-powered robots provide precise and quiet motion. This type of robot is usually used for assembly work demanding fine movement. Most robots are powered by electric motors. Detailed discussions of these power sources are found in Chapter 9.

11.3 ROBOTIC SENSORS

To perform some of the tasks presently done by humans, robots must be able to sense both their internal and external states (the environment). A sensor is a measurement device that can detect characteristics through some form of interaction with the characteristics. The fact that only rudimentary sensors are currently applied to robots on factory floors, reduces the flexibility, accuracy, and repeatability of robots. However, with the newly developed sensors, especially visual sensors, much more accurate and intelligent robots are expected.

Sensors for robotics can be classified in different ways, such as contact or noncontact, internal sensing versus external sensing, passive versus active sensing, and so on. In the following, some typical robotic sensors are introduced.

A range sensor measures the distance from a reference point to a set of points in the scene. Humans can estimate range values based on visual data by perceptual processes that include stereopsis and comparison of image sizes and classified projected views of world-object models. Basic optical range-sensing schemes are according to the method of illumination (passive or active) and the method of range computation. Range can be sensed with a pair of TV cameras or sonar transmitters and receivers. Range sensing based on triangulation has the drawback of missing data of points not seen from both positions of the transmitters. This problem can be reduced, but not eliminated, by using additional cameras.

A proximity sensor senses and indicates the presence of an object within a fixed space near the sensor without physical contact. Different commercially available proximity sensors are suitable for different applications. A common robotic proximity sensor consists of a light-emitting-diode (LED) transmitter and a photodiode receiver. The major drawback of this sensor stems from the dependency of the received signal on the reflectance and orientation of the intruding object. The drawback can be overcome by replacing proximity sensors with range sensors.

As its name implies, an acoustic sensor senses and interprets acoustic waves in gas, liquid, or solid. The level of sophistication of sensor interpretation varies among existing acoustic sensors, from a primitive detection of the presence of acoustic waves, to frequency analysis of acoustic waves, to recognition of isolated words in continuous speech.

A touch sensor senses and indicates a physical contact between the object carrying the sensor and another object. The simplest touch sensor is a microswitch. Basically, touch sensors are used to stop the motion of a robot when its end-effector makes contact with an object.

A force sensor measures the three components of the force and three components of the torque acting between two objects. In particular, a robot-wrist force sensor measures the components of force and torque between the last link of the robot and its end-effector by transducing the deflection of the sensor's compliant sections, which results from the applied force and torque.

Human workers effectively use their ability to sense the presence and outline of an object with the sense of touch. Researchers are also developing artificial tactile sensors for robots. Whereas vision may guide the robot arm through many manufacturing operations, it is the sense of touch that will allow the robot to perform delicate gripping and assembly. Tactile sensors will provide position data for contacting parts more accurately than that provided by vision.

11.4 ROBOT GRIPPERS

In order for a robot to perform an assembly task, it must be equipped with an application-dependent device, often called an end-effector. An end-effector either can be a tool (e.g., a screwdriver) or a grasping device, commonly called a gripper. In line with industrial practice, the term gripper is used to mean a grasping device, tool, or any other end-effector.

Robots are usually specified without grippers because grippers are very much task- and environment-dependant. In other words, the selection of a robot gripper depends on the nature of the task to be performed. Consequently, grippers are normally part of the customizing package along with other auxiliary equipment and installation.

It is usually assumed that a gripper has no independent degrees of freedom, as it is anticipated that all degrees of freedom are provided by other robot elements. It has been recognized, however, that certain devices (e.g., autoscrewdrivers), because of their inherent degrees of freedom, duplicate certain capabilities of a robot.

The tasks performed during operation often require precise movements of the objects being handled or assembled. There are two alternative methods of achieving precise motions robotically. The first is to use a very sophisticated robot and a simple gripper. The advantage is that the gripper does not have to be technically complex; hence, its inherent reliability will be high and its cost low. The disadvantage is that the investment on the robot is significant. The second alternative is to use a simple robot and a sophisticated gripper. The main drawback is that the gripper has to be specially designed for the task.

Although a gripper action is essentially one of opening or closing, both the design of action and the structure of the gripper are very task-specific, though not always product-specific. Grippers have many actions: (1) parallel motion; (2) scissors motion; (3) one jaw may be fixed, the other moving; and (4) they can be sprung open or closed. It is generally recognized that there are five classifications of grippers:

1. Mechanical clamping—the most common mechanism, whereby pneumatic or hydraulic devices apply a surface pressure on a component.
2. Magnetic clamping—applying electromagnetism to hold the component.
3. Vacuum clamping—applying negative pressure to components so that they adhere to the grippers.
4. Piercing grippers—puncturing the component to lift it. The technique is only used where slight damage to the component is acceptable.
5. Adhesive grippers—used for components that do not permit any of the preceding methods. These grippers use sticky tape to pick up and hold the component.

11.5 ROBOT SAFETY

A robotic system is an integration of robots, machines, computerized information channels, and humans, no element of which can be considered perfect or immune from eventual failure and malfunction. The proximity of humans to the robots allows the risk of mutual damage, resulting in the formulation of safety guidelines that indicate how the conditions of conflict can be minimized. The high productivity levels associated with robotic systems can be only realized if all the system elements are functioning safely and reliably.

However, until definitive regulations are imposed by law, attempting to determine the safety hazards of a robotic assembly system is best done on a piecemeal basis, whereby each element is analyzed for risk. The relationships between elements are known on a quantitative or qualitative basis. Therefore, the risk factors can be transferred from one element to the others.

There are four groups of humans at risk from direct personal injury from a robot:

1. *Programmers.* A robot programmer using any one of the previously mentioned programming methods is in direct contact with the robot. This closeness with the robot's work envelope, with its inherent danger of injury, distinguishes robotics from any other form of automation.

2. *Maintenance engineers.* A maintenance engineer is at risk from much the same dangers as programmers, with the added risk of electrocution. Also, because maintenance procedures often require that safety interlocks be disconnected, the inherent risk of injury is greater.

3. *Casual observers.* To the casual observer, robots are often seen standing still, apparently doing nothing, for long periods of time. The programmer, of course, would know whether or not these pauses are intentional: the robot may be performing a programmed delay or waiting. However, if, as is usually the case, the assembly robot is not rigidly guarded, then a casual observer may move toward a seemingly stationary robot and be injured when it continues its operation.

4. *Others outside the assumed danger zone.* Even though a robot has a known maximum work envelope, the risk of injury is not limited to encounters within this envelope. If components manipulated by the robot are not properly secured, then it is possible for them to fly out of the grippers and strike personnel well outside the assumed danger zone of the robot.

In a practical sense, safety procedures and devices allow the authorized entry of humans into a robot's work envelope with minimum risk of injury. Hardware devices and sensors monitor all anticipated reasonable access to a robot's work envelope.

Physical safeguards are many and varied. They include the following:

1. simple contact switches
2. restrained keys
3. pressure mats
4. infrared light beams
5. vision systems
6. flashing red lights within a work zone indicating that an apparently stationary robot is activated, but awaiting an input, or performing a time-delayed operation

11.6 ROBOT PROGRAMMING

Programming conventional robots normally takes one of three forms: (1) walking through, or pendant, teaching, (2) lead-through teaching, or (3) textual language programming. Each has advantages and disadvantages depending on the application being considered.

Pendant programming uses a teach pendant to instruct a robot to move in working space. A teach pendant (see Figure 11.16) is a device equipped with switches and dials used to control the robot's movements to and from the desired points in the space.

Figure 11.16   A teach pendant. (Courtesy of MOTOMAN.)

These points are recorded into memory for subsequent playback. This is the most common programming method for playback robots.

Lead-through programming is for continuous-path playback robots. In pendant programming, if we decided to program a straight-line path between two points, we could employ the teach pendant to teach the robot the locations of the points. The trajectory between the two points to be followed is computed by the robot controller. In lead-through programming, on the other hand, the programmer simply physically moves the robot through the required sequence of motions. The robot controller records the position and speed as the programmer leads the robot through the operation.

Textual language programming methods use an English-like language to establish the logical sequence of a work cycle. To input the program instructions, a computer terminal is used, and to define the location of various points in the workplace. A teach pendant might be used. When a textual language program is entered without a teach pendant defining locations in the program, it is often called off-line programming.

11.6.1 Robot Programming Languages

This section discusses robot programming languages for computer-controlled manipulators. A manipulator of this kind moves through a path in space under the direction of a program. Other actions included in the path are controlling the end-effector and receiving signals from sensors. Different languages can be used for robot programming, that are useful to teach the robot how to perform these actions. Most robot languages implemented today are a combination of textual and teach-pendant programming.

In 1973, WAVE, the first experimental language for research, was developed (Groover et al., 1986). AL (Arm Language) was developed during research to develop a robot to interface with a machine-vision system. This was accomplished using the WAVE language at the Stanford Artificial Intelligence Laboratory. AL can be used to control multiple arms in tasks requiring arm coordination. AL is the language that probably has undergone the most important development. In its first version, it had a planning module, compiled programs on a PDP-10 computer, and generated trajectories. An intermediate code was then executed, on the execution module, using a PDP-11/45 computer.

In 1981, RAIL was developed by Automatix for robotic assembly and arc welding as well as machine vision. MCL (Manufacturing Control Language) was developed by McDonnell Douglas and sponsored by the U.S. Air Force as an enhancement to the APT NC part-programming language. Specifically, MCL was developed within the frame of the ICAM projects (Integrated Computer-Aided Manufacturing, sponsored by the U.S. Department of Defense) to resolve all the problems associated with robot programming in a unified way. The project was carried out by McAuto, which offers a commercial interactive version (MCL/11) using a PDP-11 computer, MCL is an extension of APT and its aim is the programming of flexible units, that is, of a set of machines served by one or more robots.

POINTY, a language similar to AL, was first developed in 1975 on a PDP-11 so as to be more interactive in terms of programming.

IRL (Intuitive Robot Language) was developed by Microbot, a company affiliated with the large watchmaking companies because of its high-precision assembly robots. These robots include the electric model Souris with 6 degrees of freedom (precision of $\frac{1}{100}$ mm), the hydraulic model Castor, and the Ecureuil model introduced in 1983.

In RAIL, points, paths, and reference frames are the three types of data for robot locations. The tool-tip position is oriented and positioned relative to a world reference frame commonly located at the robot base. The point defines the X, Y, and Z coordinates for the location in the space and the orientation angles, indicating the orientation of the tool tip. The angles are expressed in degrees, and the coordinates can be expressed in millimeters or inches. Both measurements are relative to the world reference frame. A path is specified by indicating a connected series of points. When the robot is instructed to move along a path, it moves through each point in the path without stopping or slowing down at any intermediate point.

Two of the features that RAIL provides with respect to welding is that the robot can be moved along a certain path while the welding-process parameters are controlled, and variables or parameters can be adjusted at each step.

VAL II is a computer-based control system and language developed by Unimation for its PUMA industrial robots.

A computer-based system provides the ability to easily define the tasks a robot is to perform by user-written programs. The VAL II robot language is permanently stored as a part of the VAL II system. This includes the programming language used to direct the system for individual applications. The VAL II language is easily learned. Its instructions are clear, concise, and generally self-explanatory. Control programs are written on the same computer that controls the robot.

As a real-time system, continuous trajectory computation by VAL II permits complex motions to be executed quickly, with efficient use of system memory and reduction in overall system complexity. The VAL II system continuously generates robot control commands and can simultaneously interact with a human operator, permitting on-line program generation and modification.

A convenient feature of VAL II is the ability to use libraries of manipulation routines. Thus, complex operations may be easily and quickly programmed by combining predefined subtasks. For example, a typical palletizing task can be simply programmed by combining two or three standard routines. Figure 11.17 illustrates a VAL II program that commands a PUMA robot to perform spot welding. The program explanation follows:

- The home position is located well out of the way of the line and all obstructions.
- The pounce position is a central position inside a side frame.
- Input signal 1003 is generated by shot pins on an indexing line to indicate that the side frame is locked into position.

```
PROGRAM weld.style247
1         SIGNAL 5
2         MOVE home
3         MOVE pounce
4         WAIT SIG(1003)
5         APPRO spot. number[1]
6         CALL weld.spots
7         TIMER 1 = 0
8         SIG 6
9         WAIT TIMER(1) > 5
10        SIG -6
END


Program weld. spots
1         FOR points 1 TO 18
2             TIMER -1 = 0
3             MOVES spot.number[points
4             WAIT TIMER(-1) < .25
5             PULSE
6             WAIT WELD.DONE
7         END
8         RETURN
END
```

Figure 11.17. A VAL II program.

- All move steps were entered using the REC button on the teach pendant in the teach mode.
- Sig 6 is sent out as a 500-ms pulse to indicate to a controller that this particular robot has completed welding.

AML (A Manufacturing Language) was developed in 1976 at IBM's T. J. Watson Research Labs for assembly and related tasks.

There are three forms of statements in AML: executable statements, variable declaration statements, and subroutine statements. With the exception of certain special cases, all AML statements end in a semicolon (;).

Executable statements constitute the logic for the interpreter to execute. The executable statements perform calculations, comparisons, and other similar operations, which differ from the other two types of statements because executable statements do not reserve storage or provide names for variable or subroutines.

A variable declaration statement is composed of the name (or "id") of the variable and a keyword, either NEW or STATIC, which identifies the statement as a declaration statement.

A subroutine declaration statement is used to reserve space in storage for a collection of AML statements. SUBR is the keyword used to declare the beginning and END to declare the end of a subroutine.

AML/E is an entry-level language for programming the IBM 7535 manufacturing system (robot). A sample program in AML/E is illustrated in Figure 11.18. The objective of the program is explained as follows.

A robotic cell is composed of an IBM 7535 manufacturing system, two machines (M/C 1 and M/C 2), and two queues (Q_1 and Q_2), as shown in Figure 11.19.

```
ROBOCELL: SUBR:
Q1: NEW PT (50.00. 450.00. 0);
Q1H: NEW PT(50.00. 380.00. 0);
MC1: NEW PT(-250.00. 380.00. 0);
MC1H: NEW PT(-200.00. 350.00. 0);
MC2: NEW PT(-400.00. 100.00. 0);
MC2H: NEW PT(-350.00. 90.00. 0);
Q2: NEW PT(-350.00. -200.00. 0);
Q2H: NEW PT(-250.00. -100.00. 0);
PMOVE( Q1H ); PMOVE( Q1 ); DOWN; GRASP; UP;
PMOVE( MC1H ); PMOVE( MC1 ); DOWN; RELEASE; UP;
PMOVE( MC1H ); DELAY( 14.33 ); CYCLE: PMOVE( MC1 ); DOWN; GRASP; UP;
PMOVE( MC2H ); PMOVE( MC2 ); DOWN; RELEASE; UP;
PMOVE( Q1H ); PMOVE( Q1 ); DOWN; GRASP; UP;
PMOVE( MC1H ); PMOVE( MC1 ); DOWN; RELEASE; UP;
PMOVE( MC2H ); DELAY( 12.64 ); PMOVE( MC2 ); DOWN; GRASP; UP;
PMOVE( Q2 ); DOWN; RELEASE; UP;
PMOVE( Q2H ); PMOVE( MC1H ); BRANCH( CYCLE );
END;
```

Figure 11.18   An AML/E program.

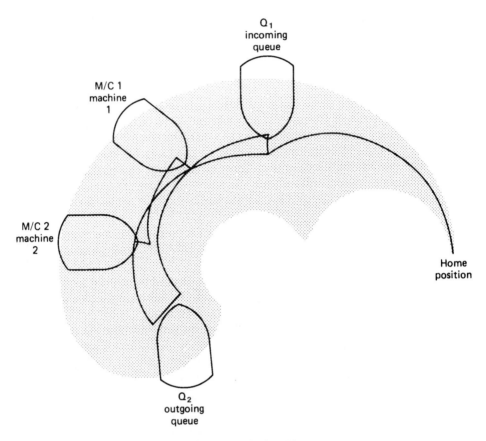

Figure 11.19 A robotic cell layout.

The cell handles only one product in the following process sequence:

$$Q_1 \Rightarrow M/C\ 1 \Rightarrow M/C\ 2 \Rightarrow Q_2$$

M/C 1 requires 15 time units and M/C 2 requires 20 time units.

TL-10, Toyota robot language—10, is a BASIC-like robot language, developed at Toyota Central Research & Development Laboratories. It has functions to define locations and subroutine parameters. It also has functions to communicate with other computers such as those for vision systems.

SIGLA (SIGma and LAnguage) was developed in 1974 by Oliveti for its Cartesian Sigma robots. The language allows control of several arms with loops and tests on the sensors, and is influenced by numerical-control languages. The grippers may be equipped with strain gauges, with allow assembly operations to be monitored. Sigma robots are intended for three main application: assembly, drilling, and welding. Sigma robots are manufactured in the United States by Westinghouse in parallel with PUMA robots.

PLAW (Programming Language for Arc Welding) is designed for sensor-based welding, that is, welding that involves the use of vision and sensors. It was developed by Komatsu for its series RW Cartesian robots, equipped with arc current and television cameras.

11.7 ROBOT APPLICATIONS

Robotics has rapidly moved from theory to application during the past two decades, primarily due to the need for improved productivity and quality.

One of the key features of robots is their versatility. A programmable robot used in conjunction with a variety of end-effectors can be programmed to perform specific tasks, then later reprogrammed and refitted to adapt to process or production line variations or changes.

The robot offers an excellent means of utilizing high-technology to make a given manufacturing operation more profitable and competitive. However, robot technology is relatively new to the industrial scene, and the prospective buyer of robot technology who is accustomed to buying more conventional items will find robot applications a highly complex subject.

Robots are used today primarily for welding, painting, assembly, machine loading, and foundry activities. The number of robots used for welding accounts for about 50% of the applications in the United States, primarily because the automotive industry is the major user of robots. The sharp visibility given to the automotive industry's robotic applications and its declared intention to even more aggressively increase the installation rates have made that industry a major focus for robot builders.

In the U.S. metalworking industry, machine loading and unloading appears to be the biggest single area of application of robots. Assembly is another extremely important application area for robots.

Arc welding by robots is a growing application, but rudimentary vision for seam tracking needs to be developed before its full potential is realized. Also coming into its own is the use of robots for stamping; the robot's lack of speed has been the deterrent up to now, but that is expected to improve.

One manufacturing process that owes much of its current growth to robotics is investment casting. The series of steps in patternmaking can now be performed easily and consistently. The assembly robot is getting intense attention in the United States and Japan. In assembly, the driving impetus is economics, and the multishift capabilities of robots may revolutionize one-shift assembly operations. Die casting, injection molding, heat treating, and glass handling are other application areas of robotics.

11.7.1 Principles for Robot Applications

There are four principles for robot applications, as follows (Heginbotham et al., 1973):

- If the conditions of dimension and state at the workplace repeat without significant unstructured variability, then a simple robotic solution is possible. For this principle, two categories of problems are considered: (1) first-order problems— position variations; (2) second-order problems—position and orientation variations; and repeatability of the gripping device.

- If the machine can be deceived into thinking that it is handling the same thing when it is not, then the third-order robot assembly or handling problem can be reduced to a second-order problem. For this principle, smart engineering design or complex sensory systems are required.
- For all changes of state or dimension (either structure or unstructured) that are imposed on a robot installation, the robot behavior and the workplace must be capable of change. It is important not to try to use robots to imitate human functions.
- Recognize and exploit or create robot-compatible mechanical states or environments. That is, eliminate or reduce the need for human skill and judgment and/or the drudgery of a function by using robot-compatible mechanical states or environments.

11.7.2 Application Planning

The planning for a robot application involves several stages of consideration.

1. *Workpiece analysis and evaluation:* a thorough study of what is to be produced, including parts breakdown, process plans, and accessibility analysis.
2. *Establishment of alternative methods for automation:* the layout of the workplace and the interlink of workplaces are major issues.
3. *Selection of optimum method:* simulation and graphical emulation are commonly used tools at this stage.
4. *Search for solutions to implement the selected methods:* the selection of the robot and the selection of peripheral devices such as parts feeder, gripper, and fixtures.
5. *Cost analysis:* this is discussed in the next section.
6. *Measures taken to implement the overall method solution:* popular tools for project management such as PERT, CPM, and Gantt charts are commonly used.

11.8 ECONOMIC CONSIDERATIONS OF ROBOTIC SYSTEMS

Several U.S. industries have shown good foresight by investing in high-tech production equipment. Part of these investments include robots for welding and assembly. However, as with any capital-intensive production investment, these systems must be economically justified before they can be purchased. Installation, however, does not end the economic justification considerations of a system. As products are redesigned, a different mix of parts enters the production system, and a new problem must be resolved: What parts can be produced economically with robotic equipment?

The economical consideration for robot applications includes the following:

- plant and equipment
- operation and maintenance
- product
- parameters and analysis

11.8.1 Plant and Equipment

In this category, what we have to be concerned about are (1) the robot(s), associated tooling, and spare parts; (2) taxes and tax consequences such as investment tax credits and tax savings due to depreciation; (3) energy requirements; (4) space requirements; (5) safety equipment; (6) programming; and (7) compatibility of current equipment with the robot(s).

11.8.2 Operation and Maintenance

In the category of operation and maintenance, key issues are (1) operating and maintenance labor costs; (2) direct cost of illness, absenteeism, insurance, and injuries; (3) training costs; (4) supervision costs; (5) retooling and setup costs for batch processing; and (6) maintenance costs.

11.8.3 Product

In this category, we focus on the cost issues associated with the product. Those issues are (1) changes in product design, (2) material costs such as raw material and in-process inventory, (3) production rates (productivity, scrap rate, defective items), (4) handling and reworking of defective products, and (5) costs due to undetected defective product released to the customer (loss of good will and complaints).

11.8.4 Parameters of Analysis

The parameters for cost analysis involve (1) income tax rates (federal, state, and local), (2) engineering and consulting costs not considered in the previous (3) cost of capital (discount rate).

For examples of cost justification, see Section 5.8 in Chapter 5.

11.9 ROBOT KINEMATICS AND DYNAMICS

Robot arm kinematics involves the analytical study of the geometry of motion of a robot arm with respect to a fixed reference coordinate system without regard to the forces/momenta that cause the motion. In other words, robot kinematics deals with the analytical description of the spatial displacement of the robot as a function of time, in particular, the relations between the joint-variable space and the position and orientation of the end-effector of a robot arm.

There are two fundamental problems in robot arm kinematics. The first is usually referred to as the direct (or forward) kinematics problem and the second is the inverse kinematics problem. If the locations of all of the joints and links of a robot arm are known, it is possible to compute the location in space of the end of the arm. This is defined as the direct kinematics problem. The inverse kinematics problem is to determine the necessary positions of the joints and links in order to move the end of the robot arm to a desired position and orientation in space.

Vector and matrix algebra are used to develop a systematic and generalized approach to describe and represent the locations of the links of a robot arm with respect to a fixed reference frame. Since the links of a robot arm can rotate and/or translate with respect to a reference (world) coordinate frame, a body-attached (joint) coordinate frame is established along the joint axis for each link. In general, the direct kinematics problem reduces to finding a transformation matrix that relates joint coordinates to world coordinates. Matrix manipulation, discussed in Chapter 3, applies here.

Computer-based robots are usually servo controlled in the joint-variable space, whereas objects to be manipulated are usually identified in the world or part coordinate system. In order to control the position and orientation of the end-effector of a robot to reach the target object, the inverse kinematics solution is necessary to obtain the correct joint angle. In other words, given the position and orientation of the end-effector of a six-axis arm and its joint and link parameters, we would like to find the corresponding joint angles of the robot so that the end-effector can be positioned as desired.

11.9.1 Basics

11.9.1.1. Translation and rotation.
Translation of a vector from one coordinate system to another is usually accomplished by multiplying a matrix that defines the linear translations of two coordinate systems on the three major axes.

Rotation is accomplished by rotation matrices in homogeneous coordinates. Matrices performing linear translations or rotation about the X, Y, or Z axes by an angle θ are given in Chapter 3 (object transformation).

The transformation matrices used are T_{to}, T_{xo}, T_{yo}, T_{zo}, To transform a point P:

$$P' = PT$$

where P and P' are row vectors $[x\ y\ z\ 1]$ and $[x'\ y'\ z'\ 1]$.

Example 11.3

Suppose there is a vector, $\mathbf{A} = 5i + 2j + 4k$, in space. We wish to find the new vector that results from rotating $\mathbf{A}$ through 90° around the $\mathbf{Z}$ axis, $-90°$ around the $\mathbf{X}$ axis, and translating through the vector value $2i + 2j + 2k$.

Solution   The three transformation matrices are

$$T_{zo} = \begin{bmatrix} 0 & 1 & 0 & 0 \\ -1 & 0 & 0 & 0 \\ 0 & 0 & 1 & 0 \\ 0 & 0 & 0 & 1 \end{bmatrix}$$

$$T_{xo} = \begin{bmatrix} 1 & 0 & 0 & 0 \\ 0 & 0 & 1 & 0 \\ 0 & -1 & 0 & 0 \\ 0 & 0 & 0 & 1 \end{bmatrix}$$

$$T_{to} = \begin{bmatrix} 1 & 0 & 0 & 0 \\ 0 & 1 & 0 & 0 \\ 0 & 0 & 1 & 0 \\ 2 & 2 & 2 & 1 \end{bmatrix}$$

$$A' = A\, T_{zo}\, T_{xo}\, T_{to}$$

$$= \begin{bmatrix} 5 & 2 & 4 & 1 \end{bmatrix} \begin{bmatrix} 0 & 0 & 1 & 0 \\ -1 & 0 & 0 & 0 \\ 0 & -1 & 0 & 0 \\ 2 & 2 & 2 & 1 \end{bmatrix}$$

$$= \begin{bmatrix} 0 & -2 & 7 & 1 \end{bmatrix}$$

We obtain the new vector, which is

$$0i - 2j + 7k$$

11.9.2 Robot Coordinate Systems

Let us use the information learned to construct coordinate systems for robot elements. First, let us look at a robot lower arm (Figure 11.20). We construct two coordinate systems for the arm: one relates to the robot waist and the other relates to the upper arm. We call these coordinate systems $X–Y–Z$ and $U–V–W$, as shown in the figure. How can we get the transformation matrix $[L]$, which translates the location of a point from one coordinate system to the other? By observing the figure, this transformation is a linear translation. The distance between the two coordinate frames is S. The generic form of a translation matrix is

$$T_{to} = \begin{bmatrix} 1 & 0 & 0 & 0 \\ 0 & 1 & 0 & 0 \\ 0 & 0 & 1 & 0 \\ \Delta x & \Delta y & \Delta z & 1 \end{bmatrix}$$

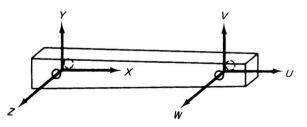

Figure 11.20   Lower arm of a robot.

In this case, $\Delta_x = s$, $\Delta_y = \Delta_z = 0$; therefore, the translation matrix relating $U–V–W$ to $X–Y–Z$ is

$$T = \begin{bmatrix} 1 & 0 & 0 & 0 \\ 0 & 1 & 0 & 0 \\ 0 & 0 & 1 & 0 \\ S & 0 & 0 & 1 \end{bmatrix}$$

In other words, a point P in $U–V–W$ can be transformed to $X–Y–Z$ as follows:

$$P_{X-Y-Z} = P_{U-V-W}T$$

For example, if P_{u-v-w} is $[1\ 0\ 2\ 1]$, P_{x-y-z} can be found:

$$P_{X-Y-Z} = [1 \quad 0 \quad 2 \quad 1] \begin{bmatrix} 1 & 0 & 0 & 0 \\ 0 & 1 & 0 & 0 \\ 0 & 0 & 1 & 0 \\ S & 0 & 0 & 1 \end{bmatrix}$$

$$= [1 + S \quad 0 \quad 2 \quad 1]$$

Another important transformation usually occurs on a robot waist, as shown in Figure 11.21. Let us construct two coordinate systems for the robot body and let these two systems be $(X–Y–Z)_1$ and $(U–V–W)_1$. By observing the figure, we realize that the relation between $(X–Y–Z)_1$ and $(U–V–W)_1$ includes two transformations: (1) rotate 90° about the X_1 axis, and (2) translate h along the Z_1 axis. Based on the discussion in the previous section, we formulate the matrices as follows:

$$T_{xo} = \begin{bmatrix} 1 & 0 & 0 & 0 \\ 0 & 0 & 1 & 0 \\ 0 & -1 & 0 & 0 \\ 0 & 0 & 0 & 1 \end{bmatrix}$$

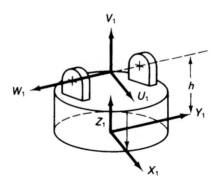

Figure 11.21   A robot base.

$$T_t = \begin{bmatrix} 1 & 0 & 0 & 0 \\ 0 & 1 & 0 & 0 \\ 0 & 0 & 1 & 0 \\ 0 & 0 & h & 1 \end{bmatrix}$$

The transformation matrix can be obtained by multiplying these two matrices (be careful with the sequence). The matrix is

$$T = T_{xo}T_t = \begin{bmatrix} 1 & 0 & 0 & 0 \\ 0 & 0 & 1 & 0 \\ 0 & -1 & 0 & 0 \\ 0 & 0 & h & 1 \end{bmatrix}$$

How do we validate the transformation matrix? We know that the determinant of a rigid-body transformation is 1. The determinant of T, $\det[T]$, is calculated as follows:

$$\begin{bmatrix} 1 & 0 & 0 & 1 & 0 \\ 0 & 0 & 1 & 0 & 0 \\ 0 & -1 & 0 & 0 & -1 \end{bmatrix}$$

Then $\det[T] = 0 - (-1) = 1$. If $\det[x]$ does not equal 1, the transformation is deformed. If $\det[x]$ equals -1, this means a mirror transformation.

11.9.3 Generic Formulas for Coordinate Transformation

We have constructed several coordinate systems for robot elements. Now let us consider a complete robot system. We use the following generic matrix representation describing two types of matrix:

> L is a link matrix describing location of joints on a body
> J is a joint matrix describing relative location or orientation across joints

and

> L must be a translation transformation matrix
> J could be a translation or a rotation-transformation matrix

The most general form of coordinate transformation from the end-of-tool to a global coordinate system is as follows:

$$O = L_{TOOL} J_Y L_5 J_R L_4 J_P L_3 J_E L_2 J_S L_1 J_W L_B T \tag{11.13}$$

where X_G, Y_G, Z_G and X_T, Y_T, Z_T are global and tool coordinate system representations, respectively.

T is a transformation matrix from the base coordinate to a global coordinate

L_B is a base-body-link transformation matrix describing where the first (waist) joint is on a robot

J_W is a transformation matrix for the waist joint

L_1 is a waist-link transformation matrix describing where the second (shoulder) joint is

J_S is a transformation matrix for the shoulder joint

L_2 is a lower-arm-link transformation matrix describing where the third (elbow) joint is

J_E is a transformation matrix for the elbow joint

L_3 is an upper-arm-link transformation matrix describing where the fourth (wrist pitch) joint is

J_P is a transformation matrix for the wrist pitch joint

L_4 is a wrist pitch link transformation matrix describing where the roll joint is

J_R is a transformation matrix for the roll joint

L_5 is a roll-joint transformation matrix describing where the yaw joint is

J_Y is a transformation matrix for the yaw joint

L_{TOOL} is the end-of-tool-link transformation matrix describing where the end-of-tool point is

Let us establish coordinate systems for the robot. The following rules are to be followed in the construction of such coordinate systems:

1. Always use the right-hand coordinate system.
2. The *Z* and *W* axes must be aligned with the axis of motion.
3. Construct two coordinate systems for each body.
4. Construct two coordinate systems for each joint.

Figure 11.22 illustrates an articulated robot as four (4) separate rigid bodies: base, waist, lower arm, and upper arm. The coordinate representations are also specified in the figure. Based on the general form of coordinate transformation and the given robot configuration, the transformation matrices are as follows:

$$T = \begin{bmatrix} 1 & 0 & 0 & 0 \\ 0 & 1 & 0 & 0 \\ 0 & 0 & 1 & 0 \\ x_t & y_t & z_t & 1 \end{bmatrix}$$

$$L_B = \begin{bmatrix} 1 & 0 & 0 & 0 \\ 0 & 1 & 0 & 0 \\ 0 & 0 & 1 & 0 \\ 0 & 0 & t_b & 1 \end{bmatrix}$$

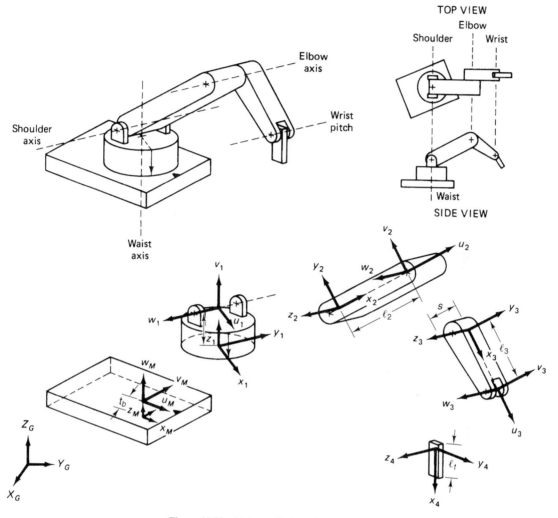

Figure 11.22   Links and joints of an articulated robot.

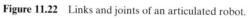

$$J_w = \begin{bmatrix} c\alpha & s\alpha & 0 & 0 \\ -s\alpha & c\alpha & 0 & 0 \\ 0 & 0 & 1 & 0 \\ 0 & 0 & 0 & 1 \end{bmatrix}$$

$$L_1 = \begin{bmatrix} 1 & 0 & 0 & 0 \\ 0 & 0 & 1 & 0 \\ 0 & -1 & 0 & 0 \\ 0 & 0 & t_w & 1 \end{bmatrix}$$

$$J_s = \begin{bmatrix} c\beta & s\beta & 0 & 0 \\ -s\beta & c\beta & 0 & 0 \\ 0 & 0 & 1 & 0 \\ 0 & 0 & 0 & 1 \end{bmatrix}$$

$$L_2 = \begin{bmatrix} 1 & 0 & 0 & 0 \\ 0 & 1 & 0 & 0 \\ 0 & 0 & 1 & 0 \\ l_2 & 0 & 0 & 1 \end{bmatrix}$$

$$J_E = \begin{bmatrix} c\gamma & s\gamma & 0 & 0 \\ -s\gamma & c\gamma & 0 & 0 \\ 0 & 0 & 1 & 0 \\ 0 & 0 & -s & 1 \end{bmatrix}$$

$$L_3 = \begin{bmatrix} 1 & 0 & 0 & 0 \\ 0 & 1 & 0 & 0 \\ 0 & 0 & 1 & 0 \\ l_3 & 0 & 0 & 1 \end{bmatrix}$$

$$J_P = \begin{bmatrix} C\eta & S\eta & 0 & 0 \\ -S\eta & C\eta & 0 & 0 \\ 0 & 0 & 1 & 0 \\ 0 & 0 & 0 & 1 \end{bmatrix}$$

$$L_{\text{TOOL}} = \begin{bmatrix} 1 & 0 & 0 & 0 \\ 0 & 1 & 0 & 0 \\ 0 & 0 & 1 & 0 \\ l_t & 0 & 0 & 1 \end{bmatrix}$$

where

$C\alpha = \cos\alpha$	$C\beta = \cos\beta$	$Cr = \cos r$	$C\eta = \cos\eta$
$S\alpha = \sin\alpha$	$S\beta = \sin\beta$	$Sr = \sin r$	$S\eta = \sin\eta$

α = waist-rotation angle
β = shoulder-rotation angle
γ = elbow-rotation angle
x_l = X translation between the base and global origin
y_t = Y translation between the base and global origin
z_t = Z translation between the base and global origin
t_b = base thickness
t_w = waist thickness
l_2 = length of lower arm

l_3 = length of upper arm

s = offset on Z at the elbow joint

l_t = length of tool

η = pitch of angle

The final transformation matrix from the end of the tool coordinate system to the global coordinate system is

$$O = L_{TOOL} J_P L_3 J_E L_2 J_S L_1 J_W L_B T$$

Example 11.4

Let us use the same robot shown in Figure 11.22. Suppose that the waist joint rotates 90°, the shoulder joint rotates 90°, the elbow joint rotates 0° and that the X, Y, and Z translations between the base and the global origin are 10, 10, and 0, respectively. Let us assume that the base thickness is 5, the waist thickness is 10, the offset on Z is 2, the length of the lower arm is 12, and the length of the upper arm is 8. Also, suppose that the location of an arbitrary point is $(5, 5, 5)$ with respect to the $(U–V–W)_3$ coordinate system. What is the location of the point with respect to the global coordinate system?

Solution   Based on the data given in the problem description, the transformation matrices are

$$[T] = \begin{bmatrix} 1 & 0 & 0 & 0 \\ 0 & 1 & 0 & 0 \\ 0 & 0 & 1 & 0 \\ 0 & 0 & 0 & 1 \end{bmatrix}$$

$$[L_B] = \begin{bmatrix} 1 & 0 & 0 & 0 \\ 0 & 1 & 0 & 0 \\ 0 & 0 & 1 & 0 \\ 0 & 0 & 5 & 1 \end{bmatrix}$$

$$[J_W] = \begin{bmatrix} 0 & 1 & 0 & 0 \\ -1 & 0 & 0 & 0 \\ 0 & 0 & 1 & 0 \\ 0 & 0 & 0 & 1 \end{bmatrix}$$

$$[L_1] = \begin{bmatrix} 1 & 0 & 0 & 0 \\ 0 & 0 & 1 & 0 \\ 0 & -1 & 0 & 10 \end{bmatrix}$$

$$[J_S] = \begin{bmatrix} 0 & 1 & 0 & 0 \\ -1 & 0 & 0 & 0 \\ 0 & 0 & 1 & 0 \\ 0 & 0 & 0 & 1 \end{bmatrix}$$

$$[L_2] = B \begin{bmatrix} 1 & 0 & 0 & 0 \\ 0 & 1 & 0 & 0 \\ 0 & 0 & 1 & 0 \\ 12 & 0 & 0 & 1 \end{bmatrix}$$

$$[J_E] = \begin{bmatrix} 1 & 0 & 0 & 0 \\ 0 & 1 & 0 & 0 \\ 0 & 0 & 1 & 0 \\ 0 & 0 & -2 & 1 \end{bmatrix}$$

$$[L_3] = \begin{bmatrix} 1 & 0 & 0 & 0 \\ 0 & 1 & 0 & 0 \\ 0 & 0 & 1 & 0 \\ 8 & 0 & 0 & 1 \end{bmatrix}$$

The transformation matrix relating the tool coordinate frame to the global frame $[O]$ is

$$O = \begin{bmatrix} 0 & 0 & 1 & 0 \\ 0 & -1 & 0 & 0 \\ 1 & 0 & 0 & 0 \\ 8 & 10 & 35 & 1 \end{bmatrix}$$

$$[5 \quad 5 \quad 5 \quad 1] \begin{bmatrix} 0 & 0 & 1 & 0 \\ 0 & -1 & 0 & 0 \\ 1 & 0 & 0 & 0 \\ 8 & 10 & 35 & 1 \end{bmatrix} = [13 \quad 5 \quad 40 \quad 1]$$

By multiplying the matrices and the point location $(5, 5, 5)$, we know that the coordinates of the point with respect to the global coordinates system are $(13, 5, 40)$.

11.10 ROBOT-ARM DYNAMICS

Robot-arm dynamics, on the other hand, deals with the mathematical formulation of the equations of robot-arm motion. Specifically, dynamics is concerned with the use of information about the loads on a robot arm to adjust the servo operation to achieve optimum performance. The information includes inertia, friction, gravity, velocity, and acceleration. The dynamic equations of motion of an arm are a set of mathematical equations describing the dynamic behavior of the manipulator. Such mathematical formulation is useful for computer simulation of the robot-arm motion, the design of suitable control equations for a robot arm, and the evaluation of the kinematic design and structure of the robot (Fu, Gonzalez, and Lee, 1987).

In this section, we derive the dynamics for the θ–r robot arm. Figure 11.23 shows the θ–r robot and its schematic representation. This robot arm includes three parts: a fixed-length body, an extended part, and a gripper. Let the mass of the fixed-length body be m_1, as shown in the figure. The extended part and the load are modeled as mass m_2. The Cartesian location of mass m_1 is

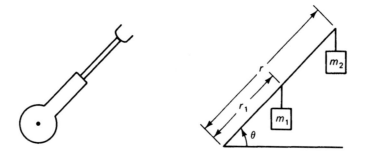

Figure 11.23   Schematic of a θ–r arm.

$$x_1 = r_1 \cos \theta \tag{11.14}$$

$$y_1 = r_1 \sin \theta \tag{11.15}$$

We differentiate these equations with respect to time to obtain the Cartesian velocities.

$$\dot{x}_1 = -r_1 \sin \theta \dot{\theta} \tag{11.16}$$

$$\dot{y}_1 = r_1 \cos \theta \dot{\theta} \tag{11.17}$$

The magnitude of the velocity vector can be expressed as follows:

$$\begin{aligned} V_1^2 &= \dot{x}_1^2 + \dot{y}_1^2 \\ &= r_1^2 \sin^2 \theta \dot{\theta}^2 + r_1^2 \cos^2 \theta \dot{\theta}^2 \\ &= r_1^2 \dot{\theta}^2 (\sin^2 \theta + \cos^2 \theta) \\ &= r_1^2 \dot{\theta}^2 \end{aligned} \tag{11.18}$$

The kinetic energy of m_1 is

$$K_1 = 0.5 m_1 (r_1^2 \dot{\theta}^2) \tag{11.19}$$

Similarly, the kinetic energy of mass m_2 is

$$K_2 = 0.5 m_2 (\dot{r}^2 + r^2 \dot{\theta}^2) \tag{11.20}$$

The total kinetic energy of the robot arm is

$$\begin{aligned} K &= K_1 + K_2 \\ &= 0.5 m_1 (r_1^2 \dot{\theta}^2) + 0.5 m_2 (\dot{r}^2 + r^2 \dot{\theta}^2) \end{aligned} \tag{11.21}$$

The potential energy is

$$P = m_1 g r_1 \sin \theta + m_2 g r \sin \theta \tag{11.22}$$

where g is acceleration due to gravity.

The Lagrangian energy for this θ–r arm is

$$L = 0.5m_1(r_1^2\dot\theta^2) + 0.5m_2(\dot r^2 + r^2\dot\theta^2) - m_1gr_1 \sin \theta - m_2gr \sin \theta \qquad (11.23)$$

The torque about the rotational actuator is

$$T_\theta = m_1r_1^2\theta + m_2r^2\theta + 2m_2r\dot r\dot\theta + g \cos \theta(m_1r_1 + m_2r_2) \qquad (11.24)$$

The force applied by the linear actuator is

$$F_r = m_2\ddot r - m_2r\dot\theta^2 + m_2g \sin \theta \qquad (11.25)$$

We have derived several basic dynamics formulas about the θ–r arm. The information about the dynamic situation of a robot arm is useful in any one of the following applications:

- *Robot-arm design.* A robot-arm designer may want to enter the geometry of a proposed arm design along with estimates of masses, loads, and so on, and simulate the dynamic performance of the arm.
- *Path planning.* Basic path-control techniques provide a robot programmer with a tool to plan the desired path for a robot. However, as the robot moves, and speeds and accelerations increase, kinetic effects may result in an unexpected deviation from the planned path. Path simulation taking into consideration the dynamic model can be used to develop worst-case estimates of path deviations at high speeds.
- *Real-time control.* It is known that no single choice of servo gains is appropriate to provide the best performance of a robot. With the dynamic model of the arm, we can have the potential of attaining such optimal control because we can now describe the interaction of the joints.

In summary, with the knowledge of kinematics and dynamics, one is able to control an arm actuator to accomplish a desired task following a desired path. Trajectory planning and motion control are of considerable interest and importance, as these issues involve the degree of automation and intelligence of the robot.

11.11 COMPUTER VISION

Computer vision has become an indispensable part of an "intelligent" robotic system. As is true with humans, vision endows a robot with a sophisticated sensing mechanism that allows the machine to respond to its environment in an intelligent and flexible manner. The use of vision and other sensing schemes is motivated by the continuing need to increase the flexibility and scope of applications of robotic systems. Although proximity, touch, and force sensing play a significant role in the improvement of robot performance, vision is recognized as the most powerful robot sensory capability.

Robot vision may be defined as the process of extracting, characterizing, and interpreting information from images of a three-dimensional world. This process, also commonly referred to as machine or computer vision, may be subdivided into six principal areas: (1) sensing, (2) preprocessing, (3) segmentation, (4) description, (5) recognition, and (6) interpretation. It is convenient to group these various areas according to the sophistication involved in their implementation. One may consider three levels of processing: low-, medium-, and high-level vision. Although there are no clear-cut boundaries between these subdivisions, they do provide a useful framework for categorizing the various processes that are inherent components of a machine-vision system.

In this section, robot vision is divided into three fundamental tasks: image transformation, image analysis, and image understanding. Image transformation involves the conversion of light images to electrical signals that can be used by a computer. Once a light image is transformed to an electronic image, it may be analyzed to extract such image information as object edges, regions, boundaries, color, and texture. This process is called image analysis. The last and most difficult process in robot vision is that once the image is analyzed, a vision system must interpret what the image represents in terms of information about its environment. This is called image understanding.

11.11.1 Image Transformation

Image transformation is the process of electronically digitizing light images using image devices. An image device is the front end of a vision system, which acts as an image transducer to convert light energy to electrical energy. In humans, the image device is the eye. In a vision system, the image device is a camera, photodiode array, charge-coupled device (CCD) array, or charge-injection device (CID) array.

The output of an image device is a continuous analog signal that is proportional to the amount of light reflected from an image. In order to analyze the image with a computer, the analog signals must be converted and stored in digital form. To this end, a rectangular image array is divided into small regions called picture elements, or pixels. Figure 11.24 illustrates the idea. With photodiodes or CCD arrays, the number of pixels equals the number of photodiodes or CCD devices. The pixel arrangement provides a

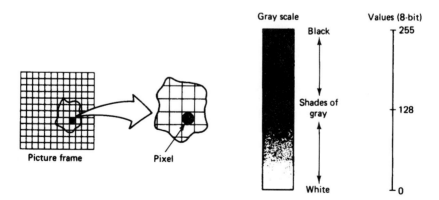

Figure 11.24   A picture frame is divided into picture elements, called pixels, for conversion to gray-scale values. (Andrew C. Staugaard, Jr., *Robotics and AI: An Introduction to Applied Machine Intelligence,* © 1987, p. 207. Reprinted by permission of Prentice Hall.)

sampling grid for an analog-to-digital (A/D) converter. At each pixel, the analog signal is sampled and converted to a digital value. With an 8-bit A/D converter, the converted pixel value will range from 0 for white to 255 for black. Different shades of gray are represented by values between these two extremes. This is why the term gray level is often used in conjunction with the converted values. As the pixels are converted, the respective gray-level values are stored in a memory matrix, which is called a picture matrix.

11.11.2 Image Analysis

A computer needs to locate the edges of an object in order to construct drawings of the object within a scene. Line drawings provide a basis for image understanding, as they define the shapes of objects that make up a scene. Thus, the basic reason for edge detection is that edges lead to line drawings, which lead to shapes, which lead to image understanding. This is illustrated in Figure 11.25.

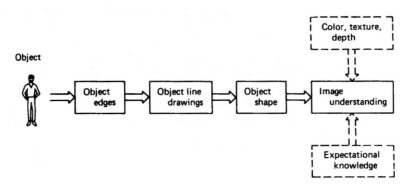

Figure 11.25   Edges lead to line drawings, which lead to shapes, which lead to image understanding. (Andrew C. Staugaard, Jr., *Robotics and AI: An Introduction to Applied Machine Intelligence,* Prentice Hall, 1987, p. 209.)

11.11.2.1 Edge detection.   The edges are usually represented by the points that exhibit the greatest difference in gray-level values within a smoothed picture matrix. Let us look at the graphs of Figure 11.26. Figure 11.26(a) is a gray-level intensity function and Figure 11.26(b) is the slope function of the intensity function. From calculus, we know that the slope of a step edge approaches infinity, as illustrated in the figure. Using this idea, all we have to do is to calculate the first derivative between adjacent gray-scale values, which is usually called the gradient. The technique is called pixel differentiation.

A pixel differentiator must operate on the digital gray-level picture matrix stored in memory. The obvious question at this point is how to differentiate a digital image. The Roberts cross operator provides a good approximation of the first derivative, or gradient, of a digital image. The Roberts cross operator is defined as

$$R(m, n) = \{[i(m + 1, n + 1) - i(m, n)]^2 + [i(m, n + 1) - i(m + 1, n)]^2\}^{1/2} \quad (11.26)$$

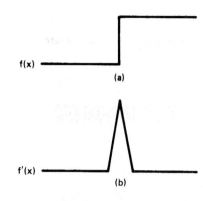

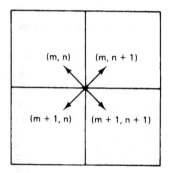

f(x)

(a)

f'(x)

(b)

Figure 11.26   (a) An ideal step edge has (b) a first derivative approaching infinity. (Andrew C. Staugaard, Jr., *Robotics and AI: An Introduction to Applied Machine Intelligence,* Prentice Hall, 1987, p. 212.)

where $i(m, n)$ is the image intensity of pixel (m, n).

As illustrated in Figure 11.27, the operator is applied to diagonal pixels within a 2×2 window of a single picture matrix. The following example shows the procedure.

(m, n)   (m, n + 1)

(m + 1, n)   (m + 1, n + 1)

Figure 11.27   A 2×2 window needed for the Roberts cross operator. (Andrew C. Staugaard, Jr., *Robotics and AI: An Introduction to Applied Machine Intelligence,* Prentice Hall, 1987, p. 213.)

Example 11.5

Given the gray-level values of the following picture matrix, construct the gradient matrix.

$$
\begin{bmatrix}
9 & 9 & 9 & 3 \\
9 & 7 & 5 & 3 \\
9 & 5 & 4 & 3 \\
3 & 3 & 3 & 3
\end{bmatrix}
$$

Solution   By applying the Roberts cross operator to each 2×2 pixel window in the matrix, the gradient matrix is shown as follows:

$$
\begin{bmatrix}
2.0 & 4.5 & 6.3 & x \\
4.5 & 3.0 & 2.2 & x \\
6.3 & 2.2 & 1.0 & x \\
x & x & x & x
\end{bmatrix}
$$

11.11.2.2 Thresholding. The function of thresholding is to decide which elements of the differentiated picture matrix should be considered as edge candidates. Edges are found by applying the Roberts cross operator to each intensity value and comparing the resulting gradient approximation, $R(m, n)$, to a threshold level, T. An edge is present if the gradient is greater than T. It is needless to say that the selection of the threshold level is very important. During the thresholding operation, the differentiated (gradient) matrix is converted to a binary picture matrix as follows:

> If the Roberts operator value exceeds the threshold level for a given pixel, that matrix element is set to a value of 1; otherwise, a value of 0 is assigned.

Example 11.6

Using the gradient matrix obtained in the Example 11.5, construct a binary matrix using a threshold level of 4.

Solution   *A* pixel value is set to 1 if the Roberts operator value is greater than 4; otherwise, a 0 is given to that pixel.

$$\begin{bmatrix} 0 & 1 & 1 & x \\ 1 & 0 & 0 & x \\ 1 & 0 & 0 & x \\ x & x & x & x \end{bmatrix}$$

Lines then might be identified from the binary matrix that is thresholded. Some popular techniques for finding lines from an edge-point matrix are tracking, model matching, and template matching.

11.11.3 Image Understanding

The final task of robot vision is to interpret the information obtained during the image-analysis process. This is called image understanding, or machine perception.

Most image-understanding research is centered around the "blocks world." The blocks world assumes that real-world images can be broken down and described by 2-D rectangular and triangular solids. Several AI-based image-understanding programs, which can interpret real-world images, have been successfully written under this blocks-world assumption.

11.12 CONCLUDING REMARKS

This chapter covers useful material of different technologies that go into a modern robotic system. It is an introduction for engineering students, technology students, and practicing engineers who are interested in obtaining some knowledge of industrial robotic systems.

With that in mind, we presented some fundamental information such as robot classification, robot kinematics and dynamics, sensory systems, power sources, and robot grippers.

There has been some growing interests in enhancing a robotic system by interfacing it to computer-vision equipment. Because of this, we thought it necessary to discuss some basics about computer vision: image transformation, processing, and understanding.

The application aspects of industrial robots are what is most important from a manufacturer's point of view. Therefore, we discussed robot programming, safety issues, application planning, and economical considerations of robotic systems.

REVIEW QUESTIONS

11.1. Using R = revolute and P = prismatic, kinematically describe the following basic robot geometries; (a) Cartesian, (b) cylindrical, (c) spherical, (d) articulated, and (e) SCARA.

11.2. The three primary DOF of a robot are used to achieve the correct ____ of the end-effector in space, whereas the three wrist DOF are needed to achieve part ____ in space.

11.3. Find the inverse kinematic solution for the cylindrical robot arm in Figure 11.4. That is, find the expression for α, a, and c as functions of X, Y, and Z.

11.4. Find the inverse kinematic solution for the spherical robot arm in Figure 11.5. That is, find the expressions for α, β, and a as functions of X, Y, and Z.

11.5. Find the inverse kinematic solution for the articulated robot arm in Figure 11.6. That is, find the expressions for α, β, and γ as functions of l_1, l_2, X, Y, and Z.

11.6. As viewed from above, a SCARA robot has the configuration shown in Figure 11.28).
  (a) Find the homogeneous transformation relating the gripper position and orientation to the base.
  (b) Assuming θ_3 is 0, find θ_1 and θ_2 to position the gripper at coordinates $(1, 1)$.

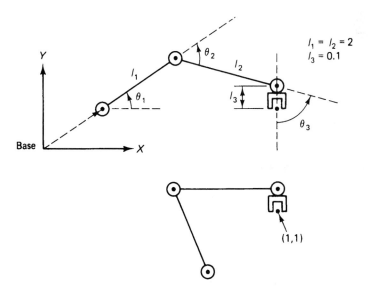

Figure 11.28   A SCARA robot.

(c) We would like to position the gripper at $(1, 1)$ with the orientation of the gripper being vertical as shown. Set up the equations that would be required to find angles θ_1, θ_2, and θ_3.

(d) Find θ_1, θ_2, and θ_3.

11.7. An articulated robot has a vertical waist axis, a horizontal shoulder axis, and a horizontal elbow axis, as shown in Figure 11.29. The shoulder axis is 6 in. above and 4 in. forward of the base of the waist axis. The shoulder-to-elbow distance is 13 in. and the elbow-to-wrist-link distance is 5 in. The waist-axis joint limits allow $\pm 90°$ motion centered on the X_M axis. The shoulder-axis joint limits allow 0 to $+90°$ motion up from the horizontal. The elbow-axis joint limits allow $\pm 135°$ motion centered about the center line of the shoulder-to-elbow link.

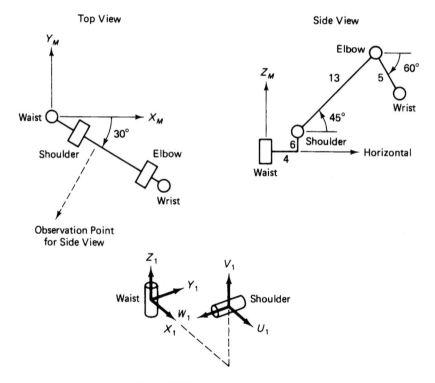

Figure 11.29 An articulated robot.

(a) Calculate the X_M–Y_M–Z_M coordinates of the wrist center for the robot position shown in the figure.

(b) Sketch the outer envelope of this robot's work space. Show both top and side views.

(c) What is the transformation matrix describing the relative pose of the waist and shoulder axes using the X_1–Y_1–Z_1 and U_1–V_1–W_1 coordinate systems, as shown in the figure?

11.8. You are requested to prepare specifications for robot selection for two different applications. As a preliminary step, you have to indicate the recommended drive system, the control type, and the programming capabilities. Indicate your selections and briefly explain your choices.

    (a) Palletizing and depalletizing of boxes on pallets. Average box weight is 3 pounds. The boxes are placed in seven layers, 20 boxes in each layer.

    (b) Spray painting of car bodies in a closed paint booth. The brand of paint used contains flammable materials.

11.9. A robot is considered for assembly of two different pegs into the bracket shown in Figure 11.30. It is suggested that the use of a RCC (remote center of compliance) device will help to successfully implement the robot for this application. Do you agree with this suggestion? Comment on how you would implement the suggested device, and indicate any problems related to such implementation.

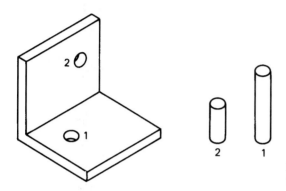

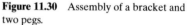

Figure 11.30 Assembly of a bracket and two pegs.

11.10. A cylindrical robot was selected to pick 80-mm by 100-mm boxes from a conveyor line and place the boxes on a pallet, as shown in Figure 11.31. Specify the degrees of freedom that

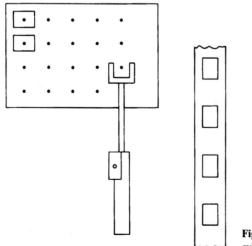

Figure 11.31 Palletizing boxes using a cylindrical robot.

will be needed on the wrist to perform this task. There is a price that will be paid for each degree of freedom on the wrist—do not overspecify!

11.11. Why is an accumulator required in a hydraulic robotic system?

11.12. Find a repetitive task that a robot might perform. Choose a robot and design the related tooling for the application.

11.13. Determine if the design developed in Review Question 11.12 is economic for the robot.

REFERENCES/BIBLIOGRAPHY

ANON. (1984a). *Robotics Industrial Directory.* Conroe, TX: Technical Database Corporation.

———. (1984b). *The Specifications and Applications of Industrial Robots in Japan.* Tokyo: Japan Industrial Robot Association.

ASADA, H., and J. E. SLOTINE (1986). *Robot Analysis and Control.* New York: John Wiley.

AYRES, R. U., and S. M. MILLER (1983). *Robotics: Applications and Social Implications.* Cambridge, MA: Ballinger.

BALESTRINO, A., G. DE MARIA, L. SCIAVICCO, and B. SICILIANO (1988). "An Algorithmic Approach to Coordinate Transformation for Robotic Manipulators," *Advanced Robotics,* 2, 315–404.

CHIU, S. L. (1988). "Task Compatibility of Manipulator Postures," *International Journal of Robotics Research,* 7(5) 13–21.

CRAIG, J. J. (1989). *Introduction to Robotics: Mechanics and Control,* 2nd ed. Reading, MA: Addison-Wesley.

CRITCHLOW, A. (1985). *Introduction to Robotics.* New York: Macmillan.

CSAKVARY, T. (1985). "Planning Robot Applications in Assembly," in S. Y. N of, Ed., *The Handbook of Industrial Robotics.* New York: John Wiley, pp. 1054–1083.

DORF, R. C. (1983). *Robotics and Automated Manufacturing.* Reston, VA: Reston Publishing.

ENGELBERGER, J. F. (1980). *Robotics in Practice.* New York: AMACOM.

FU, K. S., R. C. GONZALEZ, AND C. S. G. LEE. (1987). *Robotics: Control, Sensing, Vision, and Intelligence.* New York: McGraw-Hill.

GROOVER, M. P. (1986). *Industrial Robotics: Technology, Programming, and Applications.* New York: McGraw-Hill.

HARTENBERG, R. S., and J. DENTAVIT (1964). *Kinematic Synthesis of Linkages.* New York: McGraw-Hill.

HEGINBOTHAM, W. B., A. PUGH, C. J. PAGE, D. W. GATEHOUSE, and P. W. KITCHEN (1973). "The Nottingham SIRCH Assembly Robot," in *Proceedings of the First CIRT.* Bedford, UK: IPS, pp. 129–142.

KLEIN, C. A., and C. H. HUANG (1983). "Review of Pseudoinverse Control for Use with Kinematically Redundant Manipulators," *IEEE Transactions of Systems, Man, and Cybernetics,* 13, 245–250.

KOHLI, D., and A. H. SONI (1963). "Kinematic Analysis of Spatial Mechanisms via Successive Screw Displacements," *Journal of Engineering for Industry,* New York: ASME, 2B, 739–747.

LEE, C. S. G. (1982). "Robot Arm Kinematics. Dynamics. and Control," *Computer,* 15(12) 62–80.

————. (1985). "Robot Arm Kinematics and Dynamics," in *Advances in Automation and Robotics: Theory and Applications.* Greenwich, CT: JAI Press.

LIEGEOIS, A. (1977). "Automatic Supervisory Control of the Configuration and Behavior of Multi-body Mechanisms," *IEEE Transactions of Systems, Man, and Cybernetics,* New York: IEEE, 7, 868–871.

LIN, S. K. (1989). "Singularity of a Nonlinear Feedback Control Scheme for Robots," *IEEE Transactions for Systems, Man, and Cybernetics,* 19(1), 134–139.

LUH, J. Y. S., M. W. WALKER, and R. P. C. PAUL (1980). "Resolved-Acceleration Control of Mechanical Manipulators," *IEEE Transactions on Automatic Control,* 25(3), pp. 468–474.

MACIEJEWSKI, A. A., and C. A. KLEIN (1985). "Obstacle Avoidance for Kinematically Redundant Manipulators in Dynamically Varying Environments," *International Journal of Robotics Research,* 4(3), 109–117.

MARSH, P. (1981). "American's Factories Race to Automation," *New Scientist,* June 25, 845–847.

MCCORMICK, D. (1982). "Making Points with Robot Assembly," *Design Engineering,* August, 24–28.

MEACHAM, J. (1981). "TIG Welding and Robotics," *Robotics Age,* March, 28–31.

MILENKOVIC, V., and B. HUANG (1983). "Kinematics of Major Robot Linkages," in the *Proceedings of the 13th International Symposium on Industrial Robots.* Chicago: pp. 16–31 to 16–47.

NAKAMURA, Y., H. HANAFUSA, and T. YOSHIKAWA (1987). "Task-Priority Based Redundancy Control of Robot Manipulators," *International Journal of Robotics Research,* 6(2), 3–15.

————. (1991). *Advanced Robotics: Redundancy and Optimization.* Reading, MA: Addison-Wesley.

NAKAMURA, Y., and H. HANAFUSA (1986). "Inverse Kinematic Solutions with Singularity Robustness for Robot Manipulator Control," *ASME Journal of Dynamic Systems, Measurement, and Control,* 108, 163–171.

————. (1987). "Optimal Redundancy Control of Robot Manipulators." *International Journal of Robotics Research,* 6(1), 32–42.

NEVINS, J. L., and D. E. WHITNEY (1978). "Computer-Controlled Assembly," *Scientific American,* 238(2), 62–74.

NOF, S. Y. (Ed) (1985). *Handbook of Industrial Robots.* New York: John Wiley.

NOF, S. Y., and E. L. FISHER (1982). "Analysis of Robot Work Characteristics," *Industrial Robot,* September, 166–177.

ORIN, D. E., R. B. MCGHEE, M. VUKOBRATOVIC, and G. HARTOCH (1979). "Kinematic and Kinematic Analysis of Open-Chain Linkages Utilizing Newton-Euler Methods," *Mathematical Bioscience,* 43, 107–130.

ORIN, D. E., and W. W. SCHRADER (1984). "Efficient Computation of the Jacobian for Robot Manipulators," *International Journal of Robotics Research,* 3(4), 66–75.

OTTINGER, L. V. (1981). "A Plant Search for Possible Robot Applications," *Industrial Engineering,* December, 26.

————. (1985). "Evaluating Potential Robot Applications in a System Context," *Industrial Engineering,* January, 80–87.

OWEN, T. (1985). *Assembly with Robots.* Englewood Cliffs, NJ: Prentice Hall.

PARENT, M., and C. LAURGEAU (1985). *Robot Technology: Logic and Programming.* Englewood Cliffs, NJ: Prentice Hall.

PAUL, R. P., B. E. SHIMANO, and G. MAYER (1981). Kinematic Control Equations for Simple Manipulators," *IEEE Transactions on Systems, Man and Cybernetics,* SMC-11(6), 449–455.

PENINGTON, R. A., E. L. FISHER, and S. Y. NOF (1986). "Survey of Industrial Characteristics: General Distributions, Trends, and Correlations," in Ed., *Robotics and Material Flow.* Amsterdam: Elsevier, pp. 37–54.

PERA ROBOTS (1983). *A Further Survey of Robots and Their Current Applications in Industry,* Report 337. London: Melton Mowbray.

PIEPER, D. L. (1968). *The Kinematics of Manipulators Under Computer Control,* Artificial Intelligence Project Memo No. 72, Palo Alto, CA: Stanford University Computer Science Department.

ROBOT INSTITUTE OF AMERICA (1982). *Worldwide Robotics Survey and Directory.* Dearborn, MI: RIA.

ROMEO, G., and A. CAMERA (1980). "Robots for Flexible Assembly Systems," *Robotics Today,* Fall, 23–43.

SALISBURY, J. K., and J. J. CRAIG (1982). "Articulated Hands: Force Control and Kinematic Issues," *International Journal of Robotics Research,* 1(1), 4–17.

SAVERIANO, J. W. (1980). "Industrial Robots Today and Tomorrow," *Robotics Age,* X(Y), 4–17.

SCIAVICCO, L. and B. SICILIANO (1996). *Modeling and Control of Robotic Manipulation.* New York: McGraw-Hill.

———. (1988). "A Solution Algorithm to the Inverse Kinematic Problem for Redundant Manipulators," *IEEE Journal of Robotics and Automation,* 4(4), 403–410.

SICILIANO, B. (1986). *Algoritmi di Soluzione al Problema Cinematico Inverso per Robot di Manipolazione* [in Italian], Tesi di Dottorato di Ricerca, Universita degli Studi di Napoli.

———. (1990). "Kinematic Control of Redundant Robot Manipulators: A Tutorial," *Journal of Intelligent and Robotic Systems,* 3, 201–212.

SPONG, M. W., and M. VIDYASAGAR (1989). *Robot Dynamics and Control.* New York: John Wiley.

STADLER, W. (1995). *Analytical Robotics and Mechanics.* New York: McGraw-Hill.

STAUGAARD, Jr., A. C. (1987). *Robotics and AI: An Introduction to Applied Machine Intelligence.* Englewood Cliffs, NJ: Prentice Hall.

SUH, C. H., and C. W. RADCLIFFE (1978). *Kinematics and Mechanisms Design.* New York: John Wiley.

TANNER, W. (1978). *Industrial Robots.* Dearborne, MI: Society of Manufacturing Engineers.

THOMPSON, T. (1981). "Robots for Assembly," *Assembly Engineering,* July 32–36.

WAMPLER, C. W. (1986). "Manipulator Inverse Kinematic Solutions Based on Damped Least-Squares Solutions," *IEEE Transactions on Systems, Man, and Cybernetics,* 16(1), 93–101.

WARNECKE, H. J., and R. D. SCHRAFT (1982). *Industrial Robots: Applications Experience.* Bedford, UK: I. P. S. Publications, pp. 202–206.

WARNECKE H. J., R. D. SCHRAFT, and U. SCHMIDT-STREIER (1981). Computer Aided Planning of Industrial Robot Application in Workpiece Handling," in *Proceedings of the Eleventh International Symposium on Industrial Robots.* Tokyo: Society of Biomechanisms of Japan and Japan Industrial Robot Association, pp. 349–3S9.

WHITNEY, D. E. (1969). "Resolved Motion Rate Control of Manipulators and Human Prostheses," *IEEE Transactions of Man-Machine Systems,* 10, 47–53.

WYSK, R. A., and P. I. PHEFFENBERGER (1986). A Computerized Time Cycle Sheet for Welding Robot Justification," in *Proceedings of the 1986 Spring IIE Conference.* Dallas: IIE.

YOSHIKAWA, T. (1985). "Manipulability of Robotic Mechanisms," *International Journal of Robotics Research,* 4(2), 3–9.

———. (1990). *Foundations of Robotics.* Cambridge, MA: MIT Press.

YUAN, J. S. C. (1988). "Closed-Loop Manipulator Control Using Quaternion Feedback," *IEEE Journal of Robotics and Automation,* 4(4), 434–440.

YUAN, M. S. C., and R. FREUDENSTEIN (1971). "Kinematics Analysis of Spatial Mechanisms by Means of Screw Coordinates." *Transactions of the American Society of Mechanical Engineers, Journal of Engineering Industry,* 93(1), 61–73.

12

Group Technology

12.1 INTRODUCTION

Since the beginning of human culture, people have tried to apply reason to their actions. One important way to apply reason is to relate similar things. Biologists classify items into genus and species. We relate to such things as mammals, marsupials, batrachians, amphibians, fish, mollusks, crustaceans, birds, reptiles, worms, insects, and so on. A chicken is a bird with degenerated wings. Tigers, jaguars, and domestic cats are all members of a single family.

The same concept applied to natural phenomena also can be applied to fabrication and information phenomena. When a vast amount of information has to be kept and ordered, a taxonomy is normally employed. Librarians use taxonomies to classify books in libraries. Similarly, in manufacturing, thousands of items are produced yearly. When one looks at the parts that construct the product, the number is exceptionally large. Each part has a different shape, size, and function. However, when one looks closely, one may again find similarities among components (Figure 12.1); a dowel and a small shaft may be very similar in appearance but different in function. Spur gears of different sizes need the same manufacturing processes and vary only in size. Therefore, it appears that manufactured components can be classified into families similarly to biological families or library taxonomies. Parts classified and grouped into families produce a much more tractable database for management.

Although this simple concept has been in existence for a long time, it was not until 1958 that S. P. Mitrofanov, A Russian engineer, formalized the concept in his book *The Scientific Principles of Group Technology*. Group technology (GT) has been defined (Solaja and Urosevic, 1973) as follows:

> Group technology is the realization that many problems are similar, and that by grouping similar problems, a single solution can be found to a set of problems thus saving time and effort.

Although the definition is quite broad, one usually relates group technology only to production applications. In production systems, group technology can be applied in

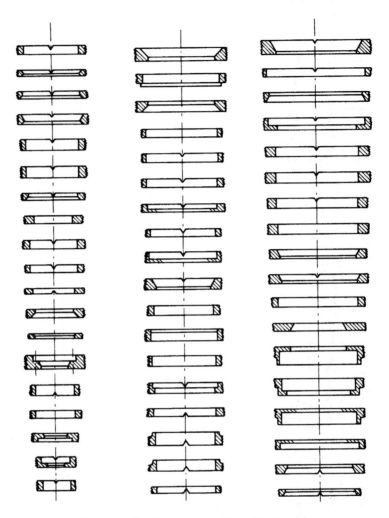

Figure 12.1   A family of components with similar design features.

different areas. For component design, it is clear that many components have a similar shape (Figure 12.1). Similar components, therefore, can be grouped into design families and a new design can be created by simply modifying an existing component design from the same family. By using this concept, composite components can be identified. Composite components are parts that embody all the design features of a design family or design subfamily. An example is shown in Figure 12.2. Components in the family can be identified from features of the composite components.

For manufacturing purposes, GT represents a greater importance than simply a design philosophy. Components that are not similar in shape may still require similar manufacturing processes. For example, in Figure 12.3, most components have different shapes and functions, but all require internal boring, face milling, hole drilling, and so

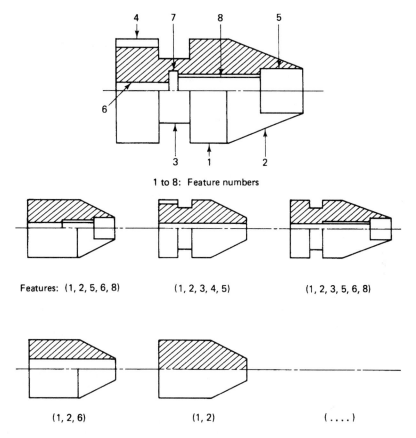

Figure 12.2   A composite component.

on. Therefore, it can be concluded that the components in the figure are similar. The set of similar components can be called a production family. From this, process-planning work can be facilitated. Because similar processes are required for all family members, a machine cell can be built to manufacture the family. This makes production planning and control much easier, because only similar components are considered for each cell. Such a cell-oriented layout is called a group-technology layout or cellular layout.

The following techniques are employed in GT:

1. Coding and classification
2. Production-flow analysis
3. Group layout

Although both production-flow analysis and group layout are based on coding and classification methods, they still can be distinguished as different activities. In the following sections, basic group-technology concepts are discussed in detail.

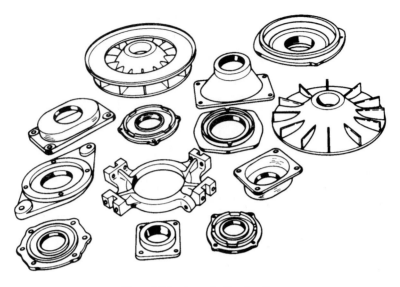

Figure 12.3 A production family.

12.2 CODING AND CLASSIFICATION

Coding is a process of establishing symbols to be used for meaningful communication. Classification is a separation process in which items are separated into groups based on the existence or absence of characteristic attributes. Coding can be used for classification purposes, and classification requirements must be considered during the construction of a coding scheme. Therefore, coding and classification are closely related.

Before a coding scheme can be constructed, a survey of all component features must be completed and then code values can be assigned to the features. The selection of relevant features depends on the application of the coding scheme. For example, tolerance is not important for design retrieval; therefore, it is not a feature in a design-oriented coding system. However, in a manufacturing-oriented coding system, tolerance is indeed an important feature.

Because the code structure affects its length, the accessibility and the expandability of a code (and the related database) is of importance. There are three different types of code structure in GT coding systems: (1) hierarchical, (2) chain (matrix), and (3) hybrid.

A hierarchical structure is also called a monocode. In a monocode, each code number is qualified by the preceding characters. For example, in Figure 12.4, the fourth digit indicates threaded or not threaded for a 322X family. One advantage of a hierarchical structure is that it can represent a large amount of information with very few code positions. A drawback is the potential complexity of the coding system. Hierarchical codes are difficult to develop because of all the branches in the hierarchy that must be defined.

A chain structure is called a polycode. Every digit in the code position represents a distinct bit of information, regardless of the previous digit. In Table 12.1, a chain-

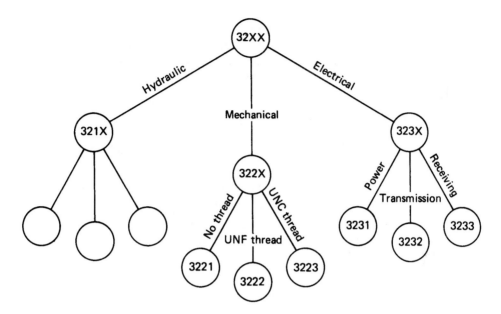

Figure 12.4   A hierarchical structure.

structured coding scheme is presented. A 2 in the third position always means a cross hole no matter what numbers are given to positions 1 and 2. Chain codes are compact and are much easier to construct and use. The major drawback is that they cannot be as detailed as hierarchical structures with the same number of coding digits.

The third type of structure, the hybrid structure, is a mixture of the hierarchical and chain structures (Fig 12.5). Most existing coding systems use a hybrid structure to obtain the advantages of both structures. A good example is the widely used Opitz (1970) code (Figure 12.6)

There are more than 100 GT coding systems used in industry today. The structure selected is based primarily on the application. Table 12.2 provides comprehensive guidelines for code-structure selection.

The physical coding of a component can be shown best by example. In Figure 12.7, a rotational component is coded using the Opitz system. By going through each code

TABLE 12.1   CHAIN STRUCTURE

Digit position	1	2	3	4
Class of feature	External shape	Internal shape	Holes	...
Possible value				
1	Shape 1	Shape 1	Axial	...
2	Shape 2	Shape 2	Cross	...
3	Shape 3	Shape 3	Axial and cross	
:	:	:	:	:

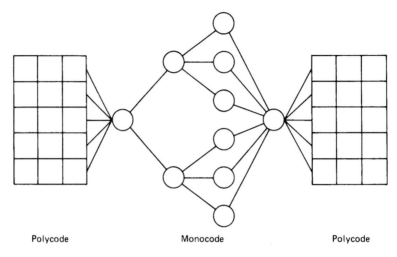

Polycode   Monocode   Polycode

Figure 12.5   A hybrid structure.

position, the resulting code becomes 11102 (see Table 12.4). This code represents this component and all others with similar shape and diameter. A definition of the specific Opitz code attributes is given later in Figure 12.9.

12.2.1 Group Technology Coding Systems

Both drafting and geometric modeling are detailed representations of an engineering design. They provide detailed information concerning the component to be made and are essential in conveying the design for manufacturing However, as with many decision-making processes, too much information may make the decision difficult. For example, when reading a magazine or journal, one seldom begins by reading each sentence on successive pages. Instead, one peruses the table of contents first in order to locate interesting technical information. By doing so, candidate articles can be located more quickly. However, a title may not convey all of the necessary information. Therefore, the reader would typically scan the abstract. The abstract is a summary that represents the article without great detail. Reading the abstract of an article normally provides one with the insight to continue reading. Parts lists corresponding to a table of contents have been around for a long time, and although it is impractical to write abstracts for a CAD model, a similar concept can be applied using coding.

Group technology (GT) is an appropriate tool for this purpose. Coding, a GT technique, can be used to model a component without all the detail. When constructing a coding system for a component's representation, there are several factors to be considered. They include

1. the population of components (i.e., rotational, prismatic, deep-drawn, sheet metal, and so on
2. the detail the code should represent

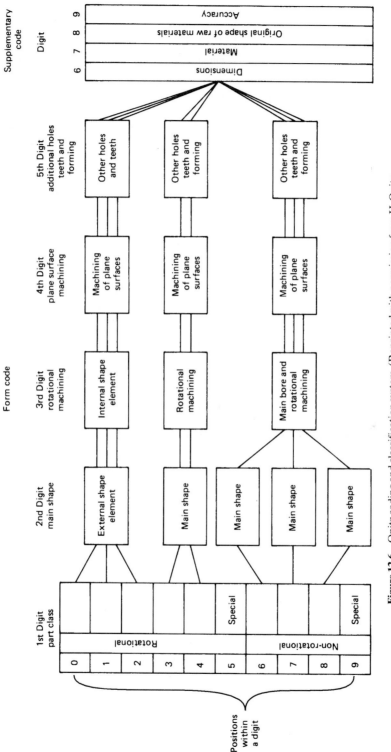

Figure 12.6 Opitz coding and classification system. (Reprinted with permission from H. Opitz. *A Classification System to Describe Workpieces*, Pergamon Press.)

TABLE 12.2 CODE-STRUCTURE SELECTION

Major item class	Resolution required	Flexibility needed	Code-system type[a]
Raw materials	Moderate	Low	Hybrid (H/C)
Commercial items	High	Low	H
Designed piece parts	Moderate	High	C
Assemblies models	Moderate	Moderate	Hybrid (H/C)
Machinery	Moderate	Moderate	Hybrid (H/C)
Technical information	Moderate	Low	H
Tools			
Commercial	Moderate	Low	H
Proprietary	Moderate	Low	C
Gauges/fixtures	Moderate	Low	H
Supplies	High	Low	H

[a]H, hierarchical; C, chain.

Source: Krag, 1978. (Courtesy of Numerical Control Society/AIM Tech.)

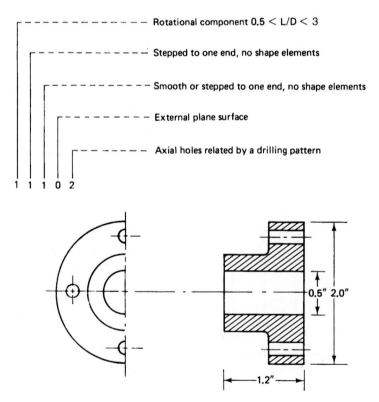

Figure 12.7 Rotational component. (Reprinted with permission from H. Opitz, *A Classification System to Describe Workpieces,* Pergamon Press.)

3. the code structure: chain, hierarchical, or hybrid
4. the digital representation (i.e., binary, octal, decimal, alphanumeric, hexadecimal, and so on)

The population of the component contributes to the variety of shapes. For example, the population of the United States includes virtually all races. In a sense, it is necessary to distinguish race, hair color, eye color, and so on. However, in a nation such as Japan, it is not worthwhile to record skin color, hair color, and so on, because these items are virtually invariant. In component coding, it is also true that only those features that vary have to be included in the code. When a coding scheme is designed or used, two properties must hold true: the code must be (1) unambiguous and (2) complete.

We can define coding as a function of H that maps components from a population space P into a coded space C (Figure 12.8). An unambiguous code can be defined (for component i) as

$$i \in P \Rightarrow \exists \text{ only one } j \in C \Rightarrow j = H(i)$$

Completeness can be defined as

$$\forall i \in P \exists j \in C \Rightarrow j = H(i)$$

The two properties suggest that each component in a population has its own unique code. However, normally, it is desirable to have several components in the population share one code.

The code has to be concise. If a 100-digit code and a 10-digit code can both represent components in P completely and unambiguously, the 10-digit code is more desirable. However, when more detail is required, a longer code is normally necessary. For example, the basic Opitz code (shown in Figure 12.6) uses five digits to describe the shape. Five digits can represent 10^5 combinations. With this set, it is not possible to show a large amount of detail of a component. Some codes are significantly longer; for

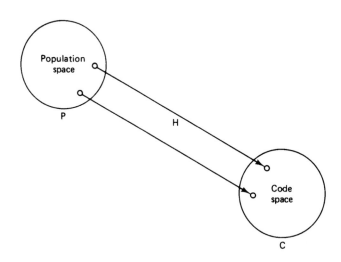

Figure 12.8   Mapping from a population space to a code space.

example, the KK-3 of Japan (Japan Society, 1980), which has 21 digits and contains multiple digits for single features, and MICLASS of TNO (Houtzeel and Schilperoort, 1976), which has a 12-digit code. For some computer-aided process-planning systems (e.g., APPAS [Wysk, 1977]), a detailed surface code is used instead of a code for the entire component. The decision on how much detail the code should represent depends solely on the application. The selection of a code structure again depends on the application. Table 12.2 provides comprehensive selection criteria.

The last consideration in coding-system construction is the code digits. Several positional alternatives can be selected (from binary to alphanumeric). However, this selection yields different precisions for the different schemes. For example, an N-digit code with different coding features yields the following combination of code:

Binary	2	$(0, 1)$
Octal	8	$(0, 1, \ldots, 7)$
Decimal	10	$(0, 1, \ldots, 9)$
Hexadecimal	16	$(0, 1, \ldots, 9, A, \ldots, F)$
Alphanumeric	$(26 + 10)$	$(0, 1, \ldots, 9, A, \ldots, Z)$

Although alphanumeric systems are the most compact (the same amount of information can be represented by fewer digits), the difficulty of handling both numerical and alphabetical characters makes alphanumerics less attractive.

12.2.2. Code contents. When using a code to represent an engineering design, it is important to represent the basic features of the design. Similar to a human represented by height, weight, color, hair, eye color, and sex, and engineering component can be represented by its basic shape, secondary features, size, tolerance, critical dimensions, material, and so on. For process planning, it is desirable to have codes that can distinguish unique production families.

Fortunately, most components of similar shape can be produced by the same set of processes. However, the opposite is not true as frequently. Shape elements normally dictate the manufacturing process. Secondary features such as auxiliary holes, gear teeth, threads, and chamfers are also important and can dictate a different set of process plans. From only the shape, there is no way of telling how large or small a component is. The production methods for a 2-cm^3 model airplane engine block are definitely different from those for the engine block of a 6-liter V-8 engine. Although similar processes may be applied to both engine blocks, the machines, tools, and material-handling methods will probably be very different. Size, tolerance, and surface finish also can affect the required processes. The price of a precision component increases as the tolerance is tightened. This is usually the result of a precision component requiring several more processes than a component of standard tolerance specification. For example, a milled workpiece does not require an additional finishing process if the specified surface finish is 125 μin. or above on a flat surface. However, if the surface-finish requirement is specified as 4 μin. a careful finishing cut on the last milling pass followed by grinding, polishing, and lapping may be necessary.

The workpiece material is also a factor that must be considered. Tools for machining aluminum are not appropriate for the machining alloy steel. Feeds and speeds used for machining also depend on the material.

Because a coding system transforms the properties and requirements listed previously into a code, this information should somehow be tied into a process-planning system. Some of the process-planning systems that have been successfully implemented are introduced in Chapter 13.

The length of a part code normally dictates the detail that is captured by the code. In general, the longer the code, the more detail that can be extracted. However, the key to any GT application is to only include detail that is relevant. In a manufacturing environment, the key is to use only descriptive data that can or will change from part to part. We mentioned that in Japan, virtually the entire populations are of the same race and have the same hair color and eye color. To include this information on a driver's license for identification purposes does not accomplish anything. Similarly, in a plastics industry, to include a material code that indicates plastic accomplishes nothing.

The length and detail of a code depend on the specific application, industry, and product mix. Codes ranging from a few digits to 50 or more digits have been successfully used in industry. For simple part classification, a few digits are adequate, whereas for process planning, more digits may be required. Two public domain codes that illustrate the "short and long" of codes are the Vuoso–Praha code and the KK-3 code. Some coding systems are discussed in the following sections.

12.2.3. The Vuoso–Praha system.

The Vuoso–Praha code is a four-digit coding system that characterizes a part by kind, class, group, and material. The code is illustrated in Table 12.3. This type of code is typically used for rough part classification so as to identify the type of department that would produce the part. For example, the part shown in Figure 12.7 would be classified as

3	Rotational workpiece, with through hole
3	$D = 51.2$ mm; $L/D = 0.6$
0	Smooth
?	Material not specified

12.2.4 The Opitz System

The Opitz coding system (Opitz, 1970) is probably the best known coding system. It was developed by H. Opitz of the Aachen Tech University in West Germany. The code uses a hybrid code structure. However, except for the first digit, it resembles a chain structure more closely (Table 12.4).

The Opitz code consists of a form code and a supplementary code. The form code can represent parts of the following variety: rotational, flat, long, and cubic. A dimension ratio is further used in classifying the geometry: the length/diameter ratio is used to classify the rotational components and the length/width and length/height ratios are

TABLE 12.3　THE VUOSO–PRAHA CODE

Vuoso-Praha　　Workpiece classification system

	Rotational workpieces			Flat and irregular	Box-like	Other mainly non-machined	Materials
	Hole in axis	Geared and splined					Plain steel STL　1

(Rotational workpieces — Hole in axis: None / Blind / Trough; Geared and splined — Hole in axis: None / Trough)

Columns: 1 None, 2 Blind, 3 Trough, 4 None, 5 Trough, 6 Flat and irregular, 7 Box-like, 8 Other mainly non-machined

Kind	D	L/D	Rough form		Rough form	Lmax	Rough weight	Made of	
0		~1			Gib-like L/B ≥ 5	mm 0-200	0-30 kg	Extruded forms	
1	0-40	1-6				mm 200-	30-200 kg	Bars	
2		~6			Platforms L/B ≤ 5	mm 0-200	200-500 kg	Tubes	
3		~1				mm 200-	500-1000 kg	Sheets	
4	40-80	1-4			Lever-like	mm 0-200	1000- kg	Wires	
5		~4				mm 200-			
6	80-200	~3			Irregular	mm 0-200			
7	80-	~3				mm 200-			Grey iron 4224
8	200-	~3			Prism-like	mm 0-200			Maleable 4225 / Iron 4226 / Cast steel 4227-29
9	Various	~30				mm 200-			Non ferrous

Group of workpiece (rows 0–9):

	Group	Hole in axis	Geared and splined	Flat and irregular	Box-like	Other mainly non-machined
0	Smooth		Spur geared / Splined	Flat Parallel	Boxes Spindlestocks Frames	Non mach
1	Thread in axis		Other	Flat Other	Columns	Part mach
2	Holes not in axis		Taper geared / Splined	Rotat Parallel	Beds Bridges	Non mach
3	Splines or grooves		Other	Rotat Other	Outriggers Knees	Part mach
4	Comb. 1+2		Wormgeared / Splined	Flat Parallel Rotat Parallel	Tables Slides	Non mach
5	Comb. 1+3		Other	Flat Parallel Rotat Other	Lids	Part mach
6	Comb. 2+3		Splined	Flat Other Rotat Parallel	Basins Containers	Non mach
7	Comb. 1+2+3		Multiple gears / Other	Flat Other Rotat Other		Part mach
8	Taper		Splined / Other	Geared		
9	Unround		Other		Counterweights	

Example of a class number: 3 3 7 2

- 3 – rotational trough hole
- 3 – max ⌀ 40-80 L/D ~1
- 7 – threaded, holes not in axis, splines
- 2 – alloy steel

(Column headers for example: Kind | Class | Group | Material)

Source: Gallagher and Knight (1973).

TABLE 12.4 FORM CODE (DIGITS 1–5) FOR ROTATIONAL PARTS IN THE OPITZ SYSTEM. PART CLASSES 0, 1, AND 2

Code	Digit 1 Part class	Digit 2 External shape, external shape elements	Digit 3 Internal shape, internal shape elements	Digit 4 Plane-surface machining	Digit 5 Auxiliary holes and gear teeth
0	L/D ≤ 0.5 (Rotational parts)	Smooth, no shape elements	No hole, no breakthrough	No surface machining	No auxiliary hole (No gear teeth)
1	0.5 < L/D < 3	No shape elements (Stepped to one end or smooth)	No shape elements (Smooth or stepped to one end)	Surface plane and/or curved in one direction, external	Axial, not on pitch circle diameter
2	L/D ≥ 3	Thread	Thread	External plane surface related by graduation around a circle	Axial on pitch circle diameter
3		Functional groove	Functional groove	External groove and/or slot	Radial, not on pitch circle diameter
4		No shape elements (Stepped to both ends)	No shape elements (Stepped to both ends)	External spline (polygon)	Axial and/or radial and/or other direction
5	(Nonrotational parts)	Thread	Thread	External plane surface and/or slot, external spline	Axial and/or radial on PCD and/or other directions
6		Functional groove	Functional groove	Internal plane surface and/or slot	Spur gear teeth (With gear teeth)
7		Functional cone	Functional cone	Internal spline (polygon)	Bevel gear teeth
8		Operating thread	Operating thread	Internal and external polygon, groove and/or slot	Other gear teeth
9	(Nonrotational parts)	All others	All others	All others	All others

Source: Courtesy of Pergamon Press.

TABLE 12.4 (continued)

Code	Digit 1 — Component class	Digit 2 — Overall shape	Digit 3 — Rotational machining	Digit 4 — Plane surface machining	Digit 5 — Auxiliary hole(s), gear teeth, forming
0		(Around one axis, no segments)	No rotational machining	No surface machining	No auxiliary hole, gear teeth and forming
1		Hexagonal bar	Machined — *External shape*	External plane surface and/or surface curved in one direction	Axial hole(s) not related by drilling pattern — *No forming, no gear teeth*
2		Square or other regular polygonal section	With screw thread(s) — *External shape*	External plane surfaces related to one another by graduation around a circle	Holes, axial and/or radial and/or in other directions, not related
3	*L/D ≤ 2 with deviation* (Rotational components)	Symmetrical cross section producing no unbalance	Smooth — *Internal shape*	External groove and/or slot	Axial holes — *Related by a drilling pattern*
4	*L/D > 2 with deviation*	Cross sections other than 0 to 2	Stepped toward one or both ends (multiple increases) — *Internal shape*	External spline and/or polygon	Holes axial and/or radial and/or in other directions
5		Segments after rotational machining	With screw threads — *Internal shape*	External plane surface and/or slot and/or groove, spline	Formed, no auxiliary hole — *Forming, no gear teeth*
6		Segments before rotational machining	Machined — *External and internal shape*	Internal plane surface and/or groove	Formed, with auxiliary hole(s)
7		Rotational components with curved axis — *(Around more than one axis)*	Screw thread(s) — *External and internal shape*	Internal spline and/or polygon	Gear teeth, no auxiliary hole — *gear teeth*
8		Rotational components with two or more parallel axes	External shape elements	External and internal spline and/or slot and/or groove	Gear teeth, with auxiliary hole(s)
9		Rotational components with intersecting axes / Others	Other shape elements	Other	Other

484

TABLE 12.4 (continued)

	Digit 1			Digit 2		Digit 3		Digit 4
	Diameter D or edge length A			Material		Initial form		Accuracy in coding digits
	mm	inches						
0	≤ 20	≤ 0.8	0	Cast iron	0	Round bar, black	0	No accuracy specified
1	> 20 ≤ 50	> 0.8 ≤ 2.0	1	Modular graphitic cast iron and malleable cast iron	1	Round bar, bright drawn	1	2
2	> 50 ≤ 100	> 2.0 ≤ 4.0	2	Mild steel ≤ 26.5 tonf/in.² not heat treated	2	Bar: triangular, square, hexagonal, others	2	3
3	> 100 ≤ 160	> 4.0 ≤ 6.5	3	Hard steel > 26.5 tonf/in.² heat-treatable low-carbon and case-hardening steel, not heat treated	3	Tubing	3	4
4	> 160 ≤ 250	> 6.5 ≤ 10.0	4	Steels 2 and 3 heat treated	4	Angle, U−, T−, and similar sections	4	5
5	> 250 ≤ 400	> 10.0 ≤ 16.0	5	Alloy steel (not heat treated)	5	Sheet	5	2 and 3
6	> 400 ≤ 600	> 16.0 ≤ 25.0	6	Alloy steel heat treated	6	Plate and slabs	6	2 and 4
7	> 600 ≤ 1000	> 25.0 ≤ 40.0	7	Nonferrous metal	7	Cast or forged components	7	2 and 5
8	> 1000 ≤ 2000	> 40.0 ≤ 80.0	8	Light alloy	8	Welded assembly	8	3 and 4
9	> 2000	> 80.0	9	Other materials	9	Premachined components	9	2 + 3 + 4 + 5

Source: Courtesy of Pergamon Press. Opitz (1970)

used to classify nonrotational components. The Opitz form code uses five digits, representing (1) component class, (2) basic shape, (3) rotational-surface machining, (4) plane-surface machining, and (5) auxiliary holes, gear teeth, and forming. Primary, secondary, and auxiliary shapes can be represented using the five geometric digits.

A supplemental code containing four digits is usually appended to the Opitz form code. The first digit represents the major dimension (either diameter or edge length). The approximate component size then can be determined by using the dimension ratio specified in the geometry.

Dimensions of less than 0.8 in. and greater than 80 in. are represented by a 0 or 9 code, respectively. The material type, raw material shape, and accuracy are represented by digits, 2, 3, and 4, respectively. The first three digits of the supplementary code are self-explanatory. The fourth digit, accuracy in coding digits, deserves some explanation.

The coding digits of the form code, in which a defined level of accuracy in the machining of the component is required, are comprised under this heading; for example, the indication here of the fourth coding digit in position 3 means a degree of accuracy in the machining of that surface. Accuracy may be comprised of clearance tolerances—H7 and better; surface quality—32 μ in. and better, and so on. Note that the accuracy standards used in the original Opitz system may not be implemented in or appropriate for the reader's manufacturing setting. Therefore, the reader is encouraged to define an accuracy scheme or range tailored to the manufacturing environment.

The Opitz code is concise and easy to use. It has been adopted by many companies as their coding subsystem. Several CAM-I-CAPP systems currently used an Opitz-based coding system.

12.2.5 The KK-3 System

The KK-3 coding system is a general-purpose classification and coding system for machined parts. KK-3 was developed by the Japan Society for the Promotion of the Machine Industry (JSPMI) (Japan Society, 1980). KK-3 was first presented in 1976 and uses a 21-digit decimal system. The code structure for rotational components is shown in Tables 12.5 and 12.6. Because KK-3 is much greater in length than Opitz, more information can be represented. The KK-3 code includes two digits for the component-name (functional-name) classification. The first digit classifies the general function, such as gears, shafts, drive and moving parts, and fixing parts. The second digit describes more detailed functions. For example, included in a single family, there are spur gears, bevel gears, worm gears, and so on. With two digits, KK-3 can classify 100 functional names for rotational and nonrotational components. However, at times, this can be as confusing as it is complete. KK-3 also classifies materials using two code digits. The first digit classifies material type and the second digit classifies shape of the raw material. Dimensions and dimensional ratios are also classified. Some redundancy can be found, that is, length, diameter, and length diameter ratios are classified for rotation components. Shape detail and process type are classified in KK-3 using 13 digits of code (much more detail than the Opitz system). An example of coding a component using KK-3 is illustrated in Figure 12.9. A modified version of KK-1 (an earlier version of KK-3) is in

TABLE 12.5   STRUCTURE OF THE KK-3 CODING SYSTEM
(ROTATIONAL COMPONENTS)

Digit	Items	(Rotational components)	
1	Parts name	General classification	
2		Detail classification	
3	Materials	General classification	
4		Detail classification	
5	Chief dimensions	Length	
6		Diameter	
7	Primary shapes and length diameter ratio		
8	Shape details and kinds of processes	External surface	External surface and outer primary shape
9			Concentric screw threaded parts
10			Functional cut-off parts
11			Extraordinary shaped parts
12			Forming
13			Cylindrical surface
14		Internal surface	Internal primary shape
15			Internal curved surface
16			Internal flat surface and cylindrical surface
17		End surface	
18		Nonconcentric holes	Regularly located holes
19			Special holes
20		Noncutting process	
21	Accuracy		

Source: Courtesy of the Japan Society for the Promotion of the Machining Industry.

use for computer-aided process planning (Japan Society, 1980). A complete set of definitions and vocabulary for KK-3 is presented in appendixes D to G.

12.2.6 The MICLASS System

The MICLASS system was originally developed by TNO of Holland, and is currently maintained in the United States by the Organization for Industrial Research (Houtzeel, 1976, 1980, 1981). It is a chain-structured code of 12 digits. The code is designed to be universal; therefore, it includes both design and manufacturing information. Information such as the main shape, shape elements, position of shape elements, main dimensions, ratio of the dimensions, auxiliary dimension, form tolerance, and the machinability of the material is included (Figure 12.10). An additional 18 digits of code

TABLE 12.6 FUNCTIONAL DELINEATION OF THE KK-3 CODING SYSTEM

I	II	0	1	2	3	4	5	6	7	8	9	II
0	Gears	Spur, helical gear(s)	Internal gear(s)	Bevel gear(s)	Hypoid gear(s)	Worm gear(s)	Screw gear(s)	Sprocket wheel	Special gear	Round vessel	Other(s)	Gears
1	Shafts, spindles	Spindle, arbor, main drive	Counter shaft	Lead screw(s)	Screwed shaft	Round rod(s)	Eccentric shaft(s)	Splined shaft	Cross shaft	Round column	Round casting	Shafts, spindles
2	Main drive	Pulley(s)	Clutch	Brake(s)	Impeller(s)	Piston(s)	Round tables	Other(s)	Flange	Chuck(s)	Labyrinth seal(s)	Main drive
3	Guiding parts	Sleeves, bushing	Bearing metal	Bearing(s)	Roller(s)	Cylinder	Other(s)	Dial plate(s)	Index plate(s)	Cam(s)	Others	Guiding parts
4	Fixing part	Collar(s)	Socket, spacer	Pin(s)	Fastening screws	Other(s)	Handles	Spool(s)	Round links	Screw(s)	Others	Fixing part
5												
6												
...												
9												

Rotational components: I = 0–4. Nonrotational: I = 5, 6, ..., 9.

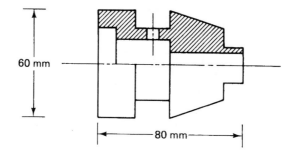

Code digit	Item	Component condition	Code
1 2	} Name	Control valve (others)	0 9
3 4	} Material	Copper bar	7
5	Dimension length	80 mm	2
6	Dimension diameter	60 mm	2
7	Primary shape and ratio of chief dimension	L/D 1.3	2
8	External surface	With functional tapered surface	3
9	Concentric screw	None	0
10	Functional cutoff	None	0
11	Extraordinary shaped	None	0
12	Forming	None	0
13	Cylindrical surface ≥ 3	None	0
14	Internal primary	Piercing hole with dia. variation, no cutoff	2
15	Internal curved surface	None	0
16	Internal flat surface	None	0
17	End surface	Flat	0
18	Regularly located hole	Holes located on circumferential line	3
19	Special hole	None	0
20	Noncutting process	None	0
21	Accuracy	Grinding process on external surface	4

Figure 12.9   Example of a KK-3 coding system.

are also available for user-specified information (i.e., part function, lot size, major machining operation, and so on). These supplemental digits provide flexibility for system expansion. MICLASS is also one of the earliest interactive coding systems (Figure 12.11 illustrates an interactive coding session). MICLASS has been adapted by many U.S. industries. Several application programs based on MICLASS are currently available, such as the MULTIPLAN and MULTICAP variant process-planning systems.

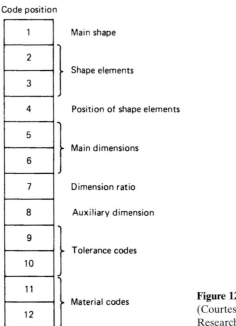

Code position

1	Main shape	
2	Shape elements	
3		
4	Position of shape elements	
5	Main dimensions	
6		
7	Dimension ratio	
8	Auxiliary dimension	
9	Tolerance codes	
10		
11	Material codes	
12		

Figure 12.10   MICLASS code structure.
(Courtesy of the Organization for Industrial
Research/Prime Computer.)

12.2.7 DCLASS Systems

The DCLASS system was developed by Del Allen at Brigham Young University (Allen and Smith, 1980). DCLASS was intended to be a decision-making and classification system (thus the name DCLASS). It is a tree-structured system (Figure 12.2) that can generate codes for components, materials, processes, machines, and tools. For components, an eight-digit code is used:

Digits 1–3	Basic shape
Digit 4	Form feature
Digit 5	Size
Digit 6	Precision
Digits 7 and 8	Material

In DCLASS, each branch represents a condition, and a code can be found at the terminal (junction) of each branch. Multiple passes of the decision tree allow a complete code to be found. Figure 12.12 illustrates the process by showing a portion of the decision tree for components. One pass on this tree generates the first three digits of the code. Code construction is established using certain roots.

The DCLASS system is not only a coding system, but also a decision-support system. A generative process-planning system using DCLASS has also been reported by Allen (Allen and Smith, 1980).

```
RUN $MICLAS
MICLAS VERSION 2.0

ENTER THE CLASSIFICATION ROUTE (1 TO 9) > 1
3 MAIN DIMENSIONS (WHEN ROT. PART D, L AND O) > 2 9375 2.0
 DEVIATION OF ROTATIONAL FORM > NO
 CONCENTRIC SPIRAL GROOVES > NO
TURNING ON OUTERCONTOUR (EXCEPT ENDFACES) > YES
 SPECIAL GROOVES OR CONE(s) OR PROFILE(S) ON OUTERCONTOUR > NO
 ALL MACH. EXT. DIAM. AND ROT. FACES VISIBLE FROM ONE END
 (EXC. ENDFACES + GROOVES(S) > YES
TURNING ON INNERCONTOUR > YES
 INTERNAL SPECIAL GROOVES OR CONE(S) OR PROFILE(S) > NO
 ALL INT. DIA. + ROT. FACES VISIBLE FROM 1 END (EXC. GROOVES > YES
ALL DIA. + ROT. FACES (INC. ENDFACES) > YES
ECC. HOLING AND/OR FACING AND/OR SLOTTING > YES
 ON INNERFORM AND/OR FACES VISIBLE FROM ONE END (EXCL. ENDFACES > YES
 ON OUTERFORM > NO
ONLY ENCLOSED INTERNAL SLOTS > NO
ECC. MACHINING ONLY ONE SENSE > Y
 ONLY HOLES ON A BOLTCIRCLE (AT LEAST 3 HOLDS) > YES
FORM-OR THREADING TOLERANCE > NO
DIAM. OR ROT. FACE ROUGHNESS LESS THAN 33 RU (MICRO-INCHES) > YES
 SMALLEST POSITIONING TOL. FIELD > .016
 SMALLEST LENGTHTOL. FIELD > .0313

CLASS. NR. = 1271 3231 3100 0000 0000 0000 0000 00
*********************************************************

DIGIT TO CHANGE >
CONTINUE [Y/N] > N
TTO—STOP
>
```

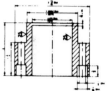

DRAWING TITLE	TOLERANCES	MATERIAL:
BUSHING	Fractional · 1 64	CC 15
DRAWING NO:	Decimal · 003	125 / (25)
7		ALL OVER EXCEPT AS NOTED

Figure 12.11   Coding session of MICLASS. (Courtesy of the Organization for Industrial Research/Prime Computer.)

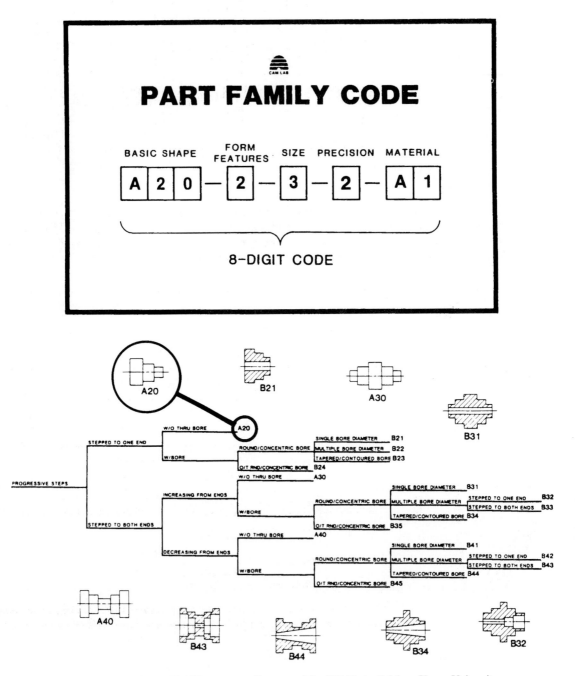

Figure 12.12   DCLASS structure.   Courtesy of the CAM Lab., Brigham Young University.

12.3 BENEFITS OF GROUP TECHNOLOGY

Coding and classification are two elements of a GT system. However, coding and classification provide little benefit to the user if the GT application ends there. Coding is a means of quantifying the geometry and material content of a part.

One immediate and somewhat obvious use of GT is to code potential designs before they are formerly designed. A designer sketches a concept and then codes the sketch. Identical and similarly coded parts then can be retrieved from the parts archives. If an existing part can be used to satisfy the design needs, the process ends here, without requiring the designer to detail the design idea and develop a set of process plans for the part. If a similar part will suffice, hundreds of engineering man-hours can be saved. If an existing part cannot be used, perhaps a variant can be used. If this is the case, the existing part drawing simply can be modified. Existing production plans may also only require minor modifications. Many companies have found that they produce identical parts with different names. Duplicate tooling, fixtures, and engineering time are all required when this duplication occurs. In many instances, a minor modification of a single part can be made to accommodate more than one application. The basic process is illustrated in Figure 12.13.

12.3.1 Machine Selection

A common characteristic of U.S. industry is the underutilization of expensive processing equipment. The underutilization can take two forms:

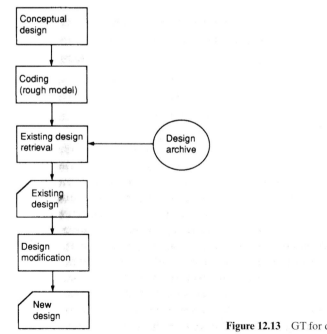

Figure 12.13   GT for design applications.

1. Much of the machine time is idle and totally unproductive.
2. Many of the parts assigned to a specific machine are far below the capacity of the machine.

By grouping closely matched parts into a part family, machines can be more fully utilized from both a scheduling as well as a capacity standpoint.

By using a part coding system, similar parts with similar feature dimension specifications can be assigned to the same part family, and machines corresponding to the minimum product specification can be selected rather than overspecifying (and overpaying) the processing. Figure 12.14 illustrates this phenomenon for lathe parts. In the figure, it can be seen that only a few percent of the parts being machined require the full lathe swing or length. Furthermore, the speed and feed capacity of the lathe can also be overspecified. See Figure 12.15. Because additional features on machine tools require additional costs, be careful not to overspecify a machine and not to use the features.

12.3.2 Part-Family Formation

One of the major benefits derived from GT applications is part-family formation for efficient work flow. Efficient work flow can result from grouping machines logically so that material handling and setup can be minimized. Parts can be grouped so that the same tooling and fixtures can be used. When this occurs, a major reduction in setup results. Machines can also be grouped so that the amount of handling between machining operations also can be minimized.

One of the most common machine layouts used in industry is a "functional layout." This type of layout is illustrated in Figure 12.16. As can be seen, machines are laid out with respect to type. Mills, lathes, drills, and grinders are separately clustered so that same machines reside in a single department. This layout is efficient in the allocation of tooling and fixturing within departments. It also allows a supervisor to accumulate a significant amount of information concerning a limited set of operations within the department. Unfortunately, functional layout also requires that the product flows throughout the entire system in a somewhat random manner. This flow is also illustrated in Figure 12.16. Material handling can be significantly reduced if parts requiring a similar set of operations are clustered into a "part family," and the machines required to produce the family are organized into a cell. This process is known as cellular layout and is illustrated in Figure 12.17. As can be seen from the figure, the flow of product through the system is much more direct and material handling can be reduced significantly.

The basis of cellular, of GT, layout is part-family formation. Family formation is based on production parts or, more specifically, their manufacturing features. Components requiring similar processes are grouped into the same family.

Because a part family is loosely defined, there is no rigid rule that can be applied to form families. Users must set their own definitions of what a family is or should be. A general rule for part-family formation is that all parts in a family must be related. For production-flow analysis, all parts in a family must require similar routings. A user may want to put only those parts having exactly the same routing sequence into a family. Minimum modification on the standard route will be required for such family members.

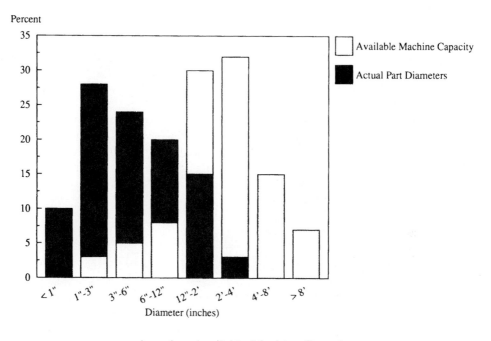

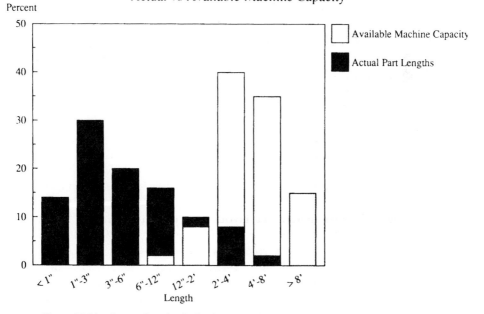

Figure 12.14   Comparison (typical) of a turned-part dimension as a function of machine capacity.

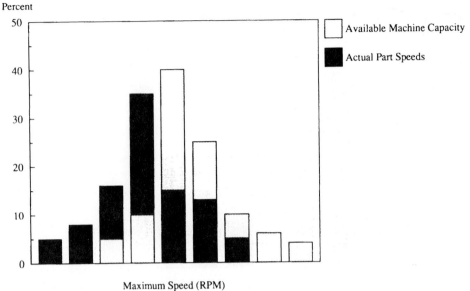

Maximum Speed (RPM)

Actual vs Available Machine Capacity

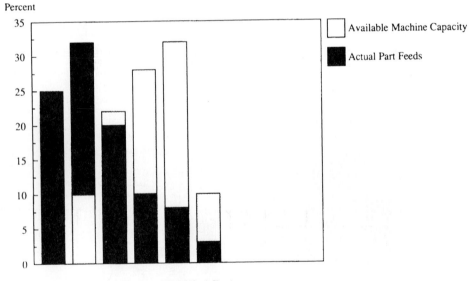

Maximum Feed (Inch/Rev)

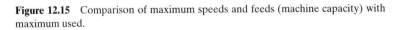

Figure 12.15 Comparison of maximum speeds and feeds (machine capacity) with maximum used.

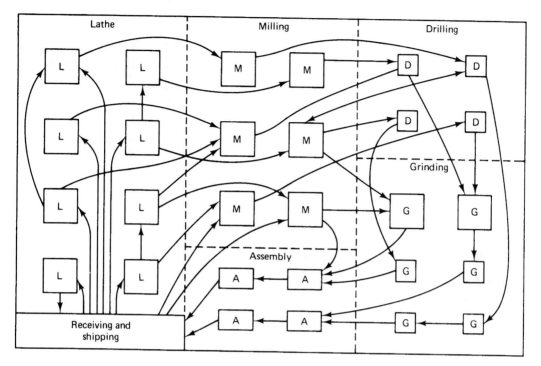

Figure 12.16   Functional (process-type) layout.

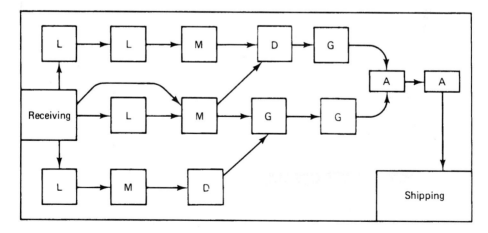

Figure 12.17   Cellular (group-technology) layout.

However, few parts will qualify for family membership. On the other hand, if one groups all the parts requiring a common machine into a family, large part families will result.

Before grouping can start, information concerning the design and processing of all the existing components must be collected from existing part and processing files. Each component is represented in a coded form, called an operation-plan code (OP code; Table 12.7). An OP code represents a series of operations on one machine and/or

TABLE 12.7 OPERATION PLAN, OP CODE, AND OP-CODE SEQUENCE

Operation code	Operation plan
01 SAW 01	Cut to size
02 LATHE 02	Face end
	Center drill
	Drill
	Ream
	Bore
	Turn straight
	Turn groove
	Chamfer
	Cutoff
	Face
	Chamfer
03 GRIND 05	Grind
04 INSP 06	Inspect dimension
	Inspect finish

(a) Operation-plan code (OP code) and operation plan

    01   SAW 01
    02   LATHE 02
    03   GRIND 05
    04   INSP 06
(b) OP-code sequence

one workstation. For example, we can use DRL01 to represent the sequence; load the workpiece onto the drill press, attach a drill, drill holes, change the drill to a reamer, ream holes, and unload the workpiece from the drill. Operations represented by an OP code are called an operation plan. An OP code does not necessarily include all operations required on a machine for a component. It is used to represent a logical group of operations on a machine, so that a process plan can be represented in a much more concise manner. Such a representation is called an OP-code sequence.

The basic premise of an OP code is to simplify the representation of process plans. A simplified process plan can be stored and retrieved by a computer easily when represented in this way. It can also contribute to the family-formation process. For example, we have a total of 24 components in our minishop. After coding them, we can obtain a summary in table form, as shown in Table 12.8. There are two methods to group parts into families: (1) observation and (2) computerized methods such as production-flow

TABLE 12.8 PARTIAL COMPONENT PROCESS SUMMARY

Component	Code	OP-code Sequence			
A-112	1110	SAW01,	LATHE02,	GRIND05,	INSP06
A-115	6514	MILL02,	DRL01,	INSPO3	
A-120	2110	SAW01,	LATHE02		INSP06
A-123	2010	SAW01,	LATHE01,	INSPO6	
A-131	2110	SAW01,	LATHE02,	INSP06	
A-212	7605	MILL05,	INSP03		
A-230	6604	MILL05,	INSP03		
A-432	2120	SAW01,	LATHE02,	INSP06	
A-451	2130	SAW01,	LATHE02,	INSP06	
A-510	7654	MILL05,	DRL01,	GRIND06,	INSP06
A-511					
A-512					
A-550					
A-556					
B-105					
B-107					
B-108					
B-109					
B-115					
B-116					
B-117					
B-118					
B-119					
B-120					

analysis. It is obvious that when we have many components, the first method (observation) will be difficult to use.

Production-flow analysis (PFA) was introduced by J. L. Burbidge to solve the family-formation problem for manufacturing cell design (Burbidge, 1971, 1975). Many researchers have subsequently developed algorithms to solve the problem. In PFA, a large matrix (incidence matrix) is constructed. Each row represents an OP code, and each column in the matrix represents a component (Figure 12.18). We can define the matrix as M_{ij}, where i designates the OP codes, and j designates components ($M_{ij} = 1$ if component j has OP code i; otherwise, $M_{ij} = 0$). The objective of PFA is to bring together those components that need the same or a similar set of OP codes in clusters.

12.3.3 Rank-Order Cluster Algorithm

King (1979) presented a rank-order cluster algorithm that is quite simple. We use his method to show how component families can be determined in our shop. King's algorithm can be stated as follows:

Step 1. For $\forall j$, calculate the total weight of column w_j:

$$w_j = \sum_{\forall j} 2^i M_{ij}$$

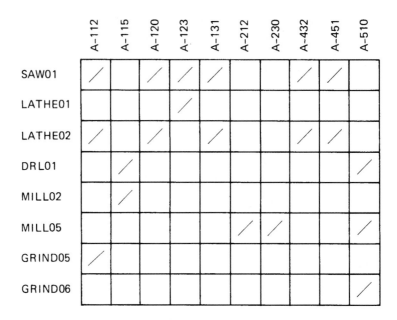

Figure 12.18   A PFA matrix.

Step 2. If w_j, is in ascending order, go to step 3. Otherwise, rearrange the columns to make w_j, fall in ascending order.

Step 3. For $\forall i$, calculate the total weight of row w_i:

$$w_i = \sum_{\forall j} 2^j M_{ij}$$

Step 4. If w_i, is in ascending order, stop. Otherwise, rearrange the rows to make w_i fall in ascending order. Go to step 1.

The rank-order clustering algorithm sorts the matrix into a diagonal block structure. The diagonal blocks are not always mutually exclusive. Final judgment has to be made by the user.

One of the major drawbacks of applying this algorithm is the need of storing the binary word. The word length is max (n, m), where n is the number of machines, and m is the number of components. For a moderate problem with 50 machines and 2000 components, it is impossible to calculate the weights before sorting. For the machine weights, 50 words of 2000 bits are needed! A word of 2000 bits requires 250 bytes. To overcome this problem, direct comparison of elements, either row or column, can be used. A digit-by-digit comparison is performed, beginning from the most significant digit. Each row or column of the matrix is treated as a binary number; no weight is ever calculated. Unfortunately, this procedure has a computational complexity of a cubic order, namely, $O[ij(i + j)]$ (King and Nakornchai, 1982), where i and j are the number of rows and columns, respectively.

Figure 12.19 shows the procedure of rearranging the PFA matrix in Figure 12.18.

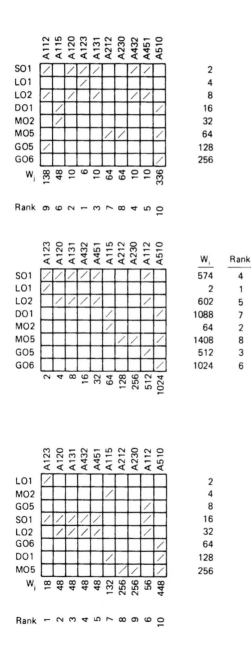

Figure 12.19   Rank-order cluster algorithm.

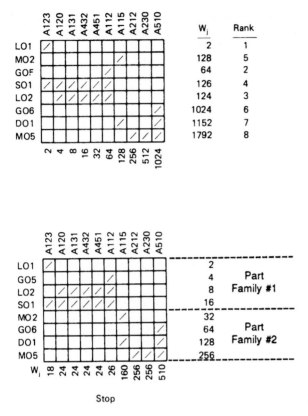

Figure 12.19   (Continued)

After we obtain the final matrix, we can determine (arbitrarily) that components A123, A120, A131, A432, A451, and A112 form a family that needs SAW01, LATHE01, LATHE02, and GRIND05. A115, A212, A230, and A510 form the second family.

12.3.4 The Direct Clustering Technique

An improvement over the rank-order clustering algorithm is the direct clustering technique. This technique was proposed independently by Chan and Milner (1982) and King and Nakornchai (1982). The algorithms proposed in both papers are almost identical.

The technique is based on the idea of using blocks and rods, and by changing the sequence in which components and machines are listed in the matrix. For convenience, we denote those cells requiring a particular operation (/) as positive cells, and those with blank entries as negative cells. The direct cluster algorithm consists of going through the matrix sequentially, and moving the columns with the topmost negative cells to the left and the rows with the leftmost positive cells to the top of the matrix. In repeated trips, the positive cells move toward the diagonal of the matrix in a clustered pattern.

The basic rule is that each component or machine must be moved together with its respective row or column entries during matrix transformation, as if the cells or the blocks were linked together by imaginary rods. The algorithmic procedure is as follows.

Step 1. For $\forall i$, calculate the total number of positive cells in row w_i:

$$w_i = \sum_{\forall i} M_{ij}$$

Sort rows in descending order.

Step 2. For $\forall j$, calculate the total number of positive cells in column w_j:

$$w_j = \sum_{\forall j} M_{ij}$$

Sort columns in ascending order.

Step 3. For $i = 1$ to n, move all columns j, where $M_{ij} = 1$, to the right, maintaining the order of the previous rows.

Step 4. For $j = m$ to 1, move all rows i, where $M_{ij} = 1$, to the top, maintaining the order of the previous columns.

Step 5. If the current matrix is the same as the previous matrix, stop, or else go to step 3.

The same PFA matrix in Figure 12.18 is rearranged using the direct clustering algorithm. The procedure and the result are shown in Figure 12.20. As can be seen, the result in this figure is the same as that obtained by the rank-order clustering algorithm. However, the direct clustering algorithm does not always work. When one or several of the machines are bottleneck machines, the iteration stops very quickly. A bottleneck machine is a machine that is used by a large number of components and prevents the further rearrangement of columns. The rest of the matrix is not rearranged because bottleneck machines block them. It happens especially in large matrices. To solve the bottleneck problem, human intervention is needed. When the iteration stops prematurely, identify the bottleneck machines and continue the iteration, disregarding the order of those rows.

We also may have a final matrix with blocks not mutually exclusive. When closely investigating the matrix, we may find that only a few cells caused this problem. Those cells can be considered as exceptional cells. Mark the exceptional cells with an asterisk (*), treat them as negative cells and then reapply the algorithm. Another technique increases the number of machines of a specific type and merges machines of the same type. This can be done by adding new rows and merging two rows, respectively . More elaborate examples of the direct clustering algorithm can be found in Chan and Milner (1982) and King and Nakornchai (1982).

So far, we have illustrated two algorithms for part-family formation. Many other methods have been developed, such as the similarity coefficient method, the set-theoretic method, and the evaluative methods. None of these methods is as simple as

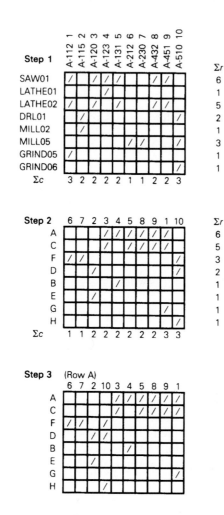

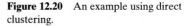

Figure 12.20 An example using direct clustering.

the ones introduced here. The results also vary. Family formation is not always objective; many other factors such as the cost of implementing the machine cell and material-handling costs have to be considered. The problem should not be considered as just clustering cells in an incidence matrix. The methods discussed here provide a starting point for further improvement.

12.3.5 Mathematical Programming in Group Technology

In solving the group-technology problem, there are two approaches that have been used extensively: heuristic algorithms and mathematical programming models. Mathematical programming deals with the optimization of a function consisting of several variables. In addition, the variables must satisfy a set of constraints that are inequalities and/or equalities (Zoutendijk, 1976).

Step 3   (Row C to H)

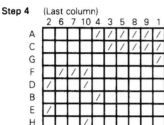

Step 4   (Last column)

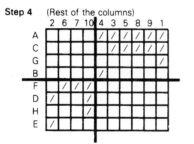

Step 4   (Rest of the columns)

Family 1

Family 2

Figure 12.20   (Continued)

When applying mathematical programming models to group-technology problems, most models consider a measure of the distance, d_{ij}, between part i and part j. Some of the measures used most often are the Minkowski distance measure, the weighted Monkowski distance measure, and the Hamming distance (Kusiak, 1990).

Given the distance between parts, the objective function can be defined as consisting of a set of variables satisfying the constraints that minimizes the total sum of distances between any two parts i and j. Two models that have been applied to the group-technology problem are the p-median model and quadratic programming (Kusiak, Boe, and Cheng, 1993). Both models are utilized to group n parts into p families. Unlike the p-median model, however, the quadratic programming model requires that both the number of part families and the number of parts in a family be specified beforehand.

There are two general categories of mathematical programming models: ones that are prescriptive and ones that are descriptive. Linear programming models are prescriptive because the objective function is predefined and once the model is "turned on," the decision variables that optimize the objective function are determined. On the other hand, descriptive models start with a definition of the decision variables, and during simulation, for example, an estimate of the overall system performance is provided (Askin and Standridge, 1991).

Askin and Standridge (1991) developed a mathematical statement for assigning part operations and machines to group utilizing binary ordering of the machine-part matrix to determine independent groups. Boctor (1991) proposed a mixed-integer linear program to minimize the number of exceptional elements in the machine-part group formulation problem. Another mathematical approach in solving the problem of exceptional elements in cellular manufacturing was presented (Shafer, Kern, and Wei, 1992). The model dealt with the minimization of three costs: (1) intercellular transfer, (2) machine duplication, and (3) subcontracting. Srinivasan, Narendran, and Mahadevan (1990) developed an improvement over the p-median model in the problem of creating part families in group technology. The assignment method was found to be superior in the quality of the solution, as well as computational time. The problem of grouping parts and tools was solved using 0–1 linear integer problem and the Lagrangian dual problem (Ventura, Chen, and Wu, 1990).

12.4 CONCLUDING REMARKS

Group technology is a practice that most engineers employ daily whether they realize it or not. Unfortunately, as manufacturing systems become larger and the number of parts in these systems increases, our ability to apply GT intuitively to everyday problems decreases. In order to take advantage of GT principles, coding systems have become common in industry. GT systems are currently in use in most U.S. and international industries involved in discrete-part manufacture. The application of GT is not limited to shop layout, process planning, design (design retrieval and parametric design), fixture design, but is also used in scheduling, NC part programming, and cost estimation. GT is a simple concept, however, its application is limited only by one's imagination.

REVIEW QUESTIONS

12.1. The engineering drawings of four manufactured components are shown in Figure 12.21. Using the Opitz geometrical code, code each of the four parts. Assuming that there are only 6 to 10,000 items, propose a means of obtaining families besides a manual sort. All dimensions in the figure are in millimeters.

12.2. Code the two parts in Figure 12.22 and 12.23 using the Vuoso–Praha, Opitz, and KK-3 coding systems.

12.3. Create the part families for the machine matrix in Fig. 12.23 using both King's algorithm and the direct cluster algorithm.

12.4. What are the major benefits of group technology?

12.5. Explain why group technology reduces production time.

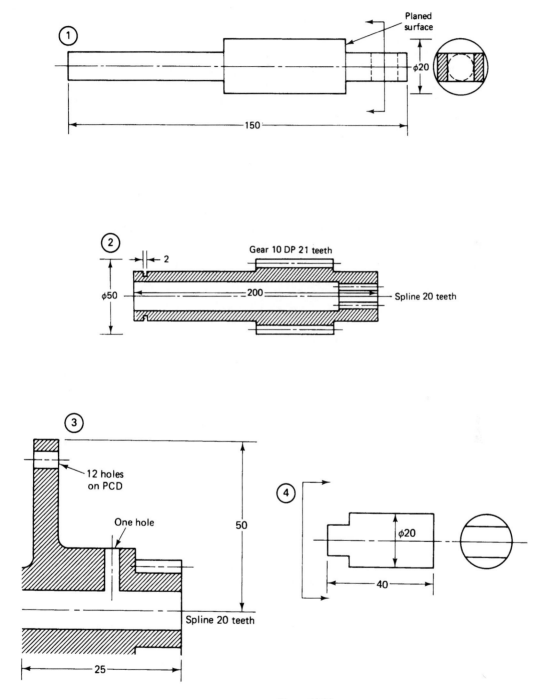

Figure 12.21

Part name: Bracket
Material: Aluminum sheet (A–2024–0, clad), 5-mm thick
Treatment: Heat treatment
Operations: Shear, breakform, trim, deburr

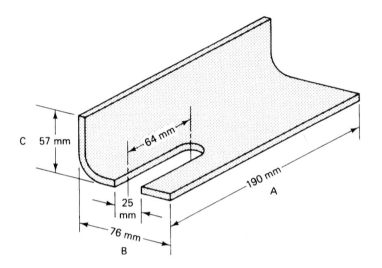

Opitz

Vuoso-Praha

KK-3

Figure 12.22

Part name: Pin
Material: Mild steel, forged round bar
Treatment: Surface hardening by carbonizing
Operations: Turning of surface, drilling a hole

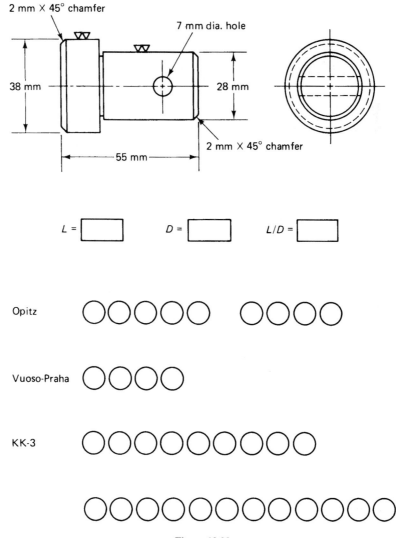

$L =$ ☐ $D =$ ☐ $L/D =$ ☐

Opitz

Vuoso-Praha

KK-3

Figure 12.23

12.6. Design a classification and coding system for printed-circuit boards.

12.7. How are group technology and cellular manufacturing related?

12.8. How does group technology help improve plant layout?

12.9. The rank-order clustering method and direct clustering method are not designed to handle matrices where there are "exception" entries. A number of methods have been proposed as remedies. Search the literature and prepare a summary of your findings.

12.10. How may group technology be used in a design process to reduce design effort and time.

REFERENCES/BIBLIOGRAPHY

ALLEN, D. K. (1974). "Implications for Manufacturing Process Taxonomy in Process Selection." Paper read at the International CAM Congress, McMaster University, Hamilton, Ontario, May 14–16.

———. (1978). *Computer Aided Process Planning Opcodes and Work Elements for Machined Parts,* final report. Arlington, TX: CAM-I, Inc.

———. (1979) *Generative Process Planning Using the DCLASS Informative System,* Monograph 4. Provo, UT: Brigham Young University, Computer Aided Manufacturing Laboratory.

———. (1981) *Classification and Coding—Theory and Application,* Monograph No. 2. Provo, UT: Brigham Young University, Computer-Aided Manufacturing Laboratory.

———. (1994) "Group Technology." *Journal of Applied Manufacturing Systems,* 6(2), 37–46.

ALLEN, D. K. and P. R. SMITH (1980). "Computer Aided Process Planning," Provo, UT: Brigham Young University, Computer-Aided Manufacturing Laboratory.

ASKIN, R., and C. STANDRIDGE, (1991). *Modeling and Analysis of Manufacturing Systems,* New York: John Wiley.

BEN-ARIEH, D., S. E. LEE, and P. T. CHANG (1994). "Fuzzy Part Coding for Group Technology, Computers in Engineering," in *Proceedings of the International, Conference and Exhibit of the ASME,* New York: ASME, 1: pp. 293–301

BOCTOR, F. (1991) "A Linear Formulation of the Machine-Part Cell Formulation Problem," *International Journal of Production Research,* 29(2), 343–356.

BURBIDGE, J. L. (1971). "Production Flow Analysis." *Production Engineer,* April 1971, 31–40.

———. (1975). *The Introduction of Group Technology.* New York: John Wiley.

CHAN, A. H., and D. B. MILNER (1982). "Direct Clustering Algorithm for Group Formation in Cellular Manufacturing," *Journal of Manufacturing Systems,* 1(1), 65–74.

CHANG, T. C. (1980). "Interfacing CAD and CAM—A Study of Hole Design." M.S. thesis, Virginia Polytechnic Institute and State University, Blacksburg, Virginia.

———. (1982). "TIPPS—A Totally Integrated Process Planning System." Ph.D. thesis, Virginia Polytechnic Institute and State University, Blacksburg, Virginia.

———. (1983). *Advances in Computer-Aided Process Planning,* NBS-GCR-83-441. Washington, DC: U.S. Department of Commerce, National Bureau of Standards.

CHANG, T. C., and R. A. WYSK (1981). "An Integrated CAD/Automated Process Planning System," *AIIE Transactions,* 13(3), pp 259–267.

GALLAGHER, C. C., and W. A. KNIGHT (1973). *Group Technology.* London: Butterworth.

HAAN, R. A. (1977). "Group Technology Coding and Classification Applied to NC Part Programming," in *Proceedings of the Fourteenth Numerical Control Society Annual Meeting and Technical Conference.* Post Printing.

HAM, I. (1988). "Course Notes and Handouts.": Pennsylvania State University, University Park.

HON, K. K. B., and H. CHI (1994). "New Approach of Group Technology Part Families Optimization," *CIRP Annals,* 43(1), 425–428.

HOUTZEEL, A. (1980). "Computer Assisted Process Planning—A First Step Toward Integration." *Proceedings of AUTOFACT WEST,* Anaheim, CA: Society of Manufacturing Engineers, pp. 801–808.

————. (1981). "Integrating CAD/CAM through Group Technology," in *Proceedings of the 18th Numerical Control Society Annual Meeting and Technical Conference,* Pittsburgh, PA: pp. 430–444.

HOUTZEEL, A., and B. A. SCHILPEROORT (1976). "A Chain Structured Part Classification System (MICLASS) and Group Technology," *Proceedings of the 13th Annual Meeting and Technical Conference,* Pittsburgh, PA:383–400.

JAPAN SOCIETY FOR THE PROMOTION OF MACHINE INDUSTRY (1980). *Group Technology.* Tokyo: University of Tokyo Press.

KAMRANI, A. K., P. SFERRO, AND J. HANDELMAN (1995). "Critical Issues in Design and Evaluation of Computer Aided Process Planning Systems,: *Computers and Industrial Engineering,* 29(1–4), 619–623.

KAO, Y., and Y. B. MOON (1995). "Feature-Based Memory Association for Group Technology," *Computers and Industrial Engineering,* 29(1–4), 171–175.

KING, J. R. (1979). "Machine-Component Group Formation in Group Technology," Paper presented at the Fifth International Conference on Production Research, Amsterdam, August.

KING, J. R., and V. NAKORNCHAI (1982). "Machine-Component Group Formation in Group Technology: Review and Extension," *International Journal of Production Research, 20(2), 117–133.*

KRAG, W. B. (1978)."Toward Generative Manufacturing Technology," in *Proceedings of the 15th Numerical Control Society Meeting and Technical Conference,* Pittsburgh, PA.

KUSIAK, A. (1990). *Intelligent Manufacturing Systems.* Englewood Cliffs, NJ: Prentice Hall.

KUSIAK, A., W. BOE, and C. -H. CHENG (1993). "Selection of Manufacturing Equipment for Flexible Production Systems,"*IIE Transactions,* July, 25(4).

KUSIAK, A. and C. H. CHENG (1991). "Group Technology; Analysis of Selected Models and Algorithms, Design, Analysis, and Control of Manufacturing Cells." 53, 99–114.

MIN, HOKEY, SHIN (1994). "Dooyoung, Group Technology Classification and Coding System for Value-Added Purchasing," *Production and Inventory Management Journal,* 35(1), 39–42.

MITROFANOV, S. P. *Scientific Fundamentals of Group Technology,* USSR.

OPITZ, H. (1970). *A Classification System to Describe Workpieces.* Elmsford, NY: Pergamon Press.

OZDEMIREL, N. E., G. T. MACKULAK, and J. K. COCHRAN (1993). "Group Technology Classification and Coding Scheme for Discrete Manufacturing Simulation Models," *International Journal of Production Research,* 31(3), 579–601.

PORAZYNSKI, R. J. (1977). "Using Group Technology Concepts in Manufacturing," in *Proceedings of the AIIE System Engineering Conference.* Kansas City: IIE Press.

SCHILPEROORT, B. A. (1975). "Classification, Coding and Automated Process Planning," in *Proceedings of CAM-1,* P-76-MM-01. Arlington, TX.

SHAFER, S., G. KERN, and J. WEI (1992). "A Mathematical Programming Approach for Dealing with Exceptional Elements in Cellular Manufacturing," *International Journal of Production Research,* 30(5), 1029–1036.

SEDQUI, A., P. BAPTISTE, J. FAVREL, and M. MARTINEZ (1995). "Manufacturing Sequence Family Grouping for FMS Design—A New Approach," in *IEEE Symposium on Emerging Technologies & Factory Automation.* Piscataway, NJ: IEEE, pp. 1:419–437.

SMART, H. G. (1980). "Group Technology and the Least Cost Method," in *Proceedings of AUTO-FACT WEST.* Society of Manufacturing Engineers, Dearborn, MI.

SNEAD, C. S. (1989). *Group Technology: Foundation for Competitive Manufacturing.* New York: Van Nostrand Reinhold.

SOLAJA, V. B. and S. M. UROSEVIC (1973). "The Method of Hypothetical Group Technology Production Lines," *CIRP Annals,* 22(1), 145–148.

SPUR, G. (1974). "Automation of Manufacturing Planning," Paper read at the CIRP Conference, Chicago, July 9.

SRINIVASAN, G., T. NARENDRAN, and B. MAHADEVAN (1990). "An Assignment Model for the Part-Families Problem in Group Technology," *International Journal of Production Research,* 28(1), 145–152.

SU, C. T. (1995). "Fuzzy Approach for Part Family Formation," in *Proceedings of the International IEEE/IAS Conference on Industrial Automation and Control: Emerging Technologies.* Piscataway, NJ: IEEE, pp. 289–292.

VENTURA, J., F. CHEN, and C. -H. WU (1990). "Grouping Parts and Tools in Flexible Manufacturing Systems Production Planning," *International Journal of Production Research,* 28(6), 1039–1056.

WYSK, R. A. (1977). "An Automated Process Planning and Selection Program: APPAS." Ph.D. thesis, Purdue University, West Lafayette, Indiana.

————. (1979) "Process Planning Systems," in *MAPEC Module,* West Lafayette, IN: Purdue University, School of Industrial Engineering. Editor, Colin Moodue

WYSK, R. A., T. C. CHANG, and R. P. DAVIS (1980). "Analytical Techniques in Automated Process Planning," in *MAPEC Module,* West Lafayette, IN: Purdue University, School of Industrial Engineering.

WYSK, R. A., D. M. MILLER, and R. P. DAVIS (1977). "The Integration of Process Selection and Machine Requirements Planning," in *Proceedings of the AIIE 1977 Systems Engineering Conference,* Kansas City: Industrial Engineering Press.

ZOUTENDIJK, G. (1976). *Mathematical Programming Methods.* New York: Elsevier.

13

Process Planning

13.1 INTRODUCTION

Manufacturing planning, process planning, process engineering, and machine routing are only a few of the titles given to the topic referred to here as process planning. Similarly, process engineers and process planners are only two of the titles given to those who actually perform this function. Because these titles and descriptions are often confused, we will spend some time defining process planning and using this terminology. Process planning is the function within a manufacturing facility that establishes which processes and parameters are to be used (as well as those machines capable of performing these processes) to convert a part from its initial form to a final form predetermined (usually by a design engineer) in an engineering drawing. Alternatively, process planning could be defined as the act of preparing detailed work instructions to produce (machine, weld, assemble, and so on) a part. The initial material can take a number of forms, the most common of which are bar stock, plate, castings, forgings, or maybe just a slab (of any geometry) of metal (see Figure 13.1). The slab of material is normally a burnout cut to some rough dimensions. This metal slab can consist of almost any geometry. The selection of raw stock requires some study to ensure its specified engineering properties and economical viability.

With these raw materials as a base, the process planner must prepare a list of processes to convert this normally predetermined material into a predetermined final shape. The processes used by a process planner in a discrete-part metal-manufacturing industry are listed in Table 13.1 Some of the operations given in the figure are often considered subsets of some major category (e.g., facing can be considered a subset of turning and reaming can be considered a subset of drilling).

The process plan (Figure 13.2) is sometimes called an operation sheet, route sheet, or operation planning summary. A detailed plan usually contains the route, processes, process parameters, and machine and tool selections. In a more general sense, a process is called an operation (including manual operations). (The route is the operation sequence.) The process plan provides the instructions for producing the part. These instructions dictate the cost, quality, and rate of production; therefore, process planning is of utmost importance to the production system.

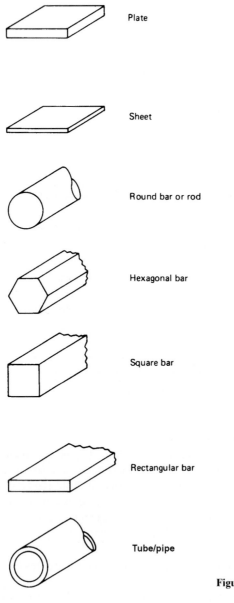

Plate

Sheet

Round bar or rod

Hexagonal bar

Square bar

Rectangular bar

Tube/pipe

Figure 13.1 Standard material shapes.

TABLE 13.1 OPERATIONS AND MACHINES FOR THE MACHINING OF SURFACES

Operation	Block diagram	Most commonly used machines	Machines less frequently used	Machines seldom used
Shaping		Horizontal shaper	Vertical shaper	
Planing		Planer		
Milling	slab milling	Milling machine		Lathe (with special attachment)
Facing	face milling	Lathe	Boring mill	
Turning		Lathe	Boring mill	Vertical shaper Milling machine
Grinding		Cylindrical grinder		Lathe (with special attachment)
Sawing		Contour saw		
Drilling		Drill press	Lathe	Milling machine Boring mill Horizontal boring machine

TABLE 13.1 (continued)

Operation	Block diagram	Most commonly used machines	Machines less frequently used	Machines seldom used
Boring		Lathe Boring mill Horizontal boring machine		Milling machine Drill press
Reaming		Lathe Drill press Boring mill Horizontal boring machine	Milling machine	
Grinding		Cylindrical grinder		Lathe (with special attachment)
Sawing		Contour saw		
Broaching		Broaching machine		
ECM				ECM machine
Laser				CO_2 laser YAG laser

Source: Reprinted with permission of the Macmillan Publishing Company from *Materials and Processes in Manufacturing* by E. Paul Degarmo. Copyright © 1988.

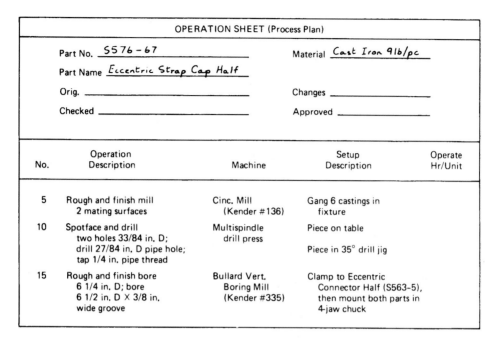

Figure 13.2 A process plan.

In a conventional production system, a process plan is created by a process planner who examines a new part (engineering drawing) and then determines the appropriate procedures to produce it. The previous experience of the process planner is critical to the success of the plan. Planning, as practiced today, is as much an art as it is a formal procedure.

As mentioned previously, there are numerous factors that affect process planning. The shape, tolerance, surface finish, size, material type, quantity, and the manufacturing system itself all contribute to the selection of operations and the operation sequence. These factors are discussed in detail in Chapter 4.

In addition to operation sequencing and operation selection, the selection of tooling and jigs/fixtures (sometimes the design of jigs/fixtures) is also a major part of the process-planning function. The tooling portion includes selection of both the tool itself and the machine on which the tool is used. (See Chapter 5.) There is a limited set of commercially available tools, with different shapes, diameters, lengths, numbers of teeth, and alternative tool materials. All these conditions have to be taken into account to select an appropriate tool.

Jigs/fixtures are devices to guide a tool or hold a workpiece for better machining. Very few standard devices are available. Even with standard devices, application is normally left to the machine operator. Process planning, however, should consider the impact of tooling and jigs/fixtures on the quality of the product during the selection of the production operations. The sophistication of the fixture will depend on the part complexity and volume.

Process planning is a task that requires a significant amount of both time and experience. According to an Air Force study, a typical process planner is a person approximately 50 years of age with significant experience in a machine shop. Although U.S. industry requires about 200,000 to 300,000 process planners, only 150,000 to 200,000 are currently available. Automating process planning is an obvious alternative to alleviate this problem. Although we emphasize the use of computers in manufacturing, we will first show how a process plan is prepared manually. In subsequent sections, computer-aided process-planning approaches are discussed in detail.

13.2 MANUAL PROCESS PLANNING

In industry, most process plans are still prepared manually. Depending on the shop environment, the process plan can be very elaborate or just an aggregated set of operation descriptions. For a model shop, where all the machinists are highly skilled in running several machines and most parts produced are one of a kind, the process plan is usually nothing but a list of workstation routes. The remaining detail is left to the machinists. In the case where a part is produced in an entirely automated transfer line, the process plan contains a breakdown of every detail. Machines, tools, and fixtures are designed to execute the required operations. However, these are extreme cases; in most machine shops, small-batch production is the norm.

In order to prepare a process plan, a process planner has to have the following knowledge:

- ability to interpret an engineering drawing
- familiarity with manufacturing processes and practice
- familiarity with tooling and fixtures
- know what resources are available in the shop
- know how to use reference books, such as machinability data handbooks
- ability to do computations on machining time and cost
- familiarity with the raw materials
- know the relative costs of processes, toolings, and raw materials

To prepare a process plan, the following are some steps that have to be taken.

- Study the overall shape of the part. Use this information to classify the part and determine the type of workstation needed.
- Thoroughly study the drawing. Try to identify all manufacturing features and notes.
- Determine the best raw material shape to use if raw stock is not given.
- Identify datum surfaces. Use information on datum surfaces to determine the setups.
- Select machines for each setup.

- Determine the rough sequence of operations necessary to create all the features for each setup.
- Sequence the operations determined in the previous step. Check whether there is any interference or dependency between operations. Use this information to modify the sequence or operations.
- Select tools for each operation. Try to use the same tool for several operations if possible. Keep in mind the trade-off on tool-change time and estimated machining time.
- Select or design fixtures for each setup.
- Evaluate the plan generated thus far and make necessary modifications.
- Select cutting parameters for each operation.
- Prepare the final process-plan document.

One has to keep in mind that during each of these steps, decisions are made based on an evaluation of many factors. For example, tool selection is based on the feature to be created and other related features as well as the machine to be used. Operation selection depends on the features to be created and the capability of the machine selected. Machine selection is normally determined by the operations required.

We now show how a process plan is prepared for a sample part. Due to the length needed to present this task, only a rough, abbreviated plan is shown.

Example 13.1

Five pieces of the part in Figure 13.3 have been ordered. Prepare a process plan for the part.

Solution   First, from the drawing, one can see that the part is a rotational component and a lathe should most likely be used. The following features are identified (see Figure 13.4):

     S1: end surface/face
     S2: 2.752-in. cylindrical surface
     S3: flat surface/face
     S4: large diameter, 5.25-in. diameter with chamfer of 0.25 in. radius
     S5: threaded cylinder with 0.25 in. $\times$ 0.25 in neck recess
     S6: flat surface/face
     S7: 1.627-in.-diameter bore
     S8: four counterbored holes

The part datum surface is the turning axis for the part (datum A). (*Note:* The turning surfaces (S1 and S8) are located from Datum A). (There is no surface-finish requirement on the surfaces and they are secondary surfaces created when machining S5.)

Precut bar stock is used. Because bar stock is used, a minimum of two setups is required. The threaded area cannot be chucked. Therefore, we must cut S1, S2, S3, and S4 in the first setup and S5 and S6 in a second setup. S7 can be drilled in either or both setups. S8's cannot be drilled on a lathe. A drill press is needed for these holes. Thus, another setup; setup 3, is required.

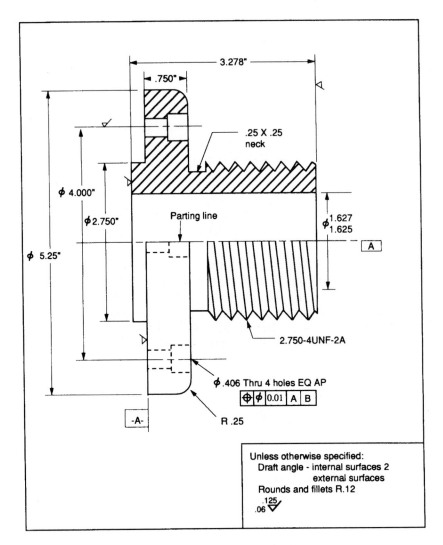

Figure 13.3   A part drawing.

S1, S3, and S6 require facing operations. S2 and S4 require turning. S5 requires turning followed by threading and an undercut. Drilling operations are needed for S7 and S8. The following is the sequence of operations determined to produce the part.

```
Setup 1:
  Chuck the workpiece.
  Turn S4 to a 5.25-in. diameter.
  Turn S2 to a 2.750-in. diameter.
  Face S1 and then S3.
  Core drill and drill S7.
```

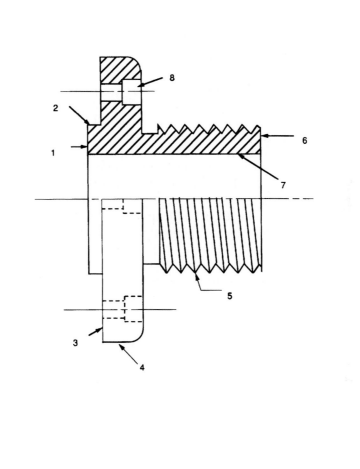

Figure 13.4   Surfaces to be machined.

```
Setup 2:
   Chuck the workpiece on S4.
   Turn S5 to 2.75-in. diameter.
   Thread S5.
   Undercut the neck.
   Face S6.
Remove the part and move it to a drill press
```

```
Setup 3:
Locate the workpiece using S2 and S7.
Mark and center drill four holes, S8.
Counterbore four holes, S8.
```

We stop our planning here and let the reader work out the tool and parameters selection for each operation.

13.3 COMPUTER-AIDED PROCESS PLANNING

Early attempts to automate process planning consisted primarily of building computer-assisted systems for report generation, storage, and retrieval of plans. A database system with a standard form editor is what many early systems encompassed. Formatting of plans was performed automatically by the system. Process planners simply filled in the details. The storage and retrieval of plans are based on part number, part name, or project ID. When used effectively, these systems can save up to 40% of a process planner's time. A typical example can be found in Lockheed's CAP system (Tulkoff, 1981). Such a system by no means can perform the process planning tasks; rather, it helps reduce the clerical work required of the process planner. See Figure 13.5.

Recent developments in computer-aided process planning have focused on eliminating the process planner from the entire planning function. Computer-aided process planning can reduce some of the decision making required during a planning process. It has the following advantages:

1. It can reduce the skill required of a planner.
2. It can reduce process-planning time.
3. It can reduce both process-planning and manufacturing costs.
4. It can create more consistent plans.
5. It can produce more accurate plans.
6. It can increase productivity.

The benefits of computer-aided process-planning systems have been documented (Dunn and Mann, 1978; Kotler, 1980a, 1980b; Vogel, 1980; Tulkoff, 1981).

Two approaches for computer-aided process planning have been pursued: variant and generative. The variant approach uses library retrieval procedures to find standard plans for similar components. The standard plans are created manually by process planners. The generative approach is considered more advanced as well as more difficult to develop. In a generative process-planning system, process plans are generated automatically for new components without referring to existing plans. The details of these two approaches are discussed in the following sections.

Figure 13.6 represents the structure of a complete computer-aided process-planning system. Although no existing turnkey system integrates all of the functions shown in the figure (or even a goodly portion of them), it illustrates the functional

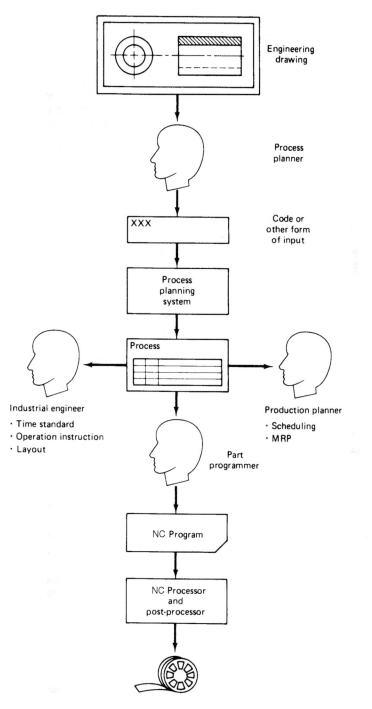

Figure 13.5   A typical process-planning system.

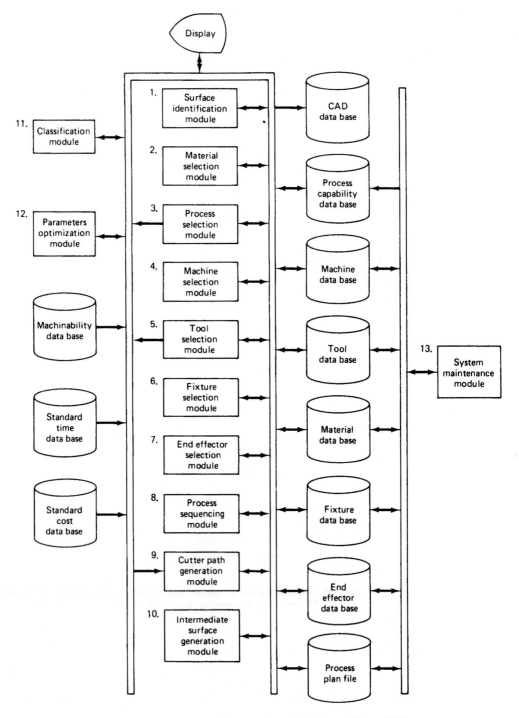

Figure 13.6   Process-planning modules and databases (Chang, 1983).

dependencies of a complete process-planning system. It also helps to illustrate some of the constraints imposed on a process-planning system (e.g., available machines, tooling, and jigs).

In Figure 13.6, the modules are not necessarily arranged based on importance or decision sequence. The system monitor controls the execution sequence of the individual modules. Each module may require execution several times in order to obtain an "optimum" process plan. Iterations are required to reach feasibility as well as good economic balance.

The input to the system will most probably be a three-dimensional model from a CAD database. The model contains not only the shape and dimensioning information, but also the tolerances and special features. The process plan can be routed directly to the production-planning system and production-control system. Time estimates and resource requirements can be sent to the production-planning system for scheduling. The part program, cutter-location (CL) file, and material-handling control program can also be sent to the control system.

Process planning is the critical bridge between design and manufacturing (Figure 13.7). Design information can be translated into manufacturing language only through process planning. Today, both computer-aided design (CAD) and manufacturing (CAM) have been implemented. Integrating, or bridging, these functions requires automated process planning.

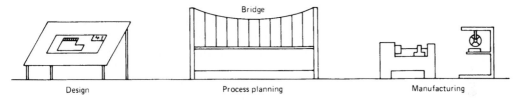

Figure 13.7   Process planning bridges design and manufacturing.

13.4 VARIANT PROCESS PLANNING

A variant process-planning system uses the similarity among components to retrieve existing process plans. A process plan that can be used by a family of components is called a standard plan. A standard plan is stored permanently in the database with a family number as its key. There is no limitation to the detail that a standard plan can contain. However, it must contain at least a sequence of fabrication steps or operations. When a standard plan is retrieved, a certain degree of modification is usually necessary in order to use the plan on a new component.

The retrieval method and the logic in variant systems are predicated on the grouping of parts into families. Common manufacturing methods then can be identified for each family. Such common manufacturing methods are represented by standard plans.

The mechanism of standard-plan retrieval is based on part families. A family is represented by a family matrix that includes all possible members. The structure of this family matrix is discussed later.

In general, variant process-planning systems have two operational stages: a preparatory stage and a production stage.

13.4.1 The Preparatory Stage

Preparatory work is required when a company first starts implementing a variant system. During the preparatory stage, existing components are coded, classified, and subsequently grouped into families. The first step is to choose an appropriate coding system. The coding system must cover the entire spectrum of parts produced in the shop. It must be unambiguous and easy to understand. Special features that exist on the parts must be clearly identified by the coding system. An existing coding system may be adopted and then modified for a specific shop. The coding of existing components can be a tedious task. Before it can be done, a thorough study of the inventory of drawings and process plans has to be completed so that an orderly coding task can be conducted. The personnel involved in coding must have a precise understanding of the coding system. They must generate identical code for the same component when they work independently. Inconsistent coding of components results in redundant and erroneous data in the database.

After coding is completed, part families can be formed. The techniques of grouping part families are discussed in Chapter 12. A family matrix is then constructed for each part family. Due to the large number of components involved, a computer should be used to help construct family matrices. The next step is to prepare standard process plans for part families. By summarizing the process plans, a set of standard operation plans (OP plans) can be identified. An operation plan contains a sequence of manufacturing operations that are normally performed together in a workstation. An identifier, an OP code, is assigned to each OP plan. A standard process plan is written in terms of OP codes and OP plans. Standard plans are then stored in a database and indexed by family matrices (Figure 13.8). In many systems, individual process plans are also stored in the database. However, only plans for frequently produced parts are stored. The preparatory stage is a labor-intensive process. It requires a tremendous amount of effort. Whatever is prepared for shop A can be used only for shop A. The system structure and software can be used by other shops, but the database must be prepared uniquely by and for each shop.

13.4.2 The Production Stage

The production stage occurs when the system is ready for use. New components now can be planned. An incoming component is first coded. The code is then input to a part-family search routine to find the family to which the component belongs. The family number is then used to retrieve a standard plan. The human planner may modify the standard plan to satisfy the component design. For a frequently produced part, it might be desirable to perform the search by direct code matching. In this case, a process plan (not a standard plan) for an existing part is retrieved. Figure 13.9 shows the flow of the

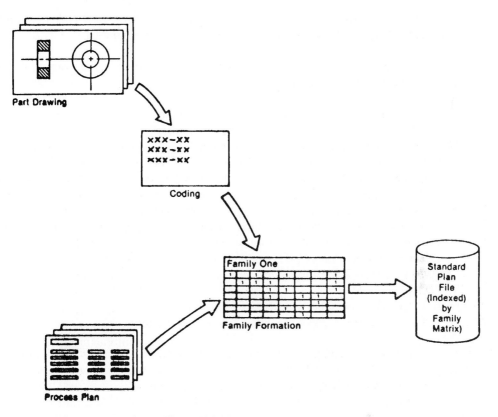

Figure 13.8   The preparatory stage.

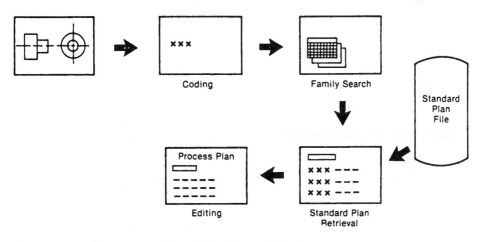

Figure 13.9   The production stage.

production stage. Some other functions, such as parameter selection and standard time calculations, can also be added to make the system more complete.

13.5 THE GENERATIVE APPROACH

Generative process planning is a second type of computer-aided process planning. It can be concisely defined as a system that synthesizes process information in order to create a process plan for a new component automatically. In a generative planning system, process plans are created from information available in a manufacturing database without human intervention. Upon receiving the design model, the system can generate the required operations and operations sequence for the component. Knowledge of manufacturing must be captured and encoded into efficient software. By applying decision logic, a process planner's decision-making process can be imitated. Other planning functions, such as machine selection, tool selection, and process optimization, can also be automated using generative planning techniques.

The generative planning approach has the following advantages:

1. It can generate consistent process plans rapidly.
2. New components can be planned as easily as existent components.
3. It can potentially be interfaced with an automated manufacturing facility to provide detailed and up-to-date control information.

Decisions on process selection, process sequencing, and so on, are all made by the system. However, transforming component data and decision rules into a computer-readable format is still a major obstacle to be overcome before generative planning systems become operational. Successful implementation of this approach requires the following key developments:

1. Process-planning knowledge must be identified and captured.
2. The part to be produced must be clearly and precisely defined in a computer-readable format (e.g., three-dimensional model or GT code).
3. The captured process-planning knowledge and the part description data must be incorporated into a unified manufacturing database.

Today the term "generative process planning" is often loosely used. Systems with built-in decision logic are often called generative process-planning systems. The decision logic may consist of the ability to check some conditional requirements of the component and select a process. Some systems have decision logic to select several "canned" process-plan fragments and combine them into a single process plan. However, no matter what kind of decision logic is used and how extensively it is used, the system is usually categorized as a generative system.

There are several generative process-planning systems (based on the loose definition) used in industry [e.g., AUTOPLAN OF METCUT (Vogel, 1979; Vogel and Adlard, 1981), and CPPP of United Technology (Dunn and Mann, 1978)].

Ideally, a generative process-planning system is a turnkey system with all the decision logic coded in the software. The system possesses all the necessary information for process planning; therefore, no preparatory stage is required. This is not always the case, however. In order to generate a more universal process-planning system, variables such as process limitation, process capabilities, and process costs must be defined prior to the production stage. Systems such as CPPP (Kotler, 1980a, 1980b) require user-supplied decision logic (process models) for each component family. A wide range of methods have been and can be used for generative process planning.

13.6 AN EXAMPLE OF A VARIANT PLANNING SYSTEM

An example illustrates the step-by-step construction of a variant process-planning system. A simplified coding system is used. The code table is shown in Table 13.2. Because it is overly simplified for illustration purposes, this system lacks detail and is not appropriate for actual application. However, it is sufficient to represent the principles of coding for process planning. We call our coding system S-CODE (Simple CODE) and the process-planning system VP (Variant Planning).

VP is used in a machine shop that produces a variety of small components. These components range from simple shafts to delicate hydraulic-pump parts. We discuss the construction of VP in the following sequence:

1. family formation
2. database structure
3. search algorithm
4. plan editing
5. process-parameter selection

13.6.1 Family Formation

In a process-planning system, family formation is based on production parts or, more specifically, their manufacturing features. Components requiring similar processes are grouped into the same family. In Chapter 12, different ways to group parts into families are presented, Similar methods can be used for a variant process-planning system. The example in Chapter 12 can be used to illustrate how to develop a family matrix with a standard process plan.

The family matrix must then be represented in a manner that is consistent with the S-CODE. A part-family matrix is a binary matrix similar to a PFA matrix. We can use P_{ij}^l to represent a part-family matrix for family l, $i = 1, \ldots, I$, where I is the number of attributes in each code position, and $j = 1, \ldots, J$, where J is the number of digits (code length). In the S-CODE, I is equal to 8 and J is equal to 4. $P_{ij}^l = 1$ implies that, for part family l, code position j is allowed to have a value i.

A part-family matrix can be constructed in the following manner. Let C_j^{kl} be the value of code position j for component k in family l, $k = 1, \ldots, K$ (K is the number of components).

TABLE 13.2 S-CODE

		Digit 1	Digit 2	Digit 3	Digit 4
		Primary shape	Secondary shape	Auxiliary shape	Initial form
Rotational	0	$\dfrac{L}{D} \leq 0.05$	No shape element	No shape element	Round bar
	1	$0.05 < \dfrac{L}{D} < 3$	Steps with round cross section — No shape element	Holes — No shape element	Hexagonal bar
	2	$\dfrac{L}{D} \geq 3$	With screw thread	With screw thread	Square bar
	3	$\dfrac{L}{D} \leq 2$ with deviation	With functional groove	With functional groove	Sheet
	4	$\dfrac{L}{D} > 2$ with deviation	Rotational cross section	Drill with pattern	Plate and slabs
Nonrotational	5	Flat	Rectangular cross section	Two or more from 2–4	Cast or forged
	6	Long	Rectangular with chamfer	Stepped plane surface	Welded assembly
	7	Cubic	Hexagonal bar	Curved surface	Premachined

532

$$\text{For } k : = 1 \text{ to } K$$
$$\text{For } j : = 1 \text{ to } J$$
$$i : = C_j^{kl}$$
$$P_{ij}^1 : = 1$$
$$\text{enddo}$$
$$\text{enddo}$$

Using this procedure, we can obtain a part-family matrix for family 1 (Figure 13.10) Thus far, we have a complete set of OP code sequences, OP plans, and a family matrix. The next step is to store them in a computer-interpretable format so that the information can be used later for new components.

13.6.2 Database Structure

The VP system contains only a small amount of information as compared to an industrial application, where thousands of components and process plans usually have to be stored and retrieved. Because of the large amount of information, database systems play an important role in variant process planning. A database is no more than a group of cross-referenced data files. The database contains all the necessary information for an application and can be accessed to by several different programs for specific

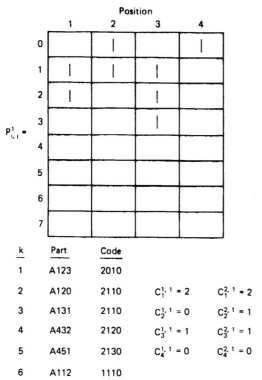

k	Part	Code		
1	A123	2010		
2	A120	2110	$C_1^{1,1} = 2$	$C_1^{2,1} = 2$
3	A131	2110	$C_2^{1,1} = 0$	$C_2^{2,1} = 1$
4	A432	2120	$C_3^{1,1} = 1$	$C_3^{2,1} = 1$
5	A451	2130	$C_4^{1,1} = 0$	$C_4^{2,1} = 0$
6	A112	1110		

Figure 13.10   A part-family matrix.

applications. There are three approaches to construct a database: hierarchical, network, and relational. Although the concept and structure for these approaches are very different, they can serve the same purpose.

For commercial programming, there are several available database management systems, such as CODASYL, ORACLE, ACCESS, dBASE, and Lotus 1-2-3. These systems are high-level languages for database construction and manipulation. Of course, a database can always be written using procedural languages such as COBOL, FORTRAN, and C. No matter what approach and language are used, the basic structure of the database is the same.

The hierarchical approach is used to construct the database in the design of the VP system. Figure 13.11 shows the hierarchy of the data. Each family is accessed by its family member. A standard plan is associated with each family and is represented by an OP-code sequence. In the sequence, each OP code has an associated OP plan stored on a lower level. Data for each level are stored in a file; therefore, VP requires three files: (1) a family-matrix file, (2) a standard-plan file, and (3) an OP file.

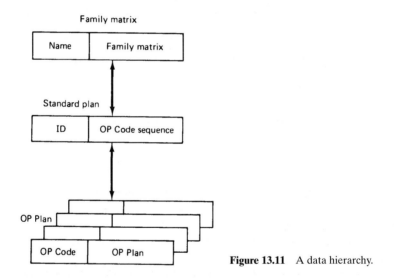

Figure 13.11   A data hierarchy.

The family name and family matrix are stored as a record in the database. A forward pointer is used to link the next record and another pointer is used to locate the associated standard plan in the standard-plan file. We can assign two words for the family name: two words for pointers, and $I \times J$ (8×4) words for the family matrix. A total of 36 ($8 \times 4 + 4$) words are required for each record. Figure 13.12 illustrates the structure of a family-matrix file.

Because the OP-code sequence has a variable length, the structure for a standard-plan file must include variable record lengths. In the file, a director is used to locate OP-code sequences. The rest of the file is divided into segments, with each storing up to five OP codes. The last word is used to indicate the continuation of the sequence. Expansion, deletion, and modification of a record are made possible by pointers in the directory and the continuation flag.

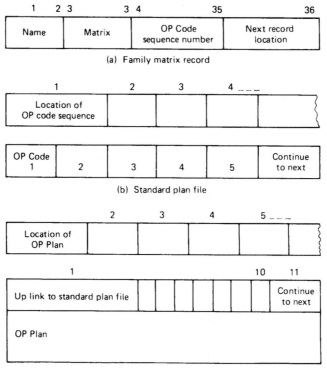

Figure 13.12   Data records content.

The OP-plan file has a structure similar to the standard-plan file except that it maintains link pointers to the standard-plan file. Because records in the standard-plan file have a one-to-many relationship with those in the OP-plan file, it is necessary to keep "where-it-comes-from pointers" in the OP-plan file. This organization makes file maintenance easier.

Figure 13.13 shows the overall structure of the VP database. The storage of families 1 and 2 is shown in Figure 13.14.

13.6.3 Search Procedure

Once the preparatory stage has been completed, the variant planning system is ready for production. The basic idea of a variant system is to retrieve process plans for similar components. The search for a process plan is based on the search of a part family to which the component belongs. When the part family is found, the associated standard plan can be easily retrieved.

A family-matrix search can be seen as the matching of the family matrix with a given code. Family matrices can be considered as masks. Whenever a code can pass through mask testing successfully, the family is found. The search procedure can be described as follows:

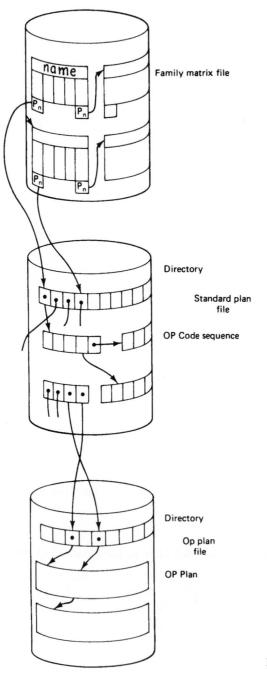

Family matrix file

Directory

Standard plan
file

OP Code sequence

Directory

Op plan
file

OP Plan

Figure 13.13   A database structure.

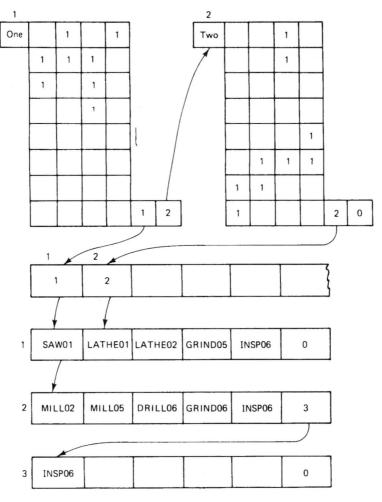

Figure 13.14   VP system data.

Let C_j be a value of code position j for the given component.

P_n^l is a pointer for family matrix l, which links to the next family matrix.

P_s^l is a pointer for family matrix l, which links to the directory of the standard-plan file.

P_{ij}^l is the content of family matrix l; when it equals 1, code position j is allowed to have a value of i.

The following algorithm can be used to find a standard plan.

Step 1. For all, do step 2. End step.

Step 2. For $j = 1$ to J, do step 3; end, go to step 5.

Step 3. $i = C_j$; if $P^l_{ij} \neq 0$, end step; otherwise,

Step 4. $l = P^l_n$; go to step 2.

Step 5.   Standard plan found; P^l_s is the pointer to the standard plan. Terminate process.

In some commercial systems, a "matrix search" is also used. In a matrix search, C^*_j is allowed to be a range of values instead of a single value. The previous algorithm can be modified to perform a matrix search as follows.

Let C^*_j be a range $C^*_j = C_j \pm \varepsilon$

Step 3. $\underset{l \in C_i}{\Sigma} \; P^l_{ij} \neq 0$, end step; otherwise, next j.

This search procedure can be demonstrated by an example. The mounting bracket shown in Figure 13.15 will be planned using the VP system. Based on the S-CODE in Table 13.2, a code (6514) can be developed for the component. (To make VP even more effective, we could develop an interactive coding system for component coding. This interactive system could eliminate the use of the manual table. $C_1 = 6, C_2 = 5, C_3 = 1$, and $C_4 = 4$.) Referring to Figure 13.14, we can start the family search. Figure 13.16 shows the step-by-step search procedure. The search results in the retrieval of a standard plan represented by an OP-code sequence. This standard plan normally requires some modification before it can be used. OP plans can be retrieved and substituted for OP codes in the OP-code sequence. Manual modification of the final process plan is also needed.

13.6.4 Plan Editing and Parameter Selection

Before a process plan can be released to the shop, some modification of the standard plan is necessary, and process parameters must be added to the plan. There are two types of plan editing: one is the editing of the standard plan itself in the database, and the

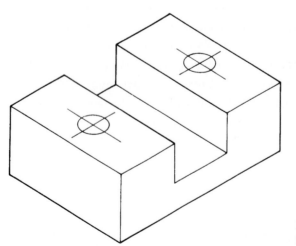

Figure 13.15   The component to be planned: workpiece.

C = 6514

Step 1 $\ell = 1$

2    $j = 1$

3    $i = C_1 = 6, P_{6,1}^1 = 0$ next

4    $\ell = P_n^1 = 2$, go to 2

2    $j = 1$

3    $i = C_1 = 6, P_{6,1}^2 = 1$ end step

2    $j = 2$

3    $i = C_2 = 5, P_{5,2}^2 = 1$ end step

2    $j = 3$

3    $i = C_3 = 1, P_{1,3}^2 = 1$ end step

2    $j = 4$

3    $i = C_4 = 4, P_{4,3}^2 = 1$ end step

2    $j = 5$ go to step 5

5   plan found

$P_s^2 = 2$

	OP Code
1	Mill 02
2	Mill 05
3	Drill 01
4	Grind 06
5	Insp 03
6	Insp 06

Figure 13.16   The search procedure.

other is the editing of the plan for the component. Editing a standard plan implies that a permanent change in the stored plan be made. This editing must be handled very carefully because the effectiveness of a standard plan affects the process plans generated for the entire family of components. Aside from the technical considerations of file maintenance, the structure of the database must be flexible enough for expansion and additions and deletions of data records. As a result, the pointer system in VP may even prove to be efficient.

Editing a process plan for a component requires the same expertise as editing a standard plan. However, it is a temporary change and, therefore, does not affect any other component in the family. During the editing process, the standard plan has to be modified to suit the specific needs of the given component. Some operations or entire OP records have to be removed and others must be changed. Additional operations also may be required to satisfy the design. A text editor is usually used at this stage.

A complete process plan includes not only operations, but also process parameters. As discussed in Chapter 4, process parameters can be found in machining data handbooks or can be calculated using optimization techniques. The first approach is easier and more appropriate for the VP systems.

Figure 13.17 shows the structure for the parameter file. Data in the file are linked so that we can go through the tree to find the feed and speed for an operation. For example, MILL02 for the mounting bracket in Figure 13.15 uses a face-milling process. The workpiece material is cast iron (BHN = 180). The depth of cut for roughing is 0.25 in. and a 0.5-in.-diameter cutter is used. Using pointers, we can then locate from this information a velocity ($V = 55$ sfm) and a feed ($f = 0.001$ ipt).

This parameter file can be integrated into VP to select process parameters automatically. Information such as depth of cut and cutter diameter can be retrieved directly from the OP plan for each operation. The same approach is also appropriate for standard time selection.

With this example, we have completed our discussion of the variant process-planning approach.

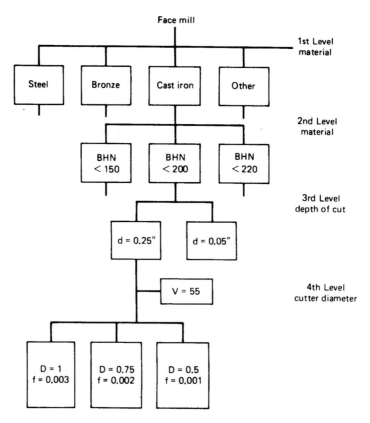

Figure 13.17 A process-parameter file.

13.7 ADVANCED TOPICS IN GENERATIVE PROCESS PLANNING

13.7.1 Forward and Backward Planning

In variant process planning, process plans are retrieved from a database. A direction for the planning procedure does not exist because plans are simply linked to a code. However, in generative process planning, when process plans are generated, the system must define an initial state in order to reach the final state (goal). The path taken (initial $\rightarrow$ final or final $\rightarrow$ initial) represents the sequence of processes. For example, the initial state is the raw material (workpiece) and the final state is the component design. If a planner works on modifying the raw workpiece until it takes on the final design qualities, the type of component is shown in Figure 13.18. The raw workpiece is a 6.0-in. $\times$ 3.0 in. $\times$ 2.5 in. block. Using forward planning, we start from the top surface, S_1. A milling process is used to create the final dimension for S_1. After S_1 has been planned, S_2 can be planned. For S_2, a chamfering process is first selected, and then the

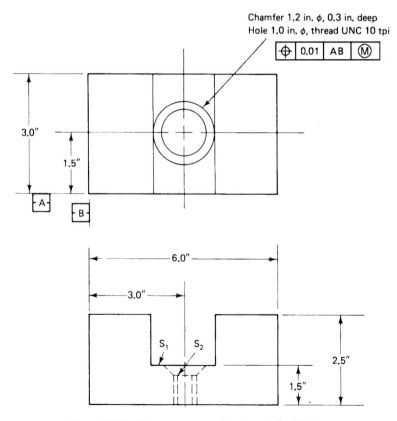

Figure 13.18   The component to be planned: final design.

hole is drilled and tapped. The progression begins from the raw material and proceeds to the finished requirements.

Backward planning uses a reverse procedure. Assuming that we have a finished component, the goal is to fill it to the unmachined workpiece shape. Each machining process is considered a filling process. A drilling process can fill a hole; a reaming process can fill a thin wall (cylinder); and so on. When applied to the example component, the bottommost surface is planned first. A tapping process is selected (this reduces the threaded surface to a smaller-diameter hole with a rough surface finish). Drilling is then selected to fill the hole, and so forth, until we finally obtain the block.

Forward and backward planning may seem similar; however, they affect the programming of the system significantly. Planning each process can be characterized by a precondition of the surface to be machined and a postcondition of the machining (its results). For forward planning, we must know the successor surface before we select a process, because the postcondition of the first process becomes the precondition for the second process. For example, when we selected drilling for the threaded hole, we knew that the thread was going to be cut. Therefore, we rough drilled the hole using a smaller drill. Otherwise, we might have chosen a larger drill and no thread could be produced. Backward planning eliminates this conditioning problem because it begins with the final surface forms and processes are selected to satisfy the initial requirements. The transient surface (intermediate surface) produced by a filling process is the worst precondition a machining process can accept (i.e., depth of cut left for finish milling, and so on). Any filling process that can satisfy the transient surface can be selected as the successor process.

In forward planning, the objective surface always must be maintained even though several operations must be taken to guarantee the result. On the other hand, backward planning starts with the final requirements (which helps to select the predecessor process) and searches for the initial condition or something less accurate (which is easy to satisfy).

13.7.2 The Input Format

The input format of a process-planning system affects the ease with which a system can be used and the capability of the system. A system using a very long special description language as its input is more difficult to use. The translation from the original design (either an engineering drawing or a CAD model) to a specific input format may be tedious and difficult to automate. In this case, it is probably easier and faster to plan a component manually than to prepare the input. However, such input can provide more complete information about a component, and more planning functions can be accomplished using the input. This does not imply that a system using a long and special descriptive language always provides more planning functions.

Many different input formats have been used in process-planning systems. Although no or few systems use the same input format, we can categorize the input for these systems into the following classes: code, description language, and CAD model.

13.7.2.1 Code.   As discussed in the variant approach, GT codes can be used as input for variant process-planning systems. Some generative systems such as APPAS (Wysk, 1977) and GENPLAN (Tulkoff, 1981) also use part codes as input. Codes used in generative systems are more detailed and sometimes mix code digits with explicitly defined parameter values. Because a code is concise, it is easy to manipulate. When process capabilities are represented by a code, a simple search through the process capability to match the component code will return the desired process. In order to determine the process sequence, a code for the entire component is appropriate because it provides global information. However, when processing detail is required, surface coding is unavoidable. A surface code normally describes the surface shape, dimensions, surface finish, and tolerances (both dimensional and geometric) rather than characterizing the entire part.

Although a surface code is easy to manipulate and store, it is difficult to generate automatically through software. A human interface between design and process planning facilitates the translation of information from one system to another.

13.7.2.2 Description languages   Specially designed part-description languages can provide detailed information for process-planning systems. A language can be designed to provide all of the information required for the necessary functions of a process-planning system. The format can be designed such that functions can easily accomplish their task from the information provided.

AUTAP system (Eversheim, Fuchs, and Zons, 1980) uses a language similar to a solid modeling language. A component is described by the union of some primitives and modifiers. Figure 13.19 shows the description of a rotational component. CYCLE (cylinder), CHAL (chamfer left), CHAR (chamfer right), UNCUL (undercut), and RADIR (radius right-curved chamfer) are primitives and modifiers. A process planner can model a component using the language. Materials, processes, machine selection, and time estimates can be selected by the system using the input model. Although reasonably complex components can be modeled, this language lacks a complete set of Boolean operators, and modeling a complex component may be difficult. The process sequence is also affected directly by the sequence with which a component is modeled. Although the system models a component from left to right, it does not reduce the number of possible models for a component to a single description.

Another system, CIMS/PRO, developed by Iwata et al. (1980), uses an input language called CIMS/DEC (Kakino et al., 1977). In the CIMS/DEC system, component shape is modeled by sweeping (translation or rotation) to generate surfaces (Figure 13.20). In CIMS/PRO, a pattern-recognition module automatically identifies machined surfaces, such as planes, cylinders, threaded shafts, holes and grooves. Twenty-six different types of machined surfaces can be characterized. Tool approach also can be determined (every machined surface has a set of approach directions predefined). This input language can model both rotational (by rotation sweep) and boxlike (by translation sweep) components. It is most powerful for modeling rotational components without axial-shape elements. However, if the component is very complex, it can be difficult to model.

GARI (Descotte and Latombe, 1981) is an artificial-intelligence (AI) problem solver. It is one of the earliest attempts to use AI in process planning. A component can

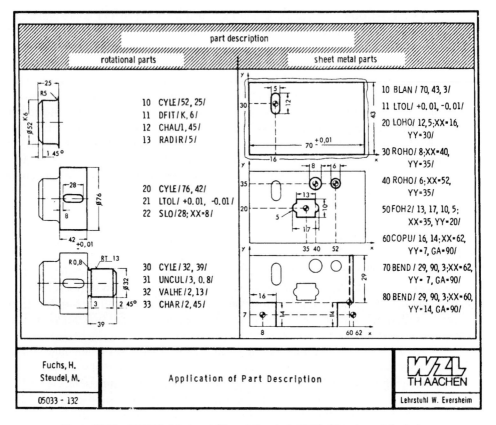

Figure 13.19 AUTAP data input (Eversheim et al., 1980). (Courtesy of the Laboratory for Machine Tools and Production Engineering of the Technical University of Aachen.)

be described by some system words such as diameter and surface finish (Figure 13.21). Rules then can be applied to determine the processes and machines needed to produce a part. The knowledge base (where process and machine capabilities are stored) uses the same set of system words; therefore, decisions can be reached by searching the knowledge base in order to satisfy the input description. The input description, however, must be prepared by a human operator. For a complex component, the translation of the original design to this input language can be very tedious and difficult.

There are many other systems [such as CPPP (Kotler, 1980a, 1980b) and AUTO-TECH (Tempelhof, 1979)] that use their own special description language. Basically, all of these systems contain a surface-shape code, dimensions, and technological data. Although description languages can provide complete information for process-planning functions, the main problem (the difficulty to generate the original design automatically) is still unresolved. The next class of input format is aimed at eliminating this problem.

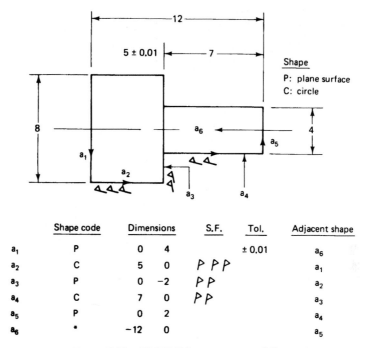

	Shape code	Dimensions		S.F.	Tol.	Adjacent shape
a_1	P	0	4		± 0.01	a_6
a_2	C	5	0	P P P		a_1
a_3	P	0	−2	P P		a_2
a_4	C	7	0	P P		a_3
a_5	P	0	2			a_4
a_6	*	−12	0			a_5

Figure 13.20   CIMS/DEC component modeling.

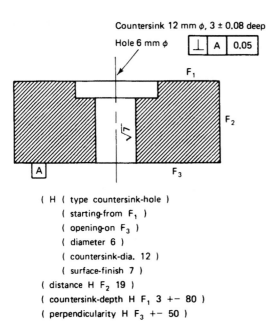

```
( H ( type countersink-hole )
    ( starting-from F₁ )
    ( opening-on F₃ )
    ( diameter 6 )
    ( countersink-dia. 12 )
    ( surface-finish 7 )
( distance H F₂ 19 )
( countersink-depth H F₁ 3 +− 80 )
( perpendicularity H F₃ +− 50 )
```

Figure 13.21   GIRI component modeling.

13.7.2.3 CAD models.   Because a design can be modeled effectively in a CAD system, using a CAD model as input to a process-planning system can eliminate the human effort of translating a design into a code or other descriptive form. The increased use of CAD in industry further points to the benefits of using CAD models for process-planning data input.

A CAD model contains all the detailed information about a design. It can provide information for all planning functions. However, an algorithm to identify a general machined surface from a CAD model does not exist currently. Additional code is needed to specify the machined surface shape from the raw material shape.

CADCAM (Chang and Wysk, 1981) uses a CAD model for its input. Several other systems [AUTOPLAN (Vogel and Adlard, 1981) and GENPLAN] also use a CAD database interactively for tool and fixture selection. There is tremendous potential for using CAD data for process-planning input. However, substantial work has to be done. The new feature-based CAD systems have created a renewed enthusiasm for automated process planning using CAD feature input.

13.7.3 Decision Logic

In a generative process-planning system, the system decision logic is the core of the software and directs the flow of program control. The decision logic determines how a process or processes are selected. The major function of the decision logic is to match the process capabilities with the design specification. Process capabilities can be described by "IF . . . THEN . . ." expressions. Such expressions can be translated into logical statement in a computer program. Perhaps the most efficient way to translate these expressions is to code process-capability expressions directly into a computer language. Information in handbooks or process boundary tables can be easily translated using a high-level computer language. However, such programs can be very long and inefficient. Even more disadvantageous is the inflexibility (difficulty of modification) of such software—this inflexibility leaves customized codes of this type virtually useless in process planning.

In Chapter 4, process-capability representation methods were discussed. Several methods can be used to describe the decision structure of process planning. The knowledge-representation methods are related directly to the decision logic in these systems. The static data are the representation and the dynamic use of the data becomes the decision logic. In the remainder of this section, we discuss the following decision logic as applied to process-planning systems:

1. decision trees
2. decision tables
3. artificial intelligence

This list is by no means complete. However, this classification forms a handy framework for discussion.

13.7.3.1 Decision trees.   A decision tree is a natural way to represent process information. Conditions (IF) are set on branches of the tree and predetermined actions can be found at the junction of each branch.

A decision tree can be implemented as either (1) computer code or (2) presented as data. When a decision tree is implemented in computer code, the tree can be directly translated into a program flow chart. The root is the start node (Figure 13.22), and each branch is a decision node. Each branch has a decision statement (a true condition and a false condition). At each junction, an action block is included for the true condition. For a false condition, another branch might be taken or the process might be directed to the end of the logic block. When the false condition includes another branch, these two branches are said to branch from an OR node. When the false condition goes

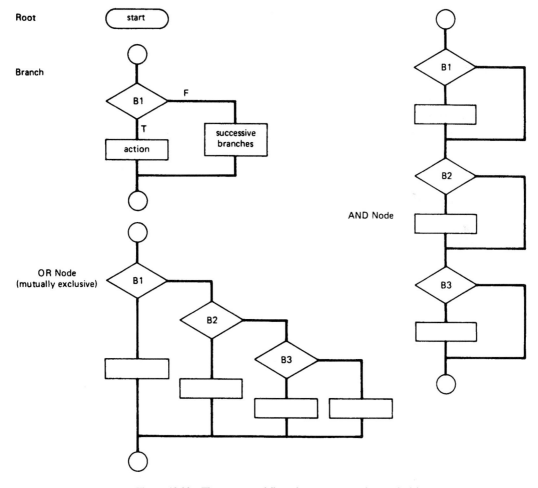

Figure 13.22   The structured flow chart corresponds to a decision tree.

directly to the end of an action block (which is rooted from the same decision state-ment), the current branch and the following branch are part of the same AND node. A decision statement can be a predicate or a mathematical expression.

Figure 13.22 shows a sample decision tree and its flow-chart representation. It can be written in a programming language (pseudocode) as follows:

```
;root
            if E1 then do N1 enddo
            else if E7 then do A5 enddo
            else endif endif stop
;node N1
;
procedure N1
if E2 then do N2 enddo
            else if E3 then do A4 enddo
            else endif endif return
; node N2
;
procedure N2
if E4 then do A1 enddo
            else if E5 then do A2 enddo
            else if E6 then do A3 enddo
            else endif endif endif return.
```

This language (or interpreter) format allows for the easy construction of decision trees that are frequently used in generative process-planning systems. Similar language formats using FORTRAN, PASCAL, C, and so on, have been developed for general-purpose algorithms. APPAS (Wysk, 1977) is a typical example of decision-tree logic used for process planning. Although the approach is easy to implement, system-expansion and maintenance work can be difficult, especially for a programmer other than the original author of the system.

When implementing a decision tree in data form, another program (system pro-gram) is required to interpret the data and achieve the decision-tree flow. This approach is more difficult to develop (for the system program). However, once the system pro-gram has been developed, the implementation and system maintenance are signifi-cantly lessened. Again, however, it can be extremely difficult to add a function that was not originally included in the system program. There are many methods that can be used to design such a system program. A simple example is presented to demonstrate a ba-sic structure that one can use.

We call the example system DCTREE. DCTREE uses a query procedure to ob-tain design information and then print the final conclusions. In DCTREE, there are three major components: (1) the decision-tree data, (2) a compiler, and (3) a system run-time module. Part (1) is supplied by a user who translates a decision tree from graph form into DCTREE input-language format. The DCTREE compiler compiles the input and saves it in a computer-usable format. Finally, the system run-time module uses the com-piled decision tree to generate questions, make decisions, and print out conclusions.

We first look at the input language. These are two parts of each input: (1) expression definition and (2) tree-structure definition (Figure 13.23). In the expression definition, each expression is preceded by an expression identifier (ID). Each ID must be unique. An expression with an ID initial of Q or A (query or action) is simply stored in a buffer. Other expressions are compiled as condition expressions. A condition expression (such as $\&1 \leq .002$) uses a postfix notation and stack operations. A variable ($\&1$) causes the run-time module to input a real number and store it on a stack. Therefore, these expressions can be compiled as a simple code instead of using a simple constant or a variable datum.

The tree structure is represented by expression IDs and pointers. For instance, an arrow ($\rightarrow$) represents "point to." The syntax is

$$E_{n0} \rightarrow \begin{bmatrix} \text{AND} \\ \text{OR} \end{bmatrix} (E_{n1}, E_{n2}, \ldots, E_{n_m}) \,|\, A_i$$

where

E_{n0} = root branch (source)
E_{ni} = expression number (destination action)
A_i = execution action
$|$ = either E's or A's, but not both

During compilation, each is assigned an address in the tree structure file. E_{ni}'s in parentheses are substituted by pointers. A_i's are marked with negative values to indicate their actions. Figure 13.24 shows how a decision tree can be represented by DCTREE.

The system run-time module performs the I/O and decision making. In Figure 13.25, a run-time module algorithm is shown. $E_{ni} \rightarrow$ represents the expression pointed to by the root branch. Each time $E_{ni} \rightarrow$ is called in a procedure, it increments forward to the next branch (i.e., $E_{n0} \rightarrow$ yields AND or OR, $E_{n0} \rightarrow$ again yields E_{n1}, $E_{n1} \rightarrow$ yields $E_{n2}, \ldots$). A(K) and Q(K) are obtained from expression definitions. E(K) signals the system to evaluate expression definition E_{nk}. The recursive algorithm can evaluate the entire tree structure and return conclusions.

13.7.3.2 Decision tables. Decision tables long have been used to present complex engineering data. Decision tables can also be easily implemented on a computer. Using decision tables for process planning, however, normally requires a special preprocessor program or computer language to implement the table and control the operation of the table. Such software is generally called a decision-table language. A decision-table language consists of

1. base language
2. a decision table
3. an outer language

A base language is the foundation of a decision-table language. For example, FORTAB of the RAND Corporation and S/360 DLT of the IBM Corporation use

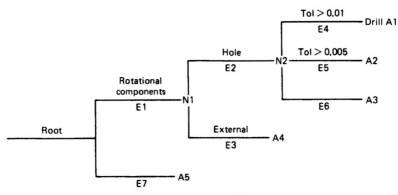

E$_i$ represents an expression or a series of expressions

A$_i$ represents an action

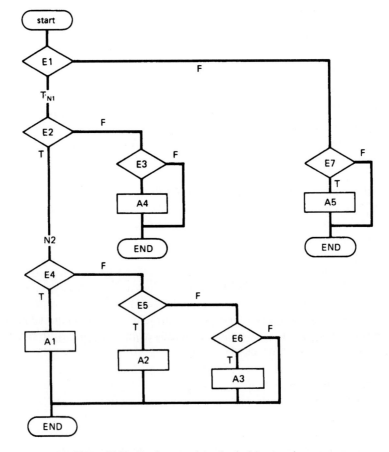

Figure 13.23   Implementation of a decision tree in a program.

Expression definition

Decision tree

Q1   Hole diameter ?

E1   &1 > 0.0

Q2   True position ?

E2   &1 ≤ 0.002

E3   (&1 ≤ 0.01) . AND . (0.002 < &1)

E4   &1 > 0.01

Q5   Tolerance ?

E5   &1 ≤ 0.002

E6   (&1 ≤ 0.01) . AND . (0.002 < &1)

E7   0.01 < &1

A1   Rapid travel out, true position = 0.01

A2   Finish bore, true position = 0.02

A3   Finish bore, tolerance = 0.01

A4   Semifinish bore, tolerance = 0.02

A5   Drill, diameter = 0

Q8   Slot ?

Q9   Internal thread ?

E8   &1

E9   &1

A6   Mill

A7   Tap

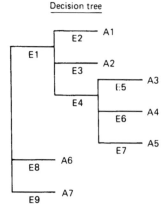

Tree structure definition

```
 0  →  OR (E1 E8 E9)
E1  →  AND (E2 E3 E4)
E2  →  A1
E3  →  A2
E4  →  AND (E5 E6 E7)
E5  →  A3
E6  →  A4
E7  →  A5
E8  →  A6
E9  →  A7
```

Figure 13.24   Input to DCTREE.

FORTRAN as their base language (McDaniel, 1970). DETAB/65 (Silberg, 1971) of SIGPLAN of the ACM (Association of Computing Machinery) uses COBOL as its base language. A base language is extended to include statements that can describe a decision table in a more easily implemented manner. A preprocessor is occasionally written to translate the decision-table language program into its base-language program.

The decision table is the most essential part of a decision-table-language program. It is represented in its original table format. For example, the decision tree in Figure 13.24 can be represented by the decision table of Table 13.3. By using a pseudo language, this decision table can be written as shown in Figure 13.26. Decision-table techniques can be used to simplify and/or parse a complex table.

```
Procedure DCTREE
Do tree (0, J) enddo
   (: 0: root)
stop
:
procedure tree (E₁,J)
set J := 'F' (:J = 'T' search successful)
set iflag := 'T' (:iflag = 'T' or node)
set K : = Eᵢ → (:K pointer to first object)
while K ≠ 0 do
  if K < 0 then write A(-K) and set J := 'T'
     (: reach the terminal)
  else if K = 'and' then set iflag := 'F'
             (: define and node)
             endif
             else write Q(K) and
             if E(K) then do tree (K, J) and
                 if J iflag then set K := 0
                 else K := Eᵢ → endif enddo
             endif endif endif
enddo return
```

Figure 13.25 A run-time module algorithm.

The third element (the outer language) is used to control the decision table. Figure 13.26 illustrates that a decision table does not contain any input/output or control statements; therefore, it is not a complete program. An outer language can eliminate this void. Again, we use the example to show how this can be done; DCTABLE is the name given the decision-table language. The table program in Figure 13.26 is written in DCTABLE. A procedure, TAB(N), evaluates a table N. All variables in DCTABLE are global variables; therefore, no parameters are passed. When table parsing is required a TAB(N1) can be added to the stub of a table N; therefore, several tables can be connected. The following program demonstrates the control of a decision table.

In this program, shape, diameter, true position, and tolerance data are input. A process array P, which stores a selected process name, is set to empty. Flag IFIND is set to 1. When none of the rules in the table is true, IFIND becomes zero. A procedure, while . . . do . . . enddo, is executed until no rule is true.

A simple algorithm for TAB(N) can be shown as follows. Let

C_i be the condition stub expressions, $i = 1, 2, \ldots, n$.

A_j be the action stub expressions, $j = 1, 2, \ldots, m$.

R_{kl} be the rule entries, $k = 1, 2, \ldots, n + m; l = 1, 2, \ldots, M$.

Step 1. Set $l: = 0$; while $l < M$, do steps 2 through 5 enddo.

Step 2. Set k: = 0; set LOGIC: = .T.; set $l: = l + 1$.

Step 3. Set k: = k + 1 while $R_{kl} \neq b$; do set 4 enddo.

Step 4. If $C_k \neq R_{kl}$, then set k : = n + 1; else LOGIC: =.F.endif.

Step 5. If LOGIC = .T., then set $l: = M + 1$ and do step 6; else, endif.

TABLE 13.3   DECISION TABLE

Hole	X	X	X	X	X		
Diameter < 0.0	X	X	X	X	X		
Slot						X	
Internal thread							X
T.P. ≤ 0.002	X						
0.002 < T.P. ≤ 0.01		X					
0.01 < T.P.			X	X	X		
Tol ≤ 0.002		X					
0.002 < Tol ≤ 0.01				X			
0.01 < Tol					X		
Rapid travel out	X						
Finish bore		X	X				
Semifinish bore				X			
Drill					X		
Mill						X	
Tap							X
T.P. = 0.01	X						
T.P. = 0.02		X					
Tol = 0.01			X				
Tol = 0.02				X			
Diameter = 0					X		

Step 6. For j = 1 to m, do step 7 enddo.

Step 7. If $R_{j+n,1} \neq \emptyset$; then do A_j enddo; else. endif.

In the example shown in Figure 13.24, we assume that a decision-table language is used. However, one may not find a formal decision-table language appropriate for the programming of an entire process-planning system. One can always implement decision-table logic using a procedure-oriented language, such as FORTRAN, CPL/I, or PASCAL. Although the implementation is not as easy as using a decision-table language, it is not so difficult as to prohibit the use of decision-table logic. The algorithm for TAB can be used with minor modification. C can be a procedure (subprogram) that consists of n expressions and A another procedure that consists of m expressions (Figure 13.27). The variables used are global variables stored in common blocks. Each time C is called, a parameter, k, is required to index the expression. The logic returns a

```
(:Decision table program for the process selection)
read shape, dia., TP,TOL
Set IFIND : =1 set P: = ;mb;
while IFIND = 1 DO TAB (100) and
write 'Process selected', P
and if P: = ;mb; then set IFIND : = 0
else set IFIND : = 1 endif and
set P: =;mb; enddo
stop
(: ;mb; is an empty entry)
$ 100 table
```

C									
Shape = hole	.T.	.T.	.T.	.T.	.T.				
Dia > 0.0	.T.	.T.	.T.	.T.	.T.	.T.	.T.		
Shape = slot						.T.			
Shape = I thread							.T.		
TP # 0.002	.T.								
(0.002 < TP) .and. (TP $ 0.01)		.T.							
0.01 < TP			.T.	.T.	.T.				
Tol < 0.002			.T.						
(0.002 < TOL) .and. (TOL # 0.01)				.T.					
0.01 < TOL					.T.				

C								
P := Rapid travel out	X							
P := Finish bore		X	X					
P := Semi-finish bore				X				
P := Drill					X			
P := Mill						X		
P := Tap							X	
TP := 0.01	X							
TP := 0.02		X						
TOL := 0.01			X					
TOL := 0.02				X				
DIA := 0						X	X	X

```
C
$ ENDT
```

Figure 13.26   A decision-table program.

```
LOGIC FUNCTION C(k)

    Common ISHAPE, TP, TOL, DIA, P

    INTEGER DATA HOLE/'HOLE'/,SLOT/'SLOT'/,THREAD/'THREAD'/

    Go To (10, 20, 30, 40, 50, 60, 70, 80, 90, 100) ,k

10  C = ISHAPE .EQ. Hole
    RETURN

20  C = DIA .GT. 0.0
    RETURN

30  C = ISHAPE .EQ. SLOT
    RETURN

40  C = ISHAPE .EQ. THREAD
    RETURN

50  C = TP .LE. 0.002
    RETURN

60  C = TP. GT. 0.002 .AND. TP .LE. 0.01
    RETURN

70  C = TP .GT. 0.01
    RETURN

80  C = TOL .LE. 0.002
    RETURN

90  C = 0.002 .LT. TOL .AND. TOL .LE. 0.01
    RETURN

100 C = 0.001 .LT. TOL
    RETURN

    END
```

Figure 13.27   A condition stub implemented in a function subprogram.

```
C ACTION STUB

   SUBROUTINE A(K)

   COMMON ISHAPE, TP, TOL, DIA, P
   INTEGER DATA RTO/'RTO'/.FB 'F-B'/.SFB 'SFB'/.
   DRL/'DRL'/.MILL/'MILL'/.TAP 'TAP'/

   GO TO (10, 20, 30, 40, 50, 60, 70, 80, 90, 100, 110), K

10 P = RTO
   RETURN

20 P = FB
   RETURN

30 P = SFB
   RETURN

40 P = DRL
   RETURN

50 P = MILL]
   RETURN

60 P = TAP
   RETURN

70 TP = 0.01
   RETURN

80 TP = 0.02
   RETURN

90 TOL = 0.01
   RETURN

100 TOL = 0.02
    RETURN

110 DIA = 0
    RETURN

   END
```

Figure 13.28   An action stub implemented in a subroutine.

Boolean value, .T. or .F. A is similar to C except that it does not return any value. Figures 13.27 and 13.28 show an implementation using FORTRAN. Entries in the table can be assigned as either data statements or input as data.

13.7.3.3 M-GEPPS, a Generative Process-Planning System using a decision tree.   In this section, a generative process-planning system called M-GEPPS (Wysk et al., 1988) is introduced as an example. The M-GEPPS system is used for turned-part process planning. It uses KK-3 code (see Chapter 12) as the input. Additional attributes such as diameter and tolerance are prompted by the system and used as input. Because KK-3 does not provide very detailed description for complex parts, M-GEPPS is limited to generate process plans for simple turned parts. The M-GEPPS system uses decision trees for decision making. A decision tree for a turning process is shown in Figure 13.29. Currently, eight lathe operations are plannable by the system. They are cutoff, facing, turning, drilling, boring, reaming, thread cutting, and tapping.

The following shows the planning operation of M-GEPPS. The part being planned is shown in Figure 13.30. After entering the system, one inputs the KK-3 code of the part, 133052621000000000001, by selecting the "Input Part Code Directly" item in the main menu. The system prompts the user for header data. The header data include the part name, part number, work material, material code, designer, drawing number, release number, lot size, order number, cost, process planner, and plan approver. In the next screen, the length and the diameter of the raw material as well as the finished part are input. The system then prompts for the length of rough turn, surface finish, and diameter tolerance. Because a screw thread exists, the system prompts for the pitch number and the length of the thread. After all that information has been input, Figure 13.31 shows the finish process plan.

The Micro-GEPPS system is a prototype generative process-planning system for lathe operations. It implements some of the ideas discussed in this chapter. The same ideas can be applied to other problem areas such as milling. When compared to manual process planning, the ease of generating a process plan with a generative system will be appreciated.

13.8 CAPP SYSTEM IMPLEMENTATION CONSIDERATIONS

From the previous sections, we can conclude that the process-function is dependent on the manufacturing facility. This implies that not one process-planning system can satisfy all manufacturing needs. A process-planning system could be used at different production facilities with little modification of the knowledge base, provided these facilities are similar (equipment and products). However, this is not true when production requirements and/or production methods are significantly different.

13.8.1 Factors Affecting CAPP Implementation

There are several factors that must be considered when one attempts to implement a computer-aided process-planning (CAPP) system. These include

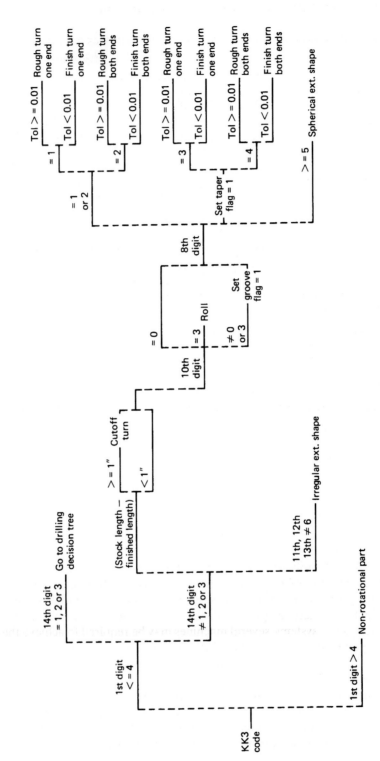

Figure 13.29 A turn decision tree.

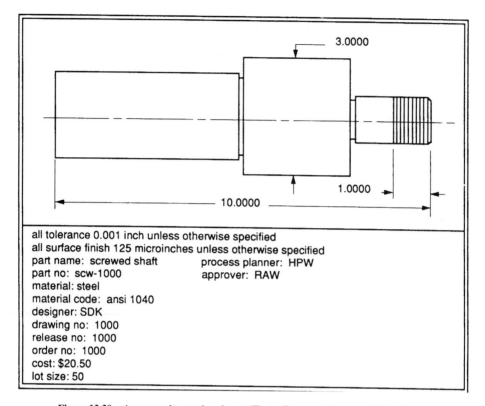

Figure 13.30   An example rotational part. (From *Computer Integrated Manufacturing—Student Manual,* R. A. Wysk, T. C. Chang, and H. P. Wang, Delmar Publishers, 1988.)

- manufacturing system components
- production volume/batch size
- number of different/production families

13.8.1.1. Manufacturing system components.   The planning function is affected directly by the capabilities of the manufacturing system where the process-planning system is to be implemented. A manufacturing system equipped with precision machining centers can produce most of its products on a single machining center. However, in other systems, several machines may be required to achieve the same geometric requirements and precision. This is true for both process and machine selection, and is also true for machine-parameter selection. Indeed, the process knowledge database depends on the manufacturing facility.

A variant process-planning system contains no process knowledge per se. Process plans are retrieved from a database. The standard process plans in the database are prepared manually by human process planners. The capabilities of the manufacturing system are embedded in the process plans created by process planners when the system

♦ ♦ ♦ ♦ ♦ ♦ ♦ ♦ ♦ ♦ Operation Sheet ♦ ♦ ♦ ♦ ♦ ♦ ♦ ♦ ♦ ♦ ♦

Part Code	:	13305262100000000000001	:	Process plan : 000.DAT
Part Name	:	scw shaft	:	Part # : scw-1000
Material	:	steel	:	Mtl Code : ansi 1040
Designer	:	sdk	:	Drawing # : 1000
Planner	:	hpw	:	Approver : raw
Date	:	06/15/1987	:	Rls. # : 1000
Unit cost	:	$20.50	:	Order # : 1000
Length	:	10.0	:	Diameter : 3.0
Lot Size	:	50		

Pause.

Please press <return> to continue.

Op #	Op-Code	Description	Feed	Speed	M/T
10	face	face both ends	.006	260	2.3
20	turn	rough turn 1st end	.007	200	1.4
20	turn	rough turn 2nd end	.007	200	1.4
20	turn	finish turn 1st end	.004	259	1.8
20	turn	finish turn 2nd end	.004	259	1.8
60	thrd	external threading	.083	40	.6

Pause

Please press <return> to continue.

Figure 13.31   A process plan generated by M-GEPPS. (From *Computer Integrated Manufacturing—Student Manual,* R. A. Wysk, T. C. Chang, and H. P. Wang, Delmar Publishers, 1989.)

was erected. Consequently, the standard plans must be changed when major factory renovation takes place. Variant process-planning structures have been adopted by different manufacturing systems; however, the database must be rebuilt for each implementation. The lengthy preparation stage is unavoidable. Implementation of a variant planning system requires that a unique database of component families and standard plans be constructed.

On the other hand, a generative process-planning system has its own knowledge base, which stores manufacturing data. The user modifies the knowledge base in order to suit a particular system. A generative process-planning system provides the user with a method to describe the capabilities of the manufacturing system. The process-knowledge representation, as described in Chapter 4, can be created and stored using several methods. It is essential, however, that the user interacts with the system so that the process-knowledge base can be changed easily. This must be considered when purchasing or creating a generative process-planning system.

13.8.1.2 Production volume/batch size.

Production volume is a major consideration in the selection of production equipment. As a basic rule of thumb, special-purpose machines and tooling are used for mass production, and general-purpose equipment is used for small-batch production. The economics of production determines this decision. These same "economies of scale" must also be applied to process planning.

Different process plans may be required for the same component design if the production volume is significantly different. For example, it is appropriate to turn a thread on an engine lathe if only a few screws are to be made. However, when 10,000 screws are to be produced, a threading die should be considered. Similarly, machining a casting is more desirable than complete part fabrication for large production volumes of complicated geometries.

In a variant process-planning system, the production volume can be included as a code digit. However, standard plans must be prepared for different levels of production. Preparing standard plans for each production level may not be feasible, because components in the same family may need quite different processes when the production volume increases. When the batch size is not included in the family formation, manual modification of the standard plan for different production volumes is necessary.

In a generative process-planning system, the production volume can be considered a variable in the decision model. Ideally, the knowledge base of a system includes this variable. Processes, as well as machine and tooling selection, are based not only on shape, tolerance, and surface finish, but also on the production volume.

13.8.1.3 Number of product families.

The number of different product families is directly influenced by the differences among the components being planned. A variant process-planning system is of little value if there are many families and few similar components (family members), because a major effort will be required to add new families and standard plans. A generative process-planning system is more desirable for this type of manufacturing environment.

Certain manufacturing systems specialize in making similar or identical components for different assemblies. These components usually can be designated by their features. These components are typically called composite components. Because each feature can be machined by one or a series of processes, a model can be developed for each family. In the model, processes corresponding to each feature are stored. A process plan can be generated by retrieving processes corresponding to the features on a new component. This type of generative process-planning system utilizes the concept of group technology. It is easier to build this type of system than a generative process-planning system; and it can provide very detailed plans (depending on the part families being produced).

For a moderate number of sizable families, a variant process-planning system is usually the most economical alternative. Although a long preparation stage is still required, a variant process-planning system is much easier to develop than a generative system. Such a system can be used very effectively when there are many similar components. On the other hand, significant product variation usually dictates generative process planning as the most economical alternative. Figure 13.32 illustrates the economic regions for the different planning alternatives.

13.8.1.4 Models for CAPP implementation considerations. We have discussed the general guidelines for factors that affect CAPP implementation. From the discussion, we realize that CAPP implementation not only involves quantitative issues (e.g., costs and benefits), but also qualitative considerations (e.g., approach selection and product variation). Furthermore, the implementation is largely company-dependent. It is, therefore, difficult to develop a model for generic CAPP implementation consideration. In the following, we introduce some specific implementation issues: quantitative and qualitative.

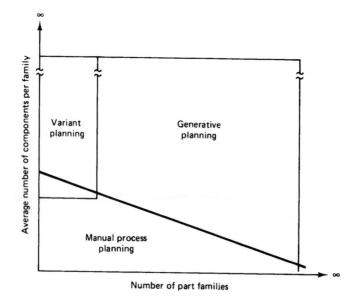

Figure 13.32   Economic regions for different process-planning systems.

13.8.1.5 CAPP cost justification.   Although we are not intelligent enough to capture the seemingly infinite number of variables associated with process planning, CAPP systems are maturing and becoming economically useful. As these systems grow in power and sophistication, they are becoming recognized as a "necessity" for those companies that wish to stay competitive. Many large companies have delved into CAPP and found it to be economical in spite of its current limitations and cost. As an increasing number of larger companies use CAPP systems purchased from a growing number of vendors, a trend takes place that drives the cost and availability of such systems down to within the grasp of medium- and small-size companies. Regardless of size, there comes a time when a company in the market for a CAPP system needs to justify the cost of such a system. Before management commits significant dollars or resources in obtaining and implementing a CAPP system, it wants to know if the benefits will outweigh the costs. For this reason, two questions have to be answered. How much is it going to cost? What savings can be expected?

Information regarding acquisition costs of hardware, software, maintenance, and training is available from the vendors. If the CAPP system is to be built in house, then software development cost, dedicated human resources, implementation lead time, and so on, are less predictable. Some form of a project-management system is usually employed to estimate costs. The resources needed to support the work are estimated. From these estimated resources, a ballpark figure can be arrived at for the total system.

However, the question of savings becomes even more elusive than defining the in-house development cost. Some companies that have a cost-tracking system are able to accurately estimate the expected savings. The majority of companies, however, are not as advanced in their accounting methods and do not separate many necessary cost categories. Estimating expected savings can be a challenge.

A simple procedure for a preliminary cost analysis is as follows:

1. Select a representative family of parts for analysis. This part family should represent a typical product type that the company is manufacturing. Otherwise, several families should be modeled and analyzed.
2. Develop a standard routing for that family (using production-flow analysis).
3. Compare and contrast the standard routing with the existing routings.
4. Carefully document all differences.
5. Analyze those differences to see what, if any, would be the cost impact.
6. Apply actual cost data for a projected cost savings.

13.8.1.6.   Qualitative considerations for CAPP evaluation.   A decision-table-based method focusing on the engineering-management-decision variables of CAPP implementation was developed by Steudel and Tollers (1985). The objective of the project was to provide perspective CAPP users with a guide that aids them in identifying, weighing, and comparing the various interrelated factors associated with CAPP evaluation. This method provides a systematic presentation, including the use of five decision tables (DTs): (1) general environment DT, (2) organizational DT, (3) technical DT, (4) need/objectives DT, and (5) summary DT.

The basic decision variables that determine if the concepts of CAPP are applicable to a company are related in the general environment DT, as shown in Table 13.4. The conditions focus on such items as the size of the company, problems the company is having with process-planning-related activities, and the characteristics of the product(s) it manufactures.

Once it has been determined that conditions are sufficient to warrant further CAPP investigation, the evaluation of the organizational decision variables is appropriate. The organizational DT is presented in Table 13.5.

The technically related decision variables are analyzed within the technical DT, as shown in Table 13.6. Within the condition stubs of this table, questions exist that segment discrete-parts manufacturing into categories of part families. These categories, in turn, relate to the current state of the art of CAPP development, and, therefore, provide a good indication of the technical work and risk that lie in store for a company that hopes to implement a CAPP system.

The objective DT, as shown in Table 13.7, has the greatest effect on determining which particular type of CAPP system a company should investigate. Responses to conditions here result in specific actions such as looking into manual, variant, or generative CAPP systems.

The last table is the summary DT, shown in Table 13.8. Its purpose is to draw together the ideas of the other segmented tables to achieve the effect of interrelating, weighing, and comparing the decision factors of different tables all at one time. From this table comes a set of final recommendations based on the cumulative actions of the previously evaluated tables.

13.9 A GENERALIZED CAPP MODEL

Computer-aided process planning is a key issue in implementing computer-integrated manufacturing (CIM). Several evolving systems have employed artificial-intelligence (AI) procedures to capture the basic logic used by a process planner. However, no effort has been directed to systemize the knowledge in the field of process planning. In the following, a framework for developing an intelligent computer-aided process planning system is presented (Figure 13.33). The information flow and the relationships among the various categories of the knowledge are illustrated in the figure. In the following sections, process-planning knowledge is examined in detail.

13.9.1 Process-Planning Knowledge Representation

The amount of knowledge related to the planning of manufacturing processes is extensive; however, very little is well organized in the field of CAPP. In its research, a significant amount of process-planning knowledge is systematically extracted (from experienced process planners), classified, refined, and formalized. The knowledge formalism schemes mentioned in the previous section have been carefully investigated and evaluated. Two of these, frames and productions, were judged most suitable for

TABLE 13.4 A GENERAL ENVIRONMENT DECISION TABLE

GENERAL ENVIRONMENT DECISION TABLE	R U L E S												
	1	2	3	4	5	6	7	8	9	10	11	12	13
CONDITION STUBS	CONDITION ENTRIES												
1) Is the company a manufacturer of discrete parts ?	N	Y	Y	Y	Y	Y	Y	Y	Y	Y	Y	Y	Y
2) Is the company relatively small in size ? (e.g. annual sales < $10 M might be considered Small)	-	-	-	-	-	N	N	N	N	Y	Y	Y	Y
3) Are any of the following frequent and costly activity? - Development and/or Maintenance of Process Plans (PPs) - Development and/or Maintenance of Cost Estimates - Hiring and Training of Process Planners - Generation of "On-demand" Routing Sheets or PPs - Cost Comparison of Different PP Methods - Implementation of New Mfg Technologies into PPs - Redesign of parts for manufacturability or automation	-	N	N	N	N	N	N	Y	Y	N	N	Y	Y
4) Are there extensive inconsistencies between existing process plans ?	-	N	N	N	N	Y	Y	-	-	Y	Y	-	-
5) Is the development and maintenance of time standards a frequent and costly activity ?	-	N	N	Y	Y	-	-	-	-	-	-	-	-
6) Is the development and maintenance of N/C (or Robotics) programs a frequent and costly activity ?	-	N	Y	N	Y	N	Y	N	Y	N	Y	N	Y
ACTION STUBS: The company should:	ACTION ENTRIES												
1) Discontinue the formal analysis of CAPP.	X		X	X	X								
2) Discontinue the CAPP project, there does not appear to be a "real" need for any technological change.		X											
3) Investigate stand alone CAD/NC system.			X		X		X		X		X		X
4) Investigate micro-computer or programmable-calculator based time standard development and maintenance.				X	X								
5) Continue with CAPP investigation, focus on small company type solutions.										X	X	X	X
6) Continue with CAPP investigation, stay open to all possible types of solutions.						X	X	X	X				

Source: Tables 13.4 to 13.8 are reproduced from H. J. Steudel, and G. V. Tollers. *A Decision Table Based Guide for Evaluating Computer-Aided Process Planning Systems," Proceedings of 1985 ASME Winter Meeting,* Miami Beach, pp. 109–119. By permission of The American Society of Mechanical Engineers.

TABLE 13.5 AN ORGANIZATIONAL DECISION TABLE

ORGANIZATIONAL DECISION TABLE

	RULES

CONDITION STUBS	1	2	3	4	5	6	7	8	9	10	11	12	13	14	15	16	17	18	19	20	21	22	23
1) Are all of the people associated with the project knowledgable about CAPP's current state-of-the-art ?	N	N	N	N	N	N	N	N	N	N	Y	Y	Y	Y	Y	Y	Y	Y	Y	Y	Y	Y	Y
2) Is Management supportive and able to provide sufficient resources for the project ?	N	N	N	N	Y	Y	Y	Y	Y	Y	N	N	N	N	N	Y	Y	Y	Y	Y	Y	Y	Y
3) Is there sufficient expertise within the company to analyze processing planning needs and possible systems ?	N	N	Y	Y	Y	N	N	N	Y	Y	Y	N	N	Y	Y	Y	N	N	N	N	Y	Y	Y
4) Are the organizations potentially affected by this project adaptable to change as well as supportive ?	N	Y	N	Y	Y	N	Y	Y	N	N	Y	N	Y	N	Y	Y	N	N	Y	Y	N	N	Y
5) Is this a "one-plant", rather than a "multi-plant" project ?	-	-	-	N	Y	-	N	Y	N	Y	-	-	-	-	N	Y	N	Y	N	Y	N	Y	-

ACTION STUBS: The company should:	1	2	3	4	5	6	7	8	9	10	11	12	13	14	15	16	17	18	19	20	21	22	23
1) Research CAPP and develop a basic knowledge of the three types of systems: Manual, Variant, and Generative.	X	X	X	X	X	X	X	X	X	X													
2) Secure management support through a program of education and promotion. Emphasize the potential strategic nature of the technology. Work closely with management to develop an awareness and appreciation of their goals and objectives for the project.	X	X	X	X	X						X	X	X	X	X								
3) Consider hiring a consultant to assist in the CAPP system evaluation.	X	X				X	X	X				X	X				X	X	X	X			
4) Involve all those directly affected by the potential implementation of CAPP in an education program. Make them aware of the possible benefits, encourage them to share their thoughts and concerns.	X		X			X			X	X		X		X			X	X			X	X	
5) Allocate "extra" time within the study phase to gather requirements from all the participating parties.	X	X	X	X		X	X		X		X	X	X	X		X	X	X		X			
6) Anticipate "High" risk, in terms of organization	X	X	X	X	X	X	X		X		X	X	X	X	X	X							
7) Before continuing, complete the recommended actions.	X	X	X	X	X	X	X		X		X	X	X	X	X	X	X	X		X			
8) While continuing, perform the recommended actions.								X		X									X		X	X	X

TABLE 13.6 A TECHNICAL DECISION TABLE

TECHNICAL DECISION TABLE	1	2	3	4	5	6	7	8	9	10	11	12	13	14	15
CONDITION STUBS	CONDITION ENTRIES														
1) Is there a scheme currently in use to group parts in families by geometry or manufacturing requirement?	N	Y	Y	Y	Y	Y	Y	Y	Y	Y	Y	Y	Y	Y	Y
2) Is the fabrication of machined rotational, prismatic or sheet metal parts a significant portion of the company's business?	-	N	N	N	N	N	Y	Y	Y	Y	Y	Y	Y	Y	Y
3) Is final assembly, sub-assembly, fabrication of castings, electrical components, or plastic parts a significant portion of the company's business?	-	N	Y	Y	Y	Y	N	N	N	N	N	Y	Y	Y	Y
4) Is there extensive process planning technical expertise within the company?	-	-	N	N	Y	Y	N	N	Y	Y	Y	N	N	Y	Y
5) Is the data currently used to develop PP accurate?	-	-	N	Y	N	Y	N	Y	N	N	Y	N	Y	N	Y
6) Is there extensive software engineering technical expertise within the company?	-	-	-	-	-	-	-	-	N	Y	-	-	-	-	-
ACTION STUBS: The company should:	ACTION ENTRIES														
1) Before continuing, analyze the product/part make-up.	X														
2) Before continuing, reevaluate part family make-up, if no part family is the most significant assume all the families are significant and go back through this decision table.		X													
3) Investigate needs across all families of products before starting development effort.												X	X	X	X
4) Plan on reviewing published material related to CAPP. In these part families, CAPP has been attempted to various degrees, in general there is amble material to use for reference information.							X	X	X	X	X	X	X	X	X
5) Plan on doing extensive new research before starting on any development effort. Few attempts have been made at implementing CAPP in these product families.			X	X	X	X						X	X	X	X
6) Plan on developing ones own system, or possibly work with someone to jointly develop the system.					X	X			X	X	X			X	X
7) Plan on contracting-out the CAPP system development.			X	X			X	X				X	X		
8) Consider spending time to "clean-up" the basic data in the active PP before attempting implementation.			X		X		X		X	X		X		X	
9) Anticipate the technical risks to be "High".			X	X	X	X			X			X	X	X	X
10) Continue on to the Objectives Decision Table.			X	X	X	X	X	X	X	X	X	X	X	X	X

TABLE 13.7 AN OBJECTIVE DECISION TABLE

OBJECTIVES DECISION TABLE

RULES

CONDITION STUBS	1	2	3	4	5	6	7	8	9	10	11	12	13	14	15	16	17	18	19	20	21	22	23	24	25	26	27	28	29
1) Are there written objectives for the project?	N	Y	Y	Y	Y	Y	Y	Y	Y	Y	Y	Y	Y	Y	Y	Y	Y	Y	Y	Y	Y	Y	Y	Y	Y	Y	Y	Y	Y
2) Do the major objectives of CAPP implementation include – Increased process planner productivity – To computerize the current Process Planning System	-	N	-	-	-	-	-	-	-	-	-	-	Y	Y	N	N	N	N	N	N	N	Y	Y	Y	Y	Y	Y	Y	Y
3) Do the major objectives of CAPP implementation include – Efficient and effective development of Process Plans – Improved consistency or increased standardization	-	N	-	-	-	-	-	-	-	-	-	-	Y	N	Y	Y	Y	Y	Y	Y	Y	N	-	Y	Y	N	N	N	N
4) Do the major objectives of CAPP implementation include – Efficient and effective maintenance of Process Plans by using automated "mass change" type functions. – Creation of on-demand Rtgs for dynamic scheduling – Creation of on-demand N/C and Robotics programs – Systematic introduction of new mfg technologies – Major Time reductions in product development cycle – Aiding Design Engineering to evaluate part manufacturability, or automation capability	-	N	Y	Y	Y	Y	Y	Y	Y	Y	Y	Y	Y	N	N	N	N	N	N	N	N	N	N	N	N	N	N	N	N
5) Do the major objectives include satisfying process planning needs for a large family of products/parts?	-	-	N	N	N	N	Y	Y	Y	Y	Y	Y	N	N	N	N	N	N	N	Y	Y	Y	-	N	-	-	Y	N	Y
6) Do the major objectives include satisfying process planning needs for a large number of unique parts in each product/part family?	-	-	N	Y	Y	Y	N	N	N	Y	N	Y	Y	N	N	N	N	N	Y	-	-	-	-	-	Y	N	Y	Y	N
7) Is the company looking to ultimately eliminate the need for process planners, rather than just aid them? (i.e. "computer-automated" versus "computer-aided" PP)	-	-	-	N	-	Y	N	N	Y	N	N	Y	N	N	N	N	Y	-	N	N	Y	N	N	Y	N	N	N	N	N
8) Is implementing CIMs a major company objective?	-	-	-	N	Y	N	N	Y	-	N	Y	-	N	N	N	Y	-	-	N	Y	-	Y	Y	-	N	N	N	-	-

ACTION STUBS: The company should:	1	2	3	4	5	6	7	8	9	10	11	12	13	14	15	16	17	18	19	20	21	22	23	24	25	26	27	28	29
1) Before continuing, work with all parties concerned to establish written needs/objectives for the project.	X																												
2) Before continuing, reevaluate the objectives.	X	X											X	X						X				X					
3) Plan on looking into Manual type CAPP systems.													X	X								X	X		X	X	X		X
4) Plan on looking into Variant type CAPP systems.								X	X				X		X	X				X	X	X	X				X	X	
5) Plan on looking into Generative type CAPP systems.			X	X	X	X	X	X	X	X	X																		
6) Focus attention on integrated CAPP systems.										X	X		X	X		X	X					X	X	X	X				
7) Anticipate "High" risk of objectives not being met.										X	X		X	X		X	X				X	X	X	X	X		X	X	X
8) Anticipate problems because of conflicting objectives.																			X	X				X			X		X
9) Anticipate unsufficient financial justification.	X	X	X	X	X	X	X						X		X	X													
10) Continue on to the Summary Decision Table.					X	X	X	X	X	X	X	X	X	X	X	X						X	X	X	X	X	X	X	X

TABLE 13.8 A SUMMARY DECISION TABLE

SUMMARY DECISION TABLE

	RULES																							
CONDITION STUBS	1	2	3	4	5	6	7	8	9	10	11	12	13	14	15	16	17	18	19	20	21	22	23	24
CONDITION ENTRIES																								
1) Is the company looking for a "small" company solution?	N	N	N	N	N	N	N	N	N	N	N	N	N	N	Y	Y	Y	Y	Y	Y	Y	Y	Y	Y
2) Is extensive new research necessary ?	N	Y	-	-	-	-	-	-	-	N	N	N	Y	Y	-	-	-	-	-	-	-	-	-	-
3) Are Generative CAPP systems to be a focus item ?	N	N	N	N	N	N	N	N	Y	Y	Y	Y	Y	N	N	N	N	N	N	N	N	N	N	Y
4) Are Variant CAPP systems to be a focus item ?	N	N	N	N	Y	Y	Y	Y	Y	-	N	-	Y	-	-	N	N	N	N	Y	Y	Y	Y	-
5) Is financial justification a major prerequisite to the introduction of any new technology ?	N	N	N	Y	Y	N	N	Y	Y	N	-	Y	-	-	-	N	N	Y	Y	N	N	Y	Y	-
6) Are two or more of the risk factors documented as being high ?	N	N	Y	N	Y	N	Y	N	Y	N	Y	N	Y	N	Y	N	Y	N	Y	N	Y	N	Y	-
ACTION STUBS: The company should:																								
ACTION ENTRIES																								
1) Take another look at the project objectives for it appears the objectives are quite short sighted. An attempt should be made to anticipate future needs.	X																							
2) Reevaluate the project objectives. For a relatively small company, generative process planning is almost impossible to justify, strategically or financially.																								X
3) Approach the implementation of CAPP aggressively. Conditions are right for a successful venture, there is relatively low risks associated with the project.	X	X													X									
4) Approach the implementation of CAPP carefully. Benefits will probably be sufficient to financial justify the system, but there is still some risk.			X	X		X		X		X		X								X	X	X		
5) Approach the implementation of CAPP with extreme caution, for the overall risk of failure is high.					X		X		X		X		X	X		X		X		X		X		X
6) Attempt to resolve the high risk factors before pursuing any type of CAPP system implementation.				X	X	X	X	X	X	X	X	X								X	X	X	X	X
7) Think about reducing the project's scope to reduce the risks. If this were done, one can anticipate the costs and benefits will be distributed over a longer time.					X		X		X		X	X	X							X	X	X	X	X
8) Anticipate a need for changes in engineering skills. Positions such as "data developers" and/or "knowledge engineers" will undoubtedly be necessary.				X	X	X	X	X	X	X	X	X	X							X	X	X	X	X
9) Place a special emphasis on identifying potential benefits, financial and strategic. Evaluators will need to work closely with management to quantify benefits normally termed intangible.							X	X		X	X		X	X		X		X			X		X	

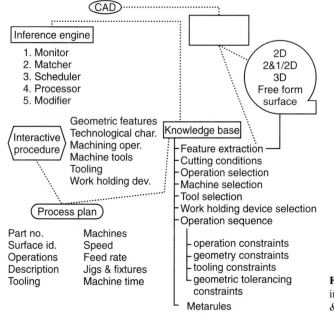

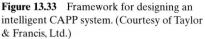

Figure 13.33 Framework for designing an intelligent CAPP system. (Courtesy of Taylor & Francis, Ltd.)

process-planning use. A combined use of both schemes can represent an intelligent reasoning process if an appropriate inference mechanism is properly applied.

Declarative facts are represented in the form of frames. A frame consists of a name and several attributes, and each attribute has an associated value. The name of a frame is used for the general identification of an object. The attributes of a frame define the special characteristics of the object. It is worth noting that an attribute may contain several features, and each feature in the next level may contain several other subfeatures, and so on. In other words, a frame may have a hierarchy of many layers of attributes to reflect a fact, as shown in Figure 13.34.

As previously mentioned, facts (declarative knowledge) are best represented as frames. These facts may be broadly classified as

- workpiece (machined surface) facts
- workpiece-qualification (surface finish and tolerances) facts
- machining-operation facts
- machine-tool facts
- tooling facts
- workholding-device facts

Procedural rules are represented in the form of productions. A production rule is basically expressed in the form of a condition/action pair. The condition part of a rule is checked every time a rule is selected for firing. If the conditions are true, the action is then executed.

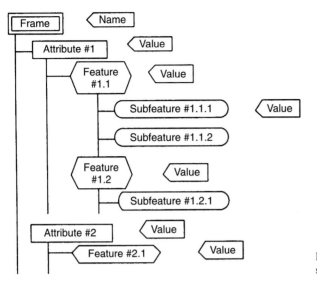

Figure 13.34 Hierarchy of a frame structure.

Rules (procedure knowledge) are best represented as productions. These rules are the real cornerstone of process planning. They may be categorized as follows:

- rules for surface-feature extraction
- rules for operation selection
- rules for operation sequence
- rules for machine selection
- rules for tool selection
- rules for jig and fixture selection
- rules for machining-parameter selection
- metarules

An extensive amount of knowledge (facts and rules) is required to describe the CAPP domain. Representation of this knowledge is discussed in detail in the following sections.

13.9.1.1 Workpiece (surface features) knowledge.   One of the most important pieces of information in a process-planning system is the geometry of the planned workpiece. The general shape, length, diameter, number of surfaces to be machined, and so on, are categorized as geometric knowledge. A workpiece is represented in the form of a frame in a knowledge base. In a fully automated CAPP system, these facts are extracted from a CAD system (Wang and Wysk, 1987). A frame for describing a workpiece is shown in Figure 13.35.

13.9.1.2 Product quality knowledge.   In addition to workpiece geometry, a description of the product quality is also important. Quality of a product for

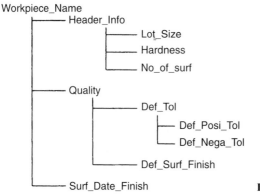

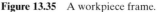

Figure 13.35 A workpiece frame.

process-planning purposes is defined by desired surface finish, maximum allowable size tolerances, and geometric dimensioning and tolerancing data.

A surface-finish notation defines the minimum surface quality of a workpiece. It is designated by the maximum allowable surface roughness, which is usually expressed in microinches (arithmetic average).

Size tolerances define an allowable range within which the produced surface dimension may vary. Unilateral and bilateral notations are usually used.

Geometric dimensioning and tolerancing provide a means of specifying engineering design and drawing requirements with respect to the actual "function" and "relationship" of part features (Foster, 1986). It is a technique that, when properly applied, ensures the most economical and effective production of these features. Thus, geometric dimensioning and tolerancing can be considered both an engineering-design drawing language and a functional production and inspection technique. The standard document governing the use of geometric dimensioning and tolerancing in the United States is ANSI Y14.5M-1982, "Dimensioning and Tolerancing," which forms the basis for the rules in the knowledge base. Details of geometric dimensioning and tolerancing are found in Chapter 2.

The size tolerances, surface-finish requirements, and geometric dimensioning and tolerancing documented in an engineering drawing define the technological characteristics of a workpiece. The definitions are translated into production instructions with which the workpiece is then produced on the shop floor. It is worth noting that most CAD systems do not have the capability of storing technological characteristics. Therefore, in a fully automated CAPP system, a procedure allowing quality description by the user is desired. The information may be attached to a workpiece frame after it is input by the user via the procedure. As a consequence, both the geometric and technological knowledge of a workpiece are integrated.

13.9.1.3 Machining-operation knowledge.   Every machining process produces a certain type of surface(s) at a certain performance level. For example, a rough turning operation can generate a cylindrical surface with a surface finish that is between 200 and 1000 μin. A finish reaming operation can produce an internal cylindrical surface with a size tolerance less than 50 μin. The performance capabilities of a specific machining process can be defined in a knowledge base as frames. An example is shown in Figure 13.36.

13.9.1.4 Machine-tool knowledge.

Every machine's output performance is bound by certain characteristics such as size, horsepower, rigidity, structure, and available tools. The characteristics decide what types of surfaces a machine can produce. Therefore, it is important to lay out the most important characteristics of a machine tool and store them in the knowledge base for process planning.

A machine's processing capability is represented in the form of frames. Figure 13.37 depicts such a frame.

13.9.1.5 Tooling knowledge.

Generally, cutting tools can be broadly classified into four categories according to their geometric shapes and basic functions. They are (1) cylindrical surface-making tools, (2) flat surface-making tools, (3) hole-making tools, and (4) others. Cylindrical surface-making tools can further be classified as right-handed tools, which are used to cut right-handed tapered surfaces; left-handed tools, which are used to cut left-handed surfaces; and neutral tools, which are used to cut straight cylindrical surfaces. Most flat surface-making tools are used on milling machines to produce flat surfaces. Hole-making tools, as the name implies, are used to produce, enlarge, and finish holes in a workpiece. The last category of tools includes gear-making tools, thread-forming tools, and so on. The characteristics of these tools can be formalized as frames and stored in a knowledge base.

13.9.1.6 Workholding-device knowledge.

Workholding devices are used to secure and locate a workpiece for producing precise machined surfaces, increasing production rates, and decreasing production costs. The supplementary production devices are extremely important in a machine shop and should be included in the work instructions. Workholding-device knowledge may also be formalized as frames.

13.9.1.7 Feature-extraction knowledge.

The extraction of surface features in a CAD database is an essential part of a fully automatic CAPP system. A feature-extraction mechanism is composed of three types of rules.

- *Rules for geometric-entity extraction in a CAD database.* These rules read entities from a workpiece using a CAD data file. Some related work in feature recognition and extraction can be found in Joshi and Chang (1988).
- *Rules for basic geometry determination.* These are used to determine the basic geometry of the workpiece. The main purpose of the rules is to determine whether the workpiece can be constructed in a 2-D, a 2½-D, or a 3-D space in the next step of inference. The reason for doing this is because rules for reconstructing a workpiece in 2-D space may be totally different from those in 3-D space. Applying irrelevant rules for object reconstruction may result in incorrect output. Therefore, it is necessary to preprocess extracted data and route this information to a group of corresponding rules for processing.

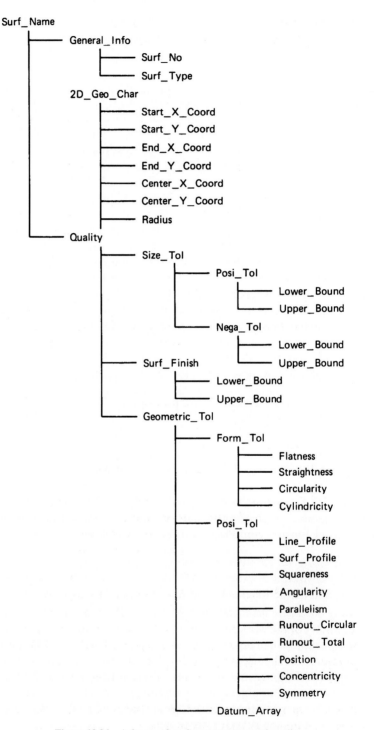

Figure 13.36   A frame of surface geometry and quality.

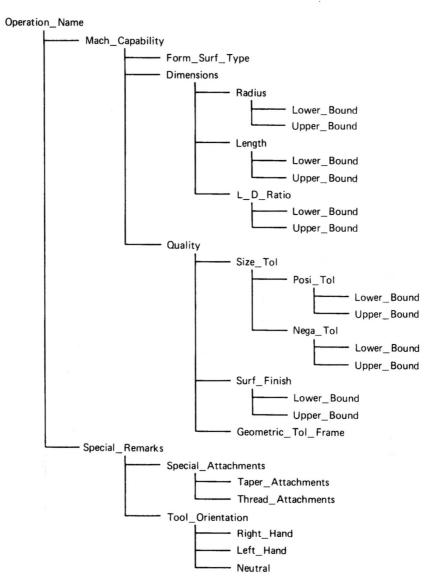

Figure 13.37   A frame of a machining operation.

- *Rules for object reconstruction and surface identification.* Extracted geometric entities are processed using these rules in order to reconstruct the shape of the workpiece, which can be recognized later by a process-planning mechanism. Algorithms and heuristics form the basis for these rules.

13.9.1.8 Operation-selection knowledge.   Most of the effort in the domain of process planning has been devoted to the extraction and formalization of the knowledge about selecting operations. The knowledge in this field is, therefore, more developed than that in other areas of process planning. Although previous investigations of process-planning knowledge have contributed to our understanding of process-planning a significant amount of work still has to be conducted before an appropriate set of formalized knowledge will be available.

A typical procedural rule for the selection of operations is shown in Figure 13.38.

13.9.1.9 Operation-sequence knowledge.

The process of extracting and formalizing rules for operation sequencing is much more complicated than that of operation selection. The logic to select appropriate operations is easily understood although the application is tedious. However, the knowledge in the realm of operation sequencing is distinctly different and subject to several categories of rules.

Rules for operation sequencing can be broadly categorized as follows:

- sequence based on operation constraints
- sequence based on geometry constraints
- sequence based on tooling constraints
- sequence based on geometric tolerancing constraints

Each of these categories of knowledge will be discussed.

Sequence Based on Operation Constraints. A special process sequence exists within a certain group of operations. For some processes, an operation must be performed before others can proceed. For example, rough boring comes before semifinish boring, and semifinish boring comes before finish boring. An order exists once the three operations are selected, and it cannot be reversed.

The operation sequence posed by operation constraints may be formulated as an analytical model and represented using a precedence graph (Chang and Wysk, 1985). The geometric features used to illustrate this category of knowledge is shown in Figure 13.39. In the figure, two concentric holes, holes #1 and #2, and hole #3 are located on a flat plane surface. Drilling, boring, and finish operations are required for producing hole #1; drilling and reaming operations are required for producing hole #2; and drilling, bor-

```
Summary_OP-selection_rule_1 (P1, P2, OP, Q2): -
        Surface (P1, P2, . . . , P38),
        Operation(OP, Q2, Q3, . . . , Q40),
        list_member (P3, Q3),
        check_previous_surf (P1, P2, P3),
        check_next_surf (P1, P2, P3)
        check_radius (P6, Q6),
        check_length (P7, Q7),
        check_LD_ratio (P6, P7, Q6, Q7),
        check_tolerances (P12, P13, Q12, Q13),
        check_roughness (P14, Q14),
        assert (P1, OP) .
```

Figure 13.38 A rule for operation selection.

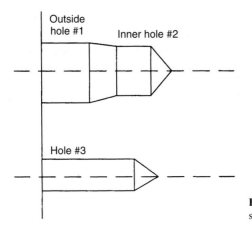

Figure 13.39   Machined features of a sample workpiece.

ing, and reaming operations are required for producing hole #3. The problem is to determine the sequence of operations to produce the three holes most efficiently. Based on the precedence relationship among the operations, a precedence graph can be constructed, as shown in Figure 13.40. A number in a circle (node) denotes the operation number and a number in a small triangle denotes the number of arrows that precede the node. The number of arrows of a certain node specifies the number of operations required prior to performing this operation. For instance, there are three arrows preceding node 6, that is, three operations are required before the inner hole can be

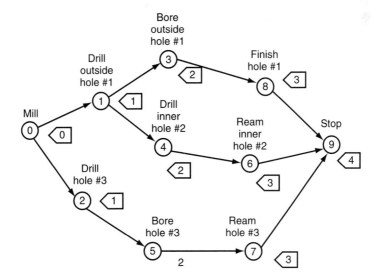

Figure 13.40   A precedence graph.

reamed. A number of alternate routes can be obtained by using different methods in the flow-line balancing problems.

As the number of operations increases, the computation requirements for determining an optimum sequence becomes more time-consuming. Moreover, when one takes into account the tools available on different machines, the problem becomes relatively complicated to solve using analytical procedures. In this case, production rules then can be used to solve this type of problem. Several rules can be formulated to describe this category of relationships.

The rule may be interpreted as

> Find an operation code OP-CODE required for a surface SURFACE-NO. Assert SUR-FACE-NO and OP-CODE into the knowledge base if OP-CODE matches an operation OP-N in the rule set of operation constraints.

Sequence Based on Geometry Constraints. A specific process sequence can be found in certain operations because of part-geometry features (Wang and Wysk, 1987). The arrangement may be violated and the part can still be made; however, the reversed order may result in extra processing time, short tool life, etc. For instance, in machining two concentric holes with different depths (see Figure 13.41), the hole with the smaller depth and larger diameter should be drilled before the other. Otherwise, deep-hole drilling will be required of the smaller-diameter hole.

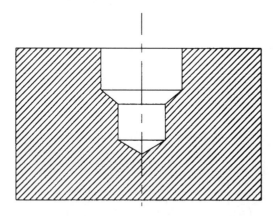

Figure 13.41 Two concentric holes with different depths.

The rules in this category can be represented as productions. Figure 13.42 is a production rule of the two-hole example.

Sequence Based on Tooling Constraints. Certain surfaces must be produced using a specific type of cutting tool. This is illustrated in Figure 13.43. In the figure, surfaces *A*, *C*, and *E* can be machined using a neutral tool; surface *B* a right-handed tool; and surface *D* a left-handed tool. A left-handed tool cannot be used to cut surface *B* simply because the tool cannot approach surface *B* appropriately. This is one of the se-

```
operation_sequence_rule_set_2: -
     operation (SURFACE_X, drill),
     operation (SURFACE_Y, drill),
     surface (SURFACE_X, CENTER_1, DEPTH_1),
     surface (SURFACE_Y, CENTER_2, DEPTH_2),
     CENTER_1 = CENTER_2,
     DEPTH_1 < DEPTH_2,
     assert (SURFACE_X),
     assert (SURFACE_Y).
```

Figure 13.42   A rule for operation sequencing.

quence-rule constraints for available tools. Grouping surfaces based on tool type may save significant tool-change time. The sequence problem sets the tool geometry constraints and is managed via pattern matches between surface types and available tools.

Sequence Based on Geometric Tolerancing Constraints.   Geometric dimensioning and tolerancing of a workpiece provide many important constraints for the selection and sequencing of operations. Four out of the 14 geometric tolerancing characteristics are related to operation selection (flatness, circularity, cylindricity, and straightness). The other 10 geometric tolerances are related to operation sequence.

Two surfaces with a strict parallelism tolerance should be machined in the same setup in order to achieve the tolerance required. Two holes with a close concentricity tolerance should be drilled in one setup. These types of constraints are used to combine selected operations into groups to simplify the operation-sequence problem.

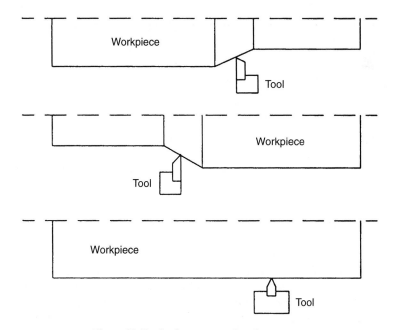

Figure 13.43   Surface types and tool geometry.

A set of rules in this category is formalized and stored in the knowledge base for the sequence of operations. A rule of this kind is as follows:

```
operation-sequence-rule-set-4:-
tolerance (SURFACE-X, PARALLELISM-X, DATUM-X),
PARALLELISM-X < 1000,
assert (group-N (SURFACE-X, DATUM-X)
```

The rule is interpreted as "If the parallelism tolerance of SURFACE-X is less than 1000, SURFACE-X should then be machined in the same setup with its reference datum surface."

13.9.1.10 Machine-tool-selection knowledge. Rules in this category are used to find a match between two types of frames, workpieces, and machine tools. Geometric features and technological characteristics are examined while machines are checked to see if there is a match between the requirements and the available equipment. Selected machines are identified and written to working memory, and the next surfaces are then examined until all surfaces are completed.

13.9.1.11 Tool-selection knowledge. Basically, tool-selection rules are used to identify the type of surface to be machined and then locate a tool that is capable of producing that surface. The procedure is almost the same as machine selection until all surfaces are completely planned.

13.9.1.12 Jig- and fixture-selection knowledge. Basically, jigs are used in hole-making processes and fixtures are used in machining operations. Rules for selecting jigs and fixtures are much more complicated than those used to select appropriate machines and tools. The shape, basic dimensions, and technological requirements of a workpiece, and machining dynamics are the basic issues in selecting an appropriate holding device.

13.9.1.13 Machining-parameter knowledge. Assigning "good" machining parameters is important with respect to increasing productivity. Geometric features, technological characteristics of a workpiece, machines, tools, and workholding devices should be included in the process of cutting condition selection. A detailed study of machining-parameter selection using an expert-systems approach is given in Wang and Wysk (1986b).

13.9.1.14 Metaknowledge. Another type of architectural innovation in the realm of knowledge-based engineering concerns the study of metaknowledge. Basically, metaknowledge is the knowledge about knowledge manipulation. It is the rationale behind an "intelligent and learning" system. Three types of metaknowledge should be included in the knowledge base in order to develop a real "learning" CAPP system. They are as follows:

- *Knowledge about the selective activation of quiescent knowledge.* Metaknowledge is required to determine what quiescent knowledge is relevant and when it should be included in inference processes. Quiescent knowledge in an intelligent process-planning system is stored on disk. Metaknowledge is responsible for the determination of which quiescent disk file is required.

- *Knowledge about the selection execution of potential actions.* The most desirable rules to execute first are those whose consequences maximize the probability of producing correct or important results while minimizing the computational cost of processing.

- *Knowledge about knowledge acquisition.* Basically, this is a process of automated learning of knowledge. An intelligent process-planning system should be able to learn from process planners who can make more efficient plans. If a human planner is not satisfied with a process plan, the planner should be able to interact with the system and "tell" the system what should be done via a specially designed procedure. The procedure ought to be fairly streamlined and interactive so that the user can teach the system new knowledge piece by piece. The taught knowledge is then stored in a knowledge base and the system should be able to make a new plan reflecting what it has been taught.

Basically, there are two levels of machine learning in terms of intelligence. The first level of learning is called "learn by told." By using this learning scheme, a system modifies its knowledge base from what it has been told by the user. In other words, the user has to explicitly instruct the system with the knowledge that the system should learn. The main advantage of this scheme is obvious: It is easy to implement. However, conflicts in the knowledge base may be created if the user presents incorrect information or several users present inconsistent knowledge. The second level of learning is called "learn by analogy." In this level of learning, the system learns new knowledge by interacting with the user, that is, the system deduces new knowledge based on user-provided examples. Moreover, an intelligent procedure that detects inconsistency in the knowledge base should be built in order to make the system more functional.

13.9.2 The Inference Mechanism

Traditional programs are highly dependent on data: initial conditions, parameters, digitized representations of signals instruments, and so on. Typically, the flow of control and the utilization of data are rigidly fixed by the program's code. The default procedure for interpreting information is sequential; branching is performed only at points—and in ways—explicitly provided for in the program code. Although this is an appropriate structure for certain kinds of computations, it is ill-adapted for others (e.g., simulating human response to a complex, rapidly changing, and unfamiliar environment). In these latter situations, branching may be the norm, not the exception. That is, the program examines the state of the world at each step and reacts appropriately. When no new important stimulus is perceived, the current "context" may be the next step. However, if an important new stimulus is detected, the program's next step will depend on the properties of that stimulus as well as on context. In these situations, the program is better viewed as a loosely organized collection of pattern-directed modules (PDMs) that are responsible both for detecting various situations and for responding appropriately to them.

Process planning can be modeled as a human cognition process. Quiescent knowledge and active knowledge are stored in long-term memory. These categories of knowledge are perceived, thought, and learned by human beings and permanently accumulated in a person's brain. The difference between the two is the immediate recall availability of knowledge in current reasoning processes. Quiescent knowledge consists of background information that is not currently accessible to the reasoning processes. Knowledge that is currently relevant and can be accessed quickly is called active knowledge. The working memory block, where the sensory data and symbolic data are shown, represents a warehouse for storing temporary knowledge. Sensory data memory holds the results of sensory stimulation (e.g., visual, auditory, and proprioceptive stimuli), whereas the symbolic data memories hold temporary or intermediate results of cognitive processing.

The proposed framework of an intelligent process planner is similar to the structure of the information-process model. The knowledge base, where rules, permanent knowledge, and temporary knowledge are stored, is a combination of long-term memory and working memory. Rules and permanent facts, which are loaded into the computer RAM upon execution, are categorized as active knowledge. The rules and permanent facts belong to the quiescent knowledge type. The quiescent knowledge is accessed by the process planner whenever it is necessary, which is decided by the meta-knowledge in the knowledge base. The temporary facts, which represent the part-dependent information, are analogical to the knowledge in working memory. This type of knowledge is erased from the working memory once a part is completely planned.

The central block in a human cognition model is the execution (or so-called rule interpreter) of a human's cognitive process. The executive has five components: (1) change monitor, (2) pattern matcher, (3) scheduler, (4) processor, and (5) knowledge modifier, that communicate with various memories to detect conditions of interests and initiate appropriate actions. The change monitor detects perturbations in the memory that may require attention and the pattern matcher compares the observed situations with those defined as warranting responses by the inference rules. Every action that is suggested by the pattern matcher is stored in an agenda (conflict set) that is used as a basis for ordering the computations. The scheduler selects the most important potential action and the processor calculates and implements the action thus selected. The knowledge modifier effects the changes to the knowledge base representing temporary modifications (knowledge activation) and assists in making permanent modifications such as rule or data reformulations.

A thorough understanding of manufacturing knowledge is a prerequisite to developing an intelligent CAPP system. In addition, a concise knowledge representation is also required. Generative process-planning knowledge has been carefully extracted, classified, and formalized in this research. The knowledge available is categorized as declarative facts and procedural rules. Knowledge is divided into sets of facts and rules, each grouped together into modules to undertake specific tasks. Basically, facts are used to describe certain objects and relationships between these objects, and rules are used to drive planning inference in order to mimic a process planner's decision-making processes.

The knowledge compiled herein is far from complete. However, it represents a structure or overview of AI-based process planning. Research in this area seems to concentrate on the selection of machine processes, which plays a less important role in the domain of process planning. Equally important characteristics that lead to the variation of process plans of the same workpiece are the rules for sequencing machine processes. They also should be carefully formalized and implemented in order to produce reasonable process plans.

13.10 CONCLUDING REMARKS

In this chapter, different types of process-planning methods are introduced. The evolution of process-planning systems from a report generator to variant process planning to generative process planning is presented. Examples of each approach are given. Although a complete view of process-planning approaches is presented, because of the rapid development in the field and the coverage of this book, no attempt was given to cover the state-of-the-art technology of automated process planning. This chapter, however, does provide basic ideas about process planning. Through examples, the various process-planning systems have been shown in usable systems.

In the last part of this chapter, we presented a generalized CAPP model that employs an expert system as its backbone. The requirements for planning knowledge, knowledge base, inference mechanism are also discussed in detail.

REVIEW QUESTIONS

13.1. What are the advantages and disadvantages of using computer-aided process-planning systems?

13.2. A company specializes in producing gears. Based on an in-house study, 85% of the gears produced over the past 10 years belong to 11 part families. Most of the drawings and process plans for those parts are available in files. What kind of approach would you recommend to the vice president of manufacturing on automating the process-planning function?

13.3. Under what kind of environment should generative process planning be used instead of variant process planning?

13.4. When variant process planning is used, a GT code may fit several part-family matrices. How can one resolve this problem?

13.5. Use an available database management system (DBMS) to develop a variant process-planning system.

13.6. Develop a standard time and standard cost package using a DBMS.

13.7. What are potential problems in using a generative process-planning system? Consider the impact of a system environment change.

13.8. What are the advantages and disadvantages of using backward planning?

13.9. Why is the input format important for generative process planning?

13.10. Implement the decision-tree processor introduced in Section 13.7 using PASCAL or C language.

13.11. The part shown in Figure 13.44 is made of high-strength steel 4340, the hardness of the material is 45 Rc. When not specified, the dimensional tolerance is 0.005 in. and the surface finish is 125 μin. Prepare a detailed process plan for the part. List machine, tools, tool material, feeds, and speeds.

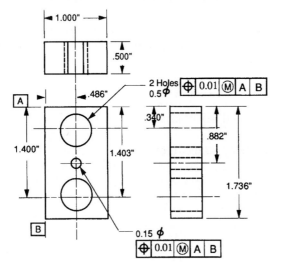

Figure 13.44 A workpiece drawing for Review Question 13.11.

13.12. Prepare a process plan for the part shown in Figure 13.45.

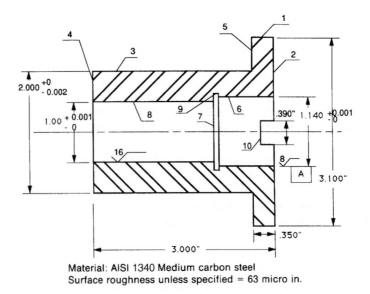

Material: AISI 1340 Medium carbon steel
Surface roughness unless specified = 63 micro in.

Figure 13.45 A part drawing for Review Question 13.12.

13.13. Discuss the potential difficulties of implementing a generative process-planning system.

13.14. List all the features a pure rotational machine part can have. You may consult a GT code table.

13.15. Write the major parameters necessary for defining the rotational features found in Review Question 13.14.

13.16. A small manufacturing company involved in the manufacture of turned parts is considering an automated process-planning system. The company is a job shop specializing in small production lots. Products are seldom repeated; however, there is a large dissimilarity in most items. What advice would you give the plant manager? What systems should be explored?

13.17. What are the difficulties of developing a generative process-planning system?

13.18. What are the advantages and disadvantages of using a decision tree and a decision table versus procedural-language implementation?

13.19. Develop a part-description (modeling) language to model rotational parts. Use the union operator to concatenate external features and the difference operator to remove internal features.

REFERENCES/BIBLIOGRAPHY

AWADH, B., N. SEPEHRI, and O. HAWALESHKA (1995). "A Computer-Aided Process Planning Model Based on Genetic Algorithms," *Computer Operations Research* 22(8), 841–856.

BURBIDGE, J. L. (1971). "Production Flow Analysis," *Production Engineer,* April/May.

———. (1975). *The Introduction of Group Technology.* New York: John Wiley.

CHANG, T. C. (1982). "TIPPS—A Totally Integrated Process Planning System." Ph.D. thesis, Virginia Polytechnic Institute and State University, Blackburg, Virginia.

———. (1983). *Advances in Computer-Aided Process Planning,* NBS-GCR-83-441. U.S. Department of Commerce, National Institute of Standards and Technology, Gaithersburg, MD.

———. (1990). *Expert Process Planning for Manufacturing,* Reading, MA: Addison-Wesley.

CHANG, T. C., and R. A. WYSK (1985). *An Introduction to Automated Process Planning System.* Englewood Cliffs, NJ: Prentice Hall.

CHANG, T. C. and R. A. WYSK. "Interfacing CAD/Automated Process Planning," *AIIE Transactions,* Vol. 13, No. 3, September, 1981.

COX, L. D., A. M. AL-GHANIM, and D. E. CULLER (1995). "A Neural Network-Based Methodology for Machining Knowledge Acquisition," *Computers and Engineering,* 29(1–4), 217–220.

DASCHBACH A., B. ABELLA, and C. MCNICHOLS (1995). "Reverse Engineering: A Tool for Process Planning," *Computers and Engineering,* 29(1–4), 637–640.

DEGARMO, E. P., J. T. BLACK, and R. A. KOSHER (1988), *Materials and Processes in Manufacturing,* 7th Edition. New York: Macmillan.

DEREK, Y. H. and D. DEBASISH (1996). "A Genetic Algorithm Application for Sequencing Operations in Process Planning for Parallel Machining," *IIE Transactions,* 28, 55–68.

DESCOTTE, Y., and J. -C LATOMBE (1981). "GARI: A Problem Solver That Plans How to Machine Mechanical Parts," in *Proceedings of IJCAI 7,* Vancouver: pp. 766–772.

DUNN, M. S., and W. S. MANN (1978). "Computerized Production Process Planning," in *Proceedings of the Fifteenth Numerical Control Society Annual Meeting and Technical Conference.* Chicago: Numerical Control Society.

EVERSHEIM, W., H. FUCHS, and K. H. ZONS (1980). "Automatic Process Planning with Regard to Production by Application of the System AUTAP for Control Problems," in *Computer Graphics in Manufacturing Systems (Proceedings of the Twelfth CIRP International Seminar on Manufacturing Systems)*. Belgrade: CIRP, pp. 779–800.

EVERSHEIM, W., and J. SCHEEWIND (1992). "Computer-Aided Process Planning—State of the Art and Future Development," *Robotics and Computer-Integrated Manufacturing*, 10(1–2), 65.

GAO, J. X, and X. X. HUANG (1996). "Product and Manufacturing Capability Modelling in an Integrated CAD/Process Planning Environment," *International Journal of Advanced Manufacturing Technology*, 11(1), 43–51.

HALEVI, G., and R. D. WEILL (1995). *Principles of Process Planning*. London: Chapman & Hall.

HETEM, V., K. CARR, M. LUCENTI, O. RUIZ, X. ZHU, P. M. FERREIRA, and S. C. Y. LU (1995). "Specification for a Process Planning Enabling Platform," *Journal of Systems Engineering*, 5, 48–59.

HUANG, S. H., and H. C. ZHANG (1994). "On the Use of Knowledge-Based Connectionist Models in CAPP Systems," *Manufacturing Science and Engineering*, 1, 65–94.

IWATA, K., Y. MUROTSU, and F. OBA (1977). "Optimization of Cutting Conditions for Multi-Pass Operations Considering Probabilistic Nature in Machining Processes," *Journal of Engineering for Industry*, 99(1), 210–217.

JOSHI, S. B., W. C. HOBERECHT, J. LEE, R. A. WYSK, and D. C. BARRICK (1994). "Design, Development and Implementation of an Integrated Group Technology and Computer Aided Process Planning System, *IIE Transactions*, 26(4), 2–8.

JUNG, M. Y., and K. H. LEE (1996). "A CAD/CAPP Interface for Complex Rotationally Symmetric Parts," *International Journal of Production Research*, 34(1), 227–251.

KAKINO, Y., F. OBA, T. MERIWAKI, and K. IWATA (1977). "A New Method of Parts Description for Computer-Aided Production Planning," in P. Blake, ed. *Advances in Computer-Aided Manufacturing (Proceedings of the Fourth International IFIP/IFAC Conference, PROLOMAT 79)*. New York: Elsevier North-Holland, pp. 197–213.

KING, J. R. and V. NAKORNCHAI (1982). "Machine-Component Group Formation in Group Technology: Review and Extension," *International Journal of Production Research*, 20(2), 117–133.

KIRITSIS, D. (1995). "A Review of Knowledge-Based Expert Systems for Process Planning: Methods and Problems," *International Journal of Advanced Manufacturing Technology*, 10(4), 240.

KOTLER, R. A. (1980a). "Computerized Process Planning—Part 1," *Army Man Tech Journal*, 4(4), 20–28.

———. (1980b). "Computerized Process Planning—Part 2," *Army Man Tech Journal*, 4(4), 29–36.

MAREFAT, M. M., and J. BRITANIK (1994). "A Case-Based Approach for Process Planning," *Manufacturing Science and Engineering*, 1, 3–12.

MCDANIEL, H. (1970). *Decision Table Software—A Handbook*. Princeton: Brandon/Systems Press.

MEI, J., and H. C. ZHANG (1994). "A Graphical Method for Datum and Setup Selection in Process Planning," *Manufacturing Science and Engineering*, 1.

MEI, J., H. C. ZHANG, and W. J. B. OLDHAM (1995). "A Neural Network Approach for Datum Selection in Computer-Aided Process Planning," *Computers in Industry*, 27, 53–64.

NAGARWALA, M. Y., P. S. PULAT, and S. R. RAMAN (1994). "Process Selection and Tolerance Allocation for Minimum Cost Assembly," *Manufacturing Science and Engineering*, 1.

SILBERG, B. (1971). "DETAB/65 in Third-Generation COBOL," *GIGPLAN Notices*, 6, 8.

TEMPELHOF, K. H. (1979). "A System of Computer-Aided Process Planning for Machine Parts," SME Technical Paper, Series MS79-154. Dearborn, MI: Society of Manufacturing Engineers.

Also in P. Blake, ed., *Advanced Manufacturing Technology (Proceedings of the Fourth International IFIP/IFAC Conference, PROLOMAT 79)*. New York: Elsevier-North Holland (1980), pp. 141–150.

TULKOFF, J. (1981). "Lockheeds GENPLAN," in *Proceedings of the Eighteenth Numerical Control Society Annual Meeting and Technical Conference*. Dallas: Numerical Control Society, pp. 417–421.

VOGEL, S. A. (1979). "Metcut Machinability Process for NC." Paper read at the First Annual Conference on Computer Graphics in CAD/CAM Systems, Massachusetts Institute of Technology, Cambridge, pp. 5–15.

———. (1980). "Integrated Process Planning at General Electric's Aircraft Engine Group" in *Proceedings of AUTOFACT WEST*. Dearborn, MI: Society of Manufacturing Engineers, pp. 729–742.

VOGEL, S. A., and E. J. ADLARD (1981). "The AUTOPLAN Process Planning System," in *Proceedings of the Eighteenth Numerical Control Society Annual Meeting and Technical Conference*. Dallas: Numerical Control Society, pp. 422–429, Pittsburgh, PA.

WANG, B., and M. CURTIS (1988). *Process Planning*. New York: John Wiley.

WANG, H. P. and R. A. WYSK (1986a). "Applications of Microcomputers in Computer Aided Process Planning," Journal of Manufacturing Systems, 5(2), 71–84.

WANG, H. P., and R. A. WYSK (1986b). "An Expert System for Machining Data Selection," *Computers in Industrial Engineering*, 10(2), 99–101.

WANG, H. P., and R. A. WYSK (1987). "Intelligent Reasoning for Process Planning," *Computers in Industry*, 8(4), 293–309.

WONG, T. N., and S. L. SIU (1995). "A Knowledge-Based Approach to Automated Machining Process Selection and Sequencing," 33(12), 3465–3484.

WYSK, R. A. (1977). "An Automated Process Planning and Selection Program: APPAS." Ph.d. thesis, Purdue University, West Lafayette, Indiana.

WYSK, R. A., T. C. CHANG, and H. P. WANG (1988). *Computer Integrated Manufacturing Software and Student Manual*. Albany, NY: Delmar Publishers.

ZHANG, H. C., and L. ALTING (1994). *Computerized Manufacturing Process Planning Systems*. London: Chapman & Hall.

14

Concurrent Engineering

14.1 INTRODUCTION

Concurrent engineering has become a frequently used term in today's manufacturing environment. Concurrent engineering is also referred to as "simultaneous engineering."

Though there are a variety of names given to concurrent engineering, the process they describe is the same—that in which a new product or significantly different existing product line is designed, developed, manufactured, and marketed. Concurrent engineering is more than a new engineering technology; it is a people and communications issue.

Concurrent engineering may be defined as a systematic approach to the integrated, concurrent design of products and their related processes, including manufacture, support, maintenance, and many other life-cycle considerations, including test, inspection, reliability, safety, human factors, and disposability.

The goal of concurrent engineering is to design and manufacture a product in such a way that the product will meet the customer's requirement to the fullest extent. In that context, it can be seen as the implementation arm of total quality management (TQM) and a modern treatment of systems engineering that combines quality engineering methods in a computer-integrated environment.

Traditionally, manufacturers have used a "serial" approach in producing a product to market. During the conceptual design and preliminary development stages, the design engineers have played a dominant, if almost exclusive, role. Prototypes developed from the initial design were given to the manufacturing engineers so that the product could be produced in the required dimensions and production volume. In order to ensure that parts and materials were available for assembly, procurement experts stepped in at the next stage of product development. Finally, marketing and sales personnel introduced the product to the consumer.

This approach leads to several drawbacks in the form of longer development cycles, increased manufacturing costs (as much as 90% of the production cost maybe specified before manufacturing engineers have a voice in process design), and a product that is not optimal for the market that exists.

With the surge in Japanese economic power over the last few decades, U.S. manufacturers have been forced to make dramatic changes. Thus, the advent of manufacturing trends such as flexible automation, just-in-time production, new scheduling practices, and increasing precision of machine tools have resulted. Although these methods have addressed some of the problems (namely, job specialization and separation of product designs; production, distribution, and field maintenance function; outdated standards and mass production techniques and principles that produce large, costly inventories and an inability to respond to market changes), they lacked a rational framework to guide implementation and fell short of modern managerial and technological capabilities.

Manufacturers have slowly realized that they need to rethink the entire engineering process in order to compete in the global marketplace. A principal focus of concurrent engineering is "accelerating time to market" by condensing the engineering and production activities required to produce production quantities of a new product.

Flexibility, another focus of concurrent engineering, aids in decreasing the time to market by allowing a quick changeover of equipment in addition to reducing lot sizes, minimizing inventories, and simplifying design.

In addition to the necessity of tighter time-to-market deadlines, increasing design complexity and intense competition have resulted in the need for concurrent engineering.

Recent data collected from the National Institute of Standards and Technology, Thomas Groups, and the Institute for Defense Analysis found that concurrent engineering methodologies can reduce product development time by 30 to 70%, result in 65 to 90% fewer engineering changes, reduce time to market by up to 90%, and contribute to quality improvement by 200 to 600%.

Concurrent engineering, as shown in Figure 14.1, may be viewed as a three-spoke wheel with the product model as the hub of all activities. The three spokes are:

1. product engineering
2. process engineering
3. production engineering

Important to this view of concurrent engineering are the interfaces between each of these spokes. Product design defines the features and their attributes, which coupled with the process-knowledge base dictates how manufacturable a product will be. The process engineering and production engineering interface defines the capabilities of a manufacturing system. The product and engineering interface dictates a product's performance in the marketplace, that is, how well it meets its functions, how reliable it is in use, how comfortable the user feels with the product, and many other product life-cycle issues.

How all these interactions and activities take place with respect to time is explained in what follows. Product design begins with the definition of global attributes of the new product by a CE product-development team. The first pass at product engineering results in an engineering design, called the current product model. The current

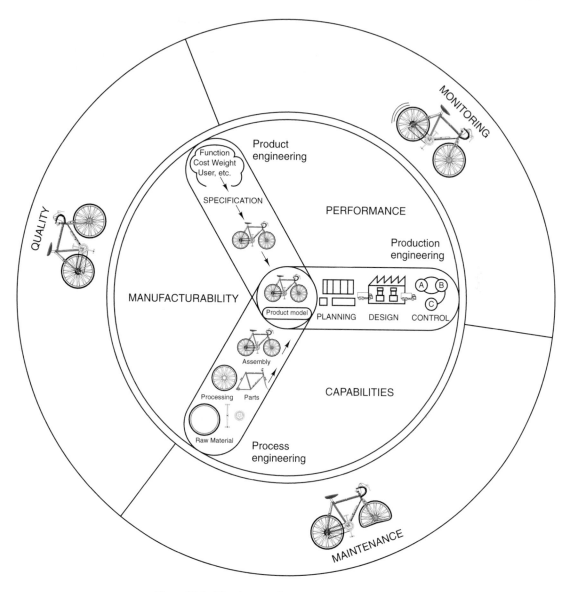

Figure 14.1   The three-spoke model of concurrent engineering.

product model is embellished at process engineering to include process-related attributes, for example, knurl surface, heat treatments, and so on. The production engineering completes the product model and fulfills the "traceability" requirements of critical components. A slot that has been broached is different from a slot that has been milled.

Concurrent design, an important aspect of concurrent engineering, has as one of its key objectives the concatenation of all relevant knowledge of an organization into the design of a product. A second objective is to decrease the product development schedule in order to maintain competitiveness in a dynamic industrial environment; a final objective is to improve product performance to better satisfy customers.

The goals of concurrent design are twofold: to enhance the effectiveness of a product by incorporating all relevant knowledge at the design stage, and to increase the efficiency of the design process by reducing turnaround time from product conception to delivery. By doing so, a company is able to meet both the market opportunities and market demands.

When applied effectively and with a companywide commitment, the following benefits of concurrent engineering are achievable:

- a high-quality, lowest-cost product that meets the customers' needs
- a decrease in the overall product-development process
- improved time to market by reducing the number of product iterations because first prototypes meet specifications and are competitive with the company's manufacturing capabilities
- higher sales and profits because a greater variety of products can be supported and targeted toward more segments of the market
- lower capital equipment costs
- greater use of automation
- less chance of redesign
- few parts to purchase from fewer vendors
- better factory availability

Many industries, eager to achieve the benefits of concurrent engineering, begin employing this process only to realize they are not achieving their goals. Why? In many cases, manufacturing companies use *some* of the concurrent engineering tools available. But in order to achieve concurrent engineering advantages, a company must have several key characteristics in its implementation of concurrent engineering:

- top–down design approach
- strong customer interface
- multifunctional and multidisciplinary teams
- continuity of the teams
- practical engineering optimization of product and process characteristics
- design benchmarking and prototyping through the creation of a digitized product model
- simulation of product performance and manufacturing and support processes
- testing to confirm high-risk predictions
- early involvement of subcontractors and vendors
- corporate focus on continuous improvement and lessons learned

Concurrent engineering has opened many doors for manufacturers seeking a rational, comprehensive plan to improve the overall operations of the firm, from design to manufacturing to delivery. However, manufacturing firms must realize that concurrent engineering may involve a total restructuring and that this restructuring cannot occur overnight. Top managers must fall out of the trap of leaning toward "quick fixes" to their problems and initiate a total commitment to the education and implementation of concurrent engineering—only then will the benefits of concurrent engineering be fully realized.

14.2 ENABLING TECHNOLOGIES FOR CONCURRENT ENGINEERING

Although it is not the only factor, technology is certainly a dominant factor in the success of any major advancement of productivity and quality. For instance, technology has played a crucial role in enabling just-in-time production, or flexible manufacturing. Likewise, technology will play a significant role in enabling the concurrent engineering process, by maintaining a global and common view of a product design to enable the parallel and integrated design of products and processes. Furthermore, with appropriate technologies, a design team is able to cut product-development cost and time even further. With less development time and cost, the design team can be proactive as opposed to reactive, as far as meeting customer demands are concerned.

Figure 14.2 depicts four stages of activities involved in the life cycle of a product. The first two stages of activities are contained in the product engineering spoke of the concurrent engineering model shown in Figure 14.1. The output of each stage of work is specified right below the stage box. For example, the global product definition is the output from product planning, prototype evaluation from product design, and so on.

Among those enabling technologies introduced in the following sections, some provide structured approaches to facilitate the concurrent engineering process, for example quality function deployment, (QFD). Others take an analysis approach for the design team member to evaluate a design, based on a certain product life-cycle attribute, such as design for assembly.

14.2.1 Quality Function Deployment (QFD)

The first step of any concurrent engineering product is to identify the needs of the customer and design a product around it.

As was pointed out earlier in this chapter, quality is one of the most important attributes that consumers take into account when acquiring a product. This quality is expressed in terms of features and performance. In QFD, quality is a measure of consumer satisfaction. Two kinds of quality are identified (Akao, 1990): (1) positive or latent quality, and (2) negative or expressed quality. Positive quality refers to consumer demand, that is, what the consumer wants. The negative quality is obtained from consumer complaints.

Quality function deployment provides a systematic and structured process for capturing the preferences of the customers and including them in the design of a given product. This technological concept can be applied either for improving an existing

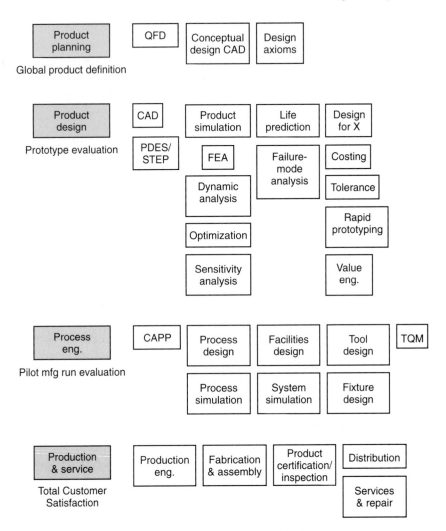

Figure 14.2   Product life-cycle activities.

product or for introducing a totally new one. The use of graphical representation (charts) in QFD facilitates it use and application.

There are several definitions of quality function deployment. The one given by Yoji Akao, creator of the QFD concept, is (Akao, 1990) "Converting the consumers' demands into quality characteristics and developing a design quality for the finished product by systematically deploying the relationships between the demands and the characteristic, starting with the quality of each functional component and extending the deployment to quality of each part and process." This definition establishes the important correlation between product and process design, although the use of QFD is not limited to only physical products; it can be used for improving the quality of services and other activities.

Since this idea was first introduced in Japan in 1966 by Yoji Akao, it has evolved to a more complex concept that includes value analysis, reliability, and bottleneck engineering. Today, many companies have integrated the tool into their product-development procedures.

Figure 14.2 also shows the route that quality follows when it is being deployed through all the stages of developing a product and the process for producing it. In order to describe the QFD method, it is necessary to understand the different parts of the product-development process and determine how they interact. In Figure 14.2, the flow downstream indicates the typical order in which a product is developed.

When QFD techniques are used to improve the design of an existing product, consumer complaints are studied and the developing process is reviewed going in an upstream direction, trying to find all possible causes for the deficient performance of the product. On the other hand, QFD helps introduce new products by analyzing the positive quality provided by the consumers and including the demands throughout the entire process. This deployment is exercised from top to bottom in a downstream direction.

The analysis of the information supplied by consumers is carried out by using quality charts. Quality charts organize the information that has been gathered by surveying the market and translate this information into more technical terms that can be associated to engineering characteristics of the product. The charts are described in Hauser and Clausing (1988). Once the information is available, its translation consist of rewording the demands, trying to break them down into single-meaning phrases. It might not be possible to do this in just one step, and there can be more than two levels of quality demands. The last level of quality demands determines a list of product characteristics, called the quality elements, that can be accessed in the product design.

The quality chart is a matrix array that shows the interdependency of consumer demands (quality demands) on engineering characteristics (quality elements). The entries of this matrix are symbols that represent the degree of dependence. An example is shown in Figure 14.3 in which a spoon is used as a hypothetical product.

In order to determine the quality elements of the quality chart, the quality demands have to be listed, analyzed, and broken down in simple phrases that can be related to one or more engineering characteristics. In Figure 14.3, for example, comfort was separated into three attributes given in the column called "Second Level." These attributes were narrower in meaning than the initial demand, but not narrow enough for obtaining the engineering characteristics; so the process of finding single-meaning expressions was continued until, under the column corresponding to the "Third-Level," the final expression of the initial demand were found. Based on these simple expressions, the quality elements are determined and the quality chart can be filled with the symbols that categorize the relationship as strong, medium, or low. Before taking this analysis one step forward, it is necessary to establish the relative importance among the consumer demand qualities. In Hauser and Clausing (1988), for example, this relative importance is expressed in terms of weight factors, which are based on either experience or on surveys.

Quality element deployment chart → Demanded quality deployment chart ↓			Handling			Product finish		
			Weight	Shape	Measurement	Material	Surface finish	Minimum radii
First level	Second level	Third level						
Comfortable	Feels nice in the mouth	No sharp edges	□	◉	△	△	△	□
		Anatomical shape	◉	△	◉	◉	□	□
	Easy to grasp	Light	□	◉	△	△		□
		Handle shape	□			□	□	□
	Easy to clean	Waterproof		□	□	◉		
		Smooth surface		△	△	△	◉	△

◉ Strong relationship

△ Medium relationship

□ Low relationship

Figure 14.3   A partial QFD chart for the spoon case.

14.2.2 Design for Manufacture

The heart of any design-for-manufacture (DFM) system is a group of design principles, guidelines, rules, and so on, that are structured to help the designer reduce the feasible region for the optimum solution of the design problem. Therefore, the probability of finding a sound design is increased.

The usefulness of these rules depends on the extent that the design team is aware of them and of the team's ability to apply them. Thus, experience in designing and manufacturing is a key factor in achieving their benefits.

Although most of this information is not new, the systematic way in which it has been recently organized in a DFM context as a solution to improving global competitiveness has given them a new value.

The principles of DFM presented here are very useful for designing products for efficient manufacturing (Stoll, 1986).

1. *Reduce the total number of parts.* The reduction of the number of parts in product design is probably the best opportunity for reducing manufacturing costs. Less parts implies less purchases, inventory, handling, processing time, development time, equipment, engineering time, assembly difficulty, service, inspection, testing, and so on. In general, it reduces the level of intensity of all the activities related to the product during its entire life. A part that does not need to have relative motion with respect to other parts does not have to be made of a different material, or that would make the assembly or service of other parts extremely difficult or impossible, is an excellent target for elimination. Some approaches to part-count reduction are based on the use of one-piece structures and selection of manufacturing processes such as injection molding, extrusions, precision castings, and powder metallurgy, among others.

2. *Develop a modular design.* The use of modules in product design simplifies manufacturing activities such as inspection, testing, assembly, purchasing, redesign, maintenance, service, and so on. One reason is that modules add versatility to product update in the redesign process, help run tests before the final assembly is put together, and allow the use of standard components to minimize product variations. However, the interfacing among modules can increase the complexity of the design, and this interconnection can be a limiting factor when applying this rule.

3. *Use standard components.* Standard components are less expensive than custom-made items. The high availability of these components reduces product lead times. Also, their reliability factors are well ascertained. Furthermore, the use of standard components transfers the production pressure to the supplier, relieving in part the manufacturer's concern of meeting production schedules.

4. *Design parts to be multifunctional.* Multifunctional parts reduce the total number of parts in a design, thus, obtaining the benefits given in rule 1. Some examples are a part to act as both an electric conductor and as a structural member, or as a heat-dissipating element and as a structural member. Also, there can be elements that besides their principal function have guiding, aligning, or self-fixturing features to facilitate assembly, and/or reflective surfaces to facilitate inspection, and so on.

5. *Design parts for multiuse.* In a manufacturing firm, different products can share parts that have been designed for multiuse. These parts can have the same or different functions when used in different products. In order to do this, it is necessary to identify the parts that are suitable for multiuse. For example, all the parts used in the firm (purchased or made) can be sorted into two groups: the first containing all the parts that are unique for a certain product or model, and the second containing all the parts that are used commonly in all products. Then, part families are created by defining categories of similar parts in each group. The goal is to minimize the number of categories, the variations within the categories, and the number of design features within each variation. The result is a set of standard part families from which multiuse parts are created. After organizing all the parts into part families, the manufacturing processes are standardized for each part family. The production of a specific part belonging to a given part family would follow the manufacturing routing that has been set up for its family, skipping the operations that are not required for it. Furthermore, in design changes to existing products and especially in new product designs, the standard multiuse components should be used.

6. *Design for ease of fabrication.* Select the optimum combination between the material and fabrication process to minimize the overall manufacturing cost. In general, final operations such as painting, polishing, finish machining, and so on, should be avoided. Excessive tolerance, surface-finish requirement, and so on are commonly found problems that result in higher than necessary production cost.

7. *Avoid separate fasteners.* The use of fasteners increases the cost of manufacturing a part due to the handling and feeding operations that have to be performed. Besides the high cost of the equipment required for them, these operations are not 100% successful, so they contribute to reducing the overall manufacturing efficiency. In general, fasteners should be avoided and replaced, for example, by using tabs or snap fits. If fasteners have to be used, then some guides should be followed for selecting them. Minimize the number, size, and variation used; also, utilize standard components whenever possible. Avoid screws that are too long or too short, separate washers, tapped holes, and roundheads and flatheads (not good for vacuum pickup). Self-tapping and chamfered screws are preferred because they improve placement success. Screws with vertical sideheads should be selected for vacuum pickup.

8. *Minimize assembly directions.* All parts should be assembled from one direction. If possible, the best way is to add parts from above, in a vertical direction, parallel to the gravitational direction (downward). In this way, the effects of gravity help the assembly process, contrary to having to compensate for its effect when other directions are chosen.

9. *Maximize compliance.* Errors can occur during insertion operations due to variations in part dimensions or on the accuracy of the positioning device used. This faulty behavior can cause damage to the part and/or to the equipment. For this reason, it is necessary to include compliance in the part design and in the assembly process. Examples of part built-in compliance features include tappers or chamfers and moderate radius sizes to facilitate insertion, and nonfunctional external elements to help detect hidden features. For the assembly process, selection of a rigid-base part, tactile sensing capabilities, and vision systems are examples of compliance. A simple solution is to use high-quality parts with designed-in compliance, a rigid-base part, and selective compliance in the assembly tool.

10. *Minimize handling.* Handling consists of positioning, orienting, and fixing a part or component. To facilitate orientation, symmetrical parts should be used whenever possible. If it is not possible, then the asymmetry must be exaggerated to avoid failures. Use external guiding features to help the orientation of a part. The subsequent operations should be designed so that the orientation of the part is maintained. Also, magazines, tube feeders, part strips, and so on, should be used to keep this orientation between operations. Avoid using flexible parts—use slave circuit boards instead. If cables have to be used, then include a dummy connector to plug the cable (robotic assembly) so it can be located easily. When designing the product, try to minimize the flow of material, waste, parts, and so on, in the manufacturing operation; also, take packaging into account, selecting appropriate and safe packaging for the product.

Design-for-manufacture rules should be expanded through a continuous process of finding good practices for a given manufacturing process and including them in the parts and process design to improve the overall manufacturing operation.

14.2.3 Taguchi Methods

Since 1960, the Taguchi methods have been used for improving the quality of Japanese products with great success. Genichi Taguchi bases his methods on conventional statistical tools, together with some guidelines for laying out experiments and analyzing the results. Taguchi's approach to quality control applies to the entire process of developing and manufacturing a product—from the concept, through design and engineering, to manufacturing.

As the first step for describing the methods, the definition of quality presented here (Taguchi, 1981): "Quality is the loss imparted to the society from the time a product is shipped." There are two loss categories: (1) the loss caused by functional variation, and (2) the loss caused by harmful effects. The first category is related to the product not performing as expected by the customer, and the second category can be associated to factors like pollution, noise, and so on. Functional variation in a product can be caused by the influence of different factors that are referred to as noise. There are three types of noise: (1) outer noise (environmental factors), (2) inner noise (function- and time-related factors), and (3) product noise (part-to-part variations). The Taguchi methods are based on the idea of making a product design robust to uncontrollable factors (noise).

The previous definition of quality helps identify low-quality products (causing loss to the customer) that have been considered a good quality (within specifications) using the conventional definition. To measure quality, Taguchi defined what he calls "loss function." This continuous function is defined in terms of the deviation of a design parameter from an ideal or target value (see Figure 14.4). Taguchi says that quality is best achieved by minimizing this function, and this is the only way of being competitive in the today's global marketplace.

The loss function can be expressed in terms of the quadratic relationship:

$$L = k(y - m)^2 \tag{14.1}$$

where:

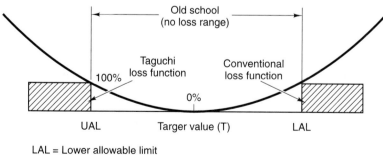

Figure 14.4   Taguchi's loss function.

L = loss associated to a particular parameter y

m = nominal value of the parameter specification

k = constant that depends on the cost at the specification limits (can be determined conservatively by dividing the cost of scrap in dollars by the square of the lower-or-higher tolerance values)

This function penalizes the deviation of a parameter from the specification value that contributes to deteriorating the performance of the product, resulting in a loss to the customer. Furthermore, the usual low and high limits for the tolerance of a given design parameter are changed to a continuous function that presents any parameter value other than the nominal as a loss. The loss function given in Equation (4.1) is referred to as "nominal is best," but there are also expressions for cases when higher or lower values of parameters are better (Ross, 1988).

If a large number of parts are considered, say, N, the average loss per part is equal to the summation of the losses given by Equation (14.1) for each part divided by N. This average loss per part is equivalent to

$$L = k[S^2 + (\psi - m)^2] \tag{14.2}$$

where

S^2 = variance around the average, Ψ

Ψ = average value of y for the group

$\Psi - m$ = offset of the group average from the nominal value m

To minimize the loss, the average has to be adjusted and the variance has to be reduced. The former is accomplished by product and process engineers in an "off-line" fashion, and the latter is realized by the production engineers during the production state in an "on-line" manner. Within the Taguchi philosophy, both quality improvement methods are considered, but building quality into the product during the design stage (off-line) represents the prized goal.

For adjusting the average as close as possible to the nominal value, Taguchi designs experiments using especially constructed tables known as "orthogonal arrays" (OAs). These fractional factorial experiments (FFE) have the ability to evaluate several factors in a minimum number of tests. The OAs to be used are selected based on the number of factors and the number of levels for the factors of interest. To design an experiment, it is necessary to select the most suitable orthogonal array, assign the factors to the appropriate columns, and, finally, describe the combinations of the individual experiments.

For reducing the variance, the influence of the noise factors over the control factors has to be studied by using what Taguchi calls "outer arrays".

Analysis of variance (ANOVA) is a statistical method used to interpret experimental data and help make decisions. By using ANOVA, the factors that influence the average and the variance of a characteristic, expressed using the loss function, can be determined.

To achieve desirable product quality by design, Taguchi suggests a three-stage process:

1. systems design
2. parameter design
3. tolerance design

The systems design stage is where new ideas, concepts, and knowledge in the areas of science and technology are utilized by the designing team to determine the right combination of materials, parts, processes, and design factors that will satisfy functional and economical specifications. Parameter design is related to finding the appropriate design-factor levels to make the system perform less sensitive to causes of variation (robust design). In this way, the product would perform better, reducing the loss to the customer. In the tolerance design stage, tolerances of factors that have the largest influence on variation are adjusted only if, after the parameter-design stage, the target values of quality have not yet been achieved.

In the parameter-design stage, control factors that may contribute to reducing variation can be quickly identified by looking at the amount of variation present as a response. This response is expressed using the signal-to-noise (S/N) ratio, which is defined as -10 times the logarithm base 10 of the mean square deviation. By conducting a standard ANOVA of the S/N ratio, the average value of S/N ratio can be increased, thereby reducing the variation. Then from S/N data, the factors that affect variation are determined, and from ANOVA, control factors that affect the average are determined. With this information, the control factors are grouped in the following way:

1. factors affecting both the variation and the average
2. factors affecting the variation only
3. factors affecting the average only
4. factors that do not affect either of them

With groups 1 and 2, the variations can be reduced. Then, with group 3, the average can be adjusted to the target value. Group 4 is set to the most economical level.

If even after the parameter-design stage, quality is not at a satisfactory level, then the tolerances of the factors that affect the variation the most should be tightened.

14.2.4 Boothroyd and Dewhurst's Handbook

Geoffrey Boothroyd and Peter Dewhurst have directed extensive research in the area of design for manufacture (DFM). They have coauthored several books and papers in the manufacturing field, including *Design for Assembly—A Designers Handbook* (Boothroyd and Dewhurst, 1983a). Their approach is based on product simplification through design for assembly (DFA) as the key to successful product design for manufacture.

The use of DFA, which is intended to reduce assembly costs by simplifying the product structure, has shown better part cost reduction than assembly cost reduction, together with other benefits such as better reliability, better product quality, and a reduction of inventory and production control costs(Boothroyd and Dewhurst, 1988a, 1988b).

In design for manufacture (DFM), different product-design alternatives are considered and compared in order to find the most economical and efficient solution to the design problem. However, the designer usually does not have the tools for obtaining an early cost estimate of the different production-scheme alternatives until the product is fully designed and detailed. This makes it too late for basic changes to be made, constraining the design to a non optimum product structure that may not be cost-effective to manufacture.

Boothroyd and Dewhurst's quantitative method is based on two basic steps: (1) to reduce the number of parts in a design, and (2) to estimate handling and assembly costs in the assembly process. To apply step 1, it is necessary to determine the number of essential parts in the assembly. This is referred to as the theoretical minimum number of parts. In order to be indispensable to the design, these parts have to satisfy one of three criteria (Boothroyd and Dewhurst, 1984a):

1. Is there relative motion between this part and all other parts already assembled?
2. Must the part be made of a different material or be isolated from all other parts already assembled?
3. Must the part be separated from all parts already assembled because necessary assembly or disassembly would otherwise be impossible?

In step 2, cost figures should be determined for the assembly process; therefore, an assembly process has to be selected. Boothroyd and Dewhurst (1983c) present a procedure for selecting the right method to assemble a given product. The method selected using this procedure is the most economical assembly process that should be used. The selection is based on projected market life, number of parts, projected production volume, and company investment policy.

There are three basic alternatives to choose from: manual (MA or MM), special-purpose machine (AI or AF), and programmable machine (AP or AR) (see Figure 14-5).

After choosing the assembly process, the efficiency of the assembly operation and the estimated cost can be calculated. In Boothroyd and Dewhurst (1988?) the present design-for-assembly rules and procedures for estimating assembly costs and for evaluating efficiency indices of automatic, manual, and robot-based processes. These DFA rules, if followed after selecting a process, can result in a manufacturing cost reduction of 20 to 40% and assembly productivity increases of 100 to 200% (Boothroyd and Dewhurst, 1983a?).

–MA	Manual Assembly
–MM	Manual assembly with Mechanical assistance
–AI	Automatic assembly machines with Indexing-transfer devices
–AF	Automatic assembly machines with Free-transfer devices
–AP	Automatic Programmable assembly machine
–AR	Automatic programmable assembly machine using Robot arms

Figure 14.5   Assembly process types.

During the analysis, special attention is paid to the possibility of reducing the number of parts either by eliminating or combining them. This is indicated by assigning a theoretical minimum number of parts to the subassemblies (if there are any) and to the entire product.

After obtaining the theoretical minimum number of parts, the design efficiency can be calculated. In the case of manual assembly, for example, the following equation should be evaluated (Boothroyd and Dewhurst, 1983c):

$$E_m = 3 N_m / T_m \tag{14.3}$$

where

E_m = manual-assembly design efficiency

N_m = minimum number of parts

T_m = total assembly time

This equation represents the ratio of the ideal assembly time/part (3s) to the actual assembly time/part, taking N_m as the actual number of parts. It is assumed that each part is easy to handle and insert, and that one-third of the parts is secured immediately after insertion.

In the redesign stage, there is an opportunity to reduce the number of parts in the operations where the theoretical minimum number of parts is less than the actual number of parts (i.e., subassemblies). Also, in this stage, excessive values in either the handling or assembly times should be studied carefully for improvement.

Boothroyd and Dewhurst's quantitative evaluation method is a useful tool for concurrent engineering because the product/process design is optimized based on good assembly practices and analytical cost estimations are made based on practical data. Also, the assembly efficiency index represents a framework for comparisons among different assembly alternatives. The use of this method is the basis of the *Handbook* (Boothroyd and Dewhurst, 1983a), which includes practical procedures and data designing products for ease of assembly.

To facilitate the use of this approach, Boothroyd and Dewhurst have developed DFA software that, by requesting the relationship between parts, helps the designer determine an efficient assembly sequence for a new product starting from a sketch.

14.2.5 Hitachi Assembly Evaluation Method (AEM)

This method was originally developed in Japan in 1976 by Hitachi. It has been used successfully by the Hitachi Group and several other companies worldwide (Miyakawa, Ohashi, and Iwata, 1990). The method is an effective tool for quantitatively evaluating the product-design quality for assembly producibility at early design stages. In the conventional product-design procedure, redesigning required so much time that products with poor producibility characteristics were manufactured. To counteract this, the AEM approach to product design includes two feedback loops to check for good producibility characteristics: one at the conceptual designing stage, and the other one at the detail designing stage. This procedure results in less product development time and in a more economical solution to the design problem.

For its application, AEM requires information available at the early stages of the product-design process. Conceptual drawings, for example, could be used to carry out this analysis.

In order to identify the weak points of a design, AEM uses two indices: the assemblability evaluation score E, and the assembly cost ratio K. The first is used in accounting for design quality or difficulty-of-assembly operations, and the second is related to assembly costs. The algorithm for calculating the indices follows (Miyakawa et al., 1990):

(a) Express the operations within a part assembly in terms of the elemental assembly operations X (approximately 20), given by the method.

(b) Assign a penalty score ε_x to each of these elemental operations proportional to their increment of difficulty with respect to the basic operation, which is the easiest of X.

(c) Determine other factors that influence each assembly operation, that is η.

(d) Express all the attached operations required for each part in terms of the AEM symbols and put them together for easy visual evaluation.

(e) Determine the evaluation score for each operation, E_i, based on the following expression:

$$E_i = 100 - g(\varepsilon_{ij}, \eta_{ij}, \ldots)$$

where i's represent the ith assembly operation of the part, and j's represent the jth factor influencing the ith operation.

(f) Determine the total assembly evaluation score E for the part based on the evaluation scores E_i of each operation.

(g) Find the cost ratio K of the assembly operation by dividing the total assembly operation cost (summation of all the part assembly costs) of the evaluated product by the total assembly operation cost of the standard product.

(h) With the same information used in step g, find the total cost C as the summation of all the individual Ci's.

The AEM procedure consists of first assuming a reasonable assembly sequence for the whole product, attaching methods for each part and then expressing the attached methods using the elementary operations given by the method. Then, based on the elementary operations selected, compute the assembly evaluation score of each part E_i and the total assembly evaluation score E. Also, determine weak points of the assembly operation by identifying low values of E and from penalty scores of the elementary operations used. Finally, establish the relative cost of the product being evaluated to the cost of the standard product by finding the cost ratio K.

It has been shown that AEM is accurate enough for practical purposes (Miyakawa et al. 1990). The more important benefits of using this method are the reduction in assembly cost, the facilitation of factory automation, the reduction in the design period, the reduction in cost of raw materials and purchased parts, and the improvement of reliability of the products and automated equipment.

14.2.6 Axiomatic Approach

The axiomatic approach is the result of a scientific search for the basic principles of design by Nam P. Suh of the Massachusetts Institute of Technology. The complete details of this approach (Suh, 1990) is the basis of the following presentation.

The axiomatic approach is based on the assumption that there exists a fundamental set of principles that determines good design practice. Phrased differently, there should exist common factors in all good designs. These factors are fundamental principles of design that can be applied to all design situations, like the natural laws in natural science problems. These principles are the basis for the solution developing process and consist of the synthesis of an overall solution and process optimization, using empirical knowledge and mathematical tools.

The use of axioms in design represents one way in which design can be converted from the art it has been treated as into a science (Suh, 1990). This conversion process agrees with traditional evolution paths followed by other sciences: from societal need, through invention and technology, to science.

It is inherent to the method that decisions be made in a hierarchical fashion. Also, special attention should be paid to the problem-definition stage, which is one of the most important and difficult tasks in design. The probability of correctness of the definition stage increases as the amount of knowledge in terms of experience and education increases in the mind of the designer.

This method is based on two fundamental principles, or axioms, that if followed adequately results in a good design. To help understand the method better, the following definitions are given (Suh, 1990):

Axioms: fundamental truths that are always observed to be valid and for which there are no counterexamples.

Theorems: a proposition that may not be self-evident but that can be proved from accepted axioms.

Corollaries: propositions that follow from axioms or other propositions that have been proven.

FRs (functional requirements): in general, a designer's characterization of the perceived needs for a product (device, process, software, system organization, and so on); also, a minimum set of independent requirements that completely characterize the design objective for a specific need.

DPs (design parameters): key variables that characterize the physical entity created by the design process to fulfill the FRs.

Constraints: limits on the specifications or on the system in which the design solution must function.

Design, within the context of the axiomatic approach, is defined as (Suh, 1990):

"the creation of synthesized solution to satisfy the perceived needs through the mapping process between FRs, which exist in the functional domain, and the DPs, which exist in the physical domain." Thus, design is a mapping operation from one domain to another where each domain is independent from the other (see Figure 14.6).

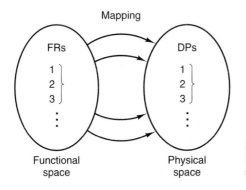

Figure 14.6 Design is a mapping operation from the functional space to the physical space.

The two axioms that rule good design practices are (Suh, 1990):

Axiom 1: *The Independence Axiom*
   Maintain the independence of FRs.
Axiom 2: *The Information Axiom*
   Minimize the information content of the design.

Axiom 1 is related to the process of translation from the functional domain to the physical domain. During this operation, the independence of the FRs must be assured. Axiom 2 states that the complexity of the design, once axiom 1 is satisfied, should be reduced. This helps decide what design alternative to choose when there are more than one that satisfy axiom 1. This is due to the nonuniqueness of the set of FRs. Within this context, design for manufacture is assured by (Suh, 1990): "When the product and process designs do not violate design axioms at all levels of the FR and DP hierarchies, then the product should be manufacturable." For example, when the FRs are dependent on each other, or the relationship between the FRs and the DPs is not clearly defined, then the products, processes, or systems are difficult, expensive, and sometimes impossible to manufacture.

The relationship between the design and manufacture activities, is shown in Figure 14.7. This relationship also can be expressed by using a mathematical model of the product-design and process-design transformation equations, which can be expressed as follows (Suh, 1990):

$$\{\mathbf{FR}\} = [\mathbf{A}]\{\mathbf{DP}\} \tag{14.4}$$

where

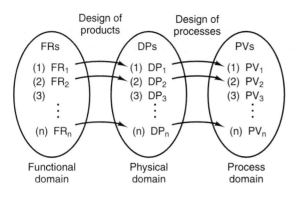

Figure 14.7   Three domains in design for manufacture.

$$\{FR\} = \text{functional requirement vector}$$
$$\{DP\} = \text{design-parameter vector}$$
$$[A] = \text{design matrix}$$

and

$$\{DP\} = [B]\{PV\} \qquad (14.5)$$

where

$$\{PV\} = \text{process-variable vector}$$
$$[B] = \text{process matrix}$$

Combining the two equations results in

$$\{FR\} = [A][B]\{PV\} \qquad (14.6)$$

$$\{FR\} = [C]\{PV\} \qquad (14.7)$$

where $[C]$ is the transformation matrix from the functional domain to the process domain

A good design depends on the form of the design matrix $[A]$. By theorem 4 (Suh, 1990), "in an ideal design the number of DPs is equal to the number of FRs"; therefore $[A]$ should be square.

There are three types of designs: uncoupled, coupled, and decoupled. An uncoupled design is characterized by having a diagonal transformation matrix. This means that each FR is influenced by only one design parameter, and, therefore, axiom 1 is automatically satisfied. On the contrary, in a coupled design, the elements of matrix $[A]$ are mostly nonzero; thus, a one-to-one relationship between the FRs and the DPs cannot be established, clearly violating axiom 1. If $[A]$ is triangular, it is called a decoupled design, and axiom 1 can be satisfied only if a specific order is followed when perturbing the design variables.

There are more readily usable versions of the design axioms. These design rules or corollaries are all derived from the axioms (as stated in the definition of corollaries) to facilitate the use of the axiomatic approach. Many corollaries can be derived from the two basic axioms, seven of which are listed here (Suh, 1990):

Corollary 1 (Decoupling of Coupled Design)
    Decouple or separate parts or aspects of a solution if FRs are coupled or become interdependent in the designs proposed.
Corollary 2 (Minimization of FRs)
    Minimize the number of FRs and constraints.
Corollary 3 (Integration of Physical Parts)
    Integrate design features in a single physical part if FRs can be independently satisfied in the proposed solution.
Corollary 4 (Use of Standardization)
    Use standardized or interchangeable parts if the use of these parts is consistent with the FRs and constraints.
Corollary 5 (Use of Symmetry)
    Use symmetrical shapes and/or arrangements if they are consistent with the FRs and constraints.
Corollary 6 (Largest Tolerance)
    Specify the largest allowable tolerance in stating FRs.
Corollary 7 (Uncoupled Design with Less Information)
    Seek an uncoupled design that requires less information than coupled designs in satisfying a set of FRs.

The axiomatic approach states that axiom 1 must be satisfied at all stages of the process of transformation from the functional domain to the process domain. Therefore, as shown in Equations (14.4) to (14.7), not only matrix **[C]** should be either triangular or diagonal, but also matrices **[A]** and **[B]**. Consequently, by theorem 9, "if either A or B represents a coupled design, the product cannot be manufactured" (Suh, 1990).

Axiom 2 is stated in terms of information, which is related to flow of knowledge and to the notion of complexity, because the more complex a thing is, the more information is required to describe it.

Usually, the final objective of DFM is to find the right combination of product design, process design, and material selection for obtaining the most economical solution to a problem while obtaining good product quality and reliability. This task, within the context of the axiomatic approach, should be done by transmitting just enough information content to maximize the probability of achieving the FRs (product design) or DPs (in the process design).

Suh (1990) states that the variance of a product does not have to be zero as long as the system range is inside the design range, although reliability is improved even more by reducing this variance.

The axiomatic approach represents a firm basis on which design knowledge can be expanded in a systematic manner. The use of the axiomatic approach in concurrent engineering is expressed as the optimization of the interaction among functional, physical, and process domains to obtain overall improvements in the manufacturing process.

14.2.7 Parameter Variations in Design

Variational simulation analysis (VSA), (Craig, 1988a) is a commercially available computer program that integrates product and process design by determining the largest tolerances that can be used without lowering the quality of the product or impairing its functioning.

A common problem in a manufacturing operation is represented by the number of defective parts that is produced. The occurrence of defective parts depends on several factors, such as the tolerances in product design, assembly methods, assembly sequences, and so on, which are either determined by some functional requirements of the product or simply chosen using engineering experience at the design stage. Therefore, the design of a particular product can be greatly improved by estimating the number of defective parts that would be produced when a given combination of tolerances, specifications, assembly methods, and sequences are utilized. This information can be fed back to the design process so that corrective actions can be taken.

A common solution to the mismatch problem in assembly is to study and specify the tolerances and dimensions of the final product (Craig, 1988a). Thus, if all the subparts are within the tolerances set by this method, then the final assembly should build to specifications. This method, called the stacking method, requires very tight tolerances allowing that in the worse case, the part can still be assembled, but resulting in an increased cost to the overall operation.

VSA represents an alternative method to the one previously described. This computer program is based on the Monte Carlo analysis that uses a random-number generator and probability curves to help determine the percentage of nonconformance for any given dimensional characteristic and the factors that influence these irregularities (Craig, 1988a). For example, in the case of manufacturing, factors such as the variations in component properties, assembly methods, and assembly sequences are responsible for product variations.

To achieve a better result, the VSA may be combined with the Taguchi methods; for example, using the assembly-tolerance result of VSA as inputs to the Taguchi methods, production problems could be eliminated before designs came off the drawing board (Craig, 1988b). Furthermore, VSA can be used to do the preliminary experiments necessary to implement the Taguchi method without having to build costly prototypes and direct difficult experiments.

14.2.8 Group Technology (GT) for Concurrent Engineering

A great deal of research has been conducted to find ways to improve mass-production systems. The main reason for this is the chances of obtaining substantial savings due to the large amount of products produced. This is not the case in batch-production systems, which represents the majority of the world's production capability, where the number of products is 50 or less. To get similar improvement with this number of products, a change of concept or idea that modifies the hole process has to be found.

The theory behind GT indicates that various situations requiring decisions can be grouped together based on preselected, commonly shared attributes, and the decision that applies to one situation in the group will apply to all of them in that group. For this reason, the system can be looked at as a collection of batch-production systems forming a more "massive-production" type system, which can enjoy the low manufacturing cost associated with mass-production systems. The implementation of GT requires information from the manufacturing system to decide what products should belong to which group or family. This same information represents an opportunity for improving not only the manufacturing activity, but also other activities such as product design, process planning, purchasing, and so on. GT is a philosophy based on a smooth, continuous, and high-quality flow of products and information from the initial conception of a product until its delivery to the customer. In order to support this philosophy, data entry and utilization have to be well structured in databases, which increases the speed of response and the productivity of a manufacturing firm with less cost and better quality.

Another important element within the GT philosophy is people. The workers should be completely involved in the process and their knowledge should be captured in databases. The concept of quality is expressed as a measure of the employees performance. It is implemented using the notion of customer satisfaction, where the next activity in the product-development process is the customer of the previous one.

To have an effective database system, it has to be consistent, structured and selective. Inconsistency is one of the most common forms of failure of database systems. These databases contain the same data, but the data are not consistent among all of them causing mistrust among their users. The data structure is very important because it helps increase the efficiency for entering and retrieving information when huge amounts of data are processed. The selectiveness of the database comes from the fact that all information cannot be stored economically; therefore, a decision about what data to store should be made. One approach to the database-development problem is the use of the production-flow-analysis (PFA) technique, which by analyzing the similarities in the production routings of all the products, determines natural divisions among them that are used to group machines for processing groups of parts. PFA is based solely on the manufacturing process and does not take the parts characteristics into account. A modified method, consisting of three parts—data collection, data sorting, and data analysis—is also available. First, the minimum amount of data is collected, all the parts with identical process numbers and sequences are assigned identification numbers, and then parts and machines are grouped into families and production facilities. Another approach is the use of classification and coding (CC). Classification means to group things with the same specific characteristic, and coding permits the development of the database because the information can be handled by computers. The data are sorted in desired groups based on the code; comparisons and synthesis of information also take place from the logic of the data.

So far, GT has been described as a concept that helps simplify the manufacturing process by identifying similar characteristics in products, grouping them and establishing manufacturing machine groups or manufacturing cells to produce them. The applications of GT are separated in two groups: family formation and retrieval, and structured analysis and decision making. In the first group, design standardization is one of the most important applications. By retrieving previous design information, designers can reduce the development time, reduce the amount of designs, and built a standardized design process with the use of standard components. Also, in the first group, the creation of manufacturing cells is present. These production units are formed based on part families and many benefits are obtained by doing so: reduced queue, reduced inventory, improved product quality, reduction in scrap, easier scheduling, and so on. Within the second group, the process-planning process is sped up and the number of plans is reduced. Also, there is a continuous process of improvement for these plans because the previous experiences are recorded and validated over and over again. Benefits in the purchasing activities also have been reported due to the existence of product families that help obtain more discounts if parts are bought as families. This principle can be taken a little bit farther by organizing vendors and suppliers into families. There are many benefits that arise from having databases to support the decision-making process, such as improvement of cost estimating, increased productivity, reduced costs, increased products standardization, reduced setup time, better product-delivery performance, and improved plant efficiency.

GT helps organize all the activities of a firm in block form with an effective interface that make CE implementation much easier.

14.3 IMPLEMENTATION OF CONCURRENT ENGINEERING

Concurrent engineering is a very broad concept based on the integration of different disciplines in the development of a product and the control of its evolution along its life cycle. Strategies that serve as tools for CE are, for example, total quality control (TQC), just in time (JIT), computer-integrated manufacturing (CIM) and human resources. These strategies utilize some of the methods that were presented earlier in this chapter, which are directed toward the improvement of product quality with lower cost, better reliability, and good availability as a means to obtain a competitive advantage in the global market. None of these CE tools represents the best solution to the transformation that manufacturing firms have to suffer to assure their survival in the marketplace; this solution has to be tailored to each firm going through a conscious analysis of its status in the market and its internal situation. Beckman et al. (1990) presents a five-step approach to manufacturing strategy development. This approach can be extrapolated to CE implementation, by using the CE tools to achieve every defined task. The steps are as follows:

1. Start with the business strategy. More specifically, understand why customers will prefer your product or service over your competitor's. Factors that influence the customers' buying decisions include low product cost, high product quality, prompt product availability, and distinguishing product features.
2. Specify manufacturing's contribution to making customers choose your product instead of your competitor's.

3. Identify manufacturing tactics to execute the strategy (CE) tools. This requires understanding how to manage and control the people, processes, materials, and information needed to deliver products in a way that meets the objectives of the strategy.

4. Organize for manufacturing success. Organization design, including structure and performance measurement, must match strategic needs or success will be limited.

5. Measure the results and initiate further change. Strategies must be continually altered to meet the needs of a constantly changing environment. Feedback loops are critical to the continuous improvement process.

The preceding steps are general actions that if taken will help the implementation problem. Again, it is difficult to give more detailed steps for implementing manufacturing strategies because they depend on each particular case.

14.4 SUMMARY

The improvement of communication systems has made possible that companies from different locations all over the globe can compete with their products and technology for a piece of market. This world competition has caused the introduction of new manufacturing methodologies and optimization of all the activities related to product development to obtain a competitive advantage. Concurrent engineering is a concept that has to be practiced in one degree or another in a manufacturing firm if it wants to survive. The methods described in this chapter are only few of many ways of achieving world-class manufacturing status, which has to be maintained through constant revisions of the customers needs and inclusion of these attributes into the evolving (or new) products. Also, in the case of DFM, several approaches were given to find the most efficient and cost-effective product/process design, but it cannot be concluded which one is best. Therefore, practical problems should be solved using the different approaches to try to determine similarities, relative advantages, drawbacks, and situations for their application to establish which method (or combination of them) suits more to a specific product/process-design problem.

REVIEW QUESTIONS

14.1. Define concurrent engineering

14.2. Is concurrent engineering a new invention in the twentieth century? Some argue that before the Industrial Revolution, most merchandise was designed and fabricated by the same person, which defines a small-scale concurrent engineering enterprise. Do you agree? If you agree with the argument, explain when and how the invisible wall between design and manufacturing began.

14.3. Concurrent engineering is gaining popularity in manufacturing industries. Is the concurrent engineering approach applicable in service industries?

14.4. What are the major benefits of concurrent engineering?

14.5. Some contend that concurrent engineering reduces product-development time, which enables a company to meet market opportunity and market demand. Elaborate.

14.6. Explain in detail why the interfaces between each of the three spokes of the concurrent engineering model in Figure 14.1 are critical to the success of concurrent engineering.

14.7. Why is it desirable to involve suppliers in a concurrent engineering project? In what way can one involve suppliers in the concurrent engineering effort?

14.8. Most companies realize that it is crucial to discover what the customers want and need as early as possible in a product-development process. Suggest different ways to find out customer needs and wants.

14.9. Prepare a list of tools and techniques, engineering and otherwise, that can be used by a concurrent engineering team.

14.10. What is quality function deployment (QFD)? Compare QFD and the value engineering approach first introduced in General Electric in the 1960s.

14.11. Form a design team of three to four people to prepare a QFD chart for an overhead projector.

14.12. Are there any CAD systems better than another when it comes to conceptual design? What are they?

14.13. Search the literature and give three successful cases employing design axioms first introduced by Suh (1990).

14.14. Use Boothroyd and Dewhurst's Handbook to analyze an overhead slide projector.

REFERENCES/BIBLIOGRAPHY

AKAO, Y. (1990). *An Introduction to Quality Function Deployment: Integrating Customer Requirements into Product Design.* Cambridge, MA: Productivity Press.

BARRON, D. D. (1988). *Simultaneous Engineering at Delco Remy,* SME Technical Paper MM88-154. Dearborn, MI: Society of Manufacturing Engineers.

BECKMAN, S. L., W. A. BOLLER, S. A. HAMILTON, and J. W. MONROE (1990). *Using Manufacturing as a Competitive Weapon: The Development of a Manufacturing Strategy.* Strategic Manufacturing, Moody, P. Dow-Jones Irwin.

BOOTHROYD, G., and P. DEWHURST (1983a). *Design for Assembly—A Designers Handbook,* University of Massachusetts, Amherst, MA: Department of Mechanical Engineering.

———. (1983b). "Design For Assembly: Manual Assembly," *Machine Design.*

———. (1983c). "Design For Assembly: Selecting the Right Method," *Machine Design.*

———. (1984a). "Design For Assembly: Automatic Assembly," *Machine Design.*

———. (1984b). "Design for Assembly: Robots," *Machine Design.*

———. (1988a). "Product Design for Manufacture and Assembly," *SME Manufacturing Engineering,* 42–46.

———. (1988b). "Early Cost Estimating in Product Design," *Journal of Manufacturing Systems,* 7(3).

CHILTON, K. W., M. E. WARREN, and M. L. WEIDENBAUM, Eds. (1990). *American Manufacturing in a Global Market.* Kluwer.

COMPTON, W. D., Ed. (1988). *Design and Analysis of Integrated Manufacturing Systems*, National Academy Press.

CRAIG, M. (1988a). "Variation By Design," *Mechanical Engineering*, Vol. 100, pp. 52–54.

———. (1988b). "Predicting Design Variations," *Machine Design*, Vol. 60 pp. 109–112.

DEL LUCAS (1987). "Concurrent Product/Process Development," SME Technical Paper MM87-219. Dearborn, MI: Society of Manufacturing Engineers.

EL-GIZAWY, A. S., et al. (1993). "Concurrent Engineering with Quality Approach for Manufacturing Industry." ASME National Design Engineering Conference, 52, 143–149.

ETTLIE, J. E., and H. W. STOLL (1990). *Managing the Design-Manufacturing Process.* New York: McGraw-Hill.

———. (1990). *Effectively Implementing a Concurrent/Simultaneous Engineering Approach in Your Organization*, SME Technical Paper MM90-368. Dearborn, MI: Society of Manufacturing Engineers.

FOREMAN, J. W. (1989). *Gaining Competitive Advantage by Using Simultaneous Engineering to Integrate Your Engineering, Design, and Manufacturing Resources*, SME Technical Paper MM89-715. Dearborn, MI: Society of Manufacturing Engineers.

GRIFFIN, A. J., and J. R. HAUSER (1993). "The Voice of the Customer," *Marketing Science*, 12(1).

GUNN, T. G. (1987). *Manufacturing for Competitive Advantage.* Cambridge, MA: Ballinger.

HARTLEY, J. R. (1992). *Concurrent Engineering*, Cambridge, MA: Productivity Press.

HAUG, E. J., Ed. (1990). *Concurrent Engineering of Mechanical Systems.*

HAUSER, J. R., and D. CLAUSING (1988). "The House of Quality," *Harvard Business Review.*

ISHIKAWA, K. (1985). *What is Total Quality Control? The Japanese Way.* Englewood Cliffs, NJ: Prentice Hall.

KUTCHINSON, G. K. (1989). *Manufacturing Competitiveness in the 1990's*, SME Technical Paper MM89-356. Dearborn, MI: Society of Manufacturing Engineers.

MILLER, L. C. G. (1993). *Concurrent Engineering Design.* Dearborn, MI: Society of Manufacturing Engineers.

MIYAKAWA S., T. OHASHI, and M. IWATA, (1990). "The Hitachi New Assembly Evaluation Method (AEM)," *Transactions of NAMRI/SME.*

MOORE, W. L., and E. A. PESSEMIER (1995). *Product Planning and Management: Designing and Delivering Value.* New York: McGraw-Hill.

ORADY, E. A., and I. SHAREEF (1993). "Expert System Design Philosophy for Application of Simultaneous Engineering in Industry." ASME National Design Engineering Conference, DE. 52, pp. 151–157.

PUGH, S. (1990). *Total Design.* Wokingham, UK: Addison-Wesley.

RANKY, P. G. (1990). *Total Quality Control and JIT Management in CIM*, CIMware Limited.

ROSS, P. J. (1988). *Taguchi Techniques for Quality Engineering: Loss Function, Orthogonal Experiments, Parameter and Tolerance Design.* New York: McGraw-Hill.

ROY, R. (1990). *A Primer on the Taguchi Method.* New York: Van Nostrand Reinhold.

SHINA, S. G. (1994). *Successful Implementation of Concurrent Engineering Products and Processes.* New York: Van Nostrand Reinhold.

SNEAD, C. S. (1989). *Group Technology Foundation for Competitive Manufacturing.* New York: Van Nostrand Reinhold.

STOLL, H. W. (1986). "Design for Manufacture: An Overview," *ASME Applied Mechanics Reviews,* 39(9), 1356–1364.

SUH, N. P. (1990). *The Principles of Design.* Oxford University Press.

TAGUCHI, G., A. E. ELSAYED, and HSIANG, T. C. (1989). *Quality Engineering in Production Systems,* New York: McGraw-Hill.

TAGUCHI, G. (1981). *On-line Quality Control During Production,* Tokyo: Japanese Standards Association.

TERPENNY, J. P., and M. P. DEISENROTH (1992). "A Concurrent Engineering Framework: Three Basic Components," in *Proceedings of the Second International FAIM Conference.* Falls Church, VA: pp. 237–247.

WESLEY, A. C. (1989). *Simultaneous Engineering: What? Why? How?* SME Technical Paper MM89-493, Dearborn, MI: Society of Manufacturing Engineers.

15

Integrated Computer-Aided Manufacturing

15.1 INTRODUCTION

Today's industry competes in a truly international marketplace. Efficient transportation networks have created a "world market" in which we participate on a daily basis. For any industrial country to compete in this market, it must have companies that provide economic high-quality products to their customers in a timely manner. The importance of integrating product design and process design to achieve a design-for-production system cannot be overemphasized. However, even once a design is finalized, manufacturing industries must be willing to accommodate their customers by allowing last-minute engineering-design changes without affecting shipping schedules or altering product quality.

Most U.S.-based manufacturing companies look toward CAD/CAM and CIM to provide this flexibility in their manufacturing system. Today, the use of computers in manufacturing is common. Manufacturing systems are being designed that not only process parts automatically, but also move the parts from machine to machine and sequence the ordering of operations in the system. Figure 15.1 contains a plot of the economic regions of manufacturing. It should be noted that manual handcrafted goods will always have a market in the United States as well as abroad. This is also true of industrial products—there will continue to be a need for special one-of-a-kind items. The spectrum of one-of-a-kind goods through high-volume goods dictates that a variety of manufacturing methods be used to meet our various industrial needs. Some of these systems will look like the factories that our grandparents labored in, whereas others will take on a futuristic look. In the following sections, a discussion of flexible manufacturing systems is presented.

15.2 FLEXIBLE MANUFACTURING SYSTEMS

A flexible manufacturing system, or FMS as they are more commonly known, is a reprogrammable manufacturing system capable of producing a variety of products automatically. Since Henry Ford first introduced and modernized the transfer line, we have been able to perform a variety of manufacturing operations automatically. However,

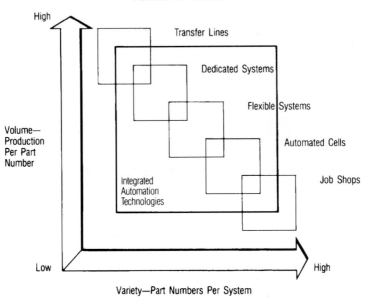

Figure 15.1   Volume versus variety regions for economic manufacturing. (Courtesy of Cincinnati Milacron.)

altering these systems to accommodate even minor changes in the product has been quite taxing. Whole machines might have to be introduced to the system while other machines or components are modified or retired to accommodate small changes in a product. In today's competitive marketplace, it is necessary to accommodate customer changes or the customer will find someone else who will accommodate the changes. Conventional manufacturing systems have been marked by one of two distinct features:

1. Job shop type systems were capable of producing a variety of product, but at a high cost.
2. Transfer lines could produce large volumes of a product at a reasonable cost, but were limited to the production of one, two, or very few different parts.

The advent of numerical control (NC) and robotics has provided us with reprogramming capabilities at the machine level with minimum setup time. NC machines and robots provide the basic physical building blocks for reprogrammable manufacturing systems.

15.2.1 FMS Equipment

15.2.1.1 Machines.   In order to meet the requirements of the definition of an FMS, the basic processing in the system must be automated. Because automation must be programmable in order to accommodate a variety of product-processing requirements, easily alterable as well as versatile machines must perform the basic processing.

For this reason, CNC turning centers (Fig. 15.2), CNC machining centers (Fig. 15.3), and robotic workstations (Fig. 15.4) comprise the majority of equipment in these systems. These machines are not only capable of being easily reprogrammed, but are also capable of accommodating a variety of tooling via a tool changer and tool-storage system. It is not unusual for a CNC machining center to contain 60 or more tools (mills, drills, boring tools, and so on), and for a CNC turning center to contain 12 or more tools (right-hand turning tools, left-hand turning tools, boring bars, drills, and so on). The automatic tool changer and storage capabilities of NC machines make them natural choices for material-processing equipment.

Parts must also be moved between processing stations automatically. Several different types of material-handling systems are employed to move these parts from station to station. The selection of the type of material-handling system is a function of several system features. The material-handling system, first, must be able to accommodate the load and bulk of the part and perhaps the part fixture. Large, heavy parts require large, powerful handling systems such as roller conveyors, guided vehicles, or track-driven vehicle systems. The number of machines to be included in the system and the layout of the machines also present another design consideration. If a single material handler is to move parts to all the machines in the system, then the work envelope of the handler must be at least as large as the physical system. A robot is normally only capable of addressing one or two machines and a load-and-unload station. A conveyor or automatic guided vehicle (AGV) system can be expanded to include miles of factory floor. The material-handling system must also be capable of moving parts from one machine to another in a timely manner. Machines in the system will be unproductive if they spend much of their time waiting for parts to be delivered by the material handler. If many parts are included in the system and they require frequent visits to machines, then the material-handling system must be capable of supporting these activities. This usually can be accommodated by using either a very fast handling device of by using several devices in parallel, for example, instead of using a single robot to move parts to all the machines in the system, a robot would only support a single machine.

15.2.1.2 Tooling and fixtures.   Versatility is the key to most FMSs, and as such, the tooling used in the system must be capable of supporting a variety of products or parts. The use of special forming tools in an FMS is not typical in practice. The contours obtained by using forming tools can usually be obtained through a contour-control NC system and a standard mill. The standard mill then can be used for a variety of parts rather than to produce a single special contour. An economic analysis of the costs and benefits of any special tooling is necessary to determine the best tooling combination. However, because NC machines have a limited number of tools that are accessible, very few special tools should be included.

One of the commonly neglected aspects of an FMS is the fixturing used. Because fixtures are part of the tooling of the system, one could argue that they should also be standard for the system. Work on creating "flexible fixtures" that could be used to support a variety of components has only recently begun. See Chapter 5. One unique aspect of many FMSs is that the part is also moved about the system in the fixture (or pallet fixture). Fixtures are made to the same dimensions so that the material-handling system can be specialized to handle a single geometry. Parts are located precisely on the

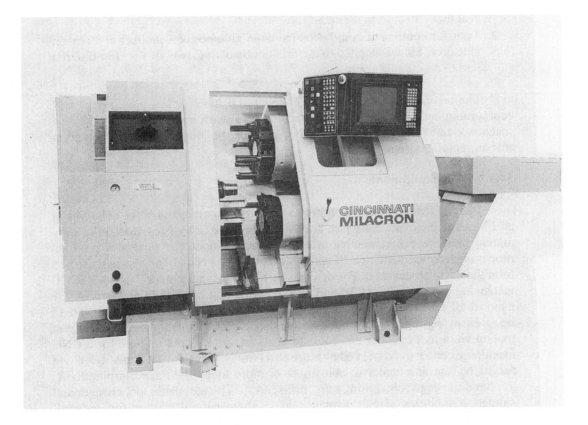

CINTURN Series 1400
4-Axis CNC Turning Centers

Brief Standard Specs

Models	1408C/1408U	1410C/1410U	1412C/1412U
Chuck Size	8"	10"	12"
Spindle rpm	40-4000	35-3500	30-3000
Thru Hole	2.06"	2.56"	3.15"
Spindle Type	A2-6	A2-6	A2-8
Horsepower	30 (50 opt.)	30 (50 opt.)	50
Z-Axis Travel	24"/44"	24"/44"	24"/44"
No. Turrets	2	2	2
No. Tools	16 OD/ID	16 OD/ID	16 OD/ID
Tailstock-Univ.	Heavy duty	Heavy duty	Heavy duty

Figure 15.2 Cincinnati Milacron Century CNC turning center. (Courtesy of Cincinnati Milacron.)

Figure 15.3 Cincinnati Milacron T-10 CNC machining center and specifications. (Courtesy of Cincinnati Milacron.)

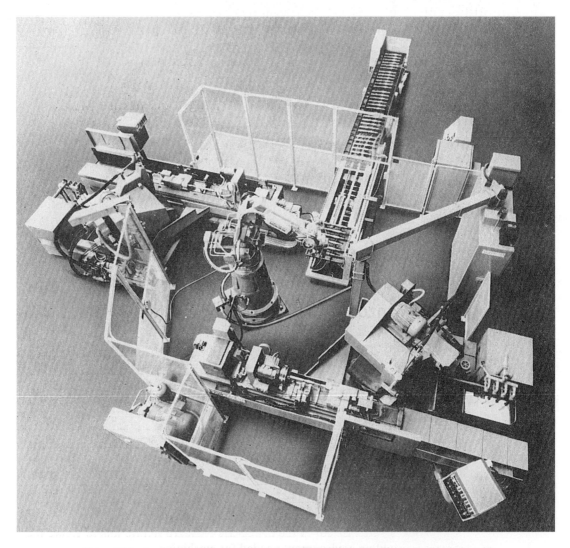

Figure 15.4 A robot-tended machining system. This integrated production cell is designed for cylindrical parts and can be the basis for thoughtful, progressive flexible automation. The two Milacron two-axis CNC step grinding machines are positioned back to back and offset. This allows full access to the front of each machine, and enables one stand-alone Milacron T³ Robot to automate loading and unloading of parts from a conveyor. Hydraulic footstocks are automatically actuated. This, and in-process gauging, makes the cell ideal for unattended operation during "lights out" shifts. (Courtesy of Cincinnati Milacron.)

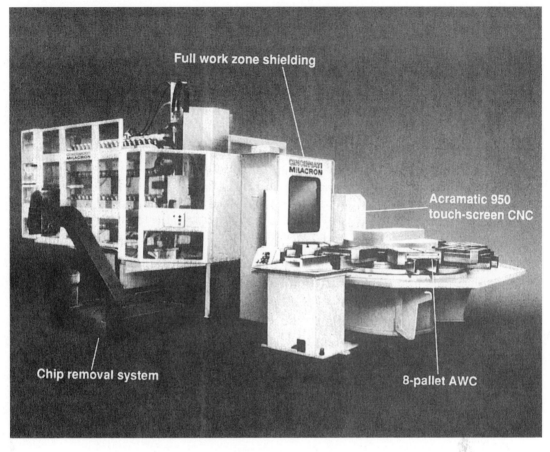

Figure 15.5   A CNC machining center with an eight-pallet workchanger. (Courtesy of Cincinnati Milacron.)

fixture and moved from one station to another on the fixture. Fixtures of this type are usually called pallet fixtures, or pallets (Fig. 15.5). Many of the pallet fixtures employed today have standard "T-slots" cut in them, and use standard fixture kits to create the part-locating and -holding environment needed for machining.

15.3 COMPUTER CONTROL OF FLEXIBLE MANUFACTURING SYSTEMS

15.3.1 FMS Architecture

An FMS is a complex network of equipment and processes that must be controlled via a computer or network of computers. In order to make the task of controlling an FMS more tractable, the system is usually divided into a task-based hierarchy. One of the standard hierarchies that have evolved is the National Institute of Standards and Technology (NIST) factory-control hierarchy. (NIST was formerly the National Bureau of Standards, NBS.) This hierarchy consists of five levels and is illustrated in Figures 15.6 and 15.7. The system consists of physical machining equipment at the lowest level of the system. Workstation equipment resides just above the process level and provides integration and interface functions for the equipment. For instance, pallet fixtures and programming elements are part of the workstation. The workstation typically provides both man–machine interface as well as machine–part interface. Off-line programming such as APT for NC or AML for a robot resides at the workstation level.

The cell is the unit in the hierarchy where interaction between machines becomes part of the system. The cell controller provides the interface between the machines and material-handling system. As such, the cell controller is responsible for sequencing and scheduling parts through the system. At the shop level, integration of multiple cells occurs as well as the planning and management of inventory. The facility level is the place in the hierarchy where the master production schedule is constructed and manufacturing resource planning is conducted. Ordering materials, planning inventories, and analyzing business plans are part of the activities that affect the production system. Poor business and manufacturing plans will incapacitate the manufacturing system just as surely as the unavailability of a machine.

15.3.2 FMS Scheduling and Control

Flexible manufacturing systems, like other manufacturing systems, can differ significantly in complexity. This complexity is not only determined by the number of machines and the number of parts resident in the system, but also by the complexity of parts and

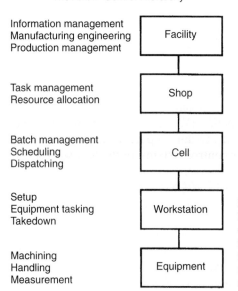

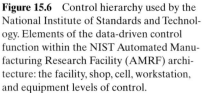

Figure 15.6 Control hierarchy used by the National Institute of Standards and Technology. Elements of the data-driven control function within the NIST Automated Manufacturing Research Facility (AMRF) architecture: the facility, shop, cell, workstation, and equipment levels of control.

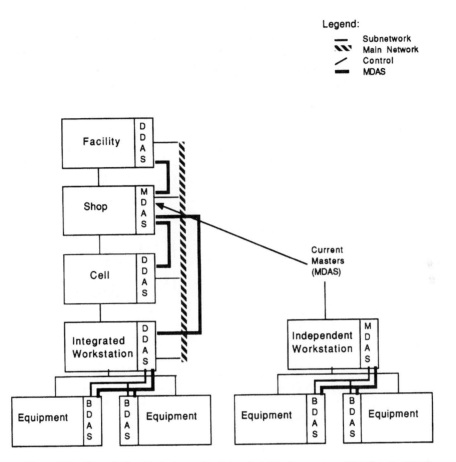

Figure 15.7   The relationship between the data-administration systems (DAS) in the NIST architecture: (1) the topologies of the Integrated Manufacturing Data Administration System (IMDAS) data-administration system; (2) the network data-communication network; (3) the hierarchical system of data-driven control; data preparation is implied in (4) the facility level of control.

control requirements of the specific equipment. Some FMSs require only a simple programmable controller to regulate the flow of parts through the system, whereas others require sophisticated computer control systems. In the following sections, examples of FMSs and their control attributes are presented.

The most simple FMS consists of a processing machine, a load/unload area, and a material handler (a one-machine system is the most simple FMS that can be constructed). This system is illustrated in Figure 15.8. Operation of this system consists of loading the part(s) that move down a conveyor to the machine. Once the part is loaded onto the machine, the robot is retracted to a "safe position" and the machining begins.

Although this is a very simple system, it illustrates several interesting design and control decisions that must be considered. If only a single part is to be processed in the

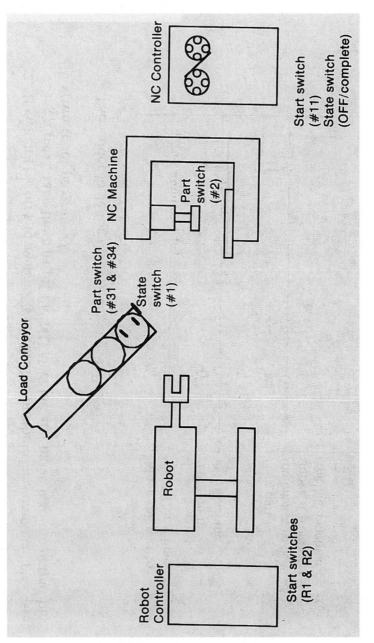

Figure 15.8 A simple one-machine FMS.

system, a minimum number of switches and sensors are necessary for the system. One requirement of the system is that the parts on the conveyor all have to be oriented in the same way. This is required so that the robot can pick up the part and deliver it to the NC machine in the same orientation every time. A proximity switch or microswitch is required at the end of the conveyor to detect when a part is resident, and on the machine for the same purpose.

This system is one that a simple programmable logic controller can easily control, as outlined in Chapter 7. The logic for the system is as follows:

1. If a part is resident at the end of the conveyor (switch 1 is on) and no part is on the NC machine (switch 2 is off), then pick up the part on the conveyor and move it to the NC machine and retract the robot to a safe point (run robot program 1). After the program is complete and switch 2 senses that the part is correctly positioned, start the NC machine (turn on relay M_1). While the machine is running, a switch signal from the NC machine, switch #2, will be on.

2. If switch 11 is off and switch # 2 is on (the NC machine has completed processing a part), take the part off the NC machine and move it to the output bin (run robot program 2).

The ladder logic for this system is as follows.

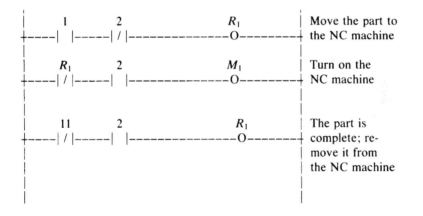

As can be seen from the diagram, the control of the system is very straightforward. Inherent in the control are several programming considerations such as the clamping mechanism for part holding can be turned on and off in an NC part program and more than one robot program can be resident on the robot controller. A Gantt chart of the flow is shown in Figure 15.9. Inherent in the figure is that there is always a part available at the load station and that there are no machine breakdowns.

If the same system were to be used to process a variety of parts, several changes in the control would be required. First, either several robot programs for handling the parts would be necessary or a common part pallet would be necessary for gripping the

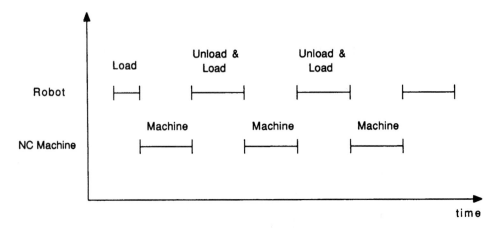

Figure 15.9   A Gantt chart of the one-machine FMS.

part. For the sake of illustration, we assume that a common pallet is used to fixture all parts. It also will be necessary to detect which part is resident at each station. Part identification is usually performed by a bar-code reader or by using a set of switches that each pallet will trigger. Each pallet type (and sometimes each pallet) then can be identified by the combination of switches that are active. For instance, if four optical switches are used for this process and the switches are off when light is unobstructed, then one pallet could have four tabs used to obstruct the light and this pallet would be identified by four closed (on) switches. Sixteen part types could be identified using four 2-state switches (2^4). For our example, these switches are numbered 31–34 (Fig. 15.8).

    The logic is the same as for the first example, except now a variety of different part programs have to be executed to machine each different part type. We assume that we have a CNC machine capable of storing and recalling the necessary part programs. (Otherwise, we would have to either control the system with a computer or front end the NC machine with a computer.) Instead of simply starting an NC program already resident in memory, the programmable logic controller ladder logic inspects each switch setting and indicates which program should be run. This logic is as follows:

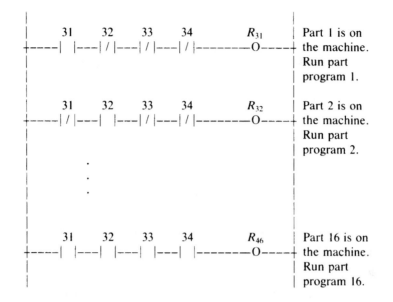

One-machine systems are the most simple case for FMSs. These systems usually can be controlled with simple switches and programmable controllers. As more machines are added, the difficulty of controlling the system increases dramatically, unless a single part type is used in the system at any time. This is illustrated using the FMS shown in Figure 15.10. The system consists of two CNC machines, a robot, a load station, and an output bin. Parts enter the system on a conveyor in a prespecified order that cannot be altered once the parts are on the conveyor.

For the first example system, a single part routing is assumed, as shown in Figure 15.10. The control logic for the system is summarized as follows:

1. If a part is at the end of the conveyor (switch 1 is on) and no part is on machine 1 (switch 11 is off), move the part from the conveyor to the machine (run robot program 1).
2. If a part is finished at machine 1 (switch 11 is on and switch 12 is off) and machine 2 is empty (switch 21 is off), move the part from machine 1 to machine 2.
3. If the part on machine 2 is complete (switch 21 is on and switch 22 is off), remove the part from the machine and place it in the output bin.

The ladder logic to control this system is as follows:

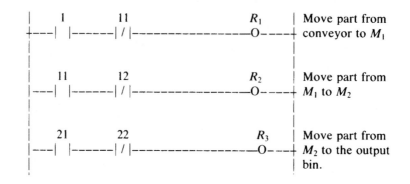

As can be seen from the ladder logic, the system is very easy to control with a single part.

If two parts are allowed to enter the system in a random order, as shown in Figure 15.11, the control of the system is increased significantly. The first characteristic of the system that is noted is that part identification is necessary. Again, if the parts are of different size, different robot programs may be required unless the parts are on a common-size pallet fixture. We once again make this assumption. Two state switches are required on each machine: one to detect if a part is on the machine and one

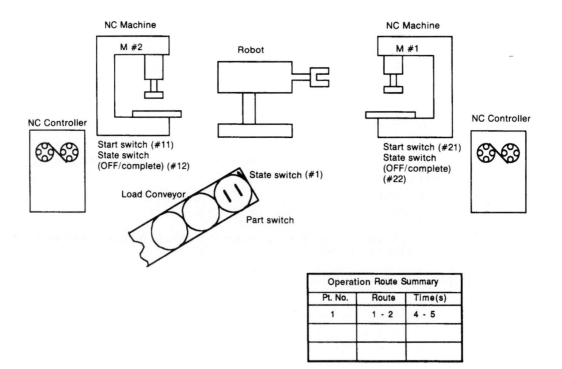

Figure 15.10   A two-machine FMS.

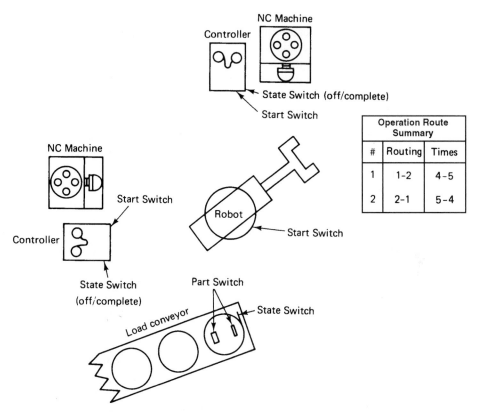

Figure 15.11   A two-machine two-part FMS.

to determine whether it is part 1 or 2. If all part 1's are in the system, the control of the system is the same as it was previously. If all part 2's are in the system, a similar control is required, changing the routing from machine 1 to machine 2 and vice versa. However, if the parts are allowed to be mixed in the system, some interesting phenomena take place. If part 1 is in the system and at machine 1 and part 2 is at the load point on the conveyor, part 2 can be moved to machine 2 and processing can begin. However, once this move is made, the system "locks" or "deadlocks." Part 1 must be moved to machine 2, which is occupied by part 2. When part 2 is complete, it must be moved to machine 1, which is also occupied. Deadlocking occurs in many operational FMSs and can only be remedied by human intervention. In order to eliminate dead-locking, one of two fixes are required: (1) either a queueing station is necessary or (2) both parts are not allowed in the system at the same time.

    In general, in order to eliminate deadlocking by adding queueing stations and if n parts are allowed in the system, then $n - 1$ queueing stations will be required to ensure that blocking does not occur. Part routing can reduce this number to zero; however, under the most severe routing conditions, $n - 1$ queueing stations are necessary. Care should be taken before a system designer arbitrarily adds queueing stations to the system, because if many different parts are allowed to enter a complex system, then the material handling system can dedicate a significant portion of its time to simply moving parts to and from these queueing stations and tie up the system. Deadlocking will be discussed more fully later in the chapter.

For our example, we use both a queueing station and then a control policy that does not allow multiple-part types in the system. For the system with a queueing station, we employ the following logic. First, if only one part type is in the system, the system control is as previously described. If mixed parts are in the system, the following logic is employed:

1. If part 1 is on machine 1 and part 2 is at the load position on the conveyor, then load a part from the conveyor to machine 2.
2. If part 2 is on machine 2 and part 1 is on the load position on the conveyor, then load a part from the conveyor to machine 1.

The processing times are given as part of the figure, and for our example, we assume that 1 min. of handling time is required for each robot operation. The Gantt chart of the system's operation is given in Figure 15.12. The Gantt chart assumes that parts are batched in groups of 2, that is, two part 1's are followed by two part 2's, and so on. It should be noted that the completion of five parts requires 44 time units given the control strategy and the additional queueing station.

The same system also can be run without a queue if the control does not allow the system to lock. To include this mechanism into the illustrated system, only a single part type is allowed in the system at any one time. It should be noted that this strategy does not always work and that a single part type can cause locking. The characteristic that indicates when locking *can* occur is that the network graph of the system forms a closed graph. The graph for this system is illustrated in Figure 15.13. Note that whenever a

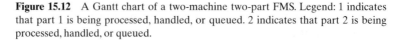

```
                |
                |1    11      11      12      22   212   12     211
       Robot    |------------------------------------------------------------
                | 1111   1111                      2222  1111  2222  1111
     Machine 1  |------------------------------------------------------------
                |      11111   11111  22222  22222       11111    111
     Machine 2  |------------------------------------------------------------
                |111111222222222222222222222222221111111111111111111112222
       Load     |------------------------------------------------------------
                |                                        22222
       Queue    |------------------------------------------------------------
     (finished) |         1       1        2          21
                |------------------------------------------------------------
                0     5    10     15    20    25    30    35    40    45
```

Figure 15.12   A Gantt chart of a two-machine two-part FMS. Legend: 1 indicates that part 1 is being processed, handled, or queued. 2 indicates that part 2 is being processed, handled, or queued.

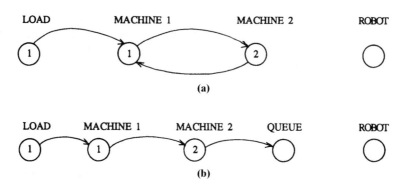

Figure 15.13   Network graph of a two-machine two-part FMS-system flow. (a) Part 1 at machine 1 and part 2 at machine 2. (b) Part 1 at machine 1 and part 2 at machine 2 and a queue.

closed circuit of arcs occurs on the network, a potential for locking occurs. When an additional queueing station is added to the system, the continuity of the circuit is broken.

Under this set of control conditions, one would expect that parts would flow through the system at a somewhat slower rate. The part flow for this system is illustrated in the Gantt chart of Figure 15.14. Note in the Gantt chart that it takes 50 time units to complete the fifth part.

For the system given, the additional queueing station improves the production rate in the system. This, however, assumes that material-handling time is constant for all part to machine operations (an assumption that would most probably *not* be valid for most real systems), and that the material-handling time is less than 25% of the average operation time. If the material-handling time were larger, the production rate may not favor having a queueing station, but favor the alternate control. Each system and part

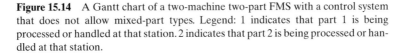

Figure 15.14   A Gantt chart of a two-machine two-part FMS with a control system that does not allow mixed-part types. Legend: 1 indicates that part 1 is being processed or handled at that station. 2 indicates that part 2 is being processed or handled at that station.

mix set of conditions have to be analyzed to determine the appropriate strategy. In addition, the batching of parts and the strategy of batching also affect the performance of the system. Either a Gantt chart of the system or a simulation of the system should be constructed before a system design and control decisions are made.

15.3.3 Flow Systems

Many FMSs are designed to produce part families that produce a *flow-system* environment rather than a *job-shop* environment. When a flow system is in order, it constrains the flow and control of the system significantly. Figure 15.15 contains an illustration of a typical flow FMS. In the system, all parts must follow the same routing. For the three-machine system illustrated, parts enter the system at the load station and are then moved to the first NC machine by robot 1. Robot 2 then moves the part from machine 1 to machine 2, and so forth. The machines need not perform an operation on all parts, but all parts must visit all machines.

The control of flow systems is usually easily accomplished, providing that a sensor to detect what part type is at each station and the NC machines and robots can store as many part programs as parts are allowed in the system. The logic control of the system is summarized as follows:

1. If a part is at the load station and machine 1 is idle, move the part to machine 1.
2. If a part is resident at machine m and complete and machine $m + 1$ is idle, move the part to machine $m + 1$.
3. If a part is at a machine and unprocessed, process that part.
4. If a part is at the last machine and complete, move it to the unload station.

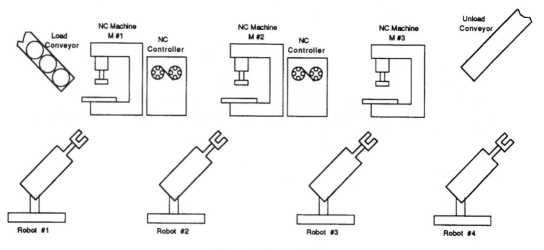

Figure 15.15 A FMS flo system.

From the description of the control, it should be noted that additional machines can be added to the system by simply adding one or two lines of ladder logic. Fairly large flow systems can be controlled using reasonable basic programmable controllers.

15.3.4 Indirect Addressing FMSs

Each of the systems illustrated up to now have been direct-address material-handling systems (systems that direct parts to specific machines rather than around a system). In many ways, indirect-addressing systems are easier to control. Figure 15.16 illustrates some different design alternatives for an identical set of machines. Figure 15.16(a) illustrates the system as a direct-address robot-handled system with no queueing stations (pallet exchangers). Figure 15.16(b) illustrates the same machines with a one-pallet queueing station in front of each machine. Figure 15.16(c) illustrates the system with a recirculating conveyor system to handle part flow in the system. One interesting aspect of the conveyor system is that the conveyor can be used as a queueing station for parts in the system. In fact, the conveyor will queue as many parts as can physically fit on it.

The conveyor system illustrated shows pop-ups (transfer mechanisms) at the corners, which are used to change the direction of part flow in the system. Pop-ups are also used to direct the parts to the individual machines. The control for this system can be summarized as follows:

1. When a part reaches the end of each corner pop-up, activate the pop-up to change the part-flow direction.
2. When a part reaches a machine pop-up, if the part is to be routed to that machine and if the machine is idle, activate the pop-up.
3. When a part reaches the end of the load conveyor, if the section of conveyor in front of it is clear of any parts, push the part onto the conveyor.
4. When a part reaches the unload station, if the part is finished, activate the pop-up and remove the part from the system.

In order to implement the control of this system, a number of sensors and switches have to be installed. However, the implementation of the system and control of the system are rather straightforward. From the previous control description, one should be able to envision the ladder logic of the system. The switches to determine the "whens," "ifs," and "ands" would have to be installed and numbered; otherwise, the task is rather direct.

15.3.5 More Complex FMSs

Certain system characteristics eventually make system control using a programmable logic controller impossible. To this point, we have assumed that adequate memory existed in the CNC machine to store all necessary part programs. As the number of parts and the associated part programs increase, eventually, the controller limit will be

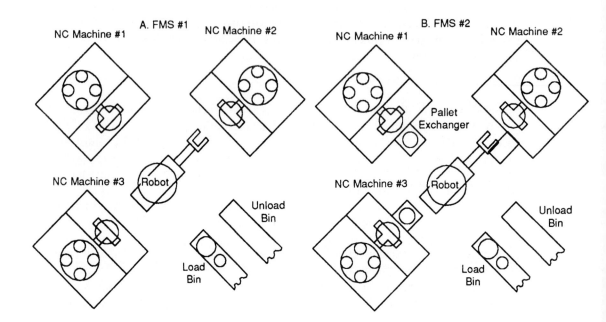

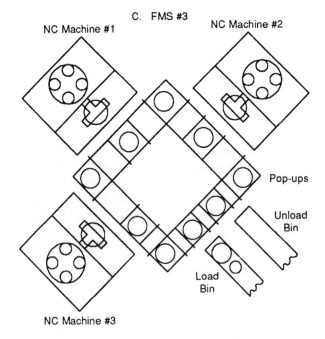

Figure 15.16 A FMS for the illustration of complex control.

exceeded. When this occurs, additional tape cassettes can be added or the individual machine can be front ended with some type of computer to download the required part programs. If a single computer is used to download part programs to a variety of NC machines, this system is referred to as a direct numerical-control (DNC) system. This computer also can (but need not) be used to download instructions to the material-handling-system equipment. The ladder logic that was used to control the systems previously described contains the logic used to sequence (as in scheduling) the machines in the system. Ladder logic is essentially the simplest form of a state table, and eventually the number of states in a system can become so large that the control using this state philosophy becomes intractable. This is illustrated in the following section.

Figure 15.17 contains the same system illustrated in Figure 15.16(a) with additional routing information. Table 15.1 contains a summary of material-handling times

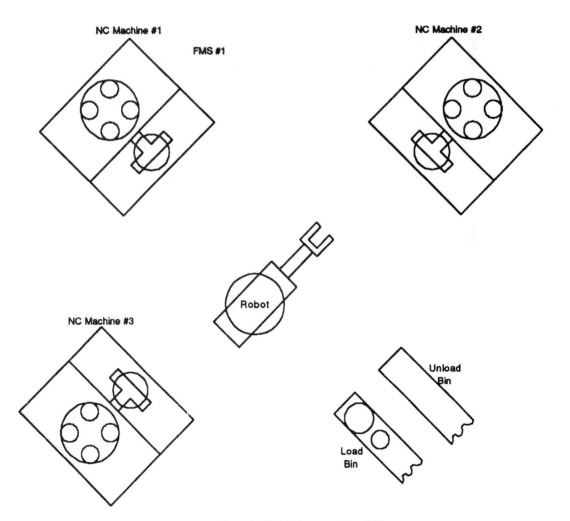

Figure 15.17   A three-machine FMS.

TABLE 15.1 TABLE OF ROBOT-HANDLING TIMES FOR FMS 1

From	To	Time
Load	Machine 1	5
Load	Machine 2	3
Load	Machine 3	2
Machine 1	Machine 2	2
Machine 1	Machine 3	2
Machine 1	Unload	5
Machine 2	Machine 3	5
Machine 2	Unload	2
Machine 3	Unload	3

for various robot tasks in the system. Note that the material-handling times for moves between each of the machines are not identical. It also should be noted that the handling time from machine 1 to machine 3 is the same as the handling time from machine 3 to machine 1, and that if a robot finishes a handling assignment at machine 3 and the next move is from machine 1 to machine 2, the robot must first move from machine 3 to machine 1. For this system, the state of the robot in terms of its position as well as its status (busy if idle) is also important. The five part routings shown in Table 15.2 are also used in this example. Note that a part can revisit a machine.

With five parts in the system and three machines, the system, by most standards, would be still considered a reasonably simple FMS. From the part routings, note that the system will dead-lock for several part/machine combinations. This dead-locking must be avoided by constructing an appropriate control strategy. Rather than summarize the control, a partial state table of the control for the system is shown in Table 15.3.

Several interesting aspects of the table and system should be noted. The variables used to describe the robot indicate which machine the robot is currently directed toward. This is necessary to plan the next activity. In addition to noting the part or direction state of the equipment, it is also necessary to depict whether the process is complete or still in process. The system response (action) to a set of conditions (states) is indicated in the table. These responses can be a chain of activities, as noted in the table.

In analyzing the equipment, note that the robot can be at any of the five stations in the system and be either busy or idle at each station. This implies that the robot position is discrete and there are 10 discrete states for the robot. At each of the machines,

TABLE 15.2 PART ROUTINGS FOR FMS 1

Part No.	Routing	Times
1	L–1–2–3–U	0–4–5–3–0
2	L–3–2–U	0–6–3–0
3	L–2–1–2–U	0–3–4–4–0
4	L–1–3–2–U	0–2–5–2–0
5	L–3–U	0–7–0

TABLE 15.3   A PARTIAL STATE TABLE OF THE CONTROL FOR THE 3-MACHINE 5-PART FMS

	System status				
Robot	Machine 1	Machine 2	Machine 3	Load	Action
L^a	0	0	0	1	$L \rightarrow M_1$
$M_1{}^a$	0	0	0	1	$M_1 \rightarrow L$
					$L \rightarrow M_1$
$M_2{}^a$	0	0	0	1	$M_2 \rightarrow L$
					$L \rightarrow M_1$
$M_3{}^a$	0	0	0	1	$M_3 \rightarrow L$
					$L \rightarrow M_1$
L	1,1	0	0	1	Wait
L	$\underline{1}^b$,1	0	0	1	$L \rightarrow M_1$
					$M_1 \rightarrow M_2$
L	3,2	0	0	1	Wait
L	$\underline{3,2}$	0	0	1	$L \rightarrow M_1$
					$M_1 \rightarrow M_2$
	.				
	.				
	.				
$\underline{M_3}$	3,2	$1,2^c$	1,3	4	Wait

[a]L denotes that the robot is currently directed at the load station. M_1 = machine 1; M_2 = machine 2; M_3 = machine 3.

[b]Underlined entries indicate that the operation is complete.

[c]1,2 indicates that part 1, operation 2 is currently being performed at that station.

a 0 indicates that no part is resident at the machine. A machine can have a part resident with an operation number currently in process also indicated. For the parts and machines noted in this system, machine 1 can be

1. idle: 0
2. busy with part 1: 1,1
3. finished with part 1: $\underline{1,1}$
4. busy with part 3: 3,1
5. finished with part 3: $\underline{3,1}$
6. busy with part 4: 4,1
7. finished with part 4: $\underline{4,1}$

In total, there are seven possible states for machine 1. Machine 2 has 11 possible states and machine 3 has 9 possible states. The load station can have 6 possible states (idle or empty is also possible). In all, there are 41,580 possible states for this simple system. This state table also reflects a reduced set of possible combinations because some part routings do not allow certain parts to visit certain machines.

It is not difficult to see that as the number of parts and machines in the system increases, the control of the system becomes very complex. Because of the requirements of constructing such state tables and the appropriate responses, procedural, or rule-based, control systems are much more desirable. Unfortunately, employing simple procedures or rules can result in the system deadlocking. In the following section, an expert-system-based control architecture to control FMSs is discussed.

INTERMEDIATE SECTION

15.4 THE GENERAL SHOP-FLOOR CONTROL PROBLEM

Shop-floor control for discrete part manufacturing has been widely described by many researchers (Albus, Barbera, and Nagel, 1981; Jones and McLean, 1986; Naylor and Volz, 1987; Duffie and Piper, 1987; Mettala, 1989; Joshi, Wysk, and Jones, 1990; Senehi et al., 1991; Smith, 1992). These descriptions have led to several frameworks to solve the overall shop-floor control problem. Many of these frameworks have been called control architectures, control structures, control models, and so on. Examples include centralized control, hierarchical control, heterarchical control, and hybrid control. However, none of these provides an adequate description of the *general* shop-floor control problem. Consequently, at best, these structures provide a solution to a single instance or a set of similar instances of the general problem.

Davis and Jones (1989) suggest that "The key to resolving these [integration] issues lies in a better understanding of each manufacturing function and how it is related to other manufacturing functions. Once we have this understanding, we can then address the questions involving the best architecture for a given manufacturing environment." We agree with this assessment and include that it is premature to describe solutions to specific instances of the shop-floor control problem, and suggest that they are of little generalizable value without first creating a formal functional description of the general problem. In this section, we will present a framework of the general shop-floor control problem. An important property of this framework is that it is independent of the methodologies used to solve the scheduling, planning, and implementation problems.

The control system and related models that are described in this section were developed for discrete manufacturing systems such as machining systems. The control system that we are working toward is intended to operate with automated equipment such as NC machines or robots; however, human-assisted or manual workstations also can be included if the human responds to prompts and commands (via a CRT, for example) in a deterministic (well-behaved) manner as the equipment would respond. In this case, the human is transparent to the other portions of the control system. Similarly, the processing equipment is assumed to be connected by an automated material-transport system, such as an AGV or conveyor system that transports items singly or in batches between the individual pieces of equipment; yet, a human parts mover could be substituted. Although the framework presented is not dependent on these assumptions, they will simplify the presentation.

15.4.1 Shop-Floor Control

A shop consists of several pieces of manufacturing equipment that are used to process, transport, and store *items*. In this case, an *item* can be a part, raw material, a tool, a fixture, or any other object that moves through the shop. The equipment includes NC machine tools, robots, conveyors, automated guided vehicles, automated storage systems, and so on. In order to process a part on a piece of equipment, a set of other items also might be required (e.g., specific cutting tools or fixtures), depending on the operation. Furthermore, between processing tasks, some or all of these items must be transported between the different pieces of equipment. The general shop-floor control problem in this environment can be illustrated, as shown in Figure 15.18. This figure shows the shop-floor control system (SFCS) as a black-box entity that receives inputs from an external (business) system(s) and generates the device-specific instructions necessary to enact the individual manufacturing tasks. In this section, we will describe the functions performed by the black box. As shown in Figure 15.18, the primary inputs to the SFCS are the *production requirements,* which describe the parts to be manufactured, and the *resources,* which describe the shared resources (items) to be used by the equipment within the shop.

Based on these inputs (which are described in more detail in the following paragraphs), the SFCS must generate a set of individual equipment-processing instructions necessary to manufacture and transport the parts specified in the production requirements. These instructions include, for example, RS-274 instructions (or CLDATA) for NC machines, VAL II, AML, or Cartesian coordinates for robots, a load/unload station, and path descriptions for AGVs, and so on. The specific format of the instructions will depend on the manufacturer/model of the equipment within the shop. Moreover, this set of individual instructions must be sequenced so that it provides a "good," or it is hoped optimal, throughput, equipment utilization,

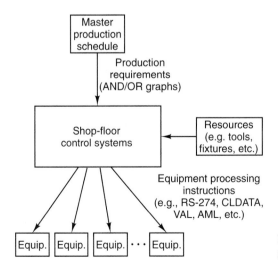

Figure 15.18 Input/output diagram for the general shop-floor control problem.

or other measure, based on some performance criteria. Note, however, that we are looking for *a* set of processing instructions rather than *the* set of processing instructions, highlighting the possible existence of alternative processing routes for parts. Also note that the term *generate* as used here in the context of equipment instructions can mean on-line creation, database retrieval, or some combination of both.

The *production requirements* input describes the technical and administrative requirements for the parts to be manufactured in the shop. The production requirements are provided by the master production schedule, the MRP system, or whatever system is used for shopwide planning and loading. The technical requirements include the processing requirements and any special handling and/or environmental requirements that affect the parts. The processing requirements for a part are specified by the *process plan,* which includes the valid part routings with the associated tooling and fixturing requirements. A process-plan representation standard similar to the ISO TC184/SC4/WG3/P11 representation standard or ALPS (Catron and Ray, 1991) is used (Joshi, Mettala, and Wysk, 1992; Cho et al., 1993). These process-plan graphs define the alternative tasks and sequence requirements for the specific equipment within the shop.

Based on this structure, we define $P = \{P_1, P_2, \ldots, P_n\}$ as a set of *n* process plans (1 for each of *n* parts), where $P_i = <V_i, E_i>$, for $i = 1,2, \ldots, n$, is the process-plan graph for part *i*. V_i is a finite set of nodes whose elements represent the individual processing steps for the part. E_i is a finite set of arcs whose elements represent precedence among processing steps. Unlike the traditional graph structure, there are two types of junctions connecting arcs and nodes in AND/OR graphs. OR junctions represent the typical case where *any one* arc within the junction may be taken out of the node. AND junctions represent the case where *all* arcs must be taken, but the sequence is unspecified (Joshi et al., 1992). So OR junctions present alternative *operations* and AND junctions present alternative *sequences* of fixed operations.

The business requirements included in the master production schedule (MPS) include due dates, priorities, and batch sizes for the parts. The SFCS uses these requirements to plan and schedule the production. The business requirements also provide some general scheduling philosophy/criteria to guide the SFCS. This philosophy is used by the SFCS to select from alternative performance measures.

The process-plan representation is demonstrated using the relatively simple part (a bracket) shown in Figure 15.19. The operation summary for the part is shown in Table 15.4. The operations summary indicates the required processes along with the equipment, tooling, and fixturing required to perform the processes. It should be noted that operations 5a and 6a are alternative processes that can be used to finish the holes shown on the part (the holes are rough drilled and then either reamed or bored to create the finish). This operation summary is based on a manufacturing workstation, which includes an NC drill, an NC machining center, and an industrial robot for loading/unloading the machines (as shown in Figure 15.20). In the table, multiple lines for an operation represent alternatives for processing that operation. For example, operation 3 (twist drill hole 1) either can be performed by the machining center, or by the drill and using either fixture 2 or fixture 3.

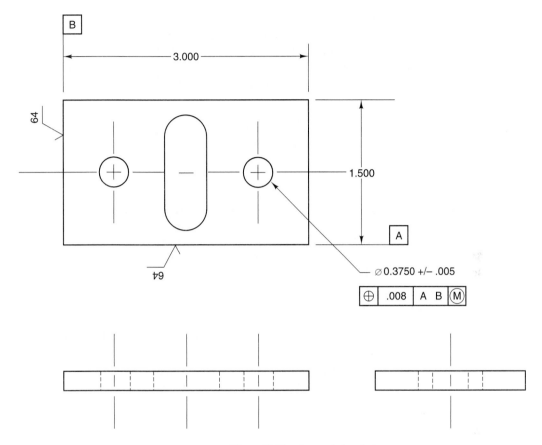

Figure 15.19 A sample bracket.

Figure 15.21 shows the feature-precedence graph for the example part. For this part, the only feature precedents are that the holes be rough drilled before they are finished (reamed or bored). In the general case, there will be significantly more feature interactions. The important point here is that the representation not only represents precedence between operations, but also alternatives where applicable. These alternatives allow the planning and scheduling functions to incorporate up-to-date information when making processing decisions.

The production control requirements include due dates, priorities, and batch sizes for the parts. The SFCS uses these requirements to plan and schedule the production. The administrative requirements also provide some general scheduling philosophy to guide the SFCS. As an example, one general scheduling philosophy might be that meeting external customer due dates is more important than achieving high equipment utilizations. This general philosophy is used by the SFCS to select from alternative performance measures in the detailed scheduling phase.

TABLE 15.4 OPERATION TASK AND RESOURCE SUMMARY FOR BRACKET ARRANGED BY FEATURE

Operation	Description	Feature	Feature spec.	Time (est.)	Tooling	Machine	Fixture
1	Side mill	Locate surf. A	Mill face A	0.6 min	1.0" end mill	Mach. Ctr.	Fxt F#1 Fxt F#2
2	Side mill	Locate surf. B	Mill face B	0.35 min	1.0" end mill	Mach. Ctr.	Fxt F#1 Fxt F#2
3	Twist drill	Hole #1	Rough drill hole #1	0.33 min	0.3595" drill	Mach. Ctr. Drill	Fxt F#2 Fxt F#3
5	Ream	Hole #1	Finish hole #1	0.25 min	0.375" ream	Mach. Ctr. Drill	Fxt F#2 Fxt F#3
5a	Bore	Hole #1	Finish hole #1	0.34 min	0.375"bore	Mach. Ctr. Drill	Fxt F#2 Fxt F#3
4	Twist drill	Hole #2	Rough drill hole #2	0.33 min	0.3595" drill	Mach. Ctr. Drill	Fxt F#2 Fxt F#3
6	Ream	Hole #2	Finish hole #2	0.25 min	0.375" ream	Mach. Ctr. Drill	Fxt F#2 Fxt F#3
6a	Bore	Hole #2	Finish hole #2	0.34 min	0.375" bore	Mach. Ctr. Drill	Fxt F#2 Fxt F#3
7	Slot mill	Slot #1	Mill slot #1	0.76 min	0.5" end mill	Mach. Ctr.	Fxt F#1 Fxt F#2

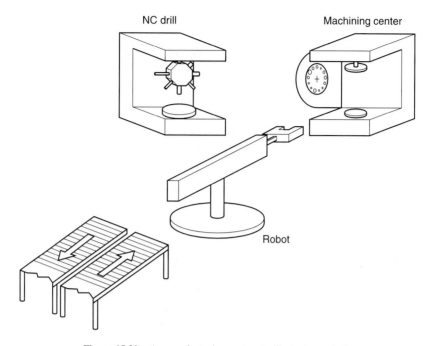

Figure 15.20   A manufacturing system to illustrate control.

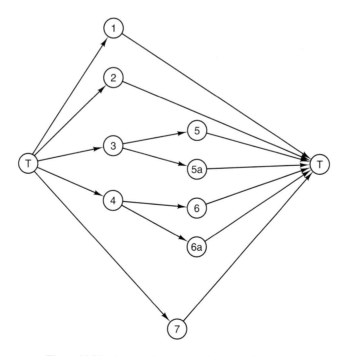

Figure 15.21   A precedence graph for a sample bracket.

The *resources* input describes the resources that are shared by all of the equipment within the shop. These resources include (but are not limited to) tooling, fixturing, maintenance, and so on. Material-transport and -processing equipment are not included in this input, even though these devices are shared resources from the point of view of the parts. Instead, this equipment is defined in a *factory model* (as described in what follows:) that is used to develop the SFCS. This distinction is made because the equipment is *controllable* and essentially permanent, whereas the shared resources are nonpermanent or perishable, and the individual requirements for these resources depend on the parts specified in the production requirements. Therefore, the availability of the nonpermanent resources (tools, fixtures, and so on) will change over a shorter time horizon than the availability of permanent resources (equipment), and we would like to create a control system independent of changes to nonpermanent resource availability. In other words, introduction of new pallets, fixtures, cutting tools, and so on, should not mandate extensive changes in the control system.

We define $R = \{R_1, R_2, \ldots, R_n\}$ as a set of available resources, where R_i, i = 1, 2, \ldots, s, describes a particular resource (e.g., a tool or a fixture). Specification of a processing task includes a set of resources from R that are required to perform that task.

The *factory model* describes the individual pieces of equipment within the shop, including the functionality and capabilities of each machine, and the relationships that exist between these individual pieces of equipment. The factory model is based on the equipment classification notation described by Smith (1992). We define $E = \{E_1, E_2, \ldots, E_m\}$ as a set of controllable equipment, where E_i, i = 1, 2, \ldots, m, is a specific piece of equipment. The factory model depends only on the physical equipment configuration and is independent of the set of parts currently being produced in the shop. This independence is necessary because the product mix will change much more frequently than the physical equipment configuration.

Figure 15.22 illustrates the generalized model of the SFCS (the resources input is not shown in this figure). In part (a) of this figure, a single part is to be produced. The process plan graph, P, defines the alternative processing sequences and describes the resource requirements for each processing step. Given the AND/OR graph $P = \langle V, A \rangle$:

$$v_j \in V$$

where $v_j : E \times R^*, j = 1, 2, \ldots, J$

$$J = |V|$$

Each node v in the process-plan graph identifies the specific piece of equipment that performs the corresponding processing task as well as the set of nonpermanent resources required for the processing (R^* represents zero or more elements from the set R). J is the total number of nodes in the graph. Arcs represent the precedence constraints between tasks. The set of equipment (E) is defined in the factory model described before. The alternatives for processing the part are represented using AND/OR junctions in the graph. As described before, the OR junctions represent alternative equipment that can perform a task, and AND junctions represent a series of tasks/equipment that all must be performed, but in no specific order. Therefore, any path through the graph represents a feasible processing route for the part. The objective of

Production requirements   SFCS

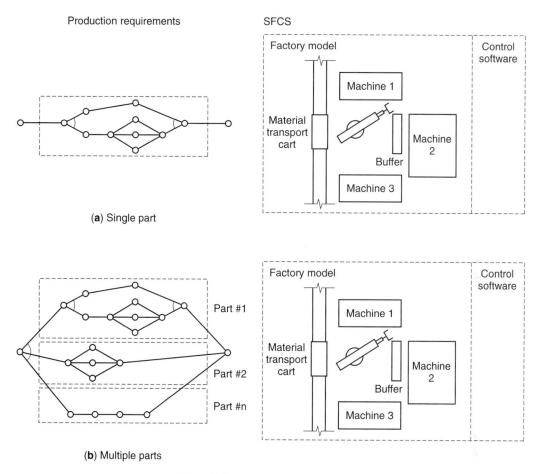

(**a**) Single part

Part #1

Part #2

Part #n

(**b**) Multiple parts

Figure 15.22   A generalized shop-floor control model.

the controller is to select a "good" path through this graph based on the state of the shop and the current scheduling criteria and then generate the instructions for the physical equipment corresponding to each node on this path.

Figure 15.22(b) illustrates the more general case in which multiple parts are assigned to the controller. In this case, all of the single parts' process plans are conjugated into a single graph by connecting the individual part graphs at a single AND junction. This conjugated graph is called the *control graph* and it formalizes the requirement that all parts be processed by the controller, but does not impose an order to the processing. In the single-part case, the control graph is simply that part's process-plan graph. As with the single-part case, the objective with the multiple-part case is to find a good path through the graph and to represent and select the corresponding equipment instructions.

A key here is that process-plan representation *can* be hierarchical in nature. In other words, subgraphs can be encapsulated inside single nodes to reduce the size of the graph. This modeling power can be exploited to represent the fact that decisions being made at one level of abstraction do not necessarily require the detailed operational characteristics needed at a lower level of abstraction. Therefore, these details can be encapsulated inside a single node. Plans and graphs of the plans may be aggregated based on the specific controller requirements. At this point, we introduce the *task graph*. A task graph is an AND/OR graph that describes the processing requirements for the individual manufacturing features of a part. Within the control graph, the task graph is normally encapsulated inside the node for the equipment that produces the features. This concept will be more fully illustrated in our examples.

It should be noted that the control and task graphs for a high-variety, multiple-machine system can become exceptionally complex. Each part in a manufacturing system has its own process-plan (task) graph derived from the ISO model of that part. For example, a system that contains 500 parts, each requiring 10 operations, contains at least 5000 task nodes. Furthermore, if alternative plans are used to enhance the flexibility of these systems, the size of the graphs grow significantly. Graphs with tens of thousands of nodes connected by both AND and OR junctions would be common for a centralized supervisory controller of a low-volume FMS.

The complexity of the process-plan graph will typically dictate the type of control architecture that will be used in a manufacturing system. An excessively complex graph would seem to dictate that some form of hierarchical control system would be in order. A reasonably straightforward graph could be controlled using most any type of architecture. We will illustrate our examples using the hierarchical control architecture of Joshi et al. (1990), in order to illustrate that planning decisions can be aggregated based on a hierarchy. However, the hierarchical model is only used to simplify the presentation and the general characterization is independent of the control architecture.

15.4.2 Functional Controller

Previous research has suggested that the shop-floor control function can be hierarchically decomposed such that each controller's functionality is partitioned into *planning, scheduling,* and *execution* tasks (see Figure 15.23) (Jones and Saleh, 1990; Joshi et al., 1990; and Smith et al., 1993). Planning in this model has been described as selecting the tasks that the manufacturing system will perform. Scheduling then identifies a "good" sequence for these planned tasks based on some performance criteria. Execution performs the scheduled tasks through the direct interfaces with the physical equipment and other external (business) systems. Information flow within the controller during normal system operation occurs in a top–down fashion from planning, to scheduling, to execution. During error recovery, the information flow is reversed and goes from execution, to scheduling, to planning (bottom–up).

The partitioning between scheduling and execution activities has been described in detail (Smith et al., 1993). The execution function is dependent only on the physical configuration of equipment, and is therefore relatively static. The scheduling function, however, is also dependent on the production requirements, and is therefore dynamic. Consequently, the performance criteria can change independently from the physical configuration in response to changes in the production requirements. By explicitly sepa-

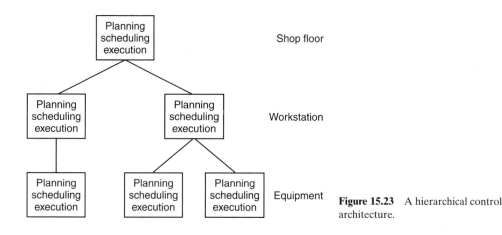

Figure 15.23 A hierarchical control architecture.

rating the scheduling and execution modules, different schedulers can be "plugged into" the execution module based on the production requirements. By using the formalism described before, the execution is responsible for performing the functions associated with each node in the process-plan graph independent of the specific path through the graph. So for each $v_j \in V$, where $v_j: E \times R^*$, the execution module is responsible for verifying the availability of each element of R^*, and for implementing the processing instructions on the device E_j.

The distinction between planning and scheduling, on the other hand, has remained convoluted throughout the manufacturing research community. Jones and Saleh (1990) and Joshi et al. (1990) provide similar qualitative distinctions between planning and scheduling, but neither provides a *formal* description of the distinction. By using the formalism described before, planning and scheduling together are responsible for determining a "good" path through the control graph. Once this path has been determined, execution is responsible for performing the individual tasks associated with each node in the path.

We partition the overall planning/scheduling problem as follows. Planning is responsible for selecting specific resources for the individual parts' process-plan graphs. By selecting the specific resources, we mean removing all of the OR junctions from the process-plan graph for each part ("DeORing" the graph). This would typically be performed by using a solution technique for some variant of the resource-assignment problem. Thus, allocation of resources would remove the OR junctions from the graph. The input to scheduling is then a list of individual part-processing routes with no operation alternatives, with all parts connected by a single AND junction. At this point, all resources have been *committed* to specific tasks, but the sequence and times of the allocation have not been specified.

For example, it is not uncommon to have a queue of parts at a single equipment resource. In the case in which a machinist is responsible for overseeing operations, the machinist chooses the sequence that is used to process the product(s). This is the function performed by out scheduler. In the case in which several parts may be loaded onto a tombstone-type fixture or an automatic pallet changer, the processing equipment can select from any of the parts to begin processing. The ordering of the process can affect the efficiency significantly. To formally model this phenomenon, the planned tasks for each part are joined to a single source and sink node in order to create an AND graph of the sequence possibilities. This process is illustrated in Figure 15.22(b). The scheduler uses this graph to make good sequencing decisions to order the parts ("DeANDing" the graph). The input to execution is then a linear sequence of tasks (a DeORed and DeANDed control graph).

15.4.3 Illustrative Examples

The functional model for planning, scheduling, and execution described before must be able to accommodate virtually all control circumstances encountered in manufacturing. We would like to illustrate the model first with a couple of traditional scheduling examples (specifically, Johnson's and Jackson's algorithms for the two-machine problem) and then provide a more detailed problem consistent with those encountered in everyday manufacturing. The examples illustrated here will be described within the three-level hierarchical control architecture illustrated in Figure 15.23 (Joshi et al., 1990).

Johnson (1954) and Jackson (1957) provided optimal solutions for the two-machine scheduling problem under several limiting assumptions. Johnson first posed a solution for problems where parts visit two machines in the same sequence (essentially a two-machine flow shop). The digraph for a set of parts that comply with the assumptions of Johnson is shown in Figure 15.24. As can be seen from the task graph in this figure, all equipment resources are determined explicitly in the initial graph. Planning, given the assumptions of Johnson, is essentially detailing the two tasks nodes for each part so that detailed processing times can be determined and conjuncting the individual part graphs with a source node and a sink node (with no OR junctions, there is

(a) Single-part task graph

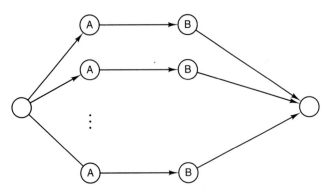

(b) Multiple-part task graph   **Figure 15.24**   Johnson's model task graph.

no DeORing). Scheduling is then responsible for sequencing the individual tasks for each part by removing the single AND junction. Johnson's rule can be applied to develop the optimal sequence of tasks for all parts (under the assumptions of all material handling and setup times equal to zero and all parts available for processing at time zero).

Jackson's algorithm further developed the two-machine problem to include parts that can be processed at both machines in either an A–B sequence or a B–A sequence, or on a single machine (essentially a two-machine job shop). The task graph for a random set of parts for Jackson's rules is shown in Figure 15.25. Again the sequence of operations at machines is fixed, and planning serves only to detail the tasks and provides a source and sink node for a cumulative parts graph.

The detail of both Jackson's and Johnson's rules is rather interesting in the functional context that we have developed. Their rules apply to an equipment-level controller where parts would be sequenced via a pallet exchanger or similar part-transfer mechanism at a processing station. Interequipment material handling is not considered, and is assumed to take zero time. In a manual environment, this might be a reasonable assumption, whereas in an automated environment, all material-handling tasks must be

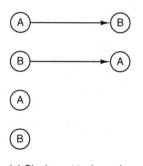

(**a**) Single-part task graph

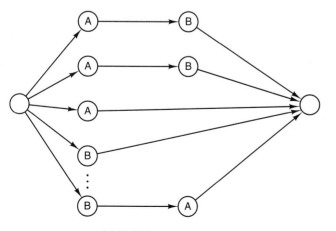

(**b**) Multiple-part task graph

Figure 15.25   Jackson's model task graph.

explicitly specified in order to control the system. In order to include material handling within the control framework, the process graph would have to be modified, and the re-source model may also require change. In this case, the system becomes essentially a three-machine system, where a robot (or some other transfer device) moves parts from one machine to another, rather than a two-machine system. The single-part graph for this modified Johnson's system is shown in Figure 15.26 (M nodes represent material-handling operations.) As can be seen in the figure, a material-handling operation is re-quired between each processing operation. The material handler becomes another equipment resource that also must be scheduled in the system. Johnson's and Jackson's rules do not provide a means for sequencing systems of this type. Therefore, although Jackson and Johnson provide optimal solutions for the two-machine case under certain restrictions, they do not provide the detail required to control these systems.

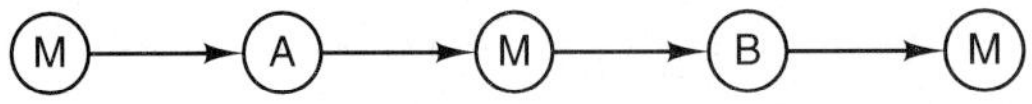

Figure 15.26   Johnson's model task graph with material handling.

For our next example, we will illustrate a single part (with multiple pieces in the same batch) flowing through the manufacturing system shown in Figure 15.21. This sys-tem consists of a single workstation containing three equipment-level devices: an NC drill (E1), an NC machining center (E2), and a robot (E3).

The process-plan task graphs for the part are shown in Figure 15.27. MT nodes in-dicate interworkstation material handling and MH nodes denote intraworkstation ma-terial handling. The resource requirements for each node are not shown on the graph, but are described in Table 15.5 The equipment-level task graph shows the alternative equipment operations (task sequences) that can be used, and the workstation task graph shows the alternative equipment sequences (Workstation Options) for the part. The operation-routing summary is used to develop detailed plans that appear in the plan graphs. There are several interesting aspects of this example. We will discuss how the functional framework that was presented can be used to develop the necessary shop-floor control required to produce a single part on a three-machine manufacturing system (where the robot is considered to be a machine in this context).

Although the part and system being illustrated are rather simple, there are a num-ber of interesting aspects associated with the part/system combination. For instance, we will assume that the part can be located and secured with a magnetic vise that makes all of the features accessible to the machine spindle. We will also assume that each machine has all the necessary tooling to produce the features. Even given both of these broad rather sweeping assumptions, the system has some rather interesting characteristics. We will begin by constructing the required control tasks for both the workstation and equipment system.

From Table 15.5 and Figure 15.27, we can infer that all of the part's tasks can be performed by the machining center (Workstation Task 2, W2), or the drilling, reaming, and/or boring can be performed by the NC drill after the machining center has per-formed the preliminary machining (Workstation Task 1, W1). If our manufacturing ob-jective is to produce the parts as quickly as possible, we may want to maintain both

SHOP-FLOOR GRAPH

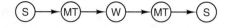

Shop-level task graph

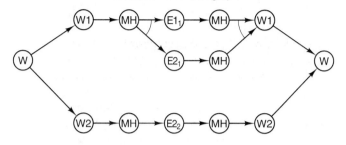

Workstation-level task graph

Equipment-level task graphs

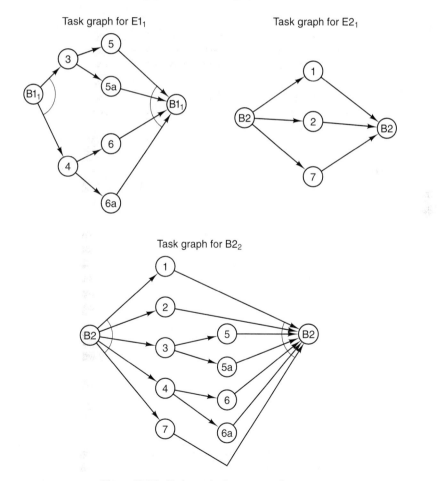

Task graph for E1₁

Task graph for E2₁

Task graph for B2₂

Figure 15.27 Task graphs for a part and system.

TABLE 15.5   TASK/OPERATIONS DERIVED FROM THE
OPERATION-ROUTING SUMMARY.

Resource	Tasks/Operations	Additional Resources
$E1_1$ - Drill	3, 4, 5, 5a, 6, 6a	Standard Fixture (F2)
$E2_1$ - MachCntr	1, 2, 7	Standard Fixture (F1)
$E2_2$ - MachCntr	1, 2, 3, 4, 5, 5a, 6, 6a, 7	Magnetic Fixture (F3)
$W1 = \{E1, E2_1\}$		
$W2 = \{E2_2\}$		

possibilities, that is, produce some parts only on the machining center and others on both the machining center and then on the NC drill. The route selected for any given part will be determined just prior to processing based on the shop status. The task graphs required for this breakdown are shown in Figure 15.27 and conjuncted as defined by the physical workstation. The bottommost graph of the figure (Workstation Task 2) illustrates producing the part only at the machining center. The graphs immediately above (Workstation Task 1) in the figure illustrate the sequence requirements to produce the part on the machine center and then on the NC drill. It should be noted that many other feasible visit possibilities exist that would entail more machine visits. These will not be illustrated.

We will begin our illustration of the decision making of the formal functional control system at the workstation-level graph where our first decisions must be made. As can be seen from the workstation-level task graph, the part can be produced using equipment E1 in conjunction with E2, or using E2 alone. The workstation-planning function will decide which alternative to use. When the plan graph is disaggregated, Workstation Task 1 (W1) is composed of equipment tasks E1 and E2, which occur at two separate pieces of equipment. Workstation Task 2 (W2) only requires the machining center. We commit (plan) our resources based on some criteria and related procedures (e.g., resource utilization, workload balance, and so on). For the sake of our example, we will fabricate a simplistic procedure to DeOR the workstation-level graph, as shown.

```
procedure Workstation_DeOR
if machine_center is_idle and magnetic_fixture available
    use Workstation Option 2
otherwise
    use Workstation Option 1
endif
endproc
```

The control process continues as defined by the formalization—planning, then scheduling, and then execution. According to the hierarchical control structure, the shop plans are first formulated and scheduled to be executed on the workstation. The workstation then plans (DeORs) its tasks and then schedules (DeANDs) the tasks to be executed at the equipment. The schema is illustrated in Figure 15.28. The planning (DeORing) and scheduling (DeANDing) procedure used is admittedly arbitrary. The

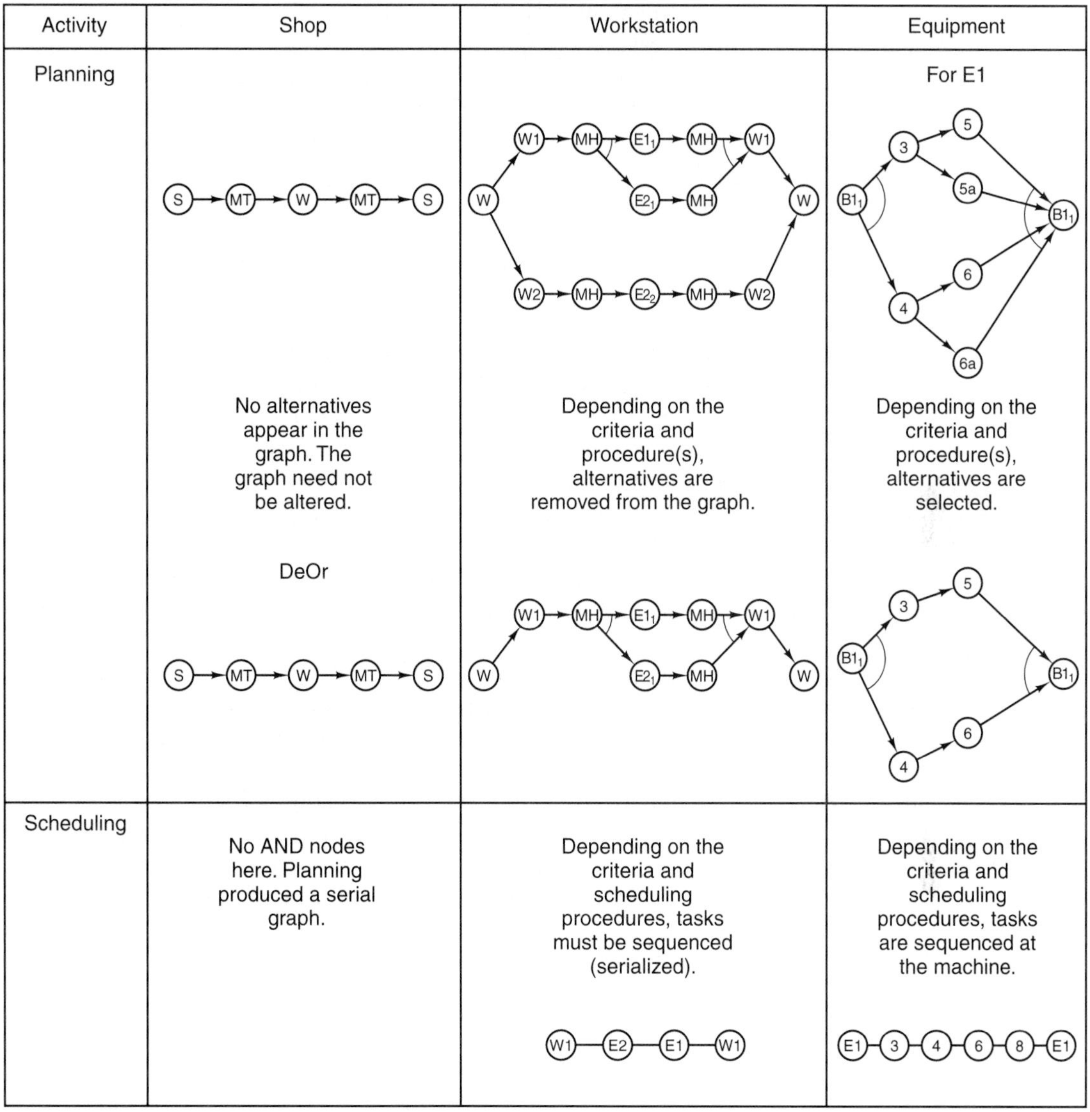

Activity	Shop	Workstation	Equipment
Planning			For E1
	No alternatives appear in the graph. The graph need not be altered.	Depending on the criteria and procedure(s), alternatives are removed from the graph.	Depending on the criteria and procedure(s), alternatives are selected.
	DeOr		
Scheduling	No AND nodes here. Planning produced a serial graph.	Depending on the criteria and scheduling procedures, tasks must be sequenced (serialized).	Depending on the criteria and scheduling procedures, tasks are sequenced at the machine.

Figure 15.28   Control specifics for multiple parts in the sample system.

intent here is to illustrate the functional separation and integration of these activities (nothing inhibits the system from planning and scheduling simultaneously). Sophisticated planning and scheduling procedures can be used to operate within this functional structure. They even can be evoked recursively. The key here is the functional structure.

The last characteristic that will be illustrated in this section is one of scheduling complexity. Suppose that the milling operations required for the part require two different setups: one for the side milling and one for the slot milling (as might be the case if the magnetic vise were not available). We further redefine the equipment-level task graphs and the workstation-level tasks graphs, as shown in Figure 15.27. As can be seen from the figure, Workstation Task 1 (W1) now consists of three tasks, which we will define to require the fixed sequence $E1_1$–$E2$–$E1_2$. Parts following this sequence will first visit the machining center, then the NC drill, and finally the machining center, with the material handling being handled by the robot. The scheduling function now becomes far more complicated, because if two parts are arbitrarily allowed in the system, a deadlock can occur (see Section 15.5). For example, the first part has completed task E1 and now resides at the NC drill. A second part with the same planned (DeORed) task graph is being processed ($E2_1$) at the machining center. Because the robot can only pick up a single part at a time, the system is in a state of deadlock. This provides an interesting case in that deadlock either can be avoided in the planning (selecting between Workstation Tasks 1 and 2)of an arriving part or through the scheduling of the parts.

15.5 DETECTION OF DEADLOCKS IN FLEXIBLE MANUFACTURING CELLS

The scheduling and control of flexible manufacturing systems (FMSs) have received significant attention because of the potential gains that can be had from significant improvements in these areas. Heuristic solutions are often the norm for real-time implementation of shop-floor control activities. Often heuristic solutions lack considerations of overall system implications, and several practical problems that arise in the control aspect of unmanned FMSs have not been studied. In this chapter, we address one specific problem of control, namely, system deadlock that can arise in an unmanned FMS. The intent of this work is to describe the system deadlock problem as it applies to FMS control and establish its credibility as a problem area of both theoretical and practical interest. The problem of FMS deadlock has been ignored by most research in scheduling and control.

An FMS is in a state of deadlock when parts are assigned to various machines in a manufacturing system such that any further part flow is inhibited. Deadlocks can occur in any "direct-address" FMS. A "direct-address" FMS is one that employs a direct-address material-handling device such as a robot or a shuttle cart (as opposed to a material-handling system like a recirculating conveyor). This configuration is often used in an FMS where a robotic device is used to service several machines in an unmanned setting (Figure 15.29). The figure shows one possible configuration of a "direct-address" FMS. A single robot is used to load/unload parts and to move parts for processing between the various machines in the system. There is no buffer or auxiliary storage device in the system. The control of the unmanned cell is executed by a control computer whose function is to coordinate and plan movement of parts in the system.

Control in an unmanned FMS is usually implemented using state tables, where the actions to be taken are implemented based on the "state" of the cell and the incoming requests from the various machines in the cell. In such a control system, suppose the following situation arises: Part 1 is loaded at machine A, part 2 is loaded at machine B, and the robot is idle. On completion of processing part 1 at machine A, a command is sent

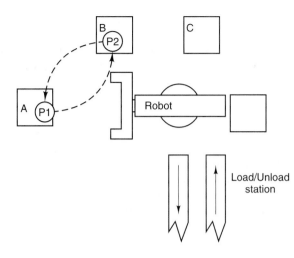

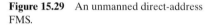

Figure 15.29   An unmanned direct-address FMS.

to the control computer indicating completion of machining. The control system then could activate the robot to move part 1 to the next destination determined by the process routing for part 1. If the next destination of part 1 is machine B, and the next destination for part 2 (currently at machine B) is machine A, then the system will be in a state of deadlock.

A solution to resolving the deadlock would be to allow a storage space that could be used to move parts temporarily to alleviate the deadlock. In the preceding example, part 1 could be moved to the storage space, part 2 moved from B to A, and then part 1 moved from storage to B. However, the presence of a storage space by itself is not sufficient to prevent a deadlock.

Consider a situation with three machines and three parts. Part 1 is currently at machine A, part 2 at machine B, part 3 at machine C, and the next requested machines are C by part 1, C by part 2, and B by part 3. If part 1 finishes processing on machine A, and is moved to the storage space while machine C is still busy, this will lead to a deadlock because no more part movement will be possible. Improper use of the available storage to alleviate deadlocking also can result in a system deadlock.

These examples indicate the relative ease with which deadlocks can occur in an unmanned FMS. The total number of deadlock possibilities in a manufacturing system with n machines is given by $\Sigma_{i=2}^{n}\binom{n}{i}$, and more than one deadlock can occur simultaneously. The existing approach to the deadlock problem is to consider it during the design phase of an FMS and try to design deadlock-free systems right from the beginning. Two approaches often used to design deadlock-free systems are

1. (ensuring that all parts flow in the same direction (this limits the type of parts that can be processed)
2. batching the parts waiting to be processed according to their flow direction (Co, 1984); once the parts are batched, the manufacturing system then can process one unidirectional batch at a time; this reduces total machine utilization

15.5.1 Deadlock Modeling

System deadlock problems occur in operating systems, in multiprocessor computer systems (Haberman, 1969; Holt, 1971; Gold, 1978), and distributed database systems (Gray, 1978; Menasce and Munz, 1979; and Gligor and Shattuck, 1980). Although techniques have been developed to handle deadlocks in computer engineering applications (Coffman, Elphick, and Shoshani, 1971; Howard, 1973), sufficient differences exist to prevent direct application to manufacturing systems.

In a computer system, tasks enter the system at random and require specific resources (memory, I/O channels, disk space, and so on). Once a task enters the system, it is allocated a share (whatever was requested) of resources until all necessary non-CPU-based resources are assigned that the task requires. Computer-system deadlocks occur when resources are assigned to tasks such that no task can obtain all the required resources for processing. Once all the necessary resources are assigned, CPU time is allocated, usually in chunks, to process the task. It may require several visits by the CPU to complete a task. Once the task is complete, the resources are released. In computer systems, resources often can be assigned fractionally and multiple tasks can share a resource simultaneously. Chained requests, where a request for a resource itself implies another resource request, frequently exist.

In a manufacturing system, jobs enter the system at random and require multiple machines for completion in a specific operation sequence (known a priori) (Figure 15.30). Each operation requires all of a particular machine resource, and this resource is held until processing is complete and the part can be moved to another machine or queue. It is the interaction of jobs that causes deadlocking.

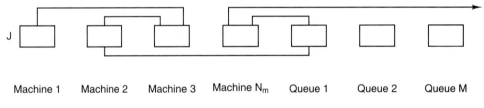

Figure 15.30   Resource allocation for a manufacturing system.

Tsutsui and Fujimoto (Gray, 1978) have defined the requirements for waiting and deadlocking in computer systems. This approach is applicable only to process-control computers, where the application programs are fixed and the time when resources are required can be easily determined in advance. Sufficient differences exist, so this cannot be directly applied to manufacturing systems. The definitions given in what follows can be made for the manufacturing-system problem. The following notation is used. $T_i (i = 1, 2, \ldots, N_T)$ is the ith task to be processed by a computer. $R_j^i (j = 1, 2, \ldots, N_R)$ is the jth common resources required by task i. $J_i (i = 1, 2, \ldots, N_J)$ is the ith job (part) to be produced, $M_j^i (j = 1, 2, \ldots, N_M)$ is the jth resource (machine) required by the ith job.

Definition 1:   Wait Relationships Among Resources

If job J_i requests machine resource M_j while holding resource M_k ($k \neq j$), it is said that resource M_k is waiting for resource M_j in Job J_i. This situation is denoted by

$$J_i$$
$$M_k \rightarrow M_j$$

This relationship is referred to as a wait relationship. Note that machine resource M_j may or may not be released until M_k is available (release would require a queue).

Definition 2:   Propagation of Wait Relationships—Blocking

Let J_1 and J_2 be two jobs simultaneously active in a manufacturing facility. If the following two wait relations

$$J_1 \qquad\qquad J_2$$
$$M_j \rightarrow M_k \text{ and } M_k \rightarrow M_l$$

(where $j \neq k \neq l$), and the usage of machine resource M_k and J_2 are true, it is said that machine resource M_j is waiting for resource M_k via resource M_l. This situation is denoted

$$J_1 \quad J_2$$
$$M_j \rightarrow M_k \rightarrow M_l$$

This relationship is referred to as propagation of wait relationships or blocking.

Definition 3:   Direct-Address Material Handling

A direct-address material system is one in which the material-handling system specifically serves a single machine resource one at a time. A robot and automated guided vehicle (AGV) are direct-address systems. Frequently, the successor resource must be released before a job can be removed from an occupied machine resource.

Definition 4:   System Deadlock (Direct-Address Systems)

When a job requests a machine resource, the manufacturing system is said to be in a deadlock state if the following condition is true. The request for a machine resource cannot be accepted unless the requesting job releases the machine resource that it currently holds and all queue resources (including the material handler if multiple parts can be handled at once) are occupied. This corresponds to a circular propagation of wait relations(see Figure 15.31).

15.5.2   Characteristics of System Deadlocks

A wait relationship also can be represented as a graph with the nodes indicating the machines and the arcs describing part flow. This is illustrated in Case A of Figure 15.31. Note that a wait relationship is created between two machines. If any one of the two

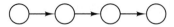

Case A. Linear wait relation – blocking

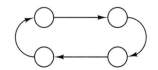

Case B. Circular wait relation – deadlocking   **Figure 15.31**   The wait relationship.

nodes is not a machine, for example, a storage, then no wait relationship can be declared. When represented by a series of wait relationships, a blocking situation appears to be linear, whereas a wait relationship associated with a deadlocking situation forms circuits. These two situations are illustrated in Case B of Figure 15.31. The circular wait relationship of a system deadlock implies that a circuit is at least a necessary condition for a system deadlock.

15.5.3 Preparation of a Graph

The basic principle of the detection procedure is to identify whether any deadlock possibility exists in a manufacturing system. If recognized, proper action can be taken to correct or avoid such a situation.

A directed graph representing the wait relationships described in Definitions 1 to 4 can be constructed for any manufacturing system.

1. For each job J_i $(i = 1, \ldots, N)$, let $M_1^i, M_2^i, \ldots, M_{ki}^i$ indicate the sequence of machine requests. This sequence corresponds to the wait relationships and can be represented as a directed graph, $G_i = (V_i, A_i)$, whose vertices V_i correspond to the resources $V_i = \{M_j^i, j = 1, \ldots, K_i\}$, and arcs A_i correspond to wait relationships

$$a_{pq} = \begin{cases} 1 \text{ if } \exists\ M_l \to M_n \text{ and } V_p = \{M_l\},\ V_q = \{M_n\} & \forall\ p, q, \in V_i \\ 0, \text{ otherwise} \end{cases}$$

2. Jobs randomly interact with each other in a manufacturing system. For such a situation, the graph of job interactions G_{int} is obtained in the following manner. Let I be a set of jobs simultaneously active. Then G_{int} is given by

$$G_{int} = \bigcup_{i \in I} G_i$$

3. The directed graph $G = (V, A)$, which represents all wait relationships between all resources and jobs, is represented as

$$G = \bigcup_i G_i$$

15.5.4 Sufficient Conditions for System Deadlock

Deadlock was graphically illustrated as circular wait relationships in a system graph. This circuit is a necessary but not a sufficient condition for deadlocking.

The following assumptions are used in the paper:

1. Each job has a unique identifier.
2. Each job occupies only one resource at any given time.
3. Each machine can process only one job at a time.

Theorem 1

Given a graph $G = (V, A)$, sufficient conditions for a system deadlock are

1. There exists at least one circuit $C = (V_c, A_c)$ in G.
2. If N_c is the number of jobs contributing arcs to circuit C, then N_c must be equal to $|A_c|$ [see Figures 15.32(a) and 15.32(b)].
3. If M_c is the number of machines in the circuit C, then M_c must be equal to $|A_c|$ [see Figure 15.32(c)].

Wait relation   Graph

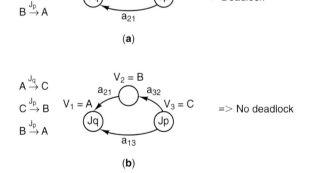

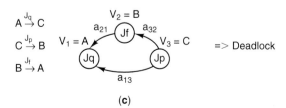

Figure 15.32 Circuits in a graph. (a) Two machines, two jobs. (b) Three machines, two jobs. (c) Three machines, three jobs.

Proof

1. If no circuits exist in the graph, there is no circular waiting and the conditions for deadlock (Definition 4) are not satisfied.

2. Suppose $|A_c| > N_c$. This implies that at least one of the jobs contributes more than one arc. Because more than one operation of a job cannot occur simultaneously, each job can only contribute one arc to a deadlock circuit, C. Hence, circuit C cannot be completed to create a deadlock [Figure 15.32(b)]. Suppose $|A_c| < N_c$. Then there exists a job J in the circuit C that does not contribute an arc to the circuit. This contradicts the definition of N_c. Hence, $N_c = |A_c|$ for circuit C to be a deadlock.

3. Suppose $|A_c| > M_c$. This implies that a machine is capable of processing and routing more than one part simultaneously to other machines. This violates assumption 3. Suppose $|A_c| < M_c$. By definition of G, each machine is represented by a vertex. Hence, $M_c = |V_c|$. If $|A_c| < |V_c|$, then C is not a circuit. Hence, $M_c = |A_c|$ for C to be a system deadlock.

15.5.5 Detection of System Deadlock

15.5.5.1 Identification of circuits. Once a graph has been created to represent a manufacturing system, circuits in the graph must be identified to indicate the parts and machines that can be involved in a deadlock. The search procedure introduced in this section applies a string multiplication algorithm (Tsutsui and Fujimoto, 1987) to identify all the circuits in a graph. Initially, a symbol matrix S is defined from a given graph. The definition of a symbol matrix is

$$S_{ij} = \begin{cases} ij, & \text{if a wait relation exists between machine i and j,} \\ 0, & \text{otherwise} \end{cases}$$

where $ij = 1, \ldots, M$. (Note that ij is a character string rather than a number.)

Let $a(uv)$ and $b(vw)$ be two strings of symbols that end and start with v, respectively. Let $*$ denote the string multiplication symbol. Then

$$a(uv) * 0 = 0 * a(uv) = 0 \tag{15.1}$$

and $a(uv) * b(vw)$ is formed by concatenating $a(uv)$ with the string that results from $b(vw)$ by removing the first symbol "v" (for example, $ubv * vexw = ubvexw$). This is extended to sums of strings by defining

$$\sum_i a_i(uv) * \sum_j b_j(vw) = \sum_i \sum_j a_i(uv) * b_j(vw) \tag{15.2}$$

For example,

$$(ubv + abc) * (vwx + vyx) = (ubv * vwx + ubv * vyx + abv * vwx + abv * vyx)$$

$$= (ubvwx + ubvyx + abvwx + abvyx)$$

The product of power of S is then defined as

$$S_{ij}^{r+t} = (S^r * S^t)_{ij} = \sum_k (S_{ik}^r * S_{kj}^t) \tag{15.3}$$

Given graph G, a symbol matrix S, and the string multiplication defined before, circuits composed of n arcs in graph G then can be found along the diagonal of S^n. (Note that two arc circuits are in S^2, three arc circuits are in S^3, and so on.)

The string-multiplication procedure requires that each node in a graph be represented by a string containing only one digit. Therefore, if a manufacturing system is composed of more than nine machines, single-digit instead of double-digit characters are used for the tenth or higher machines. For example, the twelfth machine in the manufacturing system should be labeled "C" instead of "12"; therefore, the confusion between notations for the path from node 1 to 2 and node 12 can be avoided.

Example

Given a graph as illustrated in Figure 15.33, the symbol matrix is derived as

$$S = \begin{vmatrix} 0 & 12 & 0 & 14 \\ 21 & 0 & 0 & 24 \\ 31 & 32 & 0 & 0 \\ 0 & 0 & 43 & 0 \end{vmatrix}$$

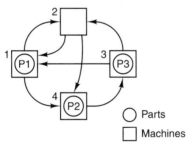

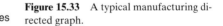

○ Parts
□ Machines

Figure 15.33   A typical manufacturing directed graph.

Given symbol matrix S of size M × M (where M is equal to the number of machines), matrix S^n is obtained as follows [see Equation (15.3)]:

$$S^n = S^{n-1} * S$$

or

$$S_{ij}^n = \sum_k S_{ik}^{n-1} * S_{kj}$$

where $i, j, k = 1, \ldots, M$.

If k is restricted to be greater than i, then the numerical value of the first character of a string will always be less than that of the rest of the characters. Therefore, only the circuits starting with the smallest number will remain, and the rest of the duplications can be excluded. Thus, Equation (15.2) is updated as

$$S_{ij}^n = \sum_k S_{ik}^{n-1} * S_{kj}$$

where $i, j = 1, \ldots, M; k = i + 1$. Actually, this restriction not only eliminates the redundant appearance of a circuit, but also curtails many of the required calculations. For example, when calculating S^2

$$S_{11}^2 = S_{12}^1 * S_{21}^1 + S_{13}^1 + S_{14}^1 * S_{41}^1$$

$$= 121$$

$S_{11}^1 * S_{11}^1$ is omitted because ($k = 1 \ngtr i = 1$). Similarly, when computing S_{21}^1, S_{21}^1, and S_{22}^1 $* S_{22}^1$ also can be omitted because ($k \ngtr i$). Also the circuit formed by $S_{21}^1 * S_{12}^1 = 212$ is redundant because it is the same as 121, which was identified in S_{11}^2.

Furthermore, there is no need to calculate the entire symbol matrix. Each symbol matrix serves two purposes. One is to expose the circuit in the diagonal entries, and the other is to facilitate the calculation of the next symbol matrix. Suppose symbol matrix S^n of size $M \times M$ is to be calculated. Only the first ($M - n + 1$) diagonal terms must be examined for circuits. For example, if symbol matrix S^2 is of size 4×4, then only the first three ($3 = 4 - 2 + 1$) diagonal terms will be calculated. For the last diagonal term (the fourth one), the circuit possibilities include 414, 424, and 434. However, these are already excluded by the restriction on k as stated previously. Therefore, in this case, only the first three diagonal entries are needed to locate possible circuits. After circuits have been collected, the S^2 matrix will be again used to calculate its successor, that is, S^3 ($= S^2 * S$). However, in an S^3 symbol matrix, only the first two diagonal entries ($2 = 4 - 3 + 1$) will store the possible circuits. To facilitate the calculation of the first two diagonal entries in S^3, only the first two rows in S^2 are required (note that the initial symbol matrix S will be kept entirely throughout the calculation). In summary, in a symbol matrix S^n of size $M \times M$, only the first $M - n$ rows and the ($M - n + 1$)th diagonal entry must be calculated and maintained.

Completing the procedures results in the following S matrices of interest (only the elements computed are shown):

$$S^2 = \begin{vmatrix} 121 & 0 & 143 & 124 \\ 0 & 0 & 243 & 0 \\ 0 & 0 & 0 & 0 \\ \cdots & \cdots & \cdots & \cdots \end{vmatrix}$$

$$S^3 = \begin{vmatrix} 1431 & \cdots & & \cdots \\ \cdots & 2432 & & \cdots \\ \cdots & \cdots & 3143 + 3243 & \cdots \\ \cdots & \cdots & \cdots & 4314 \end{vmatrix}$$

The circuits obtained from the modified string multiplication may contain an inner loop and thus need to be further examined. A string "123421" in S^5 is actually composed of two closed circuits, that is, 121 and 2342, and the two small closed circuits may have appeared already in S^2 and S^3, respectively. The large circuit 123421, in which node 2 distributes two arcs to node 1 and node 3, respectively, cannot possibly become a system deadlock, according to the theorem. Therefore, it is removed to avoid confusion in the subsequent correction procedure.

15.5.5.2 Circuit validation.   Although a circuit is a necessary condition for system deadlock, the mathematical string-multiplication procedures presented in the last section may produce circuits having no connection with system deadlocks. The sufficient conditions (2) and (3) of Theorem 1 can be used to eliminate circuits that do not correspond to a deadlock. These conditions also serve as the upper bound to the procedure for detecting circuits. The maximum depth to which the string multiplication has to be carried is $p = \min\{N_j, N_m\}$, where N_j and N_m are the number of jobs and number of machines in the system, respectively.

By inspecting Figure 15.33 and the S^2 and S^3 tables, the simple system model can provide the following information (note that the largest circuit matrix required is of order 3, $\min\{N_j, N_m\}$). S^2 reveals that one circuit, 121, can be formed with two arcs. The necessary condition for deadlock, however, requires that two jobs must be included for the system to deadlock. Because currently no job resides on machine 2, the circuit will not cause an immediate deadlock. S^3 contains two circuits, {1431} and {2432}, and both should be inspected. Circuit 1431 involved three machines and three jobs currently reside at three machines; therefore, it forms a deadlock.

15.5.6 Interaction between Circuits

In order to facilitate effective deadlock control, the interaction between the circuits must also be understood. As illustrated in Figure 15.34, the two circuits, $C_1\{A\ B\ C\}$ and $C_2\{C\ D\}$, are individually not in a state of deadlock, but together produce deadlock. Part 2 in C_1 and part 3 in C_2 both request machine C for the next operation, causing either C_1 or C_2 to become deadlocked. Such deadlocks between circuits are called second-level deadlocks.

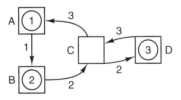

Figure 15.34   Interaction between circuits.

As shown in Figure 15.35, the two interacting circuits can be decomposed such that the first and second circuit have an arc pointing out from the node in the circuit. If each circuit is collapsed into a single node, and the outgoing arcs are connected to each other, then the second-level circuit can be represented as a circuit between two nodes, each representing a first-level circuit.

The nodes and arcs in a second-level graph are defined as follows:

Second-Level Node

A circuit identified at the first level is a second-level node.

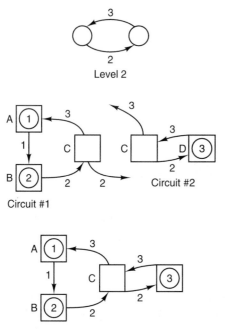

Figure 15.35   Decomposition of two interacting circuits.

Second-Level Arc

Arc *a* is defined as a second-level arc if it (1) belongs to a part that contributed an arc in the second-level node, and (2) leaves immediately for a second-level node.

The string-multiplication algorithm can be applied identically to the second-level circuits. Let M_1 and N_1 be the number of nodes and arcs, respectively, in the second-level graph. Then the power of the last symbol matrix required in searching for second-level circuits is $p = \min\{M_1, N_1\}$.

The second-level circuits thus identified also need to be validated. The following condition is used to eliminate false second-level circuits; all second-level arcs in the second-level circuit must leave from a common machine. As illustrated in Figure 15.36, three circuits can be identified at the first level, and treated as three second-level nodes. The arc labeled 1 from B → C and the arc labeled 2 from C → B are second-level arcs. Therefore, at the second level, a circuit is identified between second-level nodes 1 and 3. However, the circuit at the second level is not valid because it only repeats the circuit between B and C at the first level. Applying the validity condition eliminates the second-level circuit because there is no common machine from which the second-level arcs leave.

A second-level circuit indicates competition for a common machine by parts in two or more first-level circuits. Higher-order circuits can also be created in a similar manner.

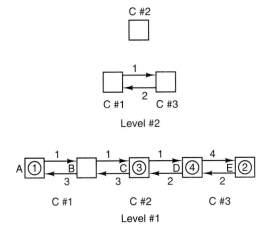

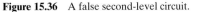

Figure 15.36   A false second-level circuit.

15.5.7 Implementation Issues

The detection procedure presented in this chapter forms the first step in the development of a deadlock-control system. Implementation of the detection algorithm involves two steps: (1) identifying potential deadlock situations and (2) checking to determine if the potential deadlock situation has or will be attained. In a system that is not currently in a deadlock state, deadlocks can arise when a part moves or a new part is introduced in the system.

```
procedure introduce_new_part
1)      Create graph Gnew for the new part
2)      Create subgraphs SGi for parts_in_system, by deleting the nodes
        corresponding to machines already visited
3)      Create complete graph G = Gnew ∪ SGi, where i ∈ {parts in system}
4)      Update parts_in_system
5)      Call DETECT_CIRCUITS (Section 15.5.5.1)
6)      For each circuit, determine arcs, nodes, and set of parts comprising the
        circuit. These circuits are potential deadlock situations.
end procedure
procedure move_part
-activated when a part already in the system requests to be moved
1)      Determine arc, destination node, and part involved in the move
2)      Determine the circuit(s) Ci to which the destination node and part belong
3)      If circuit Ci = φ, move part and update current status of parts in system,
        RETURN.
4)      For each circuit Ci (determined in (2)) check status of parts in circuit if
        addition of part to Ci completes the set of parts in Ci, then call
        DEADLOCK_RESOLUTION (a user-written procedure to resolve deadlocks)else
        move part and update current status of parts in system, and parts in
        circuit Ci, RETURN.
end procedure
```

The deadlock-detection procedure is intended for execution in real time and is currently being implemented in the FMS at Penn State. Figure 15.37 shows the position of the deadlock-detection module in a workstation/cell-controlled architecture (Joshi et al., 1990). The deadlock-detection and avoidance module interacts with the scheduler to ensure that the actions sent to the equipment controllers will not cause a deadlock.

In an unmanned FMS with no storage, deadlock is a serious problem and must be avoided. In such systems, resolution after a deadlock occurs only can be performed by human intervention. The cost of intervention is usually high, and it is advisable to keep the deadlock-detection procedure continuously active. The additional computational burden is not high, because the circuit-detection program terminates in a finite number of steps, $p = \min \{\# \text{ of jobs}, \# \text{ of machines}\}$, and is only computed when a new part enters the system. The remaining effort is simply maintaining and comparing lists.

The use of storage to break a deadlock also requires the use of the detection algorithm to establish the presence of a deadlock and to prevent any further deadlock from occurring involving storage space. Furthermore, for every reserved storage, $2mn$ more robot programs are needed to allow for the possibility of extra movement of parts between the machines and storage to resolve deadlock (where m is the number of machines, n is the number of part types). This increases the effort required at the robot programming stage, as well as the complexity of control.

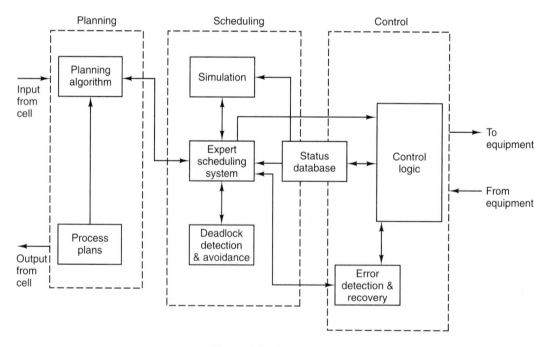

Figure 15.37   Controller architecture.

15.6 INTRODUCTION TO SHOP-FLOOR CONTROL SOFTWARE

Robust control software is a necessity for automated flexible manufacturing systems (FMSs), and plays an important role in the flexibility attainable, that is, the number of different products that can be produced, the product mix, engineering design changes, and so on. Often FMSs are built with very flexible machines (NC machines, robots, AGVs, ASRS, and so on), but the control software is unable to exploit the full flexibility of the machines or of adding new machines, parts, and changing control algorithms. Writing FMS control software is not a trivial task. The software is typically custom-written, very expensive, difficult to modify, and often the main source of inflexibility in FMSs. The primary causes of this inflexibility includes tight coupling between the functions performed by the software, hard coding of control logic, part routing and sequencing information being built into the control software, and, in general, the lack of a structured or systematic approach to FMS control-software development (Joshi et al., 1995).

Most FMSs are sold to manufacturing companies as turnkey systems by integration vendors. As a result, the software expertise does not reside at the companies and logic/software changes can be made only by the FMS vendor. A more desirable solution would allow the system operators and/or manufacturing engineers to modify the control software as mandated by changes in the physical system and production requirements, using software-development tools. Similar software tools also can be used by the systems integration vendors to reduce the time, effort, and cost to build the control software.

In this section, we will describe RapidCIM concepts and approach to the development of FMS control software and software tools to assist in the development. The focus of the discussion will be on materials developed as part of RapidCIM, a DARPA-sponsored MADE project (Smith et al., 1994; Joshi et al., 1995; Wysk, Peters, and Smith, 1995).

The tools described are intended for use by manufacturing-system engineers, who can use these tools to create control software for specific installations using freely available modeling languages (e.g., simulation languages), high-level descriptions and specifications of control activities, and factory models as data, that is, create a data-driven shop-floor control system.

15.6.1 The RapidCIM CONCEPT

RapidCIM is the embodiment of the concept that allows defining generic control elements or modules with well-defined interfaces and hooks in a manner that the control modules can be developed in an independent manner, customized based on installation-specific data, based on formal models of controller behavior, amenable to automatic generation of control-software modules, and reconfigurable to adapt to changes in the environment through changes to data and/or regeneration of control software.

The traditional approach to FMS control-software development is shown in Figure 15.38. Typically, a simulation model of the FMS is developed during the manufacturing-system design stage, and it is used to evaluate both the hardware configuration (number of machines, pallets, buffers, and so on) and the part-flow logic

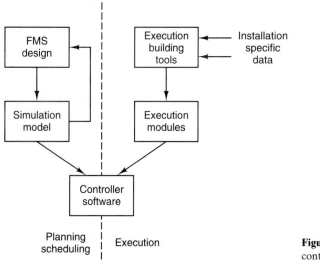

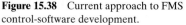

Figure 15.38   Current approach to FMS control-software development.

(dispatching rules, scheduling algorithm, and so on) with respect to some performance criteria. Once the decisions on the hardware and part-flow logic are made, the control-software-development process begins. The control logic is implemented in control code in some programming language (e.g., C, C++), and typically written from scratch. Often the control logic and execution of the logic are intertwined, along with implementation-specific details. There is no standard accepted model for structuring control software. This often leads to installation-specific, inflexible, and nonportable control software.

In the RapidCIM approach (Figure 15.39), the controller functions are partitioned so as to separate the execution functions (messaging, part status, file downloading, and so on) from the decision-making (planning and scheduling) functions. This separation allows modular development of the execution and decision-making functions. The exe-

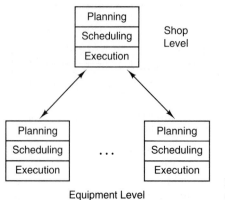

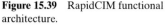

Figure 15.39   RapidCIM functional architecture.

cution functions have been formally modeled and the execution portions of the controllers can be automatically generated using the tools developed (Smith and Joshi, 1993). This provides a formal structure for the execution modules of the control software and a well-defined methodology for development that can be systematically followed, thereby reducing the development time and effort. This structuring reduces the controller-development time further by using the simulation model itself to provide the decision-making function. Thus, the simulation model can be developed once and used both for the purpose of manufacturing-system simulation analysis and then in the real-time controller, further reducing the time to build the decision-making module of the controller.

15.6.2 Components of RapidCIM

This section provides a brief overview of the control architecture, factory and process-plan model and its representation, formal models of execution and the associated tools for development of execution software, and the enhancement to simulation required to make the proposed approach a reality.

15.6.2.1 Shop-floor control architecture.   In the context of shop-floor control, a *control architecture* should provide a blueprint for the design and construction of a shop-floor control system. The functions for each controller in the system are separated into *planning, scheduling,* and *execution* functions. The details necessary to implement an operational system based on the architecture are presented in Smith, Hoberecht, and Joshi 1993. Figure 15.40 shows the generic controller structure under this architecture.

The equipment level is the lowest level in the hierarchy and there is one equipment-level controller for each piece of equipment in the system. The workstation

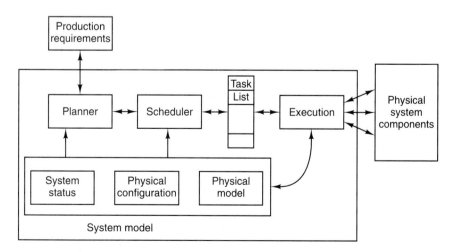

Figure 15.40   Controller structure.

level corresponds to a small subset of equipment that directly interacts (e.g., an industrial robot and the machine tools that it loads and unloads). The shop level is the highest level in the hierarchy and is responsible for coordinating the activities of the workstations. The shop level also provides the user interface to the control system. At the equipment level, the controller plans, schedules, and executes the operations that make up a traditional process plan, that is, determines which tooling to use for which feature, the sequence of operations, the preparation of the final part program, and so on. At the workstation level, the workstation controller would determine which machine would produce a product, what would be the processing sequence of machines, and coordinate the machine interactions. The shop-level controller would handle the interworkstation activities, selecting the appropriate routes for AGVs, scheduling the sequence of transport dispatches, and so on.

Within each level, functionality remains the same where the planning function determines what the controller should do to meet its requirements, the scheduling function then determines a *good* sequence for the planned tasks, and the execution function performs the individual tasks. In the RapidCIM system, the decision maker embodies the planning and scheduling functions and the executor embodies the execution function. The approach taken by RapidCIM is to develop a *plug-and-play* shop-floor control system that can be easily created and reconfigured as required by the underlying manufacturing system. Fundamental to this concept is the complete separation of the decision maker from the executor, and the interface specification between the executor and the decision maker. For further details on the architecture, see Smith et al. (1993).

15.6.2.2 Factory-resource model and process plans.

The factory-resource model and the part-process plans provide the common frame of reference between the executor and the decision maker. The factory-resource model describes the shop-floor equipment (machine tools, industrial robots, AGVs, and so on) and the associated tooling and fixturing resources. It also describes the relationships between the individual pieces of equipment. The factory-resource model is one of the primary sources of the installation-specific data required by the user to build the control system. The factory-resource model uses the shop-floor equipment class described by Smith and Joshi (1992) to describe the individual system components. This class partitions shop-floor equipment into one of four subclasses based on equipment behavior. Material processors (class **MP**) include CNC machine tools and other devices that autonomously *process* parts according to some well-defined instructions (i.e., an NC file). Material handlers (**MH**) include industrial robots and other pick-and-place devices that load and unload parts from machines, conveyors, AGVs, and so on. Material transporters (**MT**) include conveyors, AGVs, and devices that move parts from one location to another within the facility. Finally, automated storage (**AS**) equipment is a general class of automated storage and retrieval systems that store raw materials, WIP, and finished goods.

Part-process plans play an important role in shop-floor control. They form a major portion of the specifications required for control. Using process plans as another source for implementation-specific data (maintained external to the control software) provides further opportunity to decouple part flow and routing from the actual control software, thus allowing changes to part mix and part-flow data without making changes to the control software. Process plans for use in shop-floor control must be structured and represented in a manner so as to allow their use at all levels of control and provide detail consistent with the execution functions available at each level. Further, we want to represent all possible alternatives in the process plan, so alternatives can be evaluated in real time by the decision-making functions. Process plans (and alternative process plans) are represented using AND/OR graphs (Mettala and Joshi, 1993). Further details on process-plan representations and the use of process plans for control can be found in Lee, Wysk, and Smith (1995); and Wysk et al. (1995).

Formal models of execution.   As described earlier, the executor is responsible for interacting with the physical system to implement the tasks specified by the decision maker. A finite automata-based formal model called a message-based part state graph (MPSG) is used to describe this interaction (Smith and Joshi, 1993). Supervisory control in a distributed control environment is performed by sending and receiving messages to and from other controllers, and performing physical actions. In this context, examples of physical actions include sending a cycle start to a CNC machine tool, moving a robot into a machine to unload a part, and transporting a part between two locations using an AGV.

The processing protocol for a controller is the set of messages received by and sent by the controller and the set of physical actions required to process parts within the scope of the controller. For example, the processing protocol for a machine tool controller includes the messages received from the workstation controller to initiate actions, the direct interaction with the device, and the messages sent to the workstation reporting the completion of the actions. An MPSG describes this processing protocol as a modified finite automaton. Consistent with the class of equipment in the factory-resource model, *generic* MPSGs are developed for each class of equipment and workstation levels. Figure 15.41 shows an MPSG for a MP class of equipment. Software tools for automatically generating the execution portion of the controller based on the MPSG have been developed (Smith and Joshi, 1993). The software is generated by first creating a graph of the system's equipment resources, a description of their connectivity (using MPSGs), a set of transition messages; and then linking all of these to a communication system. For on-line (web) viewing of these concepts, the reader is referred to

> http://wimpy1.psu.edu/rapidcim/rapid.html, or
> http://www-tamcam.tamu.edu/rapidcim.html

15.6.2.3 Simulation for real-time control.   The RapidCIM approach is to first use the simulation to predict system performance as with the traditional approach, and then use the same simulation as the decision maker for the operational control system. The rationale for this approach is that in order for the simulation to provide accurate estimates of the system performance, it must be engendered with the same control logic as the actual control system. Given this, it would be much more attractive to *reuse* the simulation control logic than to discard the simulation and *recreate* the same logic in the control context.

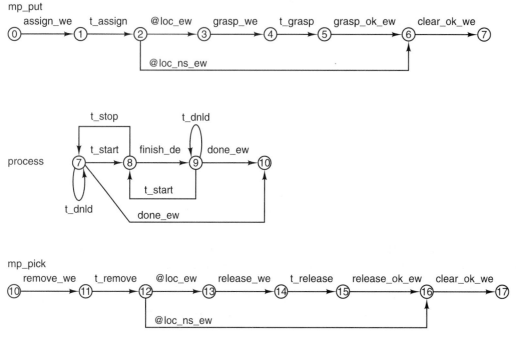

Figure 15.41   MPSG for MP class equipment.

In order to use the simulation as the decision maker in the control system, two fundamental changes must be made to the simulation system. First of all, the simulation must be at the level of commands required by the execution interface at any level. The second modification is to the simulation program itself to allow it to communicate directly with the executor in real time. The general architecture for implementing the use of simulation for creating the tasks to be used in shop-floor control is shown in Figure 15.42. The figure shows that the simulation (or task generator) utilizes a set of message (task) queues to communicate with the executor. This architecture allows any decision maker (or simulation) to hook directly to the executor.

This is accomplished using the SIMAN simulation language (Pegden et al., 1993) through the addition of a TASK element and modifications to DELAY, EXECUTE, ROUTE, MOVE, and TRANSPORT block. The EXECUTE block specifies that a physical action is to be performed, which is sent to the executor as a message. On completion of the task, the executor sends a reply message to the decision maker via the shared queue. When the entity receives the completion message, it passes through the EXECUTE block to the next statement in the code.

The CONTROL element is used to specify whether the simulation actually interacts with the execution module. If the CONTROL element is present in the experiment file, then the simulation is said to be in *real-time* mode and follows the communications sequence outlined earlier. Otherwise, the simulation is said to be in the fast mode and the message-passing sequence is replaced by a DELAY (which can be either fixed or

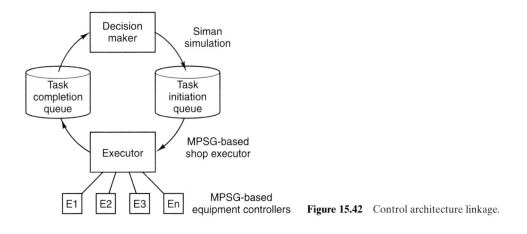

Figure 15.42   Control architecture linkage.

stochastic). By running a copy of the simulation in fast mode, different control scenarios can be evaluated while the physical system is executing tasks specified by another copy of the same simulation running in the real-time mode. At appropriate time intervals, the two simulations are *synchronized* and the results of the performance testing on the fast-mode simulation are applied to the real-time simulation.

15.6.2.4 Implementation.   The RapidCIM control system described in this chapter has been implemented in two laboratories: one at Penn State University and the other at Texas A&M University. Figure 15.43 shows an overview of the Penn State FMS lab.

Both of these implementations currently use a discrete-event simulation written in SIMAN/ARENA as the decision maker. Figure 15.44 illustrates the structure of the control system as currently implemented in the labs. In this structure, the SIMAN/ARENA simulation serves as the decision maker (or task generator) and the MPSG-based execution modules perform the execution functions. The task generator and execution modules communicate through the task-initiation queue (TIQ) and the task-completion queue (TCQ). The simulation uses the TIQ to instruct the execution module to perform specific tasks and receives completion messages through the TCQ. These queues facilitate the explicit separation for the decision maker from the execution module.

The separation of the decision maker and the execution module makes the system truly *plug and play*. Assuming the decision maker understands the physical constraints imposed on the task sequences, any decision maker can be "plugged in" to the execution module according to the current production requirements. This allows use of a decision maker most appropriate to the specific application such as an expert system, custom optimization algorithm, simulation, or other appropriate tool.

The separation between the decision maker and the execution module also makes it possible to use the decision maker in an off-line play-and-plug mode. Off-line, it can be used to *play* with different production alternatives and/or refine the production heuristics to provide improved operation. Likewise, this play mode can be used to

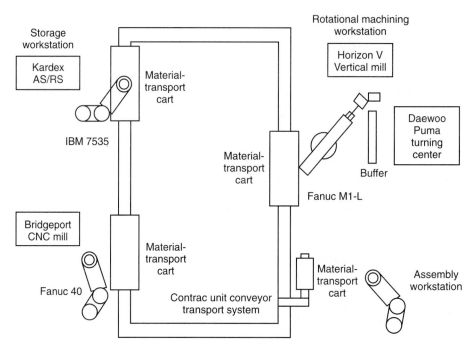

Figure 15.43 Penn State FMS Lab.

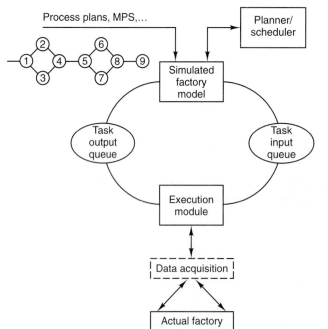

Figure 15.44 RapidCIM as currently implemented.

determine the best response to exceptions such as equipment failures. This new knowledge can then be *plugged* back into on-line operations.

It is frequently desired to emulate certain equipment. Emulation can be used to permit limited operation during installation, equipment failures, and while testing new equipment/approaches. More important, emulation allows the same control system to be used in both real-time control as well as the off-line mode discussed before.

Emulation can be accomplished in two ways. The first approach is to let the execution module simply respond with a task-completion message after a fixed time interval. This approach does not require any extra logic in the decision maker.

The second approach is to let the decision maker implement emulation logic in place of actually executing a task. For example, SIMAN can incorporate any logic necessary (from a simple delay to complex guided transporter interactions) to emulate equipment. This logic would be developed during initial system design/analysis and retained for later reuse during testing and the emulation discussed before.

15.7 CONCLUDING REMARKS

CAD/CAM and flexible manufacturing systems have arrived. These systems are capable of producing a wide range of parts. As we move closer and closer to computer-integrated manufacturing, a greater range of engineering and computer knowledge will be required by manufacturing, mechanical, and industrial engineers. If we in the United States are to continue to be world leaders in industrial productivity, future engineers must understand manufacturing science, mechanical-design principles, industrial-engineering principles, and computer science. Integration of our manufacturing environment can be achieved only through an integration of our education. Flexible manufacturing systems promise to provide the logical solution for the automatic production of low- to medium-batch-size manufacturing. However, the design and control of these systems will provide manufacturing engineers with a wealth of design and control problems during their construction.

REVIEW QUESTIONS

15.1. Briefly explain what the flexibility in a flexible manufacturing system means.

15.2. An FMS is integrated by an automatic material-handling system. What type of system would be appropriate for small parts requiring many short operations? Explain your answer.

15.3. Keeping in mind your answer to Review Question 2, what type of considerations should be made for large parts requiring a few long processing operations?

15.4. How does the process plan affect the selection of FMS equipment and control computers? Explain your answer.

15.5. Create the ladder logic to control the FMS shown in Figure 15.15.

15.6. If the parts for the FMS shown in Figure 15.17 were to be batched by part type, could the system be controlled with a programmable controller? How many ladder-logic segments or programs would be required? Create the ladder logic to control the flow of only part 1.

REFERENCES/BIBLIOGRAPHY

ALBUS, J., A. BARBERA, and N. NAGEL (1981). "Theory and Practice of Hierarchical Control," in *Proceedings of the 23rd IEEE Computer Society International Conference.* Washington, DC: pp. 18–39.

BEECKMAN, D. (1989). "CIM-OSA: Computer Integrated Manufacturing—Open Systems Architecture," *International Journal of Computer Integrated Manufacturing,* 2 (2), pp. 94–105.

BOFFEY, T. B. (1982). *Graph Theory in Operations Research.* London: Macmillan.

CATRON, B. A., and S. R. RAY (1991). "ALPS: A Language for Process Specification," *International Journal of Computer Integrated Manufacturing,* 4 (2), pp. 105–113.

CHO, H., A. DEREBAIL, T. HALE, and R. A. WYSK (1993). "A Formal Approach to Integrating Computer Aided Process Planning and Shop Floor Control," *Journal of Engineering for Industry,* November, Vol 116, No 1, pp. 108–116

CO, H. C. (1984). "Design and Implementation of Flexible Manufacturing Systems—Some Analysis Concepts." Ph.D. thesis, Virginia Polytechnic Institute and State University, Blacksburg, Virginia.

COFFMAN, E. G., M. J. ELPHICK, and A. SHOSHANI (1971). "System Deadlock," *Computing Surveys,* 3, (2).

CONWAY, R. W., B. M. JOHNSON, and W. L. MAXWELL (1960). "An Experimental Investigation of Priority Dispatching," *Journal of Industrial Engineering,* 11 (221).

CUTKOSKY, M. R., P. S. FUSSELL, and R. MILLIGNA, JR. (1984). *Precision Flexible Machining Cells within a Manufacturing System,* Paper CMU-RI-TR-84-12. Pittsburgh: Carnegie-Mellon University.

DAR-EI, E. M., and R. A. WYSK (1982). "Job Shop Scheduling—A Systematic Approach," *Journal of Manufacturing Systems,* 1 (1), 39–47.

DAVIS, R. (1976). *Applications of Meta Level Knowledge to the Construction, Maintenance, and Use of Large Knowledge Bases,* Computer Science Department Paper STAN-CS-76-564. Stanford: Stanford University.

DAVIS, W., and A. JONES (1989). "A Functional Approach to Designing Architecture for CIM," *IEEE Transactions on Systems, Man, and Cybernetics,* 19 (2), 164–189.

DUFFIE, N. A., and R. S. PIPER (1987). "Non-Hierarchical Control of a Flexible Manufacturing Cell," *Robotics and Computer Integrated Manufacturing,* 3 (2), 175–179.

GERE, W. S., Jr. (1966). "Heuristics in Job Shop Scheduling," *Management Science,* 13 (3), 167–175.

GLIGOR, V. D., and S. H. SHATUCK (1980). "On Deadlock Detection in Distributed Systems," *IEEE Transactions on Software Engineering,* SE-6 (5).

GOLD, E. M. (1978). "Deadlock Prediction: Easy and Difficult Cases," *SIAM Journal on Computing,* 7 (3).

GRAY, J. N. (1978). "Notes on Data Base Operating Systems," in W. Bayer, J. Graham, and S. Segmuller, Eds., *Operating Systems—An Advanced Course,* Vol. 60. New York: Springer-Verlag, pp. – .

GURECKI, R., and S. Y. NOF (1979). "Decision Support for a Computerized Manufacturing System," in *The Optimum Planning of Computer Manufacturing Systems,* West Lafayette, IN: Purdue University. pp. – .

HABERMANN, A. N. (1969). "Prevention of System Deadlocks," *Communications of the ACM,* 12, 373.

Hok, R. C. (1971). "Comments on Prevention of System Deadlock," *Communications of the ACM,* 14, 36.

Howard, J. H. (1973). "Mixed Solutions for the Deadlock Problem," *Communications of the ACM,* 16, 427.

Jackson, J. R. (1957). "Networks of Waiting Lines," *Operations Research,* 5, 518–521.

Johnson, S. M. (1954). "Optimal Two and Three Stage Production Scheduled with Setup Times Included," *Naval Research Logistics Quarterly,* 1 (1).

Jones, A. T., and C. R. McLean (1986). "A Proposed Hierarchical Structure for Automated Manufacturing Systems," *Journal of Manufacturing Systems,* 5 (5), 15–25.

Jones, A. T., and A. Saleh (1990). "A Multi-level/Multi-layer Architecture for Intelligent Shop Floor Control," *International Journal of Computer Integrated Manufacturing,* 3 (1), 60–70.

Joshi, S., E. G. Mettala, and R. A. Wysk (1992). "Formal Models for Control of Flexible Manufacturing Cells: Physical and System Model," *IIE Transactions,* 24 (3), pp. 84–97.

Joshi, S. B., R. A. Wysk, and A. Jones (1990). "A Scaleable Architecture for CIM Shop Floor Control," in A. Jones, Ed., *Proceedings of Cimcon 90,* Washington, DC: National Institute of Standards and Technology, 21–33, Gaithersburg, MD.

Joshi, S., E. G. Mettala, J. S. Smith, and R. A. Wysk "Formal Models for Control of Flexible Manufacturing Cells: Physical and System Model," *IEEE Transactions on Robotics and Automation,* Vol. 11, No. 4, pp 558–570, 1995.

Kumara, S. R. T., S. Joshi, R. L. Kashyap, C. L. Moodie, and T. C. Chang (1986). "Expert Systems in Industrial Engineering," *International Journal of Production Research,* 24 (5), 1107–1125.

Lee, S., R. A. Wysk, and J. S. Smith (1995). "Process Planning Interface for a Shop Floor Control Architecture for Computer Integrated Manufacturing," *International Journal of Production Research,* 33 (9), 2415–2435.

Mayer, R. J., and J. J. Talavage (1976). *Simulation of a Computerized Manufacturing System,* NSF Grant No. APR74-15256, Report No. 4. West Lafayette, IN: Purdue University.

Menasce, D. A., and R. R. Muntz (1979). "Locking and Deadlock Detection in Distributed Data Bases," *IEEE Transactions on Software Engineering,* SE-6 (3).

Mettala, E. G. (1989). "Automatic Generation of Control Software in Computer Integrated Manufacturing." Ph.D. thesis, Pennsylvania State University, University Park.

Mettala, E. G., and S. B. Joshi (1993). "A Compact Representation of Alternative Process Plans/Routing for FMS Control Activities," *International Journal of Design and Manufacturing,* 3, 91–104.

Naylor, A. W., and R. A. Volz (1987). "Design of Integrated Manufacturing Control Software," *IEEE Transactions on Systems, Man, and Cybernetics,* SMC-17 (6), 881–897.

Nilsson, N. J. (1965). *Learning Machines.* New York: McGraw-Hill.

Panwalker, S. S., and W. Iskander (1984). "A Survey of Scheduling Rules," *Operations Research,* 25, 45–61.

Pegden, C. D., et al. (1993). *SIMAN V Users Manual.* Systems Modeling Corporation, McGraw Hill, NY.

Ramswamy, S. E., and S. Joshi (1995). "Distributed Control of Automated Manufacturing Systems," in *Proceedings of the 27th CIRP International Seminar on Manufacturing Systems.* Dearborn, MI:, SME, pp. 18–27.

Sanford, J. E. (1972). "DNC Lines Link Cutting to a New Future, *Iron Age,* August, 3849.

Senehi, M. K., E. Barkmeyer, M. Luce, S. Ray, E. Wallace, and S. Wallace (1991). *Manufacturing Systems Integration Initial Architecture Document,* NIST Interagency Report NISTIR 4682. Gaithersburg, MD: National Institute of Standards and Technology.

Shapiro, S. C. (1979). "The SNePS Semantic Network Processing System," in *Associative Networks,* Ed., New York: Academic Press.

Simpson, J. A., R. J. Hocken, and J. S. Albus (1977). "The Automated Manufacturing Research Facility of the National Bureau of Standards," *Journal of Manufacturing Systems, 1, (1), 17–32.*

Smith, J. S., and S. B. Joshi (1992). "Reusable Software Concepts for Flexible Manufacturing System Control," *International Journal of Computer Integrated Manufacturing, 5* (3), 182–196.

Smith, J. S. (1992). "A Formal Design and Development Methodology for Shop Floor Control in Computer Integrated Manufacturing." Ph.D. thesis, Pennsylvania State University, University Park.

Smith, J. S., W. Hoberecht, and S. B. Joshi (1993). *A Shop Floor Control Architecture for Computer Integrated Manufacturing,* IMSE Working Paper Series. University Park: Pennsylvania State University.

Smith, J. S., W. C. Hoberecht, and S. B. Joshi (1992). *A Shop Floor Control Architecture for Computer Integrated Manufacturing,* Industrial Engineering Working Paper INEN-MS-WP-13-11-92. College Station, TX: Texas A&M University.

Smith, J. S., and S. B. Joshi (1993). *Message-Base Part State Graphs: A Formal Model for Shop Floor Control,* IMSE Working Paper Series. University Park: Pennsylvania State University.

Smith, J. S., R. A. Wysk, D. T. Sturrock, S. E. Ramaswamy, G. D. Smith, and S. B. Joshi (1994). "Discrete Event Simulation for Shop Floor Control," *Proceedings of the Winter Simulation Conference.* Orlando, FL: IEEE, pp. 418–427.

Stecke, K. E., and X. Solberg (1977). *Scheduling of Operation in a Computerized Manufacturing System,* NSF Grant APR74-15256, Report No. 10. West Lafayette, IN: Purdue University.

Swyt, D. A. (1986). *CIM, Data and Standardization within the NBS AMRF,* NBS Internal Report. Washington, DC: National Bureau of Standards.

Tsutsui, S., and Y. Fujimoto (1987). "Deadlock Prevention in Process Computer Systems," *Computer Journal, 30* (1).

Williams, V. A. (1974). "DNC for Flexibility," *Production Engineering,* August, 17–31.

Winston, P. H. (1970). *Learning Structural Descriptions from Examples,* Report No. TR-213. Cambridge, MA: Massachusetts Institute of Technology, AI Laboratory.

Wu, H. J. (1994). "Development of Execution Error Recovery Module for Shop Floor Control." Ph.D. thesis, Pennsylvania State University, University Park.

Wu, S. Y. D. (1987). "An Expert System Approach for the Control and Scheduling of Flexible Manufacturing Cells." Ph.D. thesis, Pennsylvania State University, University Park.

Wysk, R. A., B. A. Peters, and J. S. Smith (1995). "A Process Planning Schema for Shop Floor Control," *Engineering Design and Automation Journal, 1* (1), 3–20.

Wysk, R. A., S. Y. D. Wu, and N. S. Yang (1986). "A Multi-Pass Expert Control System (MPECS) for Flexible Manufactuirng Systems," in *ASME Bound Volume of the Symposium on Integrated and Intelligence Manufacturing.* Miami, FL: American Society of Manufacturing Engineers, pp. 84–97.

Wysk, R. A., N. S. Yang, and S. B. Joshi (1991). "Detection of Deadlocks in Flexible Manufacturing Systems," *IEEE Transactions on Robotics and Automation,* Vol 13, No. 2, 856–859.

16

The Planning of Manufacturing Systems

16.1 MANUFACTURING-RESOURCE PLANNING

With the advent of computerized manufacturing systems has come the need to efficiently and accurately model the performance of such systems. Several methods of planning and evaluation exist to provide a valid explanation of system behavior. The purpose of any model is to capture the essential characteristics of a system and to determine the system performance under a variety of conditions. Manufacturing-planning models are used to answer questions regarding machine-requirement planning, machine utilization, variability in operation times, and labor requirements.

Numerous types of modeling methods for manufacturing systems have been developed in recent years. Mathematical, physical, and simulation models have been developed for a wide variety of applications.

Most existing manufacturing systems models can be classified as queueing or network models. Analytical or mathematical models are available to describe the behavior of these types of systems. By using analytical models in conjunction with some necessary assumptions, a system usually can be resolved via a set of algebraic equations. A difficulty with queueing or network models develops when analyzing complex systems. Many fine intricacies found within complex systems cannot be included in mathematical models. Furthermore, the computations involved in such analyses can become quite cumbersome. Therefore, when analyzing complex systems, mathematical modeling can be used as a tool to achieve a rough measure of system performance, and, if necessary, more rigorous and detailed evaluation techniques can be undertaken.

An alternative to mathematical modeling is manipulation of the physical system itself. By physically altering the system, exact performance can be observed. Due to time and financial constraints, however, the manipulation or development of physical systems is often prohibitive.

A third method of manufacturing-system planning is by means of computer simulation. A computer-simulation model serves as an aggregate approximation of the system that can provide detail to the analysis that a mathematical model cannot. A difficulty with simulation is that as the complexity of the system grows, the time required to create a valid model and obtain meaningful results can increase rapidly. In this light, it is often preferable to analyze a system with a mathematical model initially to provide a strong base for the development of a simulation model.

16.2 PROCEDURES FOR PLANNING MANUFACTURING SYSTEMS

Planning and modeling manufacturing systems are not strictly done sequentially. However, a general approach to manufacturing-system planning is briefly described in the following and can be used for each system evaluation.

1. *Define and formulate the scope of the system.* Every study must begin with a clear statement of the planning objective. The system characteristics of interest must be determined to aid in selecting the method of analysis. The system scope is defined by establishing the complexity of the system and the degree of interaction between the machine-requirement planning problem and other facility planning/design issues such as layout, material handling, work methods, machine loading/scheduling, and resource allocation. Furthermore, the alternative system designs should be delineated and the criteria for evaluating the efficiency of these alternatives should be described.

2. *Define the model for planning the system.* The scope and complexity of the system under consideration typically will indicate the methods to be used for planning purposes. When defining a method of analysis, the amount and detail of system data that will be required also should be determined. Descriptions of several methods of analysis for planning manufacturing systems are presented in later sections of this chapter.

3. *Collect system data and evaluate its validity.* Once a model has been defined, the data should be collected on the system of interest to serve as input parameters for the model. Further, probability distributions for all random variables in the model should be defined in this stage to describe the variability of the system.

In the data-collection stage, it is essential to validate the information that is collected. It is important to involve individuals within the study who are intimately familiar with the operations and the actual system to ensure that the system parameters are accurate. In addition, the adequacy of the theoretical probability distributions fitted to the observed data should be evaluated using goodness-of-fit tests.

4. *Analyze the output data.* A typical goal of manufacturing-system planning is to determine a set of system parameters or characteristics that will optimize a particular system design relative to some specified measure of performance. Such decisions are relatively straightforward when working with deterministic models; however, statistical techniques should be used to analyze output data for simulation studies.

16.3 MACHINE-REQUIREMENT PLANNING

In the preceding chapters, we examined the problem of process/equipment selection. Having determined the manufacturing process, the type of raw materials, and the type of equipment needed, we now focus on the problem of planning the other manufacturing resources. The emphasis here is placed on machine-requirement and manufactur-

systems planning. The subsequent labor and space requirements can be determined from process-planning summaries.

Machine-requirement planning is the problem of specifying the number of each type of machine(s) to use within some planning horizon, subject to space, manpower, available financial resources, production level, and other constraints.

The solution approach for the machine-requirement planning problem depends on the complexity of the system being studied. The complexity of the system is determined by the degree of interaction between the machine-requirement planning problem and other facility planning/design issues such as layout, material-handling considerations, machine loading/scheduling, in-process inventory, lot sizing, work methods, and resource allocation.

If we consider the typical flow pattern shown in Figure 16.1, we can see that raw materials enter the system through work center 1 and exit the system at work center N, following a sequence of operations (as dictated by a routing summary). The machine-requirement planning at, say, work center 2, is determined by the input requirement of work center 3, the output to work center 1, as well as the man–machine assignments, work methods used, and the schedules employed at work center 2. Furthermore, the different work centers in a manufacturing system compete for limited resources (financial, manpower, space, and so on), thus affecting the decision of how many machines to use at each work center.

Ideally, the manufacturing-resource planning problem should be resolved within an integrated framework of analysis. However, because the interactions tend to make the analysis intractable, the different planning and implementation issues are generally resolved iteratively and sequentially. For instance, the nature of the production process greatly affects the formulation and analysis of the machine-requirement planning problem. By specifying the process plan, the machining parameters, the machine requirements, and so on, simultaneously can lead to difficulties in both model formulation and solution process.

16.3.1 Single Work Center

To begin the analysis of planning procedures, the simplest form of manufacturing systems are viewed. Consider a system of homogeneous machines or an isolated subsystem of homogeneous machines where the interaction with other facility-design and

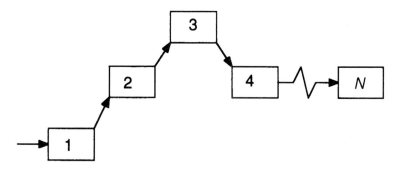

Figure 16.1   A typical manufacturing flow pattern.

production-planning decisions are disregarded. Depending on the variability of the operations being conducted at the work center, the machine-requirement planning models may be formulated as deterministic or stochastic analyses. A discussion of each type of analysis follows.

16.3.1.2 The deterministic case. To develop a deterministic analysis, let us assume that the collection of production parameters are constant and are well-defined. Let t be the average standard processing time in minutes per piece that any given part type will incur. Parameter t is computed by averaging the standard times of all parts processed in the work center, weighted by their production proportion. That is, if t_i is the standard time to perform an operation on part type i, f_i is the proportion of production that part type i maintains, and $\Sigma f_i = 1$. Then

$$t = \sum_{\text{all } i} t_i \times f_i \tag{16.1}$$

Let p be the production level in number of parts per day, h be the number of working hours per machine per day, and u be the expected efficiency factor. The expected efficiency factor is a catchall factor that may include factors such as scrap/waste, machine downtime (scheduled maintenance and machine breakdown), and idle time resulting from interaction with other work centers.

The number of machines required, x, can be determined by

$$x = \frac{(t/60) \times p}{h \times u} \text{ units} \tag{16.2}$$

Notice that x may or may not be an integer.

Example 16.1

Consider a work center where three part types are processed. Part A requires 10 min of processing per piece and comprises 50% of the total production. The other 50% of total production is divided equally between parts B and C. Part B requires 12 min of processing per piece, and part C requires 15 min of processing per piece. If the required daily production level is 100 pieces and there are 7.5 working hours per day, plot the number of machines required as a function of the expected efficiency factor, u.

Solution From Equation (16.1):

$$t = 10 \times 0.5 + 12 \times 0.25 + 15 \times 0.25 = 11.75 \text{ min}$$

From Equation (16.2):

$$x = \frac{(11.75/60) \times 100}{7.5 \times u} = \frac{2.61}{u}$$

Figure 16.2 illustrates a plot of the number of machines required versus the expected efficiency factor, u. Notice the sensitivity of the machine requirement, x, to the value of the expected efficiency factor, u.

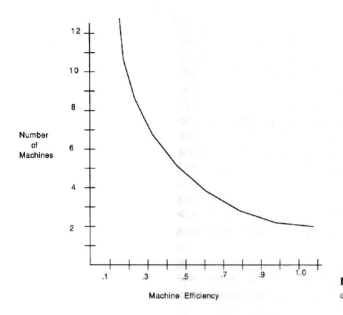

Figure 16.2   Machine requirements versus expected efficiency.

16.3.2 The Stochastic Case

In the last case, a set of constants ($t, p, u,$ and h) completely determines the machine requirements. Suppose the processing time, production level, effectiveness factor, and number of hours available are random variables ($T, P, U,$ and $H,$ respectively) instead of constants. Then the expected number of machines required is

$$E(x) = \text{EXP} \frac{(T/60) \times P}{H \times U} \tag{16.3}$$

and the variance is

$$V(x) = \text{VAR} \frac{(T/60) \times P}{H \times U} \tag{16.4}$$

The distribution of machine requirements can be used to estimate the future equipment needs. The probable number of required machines can be determined statistically. This method can aid in understanding the randomness of the production system.

Example 16.2

Suppose the standard production time of a component is a discrete random variable with the following probability density function:

PRODUCTION TIME (T)	PROBABILITY
20 min	0.6
30 min	0.3
40 min	0.1

Assume the production quantity per day depends on processing time and has the following distribution:

	p	CONDITIONAL PROBABILITY $Pr[P/T]$	JOINT PROBABILITY $Pr[P \cap T]$
$T = 20$	100 units	0.60	0.36
	120 units	0.40	0.24
$T = 30$	80 units	0.40	0.12
	100 units	0.30	0.09
	120 units	0.30	0.09
$T = 40$	95 units	1.00	0.10

The expected efficiency factor is a linear function of P and T defined by the following relationship:

$$U = 1.0 - 0.005 \times [P \times (T/60)]$$

If there are 8 working hours per day per machine, determine the expected number of machines required.

Solution   From Equation (16.3):

$$E(x) = \frac{(T/60) \times P}{8 \times [1.0 - 0.005 \times (T/60) \times P]} Pr(P \cap T)$$

$$= \frac{(20/60) \times 100}{8 \times [1 - 0.005 \times (20/60) \times 100]} \times 0.36$$

$$+ \frac{(20/60) \times 120}{8 \times (1 - 0.005 \times (20/60) \times 120)} \times 0.24$$

$$+ \cdots$$

$$+ \frac{(40/60) \times 1}{8 \times [1.0 - 0.005 \times (40/60) \times 95]} \times 0.1$$

$$= 6.92$$

$$\approx 7 \text{ units}$$

and from Equation (16.4):

$$Var(x) = E(x^2) - E(x)^2$$

$$= \left[\frac{(T/60) \times P}{8 \times (1.0 - 0.005 \times (T/60) \times P)} \right]^2 Pr(P \cap T) - E(x)^2 = 3.94 \text{ units}$$

Example 16.3

Suppose the number of machines required, X, is normally distributed. What is the probability that 8 units will be adequate? For a service level of 0.95, how many units of machines are needed?

Solution   Having determined the distribution that a given machine requirement will follow, it is necessary to evaluate how the production process will perform with different numbers of machines. Assuming that the number of machines required is normally distributed, with a mean, μ, and a standard deviation, σ, the probability that x units will be adequate can be calculated.

$$\Pr(X \ge x) = \Pr\left(\frac{X - \mu}{\sigma} \ge \frac{x - \mu}{\sigma}\right)$$

$$= \Pr\left(Z \ge \frac{x - \mu}{\sigma}\right)$$

In the previous example, the mean number of machines required was 7 units with a variance equal to 3.94 units. The probability that 8 machines will be adequate under these circumstances is

$$\Pr(X \ge 8) = \Pr\left(Z \ge \frac{8 - \mu}{\sigma}\right)$$

$$= \Pr\left(Z \ge \frac{8 - 7}{\sqrt{3.94}}\right)$$

$$= \Pr\left(Z \ge \frac{8 - 7}{1.985}\right)$$

$$= \Pr(Z \ge 0.5)$$

$$= 0.309$$

For a service level of 0.95, the number of machines required can be calculated:

$$\Pr(X \le x) = 0.95$$

$$\Pr\left(Z \le \frac{x - 7}{\sqrt{3.94}}\right) = 0.95$$

$$\Pr\left(Z \le \frac{x - 7}{1.985}\right) = 0.95$$

$$\Pr\left(Z \ge \frac{x - 7}{1.985}\right) = 0.05$$

$$Z = \frac{1.64 + 1.65}{2} = 1.645$$

$$x = 1.645 \times 1.985 + 7$$

$$= 10.265$$

$$= 11 \text{ units}$$

16.3.1.3 Flow-time and work-in-process.   The problem of determining the minimum number of machines to satisfy a production requirement has been investigated in the preceding sections. Sometimes it is necessary to consider other decision criteria such as the level of work-in-process and the make-span in determining the machine requirements.

Suppose the processing times are exponentially distributed, with expected value equal to $E(T)$, and workpieces arriving to the machine follow the Poisson distribution, with expected arrival rate equal to $E(N)$. Let

$$\rho = \frac{E(N) \times E(T)}{X} \tag{16.5}$$

where ρ is the traffic intensity of the system and is an indicator of machine utilization, and X is the number of servers at the current machine. For a stable station, $\rho < 1$. If $\rho > 1$, workpieces arrive faster than the work center can process the components and, therefore, the work-in-process will grow unbounded and become too large.

If the workpieces are processed on the basis of first in, first out (FIFO), the expected level of work-in-process (including the workpiece currently being processed) is

$$E(q) = B \times \frac{\rho}{1 - \rho} + \rho X \tag{16.6}$$

where

$$B = \frac{1 - b}{(1 - \rho) \times b} \tag{16.7}$$

$$b = \frac{(X \times \rho)^L / L!}{(M \times \rho)^2 / L!}$$

B is often referred to as the busy factor. The expected flow time is

$$E(f) = \frac{B}{X} \times \frac{E(T)}{1 - \rho} + E(T) \tag{16.8}$$

Example 16.4

Assume that parts are arriving to a work center at the rate of 1.2 parts per min. Suppose the processing time is exponentially distributed with a mean equal to 3.0 min and the arrival distribution is Poisson. Evaluate the alternatives of using 4, 5, 6, and 7 machines.

Solution The traffic intensity is $1.2 \times 3.0/X = 3.6/X$. Therefore, X must be greater than 3.6 (at least 4). Table 16.1 compares the work-in-process level and expected flow time for the four alternatives. Notice that there is a significant improvement in flow time and work-in-process between $X = 4$ (the minimum requirement) and $X = 5$.

TABLE 16.1 COMPARISON OF WORK-IN-PROCESS LEVEL AND EXPECTED FLOW TIME FOR ALTERNATIVE MACHINE LEVELS

	$X = 4$	$X = 5$	$X = 6$	$X = 7$
$E(q)$	10.6898	4.6553	3.8949	3.6913
$E(f)$	8.9082	3.8794	3.2457	3.0761
ρ	0.9000	0.7200	0.6000	0.5143
B	0.7878	0.4104	0.1966	0.0862

16.3.3 Multioperation Model

The previous section dealt with a group of elementary system descriptions. As the number of pieces of equipment increases and the interactions within a system become more complex, the methods of analysis increase in difficulty. This section focuses on multioperational systems, where several product types flow through a system with numerous equipment stations.

16.3.3.1 Serial flow systems.   Consider a serial system where each work center is visited once and only once in the same sequence. In such a system, parts flow from work center 1 to work center j, for $j = 1, 2, \ldots, m$, where m is the total number of work centers in the system.

Let t_j be the average standard work time at work center j, h be the number of working hours per machine per day, and u_j be the effectiveness factor at work center j. The machine requirements for a production level of p_j units per day, therefore, can be determined by

$$x_j = \frac{(t_j/60) \times p_j}{h \times u_j} \qquad \text{for all } j = 1, 2, 3, \ldots, m \qquad (16.9)$$

For the multiproduct case, let t_{ij} be the standard time of part type i at work center j. Then

$$t_j = \sum_{\text{all } i} t_{ij} \times f_i \qquad (16.10)$$

where f_i is the production proportion of part type i. Equation (16.9) can be used to determine the machine requirements for such a multiproduct circumstance.

16.3.3.2 Nonserial systems.   Except for pure flow shops and transfer lines, the work flow in a manufacturing system generally includes feedforward/feedback work flows and divergent/convergent work flows, as illustrated in Figure 16.3.

Let t_{ijk} be the standard time of product i at work center j for its kth operation, and v_{ij} be the number of times product i is processed at work center j. The number of operations needed to complete product i is

$$n_i = \sum v_{ij} \qquad \text{for all } j = 1, 2, 3, \ldots, m \qquad (16.11)$$

Let f_i be the production proportion of product i. Then $t_{ij} = \sum_k t_{ijk}$ is the total processing time required for product i at work center j. Further, $\sum_{\text{all } i} t_{ij} \times f_i$ is the average standard time at work center j.

The machine requirement can be determined using Equation (16.9). However, for multioperation nonserial systems, the efficiency factor, u, should take into consideration the idle time caused by scheduling related difficulties and other amenities of the interaction between work centers. Estimating the value of u is difficult. The machine requirement, x, is very sensitive to u, such that a small error in estimating u can lead to

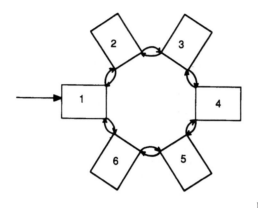

Figure 16.3 Convergent/divergent production flow.

serious error. The following section describes a queueing model that can be applied in such a situation without having to estimate the efficiency factor, u.

16.4 ANALYTICAL MODELS

16.4.1 Machine-Requirement Planning Using CAN-Q

Typical nonserial systems are quite complex in their structure. Analysis of such systems can be quite cumbersome without the use of a computational and analytical tool. A mathematical model has been established that is based on network and queueing theory. Computational efficiencies have enhanced the model's capabilities as a planning tool. The analytical tool, CAN-Q, is illustrated in the following example.

Example 16.5

Consider a nonserial system where three products are processed. The routing sequence, production proportion, and the unit investment cost of the machines are as follows:

PART	PRODUCTION PROPORTION	ROUTING
A	50%	Drill (30 min)
		Mill (10 min)
		Turn (20 min)
B	30%	Mill (5 min)
		Drill (5 min)
		Turn (10 min)
		Mill (5 min)
C	20%	Turn (15 min)
		Drill (10 min)
		Turn (5 min)

OPERATION	NUMBER OF MACHINES
Milling	3
Drilling	2
Turning	3

From the routing data, the processing time required for each product at each work center is

$$
\begin{array}{c}
\text{Work Center}\\
\begin{array}{ccc}
\text{M} & \text{D} & \text{T}
\end{array}
\end{array}
$$

$$
[t_{ij}] = \text{Part}\;
\begin{array}{c}
A\\B\\C
\end{array}
\begin{vmatrix}
10 & 30 & 20\\
10 & 5 & 10\\
0 & 10 & 20
\end{vmatrix}
$$

$$
[t_{ij}\,f_i] =
\begin{vmatrix}
5 & 15 & 10\\
3 & 1.5 & 3\\
0 & 2 & 4
\end{vmatrix}
$$

and

$$
\sum_i [t_{ij}\,f_i] = |8 \quad 18.5 \quad 17| = [t_j]
$$

Similarly, the frequency of operation per work center is

$$
\begin{array}{ccc}
\text{M} & \text{D} & \text{T}
\end{array}
$$

$$
[v_{ij}] =
\begin{array}{c}
A\\B\\C
\end{array}
\begin{vmatrix}
1 & 1 & 1\\
2 & 1 & 1\\
0 & 1 & 2
\end{vmatrix}
$$

Then

$$
[v_{ij}\,f_i] =
\begin{vmatrix}
0.5 & 0.5 & 0.5\\
0.6 & 0.3 & 0.3\\
0.0 & 0.2 & 0.4
\end{vmatrix}
$$

$$
\sum_i [v_{ij}\,f_i] = |1.1 \quad 1.0 \quad 1.2| = [v_d]
$$

The standard time per operation is

$$
\left[\frac{t}{v}\right] = \left[\frac{8}{1.1}, \frac{18.5}{1.0}, \frac{1.7}{1.2}\right] = [t_j']
$$

and the visit frequency is

$$
\left[\frac{v_j}{v}\right] = \left[\frac{1.1}{3.3}, \frac{1.0}{3.3}, \frac{1.2}{3.3}\right] = [v_j']
$$

where the expected number of operations to complete a part is

$$
V = \sum_{\text{all } j} v_j = 1.1 + 1.0 + 1.2 = 3.3
$$

Consider the following assumptions:

1. The processing times are exponentially distributed, with average processing times = t'_j for machines at work center j.
2. A fixed number of workpieces circulate in the system.
3. A new workpiece enters the system when a completed workpiece leaves the system.

Because the expected number of operations to complete a part is 3.3, the probability that a workpiece leaving a work center is a completed workpiece (and thus must leave the system) is $1.0/3.3 = 0.303$; and the probability that the workpiece goes to another work center is $1.0 - 0.303 = 0.697$.

The probability that a workpiece goes to work center j within any routing sequence is v'_j. If a work center is busy when a workpiece arrives, the workpiece will wait in a local in-process buffer until it can be processed. With regard to the interactions between material handling and the work centers, blocking is assumed to never occur.

The preceding assumptions are those of CAN-Q, a performance-evaluation package for the planning of automated manufacturing systems. CAN-Q is based on the theory developed in Jackson (1957, 1963) and Gordon and Newell (1967). The computational refinements for the model were introduced by Buzen (1973). The results pertain to the problem of determining the equilibrium distribution of parts in a queueing system of interconnected work centers. CAN-Q is described in Solberg (1976a) and a *User's Guide* (including the FORTRAN program listing) is available in Solberg (1980).

CAN-Q is based on the premise that a manufacturing system can be represented as a queueing network where flow of materials within the network occurs between each workstation through a material-handling technique. The material-handling system is central in the sense that every unit must be transported by the system before and after every operation. Further, an assumption that sets CAN-Q apart from typical simulation models is that instead of dealing with arrivals and departures of units within the system, the system is said to be closed. When a system is closed, it contains a fixed number of circulating workpieces. In order to identify completed workpieces, an additional station is created, and passage through this station is equivalent to the final completion of the workpiece.

The workloads placed on the respective stations within the system are a function of both frequency and duration of use. The frequencies are dependent only on the routing of the parts. Frequencies are represented in the model by a set of probabilities that the material handler will deliver a workpiece to an individual station. This assumption has been opposed by many critics because it implies that a workpiece may return directly to the station from which it came. This argument may be refuted by stating that if the system reaches steady state, the frequencies will produce the correct average number of visits to each station over the long run.

It is noteworthy that most of the assumptions in CAN-Q are unrealistic and are not expected to be satisfied in real systems. However, the model has been found to be robust in many empirical studies. Validation studies available in the literature include Hughes and Moe (1973); Buzen (1975); Giammo (1976); Lipsky and Church (1977); Solberg (1977); Horev, Cook, and Ward (1978); Rose (1978); Co (1984, 1986).

An important method of evaluating system performance is through a measure of the production rate of the system. A complete CAN-Q analysis produces the overall system production rate and the rates of production of each part type in the system. Another important measure of performance that is produced by CAN-Q is the average time spent in the system. This measure of performance can be used to estimate product lead times. The most important measure of performance for an individual station is its utilization. This measure indicates the average fraction of time that an individual station is busy in production. These system measures are those typically found with simulation techniques. Such measures can dictate the overall structure and control of a manufacturing system.

An executive routine that calls CAN-Q prompts the user for the input data, computes the production capacity of the configuration, and identifies the bottleneck work center.

The user is then asked:

1. Is an additional machine desired?
2. Is it desirable to drop/add a product type from the production plan?

In each iteration, the production plan, the investment cost, the number of machines at each work center, and the production capacity are updated. The program stops when the user has reached the desired production capacity or when the investment requirement exceeds the allowable budget. If desired, the user may modify the machine requirements to account for the shop/system efficiency, the limited tool-storage capacities, and the desired machine redundancy.

Table 16.2 summarizes the output of the computer program for this example. The material-handling time is assumed to be 1.2 minutes per transfer.

16.4.2 Machine-Requirement Planning Using MANUPLAN

MANUPLAN is a commercially developed software package for designing and analyzing manufacturing systems (Network Dynamics, 1986). It was created as an analytical model to overcome the disadvantages of simulation in the initial design and planning stages. The analytical model used within MANUPLAN operates on a combination of queueing networks and reliability modeling.

As with CAN-Q, MANUPLAN views a manufacturing system as a network of queues. The performance of the system results from the interaction between the products requiring service and the resources of the system. If a workpiece encounters a busy station, it must wait in a queue before it can be processed. The mathematical model used in MANUPLAN estimates the dynamics of the interactions between the resources and the workpieces in the system.

TABLE 16.2 EXAMPLE CAN-Q OUTPUT SUMMARY

WORKLOAD SUMMARY PRODUCT TYPE A

	Station	No. of Visits	Visit Freq.	Total Proc Time	Average Proc Time	Relative Workload
	1 Drill	1.00	.333	30.00	30.00	10.00
A	2 Mill	1.00	.333	10.00	10.00	3.33
	3 Turn	1.00	.333	20.00	20.00	6.67
	1 Drill	1.00	.250	5.00	5.00	1.25
B	2 Mill	2.00	.500	10.00	5.00	2.50
	3 Turn	1.00	.250	10.00	10.00	2.50
C	1 Drill	1.00	.333	10.00	10.00	3.33
	3 Turn	2.00	.667	20.00	10.00	6.67

System Performance Measures

Production Rates by Product Type

Part Number

A	4.850
B	2.910
C	1.940

Production = 9.701 Items per hour

Average time in system = 278.33 Minutes

Processing	43.50
Traveling	3.96
Waiting	230.87

Station	Number of Servers	Server Utilization	Avg No. of Busy Servers
Drill	3	.997	2.991
Mill	2	.647	1.293
Turn	3	.916	2.749
Mat. Handler	2	.320	0.640

Input required to operate MANUPLAN includes information on part routing, equipment reliabilities and capacities, as well as production requirements. The output from MANUPLAN includes a production summary for each part type and equipment group. For each given part type, the production rate, scrap quantity, flow time, and average work-in-process are detailed. With regard to each machine group, the utilization, work-in-process, and machine downtime are determined by the system. An example of a MANUPLAN model follows.

Example 16.6

Consider a manufacturing assembly line for CRT terminals that consists of the following stations:

FIXT: fixturing station

ASMN: manual assembly station

ASRB: robotic assembly station

BOND: material bond station

INSP: inspection

RWK1: continuity inspect/rework

RPR1: component inspect/repair

The manufacturing system produces two types of CRT terminals. The yearly demand for part types 1 and 2 is 18,500 and 25,000, respectively. Further, part type 1 is produced in lots of 10, and part type 2 is produced in lots of 15.

A series of system information is required to provide detail to the model. Among the required information is the demand period, the length of the workday, and the number of days worked per year. A utilization limit must be placed on all equipment groups to limit the time that any equipment can be utilized during operation, setup, and downtime. The percentage variability of the interarrival and processing times of the batches also must be entered by the user.

A section of input data defines the capabilities of all equipment within the system. The equipment name and number of each type of equipment begin this series of input. The mean time to failure (MTTF) and the mean time to repair (MTTR) must be established for historical or forecasting information for each piece of equipment. The fifth data item in the equipment range is the overtime factor. This describes the percentage of overtime in the average day that will occur on a given machine. A value of 1.2 indicates that an average of 20% overtime is scheduled on a given machine each day. Two variability factors are used to allow the user to change or vary the processing or setup times for a given group of equipment. This allows the user a great deal of flexibility in comparing alternative models.

The final area of input details the components flowing through the system. This includes the yearly demand, lot size, and a series of variability factors. The variability factors allow the user to make changes to the production characteristics without altering the baseline values of the system. The part routings for the system under consideration are presented in Table 16.3. The routings include the operation description, equipment description, setup time, and processing time for each operation.

All of the input information just given can be input to MANUPLAN using a Lotus 1–2–3 front-end interface. This facilitates flexible use of spreadsheets to drive the MANUPLAN analysis. After the model is evaluated, output is presented summarizing the equipment utilization, work-in-process, time in the system, as well as details concerning individual equipment groups. Table 16.4 describes the equipment utilization and the product summaries for the example model.

16.4.3 Optimum Operating Rates and Time of Operation

The system scope of the machine-requirement planning problem considered thus far has been confined to the question of determining the number of machines given their operating rates and times of operation per day. This section addresses the problem of simultaneously determining the optimal values of the number of machines required, their operating rates, and the duration of operation of each machine. The manufacturing system considered here is that of Figure 16.1, which conforms to a serial multi-operation

TABLE 16.3 EXAMPLE MANUPLAN INPUT SUMMARY

PART TYPE 1

Operation	Equipment	Routing Proportion	Set-up (time/lot)	Proc. Time
Fixture	FIXT	1.0		10.0
Assemble	ASRB	0.7		3.0
Assemble	ASMN	0.3	40.0	25.0
Bond jacket	BOND	1.0		4.5
Inspect	INSP	1.0	7.0	2.0
Contin. Ins.	RWK1	1.0		32.0
Compon. Ins.	RPR1	1.0		60.0

PART TYPE 2

Operation	Equipment	Routing Proportion	Set-up (time/lot)	Proc. Time
Fixture	FIXT	1.0		10.0
Assemble	ASMN	1.0	30.0	1.0
Bond jacket	BOND	1.0		4.5
Inspect	INSP	1.0	15.0	2.5
Contin. Ins.	RWK1	1.0		32.0
Compon. Ins.	RPR1	1.0		85.0

EQUIPMENT SUMMARY

Name	No. of Machines	Reliability—mins (MTTF)	(MTTR)	Overtime
FIXT	3	9600	960	1.0
ASRB	1	4800	60	1.0
ASMN	1	4800	60	1.0
BOND	−1	6000	120	1.0
INSP	1	10000	240	1.0
RWK1	2	10000	240	1.0
RPR1	1	10000	240	1.0

Note The −1 value is used to describe the number of bond machines is valid and is used to indicate that the details of capacity for a given machine are not required and need not be considered.

machining system with a different processing operation occurring at each machining center.

Within this framework, a mathematical model can be developed to determine the following:

1. the optimal number of machines in each work center
2. the optimum operating rates for the machines in each work center
3. the times that the machines should be run in each work center

TABLE 16.4 EXAMPLE MANUPLAN OUTPUT SUMMARY

PART TYPE 1

Operation	Equipment	Work In Process	Time in System	Flow Time (per good piece)
Fixture	FIXT	23.1	246.0	246.0
Assemble	ASRB	16.5	250.8	175.6
Assemble	ASMN	16.6	590.8	177.2
Bond jacket	BOND	4.5	48.3	48.3
Inspect	INSP	3.7	33.9	39.8
Contin. Ins.	RWK1	8.2	506.2	89.3
Compon. Ins.	RPR1	12.4	4239.2	144.8

PART TYPE 2

Operation	Equipment	Work In Process	Time in System	Flow Time (per good piece)
Fixture	FIXT	38.6	301.1	301.0
Assemble	ASMN	29.0	225.5	225.5
Bond jacket	BOND	9.1	71.2	71.2
Inspect	INSP	8.9	60.0	71.4
Contin. Ins.	RWK1	15.8	670.0	127.6
Compon. Ins.	RPR1	38.4	4930.4	352.2

EQUIPMENT SUMMARY

Name	% Capacity Required For: Set-Up	Run	Repair	Util.	Work in Process at: Equip.	Queue	Total
FIXT	0.0	74.1	7.4	81.5	2.22	2.66	4.9
ASRB	51.9	32.5	1.1	85.5	0.84	2.73	3.6
ASMN	0.0	70.3	0.9	71.2	0.70	0.96	1.7
BOND	0.0	0.0	2.0	2.0	1.00	0.06	1.1
INSP	11.2	29.2	1.0	41.4	0.81	0.15	1.0
RWK1	0.0	63.7	1.5	65.2	1.27	0.60	1.9
RPR1	0.0	83.7	2.0	85.8	0.84	2.96	3.8

The variation in production cost, as the rate varies, is due to such factors as tool wear, power consumption, maintenance cost, and direct labor. It is assumed that the percent defective resulting from a manufacturing process is a function of the processing parameters. Therefore, a defective rate can be associated with each discrete processing rate.

Example 16.7

Consider the following two-operation problem:

WORK CENTER 1

Production rates:	25 units/hour	30 units/hour
% Defective:	4%	6%

Processing cost:

First shift	$10/hour	$13/hour
Second shift	$12/hour	$15/hour
Fixed cost:	$80/machine-day	$80/machine-day

WORK CENTER 2

Production rates:	15 units/hour	20 units/hour
% Defective:	8%	10%
Processing cost:		
First shift	$10/hour	$12/hour
Second shift	$12/hour	$15/hour
Fixed cost:	$60/machine-day	$60/machine-day

The production level is 200 to 300 units per day. The machines in each work center are assumed to be homogeneous, and each production day is broken into two components: an 8-hour first shift and an 8-hour second shift.

The notations used in the development of the machine-requirement planning model are

N: number of stations in the system

n_i: number of machines utilized in stage i

b_i: percent defective at station i

r_i: production rate (units/hour) at station i; $r_i \in R_i$

$C_{r_i}^s$: processing cost ($/hour) for shift 1 at station i

$C_{r_i}^o$: processing cost ($/hour) for shift 2 at station i

C_i^F: fixed production cost ($/machine) at station i

$t_{r_i}^s$: production time (hours) during shift 1 at station i

$t_{r_i}^o$: production time (hours) during shift 2 at station i

S_{Oi}: number of production units output at station i

S_{Ii}: number of production units arriving at station i

Z: total production cost

R_i: set of possible production rates at station i

The objective function is designed to minimize the total cost:

$$Z = \sum_{i=1}^{N} \sum_{r_i \in R_i} (C_{r_i}^s t_{r_i}^s + C_{r_i}^o t_{r_i}^o + C_i^F n_i) \tag{16.9}$$

and is subject to the following constraints.

First, the total number of units processed at stage i must equal the quantity available for processing at that station:

$$\sum_{r_i \in R_i} r_i(t_{r_i}^s + t_{r_i}^o) = S_{Oi} \tag{16.10}$$

Second, the quantity of output product at a stage (i.e., the quantity processed less the fraction defective) must equal the quantity processed by the next stage:

$$\sum_{r_i \in R_i} r_i(1 - b_i)(t_{r_i}^s + t_{r_i}^o) = S_{Oi} = S_{I(i+1)} \tag{16.11}$$

For the final stage, this restriction takes the following form:

$$\sum_{r_n \in R_n} r_n(1 - b_n)(t^s_{r_n} + t^o_{r_n}) = S_{On} = \text{final demand} \qquad (16.12)$$

Finally, the units becoming processed at a stage cannot employ more processing time than is available on the number of machines allocated to that stage. For the first-shift operation, this is

$$\sum_{r_i \in R_i} t^s_{r_i} < 8n_i \qquad (16.13)$$

and for the second-shift operation,

$$\sum_{r_i \in R_i} t^o_{r_i} < 8n_i \qquad t^s_{r_i}, t^o_{r_i}, n_i > 0, \quad \text{and} \quad n_i \text{ an integer} \qquad (16.14)$$

This model is a fundamental linear programming problem requiring an integer domain for the subset of variables associated with the number of machines and allowing the other decision variables to have a continuous solution. A multistage system employing this model can be solved using a mixed integer linear programming algorithm with a branch-and-bound solution technique. However, the solution time and core requirements for such a procedure can become prohibitive for a problem involving a significant number of stages and operating rates. An alternative approach, using dynamic programming, may offer distinct computational advantages and result in a greater variety of decision information for the analyst. Such a procedure is illustrated here.

The processing cost per unit of good part is

$$\frac{C}{r_i(1 - b_i)} \qquad (16.15)$$

For the first operation, this unit processing cost is

RATE/SHIFT	PROCESSING COST PER UNIT	RANK	OUTPUT FOR 8 HOURS
25/first	$0.417	1	192.0 units
30/first	$0.461	2	225.6 units
25/second	$0.500	3	192.0 units
30/second	$0.532	4	225.6 units

Notice that the operating rates are ranked according to the respective unit processing costs (of nondefective parts). Higher-ranked operating rates should be considered first, and only when the production level is not reached, should lower-ranked rates be considered.

Similarly, the processing cost per unit for the second operation is

RATE/SHIFT	PROCESSING COST PER UNIT	RANK	OUTPUT FOR 8 HOURS
15/first	$0.725	2	110.4 units
20/first	$0.667	1	144.0 units
15/second	$0.870	4	110.4 units
20/second	$0.833	3	144.0 units

Notice that in the second operation, the alternative $r_2 = 15$ units/hour need not be considered because running the machines at higher rates results in a higher maximum output at a lower per-unit processing cost. Moreover, by ignoring $r_2 = 15$, the second operation involves only a single operating rate ($r_2 = 20$), the fraction defective is 0.09, and $S_{O2} = S_{I2} \times 0.91$.

Let

$$S_{I2} = \text{input to operation 2}$$

$$= \text{output of operation 1}$$

$$S_{O2} = \text{output of operation 2}$$

For a production level of $200 < S_{O2} < 300$, the input should be

$$\frac{200}{1.0 - 0.09} < S_{I2} < \frac{300}{1.0 - 0.10}$$

or

$$217.39 < S_{I2} < 333.33$$

For the first operation, the following cases must be evaluated:

CASE	NUMBER OF MACHINES	RELEVANT DECISION VARIABLES	RANGE OF S_{O1}
1.1	1	$(t^s_{r_1}, t^s_{r_2})$	$217.4 < S_{O1} < 225.6$
1.2	1	$(t^s_{r_1}, t^o_{r_1})$	$225.6 < S_{O1} < 333.3$
1.3	2	$(t^s_{r_1}, t^s_{r_2})$	$217.4 < S_{O1} < 333.3$

The reader should be convinced that there is no need to consider the other possibilities.

Case 1.1. Minimize

$$Z = 10 \times t^s_{r_1} + 13 \times t^s_{r_2} + 80 \times 1$$

subject to

$$t^s_{r_1} + t^s_{r_2} < 8$$

$$25(0.96)t^s_{r_1} + 30(0.94)t^s_{r_2} = S_{O1}$$

and

$$t^s_{r_1}, t^s_{r_2} \geq 0$$

Notice that at optimality, the first constraint must be a strict equality. (Why?) Therefore, the previous linear programming model simplifies into the problem of solving two simultaneous linear equations. The solution is

$$t^s_{r_1} = \frac{225.6 - S_{O1}}{4.2}$$

$$t^s_{r_2} = \frac{S_{O1} - 192}{4.2}$$

and

$$Z = \frac{96 + 3S_{O1}}{4.2}$$

for $217.39 < S_{O1} < 225.6$.

Case 1.2.   Minimize

$$Z = 10 \times t^s_{r_1} + 13 \times t^s_{r_2} + 12 \times t^o_{r_1} + 80 \times 1$$

subject to

$$t^s_{r_1} + t^s_{r_2} < 8$$

$$t^o_{r_1} < 8$$

$$25(0.96)t^s_{r_1} + 30(0.94)t^s_{r_2} + 25(0.96)t^o_{r_1} = S_{O1}$$

and

$$t^s_{r_1}, t^s_{r_2}, t^o_{r_1} > 0$$

However, it is obvious that for $S_{O1} > 225.6$:

$$t^s_{r_2} = 0 \quad \text{and} \quad t^s_{r_2} = 8$$

Therefore,

$$25(0.96) \times 0 + 30(0.94) \times 8 + 25(0.96) \times t^o_{r_1} = S_{O1}$$

or

$$t^o_{r_1} = \frac{S_{O1} - 225.6}{24}$$

Thus,

$$Z = \frac{S_{O1} + 142.4}{2}$$

for $225.6 < S_{O1} < 333.33$.

Case 1.3.   Minimize

$$Z = 2 \times 10t^s_{r_1} + 80 \times 2$$

subject to

$$t^s_{r_1} < 8$$

$$2 \times (25) \times (0.96)t^s_{r_1} = S_{O1}$$

Therefore,

$$t^s_{r_1} = \frac{S_{O1}}{48}$$

and

$$Z = \frac{5S_{O1} + 1920}{12}$$

for $217.39 < S_{O1} < 333.33$.

Figure 16.4 shows the intersection of the three cases. As shown, the optimal solution is

$$Z^* = \frac{96 + 3S_{O1}}{4.2}$$

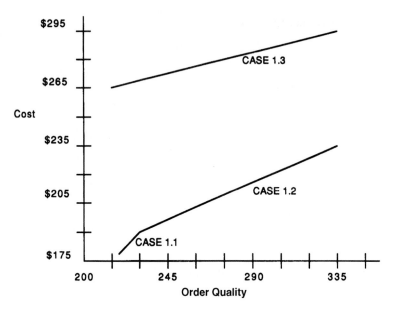

Figure 16.4   Intersection of the three planning cases.

for $217.39 < S_{O1} < 225.6$

$$t^s_{r_1} = \frac{225.6 - S_{O1}}{4.2}$$

$$t^s_{r_2} = \frac{S_{O1} - 192}{4.2}$$

and

$$Z^* = \frac{S_{O1} + 142.4}{2}$$

for $225.6 < S_{O1} < 333.33$

$$t^s_{r_1} = 0 \qquad t^s_{r_2} = 8 \qquad t^o_{r_1} = \frac{S_{O1} - 225.6}{24}$$

Only one machine is needed.

For the second operation, the following cases must be evaluated:

CASE	NUMBER OF MACHINES	RELEVANT DECISION VARIABLES	RANGE OF S_{O2}
2.1	1	$(t^s_{r_2}, t^o_{r_2})$	$200 < S_{O2} < 288$
2.2	2	$(2t^s_{r_2})$	$200 < S_{O2} < 288$
2.3	2	$(t^s_{r_2}, t^o_{r_2})$	$200 < S_{O2} < 300$
2.4	3	$(3t^s_{r_2})$	$S_{O2} < 300$

The optimal solution for this stage is

$$Z^* = \frac{5S_{O2} + 216}{6}$$

for $288 < S_{O2} < 300$.

$$t^s_{r_2} = \frac{S_{O2} - 144}{18}$$

$$t^o_{r_2} = 8$$

and

$$Z^* = \frac{5S_{O2} + 432}{6}$$

for $288 < S_{O2} < 300$.

$$t^s_{r_2} = 8 \qquad t^o_{r_2} = \frac{S_{O2} - 288}{36}$$

and $S_{O1} = S_{O2}/0.9$.

Example 16.7

For a production level of $S_{O2} = 250$, the optimal operating rate for the second operation is $t^s_{r_2} = 8$, $t^s_{r_2} = (250 - 144)/18 = 6.89$ hours, and $Z = \$244.33$. For the first operation, $S_{O1} = S_{O2}/0.9 = 277.78$ and $Z = (277.78 + 142.4)/2 = \$210.09$ plus the absorbed cost in the second operation, $\$244.33$, equals $\$454.42$.

16.5 MANPOWER AND SPACE REQUIREMENTS

For manual assembly operations, the number of employees required can be determined in the same way machine requirements are calculated by defining X as the number of operators instead of the number of machines, and u corresponds to the skill level of the operators.

For man–machine operations, however, the optimal number of operators is dependent on many factors, which may include (1) the actual work content of the operator on the machines (concurrent operations such as loading and unloading), (2) the work methods and schedules, and (3) the labor contract. The most common method of determining the number of machines assigned to an operator is the man–machine chart. Analytically, the optimal number of machines assigned to an operator can be determined by taking the ratio

$$n = \frac{\text{machine run time} + \text{concurrent activities}}{\text{operator travel time} + \text{concurrent activities}}$$

Because n, in general, may not be an integer, the question of whether to round up or to round down depends on the trade-off between the cost of the machine idle time and the cost of operator idle time.

The space requirements should take into consideration the space occupied by the equipment, the workspace for the operator, storage space for work-in-process, and space for maintenance and material handling.

16.6 MANUFACTURING PLANNING THROUGH SIMULATION

Many real-world situations are too complex to effectively evaluate analytically. Alternative methods must be used to evaluate the performance of such systems. One such alternative is performed through simulation techniques. (Simulation is said to be the most frequently used tool by industrial engineers.) Manufacturing systems can be evaluated by creating a model through a series of logical or mathematical relationships. In a simulation, a computer is used to evaluate a model numerically over a specified time period. The information that is gathered is used to estimate the true characteristics of the system.

The use of simulation as opposed to other evaluation techniques has many advantages. Simulation can provide an estimate of performance for an existing system under some projected set of operating conditions. Alternative system designs or operating policies can be compared via simulation to determine which system best meets a specific set of requirements. Simulation can provide much better control over experimental conditions than would be possible when experimenting with physical models. Finally, simulation can provide flexibility in evaluating systems over varied time frames. A system can be studied over a long time frame for economic considerations or, alternatively, the detailed workings of a system can be studied under a short time span.

Simulation is a popular and widely used technique for manufacturing-system evaluation and planning. However, two problems associated with simulation modeling have hindered its use in some circumstances. First, large-scale manufacturing systems tend to be very complex. Writing computer programs to model such systems can be a long and expensive task (on the other hand, it is impossible to develop a comparable mathematical model for such a system). Second, many complex simulation models require extensive computer time, which can be a costly exercise. The severity of these problems has been eased in recent years with the development of specialized computer simulation languages that provide many of the functions needed to model a manufacturing system (e.g., SLAM system™, SIMAN, Arena, Witness, and GPSS). Further, with continued improvements in electronics, the cost of computing has begun to fall.

Simulation of manufacturing systems takes place in one of three techniques: discrete event, continuous simulation, or a combination of both discrete and continuous methods. The method of analysis is indicative of the frequency that the state of a system undergoes changes. The state of a system is the collection of units or variables that describes the condition of the system at a given point in time. For example, the system state variables could be the number of units currently in production or the total number of finished goods output by the system or various other system descriptors. Discrete-event and continuous modeling methods are discussed in the following sections.

16.6.1 Discrete-Event Simulation

A discrete system is one in which the state of the system changes at a finite number of points in time. Discrete-event simulation involves the modeling of a system as it progresses over a period of time. For example, if a machining center produces a finished part every 3 minutes, the number of finished parts produced by the system (i.e., the state of the system) changes only at discrete instances.

Discrete-event simulation begins by mathematically and logically defining how the state of the system will change over time. A series of state variables are established to collect statistics on system performance. The time elapse of a system is simulated by a system clock that holds the current value of simulated time. Time progresses according to an event calendar that contains the list of times when each type of event will occur in the system. Events can be job_arrival, begin_operation, end_of_operation, machine_break_down, machine repaired, and so on. Random-number generators generate time values according to the prespecified probability distribution. These time values are used to determine the event time. For example, the job_arrival calls for an event, end_of_job. The time difference between these two events is the operation time. The current time, TNOW, is added to this operation time. The result is the event time for the end_of_job event. The event is then inserted into the event calendar. When the event is inserted, it must be placed according to the sequence of the event time.

On completion of a given event, time will automatically increment to the time of the next scheduled event. The occurrence of an event initiates the operation of an event subroutine to update the system when a particular type of event occurs. This simulation approach can be implemented in two different ways: written in general-purpose language or in special simulation language. Most simulation languages provide a network modeling capability. The simulation model is represented in a network. The detailed coding is hidden away from the users of the language. The user does not have to consider the event calendar, and so on, at all. However, this kind of network model has limitations on its modeling capability. For more sophisticated models, users have to write the program using general-purpose language. Most simulation languages also provide users a set of utility functions for event management, statistics collection and display, queue management, random-number generation, and so on. In this section, two examples are given. The first is a model written in C language and the second is written in SIMAN simulation language.

Example 16.8

In a one-machine system, job arrival is a Poisson process with a time between arrival, t_a. The operation time of the machine is t_m, which is exponentially distributed. A buffer is set in front of the machine. We are interested to know the queue statistics and the average time a job spends in the system.

Solution To develop the model, first, we need to determine the events. In this problem, there are two events: ARRIV (job arrival) and J_END (job completed). We need four basic functions (subroutines): EVNT_MGT (event manager), Q_MGT (queue manager), EXPT (exponential random generator), and STAT (statistic collector). We assume that these functions have been built. Here, only the parameters of these functions are defined. The reader will find that these functions are not difficult to develop.

```
EVNT_MGT (OP,TYPE,TIME,ATTR);
    where: OP: operator: 'ADD' adds an event to the event calendar,
the rest of the parameters are
    inserted to the event calendar.
    'REMOVE' removes an event from the event calendar. The
    event information is output
    TYPE: event type, 'ARRIV', 'J_END', etc.
    TIME: event time.
    ATTR: event attribute.
```

The task of the event manager is to update the event calendar. An event calendar is shown in Figure 16.5. The event manager has a built-in procedure to sort the event before it inserts a new event to the event calendar. A round-robbin type of buffer implemented by a double linked list is suitable for the event calendar.

```
Q_MGT(OP,TIME);

    where: OP can either be 'ADD' or 'REMOVE'
            TIME is a value stored in the queue.
```

The queue manager handles a queue; it also collects queue statistics. In this example, the only marking a job has is the arrival time; therefore, only one parameter is stored with each job in a queue. A global variable q_length is updated by the queue manager.

```
STAT(OP,TYPE,VALUE);

    where: OP can be 'SAVE' or 'REPORT'
      TYPE is variable type.
    VALUE is the data collected.
    STAT is a statistics collection function.

    real EXPT(T);
      where T is the average time.

    EXPT is a exponential pseudorandom-number generator.
```

The main program of the simulation model written in C language is as follows:

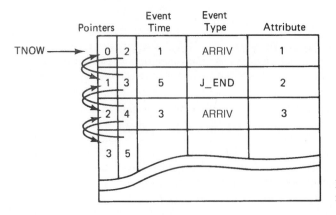

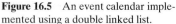

Figure 16.5 An event calendar implemented using a double linked list.

```
/*following is a simulation model for a one machine shop, functions
 EVNT_MGT, Q_MGT, EXPT, STAT are not presented.
 ta is the average time between arrival,
 tm is the average machining time.
*/


#include "event.h"
#include <stdio.h>
#define ARRIV 'A'
#define J_END 'J'

main()
{
  char *status;                       /*status of the machine*/
  float tnow, attr, t, ta, tm, t_arr: /*t_arr: arrival time, tnow:current
time*/
  int type;                           /*event type*/
  status="idle";                      /*machine status*/
  t=EXPT(ta);                         /*generate an arrival*/
  EVNT_MGT("ADD", "ARR", t, t);       /*put in event calendar,
                                      mark the arrival time in attrib*/

  while (attr !=9999){                /*simulation terminates when attr is
                                      marked 9999, otherwise repeates the
                                      cycle*/

  EVNT_MGT ("REMOVE", type, tnow, attr); /*retrieve 1st event*/
  switch (type){
  case ARRIV:                         /*Arrival event*/
    Q_MGT("SAVE",tnow);               /*put job in queue*/
    if (status == "IDLE"){            /*if machine is idle*/
        status = "BUSY";              /*set the machine busy*/
        Q_MGT ("REMOVE", t_arr);      /*remove the job from Q*/
        t-EXPT(tm) + tnow;            /*generate end of job time*/
        EVNT_MGT("ADD","J_END",t,t_arr); /*put the job in event cal*/
    }
    t-EXPT(ta) + tnow;                /*generate another job arrival*/
    EVNT_MGT("ADD","ARR",t,t);
    break;
  case J_END:                         /*end of the job*/
    status="IDLE";                    /*set the machine idle*/
    STAT("ADD","TIME_IN_SYS",tnow,attr); /*collect time in system*/
    if (q_leng > 0){                  /*if Q length is not zero*/
        Q_MGT("REMOVE",t_arr);        /*remove job from Q*/
        t=EXP_TIME(tm)+tnow;          /*generate end of job time*/
        EVNT_MGT("ADD","J_END",t,t_arr); /*schedule end of the job*/
    }
    break;
  }
  }
/*Put code for report generation here*/
}
```

Example 16.9

Consider a system where two different job types are processed within a group-technology machine cell. The cell consists of one drill and two lathes. Type 1 jobs must be processed first on the drill and then on the lathe. Type 2 jobs are processed only on the lathe. All jobs are performed with a first in, first out scheduling priority. The following data describe the production processes:

JOB TYPE	NO. OF BATCHES	NO. JOBS PER BATCH	DRILL PROC. TIME	LATHE PROC. TIME	TIME BETWEEN ARRIVALS
1	12	5	3.0	Uniform (2 to 3)	14
2	10	8	—	Uniform (1 to 2)	Exponential (3.0)

The simulation model for this system was developed using the SIMAN simulation language (Pegden, 1983). The block diagram of the model is shown in Fig. 16.6. The drill and lathes serve as resources within the system for which incoming parts compete. When a batch of parts enters the system, they are placed on the machine that is available for work. If every piece of equipment is in operation, the batch waits in a queue until the required equipment becomes available. When a batch of parts is completed on a machine, it is released from that resource and can progress through the completion of its routing sequence. The system variables that are measured in this example are the time in the system for each part type, the queue size in front of each station, and the utilization of each piece of equipment. The SIMAN summary report for this model is shown in Figure 16.7.

The summary indicates that the average time in the system for part type 1 is 31.2 min and part type 2 spends an average of 26.5 min. The average queue length behind the drill is 3.8 jobs waiting for processing, whereas, on average, 15.6 jobs wait for processing behind the two lathes. Furthermore, the utilization of the drill is approximately 99% and, on average, 1.5 lathes are busy.

An important point should be considered, however. Simulation analyses are based on probabilistic circumstances, and the results should not be interpreted as deterministic in nature. Statistical techniques should be used to analyze the output data from a series of production runs. A typical goal would be to establish confidence intervals for the system variables to compare which method of control is best with reference to some specified measure of performance.

16.6.2 Continuous Simulation

A continuous system is one in which the state of the system changes continuously over time. An example of a continuous system is the flow of rubber through a rubber mill or the concentration of a reactant within a chemical process. The flow of product within these systems is continuous and changes constantly with respect to time. Typically, continuous simulation models involve one or more differential equations that give relationships for the rates of change of the state variables with respect to time. As with

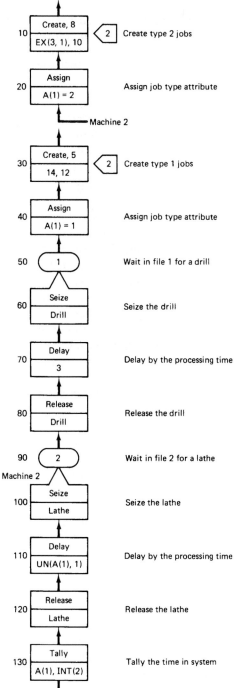

Figure 16.6   Block-diagram model for Example 16.9.

```
                        SIMIAN SUMMARY REPORT


                          RUN NUMBER 1 OF 1



        PROJECT: GT MACHINE CENTER
        ANALYST: L. PEGDEN
        DATE    : 10/30/1981


        RUN ENDED AT TIME: .1823E+03


                           TALLY VARIABLES


           NUMBER                   STANDARD    MINIMUM     MAXIMUM     NUMBER
        IDENTIFIER    AVERAGE       DEVIATION    VALUE       VALUE      OF OBS.
        1 TIME SYS   .3121E+02      .1443E+02   .1281E+02   .6639E+02     60
        2 TIME SYS   .2646E+02      .1468E+02   .1347E+01   .5019E+02     80


                      DISCRETE CHANGE VARIABLES


           NUMBER                   STANDARD    MINIMUM     MAXIMUM     NUMBER
        IDENTIFIER    AVERAGE       DEVIATION    VALUE       VALUE      OF OBS.
        1 DRL QUEUE  .3784E+01      .2901E+01      0.0      .8000E+01   .1823E+03
        2 LTH QUEUE  .1563E+02      .2060E+02      0.0      .6400E+02   .1823E+03
        3 DRILL UTIL .9872E+00      .1126E+00      0.0      .1000E+01   .1823E+03
        4 LATHE UTIL .1471E+01      .62963+00      0.0      .2000E+01   .1823E+03
```

Figure 16.7 SIMAN summary report for Example 16.9.

discrete-event simulation, continuous simulation begins by mathematically and logically defining how the state of the system changes over time. The state variables are thoroughly defined in the model to assess the statistical measures. The time change of a system is driven by the differential equations that define the change in state.

16.6.3 Manufacturing Planning Through Physical Modeling

No other method of analysis can provide a more accurate description of system behavior than actual physical manipulation of the system itself. By physically altering or constructing a system within the actual conditions under which it could operate, the system variables under considerations can be observed directly. The disadvantage of this method of planning is the enormous cost involved with the physical alteration of the system.

Two situations commonly occur when physical modeling could be considered as an alternative, but the enormous cost involved prohibits the modeling. First, the system may currently exist and be in full operating condition; however, to achieve meaningful results from the study, the current production methods will be disrupted and a loss of production time will result. The second situation commonly occurs when the purchase of equipment is being considered, but the risk of bringing the equipment on line without understanding how the system will operate under production conditions is too great.

An important advantage that physical modeling offers is the ability to perform prototyping and troubleshooting activities that will aid in the actual system implementation. Working with a physical system in the design stages can provide intangible information and valuable insight into the behavior of a system. See Figure 16.8.

Figure 16.8   Generic machining centers and a robot configured as a scaled FMS.

16.7 CONCLUDING REMARKS

With the increase in manufacturing-system complexity and the growth of competition in the marketplace has come the need for efficient and accurate planning tools. Realistic models of manufacturing systems can allow decisions to be made regarding production without disturbing the operation of an existing system or without investing the capital to build a proposed system.

This chapter has presented a series of methodologies that can be used as planning tools. Analytical models can be used to accurately predict the performance and characteristics of simple manufacturing systems. Furthermore, such models have proven to be quite robust in providing information on complex integrated systems. Often, however, many details such as equipment downtime, random process variability, and material-handling congestion cannot be reflected by analytical models. Such instances require alternatives such as mathematical models to provide significant insight. Simulation methods can add intricate details to a model that are otherwise overlooked in simple analyses. The difficulty encountered with simulation is the significant expense that is incurred in developing and analyzing the model. In this light, it is often preferable to analyze a system with a mathematical model initially, and if further detail is required for final decision making, a simulation analysis can follow.

REVIEW QUESTIONS

16.1. A capital equipment justification is being performed to determine whether a 20-ton rubber press is to be purchased. Four different part types are to be pressed and cured on this machine. Forecasting reports indicate the following production quantities along with the associated production times:

PART	QUANTITY/WEEK	PRODUCTION TIMES (min/pc)
J-431	150	8.0
J-597	175	6.0
J-604	185	9.0
J-663	125	7.5

The press will be operating for three shifts, at an average of 7 working hours/shift. Due to machine maintenance and delays, the efficiency of the equipment is estimated to be 85%. It is determined that the press will not meet the return on investment if it does not maintain 80% utilization. Determine if the press should be purchased under the current production forecasts.

16.2. A manufacturing firm receives an order for a series of shafts, which includes three different part types. All parts must be produced on a turret lathe. The estimated standards are

PART	PRODUCTION TIME (h/100)	ORDER QUANTITY
KL-1	4.80	650
KL-2	3.90	525
KL-3	4.30	625

The plant operates one shift per day at an effective 7 hours/shift. The order for the three parts under consideration arrives on the shop floor on a Monday morning and must be completed by the end of the day Friday. The average efficiency of any turret lathe is 75%. How many turret lathes must the production-planning department use to complete the order on time?

16.3. A CNC machining center is dedicated to the production of three components:

PART	PRODUCTION TIME (h/unit)
A	0.13
B	0.08
C	0.21

The machining center is operated for two shifts at an average of 7 hours/shift, with a machine efficiency of 70%. If each part type is given equal priority (total number of units produced) at the machining center, how many units, on the average, pass through the machining center in a 5-day week?

An effort is being made to reduce setup time and machine maintenance to increase machine efficiency. To what level of efficiency must the machining center be raised to produce 85 units per day?

16.4. To reduce the travel time in transporting production units from the group-technology cell to the inspection station, qualified inspectors are placed within the cell. The inspectors inspect parts immediately as they are completed on the production equipment. Within a given cell, five part types are produced. The production proportions and inspection times are

PART NUMBER	PRODUCTION PROPORTION (%)	INSPECTION TIME (min)
J22-1	10	2.2
J22-2	15	3.1
J22-3	35	6.8
J22-4	25	1.4
J22-5	15	3.7

If cell production is currently 45 parts/h, on any given 7-h shift, how many inspectors are required to keep pace with the production rate?

16.5. A chemical etching process is largely dependent on the temperature of the acidic etch solution. Past history dictates that as the acid solution decreases in temperature, the etching process must be prolonged. The temperature has an 8° range of variation and the corresponding production time of the process has been simplified to take on the following probability density function:

TEMPERATURE (°F)	PRODUCTION TIME (min/pc)	PROBABILITY
72	12	0.30
70	15	0.45
68	18	0.15
66	21	0.10

The production quantity ordered each day varies according to the processing time required for each batch.

PRODUCTION TIME (min/pc)	PRODUCTION QUANTITY	PROBABILITY
12	300	0.1
	350	0.1
	400	0.8
15	300	0.2
	350	0.3
	400	0.5
18	250	0.4
	300	0.3
	350	0.3
21	200	0.6
	250	0.3
	300	0.1

Assume the process operates three shifts at 8 hours/shift and the efficiency of the etch tank is 80%.

(a) Find the average number of machines required for production.

(b) Find the variance of the distribution.

(c) Using the mean and variance of the machine-requirement distribution, find the probability that only 6 etch tanks are required.

(d) How many etch tanks are required to assure that the production needs for a given day are met 90% of the time?

16.6. What are the inputs and outputs of manufacturing resource planning? How does it fit into the framework of concurrent engineering discussed in Chapter 14?

16.7. In addition to the machine-requirement planning methods given in the text, are there any other methods? Search the literature and prepare a summary.

16.8. Compare CAN-Q to those methods you identified for Review Question 16.7.

16.9. Prepare spreadsheet programs based on the machine-requirement planning methods, deterministic, stochastic and multioperational.

REFERENCES/BIBLIOGRAPHY

ASKIN, R. G, and C. R. STANDRIDGE (1993). *Modeling and Analysis of Manufacturing Systems,* New York: John Wiley.

BUZACOTT, J. A., and J. G. SHANTHIKUMAR (1993). *Stochastic Models of Manufacturing Systems.* Englewood Cliffs, NJ: Prentice Hall.

BUZEN, J. P. (1973). "Computational Algorithms for Closed Queueing Networks with Exponential Servers," *Communications of the Association of Computing Machinery,* 16, 527–541.

——— (1975). "Cost Effective Analytic Tools for Computer Performance Evaluation," in *Proceedings of IEEE COMPCON.* New York: Institute of Electrical and Electronics Engineers, pp. 293–296.

CASSANDRAS, C. G. (1993). *Discrete Event Systems: Modeling and Performance Analysis.* Boston: Irwin.

CO, H. C. (1984). "Design and Implementation of Flexible Manufacturing Systems—Some Analysis Concepts." Ph.D. thesis, Virginia Polytechnic Institute and State University, Blacksburg, Virginia.

CO, H. C., and R. A. WYSK (1986). "The Robustness of CAN-Q in Modeling Automated Manufacturing Systems," *International Journal of Production Research,* 6(24), 1485–1503.

DISNEY, R. L. and D. KONIG (1983). *Queueing Networks: A Survey of Their Theory and Some of Their Applications.* Blacksburg, VA: Virginia Polytechnic Institute and State University, Department of Industrial Engineering and Operations Research.

FISHMAN, G. S. (1978). "Grouping Observations on Digital Simulation," *Management Science,* 24, 510–527.

GIAMMO, T. (1976). "Validation of a Computer Performance Model of the Exponential Queueing Network Family," in *Proceedings of the International Symposium on Computer Performance Modeling, Measurement, and Evaluation.* Boston: Harvard University, pp.

GORDON, W. J., and G. F. NEWELL (1967). "Closed Queueing Systems with Exponential Servers," *Operations Research,* 15, 254–265.

HO, Y. C., and X. R. CAO (1991). *Perturbation Analysis of Discrete Event Dynamic Systems.* Boston: Kluwer.

HOREV, Y., N. H. COOK, and J. E. WARD (1978). *Discrete Simulation of Flexible Manufacturing Systems,* Report No. ESL-FR-834-4. Cambridge, MA: Massachusetts Institute of Technology.

HUGHES, P. H., and G. MOE (1973). "A Structural Approach to Computer Performance Analysis," in *Proceedings of the AFIPS National Computer Conference,* Vol. 42. Montvale, NJ: AFIPS Press, pp. 109–119.

JACKSON, J. R. (1957). "Networks of Waiting Lines," *Operations Research* 5, 518–521.

———— (1963). "Jobshop-like Queueing Systems." *Management Science,* 10(10), 131–142.

KIMEMIA, J., and S. B. GERSHWIN (1978). *Multiconductivity Network Flow Optimization in Flexible Manufacturing Systems,* Report No. ESL-FR-834-2. Cambridge, MA: Massachusetts Institute of Technology.

LAW, A. M., and W. D. KELTON (1982). *Simulation Modeling and Analysis.* New York: McGraw-Hill.

LEIMKUHLER, F. F. (1981). *Economic Analysis of CMS,* NSF Report No. APR74-15256. No. 21. West Lafayette, IN: Purdue University.

LIPSKY, L., and J. D. CHURCH (1977). "Application of a Queueing Network Model for a Computer System," *Computing Survey,* 9, 205–221.

MAYER, R. J., and J. J. TALAVAGE (1976). *Simulation of a Computerized Manufacturing System,* NSF Report No. APR74-15256, No. 4. West Lafayette, IN: Purdue University.

NETWORK DYNAMICS, INC. (1986). *MANUPLAN II Demonstration Manual.* Cambridge, MA: NDI.

PEGDEN, C. D. (1983). *Introduction to SIMAN.* State College, PA: Systems Modeling Corporation.

ROSE, C. A. (1978). "A Measurement Procedure for Queueing Network Models of Computer Systems," *Computer Surveys,* 10, 263–280.

———— (1987). "Micro-Computer Based Closed-Queue Modeling for Manufacturing Systems." B.S. thesis, Pennsylvania State University, University Park.

RUNNER, J. A. (1978). *CAMSAM: A Simulation Analysis Model for Computerized Manufacturing Systems,* NSF Report APR74-15256, Report No. 13. West Lafayette, IN: Purdue University.

SECCO-SUARDO, G. (1978). *Optimization of a Closed Network of Queues,* Report No. ESL-FR-834-3, Cambridge, MA: Massachusetts Institute of Technology, Electronic System Laboratory.

SETHI, A. K., and S. P. SETHI (1990). "Flexibility in Manufacturing: A Survey," *International Journal of Flexible Manufacturing Systems,* 2, 289–328.

SOLBERG, J. J. (1976a). *A Mathematical Model of Computerized Manufacturing Systems,* NSF Report No. APR74-15256, Report No. 3. West Lafayette, IN: Purdue University.

———— (1976b). "Optimal Design and Control of Computerized Manufacturing Systems," in *Proceedings of the AIIE Systems Engineering Conference,* Boston: IIE Press, pp. 131–142.

———— (1977). "A Mathematical Model of Computerized Manufacturing Systems," in *Proceedings of the Fourth International Conference on Production Research.* Amherst, MA: Taylor & Francis, pp. 97–14.

———— (1979). *Stochastic Modeling of Large Scale Transportation Networks,* Report No. DOT-ATC-79-2. West Lafayette, IN: Purdue University, School of Industrial Engineering.

———— (1980). *CAN-Q User's Guide,* NSF Report No. APR74-15256, No. 9, West Lafayette, IN: Purdue University.

STECKE, K. E., and J. J. SOLBERG (1981). *The Optimal Planning of Computerized Manufacturing Systems,* NSF Report No. APR74-15256, Report No. 20. West Lafayette, IN: Purdue University.

SURI, R. (1983). "Robustness of Queueing Network Formulas," *Journal of the Association for Computing Machinery,* 30, 564–571.

WARD, J. E. (1978). *Numerical Experience with a Closed Network of Queues Model.* Report No. ESL-FR-834-8. Cambridge, MA: Massachusetts Institute of Technology.

WYSK, R. A., P. CHEN, D. WU, and B. B. K. GHOSH (1988). "Advantages of Scaled and Unscaled Physical Models for FMS Research and Instruction," *Journal of Manufacturing Systems,* 6(2), 107–116.

WYSK, R. A., P. J. EGBELU, C. ZHOU, and B. K. GHOSH (1986). "Use of Spread Sheet Analysis for Evaluating AGV Systems," *Material Flow,* 3(2), 176–193.

Appendix A

Vector Algebra

In this appendix, some basic properties of vectors are introduced.

A.1 COMPONENTS OF A VECTOR

A is a vector and **i**, **j**, and **k** are unit vectors in the directions of the positive X, Y, and Z axes.

$$\mathbf{A} = A_1\mathbf{i} + A_2\mathbf{j} + A_3\mathbf{k}$$

where A_1, A_2, and A_3 are the components of **A**. See Figure A.1.

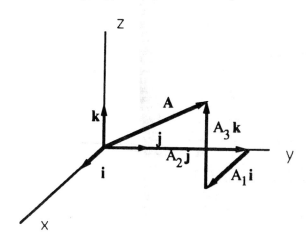

Figure A.1.

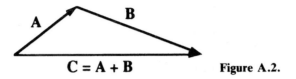

$$C = A + B$$ **Figure A.2.**

A.2 MAGNITUDE OF A VECTOR

The magnitude of a vector is

$$|\mathbf{A}| = \sqrt{A_1^2 + A_2^2 + A_3^2}$$

A.3 MULTIPLICATION OF A VECTOR BY A SCALAR

If m is a real number (scalar) and $\mathbf{A}$ is a vector, then $m\mathbf{A}$ is a vector whose magnitude is $|m|$ times $|\mathbf{A}|$.

A.4 SUM OF VECTORS

$\mathbf{C}$ is the sum of two vectors, $\mathbf{A}$ and $\mathbf{B}$. See Figure A.2.

A.5 UNIT VECTORS

A unit vector is a vector with unit magnitude. If $\mathbf{A}$ is a vector, then a unit vector in the direction of $\mathbf{A}$ is $\mathbf{A}/|\mathbf{A}|$.

A.6 LAWS OF VECTOR ALGEBRA

Commutation law for addition:	$\mathbf{A} + \mathbf{B} = \mathbf{B} + \mathbf{A}$
Associative law for addition:	$\mathbf{A} + (\mathbf{B} + \mathbf{C}) = (\mathbf{A} + \mathbf{B}) + \mathbf{C}$
Associative law for scalar multiplication:	$m(n\mathbf{A}) = (mn)\,\mathbf{A} = n(m\mathbf{A})$
Distributive law:	$(m + n)\,\mathbf{A} = m\mathbf{A} + n\mathbf{A}$
Distributive law:	$m(\mathbf{A} + \mathbf{B}) = m\mathbf{A} + m\mathbf{B}$

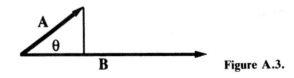

Figure A.3.

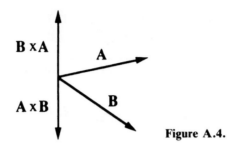

Figure A.4.

A.7 DOT OR SCALAR PRODUCT

$$\mathbf{A} \cdot \mathbf{B} = |A| \, |B| \cos \theta \qquad 0 \le \theta \le \pi$$

where θ is the angle between $\mathbf{A}$ and $\mathbf{B}$. See Figure A.3.

$$\mathbf{A} \cdot \mathbf{B} = \mathbf{B} \cdot \mathbf{A}$$

$$\mathbf{A} \cdot (\mathbf{B} + \mathbf{C}) = \mathbf{A} \cdot \mathbf{B} + \mathbf{A} \cdot \mathbf{C}$$

$$\mathbf{A} \cdot \mathbf{B} = A_1 B_1 + A_2 B_2 + A_3 B_3$$

A.8 CROSS OR VECTOR PRODUCT

$$\mathbf{A} \times \mathbf{B} = |A| \, |B| \, (\sin \theta)\mathbf{u} \qquad 0 \le \theta \le \pi$$

where θ is the angle between $\mathbf{A}$ and $\mathbf{B}$, and $\mathbf{u}$ is a unit vector perpendicular to the plane of $\mathbf{A}$ and $\mathbf{B}$. See Figure A.4. The direction of $\mathbf{u}$ is determined by the right-hand rule.

$$\mathbf{A} \times \mathbf{B} = \begin{bmatrix} \mathbf{i} & \mathbf{j} & \mathbf{k} \\ A_1 & A_2 & A_3 \\ B_1 & B_2 & B_3 \end{bmatrix}$$

$$= (A_2 B_3 - A_3 B_2)\mathbf{i} + (A_3 B_1 - A_1 B_3)\mathbf{j} + (A_1 B_2 - A_2 B_1)\mathbf{k}$$

$$\mathbf{A} \times \mathbf{B} = -\mathbf{B} \times \mathbf{A}$$

$$\mathbf{A} \times (\mathbf{B} + \mathbf{C}) = \mathbf{A} \times \mathbf{B} + \mathbf{A} \times \mathbf{C}$$

$$|\mathbf{A} \times \mathbf{B}| = \text{area of parallelogram having sides } \mathbf{A} \text{ and } \mathbf{B}$$

Appendix B

Transfer Functions and Block Diagrams

A transfer function is defined as the ratio of the output versus the input of a system in the Laplace domain. A block diagram is a way to represent a system. Figure B.1 is a block diagram showing a component of a system.

B.1 TRANSFER FUNCTIONS

The transfer function of the system shown in Figure B.1 is $T(s)$.

$$T(s) = \frac{O(s)}{I(s)}$$

where $O(s)$ is the output in the s domain, and $I(s)$ is the input in the s domain. This relation is valid under the assumption that all initial conditions are zero.

When there are multiple inputs, $I_1(s)$, $I_2(s)$, . . . ,

$$I(s) = \sum_{i=1}^{n} a_i I(s)$$

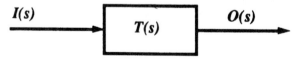

Figure B.1. A block diagram of a simple system.

where a_i is the proportion of each input.

$$O(s) = T(s)I(s)$$

$$= \sum_{i=1}^{n} a_i I(s) T(s)$$

$$= \sum_{i=1}^{n} a_i O(s)$$

B.2 BLOCK DIAGRAMS

Other than the simple block-diagram component shown in Figure B.1, there is another commonly used component—the error detector (Figure B.2). Depending on the corrective action, an error detector can be a sum operator or a difference operator. It is also sometimes called a comparator.

B.2.1 Block-Diagram Algebra

A complex block diagram can be simplified into a simple form. In this section, several rules are given.

B.2.1.1 A series of blocks.   The system shown in Figure B.3 can be simplified into the diagram of Figure B.4.

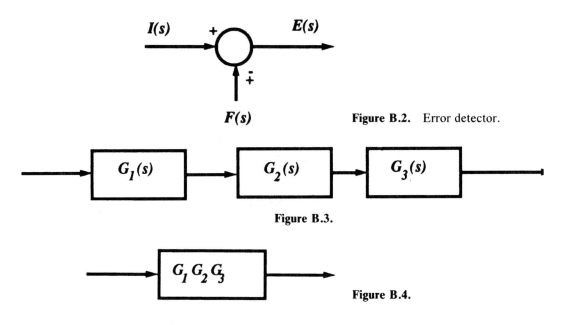

Figure B.2.   Error detector.

Figure B.3.

Figure B.4.

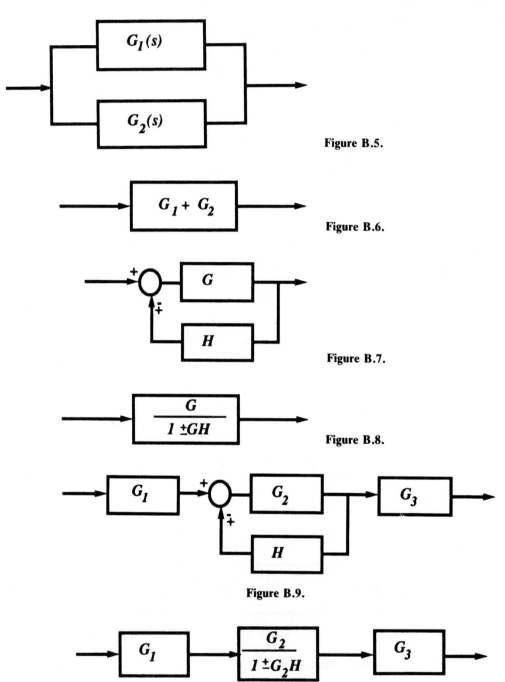

Figure B.5.

Figure B.6.

Figure B.7.

Figure B.8.

Figure B.9.

Figure B.10.

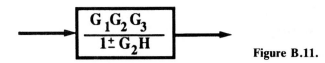

Figure B.11.

B.2.1.2 Parallel blocks.   The transfer function of the equivalent system (Figure B.5) is the sum of the original system (Figure B.6).

B.2.1.3 System with feedback.   The system of Figure B.7 can be simplified into the equivalent system of Figure B.8.

Example B.1

Simplify the block diagram of Figure B.9.

Solution   First, the feedback loop is simplified. The result is a system in series (Figure B.10).

Finally, the three blocks are combined into one block (Figure B.11). The equivalent transfer function of the system is

$$\frac{G_1 G_2 G_3}{1 \pm G_2 H}.$$

Appendix C

Laplace Transforms

C.1 DEFINITION

The definition of the Laplace transform of $F(t)$ is

$$L\{F(t)\} = \int_0^\infty e^{-st}F(t)\, dt = f(s)$$

where L is the Laplace transform operator.

C.2 DEFINITION OF THE INVERSE LAPLACE TRANSFORM

The definition of the inverse Laplace transform of $f(s)$ is

$$F(t) = L^{-1}\{f(s)\}$$

$$= \frac{1}{2\pi i}\int_{c-i\infty}^{c+i\infty} e^{st}f(s)\, ds$$

C.3 GENERAL PROPERTIES

The general properties of the Laplace transform are

$F(t)$	$f(s)$
$aF_1(t) + bF_2(t)$	$af_1(s) + bf_2(s)$
$aF(at)$	$f\left(\dfrac{s}{a}\right)$

$F(t)$	$f(s)$
$F'(t)$	$sf(s) - F(0)$
$F''(t)$	$s^2f(s) - sf(0) - F'(0)$
$\int_0^t F(u)\,du$	$\dfrac{1}{s}f(s)$

C.4 LAPLACE TRANSFORMS

The following table is a summary of commonly used Laplace transforms

$F(t)$	$f(s)$
1	$\dfrac{1}{s}$
t	$\dfrac{1}{s^2}$
e^{at}	$\dfrac{1}{s - a}$
te^{at}	$\dfrac{1}{(s - a)^2}$
$\dfrac{\sin \omega t}{\omega}$	$\dfrac{1}{s^2 + \omega^2}$
$\cos \omega t$	$\dfrac{s}{s^2 + \omega^2}$
$\dfrac{e^{at}\sin \omega t}{\omega}$	$\dfrac{1}{(s - a)^2 + \omega^2}$
$e^{at}\cos \omega t$	$\dfrac{s - a}{(s - a)^2 + \omega^2}$
$\dfrac{1}{\sqrt{1 - \zeta^2}}\,e^{-\zeta\omega t}\sin \omega\sqrt{1 - \zeta^2}\,t$	$\dfrac{1}{s^2 + 2\zeta\omega s + \omega^2}$

Example C.1

Solve the following first-order differential equation:

$$\frac{dx}{dt} + 3x = 5t$$

where $x(t) = 0$.

Solution

$$\boldsymbol{L}\left\{\frac{dx}{dt} + 3x\right\} = \boldsymbol{L}\{5t\} \tag{C.1}$$

$$s\boldsymbol{L}\{x\} - x(0) + 3\boldsymbol{L}\{x\} = \frac{5}{s^2} \tag{C.2}$$

By using the given initial condition, Equation (C.2) can be rewritten as

$$(s + 3)L\{x\} = \frac{5}{s^2} \tag{C.3}$$

so

$$L\{x\} = \frac{5}{s^2(s + 3)} \tag{C.4}$$

Using the partial-fraction expansion, we obtain

$$\frac{5}{s^2(s + 3)} = \frac{A}{s + 3} + \frac{B}{s} + \frac{C}{s^2} \tag{C.5}$$

Solving the Equation (C.5),

$$C = \frac{5}{3}$$

$$B = -\frac{5}{9}$$

$$A = \frac{5}{9}$$

Therefore,

$$L\{x\} = \frac{5/9}{s + 3} - \frac{5/9}{s} + \frac{5/3}{s^2} \tag{C.6}$$

Applying the inverse transformation,

$$L^{-1}\{x\} = L\left\{\frac{5/9}{s + 3} - \frac{5/9}{s} + \frac{5/3}{s^2}\right\} \tag{C.7}$$

$$x(t) = \frac{5}{9} e^{-3t} - \frac{5}{9} + \frac{5}{3} t \tag{C.8}$$

Rewriting Equation (C.8), we get

$$x(t) = \frac{5}{9} (e^{-3t} - 1) + \frac{5}{3} t \tag{C.9}$$

Appendix D

KK-3 Code Digit Definition
of Rotational Parts

TABLE D.1.   COLUMN VIII—GEOMETRICAL SHAPE AND MACHINING. (R)—EXTERNAL SURFACE, GENERAL EXTERNAL SHAPE

0		no center hole	recess same diameter this is a recess
1	Stepped	stepped to one end or smooth	stepped to one end non functional taper
2		stepped to both ends or multiple changes	recess not included
3	W/functional tapered plane	stepped to one end or smooth	
4		stepped to both ends or multiple changes	
5	W/spherical shape	stepped to one end or smooth	
6		stepped to both ends or multiple changes	
7	Various curved rotational shapes	stepped to one end or smooth	
8		stepped to both ends or multiple changes	
9		segment and others	

All tables in Appendixes D–G redrawn from *Classification and Coding Systems* IE550 Course Handouts from Inyong Ham, The Pennsylvania State University.

TABLE D.2.   COLUMN IX—GEOMETRICAL SHAPE AND MACHINING. (R)—EXTERNAL
SHAPE, CONCENTRIC SCREW THREAD

0	none	
1	cylindrical thread — uniform pitch thread	uniform pitch thread
2	cylindrical thread — non-uniform pitch thread	varying pitch thread
3	cone shaped thread	taper thread
4	(1) + (2)	
5	(1) + (3)	
6	(2) + (3)	
7	(1) + (2) + (3)	
8	other concentric screw thread	
9	(1 ~ 3) + (8)	

TABLE D.3. COLUMN X—GEOMETRICAL SHAPE AND MACHINING. (R)—EXTERNAL SURFACE, FUNCTIONAL GROOVE

0	none	
1	angular groove	
2	generated groove	
3	rolled	
4	(1) + (2)	
5	(1) + (3)	
6	(2) + (3)	
7	(1) + (2) + (3)	
8	other functional grooves	
9	(1 ~ 7) + (8)	

TABLE D.4. COLUMN XI—GEOMETRICAL SHAPE AND MACHINING. (R)—EXTERNAL
SURFACE, IRREGULAR SHAPE

0	none	
1	eccentric	
2	branches	
3	non-cylindrical cross-section	
4	(1) + (2)	
5	(1) + (3)	
6	(2) + (3)	
7	(1) + (2) + (3)	
8	other irregular shapes	
9	(1 ~7) + (8)	

TABLE D.5.   COLUMN XII—GEOMETRICAL SHAPE AND MACHINING. (R)—EXTERNAL SURFACE, SHAPED SURFACE

0	none	
1	precessed or notched	
2	slot	
3	groove	
4	(1) + (2)	
5	(1) + (3)	
6	(2) + (3)	
7	(1) + (2) + (3)	
8	other shaped surface	
9	(1 ~ 7) + (8)	

TABLE D.6. COLUMN XIII—GEOMETRICAL SHAPE AND MACHINING. (R)—EXTERNAL SURFACE, CYCLIC SURFACE

0	none	
1	polygonal shape	extruded
2	spline	
3	circular gear	
4	bevel gear	
5	special gear	e.g. non-circular
6	combination gear	
7	rack	
8	indexing plate	
9	others	

TABLE D.7. COLUMN XIV—GEOMETRICAL SHAPE AND MACHINING. (R)—INTERNAL SURFACE, GENERAL INTERNAL SHAPE

0	no through hole			
1	With axial hole	With through hole		no diameter change
2			with diameter changes	no functional groove
3				w/functional groove
4		Stepped to one end		no diameter change
5			with diameter changes	no functional groove
6				w/functional groove
7		Stepped to both ends		no diameter change
8			with diameter changes	no functional groove
9				w/functional

TABLE D.8.   COLUMN XV—GEOMETRICAL SHAPE AND MACHINING. (R)—INTERNAL SHAPE, CURVED INTERNAL SHAPE

0	none	
1	functional taper/rotational curved surface	
2	eccentric cylindrical surface	
3	thread	thread
4	(1) + (2)	
5	(1) + (3)	
6	(2) + (3)	
7	(1) + (2) + (3)	
8	other curved internal shapes	
9	(1 ~ 7) + (8)	

TABLE D.9. COLUMN XVI—GEOMETRICAL SHAPE AND MACHINING. (R)—INTERNAL SURFACE, INTERNAL PLANE SURFACE AND CYCLIC SURFACE

0	none	
1	groove	e.g. keyway
2	cyclic internal plane surface	e.g. spline on polygon
3	gear	e.g. gear
4	(1) + (2)	
5	(1) + (3)	
6	(2) + (3)	
7	(1) + (2) + (3)	
8	other internal plane surface/cyclic surface	
9	(1 ~ 7) + (8)	

TABLE D.10.   COLUMN XVII—GEOMETRICAL SHAPE AMD MACHINING. (R)—END
SURFACE

0	flat	
1	concentric rotational surface	
2	recess/groove	
3	curved surface cyclic surface	
4	(1) + (2)	
5	(1) + (2)	
6	(2) + (3)	
7	(1) + (2) + (3)	
8	other end surface	
9	(1 ~ 7) + (8)	

TABLE D.11.   COLUMN XVIII—GEOMETRICAL SHAPE AND MACHINING.
(R)—NONCONCENTRIC HOLE, PATTERN OF HOLE(S)

0		none	
1		axial hole	
2	Radial hole	on base line	
3		on circumference	
4		(1) + (2)	
5		(1) + (3)	
6		(2) + (3)	
7		(1) + (2) + (3)	
8		other regularly arranged holes	
9		(1 ~ 7) + (8)	

TABLE D.12.   COLUMN XIX—GEOMETRICAL SHAPE AND MACHINING.
(R)—NONCONCENTRIC HOLE, SPECIAL HOLE

0	none	e.g. single hole and irregular hole inc.
1	countersunk hole/hole with thread/thread hole	
2	deep hole	
3	odd shaped hole	
4	(1) + (2)	
5	(1) + (3)	
6	(2) + (3)	
7	(1) + (2) + (3)	
8	other special holes	
9	(1 ~ 7) + (8)	

TABLE D.13.   COLUMN XX—GEOMETRICAL SHAPE AND MACHINING.
(R)—NONMACHINING OPERATIONS

0	none	
1	bending	
2	pressing, forming	
3	welding	welding
4	(1) + (2)	
5	(1) + (3)	
6	(2) + (3)	
7	(1) + (2) + (3)	
8	other non-machining	
9	(1 ~ 7) + (8)	

Appendix E

KK-3 Classification
of Nonrotational Parts

TABLE E.1 CLASSIFICATION OF MAIN DIMENSION (N)

Column	V	VI	VII	
Position	Main Dimensions ($A \geq B$)		Primary Shapes, Ratio of Main Dimensions ($A \geq B \geq C$) C = thickness, inch, W = weight, lb	
	Edge Length A inches	Width B inches		
0	$A \leq 0.63$	$B \leq 0.63$	Cube components	$A/B \leq 3, A/C \leq 4$
1	$0.63 < A \leq 1.97$	$0.63 < B \leq 1.97$	Flat components	$A/B \leq 3, A/C \leq 4$
2	$1.97 < A \leq 3.94$	$1.97 < B \leq 3.94$		Formed component
3	$3.94 < A \leq 6.30$	$3.94 < B \leq 6.30$	Long components	$A/B > 3$
4	$6.30 < A \leq 9.45$	$6.30 < B \leq 9.45$		Formed component
5	$9.45 < A \leq 14.17$	$9.45 < B \leq 14.17$	Combination Shapes	
6	$14.17 < A \leq 23.62$	$14.17 < B \leq 23.62$	Light	$44 \text{ lb} < W \leq 220 \text{ lb}$
7	$23.62 < A \leq 39.37$	$23.62 < B \leq 39.37$	Middle	$220 \text{ lb} < W \leq 550 \text{ lb}$
8	$39.37 < A \leq 78.74$	$39.37 < B \leq 78.74$	Heavy	$550 \text{ lb} < W \leq 2200 \text{ lb}$
9	$78.74 < A$	$78.74 < B$	Extra Heavy	$2200 \text{ lb} < W$

Columns V/VI rows 0–5: Small and Medium Size Components $W \leq 44$ lb. Rows 6–9: Large Size Components $W > 44$ lb.

TABLE E.2 CLASSIFICATION OF GEOMETRICAL SHAPE AND MACHINING (IV)

Digit	VIII	IX	X	XX	XXX	XXXX	XIV	IV
	Formed Shape		Geometrical Shape and Machining				Main Hole	
			External Surface					
Classified Items	Bonding Direction	Bending Angle	External Plane Surface	External Curved Surface	Main Shaped Surface	Cyclic and Auxilliary Surface	Direction and Stop	Screw Thread and Deleted Shape
0	none	none	none	none	none	none	no main hole	none
1	simple bending	<90 deg	one side plane surface	rotational machining	recessed guiding a/o positioning groove	recessed surface	straight one side stepped	screw
2	special bending	~90 deg	one side stopped	non-rotational machining (multiple curves)	protruding guiding a/o positioning groove	miscellaneous grooves	many sides stepped	circular groove
3	simple bending	>90 deg	both sides stopped	non-rotational machining (multiple curves)	recessed guiding a/o positioning	year/ screw	parallel	axial groove spline
4	special bending	1 + 2	stepped plane surface at right angle	1 + 2	protruding guiding a/o positioning	1 + 2	right side direction	1 + 2
5	3 + 4	1 + 2	stopped plane surface at angle	1 + 3	1 + 2	1 + 3	3 + 4	1 + 2
6	simple bending		2 + 3 + 4	2 + 3	3 + 4	2 + 3	parallel	2 + 3
7	special bending	1 + 2 + 3	2 + 3 + 5	1 + 2 + 3	(1 a/o 2) + (3 a/o 4)	1 + 2 + 3	right angle direction	1 + 2 + 3
8	6 + 7		4 + 5			others	6 + 7	others
9			2 + 3 + 4 + 5			(1 7) + 6	axes with angular direction	(1 ~ 7) + 6

Notes within the table:
- VIII/IX grouping: simple; Complex (same plane surfaces, multi-plane surfaces); parallel plane surface
- External Surface grouping: linear shape; rotational shape
- Main Hole grouping: single main hole; more than one main hole (straight one side stepped, many side stepped)

TABLE E.3 CLASSIFICATION OF GEOMETRICAL SHAPE AND MACHINING (*N*)

Digit	XVI	XVII		XVIII	XIX	XX	XXX
Classified items	Geometric Shape and Machining						Accuracy
	Internal Surface Other Than Main Hole	Auxiliary Hole				Non-Machining	
		Direction		Shape	Special Hole		
0	none	no auxiliary hole		no auxiliary hole but straight hole	none	none	no accuracy specified
1	plane surface	single direction	irregular spacing	stopped hole	high accuracy, positioning hole	special machining	internal a/o external surface
2	cylindrical surface		regular spacing	threaded hole	deep hole	plastic forming	cutting — plane surface
3	other than plane/cylindrical surface	two sides opposite direction		tapered hole	irregular shaped hole	welding	1 + 2
4	1 + 2	right angle two directions		1 + 2	1 + 2	1 + 2	internal a/o external surface
5	1 + 3	right angle three directions		1 + 3	1 + 3	1 + 2	grinding — plane surface
6	2 + 3	(1 ~ 3) angular direction		2 + 3	2 + 2	2 + 3	4 + 5
7	1 + 2 + 3	no angular direction		1 + 2 + 3	1 + 2 + 3	1 + 2 + 3	higher accuracy surface finish including hand finish
8		no angular direction		others	others	others	high accuracy surface finish by special machining
9				(1 ~ 7) + 8	(1 ~ 7) + 8	(1 ~ 7) + 8	high accuracy positioning and others

INDEX

744